Cosmology

THEOLOGY AND THE SCIENCES

Kevin J. Sharpe, Series Editor

TITLES IN THE SERIES

Nature, Reality, and the Sacred
Langdon Gilkey

The Human Factor
Philip Hefner

On the Moral Nature of the Universe
Nancey Murphy and George F.R. Ellis

Theology for a Scientific Age
Arthur Peacocke

The Faith of a Physicist
John Polkinghorne

The Travail of Nature
H. Paul Santmire

God, Creation, and Contemporary Physics
Mark William Worthing

Unprecedented Choices
Audrey R. Chapman

Whatever Happened to the Soul?
Warren S. Brown, Nancey Murphy, and H. Newton Malony, editors

The Mystical Mind
Eugene d'Aquili and Andrew B. Newberg

Nature Reborn
H. Paul Santmire

Wrestling with the Divine
Christopher C. Knight

Doing without Adam and Eve
Patricia A. Williams

Nature, Human Nature, and God
Ian G. Barbour

In Our Image
Noreen L. Herzfeld

Minding God
Gregory R. Peterson

Light from the East
Alexei V. Nesteruk

Participating in God
Samuel M. Powell

Adam, Eve, and the Genome
Susan Brooks Thistlethwaite, editor

Bridging Science and Religion
Ted Peters and Gaymon Bennett, eds.

Minding the Soul
James B. Ashbrook

The Music of Creation
Arthur Peacocke and Ann Pederson

Creation and Double Chaos
Sjoerd L. Bonting

The Living Spirit of the Crone
Sally Palmer Thomason

All That Is
Arthur Peacocke

Cosmology
Robert John Russell

Creation
Fraser Watts

Cosmology
From Alpha to Omega

The creative mutual interaction of theology and science

Robert John Russell

Minneapolis
Fortress Press

COSMOLOGY
From Alpha to Omega

Cover image: Crab_Nebula, Nov. 29, 2005. NASA Image Exchange
Cover design: Paul Boenke
Book design and typesetting: Joshua Moritz

Library of Congress Cataloging-in-Publication Data

Russell, Robert J.
Cosmology : from alpha to omega / Robert John Russell.
p. cm. — (Theology and the sciences)
Includes indexes.
"Appendix: a complete listing of Robert J. Russell's publications"—P.
ISBN 978–0–8006–6273–8 (alk. paper)
1. Religion and science. 2. Cosmology. I. Title.
BL241.R88 2008
261.5'5—dc22
2007036830

The paper used in this publication meets the minimum requirements of American National Standard for Information Sciences—Permanence of Paper for Printed Library Materials, ANSI Z329.48-1984.

Manufactured in the U.S.A.

12 11 10 09 08 1 2 3 4 5 6 7 8 9 10

Contents

Part I
God and Creation *Ex Nihilo* in Light of Scientific Cosmology

Part II
Continuous Creation, Non-Interventionist Divine Action, and the Problem of Natural Evil in Physics and Biology

Part III
The Future of the Cosmos and the Eschaton

Foreword by Ian G. Barbour

Robert John Russell has made two contributions to the dialogue between science and religion, both of which are extraordinary and enduring. He is the founder and director of the Center for Theology and the Natural Sciences (CTNS) in Berkeley, California. And he has for twenty-five years written a stream of articles and book chapters that have influenced the thinking of scientists and theologians around the world. This volume makes accessible in one place some of the most significant of these articles, along with some essays not previously published.

CTNS was the setting in which most of his writing occurred. I am often asked for suggestions as to where a person might pursue study of the interaction of science and religion. The question has come from undergraduates interested in graduate study, scientists wishing to spend a sabbatical year exploring the religious implications of scientific theories, and theologians and lay persons concerned about the credibility of their religious beliefs in an age of science. In reply I usually mention half a dozen excellent centers and programs around the world, but I say that among them CTNS has the longest and the most outstanding track record. CTNS is part of the Graduate Theological Union which includes eight Catholic and Protestant seminaries as well as Jewish and Buddhist centers, and it draws on scientists and humanists from the adjacent campus of the University of California and elsewhere. It offers courses at seminary, M.A., and Ph.D. levels, and it sponsors frequent lectures, symposia, and workshops.

CTNS has also had a far-reaching influence by sponsoring conferences in many countries and by its publications, most notably a series of volumes cosponsored by the Vatican Observatory outside Rome, and more recently a quarterly journal, *Theology and Science,* of which Russell has been coeditor. Several hundred college and university professors from a wide range of disciplines have received grants (funded by the Templeton Foundation) and attended workshops at CTNS in order to develop and teach courses on science and religion in their home institutions. Another program brought together eight groups of twenty eminent scientists from diverse religious and philosophical backgrounds, each group discussing for several days the implications of a particular field of science and then sharing some of their ideas in public symposia. It is doubtful if any of this would have happened without the leadership and intellectual integrity of Bob Russell.

Most of the chapters in this volume grew out of CTNS-sponsored events, though some started as lectures under other auspices or appear here for the first time. The first part of the introduction is a brief autobiographical reflection on the path his own life has taken. Mentioning his undergraduate experience as a physics major, and his completion of graduate degrees in both physics and theology, followed by three years teaching physics, Russell points to the skepticism common among fellow scientists and his own struggles to fit together these two aspects of his life. He describes the building of the Golden Gate Bridge, visible across the bay from the GTU campus, and how it serves as a striking image for the building of intellectual bridges that will carry two-way traffic between the worlds of science and theology.

In the second part of the introduction, Russell skillfully weaves together the stages in the development of his own thought and the main themes in the chapters that follow. He starts with methodological issues in relating science and theology. Here he says he drew initially from my own writing on conceptual models and critical realism in both fields. He indicates how his more recent writing has made use of the ideas of the philosopher of science, Imre Lakatos, who maintains that the central ideas in a "research program" should be judged by their fruitfulness in suggesting new testable hypotheses as much as by their coherence and their consistency with data from the past. Russell has shown clearly that there are both similarities and differences in comparing the methods of inquiry used by the scientist and by the theologian.

Russell agrees with many previous writers that science should influence the theological interpretation of nature and the reformulation of traditional religious beliefs in the light of established scientific theories. But he is one of the few authors who also hold that theology can legitimately influence several aspects of science: underlying philosophical assumptions about nature, the selection of problems to investigate, creative ideas for the construction of new theories, and perhaps even the choice among competing theories that are equally compatible with available data (though the latter claim is more controversial). He calls for "creative mutual interaction" (CMI) between the disciplines. He envisages two-way traffic across the bridge, not a one-way flow of ideas from science to theology.

Four themes are prominent in his discussion of particular fields of science.

1. The Big Bang and the Finitude of Time. Cosmologists agree that our universe started with a Big Bang and a rapid expansion, which seems to imply the finitude of past time, in agreement with the traditional doctrine of creation *ex nihilo*. But some cosmological theories postulate an oscillating universe with alternating big crunches and big bangs, or else multiple parallel universes arising from quantum vacuum fluctuations (though we could not see other universes because light from them could not reach us). These theories assume that time is infinite—or in the case of Stephen Hawking's quantum cosmology, that time is finite but without a beginning (because time itself emerged gradually). Russell compares these theories with concepts of time and eternity in theology. He holds that the theological meaning of finitude is that the universe is dependent on God for its existence, whatever its duration, and he cautions against identifying the idea of creation too closely with the finitude of past time.

2. Non-Interventionist Divine Action at the Quantum Level. How can God act in the world if all events are governed by deterministic laws? Russell answers that events at atomic and subatomic levels are unpredictable according to quantum theory (as expressed in the Heisenberg Uncertainty Principle). He argues that this uncertainty reflects indeterminacy in nature rather than the limitations of current theories. God could realize one outcome from among the range of potentialities described by quantum equations without violating quantum laws. God does not alter what otherwise would have occurred (which is indeterminate), and no input of energy is required (since all the potentialities have the same energy). One might expect individual quantum events to average out statistically for large groups of atoms, but individual events can be amplified in biological processes to yield large-scale effects. A single photon disrupting a hydrogen bond in a strand of DNA might alter evolutionary history.

3. Order, Disorder, and the Problem of Evil. Traditional theology has associated God with order, against which disorder seems to be a threat. But disorder is prominent in some fields of science, especially thermodynamics (the study of heat and energy). Russell sees parallels between the tendency toward greater entropy (a measure of disorder) in the physical world and the presence of suffering and evil in nature. He takes up the perennial question of theodicy: Why would a good and powerful God allow suffering and evil in nature and in human life? After exploring several possible answers, Russell suggests that suffering and evil, like physical disorder, may contribute to creative new possibilities, but ultimately they will be transformed in a future life beyond death.

4. The Future of the Cosmos and Eschatology. Cosmologists expect the universe to expand indefinitely and become too cold to support life. Alternatively, the expansion may slow down and reverse itself, becoming too hot to support life as it collapses. Either prospect ("freeze or fry") seems to make life on earth transient and meaningless. In any case, our sun will burn itself out in a few tens of billions of years. Russell acknowledges that this is a very different future from that envisaged in eschatology (theological beliefs about the future transformation of this world and a future life beyond death). But he holds that the resurrection of Christ has given the Christian community grounds for hope in God's transformative power in a cosmic "New Creation" as well as in individual life beyond death.

Russell writes with clarity but he avoids giving simple answers to complex questions and he takes time to consider views that differ from his own. Some chapters require close attention to follow his reasoning, but the effort will be amply rewarded. Readers unfamiliar with this new interdisciplinary field may wish to start with some of the most accessible chapters, such as 1, 2, 4, and 8.

Preface

I would like to acknowledge with gratitude those who have supported and contributed to the research that went into the essays in this volume over the past twenty-five years. While my gratitude extends to everyone that should, ideally, be listed, I hope my limited acknowledgement will show, if nothing more, how much I have been richly blessed.

I have been shaped theologically by the ecumenical and inter-religious environment of the GTU: by interactions with colleagues in Philosophical and Systematic Theology, Ethics, and Christian Spirituality, and with members of the GTU Rostered/In Residence faculty, particularly Deans Claude Welch, Judith Berling, Margaret Miles, and Arthur Holder.

Serving on the faculty of the GTU brings with it the privilege of working with extraordinary doctoral students. I am particularly grateful to: Mark Richardson for rich insights about the philosophy of religion and Anglican theology; Nancey Murphy, whose dissertation grounded me in the philosophy of Imre Lakatos and its importance for theology; Richard Randolph for challenging conversations about environmental ethics; Wesley Wildman for fresh perspectives on christology, divine action, and inter-religious dialogue; Kirk Wegter-McNelly for exploring quantum mechanics and theology in fresh new ways, for copy-editing three of the five CTNS/VO volumes and co-editing the final one; Nathan Hallanger for the remarkable gift of the *festschrift*; and Nancy S. Wiens and Noreen Herzfeld whose dissertations, by explicitly using my "methodology of creative mutual interaction" for the first time, proved that it could achieve its intended purpose.

I have come to know numerous scholars through years of CTNS programs including the "J. K. Russell Fellowship in Religion and Science," the "Science and Religion Course Program" (SRCP), and "Science and the Spiritual Quest" (SSQ). I am particularly thankful to John Cobb, Paul Davies, Celia Deane-Drummond, Lindon Eaves, Denis Edwards, Carl Feit, Mary Gerhart, Bruno Guiderdoni, Niels Gregersen, Philip Hefner, Marty Hewlett, Wolfhart Pannenberg, Stephen Pickard, Pauline Rudd, Norbert Samuelson, Kang Phee Seng, Christopher Southgate, Ruysei Takeda, Margaret Wertheim, and Joseph Zycinski, as well as to Ted Peters, Mark Richardson, and Philip Clayton for their leadership of these programs.

The CTNS/Vatican Observatory (CTNS/VO) collaboration has been at the core of my professional career since 1987. I am grateful to George Coyne, S. J., the Director of the Vatican Observatory, for his inclusive vision and unflagging trust in the CTNS/VO working relationship, and to Bill Stoeger, S. J., and Nancey Murphy who helped plan the entire series of CTNS/VO conferences and bring them to publication, and to Michael Heller for his collaboration with the program. I am grateful for my co-editors Francisco Ayala, Michael Arbib, Philip Clayton, Chris Isham, Theo Meyering, Nancey Murphy, Arthur Peacocke, John Polkinghorne, Bill Stoeger, and Kirk Wegter-McNelly, as well as the many contributors to the series for their scholarship, vision, and dedication.

The CTNS Board of Directors and its Chairs, Bob Barr, Nancey Murphy, Ted Peters, Bill Stoeger, John Turpin, and Carl York, have helped create and guide the CTNS program and supported my position as faculty-in-residence at the GTU. I am particularly grateful to the Board for its commitment to the capital campaign to endow the Ian G. Barbour Chair in Theology and Science by 2009 and for their appointing me as the first holder of the Chair.

The staff at CTNS brings deep commitment and exceptional skill to the ongoing task of program administration. This has allowed me to focus on overall program leadership for CTNS as well as on my faculty responsibilities both at the GTU and in maintaining a continuing schedule of lectures internationally. I am particularly thankful for Bonnie Johnston who has served as the CTNS Administrative Director for the past fourteen years and to CTNS Program Directors Mark Richardson, Richard Randolph, Ted Peters, Lou Ann Trost, and Nathan Hallanger.

Ted Peters and Nancey Murphy frequently (and insistently!) encouraged me to bring this publication to fruition. Kirk Wegter-McNelly, while still a doctoral student at the GTU, helped select the essays for this volume, put together the initial table of contents, and made initial inquiries to Fortress Press. Kevin Sharpe supported the inclusion of this volume in the Theology and Science series at Fortress Press. Tom Tracy, during the CTNS/VO Capstone conference in 2005 and again during a month's sabbatical leave at CTNS in 2007, gave chapter 4 a very careful read and offered detailed suggestions for clarifying the text. Whitney Bauman initially copy-edited the revised essays. Joshua Moritz then provided more detailed and extensive copy-editing of the entire manuscript. He clarified textual ambiguities, tracked down references, compiled copy-right permissions, constructed the indices, typeset the manuscript, prepared the front and back covers, and worked with Fortress Press to bring this book to fruition.

Dedication

I dedicate this book to five cherished friends: Ian Barbour and Durwood Foster, who played pivotal roles in my intellectual life during my university and seminary days in the 1960s, and Nancey Murphy, Ted Peters, and Carl York, who have helped shape my work over these past twenty-five years.

Ian Barbour's pioneering work in bridging science and religion has had a profound influence on my life and career for nearly four decades now. I first read *Issues in Science and Religion* as an undergraduate at Stanford University and again during my theological training at the GTU. Our friendship began when I taught physics at Carleton College in the late 1970s where he helped me envision what was to become CTNS. In the decades since then, his wealth of writings and our frequent interactions at conferences and through personal correspondences have continued to stimulate and inspire my work in theology and science. I am honored to hold the Chair at CTNS named for him.

Durwood Foster was my theological mentor through four years in seminary, supporting me with patience and wisdom through my intense struggle with the relationship between science and religion. He played a central role at the founding of CTNS and has been a close colleague during my faculty career at the GTU. Throughout the years he has consistently modeled the crucial importance of rigorous scholarship, utter fairness in understanding the views of others, and an uncompromising faith in the Resurrection and from him I gained an immense appreciation for historical and contemporary Christian theology.

Nancey Murphy's GTU dissertation on methodology in theology and science has been pivotal to my own work on methodology. As a chair of the CTNS Board she helped shape the vision that CTNS embodies. Over the years of conversations, travel, and friendship I have been richly influenced by the way she consistently tackles the hardest problems in the field with care, lucidity, and vision: divine action and science, the evolution of moral agency in an anthropic universe, a consequentialist natural theodicy, and philosophical challenges to causal reductionism.

Ted Peters offered tireless and visionary leadership of the CTNS Board and two of our key international programs, the Science and Religion Course Program (SRCP) and the NIH-funded HGP. Through wonderful conversations traveling together and in team-teaching doctoral courses at the GTU, I have learned from and been inspired by his remarkable theological vision—ranging from the Trinity to temporal holism and from stem cell ethics to proleptic eschatology. I am particularly grateful to Ted and Nate for the gift of the *Festschrift.*

Carl York came to CTNS twenty years ago as a seasoned physicist and became deeply immersed in theology and science. Since then he has participated in all of the GTU courses I've offered, served as chair of the CTNS Board and has been involved weekly in the operations of CTNS. Most of all he has shared wisdom, academic critique, personal support, and trusted advice on all aspects of my academic and administrative career.

Finally, I wish to dedicate this book to my family:

My Mother, Arden Swanson Russell, who always believed in me and partnered with me financially in creating and sustaining the J. K. Russell Fellowship in Religion and Science.

My daughters, Christie Lavigne and Lisa Galicia, for gifting me with years filled with joy, laughter, and imagination, and now as adults with wonderful families of their own.

Most of all, my wife, Charlotte, for the wonder of love, mutual support for our careers in the ministry and the seminary, shared faith in the Resurrection, daily prayers, and the foundational gift of nearly four decades of marriage. Without her none of this would have been possible.

Robert John Russell
September, 2007
Berkeley, California

Acknowledgments

Chapter 1: The Contingency of Creation and Big Bang Cosmology
An earlier version was published as "Cosmology, Creation, and Contingency," *Cosmos as Creation: Theology and Science in Consonance*, Ted Peters, ed. (Nashville: Abingdon Press, 1989), 177-209.

Chapter 2: The God Who Infinitely Transcends Infinity: Insights from Cosmology and Mathematics
This chapter is a slightly revised version of a paper with the same title originally published in: *How Large is God? The Voices of Scientists and Theologians,* John Marks Templeton, ed. (Philadelphia: Templeton Foundation Press, 1997).

Chapter 3: Finite Creation Without a Beginning: The Doctrine of Creation in Relation to Big Bang and Quantum Cosmologies
Previously published in: *Quantum Cosmology and the Laws of Nature: Scientific Perspectives on Divine Action*, Robert John Russell, Nancy Murphy, and Chris Isham, eds. (Vatican City State: Vatican Observatory; and Berkeley: Center for Theology and the Natural Sciences, 1993).

Chapter 4: Does "The God Who Acts" Really Act? New Approaches to Divine Action in Light of Contemporary Science
This chapter is a significantly revised version of a shorter essay first published as "Does the 'God Who Acts' Really Act? New Approaches to Divine Action in Light of Science," *Theology Today* 54:1 (April 1997): 43-65.

Chapter 5: Special Divine Action and Quantum Mechanics: A Case for Non-Interventionist Divine Action
This is a revised version of the original paper, "Divine Action and Quantum Mechanics: A Fresh Assessment," in *Quantum Mechanics: Scientific Perspectives on Divine Action, Volume 5*, Robert John Russell, Philip Clayton, Kirk Wegter-McNelly, and John Polkinghorne, eds. (Vatican City State: Vatican Observatory; and Berkeley: Center for Theology and the Natural Sciences, 2001), 298-328. Hereafter, *QM*.

Chapter 6: Special Providence & Genetic Mutation: A New Defense of Theistic Evolution
This chapter is published in: *Evolutionary and Molecular Biology: Scientific Perspectives on Divine Action*, Robert John Russell, William Stoeger, Francisco Ayala, eds. (Vatican City State: Vatican Observatory; and Berkeley: Center for Theology and the Natural Sciences, 1998). This paper is a development of ideas previously published in "Cosmology from Alpha to Omega," *Zygon* 29.4 (1994): 557–77; "Theistic Evolution: Does God Really Act in Nature?" *Center for Theology and the Natural Sciences Bulletin* 15.1 (Winter 1995): 19–32; "Does the 'God Who Acts' Really Act?: New Approaches to Divine Action in Light of Science," *Theology Today* 54.1 (April 1997): 43–65.

Chapter 7: Entropy and Evil: The Role of Thermodynamics in the Ambiguity of Good and Evil in Nature

This chapter is abridged and expanded from the essay, "Entropy and Evil," first published in the *CTNS Bulletin* 4 (Spring, 1984) 1-12 and then in *Zygon: Journal of Religion and Science* 19.4 (December 1984). That essay was based on a lecture presented at the Twenty-Ninth Summer Conference ("Disorder and Order: A Study of Entropy and a Study of Evil") of the Institute on Religion in an Age of Science, Star Island, New Hampshire, 24-31 July 1982.

Chapter 8: Natural Theodicy in an Evolutionary Context and the Need for an Eschatology of New Creation

This chapter is based on a lecture given at a 2003 conference sponsored by the Australian Theological Forum in Melbourne and eventually published as: "Natural Theodicy in an Evolutionary Context: The Need for an Eschatology of New Creation," *Theodicy and Eschatology*, Bruce Barber and David Neville, Task of Theology Today, V (Adelaide: Australian Theological Forum Press, 2005).

Chapter 9: The Transfiguration of the Cosmos: A Fresh Exploration of the Symbol of the Cosmic Christ

The original title of this chapter is: "A Fresh Exploration of the Symbol of a Cosmic Christ: Eschatology and Scientific Cosmology." Unpublished lecture delivered to the Catholic Theological Association, 1993.

Chapter 10: Resurrection of the Body, Eschatology and Cosmology: Theology and Science in Creative Mutual Interaction

This chapter is adapted from Robert John Russell, "Eschatology and Scientific Cosmology: From Conflict to Interaction," in *What God Knows: Time, Eternity and Divine Knowledge*, ed. Harry Lee Poe and J. Stanley Mattson (Waco, TX: Baylor University Press, 2006), 95-120; and in turn from: "Eschatology and Physical Cosmology: A Preliminary Reflection," in *The Far Future: Eschatology from a Cosmic Perspective*, ed. George F. R. Ellis (Philadelphia: Templeton Foundation Press, 2002), 266-315, with permission from the Templeton Foundation Press; from Robert John Russell, "Bodily Resurrection, Eschatology and Scientific Cosmology: The Mutual Interaction of Christian Theology and Science," in *Resurrection: Theological and Scientific Assessments*, ed. Ted Peters, Robert John Russell, and Michael Welker (Grand Rapids: Eerdmans, 2002), 3-30, with permission from Eerdmans Publishing Company; and from Robert John Russell, "Sin, Salvation, and Scientific Cosmology: Is Christian Eschatology Credible Today?" in *Sin & Salvation*, ed. Duncan Reid and Mark Worthing (Australia: ATF Press, 2003), with permission from the Australian Theological Forum.

Introduction

Part I: CTNS, the Context of My Writings

1981 was, for me, a life-changing year. I was thirty-five, and after a series of shifts between distant scientific and theological communities I was moving permanently from academic physics into the unique ecumenical world of theological studies at the Graduate Theological Union, Berkeley (GTU). I had studied physics as an undergraduate at Stanford University, along with minors in music and religion. I had received an M.Div. and an M.A. in theology from the Pacific School of Religion (a member of the GTU) and an M.S. and Ph.D. in physics at the University of California (Los Angeles and Santa Cruz, respectively). I had just completed three years teaching physics at Carleton College, teaching science and religion with Ian G. Barbour, and serving in campus ministry.

My career had finally come to a pivotal turning point: Would I continue in the world of physics and perhaps write occasionally about science and religion? Or would I accept the call to create a center that would invite the religious and scientific communities out of conflict or isolation into mutually respectful, constructive, and critical dialogue for the benefit of both and for their mutual service to the world? Such an interdisciplinary interaction would require academic excellence from a wide range of disciplines including historical and contemporary theology, philosophy, ethics, spirituality, and biblical studies and the key fields of the natural sciences and mathematics, including physics, cosmology, evolutionary and molecular biology. It would require theologians who recognize the crucial role science should play in their constructive work. It would require scientists who were willing to reach beyond the limits of science and explore the philosophical, theological, and ethical implications of their research. It would flourish best in an ecumenical and inter-religious academic context with faculty colleagues and graduate students in the fields involved in the dialogue. It would mean developing an interdisciplinary methodology to enable and support the dialogue. And it would be a place where my own scholarship in theology and science could evolve. Thus was born the Center for Theology and the Natural Sciences (CTNS), "a dream worth loving, a reality worth building."[1]

From the outset I used the metaphor of a bridge to represent CTNS. The bridge itself would be the new methodology to be constructed; the traffic it would bear in both directions would be the creative interaction between scientific and religious communities. I was inspired by the Golden Gate Bridge that unites San Francisco with its neighbors to the north. It was built, not from one side to the other, but starting from both sides and meeting in the middle. Each community, scientific and religious, must first find bedrock in its own field of inquiry and according to its own intellectual standards. Each must then raise towers to soar upward into the sky above them, troll cables across the waters between them, and haul these cables to the towers' tops. Finally, bold adventurers from both communities would climb out on the slender cables hanging in space above the churning cold ocean, and while pointing across the gulf that still separates them, drop suspension cables to support an emerging highway below, hoping that in the fullness of time this highway will finally meet at the center and bear fruitful traffic in both directions. It was clearly a project that would take decades. But I believed the day would come in the not-too-distant future when, seen from a distance, a "critical displacement" would be reached and the two parts of the highway starting from distant shores would become two arms of the bridge reaching for each other, almost touching, and defining a perfect curve through the blue sky.[2]

Today, twenty-five years later, I am immensely grateful that CTNS, together with dozens of centers and programs internationally, has been instrumental in building this bridge. In many ways the bridge is now complete and we can concentrate fully on the rich opportunities and challenges brought on by the flow of knowledge and vision in both directions across the bridge: the creative mutual interaction between theology and science.

Part II: Overview of the Book

In tandem to founding and directing CTNS, I was also appointed to the doctoral faculty of the GTU by its Dean, Claude Welch. And so in 1981 I began a new academic career teaching seminary and doctoral courses in theology and science at the GTU and working directly with students on their research and doctoral dissertations. Both the many local, national, and international programs created and sponsored by CTNS and the unique research and teaching opportunities at the GTU have provided occasions for various writing projects and their publication in collections and journals. Here, I bring a selection of them together in an anthology.

The chapters of this book are organized by their theological focus following the standard arrangement of some of the doctrines in Christian systematic theology: God and creation (chapters 1–3), divine action in nature (chapters 4–6), moral evil (sin) and natural evil (suffering, death, and so on) (chapters 7–8), the redemption of life in the universe and an eschatology of New Creation (chapters 9–10). Running through these chapters are a series of *themes* (noted here in italics) that capture, in brief phrases, my own take on the novel ways these doctrines are influenced by the conversations with the natural sciences. Examples include "finite creation without a beginning," "the fall without the fall," "entropy and evil," "evolution—the biological equivalent of 'Schrödinger's Cat,'" and "Resurrection—the first instantiation of a new law of nature."

The overview, however, is organized around yet another aspect of this book: the historical development of the methodology for relating theology and science that I've explored over this period. This journey starts with Ian Barbour's work on critical realism and ranges through metaphors, consonance and dissonance, varieties of contingency, the theological appropriation of Lakatos's theory of scientific methodology, non-interventionist objective divine action, and, as including but moving beyond these, what I call "the methodology of creative mutual interaction" (CMI). This overview provides a brief narrative of that historical development. Laced throughout the narrative are short discussions of the contents of the chapters and the themes that run through them. I hope that the reader will find this overview helpful. I believe it shows that while working on specific issues and specialized areas of research, I have also used these essays as occasions to experiment with a variety of responses to the overarching question of how to relate these fields in increasingly creative and dynamic ways.

First, however, I should add a word about the relation between the material in this volume, the original published essays, and the extent of their revisions. All of the chapters begin with an endnote citing the original sources and their date of publication. For reference, the publication dates are summarized here:

By date of first publication:

1984:	chapter 7
1989:	chapter 1
1993:	chapter 3
1993:	chapter 9 (unpublished)
1995–2001:	chapters 4, 5, 6 interwoven
1997:	chapter 2
2002:	chapter 10
2005:	chapter 8

Chapters 1, 2, and 7–10 are basically in their original form. Most of the revisions are minor and were made to avoid repetitions of the same material in different chapters or to clarify the original text. Chapter 3 is a reprint of my chapter in the first CTNS/VO publication. The material in chapters 4–6 is taken from my other chapters in the CTNS/VO series and reorganized for clearer reading. I start with a general discussion of the problem of divine action, offer an assessment of several specific approaches, focus particular attention on bottom-up divine action via quantum mechanics, show its relevance for God's action in the context of biological evolution, and conclude with the problems it presents (primarily natural theodicy) and directions to address the problems (primarily via a bodily resurrection-based eschatology).

As the reader may know, Ted Peters and Nathan Hallanger honored me recently with a *Festschrift,* entitled *God's Action in Nature's World: Essays in Honor of Robert John Russell* (Aldershot, England: Ashgate Publishing Limited, 2006). Many of its essays are responses to my original essays. As a consequence, I postponed a careful reading of the *festschrift* while revising these essays in order to avoid inadvertently letting the revisions be influenced by the criticisms of (or support for) the original essays. I have made significant additions to and revisions of the original material from which chapters 4 and 5, and to a much lesser extent chapter 6, are drawn for several reasons: I am currently completing an overall analysis of the CTNS/VO series for publication in the upcoming Capstone volume, and this has led me to revisit the themes and topics surrounding divine action in chapters 4 and 5. I have also had very fruitful interactions with Tom Tracy, Philip Clayton, and Wesley Wildman in relation to their essays in the *Theology and Science* series about the divine action project. This past spring, Tom spent a month on sabbatical at CTNS, and this provided an opportunity for extensive conversations about divine action, including the materials in chapters 4 and 5. Finally, I had a remarkable exchange with Arthur Peacocke about his approach to divine action just prior to his death in the fall, 2006. All of this led me to revise, add, and clarify the original material in chapters 4 and 5. I look forward to another occasion to express my gratitude for, and response to, the *Festschrift*.

1. Background to My Methodology

The question of methodology lies at the heart of the interdisciplinary field of theology and science: How are we to relate fields as apparently different as the natural sciences, the philosophy of science, the philosophy of religion, and systematic and philosophical theology? And how are we to accomplish all this while keeping in mind that the kinds of knowledge claimed, languages used, methods of theory construction, and types of data involved seem so dissimilar? And how, once a relationship has been established at one point in time, are we to respond not only to the fact that theological doctrines and scientific theories are subject to other interpretations which will challenge that relationship but that doctrines and theories change in time, sometimes undergoing incommensurable paradigm shifts? The responses to these questions that I have developed over the past two decades are rooted, in large measure, in the pioneering work of Ian G. Barbour, dating back to his groundbreaking 1966 publication, *Issues in Science and Religion*, and continuing through a wide range of writings including *Myths, Models and Paradigms* in 1974 and his splendid 1990 Gifford Lectures, *Religion in an Age of Science*.[3] Here Barbour laid out a series of well-crafted arguments involving issues in epistemology (the kinds of knowledge we have), language (how it is expressed), and methodology (how it is obtained and justified).[4] From the outset, Barbour used the term "critical realism"[5] to stand for the specific set of arguments he first developed in 1966. I see these arguments as providing the basic components for what soon became a well-engineered and widely traveled "bridge"[6] between science and religion.

A growing number of scholars have contributed to this methodological bridge, perhaps most notably Philip Clayton, Sallie McFague, Niels Henrik Gregersen, Philip Hefner, Nancey Murphy, Wolfhart Pannenberg, Arthur Peacocke, Ted Peters, John Polkinghorne, Thomas Torrance, and Wentzel van Huyssteen. Nevertheless Barbour's pioneering scholarship, more than any other, has, in my opinion, made possible the development of what is today an international, cross-cultural, and inter-religious dialogue about science and religion.[7] It is appropriate to start with a brief summary of critical realism before exploring the ways in which my own work has presupposed and built upon it.

A. Barbour's "bridge": critical realism

It is worth noting at the outset that there are two key attractions to Barbour's work: 1) its use of nontheological arguments for the construction of the "bridge"; and 2) its compatibility with a variety of metaphysical systems. 1) Being based primarily on the secular disciplines of philosophy of science and philosophy of religion, critical realism can be used for a variety of theological purposes not only by Christian scholars seeking dialogue with science but to a large extent by scholars in any religious tradition or by those involved in inter-religious dialogue who likewise wish to engage in conversations about the natural sciences. One need not be committed to process theology, as Barbour is (and I am not), let alone be a Christian (as we both are) to employ Barbour's "bridge" in relating science and religion. 2) Critical realism is compatible with a variety of nonreductionistic metaphysical perspectives, including physicalism (cf., Murphy), emergent materialism (cf., Peacocke, Clayton), dual-aspect monism (cf., Polkinghorne), panexperientialism (cf., Ian G. Barbour), and my own choice, emergent monism. This is because its primary purpose was not to deploy a specific metaphysics to frame the science/theology dialogue. Instead it was to clear the ground for such dialogue by arguing against the strident critiques on least four fronts:[8] a) against those challenging religion as such by arguing for epistemic, ontological, causal, and eliminative reductionism; b) against those attempting to insulate religion from science by arguing for ontological dualism (including vitalism and Cartesian and Platonic forms of substance dualism) or for "two language" compartmentalizations of science and religion (as in Protestant neo-orthodoxy and existentialist theology); c) against those supporting one of several philosophical interpretations of science (including naïve realism, instrumentalism and positivism) while supporting an alternative view of religion; and d) against those claiming that scientific reasoning is radically different than theological reasoning. In their place, Barbour argued for a) anti-reductionism in all its forms, b) an overlap between scientific and theological language through the common use of metaphors and models,[9] c) a critical realist view of both science and religion, and d) an analogy between scientific and theological reasoning.[10]

Of all these arguments I view the claim for an analogy between these modes of reasoning as Barbour's most important methodological contribution to the dialogue. I see this analogy as forming the "bridge" between them. Barbour expressed it in with an elegance whose untroubled simplicity veils a complex and remarkable argument: "the basic structure of religion is similar to that of science in some respects, though it differs at several crucial points."[11] *Similarities:* Both science and religion make cognitive claims about the world using a Hempelian hypothetico-deductive method that incorporates a form of Popperian falsificationism placed within a contextualist and historicist framework complete with metaphysical commitments and criteria of theory assessment. Both communities organize observation and experience through models seen as analogical, extensible, coherent, and symbolic, and expressed through metaphors which refer even if only partially.[12] *Differences:* Still there are important differences in the "data" of religion compared to that of science.[13] Religious models serve noncognitive functions which are missing in science, such as eliciting attitudes, personal involvement, and transformation. Moreover, in science, theories tend to dominate models, whereas in religion models are more influential than theories.[14] Religion lacks lower-level laws such as those found in science, and the emergence of consensus seems "an unrealizable goal." Religion also includes elements not found in science such as story, ritual, and revelation.[15]

By the time of the Gifford Lectures (1990), the analogy was represented by a crucial set of diagrams which displayed the similarities and the differences Barbour had discovered between the rationalities in scientific and theological methods (see Figures 1 and 2 below).[16] It is his attention to the dynamic tension between similarities and differences in science and religion that make Barbour's analysis so original and fruitful. These diagrams proved to be an inspiration for my own methodological ideas culminating in what I call the methodology of "creative mutual interaction" (CMI; see section 7 below).

Barbour's Figure 1: The Structure of the Sciences

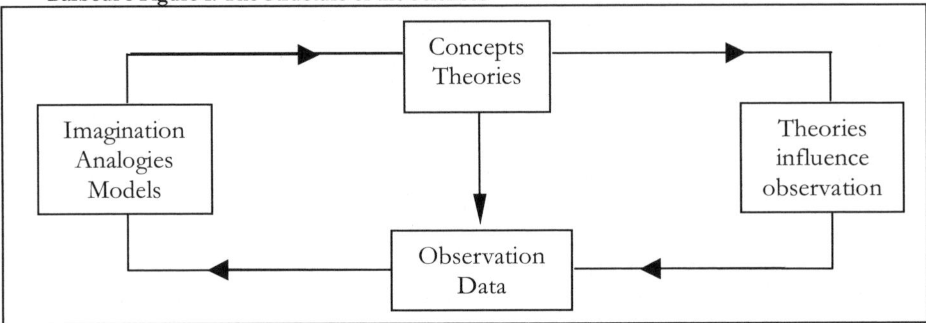

Barbour's Figure 2: The Structure of Religion

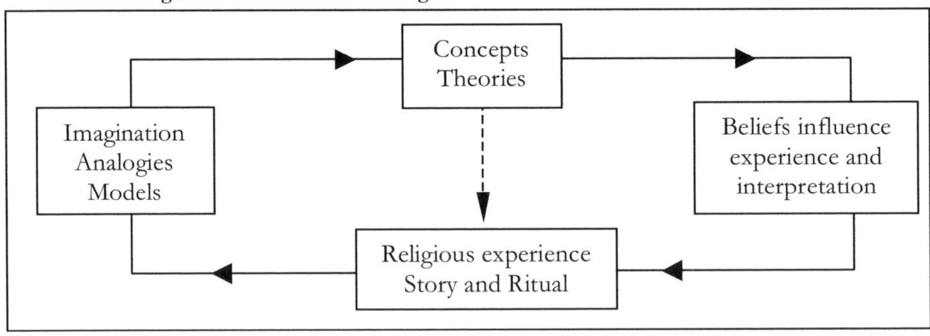

B. Peacocke's version of epistemic holism

A further key contribution to the discussion of critical realism is Peacocke's argument for epistemic holism or epistemic emergence (also known as epistemic anti-reductionism). His argument is illustrated diagrammatically by a key figure in his 1993 Gifford Lectures.[17] The vertical axis lists physical, biological, neurological, behavioral, and cultural phenomena in order of increasing complexity, ranging from atoms to human behavior, and the disciplines which study them, ranging from physics to psychology and philosophy. The horizontal axis lists phenomena lying within each phenomenological level and within each discipline describing that level and ranging in size. Thus physical entities start with elementary particles and end with galaxies, clusters of galaxies, and finally the universe.

Consider first the vertical axis in the figure (see Arthur Peacocke's Figure 3 below). According to Peacocke, epistemic holism views the disciplines of the sciences and the humanities, including theology, as a series of emergent levels that reflect the increasing complexity of the phenomena they study. It involves two claims about these levels: 1) lower levels place *constraints* on upper levels (against "two worlds" treatments that make them autonomous), but 2) upper levels are *emergent* and cannot be reduced entirely to lower levels (against "epistemic reductionism" that evacuate upper levels of novel claims about the world). For example, physics places constraints on biology: no acceptable biological theory can contradict relativity or quantum mechanics. At the same time no theory in biology can be reduced entirely to theories such as relativity or quantum mechanics in physics. Instead some of the processes, properties, and laws of the upper level are emergent in nature.

But unique to Peacocke's insight, the horizontal axis of his diagram is also very important: It ranks natural phenomena in terms of their increasing size within the same epistemic level. Thus physical systems at the bottom of the diagram range from elementary particles to galaxies. I find this one of the most important and yet underappreciated aspects of his epistemic scheme[18] for it makes abundantly clear that cosmology as a part of physics places constraints on all the supervening disciplines, including theology. Thus scholars who view the bodily resurrection of Jesus as a proleptic event of the transformation of the universe into the New Creation must face this challenge from scientific cosmology squarely and exhaustively.[19]

The discussion of epistemic holism was taken up and developed further in important ways by Nancey Murphy,[20] George Ellis,[21] and Philip Clayton,[22] among others. They all take crucial steps in the program to defeat reductionism, particularly its more virulent forms as eliminative ontological reductionism and causal reductionism. Like Barbour's argument for an analogy between science and religion, Peacocke's version of epistemic holism and these further developments have been a source of inspiration for what I am calling CMI.

C. The current status of critical realism and related open issues

In sum, the predominant school of thought among scholars in theology and science, particularly of those coming from a liberal theological perspective, is critical realism. The term has stood for a "packaged deal" whose elements were brought together from a variety of philosophical contexts.[23] They include: 1) the ubiquitous role, complex epistemic structure, and referential content of metaphors in all language (against literalism and expressivism); 2) a Hempelian hypothetico-deductive methodology embedded in a Kuhnian/Lakatosian contextualist/explanatory and historicist/competitive framework (against positivism, empiricism, and instrumentalism); 3) epistemic holism, with its hierarcy of disciplines that includes both constraints on, and the emergence of,

Arthur Peacocke's Figure 3

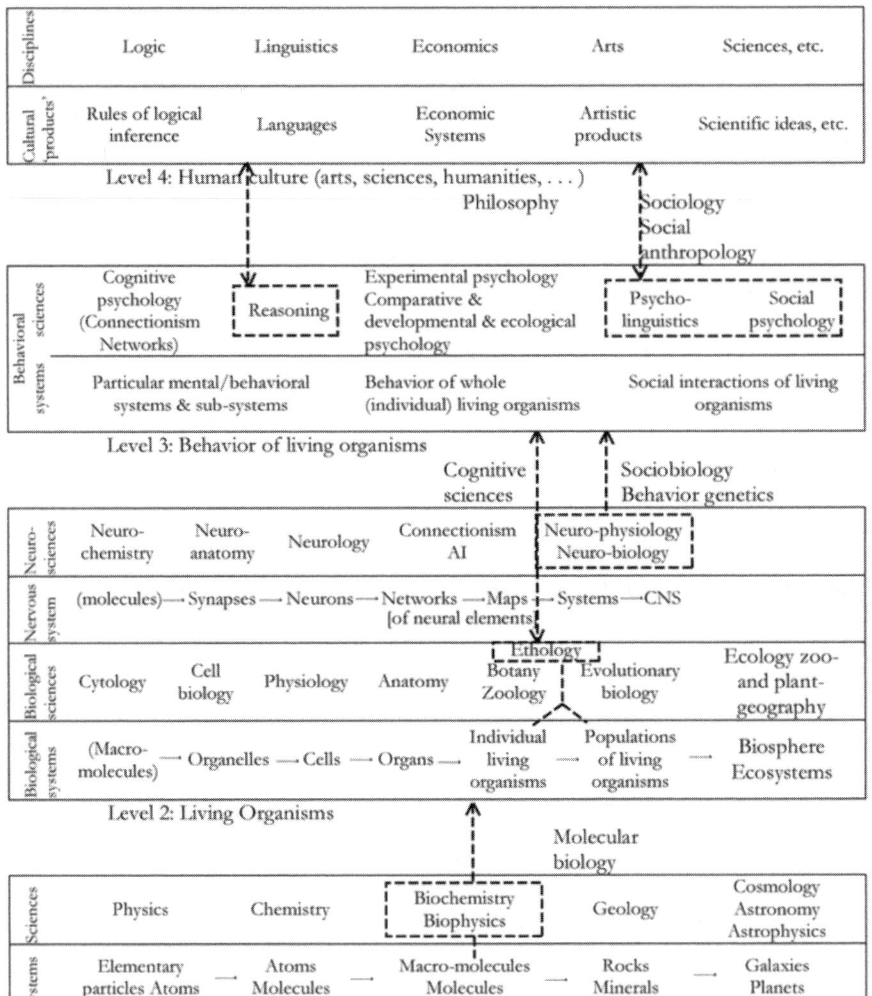

new properties and processes (against epistemic reductionism); 4) a commitment to referentiality, whether of individual terms or of entire theories (against sociologists of knowledge who claim that all theory is mere social construction), and with it a theory of truth combining correspondence, coherence, and pragmatism; and yet 5) a genuine openness to a variety of metaphysical issues.

During this period, each of these elements, of course, raised complex issues that were highly debated. A careful assessment of these debates would take us far beyond the limitations of this book.[24] Still there was sufficient agreement among most scholars for these elements to form what can be called the "consensus view" in theology and science dating back to the early 1960s. Critical realism has continued to be defended, deployed, and diversified widely in theology and science, and it continues to be presupposed both by most working scientists and by many theologians, and in much of the public discourse about both science and religion. On balance I believe it to be of enduring importance, both for its crucial role in the historical developments of the past decades and as a point of departure for future research. It constitutes the key methodological contribution of the "first generation" that makes discourse regarding theology and science possible today.

2. Stages in My Journey from Critical Realism to Creative Mutual Interaction (CMI)

My work over the past twenty-five years presupposes and has grown out of the methodological bridge that critical realism provides between theology and science. I have been particularly attracted to its focus on the epistemological structure of metaphor and I have developed it in terms of both consonance and dissonance. Epistemic holism has been the assumption behind my search for preconditions and prefigurations in biological evolution, physics, and cosmology for what emerges as fully articulated in humankind and which is described theologically in terms of the *imago dei* and sin. The referential status of theological as well as scientific concepts allows genuine exchange of ideas from science to theology even while respecting the radical differences in degrees of referentiality both within and between these fields. The problem of referentiality in quantum physics, cosmology,[25] and the doctrine of God are obvious examples. I have experimented with modeling theological methodology to some extent on scientific methodology in a number of my research programs. Most of all I have tried to construct a genuinely interactive approach to theology and science.

What about the metaphysical underpinnings for critical realist epistemology? Over the decades, Barbour has increasingly framed his integration of theology and science in terms of the metaphysics of Alfred North Whitehead and Charles Hartshorne. While I cannot follow Barbour on his own theological commitments to process thought,[26] I can certainly appreciate many of the insights they provide, including the insistence on relationality, temporality, and God's experience of the world.[27] To the extent that I have employed a metaphysics, it is a modest, pluralistic, and underdeveloped one that combines these themes with a differentiated monistic view of creation that presupposes genuine emergence both "vertically" in existing natural structures and "horizontally" in the evolutionary history of life in the universe.

3. Stage 1: Appropriating "Metaphor" as a Methodological Starting-Point

In 1982, Sallie McFague drew directly from Barbour's work in pointing to basic similarities between metaphors and models in theology and in science.[28] McFague also used Paul Ricoeur's notion of metaphor as an "is and is not": a simile and a dissimile held in creative epistemic tension.[29] She developed this understanding of metaphor into what she called "metaphorical theology" with special attention to feminist theology and ecology, offering new images of God as Mother, Lover, and Friend and the world as the body of God.[30]

McFague's work, together with that of George Lakoff,[31] against the backdrop of Barbour and Ricoeur, inspired me work with the "is/is not" concept of metaphor to build epistemic bridges between theology and science. Perhaps the most extensive use came in a very early paper based on a lecture I gave at an IRAS/Starr Island conference in 1982 where I first met Arthur Peacocke. The theme of the conference was the potential relationship between thermodynamics and the problem of natural evil (for example, suffering in nature). In my conference lecture, "Entropy and Evil," revised here as chapter 7, I developed this relationship in the form of an extended metaphor. First there is an analogy between entropy in thermodynamics, as its normal context of meaning, and a novel context, "natural evil," including such biological realities as suffering, disease, death, and extinction. Underlying each of these processes are physical processes governed by thermodynamics—in particular, entropy.

But I also point to the value of the "disanalogy" (the "is not" of Ricoeur and McFague) in which entropy underlies and contributes to those processes we understand as part of natural goodness. Because of this "double role," the ambiguity inherent in human moral good and evil can be seen as prefigured, even in quite muted form, in the physics which underlies the processes of good and evil. Wolfhart Pannenberg draws attention to this insight in Volume 2 of his *Systematic Theology*.[32] In addition, I drew on the logic of the Augustinian free-will defense as expressed by Reinhold Niebuhr—that sin is "unnecessary but inevitable"—to suggest that a "proto-logic" underlying it might be prefigured at the level of physics by the combination of necessary and contingent features that characterize the role of entropy in physical processes. My proposal is that the logic of "unnecessary but inevitable" has as its precursor the more elemental logic of the *universal contingent in physics*.[33]

I returned to the idea of the metaphorical ambiguity of the role of thermodynamics in relation to natural good and evil in a more extended treatment of suffering in nature for a conference in Melbourne, Australia in 2003 (see chapter 8). Some theologies limit the problem of evil strictly to moral evil, the result of human sin, and view pre-human nature as entirely amoral. Given an evolutionary perspective with no historical Fall, this leads to the question of why humanity should be so radically different from our evolutionary relatives and how the capacity for sin arose out of the history of evolution if there were no precursor whatsoever. I call this the problem of *the Fall without the Fall.* My response was to explore the gradual development of natural evil, the multiple precursors of moral evil, in the context of biological evolution and below that and contained within biological processes, the laws of physics. Once at that elementary level I could press backward in time in the context of physical cosmology eventually to run up against what I called *cosmic theodicy*. Here the logic of "unnecessary but inevitable" is found even at the origins of the universe and its fine-tuning for life. Now theologically my assumption is that God chose to create the universe as capable of the evolution of life and thus natural evil is an unavoidable consequence of this choice, leading me to the phrase, "cosmic theodicy." Such a theodicy, in turn, with its apparently unanswerable dilemma for the theology of creation, led me to turn to the context of redemption, rather than creation, for a response to natural and moral evil.

I also explored an alternative theodicy as articulated by Schleiermacher and developed by John Hick. In tune with other scholars, notably Barbour, Peacocke, Polkinghorne, and Holmes Rolston (but without their appeal to "kenosis"), I extended Hick's theodicy to the domain of natural evil, thus enabling us to view God's suffering through the cross of Christ to include the history of life on earth. Then I again urged that the resurrection of Jesus Christ is the most promising way to respond to natural evil as well as moral evil.

Moving then to the possibility of the universe as teeming with life, I proposed that eschatology would need to include salvation for all life in the universe through the metaphor of the "Cosmic Christ" (chapter 9). Here though we meet the most challenging question posed by Big Bang cosmology to an eschatology of New Creation—for the cosmic future predicted by science is hardly the parousia! (chapter 10). I shall return to these topics in more detail below.

4. Stage 2: Consonance *and* Dissonance as the Next Methodological Step

In 1981 Ernan McMullin published a brilliant essay in which he introduced the idea of "consonance" between theology and science.[34] The context of McMullin's essay was the relation between Big Bang cosmology and the doctrine of creation *ex nihilo*. The relation between t=0 in Big Bang cosmology and creation theology had already been widely debated, but McMullin was cautious, and rightly so in my opinion, about viewing the relationship too tightly, where t=0 might be seen as supporting or even proving the doctrine of creation, as well as the converse, viewing cosmology as irrelevant to theology. Instead McMullin offered the term "consonance" to characterize the relationship in a more nuanced way and called in general for a "coherence of worldview" to which all forms of human knowing can contribute, including science and theology—but a worldview that, as he put it in a tantalizing phrase, would involve a "constant slight shift." I was to explore one possible meaning for McMullin's phrase as I developed the idea of consonance in relation to what I began to refer to as *dissonance*.

After discussing consonance with McMullin, I began trying it out in my courses at the GTU, in public lectures, and in various publications throughout the 1980s.[35] I, too, was struck by the tantalizing fact that for the first time ever we had a scientific cosmology which viewed the universe as expanding in time and time as having an absolute beginning denoted "t=0." Clearly t=0 seemed to be remarkably coherent with our theological tradition which radically distinguishes creation, as finite, from God as infinite and understands creation as existing contingently—the gift of God who exists necessarily. The problem was that Big Bang cosmology also seemed to point to features about our universe that are actually infinite: Big Bang cosmology includes three models: closed, flat, and open (see chapters 1, 3, and 10). Now all three models involve an absolute beginning in the finite past (t=0), but only the closed model describes the universe as finite in size and with a finite future. The flat and open models, instead, are infinite in size and depict the universe as expanding forever in the future. Surely, then, if the finite past of our universe is consonant with the doctrine of creation, the infinities in size and future of the same Big Bang models undercut consonance. It seemed paramount to me that this fact be acknowledged and dealt with if we are to "play the game fairly."[36] To signal this problem I referred to it as "dissonance." To make matters worse, these early Big Bang models were already being replaced in the 1980s by inflationary Big Bang models in which the finite past of our universe was preserved but t=0 was overturned (or more technically, rendered "undecideable," to use John Barrow's phrase) and which allowed for the possibility that our universe emerged from a previous megauniverse, and so on. What then about consonance; what do we do when science changes?[37]

Perhaps McMullin's potent comment about a "constant slight shift" could point me in the right direction. And perhaps the Ricoeur/McFague understanding of metaphor, which had proved so fruitful in the context of the issue of natural evil, could be used to bring together consonance and its challenge, dissonance, into a richer epistemic relationship in which both the consonance and dissonance would be of value. The way ahead lay in interpreting consonance as one part of an epistemic metaphor—the "analogous" element following on the Ricoeur/McFague understanding of metaphor, with dissonance playing the disanologous role. By viewing "consonance" and "dissonance" as together forming a metaphorical structure convening an epistemic claim, I could allow the elements that worked against consonance, such as the actual infinities in nature, to be seen as making a positive contribution to the relation between theology and science.

There were surplus advantages to this approach as well. If dissonance is treated in a positive way it might lead to new insights and an even deeper consonance. Moreover by recognizing that what might be seen as consonant or as dissonant can change in time, we can build change directly into the relation between science and theology.[38] Finally, and perhaps most importantly, this approach avoids two extremes: on the one hand identifying the core meaning of the theological doctrine too closely to science and hence being overly vulnerable to scientific change, yet on the other hand not so insulating theology as a whole from science that no substantive relation exists. In working this way, we can make contact with science, not with the intent of proving a theological claim but of looking for a modest form of confirmation or disconfirmation that can vary in creative ways as theories change.

So for example, we can start with the consonance between the theological commitment to the finitude of creation and the finite past in all three Big Bang models. Now when inflationary Big Bang in the 1980s and, more recently, quantum cosmology removed the basis for t=0, the consonance turned to dissonance. But by acknowledging and valuing this dissonance, I then was able to find a new level of consonance of a more abstract form: Our universe still has a finite past and a specific set of physical laws and constants even without a boundary, t=0. I developed these ideas in a chapter in Ted Peters's interesting collection, *Cosmos as Creation*, republished here as chapter 1, and in a more technical form in the first volume of the CTNS/VO series on "scientific perspectives on divine action," where I coined the phrase, *finite without a boundary* (republished here as chapter 3).

Another example of dissonance between the doctrine of creation and scientific cosmology is spatial infinity: In the Big Bang models of a flat and an open universe, the universe is infinite in size (and expanding!) even though it has a finite past. This seems to undercut the consonance between cosmology and creation theology which relies on the assumption that the universe, as God's creation, is finite; only God is infinite. How to move forward? My response (chapter 2) was to explore the changing meaning of infinity from the context of Greek thought—in which the infinite is the antithesis of the finite—to modern mathematics. Here in Georg Cantor's argument for what he called the "transfinites," actual infinity (in endless varieties) is not the opposite of the finite. Instead transfinite infinities contain the finite even while they infinitely transcend the finite. Cantor also identified the Absolute Infinity in mathematics, which endlessly transcends the transfinites, as a symbol for God's attribute of Absolute Infinity. Now, rather than viewing an actual infinity as threatening the distinction between God and the world, the idea of an actual infinity in nature as a Cantorian transfinite could actually enhance theology: By using Cantor's distinctions between transfinite infinities and Absolute Infinity we can maintain the distinction between God and creation even if the universe is in some sense actually infinite. I also suggest that Cantor's ideas can enhance our understanding of the way God's self-revelation discloses the divine mystery: The transfinites form what I call *the veil that reveals,* for by veiling God as Absolute Infinity in their transfinite infinity they simultaneously point beyond the transfinite to the unknowable Absolute Infinity. Thus God as symbolized by the concept of the Absolutely Infinite is hidden in, even as God is revealed through, the actual infinities of the world, and for this reason and in this way *the God who is known is the God who is unknowable.*

The period of the 1980s was a rich time for others too to reflect on McMullin's idea. Ted Peters developed the theme of consonance in terms of what he calls "hypothetical consonance."[39] If consonance in the "strong sense" means complete harmony or accord, we might "hope to find [it], but we have not found it yet." What we do have are shared domains of inquiry or consonance in a "weak sense," but this is enough to encourage further exploration. He bases this on his critical realist assumption that theologians and scientists are seeking to understand the same reality.[40] The qualifier "hypothetical" reminds theologians to treat their assertions as fallible and subject to possible disconfirmation as well as confirmation. Willem Drees, too, entered into these conversations while working on his dissertation during an extended stay at CTNS in 1987. While approaches like the ones Ted and I were pursuing sought to discover whether there is a degree of both consonance and dissonance between theological and scientific theories, Drees took a different path. In his view the presence of dissonance along with consonance seemed to nullify their cognitive importance. Instead, he developed what he called "constructive consonance" in which consonance is "an assumption in the construction of a worldview in which theology and science come together…consonance is not found but it can be constructed."[41]

Whether consonance will continue to play a major role in research in theology and science is an open question. What is clear to me now two decades later, is the crucial role it played in my own development of methodology: Consonance would eventually lead me to explore a dynamic interpretation of the relations between theology and science, one that is interactive, that moves in both directions, and one in which science, too, has something to gain from its interactions with theology (see section 7, below). But the path to that led first through an extended analysis of the way contingency as a philosophical category mediates the relation between theology and science.

5. Stage 3: Contingency as a Philosophical Expression of Consonance

In the 1980s I began to develop the idea of contingency as a philosophical expression and mediation of the relation of consonance between the theology of creation *ex nihilo* and Big Bang cosmology (see chapters 2, 3). On the one hand, we can move from contingency in philosophy to its role in theology: Through our relative dependence on the world we can experience our absolute dependence on God as the Creator of the world—the "whence" of our existence, to use Friederich Schleiermacher's famous term for God, or with Paul Tillich, God as the "ground of being." On the other hand, philosophical contingency can be related to the scientific idea of the absolute beginning of time, t=0, in Big Bang cosmology: Here we start again with philosophical contingency but this time interpreted as finitude. Now one form of finitude is temporal finitude, one form of temporal finitude is past temporal finitude (for example, our age), and one form of past temporal finitude is having an absolute beginning (for example, our birth). With this we make contact with the age of the universe and its absolute beginning, t=0, as described by Big Bang cosmology. Thus in these multiple steps from philosophy to theology and from philosophy to science, contingency provides an *indirect* connection between creation theology and Big Bang cosmology. In short, philosophical contingency mediates between theology and science, placing them in a relation of consonance.[42]

I next explored the multiple meanings of contingency through a typology[43] I developed to analyze the meaning of contingency in the writings of Wolfhart Pannenberg (a brief summary of this typology appears as section 2, chapter 1). I chose to focus on his fundamental assertion that "the existence of the world as a whole and of all its parts is contingent. The existence of the whole world is contingent in the sense that it need not be at all. It owes its existence to the free activity of divine creation. So does every single part of the world."[44] It was this unusual double reference to contingency of the world as a whole and of its parts that fascinated me. How would this conception of contingency fare in light of science? In my typology I first distinguish between global contingency, which applies to the universe as a whole, and local contingency, which applies to a process or property within the universe. Each of these can have two forms: ontological contingency, namely why something exists per se, and existential contingency, that is, why it exists in the particular way it does. The resulting typology, as applied to the universe, includes global ontological contingency (why does the universe exist per se?), global existential contingency (why does the universe have these fundamental laws of physics and the constants of nature?), local ontological contingency (why does this particular thing exist?), and local existential contingency (why does this particular thing have its particular characteristics?). For example, t=0 addresses global ontological contingency, and the fine-tuning arguments about nature's fundamental constants are related to global existential contingency.

Using this typology it became clear to me that science actually both limits and qualifies Pannenberg's assertion about the contingency of the universe and all of its parts. Certainly it is ontologically contingent both globally and locally, but the two forms of existential contingency constrain each other, limiting their independent applicability. In the framework of theistic evolution, expanded to include cosmological fine-tuning, we can argue that God chose to create the universe such that life could evolve under the right conditions, and further that God intended that life, once capable of self-consciousness and moral freedom, could have the option of choosing freely to respond to God's invitation to covenant.

Now the mutual limitations within existential contingencies can be seen: Planck's constant, *h*, must have precisely its actual value if genetic mutations, as dependent on quantum mechanics, are to occur. Mutations, in turn, are a crucial source of biological variations which, together with natural selection, lead to the evolution of life. At the same time incompatibilist free agency requires that our bodily movement not be fully determined by physics (as it seemed to be in the worldview of Newtonian mechanism), and this in turn points to quantum mechanics as at least one source of ontological indeterminism in nature that is required for the enactment of free agency. Here, then, is the mutual constraint on contingency in the common role played by Planck's constant: Precisely the same value is independently required for both evolution and free agency, and that means that not all aspects of the universe are independently contingent. This introduces a type of dissonance into the relation between the doctrine of creation and cosmology by lessening the degree of contingency in nature. Yet this dissonance can lead to new insights and thus potentially, at least, to new consonance at a higher level of analysis when we consider the possibility of a variety of actual universes (see again chapter 1).

Pannenberg also addressed a number of ways in which the laws of nature are contingent. I decided to call the most prominent of these "first instantiation contingency." This kind of contingency is represented by the fact that most phenomena in nature appear somewhere in the universe for the first time. Unlike some elementary particles, they are not present in the very early universe. A classical example is the origin of life on earth some 3.8 billion years ago. The occurrence of the first biological phenomena coincides with what one can think of as the first instantiation of a new law of nature that describes such phenomena, such as the laws of Darwinian evolution. Hence the acronym FINLON, as one of my themes, stands for *the first instance of a new law of nature.* Barbour refers to my typology in his Gifford Lectures,[45] and Pannenberg discusses it in detail in volume 2 of his *Systematic Theology.*[46]

During this same period I used the distinction between contingency and necessity to explore the ways in which entropy in thermodynamics acts as a rudimentary component, at the level of physics, of what we can call natural evil—and natural good (see the discussion of *entropy and evil* above). I returned to this approach in very recent writings on eschatology. Here I suggested that, insofar as thermodynamics is related to natural evil it might be viewed as a contingent feature of creation to be overcome or transformed in the eschatological New Creation. In short, *thermodynamics as a form of universal contingency might itself be eschatologically contingent* (chapter 10). What kinds of consonance and dissonance will this horizon of possibilities pose for an expanded view of the doctrine of creation and the contingency of the world as we move from standard Big Bang cosmology to inflationary Big Bang and quantum cosmologies?

6. Stage 4: Gaining Rigor through Modeling Theological Method as a Lakatosian Scientific Research Program

A. Background in Murphy and Clayton

At the same time I began to explore a more complex approach: the adoption of a theory of scientific methodology in the philosophy of science as a model for theological methodology. I had been attracted to Pannenberg's use of such philosophers as Steven Toulmin and Karl Popper since reading his *Theology and the Philosophy of Science*[47] with Barbour at Carleton. However, when Nancey Murphy began her second doctorate at the GTU (her first doctorate being in philosophy of science from UC Berkeley), she quickly convinced me to adopt the methodology of Imre Lakatos. Her dissertation on Lakatosian methodology in theology, published as *Theology in the Age of Scientific Reasoning,*[48] won the American Academy of Religion's Award for Excellence in the Study of Religion in the Constructive-Reflective Studies category, 1992.

Lakatos viewed scientific theories as structured by a central or core proposal surrounded by a belt of auxiliary hypotheses. He then delineated a set of criteria by which we can decide rationally whether a given scientific research program is progressive compared to its competitors. The key criterion is a research program's ability to predict "novel facts" which are later corroborated.[49] Murphy published a crucial modification of Lakatos's conception of "novel facts" in order that it could be extended beyond natural science: "A fact is novel if it is one not used in the construction of the theory T that it is taken to confirm... [that is] one whose existence, relevance to T, or interpretability in light of T is first documented after T is proposed."[50] This modification of the concept of "novel fact" allowed Murphy to develop a theological methodology using Lakatos's work. With this methodology it would be possible to decide between competing theological research programs using criteria which transcend the programs themselves. Murphy's work thus added a crucial piece to the overall argument by Pannenberg, Thomas Torrance, and others, for the scientific status of theology.[51]

Clayton has also advocated the theological appropriation of Lakatosian methodology.[52] Clayton views "explanation" as the key concept embracing both the natural and social sciences and, ultimately, theology. In the natural sciences, where one interprets physical data, the truth of an explanation is pivotal. In the social sciences, however, where one interprets both physical data and the experience of actor-subjects (that is, the "double hermeneutic"), explanation means "understanding" (*Verstehen*). Theological explanations are subject to validation through intersubjective testability by the religious community. According to Clayton, the key is Lakatos's requirement that a previously specified set of criteria is held by the community by which competing explanatory hypotheses can be assessed.

Over the past decade, Murphy and Clayton have offered important critiques of their corresponding positions which have further revealed the layers of complexity that underlie theological rationality.[53] Meanwhile, Murphy's approach has been implemented in discussions of theological anthropology by Philip Hefner,[54] in the pragmatic evaluation of religion by Karl Peters,[55] and by a number of other scholars at the frontiers of theology and science today.[56]

B. Lakatosian research program 1: Finitude in changing models of cosmology in relation to the doctrine of creation

I first tried deploying a Lakatosian theological research program in my more technical work on Big Bang, inflation, and quantum cosmology in relation to the doctrine of creation published in the first volume of the CTNS/VO series on scientific perspectives on divine action (chapter 3).[57] In the earlier work discussed above (chapter 1) I had stressed the challenge of finding a way to continue exploring the relationship between creation theology and cosmology as cosmology changed radically from standard to inflationary Big Bang, in which the physical status of t=0 becomes "undecideable," and from there to quantum cosmology, where t=0 is eliminated by the "eternal inflation" of the megauniverses out of which our universe emerges. To make the interaction between the doctrine of creation and scientific cosmology "progressive" in Lakatos's sense I argued that there will *still* be an empirical element of finitude in these developing cosmologies and we should search for it.

It also became increasingly clear to me, that regardless of the outcome of the debates over the origin of our universe, the global characteristics of our universe constitute a kind of finitude that is unaffected by these debates. Our universe is existentially contingent through a cluster of features, such as the fine-tuning of its natural constants, which characterize it. Their role as the physical preconditions for the possibility of the biological evolution of life underscores the theological insight that God created our universe to be a home for life. The eclipse of t=0 as the "carrier" of the "finitude" argument that connected cosmology and creation theology was the result of changes in cosmology. But because of the Lakatosian structure of this approach, I came to appreciate the meaning of fine-tuning in a way that transcends the question of origins and to see it in a much wider context: the debate over the meaningfulness of life in the universe (cf. Arthur Peacocke versus Jacques Monod). In that sense we find a Lakatosian form of progress in theology in its interaction with science.

C. Lakatosian research program 2: "Predictions" based on the Cosmic Christ

I also pursue the attempt to make Lakatosian-style predictions in my discussion of extraterrestrial life (ET) and the "Cosmic Christ" (chapter 9). In my view, our inability to address cosmic theodicy adequately (chapters 7, 8) requires that we shift the problem of God's response to evil to the theology of redemption. Moreover, if the universe as a whole (including the multiverses of which it may be a part) is God's creation then from the perspective of a theology of redemption the universe as a whole will become God's New Creation. Here the redemption of humankind, begun with the cross and resurrection of Jesus, takes on universal eschatological significance. Now if it is true that the universe will be transformed into the New Creation, it implies that life in the universe needs to be redeemed. But does science give us any reason to support the idea that life in the universe needs redeeming?

I begin with the work of Francisco Ayala in which, from a Darwinian perspective, humankind's capacity for reason is adaptive and our moral capacity is a surplus gift of reason. But according to Ayala, the norms of morality are not adaptive (*pace* some sociobiologists); instead they are a "free variable" and as such they are open to determination by such sources as culture and thus religion. I then extrapolate this argument to wherever evolution has brought about intelligent life in the universe and predict that it too will have moral capacity, although the norms of morality will be determined by its culture, too. Now we humans are characterized by sin, including brokenness in our ethical actions. A likely prediction is that such brokenness is not isolated to our species but is characteristic of all ET capable of reason and thus moral behavior. This in turn leads to a second empirical prediction: ET will be neither totally benign nor totally malevolent.[58] Instead *my empirical prediction is that ET will share the ambiguity of moral behavior found in humankind.* If this is the case, it underscores the universality of the Easter event: God, who is the author of all life in the universe by means of evolutionary biology, is also the redeemer of all life in the universe as symbolized by the phrase "the Cosmic Christ."

D. Lakatosian research program 3: Non-interventionist divine action and scientific candidates (NIODA)

As Murphy, among others, has argued, three elements constitute the Newtonian mechanistic worldview: the Laplacian/deterministic view of natural causality embedded in classical mechanics, epistemic reductionism, and ontological materialism (particularly atomism).[59] Its impact, in turn, on Christian theology was to create a "forced option" between two alternatives: either 1) God really acts in nature and divine action requires that God intervene by suspending the regular flow of causal processes (and thus violate the laws of nature that physics uses to describe them), or 2) God only appears to be acting in what are in fact the ordinary processes of nature. Conservatives opted for the former and liberals the latter. But twentieth-century natural science might offer a way out of the forced option if it provides one or more well-tested theories which could be interpreted, unlike classical mechanics, in terms of ontological indeterminism. Such a possibility could then be the basis for a theological theory of *non-interventionist objective divine action (NIODA).*

A variety of proposals for NIODA are "on the table." I think this fact in itself is highly promising: it means we can seek to adjudicate between them using a Lakatosian methodology. In particular they can be assessed according to their ability to predict and explain (à la Murphy) additional issues which, while not included in the construction of each approach to NIODA, are nevertheless illuminated by it. What is first needed, however, are definitions of terms, such as "laws of nature," "ontological indeterminism," "gaps arguments," and so on, and independent criteria for assessing these competing programs (chapter 4). After offering some criteria I use them to assess two of the leading candidates for NIODA: chaos theory (supported by Polkinghorne) and whole-part divine action on the "world-as-a-whole" (supported by Peacocke).

I then devote chapter 5 to presenting and assessing a quantum mechanics-based approach to NIODA (QM-NIODA), concluding that it is the best—although still problematic—candidate so far. In the process I respond to a variety of criticisms that I frame as frequently asked questions (FAQs) since they seem inevitably to arise whenever a quantum-based approach to NIODA is discussed. For example, QM-NIODA is not a gaps argument; instead God created the world *ex nihilo* such that God can act in special ways without intervening in the flow of natural processes. It does not restrict divine action to the level of subatomic physics but is consistent with divine action in other levels of nature. It does not presuppose that the laws of nature are ontological and that quantum statistics somehow determine each individual quantum event. And granted that most quantum events "average out" to result in the ordinary processes of nature, it emphasizes that some quantum events *can* produce a macroscopic result in the world, such as a single alpha particle setting off a Geiger counter (the infamous Schrödinger's Cat experiment).

What makes QM-NIODA particularly attractive from the perspective of a Lakatosian methodology is its surplus predictions in the realm of theistic evolution: Quantum mechanics is integrally involved in genetic mutations. The making and/or breaking of a hydrogen bond which is intrinsic to such mutations is a quantum mechanical process. These mutations, in turn, make a crucial contribution to the processes of biological variation that, together with natural selection, constitute the Darwinian account of evolutionary biology. In essence, over time evolution expresses the information coded in genetic mutations through phenotypic variation in progeny, with their accompanying relative degrees of fitness. To put it metaphorically, *evolution is the long-term biological version of Schrödinger's Cat.*

Given this, QM-NIODA not only provides a preferable account of divine action in regard to its competitors. In addition, and beyond what it was specifically designed to do, QM-NIODA offers a robust version of "theistic evolution," namely that biological evolution, from the perspective of Christian theology, is "how God creates life" (chapter 6). This surplus value offered by QM-NIODA constitutes it as a richly progressive Lakatosian research program on non-interventionist divine action.

At the same time, I routinely stress that the success of this account of divine action in nature seems to exacerbate the problem of "natural theodicy" by appearing, at least, to relate God's action to the processes of suffering, disease, death, and extinction which configure the traumatic history of life on earth. Once again, this leads me to probe theological responses to natural theodicy (chapters 7 and 8), concluding with the unavoidable need to relocate the problem of evil—natural *and* moral—from the context of the doctrine of creation (such as theistic evolution) to that of redemption and an eschatology of cosmic New Creation (chapters 9 and 10).

7. Stage 5: The Culminating Approach: The Creative Mutual Interaction (CMI) *M*odel for Theology and Science

A. The methodology as such

A major challenge continues to be whether science and theology can be genuinely *interactive* in a *creative and constructive* sense in which each offers something of intellectual value to the other. Or is the relation necessarily confined to what we've seen in the past, namely a "theology of scientific culture" in which theology is limited to the interpretation of science? Actually from a historical perspective, philosophy and theology had a strong influence in the rise of modern science.[60] But do such influences continue today to play a role in theory formation and theory choice in contemporary science?[61] And can such influences, if made more explicit, be constructive and beneficial?

When I was in seminary in the 1960s, it was assumed as basically unquestionable that the most one could hope for was a one-way relation in which theology's sole role was to interpret science. But during my doctoral research in physics that followed seminary I saw firsthand the multiple ways in which key scientific concepts of nature were often rooted in the rich philosophies and theologies of individual scientists. Usually their presence was implicit but occasionally conversations and debates made them explicit. I watched in eager fascination as these concepts played a creative role in the life of theorists engaged in the process of constructing and choosing between scientific theories. I mused on the story of Fred Hoyle who had constructed steady state cosmology, in which the universe is eternally old with no t=0, and who had done so in part to undermine Big Bang cosmology which was being invoked by Christians to support the existence of God. Hoyle became my hero, for he had been willing to take his theology (that is, atheism) seriously and build a cosmology that to him represented the implications of atheism in the context of science: an eternal universe with no beginning. In my mind he had bridged the worlds of theology and science—in the way thought impossible by my seminary mentors! Why, I wondered silently, couldn't others do so too, especially those cosmologists who were theists?

In a variety of writings I have explored the possibility that theology can indeed offer creative suggestions in the form of questions, topics, or conceptions of nature[62] which scientists might find helpful in their research and as judged by their own professional criteria. In a presentation to the 1986 Annual Meeting of the American Academy of Religion I asked whether we could look for "a closer relation between theology and science [that does not] continue to restrict science to a secondary role in theology? … [Is there] any appropriate way for theology to influence choices made toward scientific research?"[63] In giving the inaugural Templeton Lecture in Atlanta, Georgia, 1994,[64] I stated that "the loftiest reward [of dialogue] would be that, having earned the right to speak by first listening, Christians might actually make a creative contribution to the ongoing research in mainstream physics, cosmology and evolutionary biology based on their [theological] insights about nature… [The value of such a contribution could] scarcely be overestimated." I have repeated this call often over the years in international conferences and in doctoral and seminary classes at the GTU.

But how was such an interaction to be achieved? By the end of the 1990s all the pieces were in place—Barbour's analogical methodology, Peacocke's epistemic hierarchy, and Murphy's Lakatosian theological research programs—but it took an *ansatz* to unite them. This came to me when I realized that Barbour's *analogical* methodology—the analogy between theological and scientific rationality particularly as he developed it in the Gifford Lectures—could be turned into an *interactive* methodology. To do so I needed to generate research not just within theology in light of science, as Barbour had, but *moving both ways between* theology and science. To do this I would extend Murphy's agenda to use Lakatosian methodology in theology *beyond theology back into the domain of science*, there to inspire scientific research programs based in part on ideas and insights drawn tentatively and hypothetically from theological doctrines.[65] At the same time I realized that Peacocke's epistemic holism of emergence with constraints suggested the correct way to order these two contexts if the interaction were to work properly, namely to place theology explicitly at the top of the hierarchy. That way theology would be *maximally constrained* by the discoveries of the sciences—as well as the humanities in his diagram—while being free to claim that emergent, novel concepts, such as the bodily resurrection, cannot be reduced to the concepts of the sciences and the humanities.[66] I also realized that the introduction of Lakatos's methodology of scientific research programs into theology by Murphy could be expanded to include work that relates theology and science as an *interdisciplinary Lakatosian research program* competing successfully against those theological or scientific programs which do not take the other field into account. A final inspiration was my growing involvement with Buddhist-Christian dialogue beginning in the 1990s through a series of conferences held at

Ryukoku University, Kyoto, Japan. The convener, Ryusei Takeda, was a long-time colleague of John Cobb Jr. I had found Cobb's work on Buddhist-Christian dialogue remarkably fruitful, particularly his method for moving beyond dialogue towards what he called a "mutual transformation of Christianity and Buddhism."[67] It served to confirm my idea that we can go "beyond dialogue" into a new form of interaction where we genuinely move across and into the world of the other.

I call the result the methodology of *creative mutual interaction* (CMI). It can be represented diagrammatically (see Figure 4 below and chapter 10 for details and references to publications): Here we can identify at least eight distinct paths taken by various scholars between theology and science.[68] The generic role of theology as critically appropriating the discoveries of science is represented by five paths which move upwards from science to theology. I label these "SRP →TRP"[69] to symbolize the way scientific research programs are taken up into theological research programs. What is novel here is that there are three paths which move downwards from theology to science (TRP → SRP).

They suggest ways in which theology can indirectly influence science as a whole as well as to inspire specific research programs in science. In short, each side can find new insights and challenges from the other while retaining their independent identities as authentic fields of discourse and discovery. Moreover, by reflecting on all eight paths *taken together* we can discern something about the interaction of theology and science as a whole which we have *not* appreciated to date by taking each path separately. Finally the overall perspective might also tell us something about the direction for "theology and science" in the future, shedding new inspiration for novel research programs that combine new work in theology as well as new work in science in a dynamic and ongoing interaction.

B. Using CMI to tackle the most serious challenge in theology and science: Christian eschatology and the cosmic far future

I have deployed this interactive methodology, CMI, to begin a response to what is arguably the most serious challenge to constructive relations between theology and science—the challenge to Christian eschatology by the scientific predictions for the cosmic far future. According to Big Bang cosmology the future of the universe is either "freeze" (expand and cool forever) or "fry" (recollapse with endlessly escalating temperatures). These predictions cannot simply be ignored by theology, although many scholars in the field have done so. Remember that the cornerstone of the "theology and science" movement, represented in CMI by the five SRP → TRP paths, is to take as a constraint the claims posed by science even while theology deploys new and emergent concepts and categories in its search for conceptual adequacy in light of, but transcending, science. Now physics lies at the bottom of the epistemic hierarchy, giving it the power of maximum constraint on theology, and Big Bang cosmology is a part of physics, as Peacocke's two-dimensional diagram so nicely conveys. Thus if Big Bang cosmology is correct, the parousia is not just delayed—it will *never* happen. If Big Bang Cosmology is right, then, following Paul's argument in 1 Corinthians 15,

Figure 4: The Method of Creative Mutual Interaction (CMI)

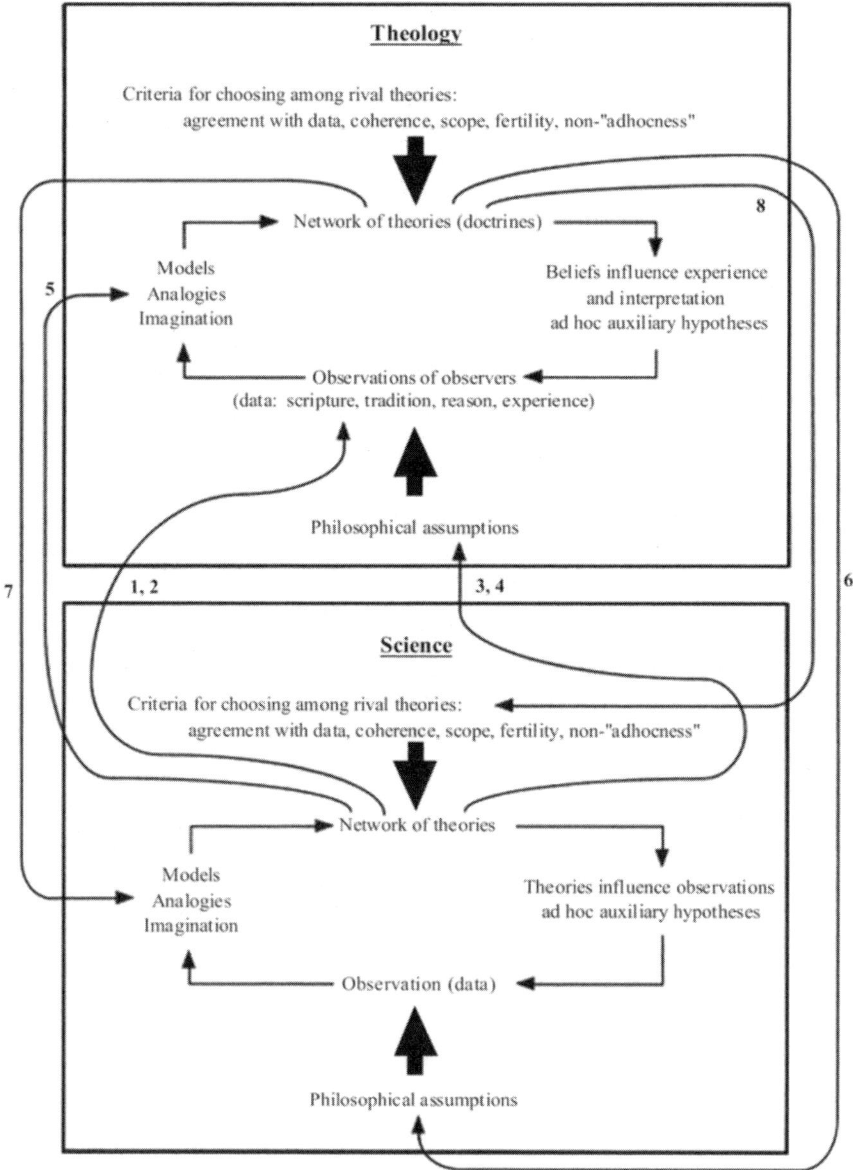

since there will be no general resurrection, Christ has not been raised from the dead and our hope is in vain. Notice, too, that the challenge also comes from theology to science: If Jesus rose from the dead, then the general resurrection will happen and the future of the universe will not be what scientific cosmology predicts. Is there any way out of this mutual challenge?

Chapter 10 is my initial response. Essentially I take path 3 in recognizing that the challenge is not technically from science but from a philosophical assumption which we routinely bring to science, namely that scientific predictions necessarily hold. This assumption is required in the practice of science since scientific theories must be empirically falsifiable, but it is not required in taking science into the theological conversation. Instead it is quite possible for theologians to accept a very different philosophical assumption about the future predictions of science while accepting what science tells us about the past history of the universe. If the processes of nature which science describes are due ultimately to God's ongoing action as Creator, and since God is free to act in radically new ways in history and in nature, then the future, shaped by God's new way of acting as begun at Easter, will not be what science predicts based on the present creation. Instead it will be based on a radically new kind of divine action which began with the resurrection of Jesus at Easter and which inaugurated the transformation of the universe into the eschatological New Creation. Drawing on my earlier discussion of contingency in Pannenberg, I have referred to this idea as the "first instantiation of a new law of nature" (FINLON) or, as I would now state more adequately, the "first instantiation of a new law of the New Creation." Another way to put this is that if it is impossible for Jesus to have risen from the dead (à la *Hume*) it cannot be true that he did. But if it is true that Jesus rose bodily from the dead (à la *the New Testament*), it must be possible, and this in turn means that God must have been created the universe such that it can be transformed by God into the New Creation without a second *ex nihilo*. Finally this idea can lead to very interesting scientific research programs, as spelled out in chapter 10.

With the ground cleared of outright conflict it was then possible to move ahead with a positive interaction between cosmology and eschatology. Returning then to CMI, I have begun to work on two aspects of the interaction between cosmology and eschatology: One aspect is to reconstruct Christian eschatology in light of science,[70] and the other is to explore new avenues in scientific research inspired by this reconstructed Christian eschatology. Needless to say, this is an ongoing research agenda, and it leads us up to the present in which this introduction is being written.

Endnotes: Introduction

[1] I wrote this for the celebration of the CTNS twenty-fifth anniversary in September 2006.
[2] The description of CTNS as a bridge was first published in Robert John Russell, "Converging Streams" in *San Francisco Examiner/Chronicle* (August 11, 1984). Revised and republished as Robert John Russell, "Christian Discipleship and the Challenge of Physics: Formation, Flux, and Focus," *CTNS Bulletin* 8.4 (1988) Autumn. And then as Robert John Russell, "Christian Discipleship and the Challenge of Physics: Formation, Flux, and Focus," *Perspectives on Science and Christian Faith* 42.3 (1990) September. See also Robert John Russell, "Bridging Theology and Science: The CTNS Logo," *Theology and Science* 1.1 (April 2003): 1–3.
[3] Barbour, *Issues in Science and Religion*; Ian G. Barbour, *Myths, Models, and Paradigms: A Comparative Study in Science & Religion* (New York: Harper & Row, 1974); Ian G. Barbour, *Religion in an Age of Science*, Gifford Lectures; 1989–1990 (San Francisco: Harper & Row, 1990). Barbour reformulated many of these arguments for diverse audiences in publications such as Ian G. Barbour, *Religion and Science: Historical and Contemporary Issues* (San Francisco: HarperSanFrancisco, 1997) and Ian G. Barbour, *When Science Meets Religion: Enemies, Strangers or Partners?* (San Francisco: HarperSanFrancisco, 2000).
[4] Barbour, *Issues in Science and Religion.* See especially Part Two: "Religion and the Methods of Science."
[5] Barbour, *Issues in Science and Religion*, ch. 6/III & IV; Barbour, *Myths, Models, and Paradigms*, 3/2; Barbour, *Religion*, 43. Note that many of the writers in theology and science described here draw on philosophers of science who defend what is more commonly called "scientific realism" though typically using Barbour's term, "critical realism." See Jarrett Leplin, ed., *Scientific Realism* (Berkeley: University of California Press, 1984) for an overview of realist positions.
[6] I discuss this metaphor in Robert John Russell, "Bridging Theology and Science: The CTNS Logo," *Theology and Science* 1.1 (April 2003): 1–3. For a critique, see W. Mark Richardson and Wesley J. Wildman, eds., *Religion and Science: History, Method, Dialogue* (New York: Routledge, 1996), xi–xiii.
[7]Most scholars in the field have adopted and developed the term, although some, while sharing one or more of its arguments, have moved away from the term. Perhaps the clearest example is Nancey Murphy, "Religion, Theology, and the Philosophy of Science: An Appreciation of the Work of Ian Barbour" in *Fifty years in Science and Religion: Ian G. Barbour and His Legacy*, ed. Robert John Russell (Burlington, Vt: Ashgate, 2004).
[8]Barbour also developed what he called a "critical realist" theory of truth. Like classical realism, the meaning of truth in critical realism is correspondence with reality (that is, reference) and the key criterion of truth is agreement of theory with data. But we often have only indirect evidence for our theories; moreover, networks of theories are tested together. Thus internal coherence and scope also serve as criteria of truth, as stressed by rationalists and philosophical idealists. Even this is insufficient when competing theories are equally coherent and comprehensive; hence fruitfulness serves as a fourth criterion of truth, as pragmatists, instrumentalists, and linguistic analysts stress. Thus intelligibility and explanatory power, and not just observableness or predictive success, is a guide to the real. Barbour, *Religion*, 34–35; Barbour, *Issues in Science and Religion*, 170, 173.
[9]Barbour argued that the language of religion is not starkly different from the language of science. Both use metaphors structured as models to convey truth claims which are intended to refer to reality even though that attempt is never entirely successful. Scientific theories yield partial, revisable, abstract, but referential knowledge of the world. They are expressed through models composed of multiple metaphors, and these models "selectively represent particular aspects of the world for specific purposes . . . [They] are to be taken seriously but not literally." Barbour, *Religion*, ch. 2/II, esp. 43; Barbour, *Issues in Science and Religion*, ch. 6/II/3; Barbour, *Myths, Models, and Paradigms*, 3/2–3. Similarly in religion, metaphors offer

open-ended analogies which are more than a useful fiction yet never a set of literal statements. Barbour, *Myths, Models, and Paradigms*, ch. 2.

[10]Barbour's approach to scientific methodology began with the empiricism of Carl Hempel, whose "hypothetico-deductive" method brought together inductivist and deductivist approaches to the construction and testing of theories *vis.* Popperian falsificationism. He then took advantage of the tremendous breakthroughs in our understanding of scientific methodology in the late 1950s and early 1960s, drawing on such philosophers of science as Norwood Hanson, Gerald Holton, Thomas Kuhn, Michael Polanyi, Steven Toulmin, and with special emphasis on the writings of Imre Lakatos. Barbour, *Religion*, ch. 2, esp. I/1, II/1, III/1; Barbour, *Issues in Science and Religion*, ch. 6/I/1,2, II/1; Barbour, *Myths, Models, and Paradigms*, ch. 6. These scholars explored the historicist and contextualist elements which characterize the scientific community. These elements include the "theory-laddenness of data," the presence of intersubjectivity rather than strict objectivity in scientific rationality, the structure of science in terms of paradigms and research programs, the competition between research programs, the occurrence of revolutions in the history of scientific paradigms, the presence of metaphysical assumptions about nature in scientific paradigms, and the role of aesthetics and values in theory choice. Scientific theories are a human construction and their conclusions are inherently tentative and subject to revision. Nevertheless, according to Barbour, they are to be assessed by four criteria which are reasonably trans-paradigmatic: agreement with data, coherence, scope, and fertility. In the philosophy of religion then Barbour constructed a similar series of arguments regarding religious epistemology, methodology, and language, drawing on the writings of John Wisdom, John Hick, Ian Ramsey, and Frederick Ferré, among others. Here Barbour argued that the methods of theory construction; the roles played by imagination, metaphor, and model; the ways data are interpreted by theory; and the presence of metaphysical and aesthetic elements in religious paradigms, are strikingly analogous to their role in the methods of the sciences. Barbour, *Religion*, chapters 2, 3; Barbour, *Issues in Science and Religion*, chapters 8, 9; Barbour, *Myths, Models, and Paradigms*, chapters 4, 5, 7, 8, 9.

[11] Barbour, *Religion*, 36.

[12] Barbour, *Religion*, ch. 2/II; Barbour, *Issues in Science and Religion*, ch. 8/I/4; Barbour, *Myths, Models, and Paradigms*, chapters 4, 5.

[13] Barbour, *Religion*, ch. 2, esp. I/1–3 and Figs. 1 and 2.

[14] Barbour, *Religion*, 46–47, 65; Barbour, *Issues in Science and Religion*, ch. 8/II, 9/I/3; Barbour, *Myths, Models, and Paradigms*, ch. 4/5.

[15] Barbour, *Religion*, ch. 2/I/3; Barbour, *Issues in Science and Religion*, ch. 8/III; Barbour, *Myths, Models, and Paradigms*, ch. 7/4.

[16] Barbour, *Religion*, Fig. 1, 32, and Fig. 2, 36.

[17] Arthur Peacocke, *Theology for a Scientific Age: Being and Becoming—Natural, Divine and Human*, Enlarged Edition (Minneapolis: Fortress Press, 1993). See particularly Fig. 3, 217, and the accompanying text.

[18]Note the difference between Peacocke's scheme and that posed by Murphy and Ellis in Nancey Murphy and George F. Ellis, *On the Moral Nature of the Universe: Theology, Cosmology, and Ethics*, Theology and the Sciences Series (Minneapolis, Minn.: Fortress Press, 1996), 268, Fig. 9.3, 204. Needless to say I agree with Peacocke here.

[19]For an initial response see Russell, "Bodily Resurrection, Eschatology and Scientific Cosmology."

[20] Nancey Murphy, *Theology in the Age of Scientific Reasoning* (Ithaca: Cornell University Press, 1990). While Murphy has contributed to development of a methodology for relating theology and science, she is highly critical of the term "critical realism." See her book *Anglo-American Postmodernity: Philosophical Perspectives on Science, Religion, and Ethics.* (Boulder, CO: Westview Press, 1997).

[21] Nancey Murphy and George F. Ellis, *On the Moral Nature of the Universe: Theology, Cosmology, and Ethics*, Theology and the Sciences Series (Minneapolis, Minn.: Fortress Press, 1996), 268.

[22] Philip Clayton, *Mind and Emergence: From Quantum to Consciousness* (Oxford: Oxford University Press, 2005).

[23]Note: Murphy argues that the term "critical realism" is strictly an epistemic theory defending a correspondence theory of truth and should not be used for the entire set of elements described here.

[24]Suffice it to say, for now, that some scholars working in theology and science have stressed the difficulties facing a realist interpretation of specific scientific theories, such as quantum mechanics Robert John Russell, "Quantum Physics in Philosophical and Theological Perspective," in *Physics, Philosophy, and Theology: A Common Quest for Understanding* (hereafter *PPT*), ed. Robert J. Russell, William R. Stoeger, S. J. and George V. Coyne, S. J. (Vatican City State: Vatican Observatory Publications, 1988), 419, 343–74; see also, for example, Robert John Russell, "A Critical Appraisal of Peacocke's Thought on Religion and Science," *Religion & Intellectual Life* (New Rochelle) II no. 4 (1985) (College of New Rochelle). Others underscore the difficulties with a realist interpretation of key theological terms, such as the concept of God: Willem B. Drees, *Religion, Science and Naturalism* (Cambridge: Cambridge University Press, 1996), 143. Some have acknowledged the diversity of realist positions taken by philosophers: Arthur Peacocke, *Theology for a Scientific Age: Being and Becoming—Natural, Divine and Human*, Enlarged Edition (Minneapolis: Fortress Press, 1993), 12. See Leplin, *Scientific Realism.* Others stress the continuing challenge to realism by the sociology of knowledge: D. Bloor, *Knowledge and Social Imagery* (London: Routledge & Kegan Paul, 1976). See Arthur R. Peacocke, *Intimations of Reality: Critical Realism in Science and Religion: The Mendenhall Lectures, 1983* (Notre Dame, Ind.: University of Notre Dame Press, 1984), 94, 19–22 for helpful references and counterarguments. Some have given increased attention to the diversity of models of rationality and their relative appropriateness for "science and religion": Mikael Stenmark, *Rationality in Science, Religion, and Everyday Life: A Critical Evaluation of Four Models of Rationality* (Notre Dame, Ind.: University of Notre Dame Press, 1995), 392. Others focus on the importance of differences, as well as similarities, between theology and science, say from the standpoint of pragmatism. Wesley Wildman, "Similarities and Differences in the Practice of Science and Theology," *CTNS Bulletin* 14.4 (Fall 1994): 1–14. Some have moved to a non-foundationalist (and in this specific sense a post-modernist) epistemology, either keeping correspondence and referentiality (see Philip Clayton, *Explanation from Physics to Theology: An Essay in Rationality and Religion* [New Haven, Conn.: Yale University Press, 1989], 230) or shifting to a pragmatic theory of truth (see Nancey Murphy, *Beyond Liberalism and Fundamentalism: How Modern and Postmodern Philosophy Set the Theological Agenda* [Valley Forge, Pa.: Trinity Press International, 1996], 162. Some working with an all-embracing philosophical system, such as Whiteheadian metaphysics, have developed a broad set of theological positions in light of science: Barbour, *Religion and Science*; Charles Birch and John B. Cobb Jr., *The Liberation of Life* (Cambridge: Cambridge University Press, 1981); John F. Haught, *Science & Religion: From Conflict to Conversion* (New York: Paulist, 1995); David Ray Griffin, ed., *The Reenchantment of Science: Postmodern Proposals*, SUNY Series in Constructive Postmodern Thought (Albany, N.Y.: State University of New York Press, 1988), 173. Others who make more limited use of metaphysics have developed a series of equally broad theological arguments. John C. Polkinghorne, *The Faith of a Physicist: Reflections of a Bottom-up Thinker* (Princeton, N.J.: Princeton University Press, 1994). There are also positions taken at increasing distances from the "consensus view." For some, a post-modernist view offers an attractive approach, drawing on Continental and/or Anglo-American sources, and for growing numbers, feminist critiques of science are crucial. Some have abandoned realism as a whole while still finding elements of the preceding helpful in relating science and religion. Drees, *Religion, Science and Naturalism*, esp. ch. 5.

[25]Bill Stoeger offers a nuanced account of this problem in William R. Stoeger, S. J., "What is the 'Universe' Which Cosmology Studies?" in Ashgate Science and Religion Series (Aldershot, England: Ashgate Publishing Company, 2004), 127–43.

[26]I am committed to the bodily resurrection of Jesus of Nazareth and an eschatology of universal transformation, as well as to creation *ex nihilo*, and so on, as the chapters in this book will—hopefully—make clear!

[27]In my view, CMI (as discussed below) allows us to achieve the goal of genuine interaction Barbour sought through the use of process metaphysics *without* requiring a metaphysical system such as theirs (a view no doubt influenced by my having thoroughly read Karl Barth in seminary even while being deeply enamored with the methodology of Paul Tillich!).

[28]McFague also stressed important differences: Metaphors provide order in theology while stimulating new discoveries in science; they more clearly carry meaning in theology than in science; and unlike in science, they are ubiquitous and hierarchical, as well as eliciting feelings and action, in theology.

[29]If the dissimile is lost, the simile is taken for an identity and interpreted literally, the classic example being that "God the Father" is taken to mean that God is male, leading to theological patriarchy. If the simile is lost, the dissimile evacuates the metaphor of its meaning, leaving it vulnerable to co-opting by other linguistic communities. One of my favorite examples is a car ad I once saw proclaiming: "Datsun saves!"

[30]These images challenge theology's patriarchical and androcentric distortions and fund her work in ecological theology. See Sallie McFague, *Metaphorical Theology: Models of God in Religious Language* (Philadelphia: Fortress Press, 1982), 225, ch. 3, esp. 101–08; see also Sallie McFague, "Ian Barbour: Theologian's Friend, Scientist's Interpreter," *Zygon: Journal of Religion & Science* 31.1 (March 1996): 21–28.

[31] George Lakoff and Mark Johnson, *Metaphors We Live By* (Chicago: University of Chicago Press, 1980).

[32]Wolfhart Pannenberg, *Systematic Theology*, vol. 2, trans. G. W. Bromiley (Grand Rapids, Mich.: Eerdmans, 1994), II/2, footnotes #253 (97) and #255 (98).

[33]Mark Worthing discussed these ideas in fruitful ways in Mark W. Worthing, *God, Creation, and Contemporary Physics*, Theology and the Sciences Series (Minneapolis: Fortress Press, 1996), 260, 146–58.

[34]Ernan McMullin, "How Should Cosmology Relate to Theology?" in *The Sciences and Theology in the Twentieth Century*, ed. A. R. Peacocke (Notre Dame, Ind.: University of Notre Dame Press, 1981), 17–57.

[35]Russell, "Entropy and Evil"; Robert John Russell, "The Theological Consequences of the Thermodynamics of a Moral Universe: An Appreciative Critique and Extension of the Murphy/Ellis Project," *CTNS Bulletin* 19.4 (Fall 1998): 19–24.

[36]The presence of these infinities in the same set of Big Bang models was routinely overlooked or discounted by most of my colleagues in theology and science, a fact which continues to puzzle me even now.

[37]It was in facing the reality of this challenge to "the gleaming goal of consonance" that I was moved to refer to the "dusty reality of dissonance." Robert John Russell, "Cosmology, Creation, and Contingency," in *Cosmos as Creation: Theology and Science in Consonance*, ed. Ted Peters (Nashville: Abingdon, 1989), 177.

[38] Russell, "Cosmology, Creation, and Contingency," esp. 188, 194, 204; Robert John Russell, "Contemplation: A Scientific Context," *Continuum* Vol. 2 (Fall 1990). See also Robert John Russell, "Theological Lessons from Cosmology," *Cross Currents: Religion & Intellectual Life* 41.3 (Fall 1991): esp. 313–14; Robert John Russell, "Finite Creation Without a Beginning: The Spiritual and Theological Significance of Stephen Hawking's Quantum Cosmology," *The Way: Review of Contemporary Christian Spirituality* 32.4 (October 1992): 268–81; Robert John Russell, "Cosmology from Alpha to Omega," *Zygon: Journal of Religion & Science* 29.4 (December 1994); Robert John Russell, "Cosmology: Evidence for God or Partner for Theology?" in *Evidence of Purpose*, ed. John Marks Templeton (New York: Continuum, 1994); Robert John Russell, "T=0: Is It Theologically Significant?" in *Religion and Science: History, Method, Dialogue*, ed. W. Mark Richardson and Wesley J. Wildman (New York: Routledge, 1996), 450, esp. 213.

[39] Ted Peters, "On Creating the Cosmos," in *PPT*, 274–76; Ted Peters, "Cosmos as Creation," 45–114; Ted Peters, ed., *Science & Theology: The New Consonance* (Boulder, Colo.: Westview, 1998), esp. 18–19.

[40]See the introduction by Ted Peters to Wolfhart Pannenberg, *Toward a Theology of Nature: Essays on Science and Faith*, ed. Ted Peters (Louisville, Ky.: Westminster/John Knox Press, 1993), 166, 5.

[41] Willem B. Drees, *Beyond the Big Bang: Quantum Cosmologies and God* (La Salle, Ill.: Open Court, 1990), 323, 29, 178. Consonance is also discussed in the valuable textbook, Christopher Southgate et al., eds., *God, Humanity and the Cosmos: A Textbook in Science and Religion* (Harrisburg: Trinity Press International, 1999), section 1.10 in particular.

[42] A central, personal image from my childhood guided my use of contingency: that of the Hawaiian Islands. Let one of these islands stand for the doctrine of creation *ex nihilo*, another t=0 in Big Bang cosmology. In this image we can relate them by a ship that moves back and forth between them—a kind of "dynamic bridge" between these idea islands. But if we disregard the Pacific Ocean we can see the islands for what they really are—not "floating rocks" but volcanoes rising up some 30,000 feet from the underlying Pacific Plate. Now if we metaphorically associate the bedrock with philosophical contingency, then the island of Big Bang cosmology is formed as contingency erupts upwards to become finitude, then temporal finitude, and finally t=0 while the island of creation *ex nihilo* arises out of the bedrock of contingency upwards through finite dependence and finally the world as absolutely dependent of God the Creator. What were seen as separate islands requiring a bridge or a boat to connect them can now be seen as "island mountains formed out of contingency bedrock."

[43] Robert John Russell, "Contingency in Physics and Cosmology: A Critique of the Theology of Wolfhart Pannenberg," *Zygon: Journal of Religion and Science* 23.1 (March 1988): 23–43. The typology discussed above has been inserted into chapter 1 here.

[44] Wolfhart Pannenberg, "The Doctrine of Creation and Modern Science," *Zygon: Journal of Religion and Science* 23 (1988): 9., republished in Wolfhart Pannenberg, "The Doctrine of Creation and Modern Science," in *Cosmos as Creation: Theology and Science in Consonance*, ed. Ted Peters (Nashville: Abingdon, 1989), 288, 152–76.

[45]Barbour suggests a "fourfold distinction." However his four types of contingency are already contained in my typology and my typology, in turn, contains additional types not included in Barbour's account. What Barbour calls type 1), contingent existence, is what I call global ontological contingency. What Barbour calls type 2), contingent boundary conditions, is what I call global empirical contingency. Barbour's type 3), contingent laws, combines two forms of what I call nomological contingency: absolute nomological contingency and first instantiation nomological contingency. Finally type 4) in Barbour's account, contingent events, is what I call local empirical contingency. His typology thus omits what I called local ontological contingency as well as the other forms of nomological contingency. See Barbour, *Religion*, 142–43.

[46]Wolfhart Pannenberg, *Systematic Theology*, vol. 2, 7.II.1, 61–76. See in particular footnotes #160 and #161 (66–67) and footnote #173 (70). It is not possible to offer a detailed response to Pannenberg's discussion of my development of the typology of contingencies here. However his critique of my view in footnote #171 (69) deserves a brief response. First I distinguish sharply between local and global contingency. Thus local contingency is *not* "basic to [my] 'global contingency.'" Secondly, I do not claim that the contingency of the universe "stands in need of the anthropic principle and that this principle offers a cogent basis for contingency." Instead I suggest that the strong form of the Anthropic Principle actually conjoins two of the otherwise distinct types of global contingency: the global ontological contingency of the universe, which as a philosophical form of contingency is grounded in sheer existence as such, and the global empirical contingency of the universe, with its evidentiary basis in the fine-tuning of our universe for life and the Anthropic claim

that our fine-tuned universe is the only actual universe. See Russell, "Contingency in Physics and Cosmology," 27–29.

[47] Wolfhart Pannenberg, *Theology and the Philosophy of Science*, trans. Francis McDonagh (Philadelphia: Westminster, 1976), 458.

[48] Nancey Murphy, *Theology in the Age of Scientific Reasoning* (Ithaca, N.Y.: Cornell University Press, 1990), regarding Toulmin, esp. 48–49, and Lakatos, ch. 3 especially 3.4. Note: Barbour was the first scholar I am aware of to comment on the importance of Imre Lakatos's ideas for theology, comparing the degree of commitment to a given theory in science versus in theology in 1974.

[49] Ibid., ch. 3, esp. 58–61.

[50] Ibid., 68. Note that without careful attention to Murphy's modification, the notion of "prediction" might seem to undercut the applicability of Lakatos to theology. See for example Polkinghorne, *The Faith of a Physicist*, 49; and Niels Henrik Gregersen, "A Contextual-Coherence Theory for the Theology-Science Dialogue," in *Rethinking Theology and Science: Six Models for the Current Dialogue*, ed. Niels Henrik Gregersen and J. Wentzel van Huyssteen (Grand Rapids, Mich.: Eerdmans, 1998), 205–12, esp. 208–09. For a substantive critique of the claim that discernment can yield novel facts see Drees, *Religion, Science and Naturalism*, 143–44.

[51]In recent years she has developed her work with a focus on the epistemological writings of Alasdair MacIntyre, but a discussion of this would take us too far afield of the present volume. See for example Murphy and Ellis, *On the Moral Nature of the Universe*, ch. 1.

[52] Clayton, *Explanation.*

[53]Nancey Murphy, "Response to Review by Philip Clayton of 'Theology in the Age of Scientific Reasoning' by Nancey Murphy," *CTNS Bulletin* (Berkeley) 11.1 (Winter 1991); Philip Clayton, "Review of 'Theology in the Age of Scientific Reasoning' by Nancey Murphy," *CTNS Bulletin* (Berkeley) 11.1 (Winter 1991): 29–31. See also Mary Hesse, "Review of 'Explanation from Physics to Theology' by Philip Clayton," *CTNS Bulletin* (Berkeley) 11.2 (Spring 1991). See also the responses to Murphy in the September, 1998, issue of *Zygon: Journal of Religion and Science.*

[54]Philip Hefner, *The Human Factor: Evolution, Culture, and Religion*, Theology and the Sciences Series (Minneapolis: Fortress Press, 1993), 317.

[55]Karl Peters, "Storytellers and Scenario Spinners: Some Reflections on Religion and Science in Light of a Pragmatic, Evolutionary Theory of Knowledge," *Zygon: Journal of Religion and Science* 32.4 (December 1997): 465–89.

[56]For additional discussion see Philip Clayton and Steven Knapp, "Rationality and Christian Self-Conception," in *Religion and Science: History, Method, Dialogue*, ed. W. Mark Richardson and Wesley Wildman (New York: Routledge, 1996), 450, 131–44; Nicholas Wolterstorff, "Entitled Christian Belief," in ibid., 145–50; Nancey Murphy, "On the Nature of Theology," in ibid., 151–60; Philip Clayton and Steven Knapp, "Is Holistic Justification Enough?" in ibid., 161–69; Gregory Peterson, "The Scientific Status of Theology: Imre Lakatos, Method and Demarcation," *Perspectives on Science and Christian Faith* 50.1 (March 1998): 22–31.

[57] Robert John Russell, "Finite Creation Without a Beginning: The Doctrine of Creation in Relation to Big Bang and Quantum Cosmologies," in *Quantum Cosmology and the Laws of Nature: Scientific Perspectives on Divine Action* (hereafter *QCLN*), ed. Robert J. Russell, Nancey C. Murphy and Chris J. Isham (Vatican City State: Vatican Observatory Publications; Berkeley, Calif.: Center for Theology and the Natural Sciences, 1993), 468, 293–329; Murphy and Ellis, *On the Moral Nature of the Universe.*

[58]Hollywood illustrates these dichotomies through such movies as *ET* with its benign alien versus *Independence Day* with its non-negotiable invaders.

[59] Murphy, *Beyond Liberalism and Fundamentalism*, ch. 3; Nancey Murphy, *Anglo-American Postmodernity: Philosophical Perspectives on Science, Religion, and Ethics* (Colorado: Westview Press, 1997), esp. ch. 5.

[60] Michael Foster, "The Christian Doctrine of Creation and the Rise of Modern Science," in *Creation: The Impact of an Idea*, ed. Daniel O'Connor and Francis Oakley (New York: Charles Scribner's Sons, 1969); Eugene M. Klaaren, *Religious Origins of Modern Science: Belief in Creation in Seventeenth-Century Thought* (Grand Rapids: Eerdmans, 1977); David C. Lindberg and Ronald L. Numbers, eds., *God and Nature: Historical Essays on the Encounter Between Christianity and Science* (Berkeley: University of California Press, 1986), 516; Gary B. Deason, "Protestant Theology and the Rise of Modern Science: Criticism and Review of the Strong Thesis," *CTNS Bulletin* 6.4 (Autumn 1986): 1–8; Amos Funkenstein, *Theology and the Scientific Imagination: From the Middle Ages to the Seventeenth Century* (Princeton, N.J.: Princeton University Press, 1986), 421; I. Bernard Cohen, ed., *Puritanism and the Rise of Modern Science: The Merton Thesis* (New Brunswick: Rutgers University Press, 1990); Roy A. Clouser, *The Myth of Religious Neutrality: An Essay on the Hidden Role of Religious Belief in Theories* (Notre Dame: University of Notre Dame Press, 1991), 330; John H. Brooke, *Science and Religion: Some Historical Perspectives* (Cambridge: Cambridge University Press, 1991), 422.

[61] James T. Cushing, *Quantum Mechanics: Historical Contingency and the Copenhagen Hegemony* (Chicago: University of Chicago Press, 1994); Henry J. Folse, *The Philosophy of Niels Bohr: The Framework of Complementarity* (Amsterdam: North Holland, 1985); Max Jammer, *The Philosophy of Quantum Mechanics: The Interpretations of Quantum Mechanics in Historical Perspective* (New York: John Wiley & Sons, 1974); Helge Kragh, *Cosmology and Controversy: The Historical Development of Two Theories of the Universe* (Princeton: Princeton University Press, 1996).

[62] Gerald Holton, *Thematic Origins of Scientific Thought: Kepler to Einstein* (Cambridge, Mass.: Harvard University Press, 1973/1980), introduction.

[63] Robert John Russell, "Steps Towards a Theology of Nature in the Thought of Ian. G. Barbour" (Atlanta, Ga.: American Academy of Religion, 1986), 11.

[64] Robert John Russell, "Cosmology and the New World of Faith," Templeton/ASA Lectures Series ((unpublished), 1994).

[65] Tillich's "method of correlation," which I had read as an undergraduate and again in seminary, offered an early hint in this direction. The figure was first published in Robert John Russell, "The Relevance of Tillich for the Theology and Science Dialogue," *Zygon: Journal of Religion & Science* 36.2 (June 2001): 269–308. Tracy offers an interesting comparison of his methodology and Tillich's in David Tracy, *Blessed Rage for Order: The New Pluralism in Theology* (Chicago: University of Chicago Press, 1975), 271, esp. ch. 3.

[66] The presence of emergent properties and processes in his epistemic hierarchy allows Peacocke to defend the integrity and semi-autonomy of theology against reductionist claims that seek to translate it entirely into psychological language. In the following quotation I see Peacocke as striking out against the vector of thought that leads from Bultmann to the Jesus Seminar by arguing that:

> The concept of "resurrection" need not be reducible to any purely psychological account and the affirmations of the New Testament that propose this concept can properly be claimed to be referring to a new kind of reality hitherto unknown because not hitherto experienced. Such a proposal is parallel to those whereby emergent realities are apprehended in any hierarchy of complex systems studied by the sciences and so given at tentative ontological status. (Peacocke, *Theology for a Scientific Age*, 280–81).

[67] John B. Cobb Jr. *Beyond Dialogue: Toward a Mutual Transformation of Christianity and Buddhism* (Philadelphia: Fortress Press, 1982). Ironically, this book emerged from Cobb's extended stay at Ryukoku University and now my own work bears, I hope, a similar imprint thanks to the discussions and hospitality of Professor Takeda. I greatly appreciate Cobb's writings on Buddhism and Christianity and I have adopted and attempted to expand his methodology to include a three-way interaction between Buddhism, Christianity, and science in Robert John Russell, "Beyond Dialogue: Toward a Mutual Transformation of Christianity, Buddhism and the Natural Sciences," ed. Ryusei Takeda (Kyoto, Japan: Ryokoku University, 2005), 71–100.

[68] I have found the diagram very helpful in overcoming some confusions in the field. As I suggest in chapter 4, Polkinghorne describes his approach as though he were following path

3, arguing for a philosophical interpretation of chaos theory as supporting a theology of divine action. Using the diagram I claim, however, that Polkinghorne is *actually* following path 7 in claiming that "holistic chaos" exists in nature and that scientific research could discover it.

[69] I am grateful to George Ellis for suggesting this label when he edited my essay Robert John Russell, "Eschatology and Physical Cosmology."

[70] Twentieth-century Christian eschatology is routinely framed in terms of classical science and ordinary understandings of space, time, matter, and causality. Hence it must first be reconstructed in light of contemporary physics (for example, relativity, quantum mechanics, cosmology) before its real potential for new visions of the universe can be assessed.

Chapter 1

The Contingency of Creation and Big Bang Cosmology[1]

> The existence of the world as a whole and of all its parts is contingent....It owes its existence to the free activity of divine creation.[2]
>
> —Wolfhart Pannenberg

We live in an age of boundless discovery. More has been learned about our world in the last few decades than had been learned over the previous millennia of recorded history. Our generation cut its teeth on Apollo 12 and the microchip, Einstein and Crick, the artificial heart, the laser and nuclear fission. Yet we are a people of tradition, rooted and growing in the biblical witness to a creator God whom we worship and proclaim in our churches and in our lives. What then does it mean to believe that the God who acts in history is the creator of the universe, "maker of heaven and earth"?

The gleaming goal of consonance with its intense joy—and the dusty reality of dissonance with its eroding disappointment—mark the lives of so many of us caught "far from equilibrium" in the intellectual and spiritual milieu of "science and religion." To continue to demark one from the other, as has been tried for centuries, no longer seems fruitful.[3] Yet what are our options?

I believe we stand at the brink of a new Reformation, one in which all we think and believe will be rethought in new terms. If it is to be faithful to its mission, the church can no longer ignore this crisis of meaning—or the opportunity for renewal. We must begin to make sense of our theology in terms of the implications of today's science if we do not want to lose our most cherished traditions. But if the risk is great so too is the reward: a new era of exchange between our knowledge of the universe and our belief in God, a new awakening of spiritual insight and ethical motivation.

Fortunately there are a few who feel the urgency of this situation. One of the leaders is Arthur Peacocke, British biochemist and Anglican theologian. Peacocke urges, "Any affirmations about God's relation to the world, any doctrine of creation, if it is not to become vacuous and sterile, must be about the relation of God to, the creation by God of, the world which the natural sciences describe. It seems to me that this is not a situation where Christian, or indeed any, theology has any choice."[4]

In this spirit I will explore the doctrine of creation in the context of contemporary physical cosmology.[5] The first step will be to survey both the creation tradition and Big Bang cosmology, looking for the role of contingency as a concept common to each, and articulated in terms of origins, finitude, dependence, and the future.

1. The Christian Creation Tradition

The central affirmation of Jews and Christians is that the God who saves is the God who creates. As the Psalmist writes, "Help comes from the Lord, who made heaven and earth" (Ps. 121:2). Throughout the Hebrew Scriptures, the God who works through the history of Israel, freeing the Jews from captivity in Egypt and bringing them to the Promised Land, hearing their prayers in Babylon, and releasing them from Exile, is not only a tribal God but the very God who created "the heavens and the earth." Christians, celebrating the New Creation in Jesus the Christ who gives victory over death, proclaim this Jesus as the same Word of God by which all things are created, the life and light of the world. Though expressed in the context of, and often opposed to, indigenous cosmologies of its period, the underlying vision of scripture is "God as creator" and "the world as creation."

In the early church the creation tradition was articulated in two distinct models: *creatio ex nihilo* (creation out of nothing) and *creatio continua* (continuing creation). The former dominated patristic thought as it sought to reject Platonic and Neoplatonic cosmology. Continuing creation was rooted in this period but remained less developed during the history of Christian thought. The difference as well as the similarity of these traditions is worth noting.

A. Creatio ex nihilo

The *ex nihilo* tradition has continued in varying forms from its inception in the patristic period through the writings of both Catholic and Protestant theologians.[6] In its contest with Greek culture, the church sought to reject both metaphysical dualism, in which the world was an eternal divine substance equal to and over against God; moral dualism, in which the world was an evil power resisting a good God; emanationism, in which the world emerged from and was the body or substance of God; and monism (or pantheism), in which the world was God.

Hence the *ex nihilo* argument first of all affirms that God alone is the source of all that is, and God's creative activity is free and unconditioned. For example, the world was not merely shaped out of pre-existing matter by the Demiurge who gazed at a set of transcendent forms, as Plato taught in the *Timaeus*. Neither the material of this world, nor the set of possible patterns it can assume, existed prior to God's creative activity; rather, these were created by God in the process of creating the world. And while God is the source of the world, the world is not just a part of God, a direct emanation of God's being. Rather it is an autonomous and distinct reality *created* by God. Hence though the world is real and good, it is neither God nor anti-God. The world is contingent, finite, temporal, and relative, for only God is necessary, infinite, eternal, and absolute. Finally as a creation by God, the world is characterized by freedom, purpose, and beauty.

A corollary to *creatio ex nihilo* that is pertinent to our subject is the point frequently made about the roots of the empirical method. Since God creates freely, under no jurisdiction or rule of necessity, the world is radically contingent: it need not be at all and it need not be the way it is. Hence for us to know the world we must set out on the path of discovery. Empirical science embodies as its methodological presupposition this Judeo-Christian view of nature framed in the doctrine of creation.

B. Creatio continua

The notion of *creatio continua* stands for God's continuing involvement with the world. Not only does God relate to creation as a whole but also to every moment, and God's fundamental relation is as creator. Hence God not only creates the world as a whole but every part of it. Though older than the *ex nihilo* tradition, *creatio continua* is a less developed doctrine of creation.

In the static cosmologies of medieval, Renaissance, and Enlightenment periods, the term "creation" was usually intended to mean "creation at the beginning," and God's present relation to the world was understood in terms of divine providence, concurrence, and government. However, with the rise of modern geology, evolutionary biology, and thermodynamics in the nineteenth century and Einsteinian cosmology in the twentieth, as well as the changing climate in philosophy, a new theological perspective is now emerging—at least in some circles. A growing number of theologians now stress the dynamics, indeterminacy, and novelty of nature *(including* human nature) as critical loci of God's participation in the universe. In this perspective God is continuously creating the world anew, guiding and urging humankind toward fulfillment and consummation in the Spirit.

So whether as a relatively separate tradition, as Ian G. Barbour[7] and Arthur Peacocke[8] suggest, or as a subordinate part of the *ex nihilo* tradition, as Phil Hefner,[9] Wolfhart Pannenberg,[10] and Jürgen Moltmann[11] suggest, an increasing number of theologians working to appropriate a scientific perspective seem to agree on the emerging vitality and importance of *creatio continua*.[12]

2. Contingency in Creation Theology

As we see in both Roman Catholic and Protestant thought, the philosophical sense of the dependence of the finite world on God is taken up into the concept of *contingency*. States of affairs or things are contingent when they are neither self-evident nor necessary. According to Karl Rahner, "Contingency is the . . . philosophical counterpart of the theological notion of createdness, since this latter more explicitly grasps the free production of the contingent and knows that the "first" creative deficient cause is identical with the living God whom man encounters in saving history."[13] Similarly, Paul Tillich identified contingency with creatureliness when he wrote: "Man is a creature. His being is contingent; by itself it has no necessity, and therefore man realizes that he is the prey of nonbeing."[14] The connection between contingency, dependence, and finitude is evident in Langdon Gilkey's summary of the creation tradition: "Creatures, that is, the finite world of created things, have a being or existence which is at one and the same time dependent upon God, and yet is real, coherent and 'good.'"[15] Wolfhart Pannenberg makes perhaps the clearest connection with science, though, in his extensive treatment of contingency in a variety of forms. According to

Pannenberg, "any contemporary discussion between theology and science should focus in the first place on the question of what modern science and especially modern physics can say about the contingency of the world as a whole and of every part in it."[16]

In *ex nihilo* theology the concept of contingency tends to denote finitude and purpose while the *continua* tradition focuses attention on the contingent in the emergence of novelty and an orientation toward future fulfillment. Of course there are important thematic differences between the two creation models. For example, *creatio ex nihilo* tends to emphasize God's transcendence of the world, while *creatio continua* underscores the presence and immanence of God at the heart of nature and human history. Yet in both traditions we find the total dependence of all-that-is on God. The finite world depends on God for its very being as such, and for its being, moment by moment.

Given the centrality of the philosophical meaning of contingency in both creation theology and contemporary natural science, we need to clarify the variety of meanings implicit in this term. In order to do so, particularly in light of the way Pannenberg writes about contingency, I recently developed a typology which sorts out these various meanings into three basic distinctions, each of which contains at least two further distinctions.[17]

A. Global contingency

By this term I mean to refer to the contingency of the universe considered as a whole. It includes a further distinction between ontological and empirical aspects. Thus *global ontological contingency* refers to the idea that the sheer existence of the universe as a whole is contingent. This form of contingency is what theology traditionally means by claiming that the world is contingent, namely that it need not exist and that its existence as such depends on God as its Creator *ex nihilo*. *Global empirical contingency* refers to the empirical features that characterize the universe as a whole—both their existence and their particular characteristics. These features include the origin of the universe with the beginning of time ($t=0$) in Big Bang cosmology, the laws of nature, the natural constants occurring in these laws such as the speed of light c and Planck's constant h, and the precise form of these laws and the precise value of these natural constants. The "Anthropic Principle" points to these features as we shall see below.

B. Local Contingency

Here I wish to refer to the contingency of each part of and process within the universe. It too includes ontological and empirical aspects. Thus *local ontological contingency* refers to the sheer existence of each and every part and process found in nature, namely that none need exist necessarily, that their very existence raises the question of "why" not in terms which can be explained by causal relations as given by science but in terms of the moment-by-moment mystery of the continued existence of anything at all. *Local empirical contingency* refers to the empirical features of each and every part and process found in nature and expresses the question implied in these features, namely why each part and process continues in existence with these specific features and whether such processes are open to causal explanation. So for example "inertia" embodied in Newton's first law offers a kind of explanation for why things remain in uniform relative motion when not acted upon by an external force but it is still a contingent feature of matter.

C. Nomological contingency

This concept includes a variety of forms of contingency reflected in the laws of nature that are not addressed fully above. In this article we will explore *absolute nomological contingency*, which starts with the contingency of the laws of nature (as above) and then moves to the next level of abstraction, the possible contingency of the laws of logic which underlie them, and so on. The most important form of nomological contingency, however, points to the fact that some, perhaps all, of the laws of nature have a first instantiation. I have called this *first instantiation contingency*.

This "first instance" contingency, in turn, can be read in a mild or an aggressive way. In the mild way, it is certainly clear that, even if there were a moment of absolute origination of the universe, not all of the laws of nature were manifest then. For example, in a cooling universe, atoms first occur when electrons are finally able to combine stably with protons; hence chemical properties and the rules they obey have a first instantiation. Similar arguments hold for macromolecules and for all the other steps in chemical and biological evolution. Mild first instantiation contingency is closely related to what many philosophers of science call "emergence" in nature: the occurrence of new processes and properties of complex systems which cannot be reduced to the processes and properties of simpler component systems. It also suggests that if new properties and processes begin in time, their meaning can only be fully disclosed through their future history.

In the aggressive way, first instantiation contingency gives a nomological framework for considering something as radically new as the resurrection of Jesus of Nazareth. The resurrection is, purportedly, the "first instantiation" of a new form of nature (the "New Creation") which represents a transformation of the present nature *beyond* what emergence refers to. It is the result of a radically new act of God in which both an event, the bodily resurrection of Jesus of Nazareth, *and* the "background conditions" of his environment, as described by the appearances traditions in the Gospels, are themselves transformed as well. If emergence is an element of novelty or discontinuity within an overarching framework of continuity (for example, the beginnings of evolutionary biology layered upon pre-existing fundamental physics), then aggressive first instantiation contingency consists primarily in discontinuity (for example, resurrection is not just resuscitation) within which a small element of continuity is maintained (for example, it is the same Jesus of Nazareth who is now the Risen Lord). Compared with emergence, it is an inverting of the relative importance of discontinuity, which becomes the key factor, and continuity, which plays a derivative role. What I am referring to as aggressive first instantiation contingency plays a crucial role in Pannenberg's argument for the historicity of the resurrection, for his claim that the meaning of contingent processes which begin with a first instance in nature will only be fully clear at the end of history (that is, eschatologically) and in his conclusion that the presence of such processes in the universe give the universe a historical character.[18]

How does contemporary science shape the meaning of these various forms of contingency and in doing so reflect both what I will call "consonance" and "dissonance" between the doctrine of creation and scientific cosmology? Let us pursue this by turning to Big Bang cosmology where at least some implications may be found for one or more aspects of the multiple forms of contingency discussed above.

3. The Big Bang: A Brief Look

In his special theory of relativity (1905), Albert Einstein took the first step in establishing modern cosmology. In this theory, space and time are put on an equal footing, combined as a four-dimensional continuum called spacetime. With the new arena of spacetime our intuitive notions of the simultaneity of events and of the lengths of objects are altered. Here space or time measurements alone, such as the size of a soaring rocket or the rate at which a moving watch ticks, lose their individual meaning, blending together in a deeper spacetime whole. Like the shadow of a rotating ruler, they seem to contract and expand—though the ruler does not.

Einstein's subsequent work on the general theory of relativity (c. 1915) is a theory of gravity. For Newton gravity was a force exerted between masses as they moved about in space. Einstein took a radically new approach. Whereas the spacetime geometry of special relativity was "flat" (or pseudo-Euclidean), in general relativity theory, spacetime is allowed to curve. Instead of particles being forced into curved paths by the force of gravity as Newton suggested, Einstein depicts the natural motion of particles by the naturally bent paths of curved spacetime. What determines the curvature of spacetime? For this Einstein turned back to matter and created a "closed circuit" between the two great ideals of natural order: form and content. In Einstein's view, the structure of space-time, its size, shape, and texture, is dependent on the distribution of matter, while the motion of matter is determined by the local curvature of spacetime. In the phrase of Misner, Thome, and Wheeler: "Space tells matter how to move; matter tells space how to curve."[19]

Given general relativity, what sort of predictions could be made about the nature and history of the universe? Imagine trying to describe a universe of a trillion trillion stars with one or two simple equations; this was precisely what scientists did early in this century. They returned to the mathematics of Einstein's theory and explored two different models that could apply to the universe as a whole. Both of them are expanding in time from a singularity of zero size and infinite density at t=0 (where t is physical time). In the so-called "open" model, a saddle-shaped surface, *infinite* in size, expands forever, while in the "closed" model, a spherical-shaped surface, *finite* in size, expands up to a maximum radius, then recontracts to the final singularity.

But these are just mathematical models. How can we relate them to the data astronomers give us? First, we shouldn't miss the fact that even the visible portion of our universe is *enormous:* There are at least 100 billion stars in our galaxy alone and easily a trillion such galaxies within the limits of present-day telescopes. Still, astronomical observations show that galaxies are grouped in the form of clusters, each containing on the average 100 million million stars, and that these clusters are distributed *evenly* throughout spacetime! Moreover in the 1920s, Edwin Hubble discovered that light from these is redshifted, and after much debate, the predominantly held interpretation was that these galactic clusters are *receding* from us and from one another. Although debate continued into the following years, it is reasonable to view this era as the one in which the expansion of the *universe* had been discovered![20]

This is a staggering fact! Modern cosmology depicts the universe as radically historical, evolving from an initial point 13–15 billion years ago. Moreover, its expansion is slowing down. If the closed, finite model is correct, the slowdown will continue until the universe reaches a maximum size, after which contraction will begin until the universe is once again arbitrarily small some 50–100 billion years from now. If, however, the universe is open and infinite in size, as most evidence currently suggests, it will continue expanding forever, growing steadily colder and more dilute.

Now I wish to try to draw out the implications of Big Bang cosmology for creation theology. I will do so by posing three questions: (1) What about the beginning? (2) Is the universe finite? (3) Is the universe necessary?

4. Implications for Creation Theology

A. "In the beginning . . ."?

"Gravitational collapse confronts physics with its greatest crisis ever. At issue is the fate, not of matter alone, but of the universe itself."[21]

To many, the most profound claim of standard Big Bang cosmology is the seeming discovery of an absolute beginning of the universe at t=0. Within science this claim is taken very seriously for several reasons. 1) As we approach the singularity at t=0, gravitational tidal forces, densities, and temperatures increase without limit. 2) t=0 is an irremovable mathematical feature of these models.[22] 3) These models, in turn, carry enormous explanatory power. They provide an integrative framework that links together the results of evolutionary biology, physical chemistry, geology, solar physics, galactic astrophysics, the relative abundances of elements in the universe, and many other disparate areas of physical science into a consistent framework. The ages of each system under study nest properly: The geological age of the earth is consistent with the age of the sun. Physical cosmology gives a unified interpretative scenario through which the universe developed from an embryonic fireball into the present composition. Recent work in high energy physics when projected back to the temperatures of the earliest epoch of the universe suggest even more unified scenarios for all of fundamental physics. 4) Physics gives little room for speculation for what could lie before t=0, where tidal forces, temperature, and density become infinite. All that *is* seems to be the outcome of initial conditions at an initial starting point which, within these models, is without physical precedent or cause, and which therefore seems outside of scientific study. Because of this, to many physicists, the embarrassing thing about modern cosmology is its seeming inability to eternalize matter. What then are we to make of the initial singularity? Should theology be enlisted in some way?

Amazingly, some secularists attribute to t=0 a direct religious implication. The June 1978 issue of the *New York Times* contained an article by NASA's Robert Jastrow, an avowed agnostic, entitled "Found God?" Here Jastrow depicts the theologians to be "delighted" that astronomical evidence "leads to a biblical view of Genesis." The article ends by describing the beleaguered scientist who, as in a bad dream, after scaling the highest peak of discovery finds a "band of theologians . . . [who] have been sitting there for centuries."[23] I recently heard him speak about this issue. Though claiming to be agnostic, he argued without reservation for the religious significance of t=0: It is beyond science and leads to some sort of creator.

A more subtle but strongly positive response came from the Vatican in 1951. In an address to the Pontifical Academy of Science, Pope Pius XII praised cosmologists for disclosing astrophysical evidence which is "entirely compatible" with theological convictions about divine creation. Although prescinding from a claim of "absolute proof" throughout the text, in a final effluence of praise the pope concluded: "Thus, with that concreteness which is characteristic of physical proofs, it has confirmed the contingency of the universe and also the well-founded deduction as to the epoch when the cosmos came forth from the hands of the Creator. Therefore, God exists!"[24] Conservative Protestant circles have also welcomed Big Bang cosmology as supporting a historical interpretation of the doctrine of creation.

On the other hand there have been numerous critics of these theological overtones within scientific *and* religious circles. Here one thinks of the Roman Catholic cosmologist and key architect of contemporary cosmology, G. Lemaitre, who disavowed the papal endorsement of its theological implications. Many other scientists rejected the religious overtones of t=0 and even challenged the scientific standing of Big Bang cosmology itself because of these overtones. Most notable among these is Fred Hoyle, who helped construct an alternative model precisely for this reason. In Hoyle's steady state model the universe has an infinite past and continues to expand forever. Since its predictions include matter spontaneously "popping" into existence from time to time to keep the cosmic density constant, this has frequently been called (ironically!) the "continuous creation" model. It was eventually abandoned after the discovery of the microwave background radiation that strongly favors the Big Bang theory. Nevertheless, the fact that a scientifically acceptable alternative cosmology was possible should make us at the very least cautious of using cosmology (Big Bang or steady state) to give direct support to *any* theological position whether that position be theistic *or*, as with Fred Hoyle, atheistic.

Indeed, one could take the approach within theology that *any* physical cosmology that science generates, including one without an initial singularity or a finite age, is at least compatible with the heart of the Christian creation tradition in its insistence on the *ontological* dependence of all-that-is on God. Neo-orthodox, existentialist, and liberal theology have stood passionately and uncompromisingly for the radical separation of science and religion and hence the complete independence of religious doctrine from secular cosmology. One need only think of Karl Barth and Paul Tillich to gauge the sweeping power of this position in contemporary theology. And such a separation is, naturally, advocated by most professional scientific societies, including the prestigious American Academy of Sciences.

There are of course deep philosophical and scientific grounds for caution. The method of science is based on causal explanation, whether deterministic (in the extreme case, Laplacian) or statistical (either for mathematical or physical reasons). From this point of view t=0 cannot finally refer to a physical state but at best it can represent a mathematical limit in the theory, suggesting the need for a new cosmology to replace it. Indeed, Newtonian cosmology gave way to Einsteinian, and the latter will eventually be replaced since it does not take into account quantum effects—the physics of the microscopic. Inflationary cosmologies are already being explored, which account for many of the "inexplicable" features of our universe, such as its homogeneity and isotropy. Though I cannot extensively discuss quantum physics in this chapter, it is clear that such effects in cosmology become critically important near t=0, precisely at the initial moments of the universe, since then the size of the universe is microscopic. Will new cosmological models influenced by quantum gravity predict a "bounce" and hence an "oscillating" universe, infinitely old already, with an infinite set of oscillations in the future? If our current views could so radically change, what is there about present cosmology that will survive the change—and how can we know what it is in advance?[25]

Alternatively, if we identify t=0 as having religious significance, how can we simply ignore other striking features of the *same model*? If the universe is describable in terms of an open Big Bang model, wouldn't we have to deal with the prediction of an infinite future? Such a model makes the universe infinite in size. What does this do to other theological issues such as the doctrine of God or eschatology? (See Figure 1.1.) We will be in a very awkward position if we "pick and choose" after the fact, selecting those features that favor our theological perspective and ignoring those that count against it.[26]

	Time (Past)	Time (Future)	Space
Closed Model	finite	finite	finite
Open Model	finite	*infinite*	*infinite*

Figure 1.1: Finitude and Infinitude in the Simplest Big Bang Models

So caution is clearly in order. Nevertheless one is still tempted to seek out some positive relation between scientific results and theological affirmations.

Notre Dame philosopher Ernan McMullin suggests what might be the narrow path between extremes. He believes we should aim at a "coherence of world-view" in which theology and cosmology are "consonant in the contributions they make to this world-view" although this consonance is always in "slight shift." Applied to the problem of the ultimate beginning, he concludes:

> What one *could* readily say, however, is that if the universe began in time through the act of a Creator, from our vantage point it would look something like the Big Bang that cosmologists are now talking about. What one cannot say is, first, that the Christian doctrine of creation "supports" the Big Bang model, or second, that the Big Bang model "supports" the Christian doctrine of creation.[27]

Can we generalize McMullin's position on consonance? In succeeding sections I will try to do so by trying out several tentative hypotheses about cosmos and creation. The first step is to reframe the question of t=0 in terms of the *spacetime* character of Einstein's work.

B. Is the universe finite?

The idea of the origin of the universe at t=0 is only one aspect of the more general concept of finitude. Related to its age, we can ask if the universe is finite or infinite in size and whether it will go on forever or someday end.

Of course we can only answer questions like these within one or another model of the universe. No data is sufficient to force us into univocal answers as to its age, size, or future. Within the two options afforded by the standard Big Bang models, most scientists presently believe that the data indicate that the universe is marginally open, though many still hope it will turn out to be closed for theoretical reasons. This conclusion is based on estimates of the average density of matter in the universe that in turn come from observing galactic clusters, estimates of dark matter, assuming that certain elementary particles such as neutrinos are massless, and other factors. If this is the case the universe is already infinite in size and will expand forever. If neutrinos are in fact massive, the universe would probably be closed. Clearly the issue is far from settled!

Yet from a spacetime perspective, the size or finitude of the universe becomes an even more intriguing and elusive concept since space and time are really more like directions on a four-dimensional "object."[28] From this perspective we can ask whether spacetime stretches in all directions to infinity, or whether it has edges along some directions or folds back smoothly onto itself like a sphere along others. Since the closed universe is spatially finite and since it has a finite past and a finite future, as a spacetime model it can be classified as *homogeneous* or strictly finite. Its spatial sections are smooth spheres, finite in size with no edges, but in reaching back into the finite past or forward into the finite future, we come to a singularity whose structure, at least in some mathematical representations, is like an edge. Hence its finitude is bought at a price; the essential singularity that poses the greatest crisis physics has ever faced, according to John Archibald Wheeler.[29]

Strange as this may be, the open model raises an even more intriguing paradox about infinity. In this model the universe is spatially infinite and its future is infinite; yet like the closed model its past age is *finite!* Therefore as a spacetime model it is *heterogeneous* or mixed, displaying both finite and infinite characteristics! (See again Fig. 1.1.)

Actually theoretical cosmology includes still other possible combinations of finitude and infinity if we modify Einstein's equations of general relativity to include a so-called cosmological constant, to which he ascribed the symbol *lambda.* This constant was originally introduced by Einstein because his initial calculations showed that even the simplest models of the universe were time-dependent: expanding or contracting, features that he considered unacceptable. Later after the redshift of distant galaxies was discovered, indicating that the universe actually was expanding, Einstein retracted the cosmological constant. Recently, however, a number of theorists have argued for its reinclusion because of technical problems with the early universe.

If we include a nonzero value for the cosmological constant, seven theoretical models are permitted by general relativity. They may be classified according to the kind of infinities they assign to the past, future, and size of the universe, as summarized in Table 1.1.

Here types I (closed) and V (open) are the standard Big Bang models (with lambda equal to zero). Types II (the closed "hesitation universe"), III (a closed contracting universe, the time-reversal of type II), and IV (the closed "turnaround universe") are extensions of the closed model type I with positive lambda. Types VI (a contracting time-reversed version of type V) and VII are extensions of the open model for nonzero lambda. Except for type I, all of these models are *heterogeneous.* Interestingly, though one can have a homogeneously finite model, no *homogeneously infinite* model, such as Fred Hoyle's steady state model (represented here as type VIII) is possible in standard general relativity![30]

The pedigree of these models is clear: They arose out of a dominant paradigm in twentieth-century physics. Their value for us lies in that they offer a set of mathematically self-consistent representations of finitude and infinity within the framework of a dominant scientific paradigm. Of course the radical differences they suggest about the kind of universe we live in could lead one to abandon the attempt to draw theological conclusions from cosmology. Moreover, since most of these models have been rejected on empirical grounds one could object that they are irrelevant to theology and science today.

However what *is* significant for our purposes is not the present empirical status of any particular model, since that *will* constantly change. Instead the advantage of inspecting a set of recent, historical models is that the lessons gained may help us with the much more complex question of working at our own present frontier. Here too there lies a wealth of competing models, but we do not have tomorrow's hindsight in weeding out weak candidates among our current competitors. Moreover the most relevant factor for theology may not—indeed should not—be linked to a precise characteristic of the model that prevails but to something more general that characterizes all those models in competition at one time. In other words my view is that, while we ought not to expect a direct relation between t=0, temporal finitude, or any other individual feature in cosmology and theology, a concept such as contingency, operating at a more abstract and general level, can provide a common framework for relating creation theology and scientific cosmology. Hence I suggest that through the element of contingency the Einsteinian models we are considering do share something in common that could offer a fruitful element of consonance with theology, something that may continue to be in consonance even as we move into the future and discover new cosmologies beyond our present horizon.

Table 1.1: Cosmologies with Finite and Infinite Features

TYPE	TIME:	TIME:	SPACE	COSMOLOGICAL	TYPOLOGY
I	finite	finite	finite	0	closed standard model
II	finite	INFINITE	finite	+	closed "hesitation" model
III	INFINITE	finite	finite	+	closed
IV	INFINITE	INFINITE	finite	+	closed "turnaround" model
V	finite	INFINITE	INFINITE	0, +	open standard model
VI	INFINITE	finite	INFINITE	0, +	open
VII	finite	finite	INFINITE	—	open
VIII	INFINITE	INFINITE	INFINITE	—	open "steady state"

Eight types of cosmological models classified by their temporal and spatial infinities. Types I-VII are consistent with Einstein's *general relativity* (if we include a nonzero cosmological constant *lambda* in some cases). Type VIII, and a special case of type V (see note 25), represent the kind of homogeneous infinity found in Fred Hoyle's steady state cosmology.[31]

In this spirit I would venture a first working hypothesis: *The particular elements of contingency in a given cosmological model both interpret and limit the theological claim that creation is contingent.* We can test this hypothesis by a specific question: If finitude is an element of contingency, how do the various types of cosmologies interpret the temporal and physical meanings of finitude and what sorts of trade-offs qualify these meanings?

To unpack this further let's start with the notion of a finite past as the correlate of the theological affirmation of finite creation. Recall McMullin's argument: If we claim that "the universe began in time through the act of a Creator," and if we work within standard Big Bang cosmology, then such a finite past might provide a fruitful interpretation of divine creation; or, as he put it, "from our vantage point [the universe] would look something like the Big Bang that cosmologists are now talking about."

However, looking more closely at our cosmological models, we find that there are not one but four different models that depict the past as finite: I, II, V, and VII. *As far as a finite past is concerned, these models are equivalent:* they would all "look something like the Big Bang that cosmologists are now talking about," to use McMullin's phrase. Yet the kind of *future* they depict includes both varieties: finite (I and VII) and infinite (II and V). Similarly their *spatial size* includes both finitude (I, II) and infinity (V, VII). (They also vary in terms of the cosmological constant, lambda; in fact, in a deeper mathematical sense this is what accounts for their variety.)

Alternatively we might start with the requirement of a *finite size* as the correlate of theological finitude and hence contingency. Now we find a different set of appropriate models: I, II, III, and IV. Moreover in this case we couldn't be guaranteed of the finitude of time since some of these models involve temporal infinity (II, finite future; IV, infinite past and future). Figure 1.2 summarizes these results.[32]

Figure 1.2: Results of Table 1.1 Using Venn Diagrams

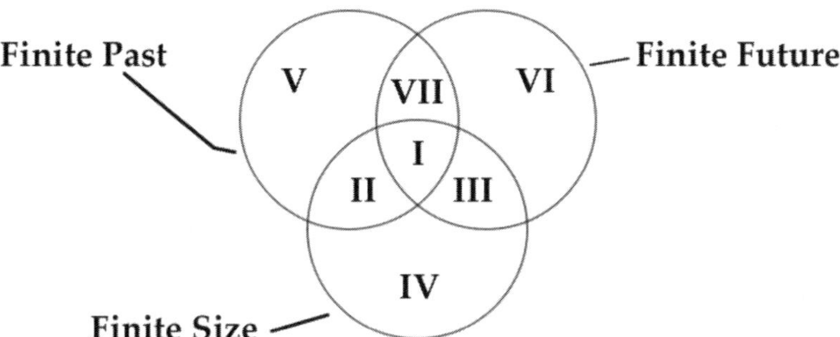

The circles in this graph represent the properties of finite past, finite future, and finite spatial size, respectively. Models lie in the areas that represent their finite properties. Hence type I, being homogeneously finite, lies in the intersection of all three circles. Types II, III, and VII are finite in two aspects; for example, type VII is finite in both past and future and hence lies in the area common to both upper circles but excluded from the lower circle. Types V, VI, and IV are finite in only one aspect.

What this analysis suggests is that we cannot equate contingency with something as loosely defined as finitude; we need to specify further what we mean by the claim that creation is finite, or that finitude is a mark of contingency. Moreover, when we specify what we mean by finitude in terms of time or space, contemporary cosmology both interprets and limits our terms: It admits temporal and spatial interpretations of finitude but it limits them by showing that we cannot claim that the universe is contingent in terms of *both* temporal and spatial finitude. The only exception is the fully finite model, type I. If we then move to identify contingency as finitude with type I uniquely, we run the perennial risk of tying creation theology to a particular physical model, the outcome we were trying to avoid by abstracting to the level of contingency.

Hence if we want to avoid a direct linkage between a specific cosmology (such as type I) and a particular interpretation of theological terms we must allow for a degree of *dissonance* as well as *consonance* between theological and scientific claims (for example, that the universe is in some respects infinite as well as finite). So we must extend McMullin's suggestion and define consonance more carefully: We may look for *consonance in terms of the temporal past*, so that the Big Bang that cosmologists are now talking about would count as a correlate to the theological concept of finitude in terms of a beginning in time through the act of a creator, but we cannot necessarily expect the future or the size of the universe to show a similar correspondence with the theological concept of finitude. In sum, we must accept the possibility of *consonance over the past but dissonance over the future and size, consonance over the future but dissonance over the past and size, and so on.*

Should the appearance of dissonance, and not just consonance, cause us to abandon our goal of constructively relating theology and science? My response is: no. Instead I see the realization of both consonance and dissonance as a positive aspect of this relationship. Its fruitfulness can best be seen by framing it as a meta-epistemological principle: *When comparing theological and scientific models of more abstract concepts, there will always be some agreement between some features of the theological and scientific models, but one cannot expect simultaneous agreement between all such features.* The contradictions (dissonances) as well as agreements (consonances) are beneficial: Without contradiction one would be open to reductionism or idolatry;[33] of course, without agreement one would be back in the problem of fully compartmentalized language games and nonintersecting spheres of rationality that we set out to overcome. The method then is to find the appropriate balance between consonance *and* dissonance.

C. The Anthropic Principle ("fine-tuning")

Just as t=0 and finitude lead to one form of contingency, so too does the idea that nothing in the universe seems totally self-sufficient or absolutely necessary. As Paul Tillich put it, "Man is a creature. His being is contingent; by itself it has no necessity, and therefore man realizes that he is the prey of nonbeing."[34]

If we generalize this same form of contingency and consider the universe as a whole we are led to ask: Why does the universe exist and why does it exist in precisely the way it does? Could things have been different?[35] The theological response, coming out of the creation tradition, has been to affirm the aseity and freedom of God as utterly distinct from the absolute dependence of all creation. In other words the church claims that the universe is contingent both *ontologically*, since nothing need be at all, and *existentially*, since the particular way it exists seems arbitrary. Traditionally anything less than this would appear to undermine the claim that God alone is both necessary being and free creator.

The consensus behind this position is underscored by a recent document of the World Council of Churches (c. 1975): "Nothing—not even space, time, matter, or the laws of physics—is self-explanatory. This is the most radical contingency imaginable. . . . The cosmos did not have to be at all. . . . Such questions have no answers within science, and their contemplation leads to some sort of theological inquiry."

But do these questions lie entirely outside of science? The surprising answer is that contemporary cosmology does seem to address this issue—and precisely by combining new scientific perspectives on the ontological and existential dimensions of global contingency! Even with the unimaginable vastness and complexity of the stars and galaxies in our universe, it now seems that the universe as a whole possesses some overall simplicity, some unifying features, that we can use to classify and compare our universe with other theoretically possible universes. If so, we can then ask whether these global features of our universe are arbitrary or whether there is some fundamental reason why they must be as they are. Perhaps the actual *existence* of our universe is connected to its own *particular* global characteristics!

First we must find a way of characterizing our universe as a whole, and then we can consider what alternative universes would be like. It turns out that there are fundamental constants scattered throughout the laws of physics which play a quixotic role in determining the most general features of, and hidden connections within, nature as a whole.[36] These include: Planck's constant, the speed of light, the charge of the electron, the proton and electron masses, the gravitational constant, and the Hubble constant. With a few simple combinations of just these fundamental constants we can characterize most of the global features of the universe. One way to approach the question of contingency, then, is to ask why the values of these constants are what they are.

Surprisingly, the answer is connected with the fact that our universe is one in which life has evolved. Pervading recent literature, the so-called Anthropic Principle[37] was first developed by Brandon Carter in 1974. According to this principle, the fundamental constants of nature must be such that "what we expect to observe must be restricted to the conditions necessary for our presence as observers. . . . The universe must be such as to admit the creation of observers within it at some stage," and this places *very stringent* restrictions on those physical constants mentioned already.[38]

To see this argument, consider a range of values for the physical constants c_1, c_2, c_3, and so on. Which of these values characterizes a universe that could, in principle, produce life—at least life as we know it? Carter argues that only a small subset of them could be such as to ever produce life. For example, the age of the universe must be consistent with the rate of stellar evolution, the production of heavy elements in stars and then novas that spill these elements into the surrounding space, the birth of a second generation of stars and planets, the evolution of life on these planets. Hence a much younger universe would not yet have produced life; a much older one would be long since barren and cooling. All of these phenomena in turn depend on the value of the physical constants falling within a very narrow range Δc_1, Δc_2, around very specific values (Figure 1.3a).

Hence the values of the constants that characterize *our* universe must fall within the small area where the dotted lines cross. In this sense our universe is "fine-tuned" for life. Perhaps Leibniz was correct in arguing that, even in spite of evil, this is the best of all possible worlds, since, if the Anthropic Principle is correct, it is the only one in which life is at all possible! In a marvelous passage from his autobiography, *Disturbing the Universe*, Freeman J. Dyson writes: "The more I examine the universe and study the details of its architecture, the more evidence I find that the universe in some sense must have known that we were coming."[39]

Does such "fine-tuning" lead to a new argument for design? Granted that life arose on earth through evolutionary processes from primordial matter, that is, through processes explained by and within the domain of science, why should such processes have occurred in the first place? Is this universe *as a whole* designed? And what kind of designer would this suggest? To put it directly, did God create *this* universe with this particular set of natural constants *ex nihilo* in order that life could evolve somewhere in it? Is God the "fine-tuner" of the universe? (See Figure 1.3b)

The Anthropic Principle points to the fine-tuning of the physics of *our* universe that makes biological life possible. Figure 1.3a illustrates the theoretical range in the values of the constants c_1 and c_2 and the tiny area where these limits cross which make life possible. Why is our universe consistent with these values? One response leads to an argument for God as the "fine-tuner" (Figure 1.3b). Another leads to a many worlds/many universes argument (Figure 1.3c). How are we to choose between them?

Although an intriguing and sophisticated case can be made for a type of generalized design argument leading to God as in more traditional forms of natural theology, I do not want to make such a case here.[40] One reason is that, like the problem of t=0, the Anthropic Principle is highly subject to changes in science. Even its standing within science remains extremely controversial, as indicated by the critical and often negative reaction to the massive study on the subject by John Barrow and Frank Tipler.[41] Another reason is that design-type arguments rarely carry significant theological "pay-dirt," since it is far from clear whether the God that emerges from them is related to the biblical witness to the Creator. John Leslie, for example, argues from the Anthropic Principle to a Neoplatonic, aesthetic/ethical divine principle and not to the biblical concept of God.[42]

Still we may now be able to find a degree of consonance between a) our theological perspective on the one hand—as informed independently of science by its primary sources in scripture, tradition, and religious experience—and b) on the other hand our evolutionary perspective on biological existence and our emerging cosmological perspective on the universe as a whole. Such a perspective might come from first appreciating the counterarguments to design that most physicists advance. Granting that our universe may be the only universe consistent with life, the real question becomes whether our universe is the only *actual* universe. The design argument seems, at face value, to assume that the only

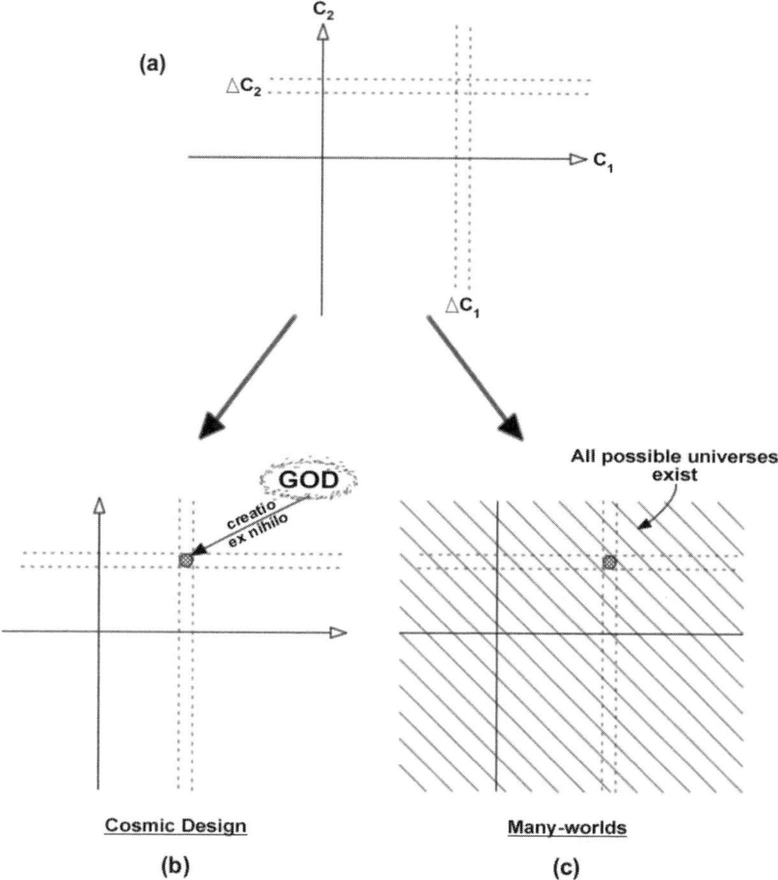

Figure 1.3: Anthropic Principle (fine-tuning): Argument for God or for many worlds?

actual universe is one that happens to be—miraculously—consistent with life. But suppose an infinity of universes actually exist: the "many-worlds" or "many-universes" scenarios proposed to overcome the apparent inference to God if ours is the only actual universe (Figure 1.3c). Inflationary cosmologies, for example, suggest that countless "bubbles" were thrown out in the early cosmic epoch, each forming its own universe. Our bubble universe, with its four dimensions and particular natural constants, is like a special, fragile, and fragrant island surrounded on all sides by an infinite lifeless sea of islands. But suppose *all such universes exist.* What would this imply about design and contingency?[43]

In my view even if such many worlds arguments receive support from science, the value of the design argument is not undercut; in essence we need not choose between a many-worlds theory and a design argument. Instead the design argument can be cast at a series of meta-levels that include the many-worlds option as part of the design! To make this explicit, we can imagine a series of levels of design contingency (Figure 1.4).

Level one, representing the standard form of the Anthropic Principle, is the space of all possible universes in which the same laws of physics apply but in which the constants vary. Each point in this space is one possible universe, and various regions of this space include universes consistent with life. Our universe is represented by a particular point in such a region, apparently of vanishingly small area, if the tight limits set by Anthropic Principle arguments on the size of the variation in the constants consistent with life are correct.

Level two, the first type of meta-Anthropic Principle, is the space of all possible laws of physics. Each point in this space represents a particular set of physical laws. Level one is thus a particular point in this space in which the physical laws are those that govern our universe. Each point in level two, being a level one-type space, contains an infinite set of possible universes consistent with those types of physical laws.[44]

LEVEL 5: ???
LEVEL 4: ???
LEVEL 3: different logical systems; same ???
LEVEL 2: different physical laws, same formal logic
LEVEL 1: varying constants; same physical laws

Figure 1.4: Levels of Design Contingency

Levels of design contingency include the space of all possible laws of physics (of which our laws, representing our universe and all other universes consistent with them, are one point); the space of all possible logical systems, each of which generates a space of possible laws of physics; and so on. Does the sequence of levels point to a designer? Is every level designed?

Now in level two we can point to a new form of the design argument, one in which God chooses not just which values of the natural constants to instantiate but, "prior" to that, which specific laws of physics to instantiate. Interestingly, physicist Jim Trefil writes: "For myself, I feel much more comfortable with the concept of a God who is clever enough to devise the laws of physics that make the existence of our marvelous universe inevitable than I do with the old-fashioned God who had to make it all, laboriously, piece by piece."[45]

And we can go further. Level three, the next level of meta-Anthropic Principles, is the space of all possible formal logical systems. Each point in this space represents one particular type of logic. The point representing traditional two-valued logic contains level two, since all known laws of physics are governed by this form of logic. Other points in level three represent multi-valued logic, nondistributive logic, and so forth. For each point there is an infinite set of possible physical laws, and for each such set an infinite set of universes distinguished by the values of the natural constants.

Similarly one could generalize to levels four, five, six, and so on. What I find interesting about this generalization of the standard Anthropic Principle is that each level involves an option between contingency (leading to design) and necessity (many-worlds); but the latter in turn leads to the next higher level with its own choice between contingency and necessity. For example, consider level one. Here one pursues the standard argument: Either our universe is the only actual universe, leading to a design-type argument to account for why this should be, or one assumes that all possible universes actually exist, consistent with the same laws of physics but differing in the values of their natural constants (the many-worlds option), thereby eliminating the novelty of our solitary existence.

But now note that we simply move to level two; after all, why should the laws of physics that govern level one be what they are? At level two these particular laws become one of an infinite set of possible laws, and again we have two options: Either they are the only set of actual laws, and a design argument is invoked to account for them, or else all possible laws are in effect, each producing their own space of level one-type possible universes.

If the latter is assumed, eliminating level-two contingency, we can still move to level three where these sets of laws are all the realization of a unique type of logic. Do other types of logic exist, leading to other types of laws, other types of constants, and other types of universes, or is only one kind of logic realized in all possible universes? If so, why? In this manner we can continue to move up the ladder of levels, finding a choice at each level: Either at a given level the series terminates in a unique point whose contingency serves as the basis of a design argument, or a given level is granted a many-worlds status, eliminating the contingency of any particular point in the level but leading to the next level and the same type of option. Even if the series of levels never ends, the series itself suggests its own form of design argument.

It is crucial to recognize that this particular series is not unique. A different, but equally valid, series could be constructed; for example, one in which we first generalize the laws of physics before the values of the constants. Clearly the levels in a particular series are not really successive abstractions from nature, since the higher levels in one series can always occur as the lower levels in another. Rather they are alternative ways to organize the meaning of contingency *within* a particular scientific theory, such as Big Bang cosmology, and they provide alternative perspectives on the complex of inherent contingency in the physical universe.

I believe this kind of analysis tells us two things about constructing a theology of creation. First, no matter how strong an explanation science can give of "the way things are," an element of the unexplained always remains; hence science will never eliminate the meaningfulness of contingency in the creation tradition. Indeed, since empirical science is based on the contingency of the world, every scientific theory will *be* compatible, at some level, with theology. In this sense one is never forced to choose between faith and science. Second, the kind of contingency which exists in each particular scientific theory provides a special context of meaning for our understanding of divine creativity. For example, if convincing arguments are given for preferring a many-worlds theory in level one, we should both accept the limitation this places on the theological meaning of contingency and yet press for the possibility of contingency at another level of generalization, perhaps one involving the laws of physics or the form of logic. In this way the discoveries of science are essential to the task of theology as *fides quaerens intellectum*, for science gives concrete language for our deepest insights about God's relation to creation.

Conclusion

In this chapter I propose that the concept of contingency is central to the doctrine of creation, both as *creatio ex nihilo* and *creatio continua*, and to contemporary scientific cosmology. Working primarily within Big Bang cosmology (and hence setting aside questions of quantum mechanics, thermodynamics, and other relevant areas of physics), I suggest various tentative hypotheses about t=0, finitude, design, and the eschatological future. These results are aimed at consonance between theology and science in which the empirical test of science will strengthen and trim the theological meaning of contingency.

The common role of contingency in both fields leads to a fresh perspective on why science and theology can be consistent with each other and need not be compartmentalized. *Every* scientific cosmology must include an element of contingency since it is precisely the role of these contingent elements in the theory to exclude that which is ultimate, absolutely necessary, *a se*, and hence to exclude "God" as part of the theoretical explanation. Hence *any* scientific cosmology must in *some* sense be consistent with the doctrine of creation since it ought not contain within it and proper to it a metascientific counterpart to the concept of God.[46]

On the other hand, if we want to move beyond consistency to consonance, the details of contingency in scientific models of the universe are *essential*. They both prune and fertilize the meaning of the doctrine of creation by providing an interpretative context with empirical pith. Hence by examining in detail the meaning of contingency in scientific cosmology, we may bring new vitality and joy to the root metaphors: "cosmos as creation" and "God as creator."

Endnotes: Chapter 1

[1]An earlier version was published as "Cosmology, Creation, and Contingency," *Cosmos as Creation: Theology and Science in Consonance*, Ted Peters, ed. (Nashville: Abingdon, 1989), 177–209.

[2]Wolfhart Pannenberg, "The Doctrine of Creation and Modern Science," *Zygon: Journal of Religion and Science* 23:1 (1988): 9, republished in Wolfhart Pannenberg, "The Doctrine of Creation and Modern Science," in Peters, *Cosmos as Creation,* 288, 152–76.

[3]Even though he stands outside the public religious circle, Stephen Weinberg closes his recent book on cosmology with a remark that I take as expressing the nihilism so characteristic of our age: "The more the universe seems comprehensible, the more it also seems pointless." Steven Weinberg, *The First Three Minutes: A Modern View of the Origin of the Universe* (New York: Basic, 1979), 154.

[4]A. R. Peacocke, *Creation and the World of Science* (Oxford: Clarendon, 1979).

[5]In this short chapter I will not examine the implications of quantum physics, quantum field theory, or nonlinear nonequilibrium thermodynamics, fruitful though these areas are, but will restrict my treatment to the specialized questions arising out of standard Big Bang cosmology and related models of the universe. Similarly, I will emphasize the meaning of creation theology in some forms of Protestant and Roman Catholic thought but leave aside the important critiques of process and deconstructionist theologies. A more extended discussion would argue that these other areas serve to relate novelty, the emergence of order from chaos, and the relation of chance and law to the creation tradition in important and differing ways.

[6]Langdon Gilkey, *Maker of Heaven and Earth* (Garden City, N.Y.: Doubleday, 1959).

[7]Ian G. Barbour, *Issues in Science and Religion* (New York: Harper & Row, 1966).

[8]Peacocke, *Creation and the World of Science.*

[9]Philip J. Hefner, "The Creation," in *Christian Dogmatics,* ed. Carl E. Braaten and Robert W. Jenson (Philadelphia: Fortress Press, 1984), 2 vols. 1:265–358.

[10]Wolfhart Pannenberg, "The Doctrine of Creation and Modern Science," *Zygon* 23:1 (March 1988): 3–21, and in altered form appearing in this volume.

[11]Jürgen Moltmann, *God in Creation: A New Theology of Creation and the Spirit of God* (New York: Harper & Row, 1985).

[12]Indeed process theologians rely exclusively on the continuous creation hermeneutic, finding no further value in maintaining *creatio ex nihilo.*

[13]Karl Rahner and Herbert Vorgrimler, *Dictionary of Theology,* 2nd ed. (New York: Crossroad, 1981), 94.

[14]Paul Tillich, *Systematic Theology,* 3 vols. (New York: Harper & Row for the University of Chicago Press, 1967), 1:196.

[15]Gilkey, *Maker of Heaven and Earth,* 47.

[16]See for example Pannenberg, "The Doctrine of Creation," 12. republished in Ted Peters, ed., *Cosmos as Creation,* 288, and Wolfhart Pannenberg, *Toward a Theology of Nature: Essays on Science and Faith*, ed. Ted Peters (Louisville, Ky.: Westminster/John Knox, 1993), 166.

[17]Robert John Russell, "Contingency in Physics and Cosmology: A Critique of the Theology of Wolfhart Pannenberg," *Zygon: Journal of Religion and Science* 23:1 (March 1988), 23–43. I added and slightly modified this short section here for convenience to the reader since this volume does not include a reprint of the *Zygon* article.

[18]See Wolfhart Pannenberg, *Jesus - God and Man*, trans. Lewis L. Wilkins and Duane A. Priebe, 2nd ed. (Philadelphia: Westminster, 1968/1977 [German: 1964]), 98; Wolfhart Pannenberg, *Theology and the Philosophy of Science*, trans. Francis McDonagh (Philadelphia: Westminster, 1976), 458, part one, section 6, esp. 66; Wolfhart Pannenberg, "Theological Questions to Scientists," in *The Sciences and Theology in the Twentieth Century*, ed. A. R. Peacocke (Notre Dame: University of Notre Dame Press, 1981), Question #2.

[19]Charles W. Misner, Kip S. Thome, and John Archibald Wheeler, *Gravitation* (San Francisco: W. H. Freeman, 1973), 5.

[20]For a careful study of the complex history of Big Bang cosmology see Helge Kragh, *Cosmology and Controversy: The Historical Development of Two Theories of the Universe* (Princeton, N.J.: Princeton University Press, 1996).

[21]Misner et al., *Gravitation,* 1198.

[22]See S. W. Hawking and R. Penrose, "The Singularities of Gravitational Collapse and Cosmology," Proceedings of the Royal Society of London A3J4 (1969), 529–48; and S. W. Hawking and G. F. R. Ellis, *The Large Scale Structure of Spacetime* (Cambridge: Cambridge University Press, 1973).

[23]For a more extended discussion, see Jastrow's *God and the Astronomers* (New York: W. W. Norton & Co., 1978).

[24] Pope Pius XII, "Mödern Science and the Existence of God," *The Catholic Mind* (March 1952): 182–92.

[25] Interestingly, an infinitely old universe takes us back to the problem of metaphysical dualism and the early battles fought over *creatio ex nihilo.* If there were a bounce, what has survived from the previous universe? According to many physicists, nothing more structured than fundamental particles could have survived the unbelievable temperatures during a bounce. Such temperatures would reduce any prior structures—galaxies, planets, civilizations, whatever—to quarks. In this sense even if the laws and elementary matter of our universe are infinitely old, our universe in all its macroscopic features is radically new since t=0! But what about the laws of physics? Do they govern all universes linked by bounces? Was God forced to work with physical laws as a modern equivalent of the Platonic forms and elementary particles as proto-matter in creating our universe? Or does even the spacetime arena, its dimensions and topological structures, and with it the particles and laws, evaporate at each bounce? What about the laws of logic, of which physics is only one form? Perhaps all these get created by a God who transcends all physical "beginnings."

[26]I still remember the scathing humor of a physics professor who caricatured theologians as "archers who first shoot their arrows, then paint the target: they can't miss—but then they can't afford to!"

[27]Ernan McMullin, "How Should Cosmology Relate to Theology?" in *The Sciences and Theology in the Twentieth Century,* Peacocke, 39–52.

[28]Is this a legitimate way to interpret physics? Many philosophers have stressed the irreducible role of time in subjectivity, and have been highly critical of any epistemology that rejects temporal passage and the distinction between past and future. Milic Capek, for example, argues that we should temporalize space, not spatialize time, as physicists do when they take spacetime to be a four-dimensional space. For a recent discussion see *Physics and the Ultimate Significance of Time,* ed. David R. Griffin (Albany, N.Y.: State University of New York Press, 1986). Actually nonequilibrium thermodynamics and quantum physics offer potentially fertile ways to reconcile subjective and physical time. See for example llya Prigogine and Isabelle Stengers, *Order Out of Chaos* (Toronto: Bantam, 1984). Since Einsteinian relativity is a classical theory in many senses, it is not surprising that it lends itself to a timeless interpretation. Nevertheless its perspective offers a way to study the question of finitude, and its timeless quality is generally accepted among physicists.

[29] Misner et al., *Gravitation*, 1198.

[30]This is not strictly correct. The Einstein-de Sitter cosmology, with type VIII infinities in time *and* space, can be interpreted as a limiting case of type V for positive lambda for very large "radius" (scale factor) and negligible matter density. For details see ibid., chapter 27, especially Box 27.5.

[31] Ibid., Box 27.5, 746–747.

[32]A similar though inverted figure could be drawn to suggest the infinities found in these models.

[33]Sallie McFague argues that when the "is not" quality of a metaphor is forgotten, the theological result is idolatry. Sallie McFague, *Metaphorical Theology* (Philadelphia: Fortress Press, 1982).

[34] Paul Tillich, *Systematic Theology*, 1: 196.

[35]When thinking about the universe in this way I am reminded of a passage from T. S. Eliot: "What might have been is an abstraction/Remaining a perpetual possibility/Only in a world of speculation./What might have been and what has been/Points to one end, which is always present." T. S. Eliot, "Burnt Norton," in *Four Quartets* (New York: Harcourt, Brace & World, 1943), 3.

[36]Sir Arthur Eddington and P. A. M. Dirac made the most significant early contributions to this argument, but there were many other persons involved in the "large numbers hypothesis" debate. For a careful history, see John D. Barrow and Frank Tipler, *The Anthropic Cosmological Principle* (Oxford: Clarendon, 1986), chapter 4.

[37]There are several versions of the Anthropic Principle, including so-called weak and strong forms. I am using the latter here. For more detailed discussion see ibid.

[38]Brandon Carter, "Large Number Coincidences and the Anthropic Principle in Cosmology," in *Confrontation of Cosmological Theories with Observation*, ed. M. S. Longair (Dordrecht: Reidel, 1974), 291–98.

[39]Freeman J. Dyson, *Disturbing the Universe* (New York: Harper & Row, 1979), 250.

[40]Tom Torrance points to yet another form of the contingency of the universe: "Since [the world] was created out of nothing, it might have been quite different from what it is, but now that it has come into being, it has a contingent necessity in that it cannot not be what it now is. Considered in itself, then, there is only *the* world, this world that has come into being, but considered from the side of God's creation it is only one of all possible worlds." Thomas F. Torrance, *Space, Time and Incarnation* (New York: Oxford University Press, 1969), 66. I am not sure whether Torrance means that all such possible worlds are actual and real, or whether they are only possibilities in the Creator's mind. It would be intriguing to explore this direction further.

[41]Barrow and Tipler, *The Anthropic Cosmological Principle.*

[42]John Leslie, "Modern Cosmology and the Creation of Life," in *Evolution and Creation*, ed. Ernan McMullin (Notre Dame: University of Notre Dame Press, 1985), 91–120. Clearly Leslie's conclusions are far removed from eighteenth-century deism, and hence ought not to be considered a design argument in the narrow sense.

[43]Taking a different tack, some believe that the universe should not be characterized by *any* arbitrary parameters. Ultimately all the laws of physics should be mutually interdeterminate. One sees this, for example, in the hermeneutic of self-consistency used so creatively in the bootstrap theory of particle physics by Geoffrey Chew. From this point of view our universe would be the *only* possible universe, and when a complete scientific cosmology is obtained, all the physical constants will fall out naturally from the theory.

[44]In many-worlds arguments based on a bounce model of the quantum-gravitational universe, Wheeler suggested that even the laws of physics, as well as the natural constants, get recycled with each bounce. This would conflate levels one and two in Figure 1.4.

[45]James S. Trefil, *The Moment of Creation: Big Bang Physics from Before the First Millisecond to the Present Universe* (New York: Collier, 1983), 223.

[46]Consequently theological programs, such as neo-orthodoxy, which separate their domains from science are not so much wrong as inadequate for both dogmatic and apologetic reasons. It would be worth exploring how substantial issues do arise between theism and naturalism or theism and pseudo-science when ultimate categories are introduced into a science-based worldview.

Chapter 2

The God Who Infinitely Transcends Infinity: Insights from Cosmology and Mathematics[1]

1. Introduction

A. Godtalk: Glimmers of Knowing Within the Horizons of Unknowing

Amidst the trappings of daily life we occasionally sense the presence of something which, though lying beyond the limits of our ordinary world, reaches up from the infinite depths that sustain our world to touch our lives and fill us with hope and compassion. In these moments, our eyes are drawn toward the boundless and mysterious horizon of our knowing and being, we become staggeringly aware of the beyond in our midst, and experience the astonishingly tender caress of that caring ultimacy in which "we live, and move, and have our being." We come away from these experiences enriched by a glimmer of understanding of what, or better yet Who, touched us, though our understanding lies within the all-encompassing mystery of its infinite, unknown source.

In seeking to articulate this numinous experience, we use the sacred and sublime word that millions of Jews, Christians and Muslims have used for centuries: "God." With this word we affirm the personal existence and ultimate reality of that which transcends us utterly—a transforming power and singular presence which has touched the innermost reaches of our self which even we can barely grasp. Our experience has left us overwhelmed with the realization, given as an irreducible datum, that this God who is absolute mystery is also our Creator and Redeemer, the source and goal not only of our life but also of the existence and destiny of the cosmos. It seems entirely fitting then that our talk about God should start with how little we know about God. Theology, which strictly speaking is "God-talk" (from the Greek word θέος for *God*, and λογος for *word*), starts with what we do not understand before it seeks to say something about that which we understand—at least in part. In the long traditions of Western monotheism, the way of unknowing leads us, and the way of knowing follows behind. These ways have come to be called the *via negativa* (the negative way of denial) and the *via positiva* (the positive way of affirmation), respectively. These ways are important when we talk about grace, creation, or atonement, for example, but they are particularly important when we attempt "God-talk" in the particular sense of discourse about the nature of God.

This means, in turn, that when we talk about God we should begin by attempting to say something about those divine attributes which we only know by negation, that is, by their utter contrast with our experience of ourselves and our universe. We should begin with what are called "apophatic" statements, from the Greek αποφ ατικος for *negative* or *denial.* The most inclusive of these attributes is the incomprehensibility of God. The word "God" stands for a self-surpassing mystery, an ineffable reality lying beyond all our thoughts and sensations, that which is wholly other. In a similar way, we speak apophatically when we refer to God's infinity and eternity as being in contrast with our finite and mortal world. Everything we experience in this visible world seems finite and limited, temporal and transitory. These phenomena come into existence, endure for a while, then pass away. They are really here now, yet soon they are gone forever. In stark contrast to this, however, is God, who alone is invisible, unlimited and infinite, everlasting and eternal, unchanging and constant. As the ground of being, God is the ultimate, unseen but ever-present reality. But this contrast, too, tells us something inestimably important about God's relation to the world: It is only by being incomprehensibly different from this world that God can be the source of this world and its final home. Thus the way of unknowing is, paradoxically, a way of knowing and a source of confident hope.

Having said that, we may also attempt to speak about what God has made known to us about God's nature and purposes, through scripture, tradition, personal experience—and now in the past three centuries and increasingly today through the great discoveries of the natural sciences. Here we can talk about God not by sheer contrast but by making a positive analogy with key experiences in our own lives and with the world in which we live. This way of speaking is called "kataphatic," from the Greek, κατάφασις, meaning *according to* or *by analogy*.

When we experience wonder and awe at the immensity and beauty of the universe we are led to think of God as utterly wondrous, terribly awesome, the source of ecstatic beauty. When we experience love in our lives, when we are forgiven our iniquities by those we have wronged, when we know the goodness of home, hearth, health, and family, we speak of God as perfect love, unconditional mercy, the source of all that is good, our final home beyond death and grief. Most importantly, when we look up from the daily routine of life and witness the sacred in our midst—as Moses did when he turned aside from tending to his sheep to go to see the burning bush (Exodus 3:1-6)—then we are compelled to confess God as utterly holy. Thus we are enveloped by the mystery of a God who surpasses all knowing; yet we know that this God seeks us and would be known by us, and so we move ahead in the light of this knowledge. To do so we must remember the poverty of faith in light of the surpassing mystery of God, and cloak all that we wish to affirm in the spreading folds of our unknowing. We explore the kataphatic on the grounds of the apophatic. The way of faith is always the way of humility.

Remarkably, many of us as scientists take a similar approach to the mystery of the universe around and in us. We find that the exploration of the universe requires that we may affirm and celebrate our discoveries only by first acknowledging an awareness of our vast ignorance of the cosmos, of all that we do not know and perhaps never will.[2] Near the end of his life, Sir Isaac Newton, one of the greatest scientists of all times, wrote:

> I do not know what I may appear to the world; but to myself I seem to have been only like a boy playing on the sea-shore, and diverting myself

in now and then finding a smoother pebble or a prettier shell than ordinary, whilst the great ocean of truth lay all undiscovered before me.[3]

And so the paths of science and theology both reflect the way of knowing as surrounded and held in perspective by the way of unknowing.

B. Godtalk: Focus on Infinity

In this chapter I want to explore the theological conversation about God and the scientific conversation about the world, to see how recent advances in cosmology and mathematics bear on this conversation. The key concept here will be *infinity*, including traditional notions of God's infinity in space and God's infinity in time, or eternity. Now, *infinity* is not a biblical term, nor does it carry a single meaning within the theological, philosophical, or scientific communities.[4] Moreover, whenever we move from the language of one community to that of another and across periods of time and history, we must recognize the differences, as well as the similarities, in meanings and connotations of languages.

Still, for the purposes of this chapter, I will assume that sufficient continuities exist between these various communities and periods of time to allow us to compare the meaning of the term *infinity* in a reasonable way. I hope to show that this term has in fact played a key role in all three communities—scientific, philosophical and theological—and that because of this, recent discoveries in the scientific community about infinity can have a direct bearing on our understanding of the concept God.

Why choose infinity? As I have already suggested, when we say that God is infinite and eternal, we normally do so by the *via negativa*: by way of utter contrast with the finite and temporal world that God created. This reflects a view of infinity which dates back to the ancient Greeks, where infinity is defined apophatically through its contrast with the finite: The infinite is called *apeiron,* meaning unbounded, unlimited, or formless. But is infinity utterly beyond our understanding, or can we know something about the meaning of infinity without exhausting all that can be true of it, reflecting the kataphatic way of knowing?

Recent developments in mathematics and in scientific cosmology may shed provocative new light on this issue. First of all mathematicians have now given us a new conception of infinity which is much more complex than previously thought, with layers of infinity leading out endlessly to an unreachable Absolute. In effect, we now can say a lot more about infinity than merely that it contrasts with the finite—indeed, an infinite amount more! How might these revolutionary discoveries in mathematics enhance our concept of God as infinite?

Secondly, we have moved from the ancient cosmologies of the Bible and the Greeks into the immensity of Big Bang cosmology, in which the universe is billions of light-years—or perhaps even infinite—in size and expanding in time. How can this revolutionary understanding of the immensity of nature help us appreciate the immensity and ineffability of the God who is its Creator?

Some see these developments as leading to pantheism, the equating of God and the universe, or to atheism, the outright rejection of God. Clearly these questions are extraordinarily complex and the relevant literature is enormous. Still in this chapter I will suggest that these fascinating developments in mathematics and cosmology actually clarify and increase our understanding of God the Creator as infinite and eternal and of the universe as dependent on God for its existence and purpose.[5]

2. A Brief History of Infinity in Mathematics and Cosmology

> It is possible to regard the history of the foundations of mathematics as a progressive enlarging of the mathematical universe to include more and more infinities.[6]

A. The concept of infinity in greek and medieval thought[7]

i) *Philosophy and mathematics.* The ancient Greek writers, who first developed both philosophy and mathematics, defined the concept of infinity as *apeiron* which means, literally, unbounded. In so doing, they gave what they thought was an unequivocal method for distinguishing the infinite from the finite: Something is infinite if it has no limit or end; it is boundless or unlimited or endless; it is chaotic, lacking any structure or order. In essence, they defined infinity by contrast to the finite: The infinite is totally different from, even opposed to, those things which make up ordinary experience.

We might balk at this definition, since there are many things in the world and in mathematics which have no end or limit or boundary but which are still finite. Think of the surface of the earth or the circumference of a ring, each of which has a definite size but no "edges" or intrinsic limits. Or think of the length of a line segment to see the irony here: The segment defined by 0 B x B 1 is finite since it is bounded at both ends (0 and 1) whereas the *smaller* interval 0 < x < 1 is unbounded. But surely the infinite is not less than the finite! Or is it?

Actually, paradoxes related to infinity such as these—and much more acute!—date back as far as ancient Greece, traceable to Zeno of Elea (490–430 B.C.E.). The classical example is the famous race between Achilles and the tortoise. Being slower, the tortoise is given a head start over Achilles, but being faster, Achilles overtakes the tortoise and wins the race. But how is this possible, since every time Achilles catches up to where the tortoise was, the tortoise has moved ahead a small amount, and so on, and so on. How is it possible for Achilles to pass the tortoise in a finite amount of time?

Through arguments like these, classical Greek thought came to view the finite world of our experience in sharp contrast with the infinite. Thus they believed that a formless and indeterminate infinity underlies the world of finite entities, and that finite entities are good precisely because they are formed, bounded, and determinate in contrast with the infinite.

Speculation concerning infinity traces back even farther into the past. Anaximander (610–547 B.C.E.) was probably the first Western philosopher to speculate in detail about infinity. For him, the infinite was understood as a spherical, limitless substance: eternal, inexhaustible, lacking boundaries or distinctions. The world of finite entities was seen as arising out of that which is infinite. Pythagoras (570–500 B.C.E.), too, rejected the infinite as having anything to do with the real world. He contended that all actual things are finite and representable by the natural numbers 1, 2, 3, and so on. Pythagoras taught that the geometrical forms—point, line, plane, and solid—arise when a mathematical limit is imposed on the underlying infinite structure. Plato (428–348 B.C.E.) believed that the Good must be definite rather than indefinite, and therefore it must be finite rather than infinite. According to Plato, God as the demiurge imposes limitations (that is, intelligible form) on pre-existent matter, giving rise to the structured world around us as an ordered whole instead of a formless, unintelligible (that is, infinite) chaos. In all these cases the infinite took on a negative quality compared with the finite.

But it was the philosopher Aristotle (384–322 B.C.E.) who provided a vital part of the conception of infinity which continued to pervade Western thought until the nineteenth century.[8] Aristotle altered the concept of infinity to mean an unending process, something unfinished or incomplete: "[T]he infinite has this mode of existence: one thing is always being after another, and each thing that is taken is always finite, but always different."[9] For example, consider the unending succession of natural numbers 1, 2, 3, . . . , the endless succession of the seasons, or the endless division of a line interval into smaller and smaller portions.[10] Aristotle apparently thought of these as potentially infinite, since the series can be continued endlessly, but not as fully or actually infinite. This is because an endless series can never be transcended by taking them serially, that is, one at a time. Going through successive elements in a series, we never get beyond the finite steps in the series to reach their term or limit—that is, the actually infinite—and view the infinite series as a whole. "It is plain from these arguments that there is no body which is *actually* infinite."[11]

This view was altered in part by Plotinus (205–270 C.E.), according to whom God, or the One, is infinite, being free of both internal and external limits.[12] Plotinus saw matter as evil because it is infinite, unbounded, and formless, following the philosophical tradition of the Greeks. But he also thought of the divine Mind as good because of its inexhaustible power, overwhelming unity, and self-sufficiency. Still the Absolute could not be considered infinite given the pejorative connotations of *apeiron*. Instead the Absolute is beyond conception or analogy with the finite world. Here, then, for the first time the infinite took on a positive quality, though it still carried the connotation of the unbounded and unlimited. With Plotinus, the notion of the infinite moves between that of Plato and that of the Christian tradition, for which the first attribute of God is infinity.

Early Christian writers were informed by this positive conception of infinity as they developed a doctrine of God based on Hebrew and Christian scripture, and in time the attribution of infinity to God became a standard cornerstone of Christian theology. Augustine (354–430), for example, was heavily influenced by Plotinus. He believed that since God is infinite, God must know all numbers and must have limitless knowledge of the world.[13] Still, the category of the infinite served to radically distinguish God from the world. Writing a millennium after Augustine and drawing on the philosophy of Aristotle, Thomas Aquinas (1225–1274) believed that only God is infinite. All creatures are finite, and even God, whose power is unlimited, "cannot make an absolutely unlimited thing."[14]

The infinity of God has also been widely assumed by philosophers and theologians in the modern period, though the meaning of God has differed widely. For example, according to pantheists such as Bruno, Spinoza, or Hegel, God and the world are both infinite and, ultimately, both identical. On the other hand, in both classical and contemporary theism a fundamental distinction is made between God and the world. Theists affirm that although God creates and sustains the world in existence, God utterly transcends it in that God's mode of existence is necessary, or to use Paul Tillich's phrase, God is the "ground of being." In terms of the finite/infinite distinction, God alone is infinite, and the world is finite. God's infinity is a mode of God's perfection and God's goodness, and at the same time, God is incomprehensible. We can know *that* God is perfect, infinite self-existence, but we cannot conceive of *how* God is perfect, infinite self-existence. Theists also affirm that God is present in the world, acting at every level of complexity from quarks to quasars to bring about God's purposes of love and life. Contemporary panentheists tend to agree with theists about the transcendence and infinity of God, but make a further claim about God's immanence in the world. According to panentheists, God is not only present in the world but the world exists *within* the being of God.

In any case, the central point here is that the concept of infinity was transformed from a negative to a positive quality by early Christian theology and almost universally attributed to God as the supreme source of being, truth, and goodness. Still, infinity was defined in terms of a contrast with the finite or in terms of a goal which the finite never attains.

ii) *Cosmology*. Moving from the context of philosophy and mathematics into cosmology, we find that the early Greek universe was seen as a mixture of finitude and infinity. According to Plato, the earth was the center of the universe. The stars were fixed on a sphere that rotated about the earth daily. What about the motion of the sun, the moon, and the planets relative to the fixed stars? Greek astronomers attempted to solve this problem by adding concentric spheres with axes angled to compensate for the planetary motions. By the time Aristotle proposed his model of the heavens in *De Caelo (On the Heavens)*, fifty-five transparent spheres were needed to accommodate the flood of increasingly accurate observations. Still, the universe was finite in size, though Aristotle believed it had existed forever and was thus infinite in (past) time.

Four hundred years later, Ptolemy (c. 83 – 160 C.E.) was to substitute a series of epicycles, deferents, and eccentrics to give even higher predictive accuracy. This system was, it seemed, endlessly adjustable, lasting until the great revolution of the sixteenth century with the new *heliocentric* cosmology of Nicolas Copernicus (1473–1543). Moreover Ptolemy's model was essentially a geometrical construct, a mathematical device highly accurate but unrealizable in nature, whereas Aristotle's model was considered as representing the physical structure of the heavens.

What is important for our purposes here, of course, is that all of these developments from the ancient Greeks to the Copernican revolution saw the universe as finite in size. They differed over the question of the age of the universe. Though Aristotle believed the universe to be eternal, Christian theology claimed it to be created by God and thus finite in age. Augustine was the clearest of the patristic theologians on this subject. It is not that God created the world at some moment in a pre-existing time. Rather, God created time as well as matter.[15] By the thirteenth century, Aquinas was to resolve the debate by arguing that the eternity of the universe cannot be settled by philosophy (for example, by appealing to Aristotle). Instead its finitude in time is given us by revelation (for example, Genesis 1). Thus the conception of the universe at the time of the Copernican revolution was one which is finite in size and age.

B. Infinity in the rise of science: examples from the mathematics of Galileo and the cosmology of Newton

i) *Galileo's arguments on infinity in mathematics.* The beginnings of the modern understanding of the mathematical concept of infinity can be traced to Galileo Galilei (1564–1642). In a delightful section of *Two New Sciences*,[16] Galileo argued that, as far as the real numbers are concerned, infinite sets do not obey the same rules as do finite sets. Consider the unending sequence of whole numbers: 1, 2, 3, . . . , and the unending sequence of the squares of the whole numbers: 1, 4, 9, . . . Intuitively we think there must be more whole numbers than their squares since the set of whole numbers *contains* the squares along with other numbers (for example, 2, 3, 5, 6, 7, 8, 10, . . .). Yet the squares can be put into a one-to-one correspondence with the whole numbers:

whole numbers:	1	2	3	...	n	...
squares:	1	4	9	...	n^2	...

Now a good working definition of equality between two sets of numbers is this: Two sets are equal if and only if each number in set A can be associated with a number in set B, and nothing is left unmatched in sets A or B. Adopting this definition we find that the series of squares 1, 4, 9, . . . is *equivalent* to the series of whole numbers 1, 2, 3, . . . ! This seems to mean that there are as many squares as there are whole numbers! Given this paradoxical result, Galileo recognized that, unlike finite quantities, "the attributes 'larger,' 'smaller,' and 'equal' have no place . . . in comparing infinite quantities with each other."[17] We shall see that Galileo's insight was to play a key role in the discovery of "transfinite" numbers by Georg Cantor (1845–1918) in the nineteenth century.

ii) *Infinity in the cosmology of Newton.* Though Copernicus gave us a heliocentric framework, it was with Sir Isaac Newton (1642–1727) a century later that one first encountered the possibility of a scientific cosmology in which the universe is infinite in size and eternal in age. Newton's cosmology was based on his theory of mechanics, his (metaphysical) assumptions about absolute space and time, and his theory of gravity. Newtonian mechanics interpreted changing motion in nature as the result of impact forces between masses: An acceleration, a, of a body, B, is produced by a force, f, inversely proportionate to the inertial mass, m, of B, or f=ma. For Newton's system to work, however, one must distinguish between real and apparent acceleration, and to do this Newton invoked what he called absolute space and absolute time. Both are infinite and passive, giving to masses their relative acceleration without being altered by the changing states of matter in the world. Newton also proposed a theory of gravity in which any two masses in the universe interact with each other with a force proportional to the product of their masses and inversely proportional to the square of the distance between them.

Turning to cosmology, where only gravity is involved, Newton faced a quandary: If the number of stars in the universe is finite, why don't the stars collapse into a single mass under their mutual gravitational force? If the number of stars is infinite, allowing them, possibly, to remain distributed evenly (pulled evenly in all directions), why isn't the night sky ablaze with starlight in every direction (that is, Olber's paradox)? For these and other technical problems, Newton's cosmology remained an ambiguous influence on culture: It was widely adopted as a description of the universe as infinite, eternal and unchanging, yet its technical scientific problems were left unsolved until the work of Albert Einstein (1879–1955) in the early twentieth century which transformed physics and cosmology.

C. The Discovery of the transfinite in modern mathematics (eighteenth to nineteenth centuries)
Galileo's insights into infinity remained dormant until the discoveries of Bernard Bolzano (1781–1848), Richard Dedekind (1831–1916), and Cantor. Before them the infinite was thought of as merely a potential infinity, the limit of an endless series, something never fully achieved either in mathematics or in nature. The birth of calculus in the seventeenth century involved complex questions about the status of infinitesimals both as minute extensions in space and durations in time. Yet even Newton, Gottfried Wilhelm Leibniz (1646–1716), and Carl Friedrich Gauss (1777–1855) adhered to the view that such infinities and infinitesimals are only abstractions or potential infinities.

At the close of the nineteenth century, however, Georg Cantor discovered that there are many kinds of mathematical infinities, and he explored their structures.[18] To do so, Cantor first showed how to apply basic mathematical principles, which we use with finite sets, to infinite sets—principles including addition, multiplication, exponentiation, and the relation "greater than." This in turn meant he could give an explicit procedure for constructing different kinds of infinity and for showing their internal consistency. In essence we could say that infinity, instead of being defined simply by contrast with the finite and remaining essentially unknown, has now been explored and we know lots about it—even an infinite amount!

To see this, we have to be clear about some basic ideas we deal with on a daily basis. Let's start with counting and from there see what we mean by saying that two (finite) sets are equivalent.

When we count something we do so by placing each element in the set of things to be counted—a "one-to-one correspondence" with the natural numbers 1, 2, 3, ... For example, suppose I want to count the number of marbles on the table in front of me. I count them one at a time, saying "one" as I touch the first marble, "two" as I touch the second, "three" for the third, and so on until I come to the last marble. The number I associate with the last marble as I touch it, say "nine," is the number I assign to the handful of marbles I began with. In counting the marbles and assigning them the number "nine," I implicitly think of the marbles as a complete set and I associate the number "nine" with that set. Mathematicians call the number "nine" the *cardinal number* of that set.

Similarly I could count the number of coins in my pocket. If I found I had nine coins, then I can think of the set of marbles and the set of coins as *equivalent.*[19] Indeed, all sets of objects of any kind which carry the cardinal number "nine" are equivalent. Moreover the cardinal number for all these equivalent sets distinguishes them from all sets with the cardinal number "eight" or "thirty-four" or "five thousand two," and so on.

Now we make Cantor's fundamental claim: *The concepts of "equivalent sets," or "counting," and of "cardinal number" can be transferred from their foundations in finite sets to infinite sets.* Cantor coined the term *transfinite* for the cardinal number of infinite sets, for reasons which will become clear shortly. Rather than assuming the infinite is in direct *contrast* with the finite, as had always been done in the past, Cantor treats an infinite set in a direct *analogy* with how he treats finite sets. The results are staggering!

Let's start with the set of natural numbers {1, 2, 3, . . . } which serves as our simplest example of an infinite set. Cantor chose $\aleph_0$ ("aleph-null") to represent its transfinite cardinal number. He thought of $\aleph_0$ as a given whole, and not just an incomplete sequence of unending numbers ascending in scale. In other words, Cantor actually distinguished between an unending sequence of elements, such as the sequence 1, 2, 3, . . . , which is potentially infinite but always, in fact, finite, and the complete infinite sequence thought of as a whole, that is, the set {1, 2, 3, . . . }. He called the potential infinite a "variable finite" and symbolized it as ∞; the actual infinite he symbolized by $\aleph_0$, as we saw above. Thus ∞ never reaches completion, never becomes $\aleph_0$. To think about ∞ is to think of an ever-increasing series of numbers continuing forever without reaching an end. To think about $\aleph_0$ is to stand outside this series, from God's point of view at it were, and to consider them as a single, unified, and determinate totality.

Cantor then extended what we know about counting finite sets to infinite sets: All infinite sets whose elements can be put in a one-to-one correspondence with the natural numbers will have the *same* cardinal number, $\aleph_0$. We call these sets *denumerably infinite* or *countably infinite.* This leads to some really surprising results. For example, recall Galileo's paradox about square numbers. Since there is a one-to-one correspondence between the natural numbers and the square numbers, it means that the set of square numbers is uncountably infinite; it has the same cardinal number, $\aleph_0$, as the set of natural numbers. Similarly the set of even numbers is equivalent to the set of natural numbers, as is the set of odd numbers.[20]

What is even more surprising is that, according to Cantor, we can generate infinities which are "bigger" than the set of natural numbers in a certain sense, though all of these still have cardinal number $\aleph_0$. Here it will be helpful to introduce the term *ordinal number* to represent the order of the elements in a set. For example, the finite set (1, 2, 3) has cardinal number 3, since there are three elements in the set, and it has ordinal number 3, since the set, as an ordered group of elements, has a third element. In the case of finite sets, the ordinal number and the cardinal number of a set is the same.

It turns out, though, that they are *not* the same for infinite sets! We start, as above, with the infinite set of natural numbers, $\{1, 2, 3, \ldots\}$; following mathematical custom, we designate its ordinal number as ω. Now let us think of this set as a whole, as complete in itself. If we do so, then it is possible to conceive of adding 1 to the set, forming a new set, $\{1, 2, 3, \ldots, 1\}$; the ordinal number of this set would be $\omega + 1$.[21] Adding 1 to this set yields another new set, $\{1, 2, 3, \ldots, 1, 2\}$, whose ordinal number is $\omega + 2$.

As we continue the process, we generate a whole ladder of increasingly complex infinities. For example, if we add the set of natural numbers to the set of natural numbers, we obtain the set $\{1, 2, 3, \ldots, 1, 2, 3, \ldots\}$ whose ordinal number is $\omega + \omega$, which we notate as $\omega \cdot 2$. Continuing from here, we can consider $(\omega \cdot 2) + 1$, $(\omega \cdot 2) + 2$, $(\omega \cdot 2) + 3$, and so on until we reach $\omega \cdot \omega$ which we can write as ω^2. Again we continue adding to this set until we conceive of ω^3, ω^4, and so on. This in turn points toward its goal: ω^{ω}—but there's still more, in fact infinitely more! We can think of an infinite series of exponential powers, raising ω to the ω power infinitely many times. What is even more astonishing is the fact that the elements in any of these transfinite sets can be put in a one-to-one correspondence with the elements in the set of natural numbers, $\{1, 2, 3, \ldots\}$. This means that all of these sets, even though differing in their ordinal number, are *denumerably* infinite: *they have the same cardinal number,* $\aleph_0$*!* Mathematicians express this fact by noting that

$$\aleph_0 + \aleph_0 = \aleph_0$$

even though it remains true that

$$\omega + \omega \neq \omega$$

Apparently the rules which infinity obeys are *both like and unlike* the rules which finite sets obey!

But there are still more surprises ahead, since we can imagine sets whose "infinity" is so great, as it were, that they *cannot* be put into a one-to-one correspondence with these sets: they are "uncountably infinite." In 1874, Cantor proved this for the set of real numbers.[22] Since the real numbers can be put in one-to-one correspondence with the points of a straight line, Cantor called the cardinal number of the set of real numbers "the power of the continuum" which is often designated by the letter *c*. It is surprising, though it is easy to show, that the number of points in any line of any length is the same. What is really surprising is that there is a one-to-one correspondence between the set of points in a plane and the set of points in a line, since one might well have thought the former to be infinitely greater than the latter. Cantor then extended this result to the points in a three-dimensional space, and then to a space of any number of dimensions. All these mathematical objects—the line, the plane, the volume, the volume in four or more dimensions—have the *same* cardinal number, *c*.

We can go further still, though a proof lies beyond the limits of this chapter. Cantor showed that one can construct a whole series of transfinite cardinal numbers $\aleph_0$, $\aleph_1$, $\aleph_2$, and so on, leading to $\aleph_\omega$. Even this is not the end, though. We can think of $\aleph_{\omega+1}$, $\aleph_{\omega+2}$, . . . , $\aleph_{\omega^\omega}$, $\aleph_{\aleph_0}$ and so on—there's never an end to the kinds of infinity we can construct. At the same time, these infinities share an important feature with finite sets since, no matter how complex they seem, the transfinite forms of infinity are at least conceivable by construction. We are thus in a better position to understand why Cantor called them "transfinite."

We are also prepared—somewhat—to take the final step and consider what lies beyond even the transfinite numbers: Cantor called it "Absolute Infinity," symbolized as Ω. In one sense the Absolute Infinity is inconceivable; it is beyond rational understanding. Yet in another sense we can know something about Ω: namely that it exists as a coherent mathematical concept. We can even know something about its properties! To make this apparent contradiction make sense, consider the converse.[23] Suppose Ω is conceivable. Then there must be some property P which is exclusively a property of Ω and Ω alone, so that we can conceive of Ω as the only number which has property P. Now in order to make Ω inconceivable, we merely have to stipulate that every property P is shared by both Ω and some transfinite ordinal. If so, then there is no property P that is unique to Ω and not shared by Ω and some transfinite ordinal. Thus we can know the properties P of Ω, since every conceivable property P is shared by some transfinite ordinal. Yet because of this, we can never differentiate Ω completely from the transfinite ordinals, since we can never describe Ω as possessing a property P which it doesn't share with a transfinite ordinal. In essence we can never tell Ω from some transfinite ordinal. We can never know if we are conceiving of Ω and not some transfinite ordinal. In short, we can never conceive of Ω alone. Therefore Ω is in itself inconceivable. Ω is inconceivable because Ω can never be uniquely characterized or completely distinguished from something which, though infinite too, is a lower order infinity than Absolute Infinity. The transfinite numbers, Cantor's endless types of infinities, lead towards Absolute Infinity Ω but never reach it, since Ω lies beyond all comprehension. This argument is often called the Reflection Principle.[24]

In the end, Cantor set up a threefold distinction regarding the infinite: the Absolute Infinity which is realized in God and the transfinite numbers which occur both in mathematics and in nature. Rudy Rucker quotes Cantor as follows:

> The actual infinite arises in three contexts: *first* when it is realized in the most complete form, in a fully independent other-wordily being, *in Deo*, where I call it the Absolute Infinite or simply Absolute; *second* when it occurs in the contingent, created world; *third* when the mind grasps it *in abstract* as a mathematical magnitude, number, or order type. I wish to mark a sharp contrast between the Absolute and what I call the

> Transfinite, that is, the actual infinities of the last two sorts, which are clearly limited, subject to further increase, and thus related to the finite.[25]

We shall pursue the question of the relation between the Absolute in mathematics and God below. But first, what about Cantor's claim about actual infinities in mathematics and in the world? These questions lead to the theme of this chapter, since if an actual infinity occurs in either mathematics or in nature it would seem to challenge the distinction between the finite and the infinite. Such a distinction has traditionally served as one of the leading ways, both theologically and philosophically, by which we may describe the world as created and describe God as its creator—in other words, to distinguish God from Creation.

3. Does an Actual Infinity Make Sense in Mathematics or in Cosmology?

Is Cantor correct in believing that the world is actually infinite? With this question we raise one of the central issues of this chapter. First, do mathematicians in general agree with Cantor on the claim that infinity is a consistent and coherent concept in mathematics? Next, do cosmologists think that the universe is actually infinite in size, and will it last forever?

A. A mixed response from modern mathematics

In fact, many contemporary mathematicians accept Cantor's theories as valid, but reject the applicability of transfinite numbers to realms beyond mathematics. In a recent survey of the issue, William Lane Craig defends the claim that, "while the actual infinite may be a fruitful and consistent concept in the mathematical realm, it cannot be translated from the mathematical world into the real world, for this would involve counter-intuitive absurdities." In support of this view he cites Bolzano, who claimed that infinite sets, such as the set of all "absolute propositions and truths," exist in the realm of mathematics alone, or what Bolzano called the "realm of things which do not claim actuality, and do not even claim possibility." According to Bolzano the only real actual infinity is God. Craig gathers additional support for this view from Abraham Robinson, Abraham Fraenkel, Alexander Abian, Pamela Huby and David Hilbert.[26]

Taking the problem one step further, Craig also describes the problems which beset Cantor's theory in the decades which followed his initial discoveries and concludes that these problems undercut a "naïve" view of the existence of actual infinities even in the realm of mathematics. To make his case, Craig first recounts four philosophical interpretations of the ontological status of mathematical sets: 1) Platonism (realism): sets have a real existence; mathematics discovers, but does not create, the infinite. 2) Nominalism: neither sets nor the numbers which are contained in them have any real existence in the world. 3) Conceptualism: sets and numbers exist as mental objects, not as physical objects, created in the mind of the mathematician. 4) Formalism: mathematics is merely a consistent way of calculating entities in the real world and nothing more. He then describes the problems which arose regarding Cantor's theory: Burali-Forti's antinomy, Cantor's antinomy, and Russell's antimony. According to Craig, these antinomies forced major revisions in set theory (logicism, axiomatization, and intutionism). Most importantly, they undercut the Platonist/realist interpretation, but not the others. In Craig's view, "even the mathematical existence of the actual infinite has not gone unchallenged and therefore cannot be taken for granted. . . . Therefore we conclude that an actual infinite cannot exist."[27]

When we turn to physics and cosmology, however, a different answer lies in store.

B. Very possibly so, according to big bang cosmology

We should first note in passing that contemporary physics is filled with infinities. Even classical fields go infinite at their point sources, but quantum fields entail a staggering variety of infinities: infinite vacuum energy; infinite charge and mass in quantum field theory requiring re-normalization to make them consistent with the empirical data; the endless production of matter/antimatter pairs and their mutual annihilations; infinities in the numbers and kinds of particles exchanged while particles interact; and so on. Perhaps these are all strictly mathematical artifices, symptoms of the transitory nature of physical theory, problems which will be removed by improvements in future theories. Perhaps not. The question of the status of infinity in physics is immense.

But here we return specifically to the theme of cosmology, where according to Einstein's general theory of relativity, space and time curve like an elastic continuum distended by matter as it moves about the universe. At the same time, the trajectories of moving matter are shaped by the curvature of the spacetime in which matter moves. The story is most striking however when we consider the universe itself. For according to Big Bang cosmology, the universe is expanding from an origin some 15 or so billion years ago described colloquially as the beginning of time, or t=0. This initial event is a genuine "singularity," a spacetime point characterized by infinite density, infinite temperature, and zero size. But is this really a description of nature as it was at the first moment, t=0, or is it merely a quirk of the mathematics which future theories will overcome?[28]

Big Bang cosmology also portrays the universe as either i) closed, shaped like a three dimensional sphere with a finite size which changes in time (first expanding then contracting), or ii) open, shaped like a three-dimensional saddle with an infinite size which expands forever. What about these features of the universe: Are they real, so that the universe may be actually infinite? Or are they, too, the spurious product of mathematics and irrelevant to nature as it actually is?

Clearly the initial singularity, t=0, may be replaced eventually by some description in which the universe has an infinite past. In some versions of inflationary cosmology, for example, the problem of t=0 is overcome along with other problems in the original Big Bang account in the technical sense that the existence of t=0 becomes formally "undecideable,"[29] and t=0 is entirely absent in several of the ongoing proposals which follow in the trajectory of Fred Hoyle's original steady state model[30] and in various formulations of quantum cosmology based on speculative approaches to quantum gravity such as popularized in Steven Hawking's book, *A Brief History of Time.*[31] Whether this undercuts the theological significance of the "finite age" of the universe in contemporary cosmology is still a matter of some debate. More interesting for our purposes here is the question of whether the universe is open or closed (that is, whether the universe will expand and cool forever or recollapse upon itself in an infinitely dense fireball). Both possibilities still hold even in the case of inflationary and quantum cosmology: After the initial moments of the universe the quantum picture must lead to the standard Big Bang scenarios. Most astronomical evidence to date strongly suggests that the universe is open. What then, are we to make of the claim that the universe is spatially infinite?

Actually this claim raises even more issues. For one thing, such a universe, though spatially infinite, is still expanding in time! Markers floating in space move apart from one another, but there is an actual infinity of markers in an endless spatial expanse. For another, the geometry of the open model, unlike that of the closed, spherical model, cannot be embedded in Euclidean space. What this means is that the closed model can be pictured as a three-dimensional sphere without much loss of accuracy, but the open model cannot really be pictured as a three-dimensional saddle. At each point in space the curvature is like that of a saddle, but the way space curves at each point extrudes out away from spacetime; it is something like a three dimensional mountain which stretches out away from a two-dimensional topological map, though the map's contour lines attempt to suggest the distortion. Language about an open universe is apophatic; it is kataphatic about a closed universe. Who would have guessed?

What does this model say about the status of infinity and its bearing on our understanding of the infinity of God? We turn to this question, along with those drawn from Cantor's astonishing work on the mathematics of infinity, in the final section below.

4. Enriching Our Understanding of the Infinity of God: "The Veil that Discloses"

We have covered a lot of territory, and yet we have barely scratched the surface. A tremendous amount of further research awaits—perhaps tapering off to infinity! Yet even with this initial foray, we can begin to collect some gems found in the process that seem worthy of further reflection. To do so, we need to recall our original discussion about the meaning of infinity. There I suggested that the early Christian world helped to transform the meaning of infinity from its negative connotations involving what is an unlimited chaos or a gnawing privation, to more positive connotations suggesting ultimate reality, the ground of being, the highest good, and the source of the world. At the same time, however, theologians retained the classical Greek distinction (captured by the Greek word for infinity, *apeiron*) between the infinite as wholly different from, and in contrast to, the finite. Thus, to say that God is infinite is really to say that we cannot comprehend God. This distinction, inherited from the Greek philosophical culture by the early church, has predominated through the centuries in Christian theology as it seeks to speak about God. We see this most clearly in the distinction theologians make between the apophatic and the kataphatic. We start with acknowledging the apophatic, that is, how *little* we know of the unseen, incomprehensible mystery that is God. Then we move to the kataphatic, that is, we seek to express something that we *do* know about God: that God intends to be known, that what we know is God's love, care, purpose, and mercy, and so on. Moreover, the term "infinity" has played a pivotal role in this history: It has been used almost exclusively to express the stark difference between the apophatic and the kataphatic. God is infinite, we are finite. God is other than, unlike, and wholly different from us. When we claim that God is infinite we intend to mean something apophatic: God is beyond, inscrutable, totally other than the known, the finite, the world as we know it.

Thus if any property of what we think of as the finite world would turn out to be, in reality, infinite, it would seem to challenge our understanding of God: Either the world would *be* God, thus leading to pantheism, or the world would simply be the infinite world and its own best explanation, and there would be *no need* for God, thus leading to atheism. The importance of the finitude of the world has resided in the fact that it has been a key defense against unbelief as well as a key constituent to the Christian distinction between Creator and creation, or more generally the Christian definition of the God-world relation in terms of Creator-creation.

In short this means that an infinite universe, either existing forever from eternity or having an infinite size, would seem to challenge Christian faith. Given that one model in the Big Bang theory is of an open universe whose size is infinite and which will continue to exist for eternity, it would seem that Big Bang theory would challenge Christian faith.

One might reply, of course, that if the universe is actually infinite, this simply means we need to adjust our concept of God, that our traditional idea of God is too small and that God is, in fact, "more infinite" than even an infinite universe. This may be the case, and here Cantor's insights about the Absolute Infinite versus the merely transfinite could be very helpful.

Alternatively, one might reply that the meaning of infinity in theology is highly ambiguous; therefore it cannot directly challenge the meaning of infinity in cosmology. Though he sees the implications of mathematical infinity for theology, Timothy Pennings highlights the ambiguity of the term nicely:

> To say that God is infinite could be referring to some attribute of God such as His omnipresence (Locke), or it could be making an absolute statement about God's being (Aquinas), or it could be contrasting God's nature with human nature (Weyl), or it could be linking God's knowledge to the set of (natural) numbers (Augustine), or it could be associating the mind of God with the Absolute Infinite (Cantor).[32]

But the argument of this chapter has been that despite these ambiguities there is a historical continuity in the way infinity has been used by scientists, philosophers, and theologians, and a common thread running through in its many meanings. It is this common thread which makes the challenge from cosmology unavoidable, or at least one which cannot be entirely diffused by appealing to the ambiguity in the term.

Now we are in a position to appreciate the radical importance of Cantor's discovery of the complexities of infinities in mathematics, and to apply them, at least by analogy, to our problem. Clearly as we pursue these leads in the future, we will have to take into account the serious problems arising from the antinomies in set theory discussed above. While I want to emphasize this, I also want to stress that these problems as such do not rule out using Cantor's work by analogy in the theological domain of discourse. What I will suggest is that Cantor's work, at least by analogy as we move across fields, enhances the meaning of God as Creator and gives new insight and energy to the proclamation of faith in God the Creator. To see this, let us turn first to mathematics and then to cosmology.

A. Mathematics: the transfinites as veils that disclose

The Reflection Principle in mathematics points to a fascinating connection between what we know and what we do not know about Absolute Infinity. In theological language we would say that the Reflection Principle combines what was otherwise kept separate, the apophatic and the kataphatic, or the way of negation and the way of affirmation. This alone is astonishing.

We begin with Cantor by defining the mathematical Absolute Infinity as beyond comprehension, lying beyond the unending ladder of the transfinite numbers which are themselves infinities but which can be fully comprehended, that is, whose properties can be formally described. Now the way we insure that the Absolutely Infinite is beyond comprehension is by claiming that if it were not so we could describe it unambiguously, and by describing it, comprehend it. Now to describe it means to state at least one property which it alone possesses and which allows us to single it out from the transfinite which share this property. We therefore reverse this and insist, via the Reflection Principle, that all of its properties must be shared by the transfinites. This alone insures that the Absolute Infinity cannot be uniquely described and is therefore incomprehensible. Since none of its properties is unique to itself, we can never point unequivocally to it by pointing to that unique property. In this sense Absolute Infinity is indescribable, incomprehensible.

But this, in turn, means that we do in fact know something about the Absolutely Infinite: All of the properties it possesses must be shared with and disclosed to us through the properties of the transfinites. The Absolute Infinite is in this sense knowable, comprehensible; each of its properties must be found in at least one transfinite number. The Absolute is disclosed through the relative, or transfinite, infinities, and yet it is through this disclosure that it remains hidden, ineffable, incomprehensible.

Another way of putting this is that the incomprehensibility of Absolute Infinity is manifested by its partial comprehensibility. What we know about the Absolute Infinite is never more than partial knowledge shared by all relative infinities. What is truly unique about Absolute Infinity is never disclosed, but forever hidden. What we do know about Absolute Infinity forms a veil hiding what is forever beyond our knowledge. Yet, something about Absolute Infinity is disclosed through what is revealed in the veil that hides Absolute Infinity. We endlessly learn more and more through endless circles of discovery of the transfinite, endlessly moving to more and more knowledge of what can never be known exhaustively.

This situation of the mutual sharing and the interpenetration of comprehensibility and incomprehensibility seems to apply preeminently well, even if only by analogy, to our knowledge of God for which we hunger and thirst. On the one hand, we want to affirm that God is both Absolute Mystery, the ineffable source lying beyond comprehension, and yet we want to affirm that we can know this God as Creator and Redeemer. How can this be? It turns out that the theological response is almost an exact parallel to the mathematical response. The incomprehensibility of God includes the infinity of God as the apophatic tradition suggests. Yet, on the other hand and as the kataphatic tradition equally suggests, this God intends on being known by us and on knowing us. This God who would be known is known to us as our Creator precisely through God's self-revelation and through the products of God's creative activity—the universe.

Now comes the analogy between the way mathematicians understand infinity and theologians speak about God: *I propose that God, as Absolute Infinity, is hidden precisely by the sharing of all God's attributes with us through all that God creates.* The Absolutely Infinite in mathematics is hidden precisely by the fact that it shares its properties with all the transfinites. The incomprehensibility of the Absolutely Infinite in mathematics is safeguarded by its reflection in all the known infinities. Thus, theologically, *the mystery of God is vouchsafed by its revelation in our experience of God and in the properties of all that God creates and science discovers.* Or once again, the Absolutely Infinite is known through the known infinities and yet being so, remains unknown in itself. Theologically, the God who is known is the God who is unknowable. What God has chosen to disclose to us, the kataphatic—God's existence as Creator, God's goodness, love, and beauty—is a veil behind which the Reality of God is endlessly hidden precisely as it is endlessly revealed. To capture this theological understanding of God's hiddenness in God's self-disclosure I have coined the metaphor "the veil that discloses."

The analogy with mathematics also has immediate connections with cosmology.

B. Cosmology: infinities in nature as veils that disclose

According to contemporary cosmology, if the universe is open it is actually infinite in size, and will continue to expand forever. Even the suggestion that the universe may be infinite in size challenges any naive view of God as somehow a God limited to terrestrial concerns or a God who is really just a super-being and not the ground, source, and destiny of all that exists. The God of the Big Bang must be thought of at least in terms of infinite presence, infinite power, and infinite compassion if this God is to be God of a universe of which even the visible portion is billions of light-years in size.

But does this lean towards the other direction and somehow undermine the distinction between God and the universe? Does it even go so far as to undercut the argument for God's existence? Though pantheists or atheists might believe so, I believe instead that this enhances our understanding of the meaning of "God." This is for two reasons.

First of all the methods and assumptions of science require us to view the universe as contingent, and this in turn raises the question of its source of being beyond itself and beyond scientific explanation.[33] Science leads in the direction of theism and away from pantheism or atheism. Thus the argument between the actual infinity of the universe (if the universe is "open") and the existence or nonexistence of God which the pantheist or the atheist wants to make is framed within the broader scientific understanding of the universe. But this scientific understanding always takes for granted the universe as contingent, and the contingency of the universe is precisely what theology points to by calling the universe "creation." This then leads to the concept of God the Creator.

The second reason starts with what we have just said about the Reflection Principle in mathematics. This time we apply the Reflection Principle to the context of scientific cosmology. Does an infinite, open universe disclose something about the meaning of the infinite nature of God? Mathematically, the infinity of the universe must be transfinite and not Absolute, for it can be specified by mathematical formalism (via Einstein's equations). But now we apply the Reflection Principle in reverse, moving from the known infinities to the Absolutely Infinite which is beyond knowledge. That is, according to the Reflection Principle, the mathematical properties of the transfinite universe must be shared by God as the Absolute Infinite, and yet in such a way that the universe as transfinite is never confused with God in God's Absolute Infinity. Thus, the spatial and temporal infinities of the universe reveal something of the God who is their source while at the same time hiding God, and leaving God as unknown and incomprehensible.

Thus, through the discoveries about the subtle nature of infinity in both cosmology and in mathematics, we are led to an even more profound understanding of the belief that God is disclosed and known through nature as her Creator precisely as that same God is hidden and veiled by nature. Surely Anselm of Canterbury (1033–1109) was leading us in the right direction when he gave us such a profound insight about God: "God is that, the greater than which one cannot conceive."[34]

5. Conclusion

Cantor's work, as we have seen, takes up the problem of what we, through human reasoning about infinity, can and cannot say. Moving beyond the previous centuries of reflection on infinity, Cantor has shown us that Absolute Infinity in mathematics utterly transcends even the infinite ladder of the transfinite infinities which he discovered and which may be embodied in the universe. Yet Absolute Infinity is revealed and known through the transfinite. It would seem then that the discoveries of science and mathematics about the universe point beyond themselves to horizons and realities whose ultimate source is the incomprehensible God. Will we follow these pointers, though keeping sharply aware of their profound limitations? Or will we be dazzled by science and stop short of that great, further exploration?

I am reminded once again of Newton with his seashells, holding the hard-won gains of his science up to scrutiny, yet barely noticing the endless and unfathomable mystery beyond. I am also reminded of the humility of those early theologians who knew that when we seek to speak of God, we do so only out of the glimmers of understanding which sparkle amidst the vast background of uncomprehensible mystery, a mystery which nevertheless shines with unquenchable light through the veil of infinity.

ENDNOTES: Chapter 2

[1] This chapter is a slightly revised version of a paper with the same title originally published in: *How Large is God? The Voices of Scientists and Theologians,* John Marks Templeton, ed. (Philadelphia: Templeton Foundation Press, 1997).

[2] We can put this more formally by claiming that the scientific method, much like the theological method, proceeds by hypotheses held tentatively, intended as true, tested by data, and subject to acceptance or rejection by the consensus of the community. All genuine knowledge—religious or scientific—is finally a small light shining in a vast darkness, a known illuminating the unknown.

[3]David Brewster's *Memoirs of the Life, Writings, and Discoveries of Sir Isaac Newton*, 2 vols, 1st edn (Edinburgh: T. Constable, 1855) vol. 2, chapter 27.

[4]As Owen Thomas points out, "although infinity is not a biblical concept, its various meanings are implied about God throughout the Bible." It includes God being present everywhere and at all time, and being unlimited in power and knowledge. He cites Deut. 33:27; Ps. 90:2, 4; Ps. 139:7-12; Ps. 147:5; Job 38-41; Isa. 40:8; Isa. 51:6; Rom. 1:20; 1 Tim. 1:17; 1 Pet. 5:10. The traditional difficulty has been to reconcile the concept that God is infinite with the concept that God is personal. Owen C. Thomas, *Theological Questions: Analysis and Argument* (Wilton: Morehouse-Barlow, 1983), 38.

[5]For readable and insightful introductions I recommend Rudy Rucker, *Infinity and the Mind: The Science and Philosophy of the Infinite* (New York: Bantam Books, 1983), and William Lane Craig and Quentin Smith, *Theism, Atheism and Big Bang Cosmology* (Oxford: Clarendon Press, 1995). For a paper which explores themes in common with the present paper, see Timothy J. Pennings, "Infinity and the Absolute: Insights in Our World, Our Faith and Ourselves," in *Christian Scholar's Review* 23.2 (1993): 159–180. In this fine paper, Pennings underscores the importance Cantor felt concerning his work on infinity and the theological tradition. Pennings also stresses the ambiguity in the theological meaning of God's infinity and the qualitative difference between the infinite and the finite.

[6] Rucker, *Infinity and the Mind*, 3.

[7] These sections draw in part from Rucker, *Infinity and the Mind*, and from Craig and Smith, *Theism*.

[8] I am using *The Basic Works of Aristotle*, edited by Richard McKeon (New York: Random House, 1941). Aristotle began, as those before him, by considering infinity as a negative quality, that is, as something lacking: ". . . [I]ts essence is privation. . ." See *Physics*, III.7.207b35.

[9] Aristotle, *Physics*, III.6.206a26-30.

[10] The only infinite considered possible is the potential infinite: something capable of being endlessly divided or added to, but never fully actualized as infinite. See Aristotle, *Physics*, III.4.204b1-206a8

[11] Aristotle, *Physics,* III.5.206a5b. Italics are in the original text. It is helpful here to distinguish between the following two ideas: 1) for every number n, there is another number n+1 and 2) there is a number n beyond every number 1, 2, 3, ... The first suggests that we can always find more numbers in the series 1, 2, 3, . . . , and thus that the series is potentially infinite (or endlessly extendable). The second suggests that there is an actual number n beyond the series as a whole, suggesting that the series as a whole is actually infinite. This second concept of an actual infinity was foreign to the Greeks.

[12] Plotinus, *Enneads*, V.5.11.

[13] Augustine, *City of God*, XII. 18.

[14] Thomas Aquinas, *Summa* Ia, 7, 2–4.

[15] In a now famous move, Augustine endorses the creation *of* time along with the world, and rejects the creation of the world *in* time, in *Confessions* XI.13 and *City of God* XI.6.

[16] Galileo Galilei, *Dialogues Concerning Two New Sciences*, trans. Henry Crew and Alfonso de Salvio (New York: Dover, 1954). See "First Day."

[17] Ibid., 33. We should note historically that underlying this paradox was the notion of space and time as continuously varying quantities and, consequently, the problem of finding the

instantaneous velocity of a moving body. The latter involves the notion of an infinitesimal quantity of time, *dt*, as developed in the calculus of Newton and Leibniz. To avoid such problems the notion of the actually infinite was replaced by the notion of a "limit."

[18] Craig gives a helpful presentation of Cantor's transfinite numbers in *The Kalam Cosmological Argument* (New York: Barnes & Noble, 1979) which I will draw upon here. Also see "Infinity" by Hans Hahn in James R. Newman, ed., *The World of Mathematics Volume 3* (New York: Simon and Schuster, 1956), 1593–1611; and Rucker, *Infinity and the Mind*, chapters 1, 2.

[19] Since I can put the elements in each set in a one-to-one correspondence with the elements in the set of natural numbers and obtain the cardinal number "nine" in each case, then I can put the set of coins and the set of marbles into a one-to-one correspondence with each other.

[20] While still a student, Cantor discovered that the set of all rational fractions (that is, the quotient of two natural numbers such as 4/7), is denumerably infinite, and the same holds for the set of all "algebraic" numbers, such as $\sqrt{3}$. All these sets have the same transfinite cardinal number, $\aleph_0$.

[21] Note that $\omega + 1$ is *not* equal to $1 + \omega$. The latter is still equal to ω. That is, $1 + \omega = \omega$ since all the symbol $1 + \omega$ means is that we add one element to the elements which taken endlessly but thought of as a whole is the set of natural numbers whose ordinal number is ω. The former, $\omega + 1$, means adding to a *given* infinite whole, namely {1, 2, 3, . . . }, a new element 1, thus forming the set {1, 2, 3, . . . , 1 }. This means that {1, 2, 3, . . . , 1}, taken as a whole, is not equivalent to the set {1, 2, 3, . . . }, taken as a whole. Thus $\omega + 1$ is not equivalent to ω.

[22] Real numbers are composed of the natural numbers, the fractions, and the irrational numbers.

[23] I am following Rucker's explanation closely here. cf. *Infinity and the Mind*, 53.

[24] Rucker puts it this way: "Every conceivable property that is enjoyed by Ω is also enjoyed by some set. . . . Every conceivable property of the Absolute is shared by some lesser entity." Rucker, *Infinity and the Mind*, 53

[25] Georg Cantor, *Gesammelte Abhandlungen Mathematischen und Philosophischen Inhalts* (Springer-Verlag, 1980), 378. This is Rucker's translation, *Infinity and the Mind*, 10.

[26] Craig and Smith, *Theism*, 9–11.

[27] Ibid., 16–24. It should become clear in what follows that I do not agree with Craig on the question of the real existence of the actual infinite.

[28] See Russell, Robert John, Nancey Murphy and C. J. Isham, eds., *QCLN* (Vatican City State: Vatican Observatory Publications and Berkeley: Center for Theology and the Natural Sciences, 1993).

[29] John D. Barrow, *Impossibility: The Limits of Science and the Science of Limits* (Oxford: Oxford University Press, 1998), ch. 6, esp. 181.

[30] Fred Hoyle, Geoffrey Burbidge, and Jayant V. Narlikar, *A Different Approach to Cosmology: From a Static Universe Through the Big Bang Towards Reality* (Cambridge: Cambridge University Press, 2000), esp. ch. 15, 191.

[31]Stephen W. Hawking, *A Brief History of Time: From the Big Bang to Black Holes* (Toronto: Bantam, 1988).

[32] Pennings, "Infinity and the Absolute."

[33] We must remember that science presupposes that the universe is contingent as a methodological commitment without which it cannot function. The universe need never have come into existence; its sheer existence points beyond itself and is unanswerable by science. Indeed, if a scientist tries to give an ultimate, necessary, and final answer as to why the universe exists, s/he would cease doing science and instead be doing metaphysics. Thus cosmology, which studies the universe as a whole, must assume that the universe need not be, and its existence calls for a reason or cause which lies beyond science to answer.

[34]St. Anselm, *Proslogion*, trans. M. J. Charlesworth (Notre Dame, Ind.: University of Notre Dame Press, 1979), 117.

Chapter 3

Finite Creation Without a Beginning: The Doctrine of Creation in Relation to Big Bang and Quantum Cosmologies[1]

1. Should Cosmology Be Important to Theologians?

With the rise of contemporary scientific cosmology this century, and especially with the triumph of the Friedmann Lemaitre Robertson Walker (FLRW) cosmology over the steady state theory in the mid-1960s, there has been growing interest in the possible theological significance of the singularity at "t=0," conventionally referred to as the "beginning of the universe" or "Big Bang" some 12–15 billion years ago.[2] During the past two decades, the original Big Bang model has been modified by inflationary scenarios to correct for a variety of technical difficulties, such as the flatness, matter/antimatter ratio, and horizon problems. Still even with inflation, if one assumes general relativity to be the correct theory of gravity, and if one makes certain reasonable assumptions about the mass-energy of the universe, then the initial singularity at t=0 is unavoidable (that is, it is an "essential singularity"), as shown by the theorems of Stephen Hawking and Roger Penrose.[3]

This situation raises a number of difficult questions, many of which require more than a strictly scientific resolution and involve interdisciplinary research: Does the initial singularity in inflationary Big Bang cosmology point to a fundamental feature of nature or is it merely an artifact of this particular cosmological model? If t=0 is of lasting scientific status, should it, in principle, bear any significance for Christian doctrine, or is it theologically irrelevant regardless of its scientific standing? If it is theologically significant, should t=0 be seen as only one aspect of God's action throughout nature and history as creator and redeemer, or does t=0 represent the sum of God's action as in deism or uniformitarianism? One of the purposes of this chapter is to explore these questions in critical interaction with other scholars who have written on the relationship between Big Bang cosmology and Christian theology.

Meanwhile, attempts are being made to obtain a quantum mechanical treatment of gravity which will replace general relativity and from which to develop quantum cosmology as a successor to Big Bang cosmology. An important, though highly speculative, approach is the Hartle/Hawking proposal, with its surprising elimination of the singularity t=0 from the scientific model. According to the Hartle/Hawking proposal the past of the universe is finite (as it is in the Big Bang model) but, unlike the past of the Big Bang, it is *unbounded* (there is no initial singularity, t=0). Although research in quantum gravity is still in a *highly tentative* stage, and the Hartle/Hawking proposal is only one of several avenues being explored, it already raises some very interesting interdisciplinary questions. For example, what effect will the move to quantum cosmology have on the ways theologians have appropriated Big Bang cosmology, particularly regarding the theological significance of t=0? How will the change in the meaning and status of temporality in the move from Big Bang to quantum cosmology affect the theological understanding of God as the creator of temporality? It is to questions like these that this chapter is also addressed.

Accordingly, this chapter is divided into two sections. In "Theological Reflections on Big Bang Cosmology," I focus on standard Big Bang cosmology and the problem of t=0. The theological reaction to t=0 has been mixed. Some theologians, such as Ted Peters, have welcomed it as evidence of divine creation; others such as Ian Barbour and Arthur Peacocke have dismissed it as irrelevant to the creation tradition. As I see it the argument on both sides has been shaped largely by the seminal work of Langdon Gilkey in his *Maker of Heaven and Earth.*[4] Although I will be quite critical of Gilkey's resolution of the problem, we owe him a great deal for his lucid insistence on its importance as such. If Gilkey is correct, the epistemological problems surrounding t=0 are well worth *our* pursuing because they are *inherent* to the theological problem of divine action, or as he later calls it, the "travail of biblical language." Thus they are not a minor issue best forgotten; instead they raise the fundamental problem of the rationality of theology in an age of scientific epistemology.

Nevertheless the resolution which Gilkey offers, and which I find inadequate, begins with his interpretation of the traditional distinction between what can be called "ontological origination" and "historical/empirical origination." Gilkey, citing Thomas Aquinas, seems to view these as *strictly dichotomous alternatives.* One then either rejects the latter as theologically irrelevant (Gilkey's position) or elevates the latter into the essential meaning of the doctrine of creation *ex nihilo* (the position Gilkey rejects). In the first case science, insofar as t=0 is concerned, plays no role in theology; in the second case it plays a normative role.

I will criticize both extremes by seeking to undermine Gilkey's assumption that the alternatives should form a *strict* dichotomy. Instead I believe that historical/empirical origination provides an important corroborative meaning for ontological origination, although it is neither its essential nor even its central meaning—a view, incidentally, which I take to be more in keeping with that of Aquinas. I then argue that an important way of relating historical/empirical origination to ontological origination is through the concept of finitude. This abstract concept, initially closely connected to ontological origination, can take on an important historical/empirical meaning in the context of cosmology, where the past temporal finitude of the universe is represented by the event t=0. Hence I will argue that t=0 is relevant to the doctrine of creation *ex nihilo* if one interprets arguments about historical origination as offering confirming, but neither conclusive nor essential, evidence for the central thesis of ontological origination. In this way science plays a more vigorous role in the doctrine of creation than many scholars today allow *without* providing its essential meaning, and certainly not its foundations. In particular, taking a cue from the writings of Ian Barbour, Nancey Murphy, and Philip Clayton, I will frame my approach in terms of a Lakatosian research program in theology. Creation *ex nihilo* as ontological origination will form the core hypothesis of this program, with t=0 entering as confirming evidence through the use of a series of auxiliary hypotheses involving the concept of finitude deployed in increasingly empirical contexts of meaning.

In the second part of this chapter, "Theological Reflections on Quantum Cosmology," I discuss the Hartle/Hawking proposal for quantum cosmology. How should their claim that the universe, though having a finite age, has no beginning event t=0, that the universe is finite but unbounded in the past, affect the theological arguments in part I? To answer this, I will first critically discuss the positions developed by Isham, Davies, and Drees regarding the theological significance of the Hartle/Hawking proposal. Next I will present Hawking's own theological views and offer a counterargument to them. My constructive position will then be that the Hartle/Hawking proposal can have much to teach us theologically, even if its scientific status is transitory. Given their work, we should distinguish between the theological claim that creation is temporally finite in the past and the further claim that this finite past is bounded by the event t=0. This leads to the important recognition that the first claim (about finitude per se) is sufficient for developing the empirical meaning of *creatio ex nihilo*. Hence we can set aside arguments *specifically* over t=0 and yet *retain* the historical/empirical sense of the past temporal finitude of creation, as developed above. I attempt to capture this insight with the phrase, *finite creation without a beginning*. Moreover, this theological insight can be maintained whether or not the Hartle/Hawking proposal stands scientifically and thus it suggests that we can in fact work with "speculative proposals" at the frontiers of science instead of *necessarily* restricting ourselves to well-established results, as most scholars cautiously advise. I view this generalization of the meaning of finitude as an additional auxiliary hypothesis to our research program, and following Lakatos again, look for novel predictions it might entail.

To do so I analyze the temporal status of the universe in terms of the relation between quantum gravity and general relativity. The variety of ways time functions here (external, internal, phenomenological) and their implications for the temporality of the universe lead to important new directions for understanding God's action as creator and the doctrine of creation. From one perspective the universe has both a temporal and a timeless domain connected by a transitional domain. From this perspective we should inquire into God's relation as Creator to each domain. Here the generalization of the concept of finitude to include an unbounded finitude might allow us to claim the occurrence of the transition domain as a Lakatosian "novel fact" of our research program. Alternatively, if quantum gravity is to be the fundamental theory replacing general relativity, God's relation to the universe as a whole will need to be reinterpreted in terms of the complex role and status of temporality and finitude in quantum gravity. In any case, God's activity as Creator is not limited to a "first moment" (whether or not one exists) but to the entire domain of nature, returning us to the general problem of divine action in light of science. I close by pointing, then, to the need now to rethink the current models of divine agency and of the relation between time and eternity in terms of a more complex understanding of temporality from a trinitarian perspective informed by quantum physics and quantum cosmology.

2. Theological Reflections on Big Bang Cosmology

A. Gilkey and his successors on theology and cosmology

Langdon Gilkey: the critical distinction between ontological and historical/empirical origination. We start with one who was strongly influenced by neo-orthodoxy and who, in turn, directly influenced many scholars in theology and science. Here I refer to Langdon Gilkey who, in 1959, wrote the ground-breaking text on the doctrine of creation, *Maker of Heaven and Earth.* Gilkey begins his detailed discussion of creation and time by reminding us that the idea of an "'originating' activity of God" has always been a part of the Christian creation tradition. It has, however, taken two distinct forms, which I will call "ontological origination" and "historical/empirical origination."[5]

Ontological origination (origin as ontological dependence):

> God originates the *existence* of each creature out of nothing, whatever its position in the time scale.

Historical/empirical origination (origin as historical narrative):

> [I]t has meant "originating" in the sense of founding and establishing at the beginning, starting the whole sequence of things at a first moment. For most Christians, creation lies not only at the base of the existence of things; it also lies *back there* in time, at the beginning of the time series. Creation was an act done "once and for all" at the beginning of the universe: it was the first event in the history of the world.[6]

Gilkey attributes this distinction to Thomas Aquinas.[7] According to Gilkey, in the *Summa Theologica*, Aquinas affirmed that the created world is ontologically dependent, drawing on philosophical arguments in several ways. Aquinas also argued for a historical interpretation of creation based on revelation, that is, that creation has a finite age, although he asserted that philosophy on its own could never prove this revealed truth. Hence Thomas could assert both a historical and a philosophical understanding of creation, but in Gilkey's opinion, he kept their biblical and philosophical warrants separate.

Gilkey supports the ontological interpretation of origination, but he finds *two* obstacles which tend to undermine the historical interpretation. The first has to do with science's challenge to the traditional, static understanding of cosmology, the second to the legitimacy of either scientific or theological talk about a moment of absolute beginning.

According to Gilkey, creation in the historical narrative sense, with its presupposition of a static cosmology, has been severely challenged by modern, evolutionary science. Instead of a creation all at once, we are called to reinterpret the meaning of God's creative act as a continuing process of bringing things into being in time. This in turn means that creation and preservation are "different aspects of the simultaneous activity of God, who continually gives to all that arises existence and form, molding the new as well as preserving the old."[8]

The second problem undermining the historical narrative sense of creation involves the status of the "beginning." Gilkey acknowledges the important role such a traditional idea had in breaking the prevailing Hellenistic belief in a cyclic view of time and in establishing time as purposive and developing. Nevertheless, Gilkey is highly critical of it. His primary argument is a priori: knowledge about a first moment of time cannot be a valid part of theology since theology does not contain *any* "facts" about the natural order. Revelation does not "inform us of its character or its constitution."[9] Since knowledge about a cosmic beginning would be just such a fact about the universe, it "cannot be a part of religious truth."

Gilkey is also dubious about science making a claim regarding a first cosmic moment, and again for a priori reasons. "Since science presumably would have to assume that there was 'something there' out of which that moment arose, albeit an existence in a very different form, science could not include the concept of an absolute beginning of the process itself."[10]

Thus Gilkey recommends that we embrace the ontological/historical-empirical distinction as a genuine dichotomy and abandon historical/empirical language as myth, choosing instead to theologize strictly in terms of ontological dependence. "The idea of a beginning to time has a great theological and cultural value; but . . . we have been forced to deny that there can be for theology any factual content to this idea."[11]

Gilkey's views have had wide-ranging effects on theologians wrestling with creation in the context of the sciences, as will become evident in the writings of Arthur Peacocke, Ted Peters, and Ian Barbour.

Arthur Peacocke: t=0 is theologically unimportant. Although science in general, including contemporary physics, cosmology, and evolutionary biology, play a crucial role in Arthur Peacocke's theology, the problem of t=0 finds marginal significance at most. This seems to stem from the fact that, without specifically referring to Gilkey's writings in this regard, Peacocke makes essentially the same distinction Gilkey makes between ontological and historical origination.

One sees this clearly in his 1978 Bampton Lectures, *Creation and the World of Science.*[12] Here Peacocke explores at length the historical and contemporary discussion surrounding the doctrine of creation as both *ex nihilo* and *creatio continua*, and the important relation of science to the doctrine. Use of the ontological/historical distinction pervades Peacocke's discussion of *ex nihilo*:

> The principal stress in the Judeo-Christian doctrine of creation . . . is on the dependence and contingency of all entities, and events, other than God himself: it is about a perennial relationship between God and the world and not about the beginning of the Earth, or the whole universe at a point in time. . . . Time, in modern relativistic physics . . . has to be regarded as owing its existence to God. . . . It is this "owing its existence to God" which is the essential core of the idea of creation.[13]

The results of science are simply not germane to the core of that doctrine:

> Scientific cosmology . . . cannot, in principle, be doing anything which can contradict such a concept of creation. From our radio-telescopes . . . we may, or may not, be able to infer that there was a point (the "hot big bang") in spacetime when the universe, as we can observe it, began, and, perhaps, what happened on the other side of that critical point. But,

> whatever we eventually do infer, the central characteristic core of the doctrine of creation would *not* be affected, since that concerns the relationship of all the created order, including time itself, to their Creator.[14]

Arguments very similar to these are found in his Mendenhall Lectures, *Intimations of Reality*,[15] and in his article, "Theology and Science Today," in *Cosmos as Creation*.[16]

Ted Peters: t=0 is theologically crucial. Ted Peters seems to accept Gilkey's distinction but opt, almost exclusively, for a historical/empirical interpretation of origins. In this sense, Peters is representative of many theologians who take Big Bang cosmology to have direct and unambiguous implications for the doctrine of creation. In several articles, Peters has focused on the importance of the *ex nihilo* tradition in Christian theology in terms of its being in "consonance" with the problem of t=0 in Big Bang cosmology.

> It simply makes sense these days to speak of t=0, to conceive of a point at which the entire cosmos makes its appearance along with the spacetime continuum within which it is observed and understood. If we identify the concept of creation out of nothing with the point of temporal beginning or perhaps even the source of the singularity, we have sufficient consonance with which to proceed further in the discussion.[17]

Peters gives both a theological reason and a scientific rationale for such a move:

> To reduce *creatio ex nihilo* to a vague commitment about the dependence of the world upon God—though accurate—does not help much. It simply moves the matter to a higher level of abstraction. We still need to ask: just what does it mean for the world to owe its existence to God? One sensible answer is this: had God not acted to bring the spacetime world into existence, there would be only nothing. Furthermore, it makes sense to talk about the temporal point of origin. The assertion that the cosmos is utterly dependent upon God is familiar to theologians, but such an assertion lies outside the domain of scientific discourse. The idea of an initial origin, however, does lie within the scientific domain. The point I am making here is this: for theologians to raise again the prospects of *creatio ex nihilo* understood in terms of a beginning to time and space is to be consonant with discussions already taking place within scientific cosmology.[18]

Peters sees himself in sharp opposition to both Barbour and Gilkey over which side of the distinction posited by Gilkey should carry the weight of *ex nihilo*. Thus Peters warns us: "If we were to follow the path led by Barbour and Gilkey, we might end up making no definitive theological commitments whatsoever regarding whether the cosmos ever had an initial origin, or, if it did, just how God was involved in this origin."[19] This certainly seems clearer in his more recent writings, where Barbour is inclined to keep something of the *ex nihilo* position. Whether he was so persuaded in 1966 remains an open question, and Peters may be correct about that part of Barbour's writings. My point is here that, assuming the distinction between ontological and historical interpretations for the sake of argument, Peters may be incorrect in his analysis that Barbour reduces ("equates") *ex nihilo* to t=0 and *then* discards the latter. Rather Barbour may be seeking to keep them separate using the ontological/historical distinction, and then to discard the latter and keep the former. The essential point here is that he seems to agree with the distinction though he disagrees over which of its interpretations is correct.

Ian Barbour: t=0 is relatively theologically unimportant. Ian Barbour's position seems to lie somewhere between Peacocke and Peters, and shifts, if I am not mistaken, from being initially closer to the position defended by Peacocke towards the interpretation advocated by Peters.[20]

Barbour's pioneering text, *Issues in Science and Religion*,[21] was written in the mid-1960s, during the competition between the Big Bang cosmology and the steady state theory of Hoyle, Bondi, and Gold. Here Barbour's theological assessment of cosmology emerges in several key passages. As Barbour points out in chapter 12, Big Bang cosmology had often been defended by theologians while naturalists opted for the steady state theory. "We would submit, however, that both theories are capable of either a naturalistic or a theistic interpretation." Both contain unexplained features and neither resolves the problem of time. "We will suggest that the Christian need not favor either theory, for the doctrine of creation is not really about temporal beginnings but about the basic relationship between the world and God."[22] He concludes that either theory is compatible with Christian theology, and only science can tell us which one is correct.

Next Barbour turns to neo-orthodoxy and its interpretation of creation. After citing Emil Brunner[23] briefly, Barbour focuses his attention on Gilkey's *Maker*, which he describes as "the best recent exposition of the doctrine by a Protestant theologian."[24] Barbour attributes to Gilkey the claim that "creation is not as such a historical account. . . . It is not really about temporal origins in the past, but about the basic relationship between God and the world in the present." Barbour admits that neo-orthodoxy leads to "a radical separation of scientific and religious questions" but he agrees with Gilkey who "emphasized that creation is a relationship, not an event; the doctrine deals with ontological dependence, not temporal history."[25]

In the concluding section of chapter 12, Barbour again seems content to accept Gilkey's formulation of the distinction without further analysis. He states clearly that "we agree with neo-orthodoxy [Gilkey] that the doctrine of creation is not fundamentally a hypothesis about origins but an affirmation of our dependence on God . . ."[26] Finally, his previous agreement with Gilkey is taken up into his general conclusions to the entire textbook, where Barbour writes: "We may have to give up *creatio ex nihilo* as an initial act of absolute origination, but God's priority in status can be maintained apart from priority in time."[27]

When Barbour's first series of Gifford Lectures were given in 1989,[28] more than two decades had passed since the demise of the steady state model and the commensurate strengthening of support for Big Bang cosmology. In this changed scientific context, Barbour returns to the problem of the status of time and the meaning of *creatio ex nihilo*. What response should theologians *now* give to the singularity at t=0, given that this event is "inaccessible" to the scientist and thus it represents "a kind of ultimate limit to scientific inquiry?"[29]

On the one hand, Barbour cites those like Pope Pius XII who found support for creation theology in Big Bang cosmology. On the other hand, he reports on those like Arthur Peacocke who claim that the topic is inconsequential to theology. Barbour's own position lies between these poles, although he again leans towards the position taken by neo-orthodoxy.

He is cautious about "gaps"-type arguments in general, although he admits that the case of t=0 is different precisely because it is inaccessible in principle to science. He is also concerned that changes in cosmology could alter the entire situation. Hoyle had avoided the problem of a beginning with his steady state model, and other models, such as an oscillating universe, could still accomplish the same. Moreover, "it is equally difficult to imagine a beginning of time or an infinite span of time."

Still Barbour's underlying reason for caution towards t=0 is basically theological.

> I do not think that major theological issues are at stake [in the case of t=0], as has often been assumed. If a single, unique Big Bang continues to be the most convincing scientific theory, the theist can indeed see it as an instant of divine origination. But I will suggest that this is not the main concern expressed in the religious notion of creation.[30]

Barbour will again locate this concern more in terms of continuing creation than in terms of creation *ex nihilo*, though a discussion of this argument would take us beyond the scope of this chapter.[31]

B. Critique and constructive proposals

Specific criticism of Peters and Barbour. First I want to offer some specific criticisms of the views of Peters and Barbour relating to t=0. Then I want to suggest a general criticism of the views of all three—Peacocke, Peters, and Barbour—by turning to the underlying source of the problem, namely the strict dichotomy between ontological and historical/empirical origination advocated by Gilkey. Finally I will propose a constructive approach to the problem which, I believe, circumvents these problems as a whole and opens the door to a detailed theological appraisal of divine action in terms of the doctrine of creation seen in the light of cosmology.

Critique of Ted Peters. Unlike Peacocke and Barbour, who seem anxious to purge *ex nihilo* of any empirical content about t=0 (though as we shall argue, Barbour shifts his position somewhat with time), Peters wants to relate, to the point of equating, *ex nihilo* with t=0. The gain would ostensibly be to achieve consonance between theology and science, and thus to secure a starting point by which further discussions can be pursued.

My concern with Peters's proposal is drawn from three distinct areas. 1) Science: If (and it is inevitably a "when" as we shall see with Hawking's research) science changes its mind about t=0, the kind of consonance sought by Peters will be lost. 2) Philosophy: It is far from clear in principle whether the "event" designated by t=0 is open to scientific investigation. Certainly if there truly were an event which was both uncaused and yet the cause of future events, its scientific status would be highly ambiguous.[32] Indeed, as Bill Stoeger argues, although a point of *absolute* beginning might have occurred, cosmology in principle would *not* be able to discover it.[33] 3) Theology: The identification of *ex nihilo* with t=0 would seem too narrow. Peters clearly wants to avoid removing all empirical content from contingency. Still, there are many forms of contingency besides the finite age of the universe.

Moreover, in seeking to avoid an overly abstract rendition of contingency, Peters, as we have seen above, writes:

> Just what does it mean for the world to owe its existence to God? One sensible answer is this: had God not acted to bring the spacetime world into existence, there would be only nothing.[34]

Unfortunately, this comment actually fails to contain any empirical content, and is no less abstract than the strict dependence argument Peters wants to dismiss. Indeed, it could be taken as a definition of the claim of ontological origination!

Critique of Ian Barbour. Ian Barbour's views on t=0 seem to move between those of Peacocke and Peters. In the 1960s he was indifferent to the theological implications of cosmology. By the time of the Gifford Lectures in 1989, Barbour seemed more willing to concede that cosmology could play a modest role in the debate over *creatio ex nihilo*. His views there, however, still seem clearly stamped by the position Gilkey set out in *Maker* more than three decades ago.

To see this, let us return to what Barbour says about *ex nihilo* in the passages we lifted up previously. In both *Issues* and the Gifford Lectures, three critical points emerge: 1) Barbour accepts the sharp ontological/historical distinction proposed by Gilkey; 2) he argues that the ontological interpretation carries the central meaning of *ex nihilo*; 3) hence t=0, being empirical, plays no role in the *ex nihilo* interpretation. This position is reflected relatively succinctly in the following passage on the contingency of the universe in the Gifford Lectures:

> I agree with the neo-orthodox authors who say that it is the sheer *existence* of the universe that is the datum of theology, and that the details of scientific cosmology are irrelevant here. The message of creation *ex nihilo* applies to the whole of the cosmos at every moment, regardless of questions about its beginning or its detailed structure and history. It is an ontological and not a historical assertion.[35]

It is only in the context of the Gifford Lectures, and not in *Issues*, that Barbour turns to the possibility of a historical interpretation of *ex nihilo* and its relation to t=0. Should an initial singularity be supported scientifically, Barbour believes this *would* provide an "impressive example of dependence on God."[36] Still he reminds us that even an infinitely old universe would be contingent.

This inclusion of even the marginal significance of t=0 in his theology of creation represents something of a shift from Barbour's earlier position. Still,

Barbour draws the distinction between ontological and historical origination very sharply and places essentially all the theological weight on the ontological interpretation, with only nodding attention to the possibility of the historical interpretation being relevant.

General criticism: Gilkey's dichotomy. My main contention with Peacocke, Peters, and Barbour is that they seem to have accepted the sharp dichotomy Gilkey makes between ontological and historical/empirical origination. They differ only in how they decide which one is theologically important. Peacocke and, to a slightly lesser extent, Barbour, accept Gilkey's distinction and, with Gilkey, abandon the historical/empirical aspect. Peters accepts Gilkey's distinction but, *contra* Gilkey, reduces the ontological meaning of creation to its historical/empirical context since, without this, ontological dependence would supposedly be a mere abstraction.

Now I agree that the critical issue at stake in the *ex nihilo* tradition is ontological origination: the radical dependence of finite being on God as the absolute source of being. The question is whether ontological origination should be seen as *devoid* of historical/empirical meaning, as Gilkey argued. To understand Gilkey's reasons and then to evaluate them, we must go back to *Maker.*

There, as I see it, Gilkey was faced with a fundamental problem which occurs throughout neo-orthodoxy and the ensuing literature in biblical theology: how to relate religious and empirical/scientific language. This problem may have been forced on him by the issue of t=0, but it is really ubiquitous to theology, as he so poignantly expressed in his now-famous article "Cosmology, Ontology, and the Travail of Biblical Language"[37] written just three years after *Maker.* There Gilkey argues that neo-orthodoxy and biblical theology consist in an unsuccessful attempt to combine biblical language and scientific cosmology. In the process it empties biblical language of its initial content, leaving it at best analogous, at worst equivocal. I would add to this that in doing so theological epistemology is isolated from secular knowledge, robbing it of explanatory, let alone predictive, power and confining it to the sphere of religious language.

Although he rejects one possible solution to the problem, that is, the attempt to incorporate facts about a beginning of the universe into the doctrine of creation, Gilkey in no way minimizes the theological importance of the question raised by t=0 nor does he dismiss t=0 as a minor topic in the pursuit of what is of "real" theological interest to the doctrine of creation, as so many theologians still do. Instead, even in *Maker,* Gilkey sees the issue of t=0 as critically important, since it forces us to confront a *foundational* problem which governs and characterizes *every* major doctrine in Christian theology. "This same dilemma dogs the heels of every major theological idea. Every doctrine of Christian faith expresses the paradoxical relation between the transcendent God and the world of facts."[38] In the writings that followed this early work, we can watch Gilkey continue to wrestle with this problem of biblical language and secular thought.

Although I will be quite critical of Gilkey's resolution of the problem, we owe him a great deal for his lucid insistence on its importance as such. If Gilkey is correct, the epistemological problems surrounding t=0 are well worth *our* pursuing because they are *inherent* to the theological agenda as such, and not a minor issue best forgotten. Indeed, they raise the fundamental and unavoidable problem of the rationality of theology in an age of scientific epistemology.

The strategy Gilkey adopted to resolve the problem of relating theological to scientific language was to view religious language about historical/empirical origins as myth, thus insulating it from scientific discourse.[39] Specifically, he argued that theological language about matters which might seem to be factual, like t=0, and thus open to scientific inquiry, is actually discourse at the level of myth having nothing in common with science. Once we recognize this, we can avoid any potential conflict between theology and science. For when properly conceived they are seen to be completely separate worlds of discourse, and thus the paradox is resolved.

Does this strategy work? In my opinion it does not, since it marginalizes theology by insulating it from the cognitive claims and discoveries of secular inquiry. Moreover, I believe we now have an alternative. Perhaps the best way to deploy the alternative will be to examine the way in which Gilkey initially approaches the problem of relating theological doctrine and empirical facts.

Gilkey bases his approach on a premise which is located at the outset of his analysis and which governs his entire line of reasoning, including his resolution of the problem in terms of myth. The crucial premise consists in what I consider to be an unnecessarily rigid distinction between ontological and historical/empirical origination. Gilkey might appear to be appropriating the traditional distinction between ontological origination and historical/empirical origination as found in Aquinas. However, in a move which is crucial for all that follows, he then *recasts* the distinction into a *sharp dichotomy*. He claims that, when properly conceived, theology is *only* concerned with one side of the dichotomy, namely ontological origination. From this it follows that language about historical/empirical origination has no valid cognitive role in theology. Where it does surface, it actually functions as myth. Since only the ontological claim is proper to theology, we should disregard the historical/empirical language and focus on the ontological meaning of creation. The result is that we avoid a conflict with science—and in the process, *any* cognitive encounter with science.

C. Overcoming Gilkey's dichotomy: a Lakatosian theological research program

I believe that Gilkey's approach ought to be set aside. In my opinion, it is based on an unnecessary premise, namely that ontological origination and historical/empirical origination *must* be seen as strictly dichotomous. Instead I propose we embed historical/empirical language within the broader context of ontological origination, thus giving a factual basis to which the core philosophical/theological generalization about ontological origination can be related without literalization *or* equivocation.

To do so I first return to the distinction as it was traditionally given. Now it is my understanding that the distinction is more complex and flexible than Gilkey allows. I take Aquinas's strategy, for example, to have been something like the following. On the one hand, if science supports an eternally old universe, as Aristotle argued, one can still maintain that the universe is ontologically dependent in the philosophical sense by the mere fact of its existence per se. Moreover, there might be other factors which would flesh out the ontological dependence of an Aristotelian universe in empirical/historical terms, involving motion, causality, agency, purpose, and so on. On the other hand, if science supports a universe with a finite age, as the Big Bang suggests, this can count as empirical evidence in support of ontological origination, although other evidence might count against it, too. Ontological dependence is thus the *crucial*, but not the *exhaustive*, meaning of creation.[40]

Next I propose that we adopt a more complex strategy for relating ontological and historical origination. To do so I will draw on recent work in theological methodology, first anticipated by Ian Barbour[41] and very recently developed in detail by both Nancey Murphy[42] and Philip Clayton.[43] These scholars appropriate current research in philosophy of science for the purposes of theological method, focusing specifically on the writings of Imre Lakatos.[44] Following their pioneering work, I propose we structure the doctrine of creation *ex nihilo* and its relation to data in cosmology in terms of a Lakatosian research program. This will include a central, or "core," hypothesis surrounded by a protective belt of auxiliary hypotheses which can be tested against relevant data, and a set of criteria agreed upon in advance by which to decide rationally between competing research programs. In this way evidence for empirical origination from contemporary science, such as the Big Bang offers in terms of t=0, could be related to a core theological hypothesis in such a way as to allow it to confirm ontological origination without the evidence being somehow directly identified with the core hypothesis.

However, lest I appear to be setting up a "no lose" scenario, I hasten to add that this method is meant to cut both ways: Evidence against empirical origination, such as offered in the 1950s and 1960s by Hoyle's steady state model or which might arise through new cosmological models of a universe with an infinite age, would count *against ex nihilo*.[45] Still ontological origination could never be absolutely disproven by *any* empirical evidence, since the sheer existence of the universe (let alone the existence of such "empirical evidence") is the foundational basis for the central philosophical argument for *ex nihilo*.

I suggest we place at the core of the theological research program the hypothesis, "*creatio ex nihilo* means ontological origination." Next we deploy a series of auxiliary hypotheses which surround the core and relate it to relevant types of data including those from cosmology. I propose as one such auxiliary hypothesis the claim, "ontological origination entails finitude." I chose "finitude" because it seems a particularly fruitful concept for relating ontological origination and t=0. By finitude I mean the traditional Aristotelian concept of something with determinate status, measure, or boundary, as opposed to the *apeiron*, that which is unbounded, unlimited, endlessly extensible.[46] We use this concept in an auxiliary hypothesis closest to the theological core theory. Thus on the one hand, finitude can function as an abstract philosophical concept located near the theological core where it will resist being reduced to a univocal, empirically testable meaning. Keeping a substantive distance between the theological core and the data from science will, in turn, at least partially address the concerns voiced by Gilkey, Peacocke, and Barbour.

Yet the concept of finitude need not be restricted to an abstract, philosophical context. Instead it can be developed in a variety of ways to make increasing contact with physics and cosmology, and thus with an empirical meaning of origination. To do so we construct a second auxiliary hypothesis, "finitude includes temporal finitude," that is, that which is bounded in time. From this we construct a third auxiliary hypothesis, "temporal finitude includes past temporal finitude," that is, the property of finite age. Now we are in a position to connect this series of hypotheses to Big Bang cosmology in which the data of astrophysics, the theory of general relativity, and other factors, assumptions, and simplifications, lead to the theoretical conclusion that the universe has a finite age and an initial singularity, t=0. In this way the concept of finitude can serve as a bridge between the core theory, ontological origination, and the data for theology, here seen in terms of the origin of the universe at t=0; this satisfies at least part of Peters's intent to make a connection (albeit *not* a direct one) between ontological and empirical origination.

Through this process I claim we can argue that the empirical origination described by t=0 in Big Bang cosmology tends to confirm what is entailed by theological core theory, "*creatio ex nihilo* means ontological origination." Moreover, to the extent that Big Bang cosmology continues to gain scientific support, the confirmation of *ex nihilo* is strengthened. Recent evidence from the COBE satellite showing the existence of minute structure in the microwave background constitutes such additional support for Big Bang cosmology, and thus indirectly it constitutes additional support for *creatio ex nihilo.* I want to emphasize again, though, that this method allows for disconfirmation as well as confirmation. Ideally, one would compare several theological and/or nontheological research programs, each of which attempt to relate *creatio ex nihilo* to cosmology in its own way, and assess which program is most progressive by the way it predicts novel facts and avoids ad hoc moves.[47] In this way, we can move theology out of its closed hermeneutical circle and allow it to make cognitive contact with empirical knowledge.[48]

Let us pause for a moment, and assess the situation. We have been focusing on the relationship between *creatio ex nihilo* and inflationary Big Bang cosmology. We know, however, that severe conceptual problems revolve around the status of t=0, problems which involve both technical issues in mathematical physics and in the philosophy of science. Moreover, Big Bang cosmology depends upon special relativity and *its* assumptions are "classical" (that is, pre-quantum mechanical). Thus much attention is now being devoted to the goal of obtaining a quantum treatment of gravity. One of the goals being pursued via quantum gravity is to obtain a quantum cosmology which will be free of the initial singularity, t=0. As such a goal is approached, what will happen to the theological research program I have sketched above which relates ontological origination with t=0, even though it does so indirectly? It is to this question that we now turn.

3. Theological Reflections on Quantum Cosmology

A. Two possible routes to quantum cosmology: quantum fluctuations versus the Hartle/Hawking model

There are a variety of approaches to quantum gravity and the cosmological models which emerge from it, that is, the models of quantum cosmology. In this chapter I will focus on the Hartle/Hawking model, first by comparing it with an alternative (quantum fluctuations) and then through a detailed look at the model itself. Much of the discussion will draw from a recent paper by Chris Isham,

"Creation as a Quantum Process,"[49] and from the Stoeger/Ellis and Isham papers in *Quantum Cosmology and the Laws of Nature*.[50] At the onset I want to underscore the *speculative* nature of such proposals, a point that Isham makes forcefully in his paper. What I hope to show is their value for theology in such a way that it is relatively independent of their long-term scientific viability.

Quantum fluctuations. One attempt at quantum cosmology begins by supposing that what is actually "created" is matter alone, and not spacetime. More precisely, one assumes: i) the existence of a background spacetime (or some other manifold), ii) filled with the appropriate quantum fields in their ground (lowest energy) state, and iii) governed by appropriate laws of nature. Now the *material* universe arises as a spontaneous quantum fluctuation of the fields in the background spacetime.[51]

Hartle/Hawking model. The Hartle/Hawking model does not assume a background spacetime out of which the universe arises. It does, however, assume a set of three-dimensional spaces out of which spacetime can be constructed. It also presupposes the existence of the appropriate laws of physics, including quantum physics (in particular the Feynman "path integral" approach) and general relativity, and it employs a mathematical trick to simplify calculations, namely the introduction of complex numbers.[52] We will look at the Hartle/Hawking model in a bit more detail below. For now the important points to note are that: i) It succeeds in describing a universe with a finite past but *no* initial singularity;[53] this accomplishes what previous theories had been unable to do, and changes the scientific mode of discussion about the origination of the universe. ii) Time arises phenomenologically in this model; it is not a given, external parameter which describes the evolution of the universe as in the FLRW model.

Exploring the Hartle/Hawking model further: the roles and status of time and space.
In the Hartle/Hawking model, time is treated as an "internal variable." A similar term is often used about general relativity, but in the quantum context the meaning is significantly different.

General relativity. For each solution to the field equations of general relativity, time and space form a *single* four-dimensional curved spacetime manifold. The spacetime manifold is *static:* it does not change in "time" since it includes time as one of the four dimensions of spacetime.

The spacetime manifold can be sliced in a variety of ways. Each set of (spacelike) slices gives a specific "history" for the universe.[54] Each history depicts the universe as a sequence of slices or three-geometries[55] sewn together smoothly by an *external* parameter, time. Now each slice can be characterized in several ways: by the value of external time (that is, through its relation to other slices) or by a property internal to the slice itself, such as the temperature of the matter field or the radius of curvature of the slice. When we use such properties as temperature or radius of curvature to serve as a temporal label, we call this label *internal* time.

There are an infinity of ways to slice spacetime, and hence an infinity of histories all explicitly different, yet all consistent with a single spacetime. Hence one can say that general relativity provides both a *dynamic* (or *temporal*) view of the universe as a three-space evolving in time, of which there are an infinity of equivalent but distinguishable versions corresponding to different slicings, and a *static* (or *timeless*) view of the universe as a unique four-geometry (spacetime) which can be decomposed to yield an infinite set of different but complete dynamic histories. So time in general relativity can be an *external* parameter which sews together an infinite set of three-geometries or an *internal* parameter which functions as a property of a three-space, like temperature or curvature.[56]

B. Hartle/Hawking model

Returning to the Hartle/Hawking model, we find a further diminution in the role and status of time in relation to space. Here we start by imagining all possible curved three-spaces, c, with all possible ways in which matter can be distributed on each of them; together these form the "configuration space" for the theory.[57] Next we define a quantum mechanical state function Y(c,f) for each curved three-space, c, and for its associated matter fields, f. Y(c,f) is a measure of the probability of finding the particular curvature and matter fields, c and f.[58] Note that time has not entered in explicitly in the definitions so far. Instead it is treated as an *internal* property of c and f.

Now comes a crucial difference between quantum and classical gravity regarding time. In some cases, the three-spaces may be sewn together to form a continuous, four-dimensional spacetime. In these cases, the path in state space would be equivalent[59] to a single four-dimensional spacetime in general relativity. However in other cases, the nonzero three-spaces will *not* fit into, or be derivable from, a single four-dimensional spacetime.

One can think of the situation as follows: A single four-dimensional spacetime, as understood in classical physics, would be represented by a single, sharply delineated path between two different three-spaces c(1) and c(2).[60] In the quantum context, however, the path is "fuzzy" and diffuse. In effect, the classical picture of a well-defined spacetime arises as the limiting case of the quantum perspective, and the sharp trajectory of the classical spacetime is just that portion of the fuzzy pattern in quantum state space where the state function Y is maximal. Hence, as Isham concludes, "the concept 'spacetime' only has an unambiguous meaning within the framework of nonquantum physics, whereas the idea of three-dimensional 'space' can be applied to both the quantum and the classical theories."[61]

In other words, in the Hartle/Hawking model *time is less fundamental than space.* Time only has an unambiguous meaning for a *given* three-space, where it is best understood as internal time. It need not have an unambiguous meaning as the external parameter characterizing the evolution of a set of three-spaces, because there may be no single four-dimensional spacetime for which all these three-spaces are sections. Without such a four-dimensional spacetime, there is no context by which to view a series of three-spaces (each characterized by some value of internal time) as linked together and thus as "evolving." *In the Hartle/Hawking model, the static view surpasses the dynamic view.*

We also have the problem of the initial singularity, t=0, in the standard cosmology. To tackle this in the context of general relativity, Hartle/Hawking first represents time by an imaginary number. This changes the formalism in such a way that time is treated on strictly the same footing as space. One can solve Einstein's field equations for matter distributed in such a four-space and obtain solutions which are *not* singular![62]

Next Hartle/Hawking looks for a *quantum* treatment using imaginary time and a state function for the universe. Its proposal is governed by the following stipulation: The spacetime must have only *one* boundary, not two as in standard Big Bang cosmology. In particular, it *cannot* have a singular initial boundary.[63] In the Hartle/Hawking model the universe has no "beginning" at the initial singular boundary, since there is *no* initial boundary at all! It simply has the "present" boundary (its current "size," to speak loosely) and a past history.[64] It is this feature of their model which led Hawking to refer to the boundary condition as the "no boundary" condition, and to the claim that, rather than being created, the universe "would just BE."[65]

The lack of an initial singularity, the "fuzzy" path problem, the mathematical treatment of time as a complex variable, and the general difficulty of giving a realist interpretation of quantum physics all make a uniform global interpretation of time in the Hartle/Hawking model very difficult.

4. Summary: Four Views of Time

A. General relativity

In general relativity one finds two interchangeable views of time: external and internal.

> a. External time: In general, Relativity labels the sequence of three-spaces that form a given four-dimensional spacetime. The sense of their being sewn together as a process in time, three-space by three-space (like sewing beads on a string), offers a dynamic description of an evolving universe. The sense of their having been sewn together, that they now exist as a whole spacetime (like a necklace), leads to a static description.
>
> b. Internal time: Internal time in general relativity is a function of a given three-space. It is transformable into some other characteristic of the three-space (such as its radius or the temperature of its matter field). It conveys a static view of the givenness of a specific geometry, losing the ordinary sense of time as passage.

However, in general relativity one can move freely between these two perspectives, since the only three-spaces admitted are those which can be sewn together (by the external time parameter) to form a unique four-dimensional spacetime. Conversely every four-dimensional spacetime can be decomposed in a variety of ways to form different sets of three-spaces. Hence dynamic (temporal) and static (spatial) views are equally fundamental.

B. Quantum gravity

In the *quantum treatment of gravity*, one expects time to have a less fundamental status than space in ways which simply do not occur in general relativity.[66] Internal time arises in quantum gravity, but in general external time does not.

Moreover, the relation between quantum gravity and general relativity leads to two interpretations of the *status* of time in quantum cosmology: as a uniform characteristic of the entire universe viewed as a single domain or as a differing characteristic of the universe seen in terms of multiple domains (see below).

Internal quantum time. In quantum gravity, as in general relativity, we start with three-spaces which have a characteristic internal time (or, equivalently, some other parameter such as size or temperature). The additional problems that surface in the quantum context, however, are clearly in evidence when we turn to quantum cosmology. Here generally speaking, one is faced with numerous three-spaces which cannot be sewn together to form an overall four-dimensional spacetime. Thus the individual internal times of these three-spaces cannot be given an external time interpretation. In this sense internal time in quantum gravity loses even more of its temporal meaning than in general relativity.

However, in some specific quantum cosmological proposals, such as the Hartle/Hawking model, one can once again obtain an overall four-dimensional spacetime into which many of the relevant three-spaces can be sewn together.[67] In this sense the internal times of many of these three-spaces *can* be given a temporal interpretation via the context of the overall spacetime in ways similar to general relativity. Still, even here, many three-spaces must be included which cannot be joined together smoothly (that is, the path of three-spaces is "fuzzy"). Thus some domains of the universe are more classical in appearance, others more quantum mechanical, even though all are generated from a strictly quantum mechanical treatment of gravity. How should we view the overall temporality of such quantum cosmologies? We seem to be led to two different interpretations of time in quantum cosmology—characterized by single or multiple domains—depending on upon the relation between quantum gravity and general relativity.

C. Single domain

Although all we have so far are tentative proposals for quantum gravity, in its eventual form as a full-blown theory it should be viewed as a *fundamental* theory replacing general relativity and thus describing the universe as a whole. This means that quantum gravity actually describes the entire universe, even the domain where its effects are negligible and where general relativity is a good approximation (that is, the classical domain from the early universe to the present and into the far future).

Thus even if the "timeless" character of quantum gravity is hidden to our macroscopic eyes, it must be taken as describing the way things really are even in our "temporal" region of the universe. Time as we know it is merely phenomenological; the entire universe is really only one timeless domain, all of it described by the three-spaces of quantum gravity. Hence the lack of a global external time parameter (that is, the problem of not being able to sew together all relevant three-geometries into a single spacetime) means that the internal time of quantum geometry gives time even less status than does the internal time of general relativity.

D. Multiple domains

In a more *phenomenological* approach, quantum gravity is taken to be limited to the very early universe, describing it in quantum terms (as, for example, in the Hartle/Hawking proposal), whereas general relativity describes the universe from a fraction of a second to the present and into the far future using classical (that is, nonquantum mechanical) terms. Hence time is domain-dependent, a real feature of the general relativistic domain but not of the quantum gravity domain.[68] We can conveniently name these the Einstein and the Hawking domains, respectively. Presumably it would be in the Einstein domain that we would also find the production of those characteristics, such as asymmetry and varying ontological status, needed for the "arrow of time," the flow from past to present into future, but this issue takes us beyond the scope of this chapter.

Thus time is neither globally present nor globally absent in this interpretation. Rather external time is a phenomenon characterizing the Einstein domain of spacetime in which we live, far from the early, Hawking domain. No longer a global feature of the model, external time is the local[69] result of the changing geometry of spacetime, that is, the change from being essentially a four-dimensional fuzzy space into being a four-dimensional well-defined spacetime.

In effect, as one thinks back from the present towards the very early universe (Hawking domain), the imaginary components of the time coordinate begin to dominate and the three-spaces become increasingly disjunct, making it increasingly hard to give a physical interpretation of time. Reversing directions and moving outward from the early universe towards the present, time as we know it seems to arise as spacetime becomes more clearly defined. In this sense, time as we know it, including time's arrow, is a phenomenon only manifested by a portion of the topology—even though in scope this domain extends from the present back to the first microseconds of the universe!

Finally, in the multiple domains interpretation one must deal with the transition between the timeless Hawking domain and the temporal Einstein domain. The key point here is that a more fundamental concept than time will be needed to describe the relation between the Hawking domain where quantum gravity predominates and the Einstein domain we inhabit. We can call the domain which connects them the transition domain.[70] Clearly in the previous, single domain interpretation, there is no need to discuss a transition domain since the entire universe is described in principle by quantum gravity as a fundamental theory.

It should be noted that the distinction between single and multiple domains does not affect the validity of the claim that the universe has a finite past in the Hartle/Hawking model, only its meaning. It suggests how difficult it is to give a consistent interpretation of the concept of a "finite past" when dealing with quantum gravity.

5. Relating Theology and Cosmology: Constructive Proposals

A. Theology as offering criteria in the choice between quantum fluctuations and the Hartle/Hawking model

How ought one to choose between these two approaches: quantum fluctuations versus the Hartle/Hawking model? The criteria are, in fact, largely philosophical in nature.[71]

Is "creation in time" reasonable? Isham illustrates this fact quite nicely when he makes his case against quantum fluctuations in favor of the Hartle/Hawking model: "These [quantum fluctuation] theories are prone to predict, not a single creation/seed-point, but rather an infinite number of them."[72] The problem stems from the fact that the background spacetime is homogeneous and infinite. "There is simply no way of distinguishing any particular instant of time" at which the material universe would spontaneously appear. Hence an infinity of universes should be created throughout the background spacetime. This obviously leads to predictions in gross contradiction with our astronomical observations,[73] and theories like this have received little sustained attention.

Isham then suggests that this problem in physics was "preempted" by Augustine in his "refutation of this demiurgic concept of God." In the famous response to the question about what God was doing before God made the universe, Augustine argued that the question itself involves a false assumption about time. God did not create the world in *time*, but rather God created time *along with the world.*[74] As Isham remarks, "it is singularly striking that, sixteen centuries later, theoretical physicists have considered precisely the same subterfuge as a means of avoiding the question of the 'when' or 'before' of creation."

A position similar to Isham was developed by Paul Davies in *God and the New Physics.*[75] In a stimulating chapter entitled "Did God create the universe?" Davies writes:

> As we have seen, modern cosmology suggests that the appearance of the universe involved the appearance of time itself. . . . [Thus] it is clearly meaningless to talk about God creating the universe in the usual causal sense, if that act of creation involves the creation of time itself. . . . This point seems to have been well appreciated by St. Augustine . . . who ridiculed the idea of God waiting for an infinite time and then deciding at some propitious moment to create a universe. . . . This [insight] is a remarkable anticipation of modern scientific cosmology.[76]

Returning to Isham's argument, if we take an Augustinian perspective we should think of the motion of matter as coincidental with the origin of time. Hence time should be a derivative of something ontologically prior, namely a derivative of the properties of matter such as temperature or field configuration, and so on. As Isham points out, the problem of the beginning of time and the universe can be avoided in principle if a physical scheme can be found to implement the Augustinian insight, such that as we approach the initial point of the universe time itself loses its fundamental status. An instance of such a scheme is realized in the Hartle/Hawking model of the universe.

Willem Drees[77] has written extensively on the topic of the Big Bang. In discussing Isham's work, Drees points out how the Hartle/Hawking model avoids the problem of the beginning of time and recalls Isham's reference to Augustine and Philo. But Drees goes further than Isham here by suggesting an important difference between the concerns of Augustine and Hawking.

> Augustine probably understood the beginning of time with the creation as an event outside the scope of natural knowledge. But Hawking holds it to be only the beginning of a co-ordinate without reference to any special event, and without a breakdown of physical describability.[78]

I think this is a valuable clarification of the difference between Augustine and Hawking. According to the former, the beginning was an event which could not be discovered by reason alone. As Drees suggests, the Hartle/Hawking model challenges this point in that in their model there simply is no such event. It is not *hidden* from view; it *doesn't exist.*[79]

Is "nothing" creative? I would like to add a second argument from a theological perspective against the quantum fluctuation model and in favor of the Hartle/Hawking model. It is related to, but not reducible to, the argument proposed by Hawking and Isham which uses Augustine's claim about creation in time.

First we must make a *philosophical* distinction between the kinds of nonbeing used in Greek metaphysics. According to Paul Tillich, there were two conceptions of nonbeing in Plato: *ouk on* and *me on*. The latter signified an undifferentiated form of potential reality out of which structures could spontaneously emerge. The former signified the utter lack of anything whatsoever, potential or actual. Tillich claimed that the classical formulation of *ex nihilo* meant creation out of *no thing*, not creation out of a reified "nothing" of any sort. Thus Christianity rejected the concept of *me on* and used *ouk on* instead to signify that there was nothing (that is, there wasn't anything) apart from God before God created, that without God nothing could exist per se.[80]

Now consider the concept of a "filled background spacetime" used in the quantum fluctuation model in terms of these two Greek categories of nonbeing. The background spacetime includes the quantum fields (albeit in their quiescent state, that is, vacuum state), the spacetime itself, and the laws of nature. It seems to me that the background spacetime would be a *meonic*, rather than an *oukonic*, form of nonbeing *on all three* counts.

Tillich then makes the *theological* claim that it is *ouk on*, or the nonbeing incapable of spontaneously creating the world, which is employed in the doctrine of creation *ex nihilo*, since God should not depend on anything (matter or form) existing prior to the act of *absolute* creation. It follows that acceptance of *creatio ex nihilo* would lead us to choose *against* the quantum fluctuation model.

Of course one should also ask whether the *ex nihilo* argument would *unilaterally support* the Hartle/Hawking model. This too would depend on the way in which our concept of nonbeing enters into *this* model. The issue has received some discussion already, notably by Wim Drees, John Barrow, Michael Heller,[81] and George Ellis.[82] Closely related arguments have surfaced before in discussions which preceded the work of Hartle/Hawking by, among others, Paul Davies and myself.[83] In the Hartle/Hawking case, the arguments tend to revolve around the idea that, although a previously existing spacetime of some sort is *not* proposed, a *preexisting set of laws of nature* are presupposed to exist. But such laws would be included in what the traditional doctrine considers as falling within God's creation and not something external to, and co-eternal with, God. Hence even the Hartle/Hawking model does not assume the creation of the universe out of *oukonic* nonbeing.

Thus although the theological commitment to *ouk on* might weigh more heavily against the quantum fluctuation model than against the Hartle/Hawking model, it certainly does not support the latter unambiguously. Indeed it drives us to look for additional ways in which even the laws of nature may be created.[84]

B. Theological appropriation of the "no-boundary" condition

The Hartle/Hawking proposal makes evident that a self-consistent scientific conception of the universe can be constructed in which the universe has a finite age but no "beginning," that is, the finite past is unbounded.[85] This may be the most important aspect of the Hartle/Hawking proposal for theologians to consider. Before turning to this discussion, however, we should consider what Hawking himself makes of the problem, since without doubt he speaks for much of secular society in finding reasons for rejecting the claim that God acts in the world.

Hawking's theological conclusions. Hawking draws two conclusions from his cosmology. 1) Since there is no beginning to the universe, there is nothing left for God to do except choose the laws of nature. 2) By understanding the underlying laws of nature as chosen by God we can, in effect, read the mind of God. We will not analyze the second conclusion here, but turn instead to the first. How does Hawking warrant this conclusion?

Hawking's argument depends on a prior argument: that if God acts at all, God can *only* act at the beginning of the universe and not during the course of natural processes. This in turn rests on two assumptions: i) that the universe runs according to scientific laws which exclude God's action except by divine intervention, and ii) that God doesn't intervene in nature. Hawking makes these assumptions clear in several passages:

> With the success of scientific theories in describing events, most people have come to believe that God allows the universe to evolve according to a set of laws and does not intervene in the universe to break these laws.[86]

These laws may have originally been decreed by God, but it appears that he has since left the universe to evolve according to them and does not now intervene in it.[87] Let us inspect both *i* and *ii* in order to understand more fully the reasons for Hawking's position.

Throughout the modern period, assumption *i* was supported in large part by the *deterministic* nature of the reigning scientific paradigm: Newtonian mechanics. Deterministic laws, such as those of Newtonian mechanics, allow one, in principle, to predict the future exactly if all physical forces are known, and if the exact present position and momentum of all particles is given. Though in practice one could never hope to know the precise initial conditions or total operative forces, in principle one thought of the future as actually determined by these conditions and forces and not open to uncertainty—in the process, leaving the meaning of human free will very much in limbo, it should be noted. Classical physics thus led to a deterministic, clock-work interpretation of nature which dominated the seventeenth through nineteenth centuries.

Hawking also assumes that God does not intervene in the orderly workings of natural processes. This too is a modern assumption, shared by many theologians and virtually all scientists. The argument usually given since Hume is that it would be irrational, unaesthetic, or suggestive of weakness or shortsightedness for God to tinker with the very laws of nature set up by God in the first place and that the Humean concept of miracle as a violation of the laws of nature is in the end theologically incoherent.

Thus, given a worldview shaped by Laplacian determinism and a rejection of the possibility of divine intervention, Hawking can draw his basic conclusion: God's only choices are: i) to select the initial conditions at t=0 which govern the universe as a whole, making it the kind of universe in which life could evolve and, of course; ii) to make such a universe actually exist at t=0. After that, God is through. But if the universe had no beginning, then Hawking draws his central theological conclusion: There is nothing *whatsoever* left for God to do—except to choose the laws of nature.

So long as the universe had a beginning, we could suppose it had a creator. But if the universe is really completely self-contained, having no boundary or edge, it would have neither beginning nor end: it would simply be. What place, then, for a creator?[88]

How might we respond to Hawking? First I want to challenge assumptions *i* and *ii* which are essential to his conclusion. In their stead I want to suggest how the "no boundary" feature of the Hartle/Hawking proposal *can* be important to theology in terms of a reinterpretation of finitude.

There are two important exceptions to the assumption that the universe runs according to deterministic laws. a) Quantum physics employs statistical laws which suggest that nature may be indeterministic, the future not entirely predictable from knowledge of the present. b) Chaos theory suggests that even classical physics may involve indeterminacy in a fundamental way, as indicated by the extreme sensitivity to initial conditions of many complex classical systems. Now both *a* and *b* are debatable, and thus, until their resolution, the question regarding the deterministic character of the laws of nature clearly remains open. Hawking even notes the possibility of *a* but rejects it because of the second assumption about intervention:

> If one likes, one could ascribe (quantum) randomness to the intervention of God, but it would be a very strange kind of intervention: there is no evidence that it is directed toward any purpose.[89]

This leads us to the problem of intervention.

There are a variety of strategies by which theologians and philosophers of religion address the question of intervention and divine action. For convenience these can be brought together under two types.[90]

Many theologians have rejected intervention but have still found ways of speaking of God as acting in the world. For example, some have identified important historical or natural events as bearing supreme religious significance and thus have attributed them subjectively to the acts of God known by faith. Others have used a variety of agential models, including embodiment and nonembodiment models, to suggest how God can act objectively in the world without violating the laws of nature.

Other theologians have seen "intervention or nothing" as a false dichotomy. Often these writers draw on the open character of nature (for example, quantum chance and/or chaos) to enhance the argument that there is plenty of room within natural processes for God to act (the "intrinsic gaps" argument). Some have challenged the assumption that the deterministic character of the laws of nature requires God to intervene in order to act directly in specific events. Instead they argue that we can never know enough to justify excluding divine action. Others have suggested that the laws of nature are descriptive, not prescriptive, and thus God's action should not be thought of in terms of a "violation" of the laws in the first place. Finally, most agree that "intervention" is a misleading term since God is present to all events as their Creator, whether or not a specific event is considered "special."

Thus the laws of nature may not imply a deterministic view of nature and even if they do God may be viewed as acting in specific events. Hence, Hawking's fundamental conclusion is undercut: Even if the universe had no beginning, God is free to act throughout nature and history as creator and as redeemer.

Finite creation without a beginning. How might theologians appropriate the possibility that the universe has a finite past but no beginning? And how might this fit into the framework we began to explore previously, that is, of a theological research program based on *creatio ex nihilo*?

My initial approach to this comes from my previous interpretation of the theological significance of t=0. Recall that, in my approach, t=0 confirms the claim that the universe is finite in the past, that is, that it has a finite age. With the Hartle/Hawking proposal, this claim is maintained in a certain sense, even though the meaning and status of time as such is radically reconceived, as we have seen already. With the Big Bang model, having a finite age was understood in terms of having had a beginning. Now with Hartle/Hawking we discover the fascinating claim that there can be a finite age without a beginning, that is, that the universe can be finite in time without being bounded in time, and that the meaning and status of temporality itself is radically altered.

What I believe this teaches us theologically is that we can and should distinguish between a first claim and a second, closely related but unnecessary, claim: i) that the universe, as God's creation, must have a finite past (that is, that it has not existed forever) and ii) that in order to have a finite past, the universe must have had a beginning. Hartle/Hawking have shown us that the latter claim is not logically or mathematically necessary to the former claim. And it is the former claim, the finitude of the past, and not the latter claim, having a beginning point, which I propose we take to be in the last analysis the real theological importance of *creatio ex nihilo* seen in this empirical context.

And so, from my perspective, Hawking's work has the effect of disabusing us of an unnecessary adumbration to the central implication about the finitude of creation as it devolves out of the doctrine of *creatio ex nihilo*. Because of his insistence on the distinction between a finite past and a beginning of time, Hawking has, in effect, helped us claim that the universe is indeed a creation of God even if it had no beginning. For this, Hawking's work, even if it represents a *transitory stage* in the pursuit of a fully developed theory of quantum gravity, will have been enormously helpful to the task of Christian theology. While engaged in purely scientific research, Hawking's results have inadvertently illuminated a subtle distinction in the concept of finitude which is highly pertinent to Christian theology. For this we ought to be very grateful.

I believe this sort of interaction between theological and scientific insights signals the promise of a new, highly creative style for discussing theology and science. Previous work has often been limited to well-established conclusions in science in order not to base theological positions on changing scientific grounds. The present approach, however, is *indifferent* to the long-term status of the Hartle/Hawking model, since the survival of the Hartle/Hawking proposal is *irrelevant* to the validity of the mathematical concept of an unbounded finitude. It is precisely this fact which allows theologians to ponder the significance of something as *controversial* as the Hartle/Hawking proposal as they theologize about time and eternity.

We might go even further. The possibility in principle of an unbounded finite past suggests that theological issues about "the beginning" might best be excised from theological discussions about creation. Since Augustine we have known that it is preferable to think of the creation of time and not creation in (pre-existing) time. Nevertheless the theological and empirical status of the beginning of time has been a continuing problem for theologians down to the present, as Gilkey emphasizes in *Maker of Heaven and Earth*. With the concept of an unbounded finitude in mind, however, theologians might now simply leave aside questions about how to treat the "moment of creation" theologically, since it seems to be an unnecessary element in the discussion of the "finite creation of the universe." We can think of the past universe as a set of events which have no past boundary, rather than a set of events with a boundary (t=0). The universe is in this sense a *finite creation with no beginning*. Every event is on a par with every other event; since time is unbounded, each event has temporal neighbors past and future (or at least in the early universe there is no "first three-space"), and we need no longer focus on t=0 in order to retain a historical/empirical sense of creation *ex nihilo*.

Finally, we might frame this point in terms of the "Lakatosian theological research program" approach advocated above. The Hartle/Hawking claim that the universe has no initial singularity would count as evidence against the theological claim that the universe has a finite past, if finitude is taken in its usual sense of requiring a boundary. Hence we are led to frame an additional auxiliary hypothesis, namely that the claim of a finite past can include either a bounded or an unbounded past. This additional hypothesis allows us to include either the bounded finitude of Big Bang cosmology or the unbounded finitude of the Hartle/Hawking cosmology as confirming evidence of the core hypothesis, "*creatio ex nihilo* means ontological origination."

However, for this to avoid being an ad hoc move, we would want it to generate some novel predictions. To do so, we must begin with some minimal understanding of the concepts of "bounded" and "unbounded" drawn from set theory. By bounded we can think of a closed set containing all points on the x-axis from, and including, 0 and 1. By unbounded we mean an open set such as the closed set just described but with its boundary deleted, that is, the set $0<x<1$. We can use an open set to describe something of the qualities of a smooth transition from one domain to another in nature, where no sharp border occurs. With this in place we should now be in a position to speak about God's action as creator not only of the universe as such but of many of its theologically crucial features, such as the origin of life, mind, and spirit, without needing to look solely for a sharp discontinuity between domains of nature (for example, the inanimate/animate distinction) that potentially signals divine agency.[91] We shall see how this might be the case in what follows.

C. Creator of the "transition to temporality"

Previously I suggested that there are two ways to view the temporal properties of the universe from a quantum gravity/cosmology perspective: as a single domain characterized by quantum gravity as the fundamental theory, or as consisting in multiple domains, characterized by quantum and classical gravity (general relativity) and the transition between them. These alternative views lead to a reconceptualization of God's action as creator of the universe. In both cases we must recognize God's action as creator of the universe as a whole. However, in the case of multiple domains, we must discuss the additional issue of God's action as creator of its domains with their specific features and of the transition between domains.

Single domain. We start with God's action as creator of the universe as a whole, viewed as a single quantum domain. This claim requires little additional discussion beyond what we have already given it above. It leads once again to viewing *ex nihilo* in terms not only of the existence but also of the finitude of the universe as such.

Multiple domains. God's action as creator of multiple domains in the universe still entails the basic *ex nihilo* insight about ontological origination as well as the finitude of the temporal past. However, the possibility of viewing the universe in terms of multiple domains brings additional issues to bear on the topic of God's action as creator.

In the Einstein domain we encounter two standard alternatives in the debate over time. We can follow the "temporalists"[92] who accept time (and time's arrow) as real and adopt theological language about God's action *in* time. This leads naturally to *creatio continua* as an additional component of *creatio ex nihilo*, although the very existence of the universe always warrants an ontological type of *ex nihilo* argument. Alternatively we can follow the "atemporalists"[93] and develop an interpretation of God's action in atemporal categories.

Regarding the Hawking domain we must think about how to conceptualize God's relation to this "timeless" domain, since God is the creator here as well. Here one has a set of separate three-geometries rather than a continuous four-geometry. We might say that God relates directly to each three-geometry, supplying its existence *ex nihilo*.[94]

Finally we focus on God's relation as creator of the transition domain from Hawking to Einstein domains, that is, from "timeless" to "temporal." Here we see the glimmerings of a model, co-opted from theoretical physics, for the theological problem of understanding God's relation to the process by which time (and time's arrow) is created. Thus God acts in the world not only to create new structures in nature, as suggested by discussions of chaos theory, thermodynamics, and quantum physics. At a more fundamental level and in certain regions of the universe, God acts to create time (and time's arrow). Hence we should not just say with Augustine that God creates time along with the universe, and that God creates new phenomena in time. We should add a *third* claim: The universe is such that in certain broad transition domains within it *God creates the transition to time and time's arrow.*

This would pick up the sense of "novel prediction" suggested above in discussing creation in terms of a Lakatosian theological research program. There we added as an auxiliary hypothesis the claim that created finitude need not be bounded. By doing so it became possible to discuss God's creative action *ex nihilo* not only in terms of the ontological dependence of all things and of their historical origin in a unique beginning event, but in terms of the radically new arising smoothly within the processes of nature. Here we have evidence of such a phenomenon, namely the transition domain from the Hawking to the Einstein domains (and with it the creation of the arrow of time in the Einstein domain as part of what God creates in certain portions of the universe). Thus the creative action of God would pertain not only to the creation of novelty within natural processes. It also involves the *creation of temporality as we know it.* The possibility of including the transition domain as *novel evidence* for the theological research program we are exploring in this chapter through the auxiliary hypothesis about finitude marks this as a *progressive* theological research program over its competitors. Those writers dismissed such issues as t=0 or other empirical aspects of *creatio ex nihilo* as anomalous or irrelevant, or disconfirmed these issues by too strictly identifying *creatio ex nihilo* with t=0.

6. Closing Reflection on Trinitarian Creation

Finally, my own view—which I will only point to here but not develop—is that we should think of the divine eternity as the source of the temporality of the universe. Here divine temporal is taken in the sense of authentic temporality, that is, divine eternity.[95] God acts eternally as God the Creator to the universe. Hence the divine eternity must be understood in a sufficiently complex fashion as to at least allow for time so understood. The challenge then to theology is to think through the meaning of divine eternity and divine action to embrace at least these meanings of creaturely time.

I would close by noting once again how closely tied are the debates over temporality in physics and cosmology, in philosophy of religion (God's action in the world), and in systematic theology (time and eternity). We need now to rethink the current models of divine agency in terms of our more complex understanding of temporality as suggested by quantum physics and quantum cosmology. This discussion in turn needs to be integrated into the systematic issues regarding time and eternity. Although highly tentative and difficult to access due to their mathematical abstraction, the scientific discussions of time ought to help theologians and philosophers of religion critically rethink their own presuppositions about time and eternity as they articulate in new ways God's action in the world.

ENDNOTES: Chapter 3

[1] Previously published in *QCLN*, Russell, Murphy, Isham, eds., (Vatican Observatory and the Center for Theology and the Natural Sciences, 1993). I want to thank Ian Barbour, Wim Drees, George Ellis, Stephen Happel, Chris Isham, Nancey Murphy, Arthur Peacocke, Ted Peters, Bill Stoeger, Claude Welch, and John Wright for their help with this manuscript.
[2] Here t stands for cosmological time. For a technical introduction see the article by Bill Stoeger and George Ellis in *QCLN*.
[3] See S.W. Hawking and R. Penrose, "The singularities of gravitational collapse and cosmology," *Proc. R. Soc. London A* 314, 529–548 (1969). This publication includes a full list of references on the singularity theorems.
[4] Langdon Gilkey, *Maker of Heaven and Earth: The Christian Doctrine of Creation in the Light of Modern Knowledge* ([Reprint] Lanham, Md.: University Press of America, 1985; [Originally published] Garden City, N.Y.: Doubleday, 1959). In recent lectures Gilkey insists that his views have changed dramatically since writing *Maker*, and that he now stands at a considerable distance from the neo-orthodoxy reflected there. However, given the influence *Maker* has had on a generation of scholars I believe it is reasonable and valuable to assess it on its own merits and in its historical context, independently of its author's current position.
[5] These are not Gilkey's exact phrases, but I believe they capture his intent. Gilkey does refer to Anthony Flew's use of the term "absolute ontological dependence" in his discussion of this distinction.
[6] Gilkey, *Maker*, 310. Italics in the original.
[7] Ibid., 313, where he cites Aquinas's *Summa Theologica*, Part I, Question 46, Article 2.
[8] Ibid., 312. One clearly sees the influence of Schleiermacher here in Gilkey's willingness to view creation and preservation as equally containing the entire meaning of the tradition.
[9] Ibid., 314.
[10] Ibid., 313.
[11] Ibid., 315.
[12] A. R. Peacocke, *Creation and the World of Science: The Bampton Lectures, 1978* (Clarendon Press: Oxford, 1979).
[13] Ibid., 78.
[14] Ibid., 79.
[15] Arthur Peacocke, *Intimations of Reality: Critical Realism in Science and Religion* (Notre Dame, Ind.: University of Notre Dame Press, 1984). See in particular 62–63.
[16] A. R. Peacocke, "Theology and Science Today," in *Cosmos as Creation: Theology and Science in Consonance*, ed. Ted Peters (Nashville: Abingdon, 1989), 28–43. See especially 33–34.
[17] Ted Peters, "On Creating the Cosmos," in *Physics, Philosophy and Theology: A Common Quest for Understanding.* Robert John Russell, William R. Stoeger, S. J., and George V. Coyre, S. J. (Vatican City State: Vatican Observatory Publications, 1988), hereafter *Physios,* 273–296, 291.
[18] Ibid., 288.
[19] Peters's criticism of Barbour may be based on an inaccurate assessment of Barbour's position. According to Peters, "what Barbour has done here is virtually equate *ex nihilo* with initial beginning, discard the idea of initial beginning, and thereby discard *ex nihilo*." As we shall see below, however, the position Barbour adopted in *Issues* was that we can discard the historical interpretation of creation in favor of the ontological interpretation for two reasons both reminiscent of Gilkey: science cannot settle the matter and revelation doesn't contain factual data of this kind. Rather than rejecting the *ex nihilo* tradition, as Peters suggests he has, Barbour wants to keep it by reducing it to its ontological interpretation. Peters, on the other hand, is intent on keeping the historical interpretation alive within *ex nihilo*; this may account for his perceiving Barbour as rejecting *ex nihilo* when rejecting a historical beginning.
[20] Here and elsewhere I am taking Peacocke and Peters to defend opposite sides of the distinction Gilkey sets up, and I am ignoring the historical sequence of the statement of their arguments. For instance, at this point in the paper I am letting Peacocke and Peters stand for opposite interpretations of the significance of the *ex nihilo* argument independent of when they wrote, and analyzing the movement of Barbour's thought between them from 1966 to 1990,

even though Peacocke and Peters themselves wrote on the subject several times during this period.

[21] Ian G. Barbour, *Issues in Science and Religion* (New York: Harper & Row, 1966).

[22] Ibid., 366–368.

[23] Further evidence of the possibility that Barbour depended on Gilkey in this discussion is the fact that Brunner is cited by both him and Gilkey; in fact they cite the same text and chapter.

[24] Barbour, *Issues*, 377.

[25] Ibid., 380.

[26] Ibid., 414.

[27] Ibid., 458. Relying on Jarislov Pelikan's arguments, Barbour is also critical of the *ex nihilo* tradition since it has historically suppressed the tradition of continuing creation. According to Pelikan, this has "made it difficult for us to interpret evolution as the means of creation" (Ibid., 384). Barbour urges that we merge continuing creation with providence, and he deploys a number of arguments in support of this move. These arguments are worth pursuing, but, however, not in the limited context of this chapter.

[28] Ian G. Barbour, *Religion in an Age of Science*, The Gifford Lectures 1989–1991, Volume 1 (San Francisco: Harper & Row, 1990).

[29] Ibid., 128ff.

[30] Ibid., 129.

[31] Barbour makes extensive use of the philosophical category of contingency to relate cosmology to *creatio ex nihilo* in the Gifford lectures. This is an important point; however, contingency tends to remain a merely philosophical category if its meaning is restricted to the existence per se of the universe. If contingency is extended to include the finite age of the universe, then contact can be made with specific cosmologies such as Big Bang (which tends to *confirm ex nihilo*) or steady state (which tends to *disconfirm ex nihilo*). Thus finitude and not contingency plays the pivotal role in subjecting *ex nihilo* to the empirical test offered by cosmology.

[32] If we mean by events open to scientific investigation those which are both the effects of previous causes (which presumably it would not be) and which in turn are the cause of future effects (which presumably it would be), then an uncaused event would be a contradiction in terms. Note that one need not limit the form of causality assumed here to Laplacian determinism; statistical determinism would be equally acceptable. Moreover, quite different examples of statistical determinism are provided by statistical mechanics and quantum mechanics.

[33] For an excellent treatment of this and other philosophical aspects of cosmology see "Contemporary Cosmology and Its Implications for the Science-Religion Dialogue" by W. R. Stoeger in *Physics*, 219–247.

[34] Ted Peters, "On Creating the Cosmos," 288.

[35] Barbour, *Religion*, 144.

[36] Ibid., 129.

[37] Langdon B. Gilkey, "Cosmology, Ontology, and the Travail of Biblical Language," *The Journal of Religion* 41 (1961), 194–205.

[38] It is worth quoting Gilkey at length here, for this point is crucial: "If religious ideas stay wholly within the world of fact and experience, they lose that saving content which is the transcendent power and love of God. . . . If, on the other hand, they transcend the world entirely, and if they describe God in the purely negative and impersonal terms of speculative philosophy, that relatedness of God to the world of which the Gospel speaks is lost. Theological truth must maintain a dialectic or tension between God's transcendent eternity and the finite world of change and time, if it is to express the Christian Gospel of God's salvation. It must continually relate to the facts of our experience what transcends fact; for what theology seeks to formulate is the activity of God who transcends our experience. . . . One of the basic problems of theology, then, is to express the relation of eternity to time as Christianity understands it, without on the one hand competing with our scientific knowledge of the origins of the natural universe of space and time, and without on the other losing all positive relation to the world of actual experience." Gilkey, *Maker*, 315–316.

[39] Ibid., 316ff.

[40] One should also note that, even in the context of strictly philosophical contingency it is, after all, the *existence* of the universe which provides the datum on which the philosophical claim is warranted. Thus the claim is never *entirely* emptied of empirical context.

[41] Ian G. Barbour, *Myths, Models, and Paradigms: A Comparative Study in Science & Religion* (New York: Harper & Row, 1974). See especially chapters 6 and 7.

[42] Nancey Murphy, *Theology in the Age of Scientific Reasoning* (Ithaca, N.Y.: Cornell University Press, 1990). See also her chapter in *QCLN*.

[43] Philip Clayton, *Explanation from Physics to Theology: An Essay in Rationality and Religion* (New Haven, Conn.: Yale University Press, 1989).

[44] See in particular, "Falsification and the Methodology of Scientific Research Programmes," in *The Methodology of Scientific Research Programmes: Philosophical Papers*, vol. I, ed. John Worrall and Gregory Currie (Cambridge: Cambridge University Press, 1978), 8–101.

[45] Even the Big Bang model can be taken as offering disconfirming evidence if we can argue that its past can be characterized as infinite. As it turns out, using temperature to define the age of the universe makes even the Big Bang model infinitely old. Finally, quantum gravity can lead to proposals in quantum cosmology which either give the universe an infinite age or which, as in the Hartle/Hawking model, redefine the meaning of a finite age to be one having no beginning, as we shall see below.

[46] I do not want to make this into a *definition* of finitude, since I want to argue that the distinction between the finite and the infinite need not include the concept of boundary. In recent mathematics, and especially since the work of Georg Cantor, we have extended the notion of finitude to include unbounded finitude. We shall see the importance of this latter concept as it surfaces in the work of Hartle/Hawking below.

[47] For an excellent example of such a comparison between theological and nontheological research programs and cosmology, see the article by Nancey Murphy in *QCLN*.

[48] In short, I believe it is better to be wrong than to be meaningless. In order to be wrong, a theory must be capable of being falsified. As long as it could be falsified, then if it isn't falsified but instead it receives partial confirmation (since it can never be verified), it must bear some resemblance to the truth. This clearly should be a goal of theology, to include as part of the domain in which it tells the truth of the world God so loved (John 3:16).

[49] Isham, "Creation as a Quantum Process," in *Physics*.

[50] Published in *QCLN*. In this chapter I focus attention on Isham's analysis of the Hartle/Hawking model, drawing primarily from his article in *Physics*. In the future, I hope to expand my arguments to include his analysis of Vilenkin's model and other proposals in quantum cosmology.

[51] To understand how this is possible, one needs to bear in mind two points. i) Gravitational binding energy is negative, since gravity is an attractive force. Rest mass and kinetic energy are positive. It is likely that in our universe the amount of gravitational binding energy just equals the total rest mass and kinetic energy of the universe, so that the universe as a whole has no net energy. ii) Quantum mechanics predicts that the lifetime of a quantum system is inversely proportional the uncertainty in its energy. The result of these two observations is that a quantum fluctuation of the background spacetime could produce a universe with a lifetime of billions of years, as ours has, without violating conservation of energy.

[52] The use of complex numbers is commonplace in mathematical physics. Complex numbers consist of real and imaginary parts, the latter involving the square root of a negative number. They have nothing whatsoever to do with the meaning of "imaginary" in artistic, literary, or personal contexts.

[53] To be accurate, we cannot simply extrapolate backwards in ordinary time to a *unique*, finite past since time, in quantum gravity, is a highly ambiguous concept. Our ordinary concept of time assumes that the universe is a single four-dimensional spacetime manifold, and that time is unambiguously defined in terms of one of these dimensions. In the case of quantum gravity, however, one is faced with a set of such four-dimensional spacetime manifolds, all of which contribute to what we consider to be ordinary time.

[54] Isham, "Creation," Fig. 4, 390.

[55] For this paper the terms "three-space" and "three-geometry" are essentially interchangeable, and both refer to a three-dimensional space with an arbitrary curvature. Ordinary Euclidean three-space is an example of a three-space with zero curvature (that is, a flat three-space).
[56] Isham, "Creation," 391.
[57] Ibid., 396.
[58] This interpretation of Y(c,f) is only one of several possible ways of understanding the wave function. This fact is deeply connected with the problem of time in quantum gravity. I am indebted to Chris Isham for this and other important comments on my treatment of quantum gravity. I refer the reader to the excellent but highly technical paper for further research: "Canonical Quantum Gravity and the Problem of Time," C.J. Isham (Lectures presented at the NATO Advanced Study Institute, "Recent Problems in Mathematical Physics," Salamanca, June 15–27, 1992).
[59] This must be understood modulo the very real problem of whether a realist interpretation of quantum mechanics in general can be sustained. To the extent that a realist interpretation is attributed to quantum physics, then the "path" linking three-spaces would be interpretable as a four-dimensional spacetime. A somewhat related issue is the measurement or observer problem, that is, to the problem of what it means for the universe as a quantum system to be "observed" and thereby to be in a single state. How can an "observer" be "outside" the universe?
[60] See Isham, "Creation," Fig. 4, 390. Strictly speaking, a single four-dimensional spacetime is represented by a whole collection of paths connecting c(1) to c(2), each path corresponding to a different foliation of the manifold whose boundaries are c(1) and c(2) (and hence to a different definition of time).
[61] Ibid., 397.
[62] Ibid., Fig. 6, 398.
[63] This is represented by the vertex of the cone in Figure 5, cf. Ibid., 391.
[64] Again one should keep in mind that, strictly speaking, there are many spacetimes involved in the Hartle/Hawking model, not just one. Their approach requires integrating over all those four geometries which are consistent with the specified three-manifold.
[65] "The quantum theory of gravity has opened up a new possibility, in which there would be no boundary to spacetime and so there would be no need to specify the behavior at the boundary. One could say: 'The boundary condition of the universe is that is has no boundary'. The universe would be completely self-contained and not affected by anything outside itself. It would neither be created nor destroyed. It would just BE." Hawking, *A Brief History of Time*, 136.
[66] Note again that these remarks about quantum gravity and time reflect only a part of the overall problem of interpreting quantum gravity. Actually, the concept of time in quantum theory compared with the concept of time in general relativity is far more complicated than can be treated here. For a recent, technical treatment see C. J. Isham, "Canonical Quantum Gravity and the Problem of Time."
[67] Technically one must note that there are multiple four-geometries which in turn incorporate the sets of relevant three-geometries in the Hartle/Hawking *ansatz*.
[68] Note however that there is a serious debate regarding the status of time even in the classical domain, as discussed below and by Polkinghorne and Isham in this volume: Should spacetime be considered a static four-geometry (a world of being) or a dynamic evolving three-geometry (a world of becoming)? The point here is that in the quantum domain, as opposed to the classical domain, *time is not even on a par with space*, rendering the static view of being *even more compelling* than the dynamic view of becoming.
[69] "Local" is meant here in a topological, not a geometrical, sense. The local region of spacetime that includes an external time includes all events from the first microsecond through the present into the far future.
[70] I resist the temptation to talk about the transition domain as the domain where time "emerges," even though this might be a natural way to think about it. Emergence seems to carry with it temporal overtones, and this is precisely what we need to avoid here. The "emergence of time" is *not* a *temporal* process, that is, it is *not* a process in time. Neither is it a sharp boundary from one domain to another, but a distributed process more like a gradual shift in character.

---

[71] As we know, philosophical and aesthetic commitments often serve as criteria of theory choice in science.

[72] Isham, "Creation," 387.

[73] In the quantum fluctuation model, the infinity of universes would all coexist, in a sense, within the same spacetime continuum. This means that we would see galaxies moving in all directions in the sky, depending on the location in spacetime of the "creation/seed-point" from which they arose. Clearly we see nothing of the sort in the visible universe. This way of speaking about an infinity of universes is to be sharply distinguished from the concept of an infinity of universes that appears in "many-universe" theories arising in inflationary quantum cosmology or from many-worlds interpretations of quantum physics, and so on. In the latter cases, the universes are each more or less distinct spacetimes, somewhat like pseudopods arising from some common source and no longer in communication.

[74] As Isham points out, Philo of Alexandria took a similar position to that of Augustine.

[75] Paul Davies, *God and the New Physics* (New York: Simon & Schuster, 1983).

[76] Ibid., 38.

[77] Willem B. Drees, *Beyond the Big Bang: Quantum Cosmologies and God* (La Salle, Ill.: Open Court, 1990).

[78] Ibid., 55–56.

[79] Drees also focuses on *creatio ex nihilo* in the context of the Hartle/Hawking cosmology. He begins with the common distinction between two meanings of *ex nihilo*: historical origination and ontological dependency. Drees claims that the former leads to deism, whereas theism, with its sense of the dependence of all moments on God, is more compatible with cosmology. He points out that the removal of the t=0 event does not undercut theism, only deism. "Theology is not necessarily tied to an absolute beginning, an edge to time. . . . Sagan's argument 'no edge, hence no God' is not decisive" (Ibid., 70–71). Thus Drees defends what I previously called the Peacocke/Barbour position, a position I criticized in some detail.

[80] "*Ouk on* is the 'nothing' which has no relation at all to being; *me on* is the 'nothing' which has a dialectical relation to being. The Platonic school identified *me on* with that which does not yet have being but which can become being if it is united with essences or ideas . . . Christianity has rejected the concept of *me-ontic* matter on the basis of the doctrine of *creatio ex nihilo.* Matter is not a second principle in addition to God. The *nihil* out of which God creates is *ouk on*, the undialectical negation of being." Paul Tillich, *Systematic Theology* (New York: Harper & Row, 1951/1967), vol. 1, 188.

[81] Drees, *Beyond the Big Bang*; J. D. Barrow, *The World within the World* (Oxford: Clarendon, 1988); Michael Heller, "Big Bang on Ultimate Questions," in *Origin and Early History of the Universe: Proceedings of the Twenty-sixth Liege International Astrophysical Colloquium, July 1-4, 1986* (Cointe-Ougree, Belgium: Université de Liege, 1986). See Drees, *Beyond the Big Bang*, 72.

[82] In private correspondence Ellis points out that the Hartle/Hawking proposal includes pre-existent Hilbert spaces, quantum operators, Hamiltonians, and so on, "whose existence is if anything more mysterious than that of the universe itself. . . . In fact the argument [about *creatio ex nihilo*] supports the idea that the old-fashioned big bang should be correct—and thus that quantum gravity, if indeed necessary, does not change the nature of the big bang from that predicted by classical theory."

[83] Davies, *God*, ch. 16, "Is the universe a 'free lunch'?" 214–217. Here Davies asks: "Does such a [quantum model of the universe] have any need for God? . . . Physics can perhaps explain the content, origin and organization of the physical universe, but not the laws (or superlaw) of physics itself. Traditionally, God is credited with having invented the laws of nature and created things . . . on which those laws operate" (216–217); Russell, "Cosmology," in Peters, *Creation*, especially 198–201.

[84] Would something still be left? Perhaps the laws of logic? It would be fascinating to explore *these* possibilities. We should keep in mind, however, the important argument raised by Stoeger against viewing the laws of nature as having an ontological standing of their own. Perhaps the laws merely describe nature, and do not act to prescribe the behavior of natural phenomena.

[85] I use the term "unbounded" here as meaning "having no boundary." Mathematicians often use the term "unbounded" in a different sense. They might instead say that the Hartle/Hawking model involves four-manifolds that are past-bounded. Similar remarks apply to e word "open."
[86] Hawking, *Brief History*, 140.
[87] Ibid., 122.
[88] Ibid., 141.
[89] Ibid., 166.
[90] For references, see the footnotes in the introduction to this volume.
[91] This additionally implies something about the internal coherence of the doctrine of creation in light of quantum cosmology, namely that we could relate the *continua* and *ex nihilo* traditions of the doctrine in a more fundamental way. I will explore this suggestion in future work.
[92] Barbour, Peacocke, Lucas, Polkinghorne, and Ward are representatives of this position.
[93] Isham and Drees represent this position—as did Einstein.
[94] See Isham, "Creation," 404.
[95] I am indebted to the recent discussion of eternity stemming from the writings of Karl Barth and Karl Rahner and picked up in various ways by Ebehard Jungel, Wolfhart Pannenberg, Jürgen Moltmann, and Ted Peters. I hope to develop this approach in future writings.

Chapter 4

Does "The God Who Acts" Really Act? New Approaches to Divine Action in Light of Contemporary Science[1]

> The "mighty acts" (Ps. 145:4), the "wondrous deeds" (Ps. 40:5), the "wonderful works" (Ps. 107:21) of God are the fundamental subject matter of biblical history, and the object of biblical faith is clearly the One who has acted repeatedly and with power in the past and may be expected to do so in the future.
>
> —Gordon D. Kaufman[2]

> Unless God acts in a special way in special events it is difficult to see how we could have religious authorities from within history with the degree of specialness which Christians do in fact ascribe to their authorities. And those very authorities in fact do speak of a God who acts in precisely that kind of way.
>
> —Maurice Wiles[3]

> [T]he Bible is a book descriptive not of the acts of God but of Hebrew religion. . . . [It] is a book of the acts Hebrews believed God might have done and the words he might have said had he done and said them—but of course we recognize he did not.
>
> —Langdon Gilkey[4]

1. Introduction

At the core of Christian faith and praxis lies the prayer Jesus taught his disciples, centered around these three supplications: "thy kingdom come, thy will be done, on earth as it is in heaven." These requests were intelligible in the New Testament era, even if they were extraordinarily challenging to personal faith by the sacrifices demanded of discipleship. But we live in the twentieth century, where their challenges are amplified almost beyond bearing by the chasmic intellectual incoherence underlying and threatening them. What could these supplications mean, how could they possibly make sense let alone be central to the truth of Christian faith, given the current context shaped by at least four tremendous features: i) scientific cosmology, with its 15 billion-year-old universe whose vastness challenges our imagination and whose uniform "secularity" makes any differentiated conception of creation ("heaven and earth") almost inconceivable; ii) a reductionist, materialist, and determinist philosophy of nature which held sway during the theological developments of the eighteenth to nineteenth centuries and by portraying nature in terms of a closed causal web undercut an integrated understanding of human or divine action in nature; iii) the real and striking divergences in the truth claims of the world religions, which seem to undercut any normative epistemology for each of them and, in particular, to undercut Christianity's language about a universal reign of God on earth; iv) and the immeasurable cost of human evil and natural peril plaguing the world this century, where the immensity and depravity of human wickedness empowered by almost unimaginable technological power has wreaked desolation, Holocaust, and threatened nuclear nightmare, where the ecosystem is threatened with massive extinctions due to human greed, where the extent of "natural evil" looms ever larger as we recognize the billion-year-old history of evolutionary nature "red in tooth and claw"? The challenges to the intelligibility of the Christian faith are truly fundamental today, especially for those for whom the solace of a Kantian or an existentialist solution, or the "oil and water" mix of neo-orthodoxy and biblical theology, or the reductionism of faith to personal or social praxis/liberation, is inadequate to the depth and extent of historical Christian witness.

This chapter is the first of three chapters (chapters 4–6) dealing specifically with the question of divine action. The task of this chapter is introduce and discuss the overall problematic of the intelligibility of divine action in light of the natural sciences. It now seems that contemporary physics, cosmology, evolutionary biology, and the psychological and neurosciences, together with recent moves in post-modern, holist philosophy, actually provide new modes of reflection on nature which allow Christians to talk coherently about God's action not only in human life but in the "immense journey" of evolution, as Loren Eisley so beautifully put it, stretching back over three billion years on earth, and back even to the beginning of the universe in the Big Bang. Moreover it can do so in a non-interventionist way if the case can be made that nature is intrinsically open at many, or at least one, level of complexity, and that "top-down" and "whole-part" as well as "bottom-up" causality is at work in complex biological systems. If the materialist reductionist interpretation of science needs to be rejected—and it does—then likewise the mentalist/spiritualist reductionist interpretation of religion should be discarded. Indeed, the latter should be abandoned on the grounds of its being based on old-fashioned and outmoded *science*! It is my observation that recent efforts in this regard are in fact rather promising and deserve further pursuit and broader recognition.

Let me put the overarching thesis of this chapter up front: The old assumption is that we are faced with a "forced option." We must choose between two understandings of special providence: 1) as the *objective* acts of God in nature and history to which we respond, where these acts are understood as divine *interventions* into the natural and historical world, or 2) as our *subjective* response to God's acts, where these acts are understood as *uniformly the same* in all events whether or not we consider them special. My thesis is that this old assumption of a forced choice no longer holds. Instead, because of developments in the natural sciences, including quantum physics, genetics, evolution, and the mind/brain problem, and because of changes in philosophy, including the move from epistemic reductionism to epistemic holism and the recognized legitimacy of including whole-part and top-down analysis, we can now view special providence as consisting in the *objective* acts of God in nature and history to which we respond through faith *and* we can interpret these acts in a *non-interventionist* manner consistent with the natural sciences. In short we can begin to do what we thought was impossible for over one hundred years—believe credibly that God really did do what the Bible testifies to—and we may in the process begin to overcome one of the basic reasons for the split between theological liberals and conservatives. Kaufmann and Wiles of all people may be right in their epigraphs above and the defeat Gilkey reports may be supplanted by a new understanding of divine action! The "strange world of the Bible," to employ Karl Barth's enticing term, might, in a surprising way, be the real world after all!

In what follows, I will first offer an overview of why a non-interventionist understanding of objective divine action is important theologically (section 2). I then delineate the terminology and assumptions underlying the search for non-interventionist objective divine action (NIODA), the criteria which a candidate theory must meet and seven FAQs or misconceptions about NIODA which one finds (all too frequently) in the literature (section 3). In section 4 I will survey two types of approaches to NIODA in detail: 1) lateral causality and chaos theory (John Polkinghorne), and 2) top-down causality, the universe-as-a-whole and cosmology (Arthur Peacocke). Bottom-up causality and quantum mechanics will be deferred to chapter 5, where I will treat them in great detail. For a more thorough discussion on NIODA I direct the reader to a much larger body of materials in the five volumes that have been published following the decade-long series of research conferences sponsored by the Vatican Observatory (VO) and the Center for Theology and the Natural Sciences (CTNS).[5] Although these publications include approximately one hundred chapters,[6] the central theme of many of them is divine action in light of such scientific topics as Big Bang and quantum cosmology, quantum physics, chaos and complexity theory, evolutionary and molecular biology, and the person in light of the neurosciences.

Take this chapter as a report from the frontiers of the problem, where pitfalls abound and blind alleys loom, but progress is actually being made in giving credible support to the *kerygma* of faith that God acts as creator and redeemer in the world God so loves.

2. Overview of Divine Action: Why is a "Non-Interventionist" View of Objective Divine Action Theologically Important?[7]

A. Historical background to the problem of divine action

The notion of God's acting in the world is central to the biblical witness. From the call of Abraham and the Exodus from Egypt to the birth, ministry, death, and raising of Jesus and the founding of the church at Pentecost, God is represented as making new things happen. Through these "mighty acts," God creates and saves.[8] Rather than seeing divine acts as occasional events in what are otherwise entirely natural and historical processes, both the Hebrews and the early Christians conceived of God as the creator of the world and of divine action as the continuing basis of all that happens in nature and in history.[9]

The view that God works in and through all the processes of the world continued throughout patristic and medieval times. For example, God was understood as the first or *primary cause* of all events—where all natural causes are instrumental or *secondary causes* through which God works. The conviction that God acts universally in all events, and that we act together with God in specific events, was maintained by the Reformers and the ensuing Protestant orthodoxy. John Calvin (1509–1564) argued that God is in absolute control over the world and at the same time maintained that people are responsible for evil deeds.[10] Questions about human freedom and the reality of evil were seen more as problems requiring serious theological attention than as reasons for abandoning belief in God's universal agency.

Moreover, faith in God the creator was articulated through two distinct but interwoven doctrines: creation and providence. The doctrine of creation asserts that the ultimate source and absolute ground of the universe is God. Without God, the universe would not exist, nor would it exist as "universe."[11] Creation theology, in turn, has often included three related but distinct claims: 1) the universe had a beginning; 2) the universe depends absolutely and at every moment on God for its sheer existence; and 3) the universe is the locus of God's continuing activity as Creator. The first two have traditionally been grouped in terms of *creatio ex nihilo*, and the third in terms of *creatio continua*.

The doctrine of providence[12] presupposes a doctrine of creation, but adds significantly to it. While creation stresses that God is the cause of all existence, providence stresses that God is the cause of the meaning and purpose of all that is. God not only creates but guides and directs the universe towards the fulfilling of God's purposes. These purposes are mostly hidden to us, though they may be partially seen after the fact in the course of natural and historical events. The way God achieves them is hidden, too. Only in the eschatological future will God's action throughout the history of the universe be fully revealed and our faith in it confirmed. General providence refers to God's universal action in guiding all events; special providence refers to God's particular acts in specific moments, whether they be found in personal life or in history.

The rise of modern science in the seventeenth century and Enlightenment philosophy in the eighteenth, however, led many to reject the traditional views of divine action. Although Isaac Newton (1643–1727) argued for the essential role of God in relation to the metaphysical underpinnings of his mechanical system, and in this way defended the sovereignty of God in relation to nature,[13] Newtonian mechanics depicted a causally closed universe with little, if any, room for God's *special* action in specific events—and then only by intervention. A century later, Pierre Simon Laplace (1749–1827) combined the *determinism* of Newton's equations with *epistemological reductionism* (the properties and behavior of the whole are reducible to those of the parts) and *metaphysical reductionism* (the whole is simply composed of its parts), to portray all of nature as a causally closed, impersonal mechanism. This in turn led to the concept of interventionism: If God were really to act in specific events in nature, God would apparently have to break the remorseless lock-step of natural cause and effect by intervening in the sequence and violating the laws of nature in the process.

The eighteenth century saw the rise and fall of deism, in which the scope of divine agency was limited to an initial act of creation. According to deism, the universe was like a clock which, once built and set in place, proceeded to run on its own.[14] David Hume (1711–1776) challenged the deistic (and theistic) arguments for God as first cause and as designer.[15] In response, Immanuel Kant (1724–1804) constructed a new metaphysical system which emphasized the mind's role in organizing sense-data through universal categories of intuition and forms of sensibility. According to Kant, the sphere of religion lies not in our knowing (the activity of pure reason) but in our sense of moral obligation (the activity of practical reason). It is our ethical system, not our knowledge of nature, that requires us to postulate God, freedom, and the immortality of the soul.[16] The consequence of Kant's thought for the West was the philosophical separation of the domains of science and religion into "two worlds"—a move which was to have an immeasurable effect on Christian theology up to the present.

As a consequence, theology in the nineteenth century was faced with a fundamental challenge not only to its contents and structure, but even to its method. The variety of responses to this challenge tend to fall into two groups: "Liberals" largely accepted and worked within the terms of the discussion that modernity dictated while "conservatives" upheld traditional formulations and tended to reject "modernity." The earliest and most influential figure among liberals was Friedrich Schleiermacher (1768–1834), who responded to Kant by locating religion as neither a knowing nor a doing. Instead religion is grounded in personal piety—the feeling of absolute dependence. Theological assertions emerge from the immediacy of the religious self-consciousness. Schleiermacher understood God's relation to the world in terms of universal divine immanence and he blurred the distinction between creation and providence by collapsing the latter into the former. In a famous move he defined miracle as "simply the religious name for event. Every event, even the most natural and usual, becomes a miracle, as soon as the religious view of it can be the dominant."[17] Schleiermacher's arguments became characteristic of liberal Protestant theology throughout the nineteenth century and continued into much of twentieth century theological work.

The second half of the nineteenth century saw the rise of Darwinian evolution, which combined random variation and natural selection to explain biological complexity. To some in the nineteenth and twentieth centuries, the fundamental role of chance in nature seemed to undercut any notion of divine action in the world; to others, such as the Anglo-Catholic liberal movement in Britain and America, Darwinian evolution could be accommodated and even integrated into theology without interventionism, since God works immanently in and through the very processes of nature.[18] In contrast, religious conservatives tended either to reject evolution as a whole or give it a limited acceptance with the proviso that the objective acts of special providence constitute divine interventions in nature.

Protestant theology in the first half of the twentieth century was largely shaped by Karl Barth. In his rejection of nineteenth-century liberal theology, Barth returned theology to its biblical roots and focused it on the God who is "wholly other." Recognizing that a religion founded exclusively on subjective experience is vulnerable to the critiques of Feuerbach and Freud, Barth and his followers held fast to the objective action of God in creating and redeeming the world. "The Gospel is . . . not an event, nor an experience, nor an emotion—however delicate! . . . [I]t is a communication which presumes faith in the living God, and which creates that which it presumes."[19] The "God who acts" became a hallmark of the ensuing "biblical theology" movement which arose in the 1940s and 1950s.[20] To many this movement seemed to offer a *tertium quid* between liberal and conservative theologies.

But do Barthian neo-orthodoxy and the biblical theology movement actually produce a credible account of divine action? In a well-known article written in 1961, Langdon Gilkey argued forcefully that they do not.[21] According to Gilkey, neo-orthodoxy is an unhappy composite of conservative, biblical/orthodox language, with its objectivist/interventionist view of divine action, and liberal theology's acceptance of modern scientific cosmology with its view of nature as a closed system and its subjectivist approach to divine action. On the one hand it attempts to distance itself from liberal theology by retaining biblical language about God acting through wondrous events and by viewing revelation as including an objective act. Yet on the other hand, it, like liberalism, accepts the modern premise that nature is a closed causal system, as depicted by classical physics. The result is that, whereas orthodoxy used language univocally, neo-orthodoxy uses language at best analogically, and, at worst, equivocally. "[T]he Bible," maintains Gilkey, "is a book descriptive not of the acts of God but of Hebrew religion. . . . [It] is a book of the acts Hebrews believed God might have done and the words he [*sic*] might have said had he done and said them—but of course we recognize he did not."[22]

Twentieth century Roman Catholic thought was burdened with similar problems. It tended to appeal to the Thomistic distinction between primary and secondary causality, thus avoiding conflict with science (which only studies the latter) in much the same way that liberal Protestant theology did. Yet Catholic theology reserved the category of miracle and an appeal to the authority of the church and philosophy even though the affirmation of miracles meant a confrontation with, or rejection of, science in much the same way as Protestant conservativism.

And so we find ourselves back once again before a key theological problem facing contemporary Protestant and Catholic theology: Should special providence be understood entirely as our subjective response to God's uniform and undifferentiated action, or can it include an objective dimension of divine agency which grounds our response to special events? The question is whether we are right to call certain events "special" because we are actually responding to God's distinctive action in, together with, and through them. This claim can be made even more sharply: Is it the case that, had God not acted in a special way in a given particular event, the event would *not* have occurred in precisely the way it did?

For those who take a subjective view, special providence tends to be absorbed into general providence and the latter is usually blended together with God's action in creation to give a single undifferentiated view of divine action. For those who hold to objective special providence, one's response to specific events or experiences is based on God's special or particular action in these events and experiences. To quote once again the inimitable Gilkey, "for those of faith [an act of God] must be objectively or ontologically different from other events. Otherwise, there is no mighty act, but only our belief in it. . . . Only an ontology of events specifying what God's relation to ordinary events is like, and thus what his relation to special events might be, could fill the now empty analogy of mighty acts."[23] Theologians such as Rudolf Bultmann, Gordon Kaufman, and Maurice Wiles represent the subjectivist interpretation which denies all claims involving God's particular action, while others such as Charles Hodge, Donald Bloesch, and Millard Erickson affirm the objectivist view.[24] (For a closer look at how Bultmann, Kaufman, and Wiles articulate this position, see appendix A.)

B. A key to the problem: the presumed link between objective divine action and divine intervention

Although divided over the choice between subjective and objective interpretations of divine action, liberals and conservatives have actually agreed on the underlying reason for *why* they are divided—because objective divine action seems to entail divine intervention. But what initially led to this perceived linkage between objective divine action and interventionism? As Nancey Murphy has stressed,[25] it was due to factors lying *outside* of theology per se: namely the combination of *deterministic* physics and *reductionistic* philosophy. If the physical world is a causally closed, deterministic system according to science, and if the behavior of the world as a whole is ultimately reducible to that of its physical parts as reductionistic philosophy demands, then the action of a free agent—whether human or divine—must entail a violation of natural processes and as a consequence, as Arthur Peacocke writes, the concept of free agency becomes unintelligible.[26] Thus, by and large the choice has been either to affirm objective special providence at the cost of an interventionist and, in some extreme cases, an anti-scientific theology (the position taken by anti-evolution creationists in the Scopes trial of the 1920s), or to abandon objective special providence at the cost of a scientifically irrelevant and, in many cases, privatized and tame theology—a theology relegated, as John Cobb writes, to an "intellectual ghetto."[27] Seen in this light, a third option which both respects the integrity of the natural sciences and honors the Judeo-Christian understanding of God as active in creation is crucial.

C. Breaking the link: non-interventionist objective divine action (NIODA)

It seems clear that any purported "third option" will require an intelligible concept of objectively special providence which does *not* entail divine intervention. Such a concept could serve as a genuine *tertium quid* to conservative and liberal notions of special providence, combining strengths borrowed from each. Specifically, we will seek to speak about special divine acts in which God acts objectively in an unusual and particularly meaningful way in, with, and through events which serve to mediate God's action. We will seek to do so without entertaining—in fact by refusing—the additional claim that God must intervene in, or at least suspend, the laws of nature (which are themselves the result of and description of God's continuous creation). I call this type of divine action *non-interventionist view of objective special providence* or *non-interventionist objective divine action* (NIODA).[28]

What is most fascinating, ironic, and even tragic is that while the cavernous divisions between subjectivist liberals and interventionist conservatives were dominating the landscape of twentieth-century theology, and while theology in turn cast a deaf ear to the world of science which had played such a fundamental role in affecting this theological landscape, science itself was undergoing an internal revolution with potentially tremendous consequences for theology. These consequences, if theologians had only paid attention, would have offered a basis for theological unity concerning the question of divine action by providing the *scientific foundation*—through a careful philosophical interpretation— for just such a new theological *tertium quid*. In essence, some form of what I am calling "NIODA" could have been constructed as early as 1930 by the very theologians—liberal and conservative Protestants and Catholics—who were divided on account of their shared assumption that nature was causally closed because science was viewed as deterministic. This division was exacerbated by their theological methodologies which, across the board, sanctioned a refusal to learn from and incorporate contemporaneous developments in and insights from the natural sciences in the twentieth century. Thus while an exponential increase and radical transformation of scientific knowledge was happening worldwide, the theological community doggedly pursued strategies designed to cope with a science *which had been long abandoned by scientists*, and in doing so theology failed, by and large, to recognize the revolution in science and its significance. As we shall see, the apex of the theological debate over divine action—whether God can act objectively without intervening in nature—is precisely the point where these changes in science offer the most promise, and it has only been in the last decade of the astonishing century in which these developments took place, that these connections are being made by a handful of scholars in "theology and science."

Here is a tiny sample of the remarkable scientific discoveries and technological inventions in the twentieth century that have changed the global intellectual and cultural landscapes forever:

- Special relativity (1905)
- Quantum mechanics (1900–1930)
- General relativity (1915)
- Big Bang cosmology, the expanding universe, and t=0 (1940s–1980s)/discovery of the cosmological microwave background (1965)

- Invention of the electron microscope (1939)
- Active galaxies (1940s–present), quasars and black holes (1960s–present)
- Manhattan Project/invention of the atomic bomb (1939–1945)
- Invention of ENIAC (1946)
- Invention of the transistor (1947) and the integrated circuit (1958)
- Invention of the maser/laser (1959–1960)
- DNA structure (1953)
- Chaos and complexity in physical and biological systems (1960s–present)
- Nonlinear, nonequilibrium thermodynamics (1950s–present)
- Quarks/Standard Model of fundamental particles (1964–1995)
- Invention of the hand-held calculator (1967) and the microprocessor (1968)
- String theory (1968), supersymmetry (1971), gravitons (1974), duality (1991–1995)
- First landing on the moon/Apollo 13 (1969)
- First Earth Day (1970)
- Invention of the CAT Scan (1973)
- First "test tube baby" (1978)
- Inflationary Big Bang and quantum cosmology (1981–present)
- World Wide Web (1989–present)
- Human Genome Project (1990–2000)
- Neuroscience and cognitive science/Decade of the Brain/emergent, nonreductive theories of mind (1990s–present)
- Bell's theorem/quantum nonlocality & nonseparability (1964–present)
- Cloning (1997–present) and stem cell research (1998–present)

In essence, by the first three decades of the twentieth century classical physics was replaced—at least as the accepted fundamental theory—by two new paradigms: special relativity and quantum mechanics. In that same period, the infinite, flat three-dimensional cosmology of Newton was eclipsed by the Big Bang universe of Einstein. In biology, the last evidences of vitalist hopes that had lingered after Darwin were to vanish with the triumph of a mechanistic account of variation through the discovery of the molecular structure of the gene in the mid-1950s by Watson and Crick. Through the combination of an increasingly robust account of biological complexity through the neo-Darwinian synthesis and an equally robust account of solar, galactic, and cosmic development through general relativity, astrophysics, and most recently particle physics, the natural sciences this century have radically and irrevocably altered our understanding of nature and our relation to the universe.

In light of contemporary, post-Newtonian science and post-reductionist philosophy, then, can we construct a non-interventionist account of objective divine action (NIODA)? Much of the current discussion in the field of theology and science regarding divine action is focused on this crucial goal.

3. NIODA: Terms and Assumptions, Criteria, and Responses to Frequent Misconceptions

Our task now is to characterize the meaning of a non-interventionist approach to a theology of objective divine action (NIODA). We will do so by stipulating a set of criteria which any potential or purported candidate for NIODA must satisfy. Following this we will assess specific proposals for NIODA (section 4 below). First, however, we need to offer some working definitions of the terms involved and the assumptions brought to the conversation. We also must respond briefly to frequent misconceptions regarding NIODA that tend to obscure the conversation and delay progress in assessing serious candidates for NIODA.

A. Terminology and assumptions

1. Laws of nature: By "laws of nature" we mean the regularities of natural processes as subsumed into scientific theories most often through mathematical formulation. Examples of these laws are the inverse square law in Newton's theory of gravity, the iterative equation in chaos theory, the Schrödinger equation in quantum mechanics, the Dirac equation in relativistic quantum mechanics, the field equations in Einstein's general relativity, and so on. Now there are several qualifications I need to make about the meaning of the term "laws of nature." First of all, most scholars recognize that the actual laws of nature—if there are such laws—are only partially and provisionally represented by the laws contained in particular scientific theories such as quantum mechanics; whether we will ever discover the actual laws is a debatable question.[29] Assuming there are such actual laws, some scholars view them ontologically, believing they exist as in the sense of Platonic realism. When understood this way, the laws of nature are then often said to "govern" natural processes prescriptively, and such processes are said to "obey" the laws of nature. Others, however, view the laws of nature as descriptions of what are either simply natural regularities or, perhaps underlying these, the causal efficacy of nature itself.[30] In either case, from a *theological* perspective the laws of nature and the kinds of causal efficacies they represent—ontological forms or immanent natural causality—are due ultimately to God's faithful and trustworthy action in creating the world *ex nihilo*. God's action as Creator is accomplished both as a whole and at each moment and, through such faithful and trustworthy action, the world is given its natural regularities as described by the laws of nature. In a trinitarian doctrine of God, these natural regularities and the intelligibility of nature are a result of the world being created through the second Person of the Trinity, the λόγος of God (John 1:3; Heb. 1:2).

I tend to view the laws of nature in the latter, descriptive sense. At times, though, I use the language of "nature obeying" such laws in order to make a specific methodological point: that I (and others in theology and science) must take seriously and stick with the consequences of a given scientific theory even if these mitigate against my theological position. If I am to "play the game" of theology and science fairly, then I had best use sparingly—as a rare fall-back strategy—any move which says "the laws are mere descriptions and cannot apply apodically or normatively in all cases." Such a move might save the day for theology, but it only does so by threatening to end the discussion with science.

2. "Ontological indeterminism": By ontological indeterminism I mean the philosophical interpretation of nature according to which there may not always be an efficient physical cause for every effect. The decision to regard nature as indeterministic is a philosophical interpretation based on the best-known scientific theories and the laws they incorporate. As essential background to this discussion we must review briefly the role of statistics, or "chance," in classical physics.[31]

In Newtonian physics, the fundamental laws—Newton's laws of classical mechanics and his law of gravity—were deterministic and implied, philosophically, that nature itself is deterministic, a closed causal system of forces acting on matter-in-motion. Laplacian determinism led to this mechanistic view of nature and the challenge to human free will and divine action, as we saw above. Classical physics, however, included statistical laws, such as in the kinetic theory of gases, but they were used for practical purposes; the underlying deterministic forces and all the relevant boundary and initial conditions were entirely too complicated to make explicit calculations possible. For simplicity we can distinguish two meanings of "chance" in classical statistics: 1) chance evident in a single causal trajectory. Here random forces deflect a single physical system along a crooked trajectory, such as with the Brownian motion of a dust mote or the bouncing of a cart wheel along a rutted road. 2) Chance due to the random juxtaposition of several causal trajectories. Here the random intersection of two causally independent trajectories leads to chance events, such as a car crash or an accidental meeting of two old friends at a totally unrelated event. The latter is often called "accidental" to distinguish it as a more complicated form of chance from the former. Yet in a fully deterministic universe, both could be predicted if one possessed sufficient knowledge of all the governing forces along with the initial and boundary conditions. A more complex form of this version of chance is found in evolutionary biology, where random mutations occur at the genetic level. Chance events also occur at the level of the environment, and the juxtaposition of these changes in genes and environment is itself random. Thus, natural selection involves a highly complex form of chance. In the theology and science literature, both forms of chance are called "epistemic chance" or "epistemic ignorance" because they refer to our lack of knowledge of the underlying causes. So chance or statistics as "epistemic ignorance" was taken routinely to indicate ontological determinism.

Does twentieth-century natural science open the possibility of chance being interpreted as a sign of ontological indeterminism in nature? This is, of course, an absolutely pivotal question, and one requiring a tremendous amount of analysis and judgment. As we shall see, scholars in theology and science have made a powerful case that various fields, including cosmology, thermodynamics, chaos theory, and quantum mechanics, do indeed suggest or point to ontological indeterminism. If this surmise is correct, it would mean that the presence of statistics in the mathematics of these fields does not arise from our ignorance of the underlying deterministic forces but from the fact that there are, in reality, no sufficient underlying forces or causes to fully determine particular physical processes, events, or outcomes. Scholars call this view of chance "ontological indeterminism" to distinguish it from chance as mere "epistemic ignorance." NIODA is a search for scientific theories that support ontological indeterminism.

3. "Objective versus subjective acts of God": Events are considered to be "objective acts of God" if God has acted differently in bringing them about than God acted in bringing about ordinary events. Put in counterfactual terms, events are considered the effect of an "objective act of God" if they would not have occurred had only the ordinary processes of nature, that is God's ordinary action, had been at work. Conservatives support the possibility of such objective divine acts. Conversely, liberals believe God acts uniformly in all events even though some may be viewed as "subjectively" special when the religious believer attributes to them specific revelatory meaning or distinctive divine agency.[32]

A nice example of an event in nature viewed subjectively as a divine act involves a typically religious response to the drama of a solar eclipse. At the moment of the eclipse, as the "diamond ring" takes place, observers gasp in awe and wonder at the extraordinary beauty of the eclipse and the way this beauty points in extraordinary ways to God as the Creator of the world. Still no one assumes that anything out of the ordinary has happened in terms of astrophysics: Two objects with the same ocular diameter have been juxtaposed by their motion which is entirely predictable according to classical physics. According to the liberal view the eclipse happened without God acting in other than God's usual way of upholding the regularities of nature. The beauty of the solar eclipse and its religious significance are truly "in the eye of the beholder" and not in the event itself.

An objective act of God, on the other hand, might involve a medical healing, being saved from a near disaster, or a sudden inspiration that leads one to decisive and unanticipated action. Such events would not have occurred without God acting in some distinctive way in relation to them. Our attribution of meaning and intentionality to God in relation to them is, or at least might be, based on our response to what God is actually doing in and through these events. We might be wrong in calling them an objective act of God but we are not wrong in employing the category of objective divine action to claim theologically that God can act in extraordinary ways in the world. Note, however, events can be considered distinctive or special acts of God only within the broader context of one's overall theology. This means that God's objective acts never contradict God's general action in creation and providence. It also means that God's objective acts will not be seen to be such without the theological presuppositions which allow for their possibility. Finally, I want to note here that NIODA is *not* meant to include miraculous divine action.

4. "Direct" or "indirect" acts:[33] I am drawing the distinction between *direct* and *indirect* acts from the context of the philosophy of action as it has developed around the problem of human agency. By a "direct act" or "basic act" I mean an act which an agent accomplishes without having to perform any prior act. By an "indirect act" I mean an act which an agent accomplishes by setting into motion a sequence of events stemming from a direct act. So, for example, when I turn on a light switch, the indirect act of my finger moving the switch is the result of a sequence of biological events in my body stemming, originally, from a direct act by which I initiate this sequence of events, presumably through a form of "top-down" causality between my mind and my brain.

In turning to divine action I will use the distinction between direct and indirect acts analogously, recognizing the severe apophatic limitations on any such analogy. This leads to the following distinction regarding divine action: An objective act of God may be either a direct act of God or an indirect act resulting from God's direct act elsewhere in nature. Note that every event in the universe, including (but not limited to) the absolute beginning of the universe at "t=0" (if it had such a beginning), is a direct act in the sense of its sheer existence, that is of its being created *ex nihilo.*

5. Mediated and immediate divine action. By *mediated,* I mean that God acts in, with, and through the existing processes of nature without thereby becoming a secondary, or natural, cause. By *unmediated* or *immediate* I mean God's action of creation *ex nihilo* which accounts for the ontological existence of the world as a whole and for the existence of the world at every moment of time. In most Christian theology[34] God does not create the universe by working with, in, and through some pre-existing medium, such as a Platonic substance. To exist is to be posited as existing by God alone. More correctly, to exist is not ontologically prior to being in relation to God. Rather to exist is to be in a relation of radical ontological dependence on God.

Thus every event in nature, in that it exists per se, is the result of the immediate creative act of God *ex nihilo.* At the same time all events in the world excepting an absolute beginning of time, t=0 (if there is such an event), are also the result of God's mediated action, that is God's action mediated in, with, together, and through, the causal processes of nature.[35] Thus within the context of creation and providence, no event, excepting t=0, comes about *only* through an unmediated act of God. If there were a genuine "moment of creation" or t=0, it would be the result solely of God's immediate action since here there is no preceding, mediating event in which God works with nature to cause t=0.

Combining 4) and 5) we can delineate the following possibilities: Events may be the result of God's immediate and direct action (for example, t=0), God's mediated and direct action (for example, objective special divine action), and God's mediated and indirect action (for example, the consequences at a later time or at another level of complexity in nature of objective special divine action). In this scheme it would make no sense to talk about God's immediate and indirect acts; all indirect divine acts are mediated. Finally, in all preceding discussion it would be more correct to refer to an event as the locus of the effect of God's action rather than an event as due to God's action. The latter sounds too close to the infamous problem of the "causal joint" and betrays the fact that God's action is so different from natural agency that even those events which we see as direct acts of special providence are at most the consequence of God acting in the forever hidden region of the "causal joint."

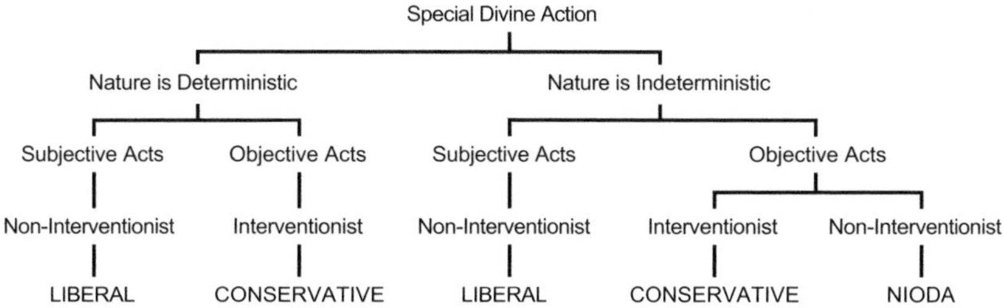

Figure 4.1: Options for divine action given either ontological determinism or indeterminism in nature

On the left half of the figure nature, viewed through the lens of classical physics, is interpreted deterministically. This in turn leads to the historical split between liberal and conservative approaches to special divine action. For liberals, the notion of subjectively special divine action reduces, in essence, to a verbal redescription of what is in fact ordinary divine action. For conservatives, objectively special divine action requires interventionism and thus amounts to "miraculous" divine action (in the Humean sense). Note that determinism, as a *philosophical* interpretation of classical *physics*, forces the *theological* split between these approaches to divine action. On the right half of the figure nature, understood through contemporary science, is interpreted indeterministically. Here we see that, while liberal and conservative approaches to divine action are still options, a third possibility arises for the first time: NIODA. NIODA combines the virtues of the liberal approach (non-interventionism) and the conservative approach (objective divine action) without their corresponding disadvantages. Note in particular that the indeterministic interpretation of nature allows us to separate out "miraculous" objective divine action from "non-miraculous" (non-interventionist) objective divine action, a move which has tremendous theological promise. The challenge is to find one or more areas in contemporary science that permit such an indeterministic ontology for nature. CTNS/VO scholars pursued a variety of areas in science in response to this challenge.

6. "Top-down," "whole-part," "lateral," and "bottom-up" causality, and their combinations. There are several distinct approaches to the problem of divine action. Their main difference lies in the relation between where God's direct act is thought to occur and the ordinary world of lived experience in which its indirect effects are experienced and understood as acts of God. a) "Top-down" refers to God's action at a higher epistemic and phenomenological level than the level of the effects. So, for example, in the "mind/brain" problem, where language about mental states cannot be entirely reduced to—although it is constrained by—language about neuroscience, God might be thought of as acting at the level of mind (for example, revelation or inspiration) and thereby affecting the pattern of neuron firings. (The converse model of revelation—God affecting neuron firings to bring about mental inspiration—would be "bottom-up": see below.) b) "Whole-part" causality or constraint refers to the way the boundary of a system affects the specific state of the system. Examples include the formation of vortices in a bucket of water being heated by a burner. The vortices form because the shape of the bucket as well as the applied heat bring about large-scale patterns of movement in the water. Another example, coming from quantum mechanics, is the set of eigenstates in a square potential well. These eigenstates are simple periodic functions because they must vanish at the boundary of the well. A final example is the universe considered as a whole, to the extent that the universe can be said to have a boundary. In these cases, God may be thought of as affecting the boundary or the container of a system, or perhaps the boundary of the universe itself and this action leads to specific states within the system/universe which we call objectively special indirect divine acts.

c) "Lateral" refers to effects lying in the same epistemic level (physics, biology, and so on) as their causes but at the end of a long causal chain. So the "butterfly" effect in chaos theory depicts small differences in the initial states of a chaotic physical system leading to large differences in later states of that same system: For example, small changes in the weather over Paris might lead to large-scale changes in the weather over Geneva. God, then, might act directly to set the initial conditions and thus bring about bulk states indirectly, all within a meteorological system. d) "Bottom-up" causality refers to the way the lower levels of organization affect the way more complex levels behave. So, for example, the temperature and pressure of a gas in classical thermodynamics arise, in the atomic theory of gases, from the kinetic energy of the atoms of the gas and their exchange of momentum with the container. Here God might act at the most elementary domains of an organism or system to achieve specific results which are manifest at the level of ordinary human experience. Quantum physics seems the most promising candidate for further inquiry into divine action through bottom-up causality.

Actually, most scholars want to combine most, or even all four, types of causality when it comes to human agency in the world and to God's action in human life and history. The challenge is to conceive of God as acting in the processes of biological evolution or physical cosmology long before the arrival of any kind of complex biological organism (let alone humanity). Here bottom-up causality may be the only approach available. Note: I will discuss a Whiteheadian approach to NIODA below (see 4D).

B. Criteria for a Successful proposal for NIODA

We are now prepared to state the criteria for deciding whether we have a successful proposal for NIODA:

For non-interventionist objective divine action to be intelligible in light of science, the events that result from God's action must occur within a domain of nature in which the appropriate scientific theory can be interpreted philosophically in terms of ontological indeterminism. *The events must be considered as* direct, mediated, *and* objective acts of God.

Hence the primary goal to reach in pursuit of NIODA is to identify and assess candidate theories in science for their capability of being given an indeterministic interpretation. When we have such a scientific theory we can claim that the objective acts of God occur without intervention.

C. FAQs: Responses to frequent misconceptions about NIODA

Before turning to some specific proposals for NIODA and their assessment, I would like to dispel some of the confusion which often accompanies these discussions. Inevitably, a number of misconceptions about NIODA frequently arise which tend to prevent or detract from a substantive assessment of these proposals. My hope is to minimize any future confusion over just what the NIODA project is, and is not, about, so that in the future the serious discussion of specific proposals can be more efficient and constructive. (Note: The reader can think of this section as a "FAQs" page on the "NIODA website," as it were! If she/he is not liable to these misconceptions I suggest skipping to section 4 below, where I present a detailed discussion of several specific proposals for NIODA.)

1. NIODA is part of a theology of nature, not natural theology ("physico-theology"). This is a project in constructive theology, with special attention to a theology of nature. (See chapter 10, Figure 10.1, paths 1–5). This hypothesis should be taken not as a form of natural theology, nor as one of physico-theology, and most certainly not as an argument from design. Instead it is part of a general constructive trinitarian theology pursued in the tradition of *fides quaerens intellectum*, whose warrant and justification lies elsewhere and which incorporates the results of science and the concerns for nature into its broader framework mediated by philosophy. Although I believe God's special action is intelligible in the context of, and coherent with, our scientific view of the world because of the indeterministic character of the natural processes as suggested by a plausible philosophical interpretation of quantum physics, such special action cannot be discovered by the natural sciences as such nor can it be based on them. Where faith will posit it, science will see only random events described, as far as they can be by science, by the theories of physics, chemistry, biology, ecology, and so on. The positive grounds for an alleged divine action are theological, not scientific. This hypothesis is not drawn from science even though it aims to be consistent with science.

Science would not be expected to include anything explicitly about God's action in nature as part of its scientific explanation of the world. Theology, however, in *its* explanation of the world, can and should include both. This is as it should be for the mutual integrity of, and distinction between, the two fields of inquiry, and for the order of containment entailed by emergence views of epistemology which requires that theology include and be constrained by, while transcending, science in its mode of explanation.

2. NIODA is not meant to "explain" how God acts or "prove" that God acts. Proposals for NIODA are not meant as an "explanation" of *how* God acts in nature and history. Whether or not one thinks of the God-world relation in terms of primary and secondary causalities, as Austin Farrer did, NIODA is not a description, let alone an explanation, of what Farrer called the "causal joint" between God's agency and creaturely agency.[36] Nor are such proposals meant as an argument to "prove" *that* God acts; instead they assume that warrants for the belief in divine action come from extended theological arguments whose sources lie elsewhere (including scripture, tradition, experience, and reason). What proposals for NIODA *are* required to do is to specify a certain area or theory in science that describes one possible location or domain where God's direct or basic acts—although ultimately mysterious and unknowable in themselves—result in an objective event effecting the course of nature *without intervention*.[37]

3. NIODA is not a gaps argument in either the epistemic or ontological sense of gaps.[38] There are two kinds of gaps arguments which I do not believe correctly describe a successful candidate for a NIODA proposal.

Type I: epistemic gaps. An *epistemic* gaps argument is based on what we do not know about the world. It invokes God to explain things that we do not yet understand. But many gaps in our current understanding of nature will eventually be filled by new discoveries or changing paradigms in science. The argument is that we ought not stake our theological ground on transitory scientific puzzles. In a moving letter from a Nazi prison cell, Dietrich Bonhoeffer urges us to reject such a "stopgap" argument as he calls it. Instead we must discuss God's activity in the world in terms of "what we know, not . . . what we don't know."[39]

I agree with this concern. Epistemic gaps as such in science *will* be filled by science, and theology should *not* be evoked as offering the type of explanation which science could eventually provide. Candidates for a successful NIODA must *not* be based on epistemic gaps. Instead they must be based on what is *known* by one branch of science within a reasonable interpretation of it, namely ontological indeterminism. Within the framework of this interpretation, what we *know* is that we cannot explain scientifically why a specific event in nature occurs.

Type II: ontological gaps. An *ontological* gaps argument assumes that natural processes are ontologically deterministic. There are no "causal gaps"[40] or breaks in the order of event causation, to use Thomas Tracy's term. Since nature itself lacks such causal gaps, God must act to create them. An account involving objective ontological gaps is therefore *interventionist:* in order to act in nature, God must intervene in these processes by suspending or violating the flow of these processes. An additional concern is that an ontological gaps argument depicts God as only occasionally acting in nature, causing gaps in the *otherwise seamless* natural processes, and it suggests that God is normally absent from the web of natural processes, acting only in the gaps which God causes. Furthermore, since God's intervention breaks the very processes of the natural order which God created and constantly maintains, it pits God's special acts against God's regular action which underlies and ultimately causes nature's regularities. Finally it undermines the "theology and science" interaction by theologically challenging the rights of science to rely on methodological naturalism and instead refer, somehow, to God as a legitimate factor in a strictly scientific account of natural processes. In sum, the key issue is whether the ontological gaps in nature are generated individually by divine intervention or created *ex nihilo* by God for nature as a whole.

Again, I agree with these concerns; we *should* avoid an approach to NIODA that depends on ontological gaps resulting from divine intervention in a world that God created as causally closed. If there are ontological gaps in nature, they must not be viewed as disruptions of what, without God's specific intervention, would otherwise have been a closed, causal process. Instead ontological gaps in nature must be a result of the way God created the world *ex nihilo*. Thus a successful approach to NIODA must claim that 1) the processes of nature are neither violated nor suspended by God's action, but maintained by God in the very way God created them *ex nihilo*. 2) It is precisely our scientific theories based on these processes and their capacity for being interpreted philosophically as pointing to ontological indeterminism that together tell us that there already are *ontological* gaps throughout the domain of nature described by these scientific theories. 3) Since these gaps are created *ex nihilo* as part of the way nature is, the God who acts through them is the same God who is universally present in and immanent to the natural processes wherein nature's causal efficacy is entirely sufficient. 4) Finally since this approach to NIODA is based on what science, philosophically interpreted, tells us about nature, it is consistent with, and not contradictory to, the commitment of the "theology and science" scholars to respect the integrity and autonomy of science and learn from its discoveries.

4. NIODA is not undermined by the fact that scientific theories can be given multiple and mutually contradictory interpretations. I agree that multiple interpretability is a real problem for NIODA, but it is in fact a real problem for any theology seeking to engage with scientific theories. Every scientific theory is multiply interpretable! For example, classical mechanics can be understood in terms of efficient causality (forces act on matter at specific points in space and time to produce the actual trajectory moment by moment) and final causality (the trajectory actually taken minimizes a single, global, integral property, termed "action," of that entire trajectory). Chaos theory can be seen as either a victory for unpredictability or a victory for determinism. However, some theories are vulnerable to much sharper and more entrenched controversies. Special relativity gives rise to the "flowing time versus block universe" debate. Quantum mechanics can lead to at least eight distinct and, in most cases, mutually contradictory interpretations,[41] whereas classical physics, and with it chaos theory, are blatantly deterministic.

Clearly we cannot avoid the reality of multiple interpretability. Instead each scholar must build a response to it directly into her/his methodology for relating theology and science. In my view, the best response is to take a "what if" stance to this problem. One must be rigorously clear in acknowledging and underscoring the multiple interpretability of a given theory and in disclosing "in broad daylight" *that* one is choosing one particular interpretation in order to explore its theological implications as a "what if" strategy. This means stressing that this approach, like any venture in theology, is hypothetical. With this stated up front, one can proceed to be as rigorous as possible about what this interpretation would tell us about the world *if it were true which it might in fact be.*

5. God's action is not reduced to the status of a natural cause. NIODA does *not* reduce God to a natural cause because, according to the philosophical interpretation of the candidate theory in science, there are no efficient natural causes for the specific events in question. If God acts together with nature to produce the events of objective divine action, God is not acting as a natural, efficient cause.

6. God's action is hidden from science. The theory of divine action being considered here is entirely consistent with the basis of science in methodological naturalism. As indicated above, neither theology nor science will view "God" as a proper part of a scientific explanation of the world.[42] More sharply, God's direct action according to NIODA will be hidden in principle from science even if science were to search for it. This is because, for each event in question, there is no natural efficient cause for science to discover, given that the scientific theory in question is interpreted philosophically as pointing to ontological indeterminism. Thus this theory of divine action supports the integrity of science and yet allows science to be integrated fruitfully into constructive theology where "God" as an explanation of natural events is appropriately and fully developed.

7. NIODA is a distinct category from that of miracle. As we have seen above, in a deterministic world, objective divine action requires that God intervenes in nature, suspending or disrupting the ordinary processes of the world and violating the laws of nature we construct to describe these processes. In short, objective divine acts are "miracles" in the Humean sense of miracle as a violation of the laws of nature. The split between liberal and conservative Christians can be seen as a split over whether or not God acts in miraculous ways in the world. (See the left side of Figure 4.1.)

When we shift to an *in*deterministic world, a new possibility opens up: One can now speak of objective acts of God that do not require God's miraculous intervention but offer, instead, an account of objective divine action that is completely consistent with science. These are the acts to which the acronym NIODA refers. Note that the liberal and conservative positions can still be articulated in an indeterministic world: Liberals can still assume that all talk about divine acts is merely religious language about ordinary events while conservatives can still insist that God objectively acts by miraculously intervening in the indeterministic processes of nature, but now there is a third alternative as well—NIODA: special acts of God that are objective but not miraculous. (See the right side of Figure 4.1.)

This remarkable distinction made possible between miracles and NIODA in an indeterministic world offers theologians for the first time the opportunity to distinguish between objective divine providence in light of science (see, for example, my version of theistic evolution in chapter 6) and those events in scripture and the life of faith which do require the language of miracle, such as the nature miracles and healing miracles in the New Testament. Note: When discussing the resurrection of Jesus, I usually refer to it as "more than a miracle" since his resurrection seems to involve the transformation of nature as a whole rather than an intervention into the processes of nature which leave them otherwise untouched (as, for example, in the miraculous resurrection of Lazarus). For further discussion see chapter 10 on the resurrection of Jesus and Christian eschatology.

4. Types of Approaches to Non-Interventionist Objective Divine Action (NIODA): Critical Assessment

With the preceding definitions, assumptions, and criteria in mind we are ready to turn to some specific candidates for scientific theories which could serve as a basis for a non-interventionist account of objective divine action.

A. Lateral causality and chaos theory: John Polkinghorne

As I understand his work, John Polkinghorne develops an approach to objective divine action by starting with the analogy, God : world :: mind : body, and then shifting it to the analogy, God : world :: human agent : world. He then asks what it is about the world that allows us to exercise free will, since the answer to this might provide a clue, via the analogy, to the way God interacts with the world. For Polkinghorne the answer lies in the new scientific understanding of nature as ontologically open. He draws in detail on recent developments in the theory of dynamic chaos to support his commitment to openness.

In the late 1980s Polkinghorne published a "trilogy" on science and theology. In the second book, *Science and Creation,*[43] Polkinghorne focused on the sensitivity to small variations in the initial conditions on the many-body problem in Newtonian mechanics. Here we find him moving from Newtonian mechanism to an indeterministic ontology:

> The apparently deterministic proves to be intrinsically unpredictable. It is suggested that the natural interpretation of this exquisite sensitivity is to treat it, not merely as an epistemological barrier, but as an indication of the ontological openness of the world of complex dynamical systems.

Finally he warrants this interpretation by appealing to his own take on critical realism in which "epistemology and ontology are always closely linked."[44]

One might suspect, with Polkinghorne, that the prevalence of chaotic phenomena in nature suggests that the world is in reality ontologically open, but his argument to ground this based on the specific connection he cites between epistemology and ontology seems wrong-headed to me for two reasons. 1) The appeal to a link between scientific epistemology and ontology goes far beyond the phenomena science studies—which taken at face value might suggest ontological openness—to the theory representing them. 2) Chaos theory is clearly deterministic and therefore points inferentially to ontological determinism, not ontological indeterminism, in nature.

1) Epistemology in science includes both the phenomenon being studied, its form as data of a specific theory, the theory which accounts for it as tested by its predictive success, and the paradigm which contextualizes the theory through exemplars and metaphysical elements. It is this entire epistemic framework, and not just the phenomena we observe, that realists use as an inferential clue to the ontological character of the physical world. It is then the standard task of "theology and science" to appropriate this philosophical interpretation of a scientific theory, and not just hints from the data being discussed, into a revised and reconstructed systematic theology. (Again, see Figure 10.1, paths 1–5.)

2) Chaos theory is indisputably a deterministic theory fully situated within classical physics even though it is expressed in terms of statistical equations. Actually Wesley Wildman and I have argued that chaos theory, while deterministic, represents something quite novel in science: a *tertium quid* between the classical "equation": "epistemic predictability in principle with unpredictability in practice → ontological determinism" (cf. Newtonian mechanics) and the quantum "equation": "epistemic unpredictability in principle → ontological indeterminism." Instead chaos theory, although squarely a part of classical physics, represents the "both/and" surprise: "epistemic unpredictability in principle → ontological determinism."[45] I believe this is a very new situation in science which we have not yet fully plumbed theologically.

In sum, then, if "epistemology models ontology," then it is the entire framework of theories with their relevant data and equations, which "models" either a deterministic or an indeterministic reality, and not just the phenomena separated from theory, instrumentation, and mathematical equations. A deterministic theory such as chaos theory points to ontological determinism in nature; for the theologian it will *not* provide a basis for a non-interventionist theory of divine action.

There is, however, an alternative way of construing what Polkinghorne is really doing—granted it is not "epistemology models ontology"! In the third volume in the trilogy, *Science and Providence,*[46] Polkinghorne seems at first reading to be making the same move from a deterministic theory to an indeterministic ontology when he writes that the data drawn from chaotic systems "reflect an intrinsic openness in the behavior of these systems."[47] Nevertheless I am convinced that Polkinghorne is actually moving in a different—and highly promising—direction: He is not moving from science through philosophy to theology but from a set of theological and experience-based convictions about the world back to science to suggest a new scientific research program: the search for what he will call "holistic chaos." In essence I see him as stipulating that nature must be intrinsically open; he is not concluding that it is so from chaos theory. Such a "metaphysical wager" about the intrinsic openness in nature leads him to view the openness of nature as an "emergent property . . . within the world of classical physics" such that Newtonian determinism is "no more than an approximation to a more supple reality." Finally if such a scientific research program is successful, and if such holistic chaos is clearly indicative of ontological indeterminism—as Polkinghorne apparently believes it will be—it could, in turn, provide a new basis for a non-interventionist account of divine action.

This approach is further developed in *Reason and Reality*.[48] Here he first suggests that the intrinsic unpredictability of chaotic systems arises because they can never be fully isolated from their environment and because their initial conditions can never be fully known. So far, of course, these points actually underscore the deterministic character of chaos theory. However, Polkinghorne once again places chaotic phenomena within the context of emergence—and now emergence of a very unusual kind. Like other scholars in the field, Polkinghorne defends emergence in terms of structural (or ontological) reductionism[49] and epistemological anti-reductionism or holism. Now, however, he adds to this a crucial possibility he has already discussed, namely that emergence is "a two-way process" and that our understanding of reality should involve *both* bottom-up thinking, where emergence in the ordinary sense applies, and, more importantly, top-down thinking, where "downwards emergence" is called for. This in turn means that inferences about reality made from lower levels might not apply universally. Instead they may be only approximations to the nature of reality which these higher levels depict. "[T]he characteristics of the elementary level (whether deterministic, or quantum mechanical, or whatever) may be as much emergent properties (in the direction of increasing simplicity) as are life or consciousness (in the direction of increasing complexity)."[50] Finally, emergence as he understands it can serve as an avenue for God's non-interventionist interaction with the world. Both the free acts of humans and God point towards these ontological gaps or openness in physical processes.[51]

It is now clear why Polkinghorne can turn to chaos theory and suggest that reality is ontologically open. Although the equations we presently use to describe chaotic phenomena are deterministic, Polkinghorne speculates that they may in fact be mere approximations to more holistic theories. Moreover, when discovered, these theories will describe a range of complex systems from meteorology to biology to the mind/brain problem in terms of *ontological indeterminism.*

> That structured chaos can arise from deterministic equations is a mathematical fact. That fact by itself does not settle the metaphysical question of whether the future is determined or, on the contrary, the world is open in its process . . . if apparently open behaviour is associated with underlying apparently deterministic equations, which is

> to be taken to have the greater ontological seriousness—the behavior or the equations. . . . It is conceivable that apparent determinism emerges at some lower levels without its being a characteristic of reality overall.[52]

In subsequent publications, Polkinghorne has continued to reiterate this approach to divine action.[53]

I applaud this approach and encourage its pursuit. A successful move from theology to research in science would provide a powerful vindication of the cognitive capability of theology and a stunning victory for its specific claims about "the God who acts." What I would urge, however, is for clarity and candor regarding the fact that the move which Polkinghorne desires to make does not follow the usual progression that goes from science to its philosophical interpretation and then to implications for theology. Examples of the standard move include starting with t=0 in Big Bang cosmology, interpreting this as evidence of the contingency of nature and framing this in a theology of creation *ex nihilo*; viewing evolutionary biology in terms of continuous creation ("theistic evolution"); drawing philosophically on quantum mechanics for a theology of divine action; and so on. Instead Polkinghorne's move is in the opposite direction: It starts with an unassailable theological conviction that the world must be open—a conviction framed in a theology of divine action and supported by religious experience. It proceeds from this back to science where it launches a new scientific research program that views *current* chaos theory as merely an approximation to *true* chaos theory, assumes that such a theory will be unambiguously interpretable as pointing to ontological indeterminism in the macroscopic world, and directs us to search for such a theory. In short the move is not the standard one from existing physics (deterministic chaos theory) through philosophy to new theology (non-interventionist objective divine action—which fails given the determinism of chaos theory) but from theology (presupposing non-interventionist objective divine action) through philosophy to a new physics (research searching for a holistic, indeterministic chaos theory)!

Beginning in the 1980s I began developing what I call the "method of creative mutual interaction" (CMI) in order to describe—and urge!—the development of research programs in theology and science that make novel moves from theology to science as well as standard moves from science to theology. Figure 10.1 captures the variety of such moves by indicating eight paths actually taken by various scholars in the field. It is clear, now, that when Polkinghorne discusses his work, he is following paths 7 and 8, and not paths 1–5. I believe that such moves are, in fact, highly justifiable and much to Polkinghorne's credit. Many distinguished scientists have been inspired by their philosophical and theological beliefs to construct, or to choose between, scientific theories and to pursue them doggedly; the history of the development of quantum mechanics is replete with such stories. It is not all that surprising that a physicist as distinguished as Polkinghorne would be guided by just such a deeply intuitive understanding of the most promising direction for future research. I await the results with excitement! Nevertheless, my conclusion here is that *lateral causality based on existing chaos theory fails to provide a successful candidate for NIODA.*

B. Top-down and whole-part causality, the mind/brain problem, and the universe-as-a-whole: Arthur Peacocke[54]

A great deal of work is ongoing in both "top-down" and "whole-part" models of causality in nature and their relation to various approaches to divine action. The former most often involve the mind/brain problem and focus specifically on the challenge of arguing for mental causation (mental states can, in principle, affect brain states) as a response to causal reductionism (mental causation is epiphenomenal, entirely reducible to bottom-up physical causality). Strategies such as emergence and supervenience are being explored by a number of scholars including Philip Clayton,[55] George Ellis,[56] Theo Meyering,[57] and Nancey Murphy.[58] While this work seems extremely promising in eventually offering a variety of successful top-down approaches to NIODA, it is too early to assess their accomplishments fairly. What we can do, instead, is turn to the work of one of the earliest scholars to attend to these ideas: Arthur Peacocke. I will focus specifically on Peacocke's work in this section.

Peacocke has developed a variety of models of God's interaction with the world within the framework of panentheism, with its stress on divine immanence as well as divine transcendence.[59] These models combine top-down and whole-part approaches in fascinating ways. Peacocke begins by challenging the mechanistic view of nature which, because of its underlying acceptance of Laplacian determinism, led to an interventionist understanding of God's actions.[60] Here, for God to act in specific events in nature, God would have to violate the causal processes of nature and God's action, in turn, would contradict the laws of nature which science uses to describe natural processes. Instead, Peacocke urges us to see God as being in "continuous *interaction* with and a continual influence on the created order . . . [rather than] 'intervening' in any way disruptive of the natural and human processes he has created."[61] He then draws on contemporary science for evidence to support his challenge to mechanism.[62] Here fields like quantum mechanics and nonlinear dynamics seem to point to "permanent gaps in our ability to predict events in the natural world." This might, in turn, lead to a new view of nature as ontologically open and thus open the way for a new approach to divine action in the world. For this to be achieved, Peacocke raises two key questions: 1) Even if we cannot predict the future, can God know it? 2) Does the new flexibility of nature provide room for God to act without intervening in the causal regularities of nature?

First Peacocke addresses these questions from the perspectives of promising new foci in classical physics, namely the many-body problem, chaos theory, and nonlinear nonequilibrium thermodynamics. Some scholars have found these new fields as offering a promising approach to non-interventionist divine action. However, since they are still in principle a part of classical physics, Peacocke's prognosis is negative. On the one hand it is true the future state of these systems is, for us, unpredictable in principle, not just in practice. Chaotic systems, for example, exponentially amplify tiny, undetectable fluctuations in the initial conditions into different future states of the system which are for us unpredictable.[63] But does this unpredictability hold for God as well? No, replies

Peacocke. Unlike us, God can know the future state of systems like these by predicting the future from the present (Question 1) because these systems, being essentially classical in nature, are determinist and if God is omniscient, God's exact knowledge of the present would allow God to predict the future.[64] Moreover for God to act to alter the future (Question 2), God would have to change the initial conditions of these systems. Although this kind of divine action would never be detectable by us it would still be a form of intervention, and thus Peacocke—in my view correctly—rejects chaos theory, and so on, as offering a non-interventionist approach to divine action.[65]

Next Peacocke turns to quantum mechanics in his search for a non-interventionist account of divine action. He acknowledges the possibility of a deterministic interpretation of quantum uncertainties (that is, a "hidden variables" view) but favors the argument that quantum mechanics points to ontological indeterminacy in nature, which he reports as the "majority view of physicists."[66] He cites radioactivity as an example of such genuine indeterminacy in nature.[67] In response to Question 1), Peacocke views quantum indeterminism as a limitation even on God's omniscience; because of quantum indeterminism, God can only know the future probabilistically. Moreover, since God has created the world this way, this limitation is "self-limited." According to Peacocke, this entails an answer to Question 2) as well. Since "God cannot know precisely the future outcome of quantum dependent situations, [God] cannot act *directly* to influence them in order to implement the divine purpose and will."[68]

Unlike my endorsement of Peacocke's critique of the appeal to new foci in classical physics as discussed above, my response to these claims about quantum mechanics is mixed. 1) In my opinion the indeterministic interpretation of quantum mechanics does not imply that God cannot know the future. Instead, quantum indeterminism only implies that God cannot foreknow the future based on God's knowledge of the present just prior to a quantum event—say the decay of a radioactive atom. But within classical theism God knows the future not by foreknowledge based on God's knowledge of the present but by knowing the future in its own present actuality. This claim is not challenged by quantum indeterminism. 2) If God acts within nature (though never as a natural cause) to provide the sufficient cause of a particular quantum event then God can foreknow the future since it is determined by the way God chooses freely to act with nature to bring about that quantum event.

Thirdly, Peacocke targets complex processes in nature which display both top-down and bottom-up causality. On the one hand, events at "lower" levels of complexity influence the behavior of the total system in a bottom-up way; yet on the other hand Peacocke claims that the system as a whole supervenes on, and thus constrains, the behavior of its lower levels, though in a way consistent with the laws describing these levels. Now he makes his key move: By applying this notion to the universe—which he calls the "world-as-a-whole"—we can think about how God interacts with the world to bring about particular events in nature while respecting and not violating the law-like processes of the world.[69] The concept of panentheism again helps Peacocke bring together God's transcendence of the world-as-a-whole with God's immanence "in, with, under and through" natural processes as suggested by his fascinating term, "transcendence-in-immanence."[70]

> Attempts to hold together the notions of God's transcendence over the world, his ultimate otherness, with that of his immanent Presence in, with and under the world often find it helpful to deploy models of the world as being, in some sense, "in God," but of God as being "more than" the world, and so as the circumambient Reality in which the world persists and exists ("pan-en-theism").[71]

The key, however, is Peacocke's focus on God's causality in a top-down manner[72] which does not involve God intervening in the laws and regularities of the lower levels. The crucial piece that makes Peacocke's approach work is his conceptual model of the world-as-a-whole; through it, Peacocke can speak of God not only sustaining the world but interacting continually with it to achieve both general and particular effects.

I am in solid theological agreement with Peacocke here in his understanding of God's relation to the world and I admire the way it offers him a unique approach to our understanding of God's interaction with the world. The former is grounded in the rich theological tradition that emphasizes the radical ontological distinction between God and "all-that-is" while at the same time it insists that God is intimately present to all-that-is. The latter is a splendid attempt to achieve the goal of a non-interventionist account of divine action in a unique way: not by identifying domains of ontological openness within nature as I do through a quantum mechanics -based non-interventionist approach to objective divine action (QM-NIODA) but by viewing God's action as directed to the world-as-a-whole. If we distinguish between the laws of nature that govern the world-as-a-whole and the initial and boundary conditions that hold for the world-as-a-whole, then God can be thought of as acting on these initial and boundary conditions without intervening in the laws of nature. Divine action conceived in this way achieves particular effects as indirect and mediated by God's direct action on that whole rather than "within" it. Using an expanded version of Figure 4.1 we could understand Peacocke's approach to objective divine action as non-interventionist whether or not nature is deterministic.[73]

The question I want to raise, however,[74] is whether the concept of the world-as-a-whole, which Peacocke uses to explore both the theological understanding of God's ontological relation to the world and a top-down non-interventionist account of divine action, makes sense when we try to interpret this concept in terms of contemporary science.[75] My worry is that it does not, and this worry might best be expressed by turning to the diagram which Peacocke used to God's interaction with the world in the Gifford Lectures and in his chapter in the CTNS/VO volume *Neuroscience and the Person*, although it is not included as such in the present essay on "A Naturalist Christian Faith."[76] The figure is meant to suggest both God's transcendence to and immanence within the universe as the world-as-a-whole.

In the figure a dashed circle represents the boundary of the world-as-a-whole. Within the circle we find all of creation, including a symbol standing for humankind at the center of the circle. God as the transcendent Creator is then symbolized as coming in from the infinite region outside the circle and acting on it. The effects of that action are transmitted by natural causes into the interior of the circle, eventually reaching humanity. God is also symbolized as acting immanently on all points of the world-as-a-whole. Here God's action is orthogonal to the paper on which the diagram is inscribed as indicated by the ⊗ at the center of the diagram.[77]

Now Peacocke is quite clear that a figure such as this can only go so far in depicting the God-world relationship since God's relation to creation is not "spatial." Instead spatiality is one of the properties of the created world. Instead, as Peacocke rightly insists, the figure is meant to represent God's ontological relation to the world as well as God's interaction with the world.

> Figure 1 attempts to express on a two-dimensional surface the relation between different modes of being—it is an ontological representation (rather like a Venn diagram representing the logic of the relation between different classes).[78]

So far we are on solid ground. My concern, however, is with the extent to which the figure relates to what science tells us about the universe, that is, the world-as-a-whole in the framework of science. On the one hand, if the dotted circle merely represents the ontological distinction between God and the universe then it leaves little room for the implications of science. After all theologians have been making this same strictly ontological distinction between God and creation in eras dominated by the vastly different cosmologies of Aristotle/Ptolemy, Copernicus/Newton, and now Einstein. If on the other hand the dotted circle is also meant to represent what science tells us about the universe, if in particular the dotted circle is meant to represent the limits or the boundary of the universe, it fails be a valid interpretation of what science tells us about the universe—in a quite remarkable way. But if this is so, and I believe it is, then it also fails to be a valid interpretation of God's relation to the universe *in light of science.*

The reason for the failure is based on the "counterintuitive" fact that, according to contemporary scientific cosmology, *the universe does not have a boundary*; it is unbounded.[79] It is relatively easy to understand this using the basic models in Big Bang cosmology.[80] In these models the topology of the universe is a three-dimensional hypersurface expanding in time. The hypersurface is either "spherical" (closed/finite in size, eventually recontracts), "flat" (open/infinite in size, expands forever) or "hyperbolic" (open/infinite in size, expands forever). The spherical three-dimensional hypersurface, for example, is analogous to a two-sphere such as a beach ball (that is, the two-dimensional surface of a beach ball, not its three-dimensional volume). Obviously the surface of a beach ball has no boundary; an ant crawling on it never comes to an "edge," although in time it might return to its starting point.

The universe then is simply not analogous to Peacocke's disk circumscribed by a dashed line. There is no boundary to the universe. Therefore there is no boundary on which God can act from "outside" and thus no top-down or whole-part divine action on the universe as a whole when the universe is understood in light of science. As long as the theological claim about the relation between God and the world is strictly ontological, there is no "boundary" problem, but then science is *irrelevant* to this theological claim. As soon as science comes into the picture at all, the dotted circle and thus the figure as a whole fails to represent what science tells us about the universe.

But wait, there is still one way that might take us out of this cul-de-sac. One might say that the "world-as-a-whole" is best thought of as the entire three-dimensional curved hypersurface of the universe considered at a specific moment of proper time τ (that is, the age of the universe) and not its boundary (of which there is none). God's action might then be thought of as immanent everywhere and at every point in the hypersurface (that is, as indicated by the ⊗ symbol). Ironically, given Peacocke's dislike of a quantum mechanical approach to divine action, this actually moves the conversation about divine action to precisely this approach: divine action at every point-like quantum event throughout the universe. Perhaps God's top-down action on every part of the universe is intimately related to God's bottom-up action "in" every part of the universe.

C. Bottom-up causality and quantum mechanics

An additional option to be explored for NIODA is "bottom-up" causality. In my opinion the most promising approach is to base NIODA on quantum mechanics (QM), with its philosophical interpretation that nature's ontology at the subatomic level is at least partially indeterministic. This approach has been explored since the early 1950s by scholars such as Karl Heim, E. L. Mascall, and William Pollard and includes very recent work by a number of participants in the CTNS/VO series of research conferences and publications.

I believe that a QM-based NIODA does in fact meet the criteria for NIODA listed above and that it is distinctively robust, responding to a variety of FAQs and opening up new insights into more complex questions including the relation between general and special providence, whether God acts in some or in all quantum events, how one deals with the challenges to human freedom and the problem of evil (theodicy), and so on. Because the extensive work done by so many contributors in this area requires a detailed discussion and assessment, I will devote all of the next chapter (5) to QM-NIODA.

D. An alternative metaphysics: process philosophy and NIODA

Finally I want to turn to process philosophy, as based primarily on the works of Alfred North Whitehead and Charles Hartshorne, and thus to NIODA from the perspective of process theology. Ian Barbour has done more than any other scholar, in my opinion, to relate process thinking to specific issues in physics, cosmology, and evolutionary biology. I will be following his most recent account here.[81]

According to Barbour's reading of process philosophy God gives order to the world as its primordial ground, God experiences the world in time through God's consequent nature, and God influences the world while respecting the freedom of each event by luring the world moment by moment towards God's highest ideals. Two of process thought's most distinctive features are the rejection of creation *ex nihilo* and the rejection of the traditional categories of primary and secondary causes. Instead, God and the world are co-eternal, and God is seen as the continuous creator acting *within* all events ("actual occasions"). Moreover, divine action is persuasive and never unilateral. Each occasion includes an irreducible element of genuine novelty, expressed through its unique response to the influence of the past and to God's lure. As Barbour puts it, "We can speak of God acting, but God always acts with and through other entities rather than by acting alone as a substitute for their actions."[82]

Another distinctive feature of process philosophy is the claim that all actual occasions have a mental as well as a physical pole. The complexity of their organization into inanimate and living organisms affects the degree to which they can respond to the mental pole and to God's lure. At the inanimate level of organization, God's influence underlies the regularities which the natural sciences study. At more complex levels, nature and eventually human nature are much more capable of responding to the creative action of God.

Historically process philosophy was formulated in light of the changes in physics and biology in the early part of the twentieth-century science. Because of this, process philosophy works with an evolutionary, historical, and emergent interpretation of the world, where both law and chance, structure and openness, are in play. Instead of a more traditional worldview of a fixed order, a substantialist metaphysics, and an anthropocentric hierarchy, process thought views the cosmos in temporal, relational, and ecological terms characterizing systems and wholes in a multi-leveled community. This worldview is seen as highly coherent with current science and it opens up new ways of thinking about God's action in the world.

Working with this metaphysics, process theologians view God's purposes as eternal while God's knowledge changes in time as God interacts in mutual relationship with the world. For them, panentheism provides an important step beyond classical theism and a crucial argument against pantheism. According to Barbour's careful and insightful analysis, process theism offers some clear advantages over other models of divine action while bearing liabilities as well.[83] On the one hand, it emphasizes a social and ecological model for the world in which God offers creative persuasion and participation. It underscores the importance of human freedom, God's suffering with the world, "masculine" and "feminine" attributes of God, and the importance of religious pluralism.

What about *special* divine acts? According to David Ray Griffin, special providence can be understood in process categories in a distinctive way. Granted that every event receives its initial aim equally from God, events which are capable of self-determination have a greater potential for being stimulated by God to achieve something truly distinctive than do more elementary events. In addition, to the extent that the divine initial aim is actualized, it contributes to the uniqueness of the event and it allows God's initial aim to be effective. Since God is internally present in all events, God's action is non-interventionist. Finally, to the extent that the response actually conforms to God's initial aim and its content, the event reflects the divine aim for the world.[84]

In his conclusions, Barbour acknowledges that process theism is tied to a complex, abstract, and speculative metaphysical system which can hinder both theological development and liturgical efficacy. With this in mind, he writes that "the theologian must adapt, not adopt, a metaphysics. Many process insights may be accepted without accepting the total Whiteheadian scheme."[85] The intrinsic limitations on God's power "call into question the traditional expectation of an *absolute victory over evil.*" In his concluding remarks, Barbour summarizes the situation with characteristic honesty and humility: "The process model thus seems to have fewer weaknesses than the other models considered here. But according to critical realism, all models are limited and partial, and none gives a complete or adequate picture of reality. . . . We need diverse models . . . to keep us from the idolatry that occurs when we take any one model of God too literally."[86]

Process theology seems to provide a candidate for NIODA: Its view of God's action is objective (the effects really occur in the actual constitution of each occasion), mediated, and direct (divine agency works in and through each occasion at every level of nature). But is it non-interventionist? According to Barbour and Griffin, God's action is non-interventionist in a *metaphysical* sense: God acts within each occasion rather than "breaking into" the flow of natural processes from an "external" vantage. It is thus a part of what constitutes an actual occasion. But for NIODA to work, we must *also* be in a position to claim that these processes are ontologically indeterministic based on a "best inference" from a specific area of science. If our best inference from one such area, for example chaos theory, is that nature at that level is deterministic, then while process philosophy might offer a metaphysical conception of nature—one in which God's persuasive action is constitutive of each occasion at that level—and even if each such occasion does indeed include intrinsic novelty, the results of divine action and intrinsic novelty are not genuine unpredictability but deterministic order. To put this another way, whether or not one wants to claim that process metaphysics makes it possible to view God as acting in processes which can be described by deterministic equations such as chaos theory, one would have to conclude *either* that any specific acts of God in these processes are of no avail *or* that God's action is, after all, merely uniformitarian. In either case we are back to the liberal/conservative forced option we began with, but without the possibility of transcending it via NIODA.

To put it still differently, for God's action to be effective, it requires that natural processes at least at some level do not include sufficient efficient causality. In process language, the prehension of the past must not fully determine the way an event concresces; instead the prehension of the past must only be partially efficacious, leaving room for intrinsic novelty and an effective divine lure. Of course one can answer this question metaphysically by saying that this is in fact the case, but this is no more than a rhetorical response. The crucial test is whether science plays an independent role in determining the question. Unless process scholars make a case-by-case claim that divine action is non-interventionist by specifically involving science, all they offer is a metaphysical framework in which NIODA is *potentially possible.* The decision requires the introduction of independent arguments for ontological indeterminism based on one or more of the theories in the natural sciences. In short, in my opinion process theology cannot deliver a genuine form of NIODA without arguing for ontological indeterminism based on science even if it does offer a helpful metaphysical framework in which to conceive the relation between divine and natural causality as "non-interventionist" in the *constitutive* sense.

Barbour actually makes such claims in relation to quantum mechanics. I will summarize and assess these claims in chapter 5.

5. Concluding assessment: the need for a detailed exploration of quantum mechanics as the most viable basis for NIODA

In this chapter I have argued for the need for NIODA. Having offered criteria for assessing potential candidates, I have discussed a number of such candidates. My conclusion is that whole-part and lateral causal approaches to date have not successfully qualified for NIODA. Top-down approaches are promising and deserve serious consideration in the future as they develop more fully. Bottom-up approaches based on quantum mechanics are extremely promising and will be treated in chapter 5. Process philosophy offers a metaphysical framework in which NIODA is *potentially possible* but specific theories in science must first be independently assessed for their support of ontological indeterminism. Barbour, in particular, has extensively developed a process approach to NIODA in light of various areas in science. His discussion of a process approach based on quantum mechanics will be assessed in chapter 5 as well.

> In sum, then, the game is afoot: "The God who acts" truly acts—not by intervening in but by acting with and in addition to the open causal processes of the natural world which God has transcendently created *ex nihilo* and with which God continuously and providentially acts as the immanent, ongoing Creator.

Appendix A: The Subjectivist Approach to Divine Action as Developed by Bultmann, Kaufman, and Wiles

Rudolf Bultmann is a clear representative of an existentialist view of divine action, and Gordon Kaufman and Maurice Wiles are two well-known representatives of the subjectivist interpretation with its underlying uniformitarian view of God's actions.

In his two volume work, *Theology of the New Testament*,[87] Bultmann develops his program of demythologization, with its focus on personal existence out of which theological assertions arise and its stress on the historical shift in cosmologies brought about by modern science which has taken place since the New Testament period. In *Kerygma and Myth*, Bultmann responds to critics by stressing that an act of God is understood "not as something that takes place *between* worldly occurrences, but rather as something that takes place in them, so that the closed continuum of worldly events that presents itself to the objectifying eye remains untouched."[88] Bultmann returned to the problem of divine action in his 1958 masterpiece, *Jesus Christ and Mythology*.[89] Here he again rejected interventionism in either nature, history, or human psychology. God's transcendence requires us to think of divine causality within, and not between, the events of the world.[90] Faith does not offer a worldview in competition with science; instead, faith understands the events interpreted by science through natural causality alone as "nevertheless" the locus of God's action,[91] the domain in which God may be said to "supervene."[92]

Although his theology is extraordinarily complex and spans three decades, a common thread runs through Kaufman's position on divine action since his systematics appeared.[93] In 1968, Kaufman argued that God relates intrinsically to every event in the same way. Thus "general providence includes what is usually called 'special providence.'"[94] The only purpose for maintaining a distinction between general and special providence is to describe the variation in our subjective response to God's uniform, general action. "The acceptance of such events as authentic expressions of divine activity—and thus a proper ground for believing in 'general providence'—is called faith; unfaith, in contrast, is that attitude which views such moments as mere chance or coincidence and of no special significance." They should not "be viewed as acts in which God discontinues or sharply alters his ordinary patterns of action." They are "break-throughs" merely by providing the "historico-psychological grounding for the appearance and continuance of faith." Even miracles should be understood as, with Schleiermacher, "simply the religious name for event."[95] Kaufman reiterated this argument in a widely read article first published in 1972.[96] Here Kaufman proposes that God enacts history as a whole. "[I]t is *the whole course of history* . . . that should be conceived as God's act in the primary sense." The act of God is "the overall movement of nature and history towards God's ultimate goal."[97]

What is crucial to notice, however, is the argument which has disposed Kaufman to reinterpret divine action this way. He accepts the "modern conception of nature and history as a web of interrelated events that must be understood as a self-contained whole."[98] Even if there is "indeterminacy" at the atomic level, and "creativity and self-determination" on the human level (both of which he asserts), the web of events means "it is no longer possible for us to think . . . of individual or particular events somehow by themselves." But the traditional understanding of a special act of God, according to Kaufman, "seems to refer to events that have their source or cause directly or immediately in the divine will and action rather than in the context of preceding and coincident finite events." Thus "the problem [is] the difficulty—even impossibility—of conceiving the *finite event itself* which is here supposed to be God's act."[99] His conclusion follows: The idea of particular acts of God is unintelligible and inconceivable.[100]

Wiles opened his 1986 Bampton Lectures by underscoring both the importance and the problematic nature of the issue of divine action.[101] Divine action is required by the doctrine of creation *ex nihilo*, which Wiles holds to be "both philosophically and religiously essential" to Christian theology.[102] Nevertheless he insists, like Kaufman to whom he acknowledges his dependence, that continuous creation is a sufficient rubric for God's action; there is no need for special action.[103] "I have argued that there is one act . . . that we may and must affirm to be God's act, namely the continuing creation of the universe. The complexity of this 'act' does not invalidate its being described as a single act . . . I have argued against the reasonableness of expecting any special divine modification of the physical ordering of the world . . ."[104]

Wiles took a similar position in an earlier publication.[105] There he described how Newtonian mechanics led to a "God of the gaps" argument. When this argument was rejected, theologians were able to achieve a more profound view of the transcendence of God. Similarly Wiles claims that a mythological view of the world led to an interventionist view of God's actions. When rejected, Bultmann's program led to a more profound view of divine action: God does not act "between" but "within" every event in the world. Are there then any reasons for speaking about God's special actions in history? The answer for Wiles lies exclusively in our capacity of " 'experiencing-as,' of experiencing what happens to us and what we achieve as being in response to an overall purpose at work in the world."[106] It is our "depth of response," and not any intrinsic difference in the event, that makes that event part of God's special providence. There is no "fundamental difference in the relation of the divine action to the particular worldly occurrences of their situation."[107]

Conservative and evangelical theology during the same period insisted that we are right to call these events "special" because we are actually responding to God's distinctive action in, together with, and through them: Subjective meaning is based on objective divine action. In essence the claim is that if God had not acted in a special way in this particular event, then that event would not have occurred precisely the way it did occur. In similar ways, the "biblical theology" of the 1950s, drawing on its roots in neo-orthodoxy, insisted that the special acts of God are ontologically different from other events, though this difference is only discernable to the "eyes of faith." As Langdon Gilkey put it, "for those of faith [the act of God] must be objectively or ontologically different from other events. Otherwise, there is no mighty act, but only our belief in it. . . . Only an ontology of events specifying what God's relation to ordinary events is like, and thus what his relation to special events might be, could fill the now empty analogy of mighty acts."[108] I will call this claim *objective special providence.*

To summarize, the essence of the debate over the meaning of special providence is the question of whether God acts "differently" in these occasions than in those falling under the rubric of general providence. For those who take a subjective view, special providence tends to be absorbed into general providence and the latter is usually blended in with creation to give a single undifferentiated view of divine action. For those who hold for objective special providence, our response to specific events or experiences is based on God's special action in these events and experiences.

Acknowledgements

I am deeply grateful for the careful reading and critical suggestions made by Philip Clayton and Tom Tracy on the latest version of this chapter.

Endnotes: Chapter 4

[1] This chapter is a significantly revised version of a shorter essay first published as "Does the 'God Who Acts' Really Act? New Approaches to Divine Action in Light of Science," *Theology Today* 54:1 (April 1997), 43–65.

[2] Gordon D. Kaufman, "On the Meaning of 'Act of God'," *Harvard Theological Review* 61 (1968): 175–210. This article was reprinted in Gordon D. Kaufman, *God the Problem* (Cambridge, Mass.: Harvard University Press, 1972), ch. 6, and in Owen C. Thomas, ed., *God's Activity in the World: The Contemporary Problem* (Chico, Calif.: Scholars, 1983) hereafter *GAW*, ch. 9. 137–161.

[3] Maurice Wiles, "Religious Authority and Divine Action," *Religious Studies* 7 (1971): 1–12; reprinted in *GAW*, edited by Thomas,181–194.

[4]4. Langdon B. Gilkey, "Cosmology, Ontology, and the Travail of Biblical Language," *The Journal of Religion* 41 (1961), 197. Reprinted in Thomas, *God's Activity*, 198.

[5] The CTNS/VO series includes: Robert John Russell, Nancey C. Murphy, and Chris J. Isham, eds., *QCLN* (Vatican City State: Vatican Observatory Publications; Berkeley, Calif.: Center for Theology and the Natural Sciences, 1993); Robert John Russell, Nancey C. Murphy, and Arthur R. Peacocke, eds., *Chaos and Complexity: Scientific Perspectives on Divine Action* (hereafter *C&C*) (Vatican City State: Vatican Observatory Publications; Berkeley, Calif.: Center for Theology and the Natural Sciences, 1995); Robert John Russell, William R. Stoeger, S. J., and Francisco J. Ayala, eds., *Evolutionary and Molecular Biology: Scientific Perspectives on Divine Action* (hereafter *EMB*) (Vatican City State: Vatican Observatory Publications; Berkeley, Calif.: Center for Theology and the Natural Sciences, 1998); Robert John Russell, Nancey Murphy, Theo C. Meyering, and Michael A. Arbib, eds., *Neuroscience and the Person: Scientific Perspectives on Divine Action* (hereafter *N&P*) (Vatican City State: Vatican Observatory Publications; Berkeley, Calif.: Center for Theology and the Natural Sciences, 1999); Robert John Russell, Philip Clayton, Kirk Wegter-McNelly, and John Polkinghorne, eds., *Quantum Mechanics: Scientific Perspectives on Divine Action* (hereafter *QM*) (Vatican City State: Vatican Observatory Publications; Berkeley, Calif.: Center for Theology and the Natural Sciences, 2001). For a brief description of these approaches, see the introductions to Russell, Murphy, and Peacocke, *C&C*, section 3.4, and Russell et al., *Quantum Mechanics*, section 2.1.

[6] Summaries of all chapters can be found online and arranged by topic, author and book, at http://www.ctns.org/books.html.

[7] For an anthology and careful analysis of the contemporary theological literature on divine action see Owen Thomas, ed., *GAW*, and idem, "Recent Thought on Divine Agency," in *Divine Action*, B. Hebblethwaite and E. Henderson, eds. (Edinburgh: T & T Clark, 1990). For a detailed analysis of the philosophical problems involved, see Keith Ward, *Divine Action* (London: Collins, 1990), and Thomas F. Tracy, ed., *The God Who Acts: Philosophical and Theological Explorations* (University Park: Pennsylvania State University, 1994).

[8] Although creation and redemption are intimately linked in biblical theologies, the relation between them is the subject of debate. It has long been held that the Exodus experience served as the basis for Hebrew faith in God the creator, a position developed by Gerhard von Rad (*Old Testament Theology*, 2 vols. [New York: Harper & Row, 1957–65], 1:138; and *idem, The Problem of the Hexateuch* [New York: McGraw-Hill, 1966], 131–43). This view was frequently incorporated in standard treatments of the doctrine of creation. See, for example, Langdon Gilkey, *Maker of Heaven and Earth* (Garden City, N.Y.: Doubleday, 1959), 70. Recent scholarship, however, has questioned this view, raising the possibility that creation theology actually permeates the historical development of Israel. See, for example, Claus Westerman, *Creation* (Philadelphia: Fortress Press, 1974); Bernhard Anderson, ed., *Creation in the Old Testament* (Philadelphia: Fortress Press, 1984); and R.J. Clifford, "Creation in the Hebrew Bible," in R. J. Russell et al., eds., *Physics, Philosophy and Theology* (Vatican City: Vatican Observatory, 1988), 151–70. For a recent theological discussion of the relation between creation, redemption, and natural science, see Ted Peters, "Cosmos as Creation," in *Cosmos as Creation*, ed. Ted Peters (Nashville: Abingdon Press, 1989), 45–113.

[9] See, for example., Gen. 45:5; Job 38:22—39:30; Ps. 148:8-10; Is. 26:12; Phil. 2:12-13; 1 Cor. 12:6; 2 Cor. 3:5.

[10] See, for example, John Calvin, *The Institutes*, II, iv, 2. In general, the topic of divine agency was treated as part of the doctrine of providence and formulated in terms of divine preservation, concurrence, and government.

[11]This is a delicate point since it is not shared with process theology.

[12] For a helpful introduction, see Michael J. Langford, *Providence* (London: SCM, 1981); see also Julian N. Hartt, "Creation and Providence," in *Christian Theology: An Introduction to Its Traditions and Tasks*, 2nd ed., Peter C. Hodgson and Robert H. King, eds. (Philadelphia, Pa.: Fortress Press, 1985).

[13] Newton's mechanics and his system of the world led to profound philosophical issues through his introduction of absolute space and absolute time to ground the distinction between uniform and accelerated motion, as well as to important theological reconstructions of the relation of God to nature in terms of the *divine sensorium* and the design of the universe. See E.A. Burtt, *The Metaphysical Foundations of Modern Science* (Garden City, N.Y.: Doubleday, 1954). Michael Buckley has argued that the reliance on Newtonian science as a foundation for theology, and the abandonment of the "God hypothesis" thereafter, were principal causes of the rise of atheism in the West. See Michael J. Buckley, *At the Origins of Modern Atheism* (New Haven, Conn.: Yale University Press, 1987). For a brief historical account see Ian G. Barbour, *Issues in Science and Religion* (New York: Harper Torchbook, 1966), chap. 3. One can also argue that the concept of inertia played an important role in deflecting attention away from the view of God as acting ubiquitously to sustain nature in being. See Wolfhart Pannenberg, "Theological Questions to Scientists," in *The Sciences and Theology in the Twentieth Century*, ed. A.R. Peacocke (Notre Dame, Ind.: University of Notre Dame Press, 1981), 3–16, esp. 5–6.

[14] In its initial forms, deism viewed reason and revelation as two routes to the same truth. By mid-century, reason and natural theology gained precedence over revelation. In the end, deism collapsed under its own incongruities: Why pray to a absent, clockmaker god?

[15] See David Hume, *Dialogues Concerning Natural Religion* (New York: Social Science Publishers, 1948). See also David Hume, *Treatise on Human Nature* (Oxford: Clarendon, 1958); David Hume, *An Enquiry Concerning Human Understanding* (Chicago: Open Court, 1927).

[16]See Immanuel Kant, *Critique of Pure Reason*, trans. Norman Kemp Smith (New York: St. Martin's Press, 1929), and Immanuel Kant, *Critique of Practical Reason*, trans. Lewis White Beck (New York: Macmillan Publishing Company, 1956).

[17.] Friedrich Schleiermacher, *On Religion: Speeches to Its Cultured Despisers* (New York: Harper Torchbook, 1958), 88. In *The Christian Faith* (Edinburgh: T & T Clark, 1968), he wrote: "[A]s regards the miraculous . . . we should abandon the idea of the absolutely supernatural because no single instance of it can be known by us. . . ."(#47.3, 183). For an excellent analysis of Schleiermacher and other important developments in the nineteenth century see Claude Welch, *Protestant Thought in the Nineteenth Century*, 2 vol. (New Haven, CT: Yale University Press, 1972).

[18] See "Evolution and Theology: Détente or Evasion?" in Claude Welch, *Protestant Thought in the Nineteenth Century, Volume 2, 1870-1914* (New Haven: Yale University Press, 1985), ch. 6.

[19] Karl Barth, *The Epistle to the Romans*, 6th ed. (London: Oxford University Press, 1968), 28.

[20] See for example G. Ernest Wright, *God Who Acts: Biblical Theology as Recital* (London: SCM Press, 1952); Bernard Anderson, *Understanding the Old Testament* (Englewood Cliffs, N.J.: Prentice-Hall, 1957).

[21.] Gilkey, "Cosmology, Ontology, and the Travail of Biblical Language," 194–205.

[22.] Ibid., 198.

[23] Ibid., 201

[24] Rudolf Bultmann, *Theology of the New Testament: Complete in One Volume,* translated by Kendrick Grobel (New York: Charles Scribner's Sons, 1951/1955); idem, *Kerygma and Myth*, ed. H. W. Bartsch, vol. 1, 197–99; idem, *Jesus Christ and Mythology* (New York: Charles Scribner's Sons, 1958), particularly chap. 5; Gordon D. Kaufman, *Systematic Theology: A Historicist Perspective* (New York, N.Y.: Charles Scribner's Sons, 1968); idem, "On the Meaning of 'Act of God'," in *God the*

Problem (Cambridge, Mass.: Harvard University Press, 1972); Maurice Wiles, *God's Action in the World: The Bampton Lectures for 1986* (London: SCM, 1986); idem, "Religious Authority and Divine Action," *Religious Studies* 7 (1971): 1–12, reprinted in *GAW*, Owen Thomas, ed., (Chico, Calif.: Scholars), 181–94; Charles Hodge, *Systematic Theology*, 3 vols. (New York, N.Y.: Scribner's Sons, 1891); Donald G. Bloesch, *Holy Scripture: Revelation, Inspiration and Interpretation* (Downers Grove, Ill.: InterVarsity, 1994); Millard Erickson, *Christian Theology*, one-volume ed. (Grand Rapids, Mich.: Baker, 1983).

[25] Nancey Murphy, *Anglo-American Postmodernity: Philosophical Perspectives on Science, Religion, and Ethics* (Boulder, Colo.: Westview, 1997). See also Nancey Murphy, *Beyond Liberalism and Fundamentalism: How Modern and Postmodern Philosophy Set the Theological Agenda* (Valley Forge, Pa.: Trinity International, 1996), chapters 3, 4, 6. I am indebted to her analysis here. See also Arthur Peacocke, *Theology for a Scientific Age: Being and Becoming—Natural, Divine, and Human*, enlarged edition (Minneapolis, Minn.: Fortress Press, 1993), 139–140.

[26] See for example, Peacocke, *Theology for a Scientific Age*, 139–140.

[27] See John B. Cobb Jr., *Beyond Dialogue: Toward a Mutual Transformation of Christianity and Buddhism* (Philadelphia: Fortress Press, 1982), ix–x.

[28] In Owen Thomas, "Chaos, Complexity and God: A Review Essay," in *Theology* Today 54:1 (April 1997): 66–76, Thomas makes the important point—with which I agree—that many authors who turn to a non-interventionist approach in theology and science treat interventionism pejoratively. This is unfortunate since it confuses the issue and undercuts a potentially useful concept. My concern here for a non-interventionist approach is not meant to disparage interventionism per se, only its unnecessary application. For key issues such as the Incarnation, the resurrection of Christ, and Pentecost, an interventionist approach will be necessary after suitable nuancing. In fact, when the domain of God's action is eschatological the "laws of nature" (that is, God's faithful action) themselves will be different and "intervention" may cease to be a useful concept, to be replaced by "transformation." See Sec. 3C.7 below regarding miracles.

[29] See for example John C. Polkinghorne, "The Laws of Nature and the Laws of Physics," in *QM*, 437–48.

[30] See for example William R. Stoeger, S.J., "Contemporary Physics and the Ontological Status of the Laws of Nature," in *QCLN*, 209–34.

[31] For a helpful summary of the following distinctions see Arthur Peacocke, "Biological Evolution—A Positive Theological Appraisal," in *EMB*, 357–76. See Sec. 2.2, 360–364.

[32] In his paper for the "Capstone" volume, Thomas Tracy describes objective divine action this way: "God acts directly to bring about an event in the world that created causes alone are not sufficient to produce." See "Special Divine Action and the Laws of Nature" in *Scientific Perspectives on Divine Action: Twenty Years of Challenge and Progress*, Robert John Russell, Nancey Murphy and William R. Stoeger, S. J., eds. (Vatican City State; Berkeley, Calif.: Vatican Observatory Publications; Center for Theology and the Natural Sciences, 2007).

[33] I am indebted to the discussion of divine action found in Thomas Tracy, "Particular Providence and the God of the Gaps," in *C&C*, particularly 294–96, and in private conversations. I am using the term "direct act" in the same way Tracy uses the term "basic act," and "indirect act" in the same way he uses the term "instrumental act."

[34] Note: Most process theologians reject the doctrine of creation *ex nihilo* while understanding themselves as engaging in Christian theology.

[35] From the perspective of "occasionalism," all events in the world occur solely through God's action. Occasionalism denies that there are natural causes in the world and undercuts the importance of science in discovering and in representing them mathematically.

[36] In *Faith and Speculation*, Austin Farrer recounts the biblical witness to God's action in particular events in nature and history. Although he conceives of God's action as "the infinitely higher analogue of our way" of acting, the problem of understanding "the causal joint . . . between infinite and finite action" is absolutely unsolvable. We can assert, however, that God's grace "should enable natural agencies to go beyond themselves in their own way, the way of

uniformity; a way neither imposed on nature, nor interrupted in nature, by the supervenient and perfecting act of God." See Austin Farrer, *Faith and Speculation: An Essay in Philosophical Theology* (London: Adam & Charles Black, 1967), esp. ch. 4 and 5, 62–63, 65, 72, 78.

[37] In a recent review essay of *C&C*, Owen Thomas makes calls for a more nuanced discussion of concepts like intervention, God of the gaps, and so on. I agree with him, and hope that my remarks here move us towards this goal. See Owen Thomas, "Chaos, Complexity and God: A Review Essay," specifically 74–75.

[38] I am using terms in a slightly different way than Tracy does. According to Tracy, there are two kinds of "explanatory gaps." In-practice gaps are holes in our current theories which we expect to fill in the future. In-principle gaps are holes in our current theories which our theories suggest can never be filled. The latter may, but need not, arise from another kind of gap, namely "causal gaps," or holes in the flow of natural processes. Quantum mechanics may be interpreted as pointing to such causal gaps, as Heisenberg first suggested. See Tracy, "Particular Providence and the God of the Gaps," 290–92.

[39] Dietrich Bonhoeffer, *Letters and Papers from Prison*, enlarged ed. (London: SCM, 1972/1979), 311. See Tracy, "Particular Providence," 289.

[40] Here I am following Tom Tracy's language in his "Particular Providence," sec. 1.1.

[41] I will explore this problem in great detail in the next chapter on a QM-based NIODA.

[42] This approach thus differs radically from that of "intelligent design" since, unlike ID, it does not introduce "agency" into physics, biology, or cosmology. Instead it introduces theories in these sciences into a Christian theology of divine action in nature.

[43] John Polkinghorne, *Science and Creation: The Search for Understanding* (Boston: Shambhala, 1989).

[44] Ibid., 43.

[45]Wesley J. Wildman and Robert J. Russell, "Chaos: A Mathematical Introduction with Philosophical Reflections," in *C&C*, ed. Robert J. Russell, Nancey C. Murphy, and Arthur R. Peacocke, Scientific Perspectives on Divine Action Series (Vatican City State; Berkeley, Calif.: Vatican Observatory Publications; Center for Theology and the Natural Sciences, 1995), 416, 49–92.

[46] John C. Polkinghorne, *Science and Providence: God's Interaction with the World* (Boston: Shambhala Publications, 1989), 114.

[47]Ibid., 28–30.

[48] John Polkinghorne, *Reason and Reality: The Relationship between Science and Theology* (Philadelphia: Trinity International, 1991). See especially ch. 3.

[49] "Physical reality is made out of the entities described by fundamental physics." Ibid., 34.

[50] Ibid., 39.

[51] Ibid., 45–47.

[52] Ibid., 39, 41.

[53] See for example John Polkinghorne, "The Laws of Nature and the Laws of Physics," in Russell, et al., *QCLN*, 437–448. John Polkinghorne, *The Faith of a Physicist: Reflections of a Bottom-Up Thinker*, The Gifford Lectures for 1993-4 (Princeton, N.J.: Princeton University Press, 1994), 67–69, 77–82. John Polkinghorne, "The Metaphysics of Divine Action," in Russell, et. al., *C&C*, 147–156.

[54] The following section on Peacocke's work is taken almost in its entirety from Robert John Russell, "Arthur Peacocke on Method in Theology and Science and His Model of the Divine/World Interaction: An Appreciative Assessment," in *All That Is: A Naturalistic Faith for the Twenty-First Century*, ed. Arthur Peacocke and Philip Clayton (Minneapolis: Fortress Press, 2007), 140–51.

[55] Philip Clayton, *God and Contemporary Science* (Grand Rapids: Eerdmans, 1997); Philip Clayton, "Neuroscience, the Person, and God: An Emergentist Account," in *N&P*, ed. Robert John Russell et al. (Vatican City State; Berkeley, Calif.: Vatican Observatory Publications; Center for Theology and the Natural Sciences, 1999), 181–214.

[56] George F. R. Ellis, "Intimations of Transcendence: Relations of the Mind and God," in *N&P*, ed. Robert John Russell et al. (Vatican City State; Berkeley, Calif.: Vatican Observatory

Publications; Center for Theology and the Natural Sciences, 1999), 449–74; Nancey Murphy and George F. Ellis, *On the Moral Nature of the Universe: Theology, Cosmology, and Ethics*, Theology and the Sciences Series (Minneapolis, Minn.: Fortress Press, 1996), 268.

[57] Theo C. Meyering, "Mind Matters: Physicalism and the Autonomy of the Person," in *N&P*, ed. Robert John Russell et al. (Vatican City State; Berkeley, Calif.: Vatican Observatory Publications; Center for Theology and the Natural Sciences, 1999).

[58] Murphy, *Anglo-American Postmodernity*; Nancey Murphy, "Supervenience and the Downward Efficacy of the Mental: A Nonreductive Physicalist Account of Human Action," in *N&P*, ed. Robert John Russell et al. (Vatican City State; Berkeley, Calif.: Vatican Observatory Publications; Center for Theology and the Natural Sciences, 1999).

[59]See ch. 4 in Peacocke, *All That Is.*

[60]*Theology for a Scientific Age*, 139–140. Peacocke lays out four of the widely shared reasons for this rejection: interventionism assumes that God is entirely external to the world except in special events; ii) it undermines the claim that God is the source of the rationality and regularity of the world as seen in the laws of nature since God apparently must abrogate this regularity to act; iii) it runs aground of Hume's arguments against evidence of the miraculous; and iv) the apparent capriciousness of special acts challenges the moral character of God.

[61] Ibid., 140.

[62]Ibid., 152–157. Note: Peacocke restates the arguments found in this section in a much clearer fashion in "God's Interaction with the World" found in *C&C*, cf. footnote #32, 276. I will follow the latter presentation, but provide page references to both sources so the reader may compare them independently.

[63]"God's Interaction," 266–272; *Theology for a Scientific Age*, 44–55, 152–155.

[64] *Theology for a Scientific Age*, 153; "God's Interaction," 277.

[65] "God's Interaction," 278. Note his criticisms of W. P. Alston and others in footnote # 34. *Theology for a Scientific Age*, 154. In passing he levels this criticism at John Polkinghorne's arguments about divine action and nonlinear dynamics.

[66] "God's Interaction," 279.

[67] Ibid., 280. *Theology for a Scientific Age*, 155.

[68] "God's Interaction," 281.

[69]See *Theology for a Scientific Age*, 158–9, including the wonderful quotation from St. Augustine.

[70]My own preference for their combination is what can be achieved through a more explicitly trinitarian conception of divine agency.

[71]*Theology for a Scientific Age*, 158. See also *Creation and the World of Science* for an earlier discussion of panentheism (45, 141, 201, 207, 352). In *Theology for a Scientific Age,* endnote # 75 (370–372), Peacocke includes a very helpful discussion on the definition of panentheism, its relative independence from any specific metaphysical system (*pace* process theologians and John Polkinghorne!), a note about his (I think very wise) intention to avoid using the term because of its frequent misinterpretations, and some comments on the way it is formulated by Hartshorne and others.

[72] In "God's Interaction" he prefers the term "whole-part constraint," cf. 282–283.

[73] I am grateful for conversations with Tom Tracy that helped clarify this point.

[74] There is the additional question of whether God's action on the initial conditions and boundary conditions of the universe—if such can be said to exist for the universe—is itself non-interventionist. Clearly the decision depends on the detailed philosophical and physical meaning of these initial and boundary conditions. In my view, a non-interventionist approach to divine action on the initial and boundary conditions is incoherent, and Peacocke's approach fails for this reason as well as for the reasons offered in the text. I hope to provide a detailed account of my view in later publications.

[75]There are, of course, rich philosophical resources for deploying the concept of the "world-as-a-whole" but in general Peacocke tends not to use them. See for example his opting out of a close connection with process metaphysics as mentioned in a previous endnote. Whether a

more developed use of such resources would actually help bring him to take advantage of the scientific view of the world is another question.

[76] *Theology for a Scientific Age*, 195, Fig. 1. Arthur Peacocke, "The Sound of Sheer Silence: How Does God Communicate with Humanity?" in *N&P*, ed. Robert John Russell et al. (Vatican City State; Berkeley, Calif.: Vatican Observatory Publications; Center for Theology and the Natural Sciences, 1999), 238, Fig. 1.

[77] The ⊗ does not appear in the 1993 version of the diagram. Peacocke added it to the 1999 version following the suggestion I made that the figure needed something to indicate divine immanence along with divine transcendence.

[78] *Theology for a Scientific Age*, 192. See also "The Sound of Sheer Silence," 235.

[79] Indeed one can formulate general relativity, on which contemporary cosmology is based, and distinguish it from other twentieth-century theories of gravity, by the aphorism, "the boundary of the boundary is zero"; written topologically, $\delta\delta = 0$. Astonishingly, Einstein's field equations, $G_{\mu\upsilon} = 8\pi T_{\mu\upsilon}$, link the geometry of spacetime ($G_{\mu\upsilon}$) with the distribution of stress-energy ($T_{\mu\upsilon}$) such that the condition $\delta\delta = 0$ on spacetime geometry implies the conservation of energy-momentum. Hence one need not impose it as a separate condition as in other competing theories of gravity in the twentieth century. All the more reason to conceive of the universe as "boundaryless." See Charles W. Misner, Kip S. Thorne, and John Archibald Wheeler, *Gravitation* (San Francisco: W. H. Freeman, 1973), ch. 15.

[80] Even in more complicated models, such as inflationary Big Bang and recent speculations in quantum gravity, the universe is unbounded.

[81] Ian G. Barbour, *Religion in an Age of Science,* Gifford Lectures: 1989-1990 (San Francisco: Harper & Row, 1990), esp. chapters 8, 9.

[82] Ibid., 233. Also see Daniel Williams, "How Does God Act? An Essay in Whitehead's Metaphysics," in *Process and Divinity*, eds. W. L. Reese and E. Freeman (LaSalle, IL: Open Court, 1964).

[83] Barbour, *Religion in an Age of Science,* especially 247–258.

[84] David R. Griffin, "Relativism, Divine Causation, and Biblical Theology," *Encounter* 36 (1975), 342–360, reprinted in Owen Thomas, ed., *GAW*, 121–130). Barbour's interpretation is more consistent with a liberal, subjectivist mode. "God's basic *modus operandi* is the same throughout, but the consequences will vary widely between levels of being. In *the human sphere* . . . God loves all equally, yet that love may be revealed more decisively in one tradition or person than another. God calls all, but people respond in diverse ways . . . Continuing creation and redemption are brought within a single framework." 235.

[85] Ibid., 263.

[86] Ibid., 270.

[87] Rudolf Bultmann, *Theology of the New Testament: Complete in One Volume,* translated by Kendrick Grobel (New York: Charles Scribner's Sons, 1951/1955).

[88] Rudolf Bultmann, *Kerygma and Myth*, ed. by H. W. Bartsch, Vol. 1 (New York: HarperCollins, 2000), 197–199.

[89] Rudolf Bultmann, *Jesus Christ and Mythology* (New York: Charles Scribner's Sons, 1958), particularly ch. 5.

[90] Ibid., 61.

[91] Ibid., 65, 72. This does not entail that God does not exist apart from our faith in God, but only that the grounds of faith are themselves the given in and through faith.

[92] Ibid., 78.

[93] Gordon D. Kaufman, *Systematic Theology: A Historicist Perspective* (New York: Charles Scribner's Sons, 1968).

[94] Ibid., 302–4. Kaufman gives two theological reasons for rejecting ontologically special divine acts: They would require interventions to alter and correct the ordering of things, and they would raise questions of the justice of a divinity who acts occasionally. Though acknowledging that changes made by contemporary science lead to a dynamic and evolving view of nature instead of a static one, Kaufman insists that an ontological view of special providence would

entail a violation of that order. Somewhat inconsistently with this point, however, Kaufman nevertheless claims that history is more than a mere unfolding of events set entirely in motion at the beginning. Instead, God responds "in particular and unique ways . . . to each new historical situation . . ." and these events do indeed create faith and sustain it through adversity.

[95] Ibid., 307.

[96] Kaufman, "On the Meaning of 'Act of God.'"

[97] Ibid., 149, 152.

[98] Ibid., 146.

[99] According to tradition, "the finite nexus apparently need not be thought of as conditioning the newly injected event in any significant way, though a chain of consequences within the finite order presumably ensues from it. Acts of God in this sense, seen from man's side, are absolute beginning points for chains of events that occur . . . *within* ongoing natural and historical processes," ibid., 147.

[100] The operative assumptions, then are that i) ontologically distinctive divine acts entail a disruption of the processes of nature (that is, intervention) and they would be events entirely disconnected from the rest of nature (a view which I will refer to as "disjunctionist"). Clearly a response to this argument will require a reconceptualization of special providence in non-interventionist and non-disjunctivist terms.

[101] Maurice Wiles, *God's Action in the World: The Bampton Lectures for 1986* (London: SCM, 1986), 2.

[102] Ibid., 16.

[103] But is it still possible to speak of God's special action in specific events? Wiles cites three possibilities: He admires Bultmann's program of demythologization and his existentialist insistence on the experiential context of theological language, but he rejects it as dualistic (ibid., 31). Process theology sees God's actions in human events and in nature as equivalent, but its use of words like "response" and "awareness" for purely physical phenomena lacks credibility. Austin Farrer speaks of divine action via the Thomistic distinction between primary and secondary causation, but in the end his argument does not go beyond a uniformitarian account of the whole process as God's single act (33). Why not, then, simply reject the attempt to speak of particular divine action "at the sub-human level"? Wiles follows this option, though with the addition of our subjective response.

[104] Ibid., 96, 100. See also 29.

[105] Maurice Wiles, "Religious Authority and Divine Action," *Religious Studies* 7 (1971): 1–12, reprinted in Owen Thomas, ed., *GAW,* 181–194.

[106] Ibid., 185. Note Wiles's use of the phrase developed by John Hick here.

[107] Ibid., 188. Wiles returned to these arguments in slightly different form in "Divine Action: Some Moral Considerations" in Thomas F. Tracy, ed., *The God Who Acts: Philosophical and Theological Explorations* (University Park: Pennsylvania State University Press, 1994), ch. 1.

[108] Gilkey, "Cosmology," 37, in Thomas, *GAW.*

Chapter 5

Special Divine Action and Quantum Mechanics: A Case for Non-Interventionist Divine Action[1]

1. Introduction

A. Overview

This is the second of three chapters (chapters 4–6) which explore the problem of non-interventionist objective divine action (NIODA) in light of contemporary science. Many of the terms used here, such as non-interventionist objective divine action, direct divine action, mediated divine action, and bottom-up divine action, have already been defined in chapter 4 (particularly section 3C). The thesis to be explored here is the following: If quantum mechanics (QM)[2] is interpreted philosophically in terms of ontological indeterminism (as in one form of the Copenhagen interpretation), one can construct a bottom-up, non-interventionist, approach to mediated, objective, and direct divine action in which God's indirect acts of general and special providence at the macroscopic level arise in part from God's direct action at the quantum level. This direct action at the quantum level occurs both in sustaining the time development of elementary processes as governed by the deterministic Schrödinger equation and in acting with nature to bring about irreversible, indeterministic interactions referred to as "quantum events."

If sustained under careful scrutiny, this thesis would provide two remarkable outcomes: 1) It would allow us to extend the domain of non-interventionist objective divine action not only to the entire 3.8 billion-year history of life on earth but to the entire 15 billion-year history of the universe. 2) It would allow us to "make good" on the promissory note of theistic evolution by showing that God's action within the evolution of life really does make a difference even while the results of God's action necessarily appear to science as "blind chance" (cf. chapter 6).

In part B of this introduction, I claim that quantum mechanics meets the criteria for a successful proposal for NIODA. In section 2 I review the early theological sources and more recent developments in QM-NIODA. Section 3 discusses *methodological* issues, including the warrant for a "bottom-up" approach to divine action and the problems of the "multiple interpretability" of quantum mechanics and "historical relativism." In section 4 I turn to two *philosophical* issues: the phenomenological domain of the measurement problem and its relation to the indeterministic form of the Copenhagen interpretation of quantum physics. I then explore a variety of *theological* issues in section 5. Background topics include how QM-NIODA responds to seven key FAQs regarding NIODA proposals drawing from the material in chapter 4. This section also explores divine action at the quantum level in relation to both general and special providence, the pervasiveness of divine action, local and global aspects of divine action, and the challenge of special relativity. Crucial theological issues include whether God acts via special providence in some or in all quantum events and relation of quantum mechanics to the problem of human freedom and the challenge of theodicy. I will also propose that a trinitarian doctrine of God is the most suitable embedding context for the QM-NIODA approach. The final section (6) lays out directions for future research on the philosophical implications of quantum mechanics and their relevance for divine action, including both a proposed architecture of philosophical issues that moves us "above" the quagmire of multiple and conflicting interpretations and an exploration of long-term implications of Bell's theorem as a response to the challenge of historical relativity. A brief appendix provides a comparison of nonlocality and (in)determinism in Bohm's formulation and the Copenhagen interpretation based on the mathematical transformation between the Schrödinger equation and Bohm's modification of Newtonian mechanics.

B. QM: meeting the criteria for a successful proposal for NIODA

In chapter 4 I offered definitions of terms and described assumptions framing the NIODA project, and then stated the criteria for deciding whether we have a successful proposal for NIODA:

> *For non-interventionist objective divine action to be intelligible in light of science, the events that result from God's action must occur within a domain of nature in which the appropriate scientific theory can be interpreted philosophically in terms of* ontological indeterminism. *The events must be considered as* direct, mediated, *and* objective acts of God.

Hence the primary goal to reach in pursuit of NIODA is to identify and assess candidate theories in science for their capability of being given an indeterministic interpretation. When we have such a scientific theory we can claim that the objective acts of God occur without incompatibilist-, or IC-intervention.

As we have seen (chapter 4), there are a number of distinct proposals for NIODA. This chapter will focus on an agential model of God's interaction with the world involving bottom-up causality. In a bottom-up approach, God is thought of as acting at a lower level of complexity in nature to influence the processes and properties at a higher level. God's acts will be taken as direct, mediated, and objective, as they must to qualify for an non-interventionist approach to NIODA. Most importantly, to qualify as an non-interventionist approach, the lower level of nature must be interpretable philosophically as ontologically indeterministic.

Quantum mechanics is the foundational theory in physics dealing with the subatomic realm of nature. Accordingly, the acts of God at the quantum level would be direct acts; more precisely, the effects of God's direct, mediated action may occur initially at the quantum level. The events we attribute to God at the macroscopic level would then be their indirect result. Thus divine acts of general and special providence at the ordinary, classical level are mediated and indirect divine acts that arise from God's direct acts mediated in, through, and by quantum processes. Such providential acts can equally be seen as a form of God's ongoing, continuous creative action. They would be mediated in, with, and through the processes of nature, since God's acts would work together with nature to bring about distinct quantum events. They would be objective because the precise way these events occur are due, in part, to God's special intentions expressed in God's particular action in and through them. Most importantly, God's action can be considered non-interventionist because quantum mechanics, as we shall discuss in detail below, can be interpreted as pointing to ontological indeterminism in the subatomic realm.

While the history of these discussions goes back at least fifty years, they intensified beginning when the Vatican Observatory (VO) convened a ground-breaking international conference and publication entitled *Physics, Philosophy and Theology: A Common Quest for Understanding* (*PPT*) and continuing into the CTNS/VO decade-long series of research conference and publications on divine action and contemporary science (see chapter 4 for references). The key scholars involved in the QM-NIODA project within the CTNS/VO series include George Ellis, Nancey Murphy, and Thomas Tracy. The work of these and other scholars, their critics, along with earlier work since the 1950s will serve as sources for the current essay where the focus will be entirely on QM and bottom-up causality as a very promising candidate for NIODA.[3]

2. Converging Theological Streams

A. Early theological sources

We begin our account of early theological sources in the 1950s with the writings of Karl Heim, E. L. Mascall, and William G. Pollard. Interestingly we will see that in several places connections were already being suggested between quantum indeterminism, genetic mutation, and divine action—the theme to be developed in detail in the next chapter here (6).

In 1953 Heim suggested that, since Laplacian determinism had been overturned by quantum indeterminism, God could now be thought of as acting at the quantum level.[4] In a paraphrase of Matthew 10:29, Heim wrote: "No quantum-jump happens without your Father in heaven." In Heim's opinion, this led to the further claim that the world of ordinary experience is entirely determined by God's action at the quantum level. "All events, however great, we now know to be the cumulation of decisions which occur in the infinitesimal realm."[5] Although appreciative of Heim's early recognition of the importance of quantum indeterminism for divine action, I do not agree with Heim's preference for divine omnideterminism, and I believe it can be avoided while relating divine action to quantum indeterminism.

In his 1956 Bampton Lectures, E. L. Mascall first focused on classical physics and its inherent determinism. The theist will account for physical events as due to finite agents acting through secondary causes. God, as primary cause, will be seen as acting by creating and conserving these finite agents and their causal efficacy. Thus the account on the physical level will be complete, while a metaphysical account will include reference to God's action as well as secondary causes.

> If now we abandon the classical standpoint and adopt that of quantum physics, we cannot give a complete account, even on the physical level, simply in terms of finite causes. The degree of autonomy with which God has endowed the finite agents is sufficient to specify the relative frequency or probability with which specified types of event occur, but nothing more . . . .The situation in fact is as if . . . God has reserved to himself the final decision as to whether a specified event occurs of not.[6]

Referring to the example of a click in a Geiger-counter, Mascall concludes that a click "may be due solely to the primary causality of God." My reservation with Mascall's position is that I see God's activity in quantum events as mediated by nature (both materially and nomologically); I would not see quantum events as due solely to primary causality.

In 1958 Pollard advanced a more complex form of the argument.[7] To the scientist, quantum processes are entirely random; to the Christian, God can be seen as choosing the outcome from among the quantum mechanically allowed options. Pollard then added two key reservations: 1) This view of God's action does not imply that God acts *as* a natural force; and 2) it is not a form of natural theology, since belief in divine action is based on theological, not scientific, grounds. "Science, for all its wonderful achievements, can of itself see nothing of God."[8]

Next Pollard made the connection between chance in science and divine causality. First he pointed out that chance is not a cause: "chance as such simply cannot be the cause or reason for anything happening." Instead it stands for our ignorance of hidden, but real, causes. Thus, since science knows it cannot discover them, it makes sense to posit God as providing the ultimate cause for particular natural events. This allowed Pollard to counter the critics of religion who claimed that chance undermines providence; instead, "those secular writers who feel that they have demolished the biblical view of creation and evolution as soon as they have established the statistical character of the phenomena involved, have unwittingly done the one thing necessary to sustain that view."[9] Pollard drove home this point by making his central claim that a link exists between quantum indeterminism with genetic mutation. "[T]he phenomenon of gene mutation is the only one so far known in these sciences which produces gross macroscopic effects but seems to depend directly on changes in individual molecules which in turn are governed by the Heisenberg indeterminacy principle."[10] I appreciate Pollard's advance over the early formulations of Heim and Mascall, but again I do *not* agree with the use of quantum indeterminism in support of divine omnideterminism.

In 1966, Ian G. Barbour, though appreciative of much of Pollard's work, raised serious questions about Pollard's endorsement of total divine sovereignty.[11] He also stressed the idea of God as acting through both order and novelty, and the extension of the domain of God's action to all levels of reality. I agree with

Barbour's insightful criticisms and in my own writings have sought to proceed along similar lines.

Several of these arguments resurfaced two decades later in the writings of Donald M. MacKay and Mary Hesse. In 1978 MacKay argued that chance is not properly a cause; instead chance "stands for the *absence* of an assignable cause."[12] Thus what appears to the scientist as a random event may be taken by the theist as the action of a supremely sovereign God. Writing three years before MacKay, Hesse used a similar argument to defend a theistic interpretation of evolution:

> Just because chance is necessary to the evolutionary history that Monod accepts, there must be irreducibly random outcomes that scientific theory cannot explain. It follows that this theory cannot refute a theistic hypothesis according to which God is active to direct the course of evolution at points that look random from the purely scientific point of view.[13]

But Hesse went further than all of those preceding her because she recognized that, in order to launch a robust response to atheist Jacques Monod, her argument would have to be housed within a systematic framework, including:

> [T]heology, ethics and a theory of knowledge that can be shown to be more intimately related to each other and to what we know of the facts than Monod and other scientific humanists have been able to show in the case of their own systems.[14]

Though I strongly agree with Hesse's insistence on the need for a systematic framework, it is noteworthy that she did not cite the role of quantum physics as a basis for chance in genetics, nor did she refer to the work of scholars such as Pollard who had already pointed to these ideas.

B. More recent developments

I have been exploring the prospects for a quantum mechanical approach to NIODA for several decades, building on the earlier work of Pollard, et al. In 1982 I suggested that quantum mechanics provides "grounds for new research in science and religion" particularly in relation to *creatio continua*, given its underlying assumption, in my view at least, to non-interventionist divine action.[15] I stressed the concern, however, that our treatment of divine action must not imply that God acts as a natural cause: "God is 'wholly other,' not a cause among the causal network (of nature), not a marauder in the dark recesses of nature's womb of chance."[16] Two years later I argued against the view that quantum indeterminism associated with the collapse of the wave function depends entirely on measurements performed by scientists. Instead, "quantum indeterminism seems to apply across the board at the microlevel, regardless of whether laboratory measurements are actually being performed. One need only think of the processes of nucleosynthesis in stars, the chemical properties such as valence, electron tunneling in semiconductors, to mention just a few broad examples of the dominant role quantum mechanics plays in forming the very structure of nature and technology."[17]

In 1988 I wrote that "quantum physics contributes a necessary—though not sufficient—piece to the explanatory puzzle of how God acts in the world." It does so by pointing to at least one level in nature—its "bottom rung"—where nature is, arguably, open-ended. Moreover God's action in light of quantum physics would be mediated through and co-operative with natural causes: It would involve "a continuous creative (divine) presence within each (quantum) event, co-determining the outcome of these elementary physical processes."[18]

Clearly the most important aspect of QM for NIODA is that it offers an indeterministic interpretation of nature at the subatomic realm. From this perspective, the use of statistics in quantum mechanics is not a mere convenience to avoid a more detailed causal description. Instead, quantum statistics is all we can have—for *there is no underlying, deterministic natural process.* As an example, consider a sample of uranium (^{238}U) in which a specific atom suddenly decays into thorium (^{234}Th) by emitting an alpha particle. We can calculate the probability of the event to occur, but we cannot explain why this particular uranium decayed when it did and why its neighbors did not. All the atoms in the sample are absolutely identical, and the decay event is independent of any physical or chemical conditions imposed on them. Similar quantum mechanical descriptions apply throughout the subatomic realm. In each case, the total set of natural conditions affecting the process, and thus the total possible set of conditions which science can discover and describe through its equations, are *necessary but insufficient* to determine the precise outcome of the process. The future is ontologically open, influenced but *under*determined by the factors of nature acting in the present. In, through, and beyond the causal conditions we can describe scientifically, things just happen.

Following Heisenberg's suggestion,[19] we can characterize a quantum system in terms of potentialities and actualities. The system starts off in a superposition of "coexistent potentialities": a variety of distinct states are simultaneously possible for the system, but none are fully actual. Suddenly one of them is realized at a specific moment in time. *The uranium atom moment by moment continues to be what it has been, uranium, and then it comes to be something else, something which it could also always have been, thorium.*

Returning to our theme of divine action, we can see the importance of Heisenberg's interpretation of quantum mechanics. If his interpretation is correct, we can view nature theologically as genuinely open to God's participation in the bringing to actuality of each state of nature in time. Where science employs quantum mechanics and philosophy points to ontological indeterminism, faith sees God acting with nature to create the future. This is neither a disruption of the natural process nor a violation of the laws of physics. Instead, it is God fulfilling what God through nature offers, providentially bringing to be the future which God promises for all creation, acting specifically in all events, moment by moment.

In a 1994 lecture I argued that:

> Nature may provide the necessary conditions for a specific quantum event to occur, but the actual quantum event happens without nature providing a sufficient cause. . . . This means that if quantum physics is correct [we can interpret it as implying that] there can never be a complete *scientific* explanation of just why specific quantum events happen as they do. Granted this view may prove to be wrong, it does seem to shed light on . . . God's action in the world. . . . It helps us understand how one can think of God as acting at the sub-atomic level without violating the laws of nature. When a quantum event occurs, it occurs by God's direct action. . . . God may indeed work at higher levels in nature as well . . . but now we can affirm that God can also act in a "bottom/up" way through the openness of nature at the quantum level.[20]

I returned to this idea in a separate publication that same year, writing:

> When a quantum event occurs, it occurs by God's direct action. In other words, since quantum physics points not just to epistemic gaps in our theory that are about to be filled, but to ontological "bubbles" in the fabric of nature, one is free to stipulate that God acts immediately in nature—and not just through secondary, instrumental causes . . . In this perspective, God can act providentially to determine the future course of the world through the openness of quantum reality.[21]

Meanwhile in 1987 I began to develop the implications of the fact that quantum chance is formative of the basic features of the classical world, features taken for granted but never really explained by classical physics.[22] As we know, in classical physics, nature is a closed causal system described by deterministic equations. Here, then, the notion of chance is purely epistemic. In general, classical chance is represented mathematically by Boltzmann statistics (the familiar "bell-curve") typifying a random distribution of data caused by hidden but deterministic underlying forces and processes. Moreover, classical chance pervades not only physics but biology as well, from Mendel's laws to the Hardy-Weinberg theorem.

Quantum physics severely challenges this understanding of chance. Quantum chance accounts for the basic features of the classical world, features taken for granted but never really explained by classical physics.[23] The statistics employed by quantum mechanics come in two varieties and both are strikingly different from classical statistics.[24] Particles such as protons and electrons are called "fermions": they obey Fermi-Dirac (FD) statistics and give rise to the Pauli exclusion principle. Their statistical properties lead to the impenetrability of matter and its "space-filling" character. They also produce the chemical properties of the elements such as valency and color, and the electrical and thermodynamic properties of solids such as conductivity and specific heat.

Particles such as photons and gravitons are called "bosons": they obey Bose-Einstein (BE) statistics and carry the fundamental forces in nature, such as electromagnetism and gravity, that "glue" the world together and create such macroscopic "quantum" phenomena as superfluidity and superconductivity. In this sense quantum statistics, with its two distinct forms and their radical differences from everyday chance, underlies and accounts for the fundamental properties of our everyday world.[25]

The fact that we use FD and BE statistics in quantum mechanics and yet Boltzmannian statistics in classical mechanics provides an additional reason to support our interpretation of quantum mechanics in terms of ontological indeterminism. The mathematical equations that represent FD and BE statistics are radically different in the quantum realm of low energies and temperatures, but as we move to room temperature, both approach the Boltzmannian equation that characterizes classical statistics (that is, a Gaussian bell curve).[26] If we look at statistics from an *epistemological* perspective, "classical chance" is grounded mathematically in and arises smoothly in the appropriate limit from quantum statistics. But if we look at statistics from an *ontological* perspective, the result is far more complex. Recall that Boltzmannian statistics give rise to bulk properties of solids, liquids, and gases, derived mathematically from a statistical treatment of the deterministic interactions between their component parts (for example, the kinetic theory of gases). On the other hand, FD and BE statistics are not easily understood as arising from the action of hidden classical forces. Even Bohm's attempt at a "hidden variable" interpretation of quantum data leads to highly nonclassical "hidden variables" (see below and the appendix). So if we are interested in *ontology* we are led in opposite directions: to *determinism* if we stay within the framework of the classical world and to *indeterminism* if we move to the quantum world of FD and BE statistics. How strange it is that the classical, everyday world, where Boltzmannian statistics point to causal determinism, is actually the product of a quantum world whose FD and BE statistics point instead to ontological indeterminism!

Does this mean, then, that the specific effects of *every* quantum event get "averaged out" by the sheer number of such events? This claim, if true, could serve as a reason against using quantum physics in a discussion of God's action.[27] Actually specific quantum processes *can* have an irreversible effect on the classical world, and they can do so in a way that is entirely consistent with quantum mechanics. A particularly vivid example is vision, in which a single photon absorbed by one's retina can produce a mental impression![28] A somewhat *artificial* but now infamous example is the "Schrödinger's cat" thought experiment.[29] The genotype-phenotype relation is its *natural* "biological instantiation," where genetic mutations may eventually get expressed in the phenotype and contribute to the evolution of species—as I'll argue in chapter 6.

Let me summarize what we have seen so far. 1) Quantum processes can be interpreted philosophically in terms of ontological indeterminism, and this in turn opens the possibility of a non-interventionist account of objective divine action. 2) Quantum statistics are dramatically different from classical statistics. They are foundational for the ordinary properties of the everyday world and they allow for individual quantum events to trigger irreversible and significant effects in that world. In doing so they offer us a clue to how things in general come to be as they are *as well as* how things in particular happen within the general environment. This in turn opens up the possibility both for non-interventionist general divine action ("general providence"), which indirectly results in creating and sustaining the world, and for non-interventionist special divine action ("special providence"), which can indirectly result in special events in the world.

We will explore these and other theological topics in the following sections in greater detail. First however we should turn to several crucial methodological issues which potentially challenge the project as a whole.

3. Methodological Issues

A. Is a bottom-up approach to divine action warranted, and does it exclude other approaches?
In my opinion it is crucial that we *not* see the present focus as a *general* limitation or restriction of divine action to bottom-up causality alone. Instead, I view the present argument as located within a much broader context, namely the theology of divine action in personal experience and human history, because that is primarily where we, as persons of faith, encounter the living God. For this, we clearly need to consider a variety of models, including both top-down, whole-part, and bottom-up causes and constraints, and their roles within both embodiment and nonembodiment models of agency, with particular emphasis on the mind/body problem and human agency. Moreover, I believe we will eventually need to work out the detailed relations between these models by integrating them into a consistent and coherent, adequate and applicable metaphysical framework.

The question here, though, is why and how God might be thought of as acting within nature via a form of bottom-up causality. First, I am presupposing that God is the creator of the universe per se, maintaining the efficacy of nature, whose regularities, which we call the laws of nature, manifest God's faithfulness and rational intelligibility as creator. Secondly, I am assuming that these laws have just the right statistical ingredients to allow for the production of "order out of chaos" as part of God's creative actions. Granting thirdly that in some situations, such as in our personal encounter through faith with God—which brings up the "mind/brain problem"—it is highly appropriate to introduce top-down language about God's action, we may ask whether we can nonetheless adequately understand God's action within the physical, astrophysical, molecular, and evolutionary processes—out of which we arose—as expressing God's intention in ways that go beyond that of maintaining the existence of these processes and allowing their built-in "potentialities" to work themselves out over time. Finally I am concerned whether such an understanding of God's action can be rendered in an intelligible way if we restrict ourselves to top-down causality or to whole-part constraint *alone.*

I believe it cannot. Top-down causality is helpful when considering the action of conscious and self-conscious creatures that are genuinely open to God's action and that have at least some capacity to respond to it. But it is hard to see what constitutes the "top" through which God acts in a top-down way when no conscious, let alone self-conscious, creatures capable of mind/brain interactions have yet evolved. Remember, we are trying to understand God's action in the universe over its full 12–15 billion-year history, including the production of first- and second-generation stars, planetary systems, and eventually the evolution of organisms, at least on earth, over a period of nearly four billion years, ranging from the simplest primitive forms to the present vastly rich profusion of life.

Moreover, if God acts at the top level of complexity at a given stage in evolutionary history, that level of complexity must be ontologically open, that is, it must be described by laws that can be interpreted in terms of ontological indeterminism. Yet, until the evolution of organisms capable of even primitive mentality, the top levels would presumably have been within the domain of the "classical" sciences and the ontological determinism of Newtonian physics. On the top-down approach special divine action would thus be unintelligible *without* intervention from the epochs of early galactic, stellar, and planetary formation on up through those early stages of evolutionary biology prior and leading to the development of a central nervous system. But if we omit this early period from our discussion of special providence, then we once again risk a radical limitation on special divine action: God's special action can only occur after a sufficient degree of biological complexity has been achieved, but it cannot be effective within the processes *by which* that degree of complexity is achieved. For both these reasons, then, the top-down strategy seems stymied.

Perhaps we should try whole-part constraint arguments instead. The challenge here is to find phenomena in nature that display holistic characteristics and that point to ontological indeterminism. The ecological web is often cited as a candidate, due to its inherent complexity and seemingly endless openness to external factors, but in my opinion it fails to be a candidate for non-interventionist divine action because of the underlying determinism of the processes involved, no matter how complex or inter-related they might be.

Thus on critical reflection, and contrary to the hopes of most previous attempts at theistic evolution, it seems unlikely that top-down or whole-part approaches are of much value for interpreting physical processes and biological evolution at the pre-cognitive and even pre-animate era in terms of special divine action. Unless one returns to the quantum level, where holism and indeterminism are displayed everywhere and at all times since t=0, I see little hope that God's action within the early stages of physical, astrophysical, and biological phenomena can be described in non-interventionist ways using either whole-part constraint or top-down causal arguments.

B. The historical relativism and multiple interpretability of quantum mechanics

The next two problems are also methodological. First, *historical relativism*: Why should we take the theological implications of quantum physics seriously if quantum physics will eventually be replaced by a new theory? Second, *multiple interpretability*: How can we take the theological implications of quantum physics seriously given the fact that quantum mechanics is subject to a variety of equally valid, and radically distinct, philosophical interpretations? Actually historical relativism and multiple interpretability regarding quantum physics are concrete examples of a very general issue that inevitably surrounds *any* scientific theory and affects the philosophical and theological discussions of that theory. How one should proceed is a *crucial* methodological issue lying at the heart of *any* conversation about "theology and science." A decision regarding them is required of every scholar in the field. I will outline my responses here, though briefly. (I gave a brief response to the problem of multiple interpretability in chapter 4, FAQ #4.)

Historical relativism: my response. In response to historical relativism, one option would be to disregard all theories that are at the frontier of science, including quantum physics, and instead stick with proven theories such as classical physics. If we did so, would we not be on surer grounds for drawing theological conclusions about the world?

I have often heard cautious wisdom such as this. However, I don't agree with it for two reasons. First, as Charles Misner has remarked, the theories which we know are "proven" are the ones which have been the most clearly falsified! For example, we know precisely the domain in which classical physics is applicable:[30] namely in the limits $h \rightarrow 0$ and $c \rightarrow \infty$. But classical physics is in principle false. As a useful theory for practical needs, like engineering or planetary exploration, it is excellent. But as a fundamental theory of nature, its explanation of the world is wrong. Second, it is within this classical view of nature as a closed causal system that the theology of previous centuries has operated—and much of contemporary theology still does! It has contributed to the divisions between conservatives and liberals over issues such as divine agency and special providence, leading to what Gilkey called the "travail" of neo-orthodoxy and biblical theology. In addition, both the atheistic challenge to theistic evolution and the religiously motivated attacks on evolution have almost without exception ignored the quantum mechanical aspects of genetic variation and presupposed classical science and a mechanistic, deterministic metaphysics as Ellis has pointed out.[31] Thus their arguments, too, are fundamentally flawed. So sticking only with proven theories is out.

My approach, instead, is to engage in the conversation with quantum mechanics, as with any scientific theory, in full realization of the tentativeness of the project—but to engage in it, nevertheless. This is warranted for three reasons. 1) We are doing constructive theology, *not natural theology let alone physico-theology*. Hence a change in science would at most challenge the constructive proposal at hand, but not the overall viability of a theology of divine action in nature, whose warrant and sources lie elsewhere in scripture, tradition, reason, and experience. 2) As the experimental violation of Bell's theorem shows us, any future theory will have to deal with some aspects of current quantum phenomena, and it is these general features and their metaphysical implications which are our focus here. 3) We should welcome the specificity of this approach and the vulnerability it produces to problems like these, for by illuminating the actual implications of a concrete example of a non-interventionist approach to objective special divine action it enhances the strengths as well as reveals the limitations of that approach, and this in turn leads to further insight and research.

Multiple interpretability. As is well known, quantum mechanics can be given a variety of philosophical interpretations.[32]

The Copenhagen interpretation is, arguably, the most widely held view by physicists and philosophers of science. According to Jim Cushing, it essentially involves "complementarity (for example, wave-particle duality), inherent indeterminism at the most fundamental level of quantum phenomena, and the impossibility of an event-by-event causal representation in a continuous spacetime background."[33] Although rooted in the work of Niels Bohr, the term "Copenhagen interpretation" includes several distinct versions. Bohr himself stressed the epistemic limitations on what we can know about quantum processes. Compared with their effortless union in classical physics, spacetime description and causal explanation become complementary (necessary but mutually exclusive) aspects of a quantum account of microscopic processes.[34] Bohr also believed that quantum formalism applies to individual systems, compared with Einstein's statistical view in which the formalism applies to ensembles only.[35] Heisenberg both supported the completeness of quantum mechanics and developed his own realist, indeterministic version of the Copenhagen interpretation in which the measurement process actualizes potential characteristics of the quantum system. His interpretation suggests that the unpredictability that arises during measurement has an ontological basis and is not simply epistemological.[36] Ian Barbour cites Henry Margenau who writes, "the uncertainty does not reside in the imperfection in our measurements, nor in man's ability to know; it has its cause in nature herself." As Barbour puts it, "if this interpretation is correct, indeterminacy is an ontological reality."[37] In sum, Cushing concludes that, "On the Copenhagen interpretation of quantum mechanics, physical processes are arguably, at the most fundamental level, both inherently indeterministic and nonlocal. The ontology of classical physics is dead."[38]

A variety of scientists have supported ontological indeterminism, including such contemporaries as Chris Isham, Paul Davies, and Ian Barbour.[39] This alone, of course, is not a warrant for adopting indeterminism, only a recommendation. In fact, from its beginnings in 1900 up to the present, physicists and philosophers of science have explored other robust interpretations of QM. These include: ontological determinism (the neo-realism of Einstein/incompleteness and Bohm/"hidden variables"); many-worlds (Everett); quantum logic (Gribb, Finkelstein); observer-free decoherence/consistent histories (Clarke, Griffiths, Omnès, Gell-Mann, Hartle); and mind-dependent idealism/consciousness which creates reality (von Neumann, Wigner, Wheeler, Stapp). With this in mind, some have argued that we modify the basic equations of quantum mechanics (for example, Shimony's philosophically motivated exploration of stochastic modifications of the Schrödinger equation[40]). To complicate matters even further, since their discovery in the 1960s, Bell's theorems have underscored the nonlocal and particularly the nonseparable character of quantum phenomena, making each of the earlier interpretations more problematic.[41] How then are we to decide which interpretation or modification is right and reliable for a discussion of divine action, and if we cannot decide, should we abandon a QM-based NIODA as some urge[42] or is there a reasonable way to proceed?

Multiple interpretability: my response. My response is fourfold. First, as I indicated above, why single out quantum mechanics? Every scientific theory is open to competing metaphysical interpretations; indeed, metaphysics is *always* underdetermined by science, although some theories, like classical physics, seem strongly to favor one interpretation (for example, determinism) over others. So this concern about quantum mechanics applies, in principle, to *any* metaphysical interpretation of *any* scientific theory. Indeed, the warrant for choosing a specific metaphysical interpretation of any scientific theory is an issue not only for theists but equally for nontheists, naturalists, and atheists! In essence, we face a truly generic problem, one that is unavoidable: We must adopt one or another philosophical interpretation *whenever* we incorporate the results of science (or any other field of knowledge) into a wider intellectual context, particularly into constructive theology. The inclusion of a philosophical interpretation is not an option; the only option is which interpretation is to be chosen.

Second, none of these interpretations returns us to an entirely classical view of the world; to one extent or another, all of them require a reconstruction of our philosophy of nature. This might seem obvious, but it actually addresses what is a subtle problem in the literature. Bohm's interpretation, being deterministic and describing nature in such classical terms as particles, forces, and trajectories, can seem like a less problematic option than Bohr's epistemology, with its wave-particle complementarity, or Everett's many-worlds ontology. But in fact Bohm's advantages are bought at a heavy price: The determinism suggested by Bohm is not classical but *nonlocal* and *nonmechanical*—a view of nature in which the force on a particle depends instantaneously on the world as an "undivided whole" through what Bohm called the "quantum potential." Thus even if we adopted Bohm's approach we would *not* simply fall back into the safe haven of classical metaphysics (if indeed it ever were so, or we ever wanted to!); instead we would inherit yet another set of thorny issues that I will label "Bohmian determinism." Indeed, this fact can actually be used to our advantage: A careful comparison of Bohmian and Copenhagen views, as suggested below, might help us understand just what is meant on both sides by (in)determinism. The details are given in the appendix.

Third, my approach is best seen as a form of constructive theology with a focus on nature (what Barbour calls a "theology of nature"), *not* a form of natural theology, let alone physico-theology. Hence a change in science or its philosophical interpretation would challenge the constructive proposal at hand, but not the overall viability of a theology of divine action in nature, whose primary warrant and sources lie elsewhere in scripture, tradition, reason and experience.

Finally, I think we should welcome the specificity of this approach and follow it as far as it can take us. By illuminating the concrete implications of a non-interventionist approach to objective special divine action in light of a particular interpretation of quantum physics, the strengths as well as the limitations of the approach are revealed, which in turn should lead to further insight and new areas of research.

C. The approach taken here

With these responses in mind, my approach will be an explicitly "what if" strategy: I will engage in the theological conversation with quantum mechanics by choosing one particular philosophical interpretation (ontological indeterminism within the general Copenhagen interpretation), stating clearly that this choice is being made, stressing that it may one day prove no longer tenable (presumably for scientific reasons—but philosophical or even theological reasons could also play a role in either initially choosing or later changing interpretations[43]), and proceeding to explore the philosophical and theological implications of this interpretation in full awareness of the tentativeness of the project—but engaged in it nevertheless. I will hold this philosophical interpretation both explicitly and hypothetically as a lens through which to ask questions about the relation between science and theology, not foundationally as the basis of one's theological position (as for example in natural theology or physico-theology). I believe, in sum, that every approach must be based on a "what if" approach such as this: an approach which takes a given interpretation of physical theory seriously and resolutely, and yet which recognizes the real possibility that such an interpretation may one day be undermined by advances in physics and philosophy.[44]

Saunders acknowledges that he does not find any problems with this approach. Of course it requires us to work within a particular philosophical position, but this is in fact unavoidable as I have repeatedly stressed.[45]

My choice of the Copenhagen interpretation means that I will need to respond to a number of key issues that arise within this interpretation. The most important issues will be the "measurement problem" and the associated "collapse of the wave equation," as well as the meaning of a "quantum event." All of these are involved in the claim of ontological indeterminism with its presupposition that quantum mechanics can be given a (critical) realist interpretation. I will then need to work out the implications of these issues for our understanding of divine action and embed it in a broader theological context. This process will occupy most of the remaining portions of this chapter.

4. Philosophical Issues: The Measurement Problem Within the Copenhagen Interpretation of Quantum Mechanics

We turn now to a key issue in the Copenhagen interpretation of quantum mechanics, the measurement problem. There are, of course, various formulations of this problem, each raising complex issues for a realist understanding of quantum mechanics. According to Chris Isham, the way we understand the measurement problem depends on our interpretation of the formalism and, in particular, on what one means by the reduction of the state vector. The measurement problem, in turn, is part of a "quaternity of problems" all posed to the realist (but avoided by instrumentalists and pragmatists): (i) the meaning of probability; (ii) the role of measurement; (iii) the reduction of the state vector;

and (iv) quantum entanglement. Although their classical analogues allow for a clear resolution from a realist perspective, Isham shows that the quantum versions do not.[46] For Jeremy Butterfield, the measurement problem is important because it illuminates and underscores the problem of quantum indefiniteness from a realist perspective. If, as realists claim, quantum physics applies to everything physical, the indefiniteness of the microrealm should be endemic in the macrorealm—it should be transmitted to the macrorealm, but apparently is not. Indeed, indefiniteness should manifest itself in macrostates that blatantly contradict our ordinary experience of definite states.[47]

For the limited purposes of this chapter, I want to distinguish between two issues regarding the measurement problem from a critical realist perspective: (i) its phenomenological domain (that is, what sorts of physical processes should be called "measurements") and (ii) its relation to ontological indeterminism. When discussing the mathematical structure of the wave function and its implications for divine action below, I will stress again the challenge posed to a realist interpretation.

A. The phenomenological domain of the measurement problem

We begin with a well-known distinction that arises in the Copenhagen interpretation between (i) the *time development* of the wave function ψ of a quantum system, as governed by the deterministic Schrödinger equation, and (ii) the *irreversible interaction* between the quantum system and other systems. *Ex hypothesis*, these systems must be of such size and complexity that their interaction with the quantum system is, at least in practice, irreversible, that is, the Schrödinger equation does not apply. Irreversible interactions are routinely called "measurements," but they are not limited to interactions with the ordinary world around us; instead, they include phenomena ranging from what we can call, for want of better terms, "micro-macro," "micro-meso," and "micro-micro" interactions.[48]

Micro-macro involves interactions between elementary particles and "classical measuring devices," such as the response of a Geiger counter to an alpha particle[49] or a photoelectric counter to a photon, but it also includes any irreversible interaction between an elementary particle and an ordinary object, such as the absorption of a photon by an animal retina or the surface of a painted solid. Clearly micro-macro interactions then entail a vast range of *natural* phenomena from the physical and biological sciences. As stated above, the evolution of life depends on such biological amplifiers as genotype-phenotype population arrangements. But, contrary to the views of some scholars (see section 5A.1.e below) I claim that the domain of the measurement problem is far more extensive than this, for it also involves irreversible micro-meso and micro-micro phenomena.[50]

Micro-meso includes all those interactions between elementary particles and (sub)microscopic objects with enough degrees of freedom to make the interaction irreversible (at least in practice). Examples include the capture of a photon by a dust particle in interstellar space, the decay of atoms in solids (such as radioactivity), the interaction between bound and free particles (such as the absorption or emission of a photon by an atomic electron in a crystal solid), and the making or breaking of atomic and molecular bonds (such as hydrogen bonding during genetic mutations of DNA). All of these, too, constitute a measurement since they are irreversible, even though their scale is micro-meso.

Micro-micro interactions would normally be considered reversible and governed by the Schrödinger equation, and thus would not constitute "measurements." Examples include proton-proton scattering in free space and pair production and annihilation in the vacuum. However, if such interactions occur within a complex environment they could well be irreversible and thus constitute "measurements." Proton-proton scattering in the presence of heavy nuclei would be an example.

In summary, the term "measurement" should *not* be restricted to micro-macro interactions, let alone to those "macro" interactions that involve laboratory experiments. Instead, the term "measurement" should include *all irreversible interactions* in nature from micro-micro to micro-macro. What is crucial, then, to making an interaction a "measurement" is not that it involve something "macro" but that it is irreversible. (It is obvious from these examples that measurements do not depend critically on, or even involve, chaotic phenomena, again contrary to the claim of some scholars; see section 5A.1.e below.)

B. The measurement problem as the basis for the indeterministic interpretation of quantum physics

The measurement problem can now be stated (but, alas, not solved!) easily: How are we to understand measurements by using quantum physics if measurements cannot be described by applying the Schrödinger equation to them and if we are not to alter quantum physics? Within the Copenhagen interpretation, the response is stark: The measurement problem is not really a "problem to be solved," but a *synonym* for those processes not governed by the Schrödinger equation. Since causes are represented by the Schrödinger equation (as formal cause) and the potential V contained in that equation (as the efficient cause), the inapplicability of the Schrödinger equation to a measurement is the basis for the philosophical claim of ontological indeterminism. Since the outcome of a measurement is not describable in terms of the Schrödinger equation, we can infer that there are necessary (for example, material) causes but not sufficient (in particular, efficient) causes to bring about the measurement.

We can also see why the phrase "the collapse of the wave function" is used to describe "what happens" during a measurement. The wave function ψ, which had evolved deterministically in time under the influence of the classical potential V and according to the Schrödinger equation, changes discontinuously from a superposition of states to a specific state. This is also a convenient place to offer a more precise definition of the term "quantum event" than one customarily finds in the literature. I propose that we restrict our usage of the term to what we are calling "measurements," that is, those interactions that are irreversible regardless of whether they are micro-macro, micro-meso, or micro-micro interactions. Conversely, the time development of the wave function between measurements is *not* to be thought of as a series of quantum events.

In this approach, then, the measurement problem and ontological indeterminism are two sides of the same coin: The measurement problem is that aspect of quantum physics to which ontological indeterminism is specifically addressed. For the purposes of this chapter we will stay within the Copenhagen interpretation. This allows us to say that for quantum events or measurements to occur, nature provides the necessary but not the sufficient causal conditions, or what Barbour calls a "weak form of causality."[51] Along with Ellis and many others I acknowledge the unresolved status of the measurement problem but I hope that by using it in this specific way we can proceed to explore the case for divine action and quantum physics.[52]

To summarize, within (at least one variety of) the Copenhagen interpretation, ontological indeterminism, the measurement problem, the collapse of the wave function, and the meaning of quantum event all merge into one conceptuality: A quantum event is an irreversible interaction (at all scales in physics from micro-micro to micro-macro), in which the Schrödinger equation ceases to govern the time-evolution of the wave function ψ describing both the system and that with which it irreversibly interacts. Instantaneously ψ collapses from a superposition of states to one state. The fact that the resulting state is unpredictable in advance, that is, that it cannot be explained by a deterministic law, is the basis for the philosophical interpretation that such an event is ontologically indeterministic. In short, we find both the determinism described by the Schrödinger equation between quantum events and the indeterminism characterizing quantum events. In the following I shall refer to "ontological indeterminism" in the strict sense as referring to quantum events.[53]

5. Theological Issues

A variety of theological issues now emerge in the general relation between divine action and the Copenhagen interpretation of quantum physics as we look more closely at the thesis we are exploring here. I will separate them into background issues and crucial issues.

A. Background theological issues

1. How QM-NIODA responds to seven key FAQs regarding NIODA proposals. First I want to respond in a bit more detail to some of the most important FAQs cited in the preceding chapter as well as two additional ones specific to QM-NIODA.

a) *Does QM-NIODA require epistemic and ontological gaps?* My response is a firm "No!" QM-based NIODA does *not* constitute either an epistemic or an ontological "God of the gaps" argument.[54] I completely agree with Thomas Tracy[55] who has argued that we should reject an epistemic gaps argument for *theological* reasons. To make his case, Tracy cites Dietrich Bonhoeffer: "[It is wrong] to use God as a stop-gap for the incompleteness of our knowledge. . . . [Instead] we are to find God in what we know, not in what we don't know."[56] But a QM-based NIODA is *not* an epistemic gaps argument; instead it relies on what we *do* know about nature, assuming that quantum physics is the correct theory. Moreover it is *not* an ontological gaps argument since it does not require God to "break into" the causally closed processes in nature. Instead, when quantum mechanics is interpreted philosophically it tells us that nature is ontologically indeterministic. By "ontologically indeterministic" I mean, again, that nature provides the necessary but not the sufficient causes for quantum events to occur. While the Schrödinger equation applies deterministically to the propagation of the wave function and includes efficient causes in the form of potential energy (representing forces at work in nature), during a quantum event or "collapse of the wave function," the Schrödinger equation does not apply and there is no efficient natural cause that brings about this event. We will explore this issue in detail below. For now, however, let us assume it holds. If so, then we have our answer to the challenge of ontological gaps:

God has created the universe *ex nihilo* such that some natural processes at the quantum level are insufficiently determined by prior natural events. One could say that nature is "naturally" indeterministic, that it is suffused with what Tracy calls "causal gaps."[57] If so, then God does not suspend natural causality but creates and maintains it as ontologically indeterministic. Because nature is indeterministic, God does not need to intervene in nature to create ontological gaps as a concommitment to objective divine action. In essence, God creates the universe *ex nihilo* such that quantum events occur without sufficient natural causes and God acts as continuous creator within these natural processes and together with nature, which supplies the material and formal causes, to bring them about. In a non-interventionist account of divine action, we can relate God's action in the world to our knowledge of the world, not our ignorance of it. With it objective special providence is achieved without contradicting general providence since God's particular acts, being non-interventionist, do not violate or suspend God's ordinary action.

Another way to make this point is to frame it in terms of "the laws of nature" or "the laws of physics." A frequently held view among physicists is that nature is said to "obey" the laws of physics, and these laws hold an ontological status modeled after Platonic forms. From this perspective we can say that in a non-interventionist account of divine action God does not violate or suspend the laws of quantum physics. Instead God acts in accordance with them even while bringing about quantum events. I prefer to think of the laws of nature as our best descriptions of the underlying causality intrinsic to nature. They are a remarkable combination of mathematical a priori logic and empirical a posteriori empirical data embedded in paradigms rich with metaphysical and aesthetic elements. Still the causalities and regularities of nature which they describe are intrinsic to nature and are due, ultimately, to the ongoing action of God as the continuous creator of the universe which God ontologically creates *ex nihilo*.[58]

Still another way to make the case against gaps is to stress that divine action is mediated. According to Murphy, God never acts (apart from creation *ex nihilo*) except through cooperation with created agents.[59] This means that "God's governance at the quantum level consists in activating or actualizing one or another of the quantum entity's innate powers at particular instants." It also means that "these events are not possible without God's action."[60]

In sum, by avoiding a "gaps" strategy, quantum-based NIODA allows us to affirm that God is the transcendent Creator *ex nihilo* of the universe as a whole and that God is the immanent ongoing Creator of each special event who acts objectively in, with, and through the processes of nature (*creatio continua*). Non-interventionist objective special divine action thus offers a robust response to atheistic challenges to the intelligibility and credibility of Christian faith in light of "chance" in nature since the presence of "chance" does not imply an absent God and a "pointless" and dysteleological world but an ever-present God acting immanently with purpose in the world.

b) *Is God's action at the quantum level in effect a natural cause?* Again, my response is "No!" A QM-based NIODA does *not* reduce God to a natural cause because, according to the philosophical interpretation of quantum mechanics deployed here, there are no efficient natural causes for a specific quantum event. If God acts together with nature to produce the event in which a radioactive nucleus decays, God is not acting as a natural cause. Whether God must act with nature in all such events for them to occur, or whether some quantum events are not caused by nature or even by divine action is an open question and will be addressed in detail below (section 5B.1).

c) *Is God's action at the quantum level hidden from science?* Here my response is "Yes!" for several reasons. 1) The theory of divine action being considered here is entirely consistent with the basis of science: methodological naturalism. Neither theology nor science will view "God" as a proper part of the scientific explanation of quantum events.[61] 2) God's direct action at the quantum level will be hidden in principle from science because, given this philosophical interpretation, there is no natural cause for each specific quantum event for science to discover. 3) Alternatively, as Tracy writes, God's action will remain hidden from science because it will take the form of realizing one of several potentials in the quantum system, not of manipulating subatomic particles as a quasi-physical force.[62] Thus this theory of divine action supports the integrity of science and yet allows science to be integrated fruitfully into constructive theology where "God" as an explanation of natural events is appropriately and fully developed. 4) The effects of God's objective non-interventionist action will be viewed by science as ensembles of chance events described by mathematical probabilities calculated using quantum theory; at the same time quantum theory can provide no further causal explanation for the specificities of each event in the ensemble. While the data of science is irreducibly statistical ("blind") chance, and while this data can be interpreted philosophically as due to nature at the quantum level lacking a sufficient efficient cause, theology sees this data as the result of God's object action at the quantum level.

In a pivotal paper written in 1993, Nancey Murphy[63] argued that any acceptable theory of divine action must allow for objectively special divine acts, giving three reasons: i) our knowledge of a person comes primarily through the person's actions; ii) without special providence, petitionary prayer would be "groundless"; iii) without special providence, God would be equally and entirely responsible for every event, thus exacerbating the problem of evil. At the same time, any such theory should "explain how God and natural causes conspire to bring about the world *as we know it*," including our scientific picture of law-like regularity and the genuine randomness of quantum events, as well as our experience of free will. It must also avoid reducing God to a natural cause while granting that God can bring about special events which would not have occurred by merely holding the set of natural causes in existence. Murphy sees the contemporary understanding of nature as a nonreducible hierarchy of increasing complexity as "absolutely crucial" for this task since according to this understanding, both top-down and bottom-up causality are at work in nature. According to Murphy, quantum physics offers a promising possibility for bottom-up causality. If we reject both a purely epistemic interpretation of quantum mechanics as well as a hidden variables interpretation, we face the fact that there is no "sufficient reason" in nature to determine a quantum event. Such ontological indeterminism allows for a bottom-up account of divine action wherein God has no need to overrule or intervene in natural processes.

I think this paragraph based on Murphy's paper succinctly responds to all three FAQs.

d) *Can even God know the outcome of a quantum process given the underlying ontological indeterminism?* Here my response is "Yes!" In his 1979 Bampton Lectures Arthur Peacocke launched a major challenge to Monod's atheistic interpretation of biological evolution to which we shall return in the next chapter. A key component in his challenge to Monod was the assertion of God's continuous and immanent creative action in, under, and through the processes of nature. Here Peacocke supported Pollard's claim that quantum phenomena represent the *only* domain of ontological indeterminacy, at least below the level of consciousness in animals: "Apart from events at the level of the fundamental subatomic particles, the [statistical character of the laws of science] represent[s] simply our ignorance of all the factors contributing to the situation—they do not imply any lack of causality in the situation itself."[64] Still, Peacocke dismissed this view as allowing one arbitrarily "to pick and choose" which chance events are to be credited to providence. He then shifted first to the thermodynamics of living organisms but here, as his agreement with Pollard implies, the determinism implied by thermodynamics undercuts what I am focusing on as non-interventionist objective divine action. He later turned to top-down and whole-part approaches, as we saw in the preceding chapter (4), emphasizing that God acts on the whole of reality and that these non-interventionist actions, as I now call them, can eventually bring about specific events which we claim for special providence.[65] Although Peacocke has published widely on these issues in recent years, he does not continue to refer to Pollard's groundbreaking work.[66]

The clue may be found in a recent essay where Peacocke explained why he rejects the relevance of quantum indeterminacy to the problem of divine action. Here Peacocke writes that "the inherent unpredictability [of quantum events] represents a limitation of the knowledge even an omniscient God could have of the values of these variables and so of the future trajectory . . . of the system."[67]

This will be a view Peacocke returns to on a variety of occasions. In my estimate this view is mistaken in two crucial ways. To see this, recall that, according to the Heisenberg interpretation, a quantum system is initially in a superposition of several distinct potential states represented by the wave function Ψ. Suddenly one of them becomes actual with the "collapse of the wave function." We can only predict the relative probabilities for which it will become actual since there is no *natural* efficient cause which determines the result; during the collapse, the quantum system is developing indeterministically.

Now according to Peacocke even God cannot know which potential state will become actual, and therefore what the future trajectory will be for that state. Let's take this claim one step at a time. While it is true that only the relative probabilities are given in the wave function Ψ (technically in the absolute square of the wave function following the Born interpretation), these probabilities can be calculated *exactly* from the wave function. Moreover, if the scientist can calculate them exactly, surely God can know them exactly, presumably even without calculation! So the fact that we are dealing with relative probabilities does *not* represent a "limitation of the knowledge even an omniscient God could have of the values of these variables."

More importantly, however, Peacocke also seems to suggest that since there is no natural efficient cause which determines the result, God cannot know which potential state will become actual. But that assumes that since there is no natural efficient cause, even God cannot play a role in determining the result. Instead I am claiming theologically that God acts together with nature to determine which quantum outcome becomes actual by providing what nature lacks as an efficient cause and that God does so without being a natural cause, efficient or otherwise. In essence, God can know which potential state will become actual since *God causes it to become actual!*

Finally, once the system is in a definite state, its future state is determined by the deterministic Schrödinger equation. Thus contrary to Peacocke, God could easily predict that future state from the actual, definite present state. More precisely, to use more traditional language, God can know the future state as its own present state; God does not need to predict the future from the present.[68] The conclusion I come to is that Peacocke's reasons for rejecting quantum indeterminism in relation to a theology of divine action are based on erroneous arguments and should be set aside as we move ahead in our assessment of QM-based NIODA.

e) *Does QM make divine action "episodic" and thus unacceptable?* In writings dating from 1986 John Polkinghorne has been skeptical about the possibilities offered by quantum physics for our understanding of divine action. In *One World* he cited Pollard's argument, but asserted it had "an air of contrivance."[69] In 1988, he again rejected Pollard's argument: "The idea of such a hole-and-corner deity, fiddling around at the rickety roots of the cosmos, has not commended itself to many."[70] A year later, however, Polkinghorne moved beyond such rhetorical comments and gave the idea a more objective response, citing two problems: 1) "[it] founder[s] on the propensity for randomness to generate regularity, for order to arise from chaos," and 2) "[If] the everyday certainties of the world of Newtonian mechanics arise from out of their fitful quantum substrate . . . [it is] unlikely [that they, by themselves] provide a sufficient basis for human or divine freedom."[71] In response to Polkinghorne's first point, I believe Pollard clearly saw that chance is not a form of causality but the lack of it. As for Polkinghorne's second point, one can claim that quantum indeterminism contributes something important to the problem of human or divine action without claiming reductively that it contributes all that is necessary to it, even if Pollard may have done so.

In 1991, Polkinghorne gave three additional reasons why he believes that the appeal to quantum physics raises real complications for the problem of divine action.[72] 1) The first focuses on chaos in classical science, where small changes in the initial conditions are amplified rapidly into large changes as the system develops in time. Some have speculated that quantum physics may be the ultimate source of these initial changes. The problem, according to Polkinghorne, is that the equations of quantum physics are not chaotic, unlike their classical counterparts; but if this is so, how can chaos arise at the classical level out of the underlying non-chaotic quantum processes? 2) Quantum physics is subject to competing interpretations, including deterministic ones. This should caution us, Polkinghorne warns, from drawing metaphysical conclusions too quickly from quantum physics. 3) Finally, Polkinghorne cites the quantum measurement problem: How can a piece of apparatus yield exact measurements on a quantum system if it too is composed of elementary particles obeying the indeterminacy principle?

Polkinghorne's reasons for not using quantum physics in the context of divine action are important and deserve a careful response. With respect to (1), Polkinghorne is certainly correct in pointing to the immense difficulties presented by "quantum chaology" to theoretical physics, but I do not believe they bear directly on the problem of interpreting divine action in light of quantum mechanics. There are, in fact, numerous ways in which quantum processes both underlie and give rise to specific effects in the classical, macroscopic world that do not depend on chaos to amplify them. Contrary to Polkinghorne's claim, quantum chaos is not necessarily (or even typically) involved even in most micro-macro irreversible interactions, let alone most micro-meso and micro-micro irreversible interactions (see section 4A above for examples of these kinds of interactions). (2) The problem of multiple interpretability, Polkinghorne's second point, was addressed above in the section on methodology. Finally, point (3) is of course just a restatement of the standard criticism of Bohr's "two worlds" approach to the problem of the collapse of the wave function: namely to treat the world as divided between classical objects (measuring apparatus) and quantum processes (the subject of measurement). It is not a criticism of the claim being made here, however, since I am not adopting Bohr's approach but Heisenberg's advocacy of ontological indeterminism.

Polkinghorne returned to these issues in 1995, referring in his footnotes to Pollard's early work.[73] Here he actually sets to rest his second concern: Though other interpretations are possible, ontological indeterminism "is a strategy consciously or unconsciously endorsed by the great majority of physicists." But

Polkinghorne reiterates point (3), drawing out the implications of the latter in a slightly different direction and leading to the oft-quoted charge that divine action related to quantum mechanics would be "episodic." According to Polkinghorne, the indeterminacies in quantum behavior only arise in "those particular events which qualify, by the irreversible registration of their effects in the macro-world, to be described as measurements. In between measurements, the continuous determinism of the Schrödinger equation applies." Because measurements only occur occasionally, this approach would limit God's action to "occasions of measurement" and suggest an "episodic account of providential agency." For these and other reasons, Polkinghorne turned from quantum physics to chaos theory as an indication that new holistic laws, carrying an undeniably indeterministic interpretation, will one day be found. Such holistic-chaotic laws, he deemed, will describe the everyday, classical world, will include current chaos theory as a "downwards emergent" limit case, and will, therefore, be consistent with non-interventionist special divine action.

Of course it is certainly true that the measurement problem is connected with tremendously complex issues in the philosophical foundations of quantum mechanics, but from this it does not follow that the measurement problem makes God's actions "episodic." To see this we need to unpack Polkinghorne's point carefully. First, Polkinghorne asserts that indeterminacies in quantum behavior *only* arise when an irreversible registration of their effects occurs in the macro-world; in essence, the concept of measurement is limited to processes that involve the quantum (micro) and the classical (macro) levels (or what I have called irreversible micro-macro interactions). I have argued instead (again see section 4A) that they occur not only at the micro-macro level of irreversible interactions but also in irreversible interactions at the micro-meso and the micro-micro levels. Polkinghorne's first assertion is thus unwarranted. This leaves his second claim, that measurements only occur occasionally, making divine action "episodic" in character. In fact, however, such measurements can occur at any time and place in the universe when the conditions are right for micro-micro, micro-meso, as well as micro-macro, irreversible interactions, as is evident from the examples given in the previous discussion. Contrary to Polkinghorne's understanding, then, the interpretation of quantum level divine action I am recommending here suggests a God who is *acting providentially everywhere and at all times* in and through all of nature—a God whose agency is hardly "episodic."

In a footnote in the original text for what is now chapter 6, I used the term "ubiquitous" to suggest this comprehensive characteristic of divine action, since the term "episodic" makes quantum events sound extremely infrequent.[74] I am now persuaded that both terms—episodic and ubiquitous—unduly emphasize distinct aspects of what is in reality a single complex situation. A term is needed that suggests that non-interventionist divine action can be related to the sudden disruptive aspect of quantum events but not to the continuous time development of the system according to the Schrödinger equation. An appropriate term for such divine action might be "pervasive," and I shall use this term in future writings. With this understanding in place, I hope that we can lay to rest any further concerns about this approach being episodic.[75]

f) *Why the Saunders/Wildman "tetralemma" argument against QM-NIODA fails in principle*[76]

1) Saunders's argument and my response. Nicholas T. Saunders has offered a lengthy analysis of the special divine action project in general (SDA) and the QM-NIODA project of Murphy, Ellis, Tracy, and mine in particular (QSDA).[77] He concludes that the case being made for "the 'traditional understanding' of God's activity in the world [is] extremely bleak . . . [and that] *contemporary theology is in crisis*"[78]—a judgment which has been quoted in various venues, notably by Peacocke who clearly "concurs" with it.[79] I will briefly discuss Saunders's views and respond to them, and then I will summarize the way Wildman has reformulated Saunders's views and respond to it, too.

In a widely read essay[80] published in 2000, Saunders offered an overview of several interpretations of quantum physics and of various theological notions of providence and divine action. He then delineated four ways of relating divine action and quantum mechanics. The first three are that God alters the wave function between measurements, that God makes measurements on a quantum system, or that God alters the probabilities of obtaining a particular result. Curiously they do not describe the actual positions of any of the principal scholars that I know of in theology and science, nor does Saunders claim that they do, so their presentation seems more of an academic exercise than a substantive argument.

The fourth approach, according to Saunders, is that "God ignores the probabilities predicted by orthodox quantum mechanics and simply controls the outcomes of particular measurements." If this approach were rephrased more carefully it could come close to what several of us want to say. My way of putting it[81] would be that God foreknows the probabilities predicted by orthodox quantum mechanics, since these after all describe possible outcomes of what are ultimately the results of the mediated acts of God in and with nature. (As we will see below, this is in fact similar to what Saunders calls a "regulative" account of the laws of nature, that is, that the laws describe the results of the underlying divine causality and have no ontological status in themselves.) Rather than unilaterally controlling the outcome of natural processes at the quantum level, as Pollard seemed to suggest, in my view God acts with nature to bring about the outcomes of particular measurements consistent with the probabilities given by quantum mechanics before the event occurs. God's action with nature is also consistent with the fact that specific outcomes might have a crucial, albeit indirect, effect at the macroscopic level which God wants to bring about and which those with faith would take correctly as objective acts of God's special providence. Saunders acknowledged that he does not find any problem with this approach. Of course it requires us to work within a particular philosophical position regarding quantum mechanics (that is, ontological indeterminism), but this is unavoidable as I have repeatedly stressed.

Saunders expanded these arguments into a full-length book published in 2002.[82] In my opinion it is a well-researched, finely crafted, highly nuanced, and quite valuable presentation and analysis of the overall problem of divine action and science with special attention to several projects, including divine action in the context of chaos theory (for example, in Polkinghorne) and quantum mechanics. I found Saunders's summary of my writings on QM-NIODA early in the volume to be quite fair.[83] All the more perplexing, then, were his conclusions about the approach Murphy, Ellis, Tracy, and I take.

In essence Saunders claims that to avoid divine intervention we must "deny that Born's probability interpretation of the wave function has an ontological priority and assert that it is simply an approximate relationship between ensembles of identical systems for a given measurement repeated a large number of times." But according to Saunders none of us interprets quantum laws in this regulative/descriptive way.[84] Moreover Saunders claims that if one takes a descriptive approach to the laws of nature, this makes quantum mechanics irrelevant to the problem of non-interventionist divine action since a regulative methodology would make divine action non-interventionist regardless of the (in)determinism of the relevant science.[85]

To the first point I actually do, in fact, prefer the regulative to the ontological view of scientific laws although I realize I may not have been entirely clear and consistent in my writings about this. While physicists often talk as though the laws of nature are ontological—and I was raised, after all, in this community—only a few of the scholars in theology and science seem to adopt a Platonic attitude toward them. Instead most see them, as Bill Stoeger argued so conclusively at the start of the CTNS/VO series, as describing what is ultimately the regular and dependable action of God in nature.[86] Actually I have no overwhelming objection to viewing quantum laws as having an ontological status as long as one asserts that God creates these laws *ex nihilo* (unlike the Platonic demiurge for whom they are an eternal given) along with the universe they govern.

Saunders also claims that a regulative view of the laws of nature undercuts the importance of quantum mechanics since any scientific law would be consistent with non-interventionist divine action. My response is that while any laws of nature, from a regulative perspective, would be consistent with both special and general divine action, that doesn't undermine the theological importance of discovering these laws. God's special and general providence "blur together" in a regulative and deterministic account of the laws of nature, but we can distinguish special and general providence when there are differences between the underlying deterministic versus stochastical laws, as is the case with classical and quantum mechanics. So, contra to Saunders, quantum mechanics provides a domain in the sciences for making a crucial theological difference even with a regulative interpretation of the laws of quantum mechanics. The reason is that classical mechanics portrays the processes of nature as though the future could be predicted from the present with arbitrary precision. Even if these laws are only descriptive of God's action, were God to bring about something genuinely new and unpredictable this would surely be a form of divine intervention, at least at the epistemic level. The same thing simply does not hold for quantum mechanics, where the radically unpredictable is "par for the course."

But the deeper criticism Saunders advances is that if the laws of quantum mechanics are thought to have an ontological status, then to act objectively God must ignore or intervene in nature. But this would only be true if *each* event is determined by the ontological probability distribution. It would *not* be true if *the ensemble as a whole, and not each event,* is determined by the ontological probability distribution. Clearly in the former view divine action by definition would be interventionist since it would clash with the fact that the wave function determines each and every event.

Actually I am not convinced that this is even an intelligible position. In any case it is certainly a "red herring" since *no one* in the divine action series, as far as I know, takes this view. Indeed why would we convene a decade of research conferences like CTNS and the VO have undertaken if even in quantum mechanics, where the striking change in quantum statistics compared with classical physics may point to a lack of efficient causality in nature, was really just equivalent to the kind of "epistemic ignorance" that characterizes chance in classical mechanics and that makes God's objective action interventionist?[87]

2) Wildman's reformation of Saunders's argument and my response. Wesley Wildman has offered a careful summary and critique of Saunders's arguments.[88] According to Wildman, Saunders believes that the success of SDA theories is to be judged according to a strict criterion. Wildman calls this criterion a "tetralemma" because it involves a conjunction of four factors: 1) objectivity, 2) incompatibilism (freedom is incompatible with determinism), 3) non-interventionism, and 4) the "strong-ontological view of the laws of nature."[89] By the last factor Wildman means that, as indicated above in discussing Saunders's position directly, not only deterministic but even stochastic laws such as those found in quantum mechanics "govern *each individual event* within an ensemble of events."[90] Wildman then claims that "all theories of SDA fail to meet the [tetralemma] criterion," that each advocate of QSDA recognizes this failure, and that they "protect" their version of QSDA by "weakening or rejecting one of the four propositions defining the criterion for success."[91] The failure, then, of these proposals to meet the tetralemma accounts for Saunders's dismissal of them.[92]

Does this then mean that Wildman agrees with Saunders? On the one hand he criticizes Saunders for failing to state why we must accept the strong-ontological interpretation of the laws of nature which plays such a crucial factor in the tetralemma. In fact he calls Saunders's silence about this point a "key lapse" in Saunders's book. On the other hand he criticizes proponents of QSDA for not providing reasons for rejecting it.[93] Then in a highly telling move Wildman shifts the focus from the ontological issue to the assumption of incompatibilism within the tetralemma. It is *this* assumption that leads Wildman to conclude that the QSDA proposals must fail, and here he discloses the lynchpin of his argument: his underlying commitment to Kantian compatibilism. In essence the failure of SDA is entirely expected because Kant's antinomy of reason shows that, unlike the tetralemma, causality in nature and human freedom requires a *compatibilist* view of freedom understood as the transcendental condition for the possibility of human experience. Wildman's *key* move then is to claim that Kant's argument "applies equally well to divine freedom to act." Hence the QSDA proposals inevitably fail the test posed by the tetralemma because it requires incompatibilism and this is ruled out by Kant.

But why should we take Kant as a given? Philip Clayton, in response to Wildman's article, listed five arguments that he takes as refuting Kant.[94] I will set aside a detailed response of my own to Kant and offer two brief comments. First if Kantian compatibilism is presupposed there would have been no reason to search for an indeterministic interpretation of science, but this was clearly a part of the overall research agenda of the CTNS/VO series of conferences. Second the fact that an indeterministic interpretation of causality in nature is made possible because of QM (and perhaps other areas in twentieth-century physics) challenges a dogmatic acceptance of Kant's metaphysical system and calls for a fresh explanation of alternative systems, as evidenced by the keen interest in Whiteheadian metaphysics by several of the participants in the series.

What then of the tetralemma? If incompatibilism is a viable assumption (*pace* Wildman), what about Saunders's strong-ontological interpretation of the laws of nature? Is it really a requirement that any successful SDA proposal must meet? Hardly. As Wildman himself remarks, if the strong-ontological interpretation were correct, "we do not need . . . two chapters of [Saunders's] book or a bunch of conferences to conclude that a non-interventionist account of QSDA is impossible." More to the point, as far as I know none of the scholars searching for QSDA view the tetralemma as representing the "criterion for success," nor do they set out to reject one of its four propositions in order to avoid failure, as charged by Wildman. The reason for this is quite simple: The tetralemma is intrinsically and self-evidently self-contradictory. An incompatibilist account of non-interventionist objective divine action requires that nature be causally indeterministic. But a strong-ontological interpretation of the laws of nature means that nature is deterministically governed event by event by these laws. Hence the flat-out contradiction at the center of Saunders's argument.

It is not surprising that Thomas Tracy[95] dismisses the tetralemma out of hand, writing that "these four assertions are logically incompatible" and that the tetralemma "cannot possibly define 'the criterion for success'" for SDA proposals. Not affirming the criterion is not a "weakening of such proposals," as Wildman claims, because "a theory is not compromised by its inability to accomplish a logically impossible task." Indeed, Tracy calls support for the tetralemma a "flatfooted mistake." I strongly concur.

g) *Does process theology provide a significantly different approach to QM-NIODA?* Ian Barbour has written on QM-NIODA from the perspective of process philosophy. My aim here is to briefly state Barbour's position, explore whether it is a successful form of NIODA, determine whether he and I differ in significant ways regarding our approaches to QM-NIODA, and assess the significance of those differences.[96]

Barbour adopts Heisenberg's version of the Copenhagen interpretation of quantum mechanics in which the uncertainty principle is an indication of ontological indeterminacy at the subatomic level.[97] According to Barbour, "quantum events have necessary but not sufficient physical causes. . . . [T]heir final determination might be made directly by God. What appears to be chance . . . may be the very point at which God acts."[98] In essence quantum events occur in part because of divine causality (the divine "lure"), and in part because of natural causality (the "prehension of past actual occasions" and "intrinsic novelty"). He then uses this interpretation to explore a non-interventionist account of divine action from the perspective of process philosophy and process theology: in short, a process approach to QM-NIODA.

In my opinion this approach succeeds in passing the crucial criteria for genuine NIODA as laid out in chapter 4: God's acts are objective, direct, and mediated. Most importantly Barbour argues for a philosophy of ontological indeterminism at the quantum level based on quantum mechanics, and such an interpretation is crucial to the definition of NIODA. What is particularly important here, however, is that this interpretation is made independently of Barbour's commitment to process philosophy as providing a metaphysical framework in which divine action is "non-interventionist." I argued (again in chapter 4) that process metaphysics in and of itself merely provides a framework for claiming that God's action is non-interventionist in what I called the "constitutive" sense: Divine action is part of what constitutes the nature of an actual occasion and thus need not "break into" nature from "outside" the world. But for NIODA to succeed, nature must also display scientific evidence at some level which can be interpreted in terms of ontological indeterminism: There must not appear to be sufficient efficient causality in nature. Without this, an appeal to a metaphysical sense of constitutive non-interventionism is at best mere rhetoric, since it could apply to classical processes displaying Laplacian determinism as well as quantum processes challenging such determinism.

Do Barbour and I then differ in significant ways in our approaches to QM-NIODA? I certainly agree with Barbour regarding many of the advantages of QM-NIODA in general. God's action at the quantum level can in some circumstances be amplified and lead to macroscopic, large-scale phenomena. God's action would not be "detectable" by science as a "skew" in routine data, nor be open to scientific or refutation.[99] But Barbour also points to several problems with this approach as it was originally developed by William Pollard. Here God is thought of as completely controlling quantum indeterminacies. The resulting position, which Barbour calls "theological determinism," is a version of predestination that Barbour rejects for several reasons: it gives God "total control over the world," it undercuts human free will, and it makes God responsible for evil (that is, the problem of theodicy). By restricting divine action to the quantum level, Barbour sees Pollard as opening the door to an "implicit reductionism." Finally, Barbour argues that without an elaborated metaphysics, which Pollard lacks, one is left to simply "juxtapose divine causation, natural causation, and free human causation."[100]

Process philosophy provides Barbour with a way to avoid these concerns. He reminds us that there are three independent principles of causation at work in each actual occasion and at every level in nature: 1) the causal past (each occasion prehends its unique set of past occasions, resulting in what we call efficient causality); 2) God's action, which provides the subjective lure or aim to each occasion but does not determine the outcome (God's lure is what Barbour calls "final causation"); and 3) an element of irreducible and genuine novelty (or "self-causation") as, during concrescence, the occasion experiences and shapes itself in light of the causal past and the divine subjective lure.[101] Thus, God's subjective lure together with the causal past influence but do not entirely determine the outcome of a quantum concrescence. Instead, intrinsic novelty is present even at the most elementary levels in nature and in all events at that level. Indeed its presence is required metaphysically. Because of this, intrinsic novelty makes an irreducible contribution to quantum indeterminism in all quantum events. Moreover, Barbour sees the metaphysical limitation on God's power as addressing his concern for human free will and as alleviating some aspects of theodicy. Given this, Barbour supports a process-based QM-NIODA instead of Pollard's approach.

Where, then, does the difference, if any, between Barbour and me lie regarding our uses of QM for NIODA?[102] I believe they lie in three related areas. 1) The first difference stems from the differing metaphysics we use. For Barbour, intrinsic novelty and interiority are *necessary* and *ubiquitous* features of nature at every level.[103] Process metaphysics offers a "thick metaphysics" which is "adequate and applicable" to all phenomena in nature.[104] I work with a "thin metaphysics" best described as "emergent monism" in which novelty, along with other features such as consciousness and agency, are *contingent* and *emergent* properties at higher levels of biological and neurophysiological complexity—a metaphysics in which the kind and degree of divine action in nature might vary from level to level. Thus, while I share his concerns about avoiding theological determinism, safeguarding human free will, and responding to theodicy, my approach to these concerns is quite different. Rather than viewing God's causal efficacy as metaphysically limited in all quantum events, Ellis, Tracy, and I are exploring an alternative in which God actualizes some but not all quantum events—specifically those few events in which mental causation is a direct or basic act initiating the body's response to volition. Moreover, our approach is open to a combination of bottom-up and top-down approaches, thus avoiding any concessions to reductionist bottom-up-only accounts.

2) A deeper difference seems to entail the essential role of science in arguing for ontological indeterminism. Granted, Barbour does appeal specifically to QM and Heisenberg's interpretation of it to make his case for NIODA at the quantum level. My concern is that Barbour goes on to claim that "indeterminacy is assumed by process thought not only in the quantum world but at all levels of integrated activity."[105] Indeed the assumption is an a priori assumption given by process metaphysics. I, however, believe that ontological indeterminism is an a posteriori inference based on specific theories in science and that this inference only holds for that particular level of complexity in nature. It is not built into the metaphysical framework as such. This means we need to make a case-by-case argument in support of this claim, inspecting the detailed scientific theories one finds as one moves up the ladder of complexity from subatomic physics to neuroscience and to ecology, and so on. When we find deterministic theories of

nature, such as chaos theory at the ordinary level of macroscopic physics, the case for *ontological determinism* is strengthened in the same way as the case for ontological *in*determinism flourishes when considering physics at the subatomic level.

One might even claim that an a priori argument for indeterminism at every level based on a metaphysics assumed in advance would seem to discount the rationale for engaging in the "theology and science" dialogue and the methodology by which theology engages the actual working theories in science. One might even argue that a metaphysics of actual occasions is *not* a sufficient, or even a clearly warranted, philosophy in light of quantum mechanics. When we consider that the deterministic Schrödinger equation governs the trajectory of elementary particles except for an occasional quantum event/measurement process, something more like the traditional substantialist metaphysics might be more strongly implied at the quantum level. In any case, the difference seems to lie in our choice of metaphysical systems and the degree to which these systems apply uniformly and universally in nature.

3) Finally the problem of theodicy leads Barbour and me into differing responses. From a Whiteheadian perspective, the metaphysical limitation on God's power is seen as a partial but helpful response to why God permits evil to exist. Barbour adds to this his support of a process eschatology including both objective and subjective immortality. From my perspective, limiting God's power only increases the problem of evil; indeed in the process approach evil is co-eternal with the world. In my view our only true hope is that evil is not co-eternal but will be overcome permanently by God in the New Creation. Hence I work with an eschatology which involves the transformation of the universe by God's action into the New Creation, an eschatology based on the bodily resurrection of Jesus of Nazareth at Easter. Thus both forms of NIODA—Barbour's and mine—address the problem of evil in ways that move beyond the confines of God's action as ongoing Creator and point towards eschatology, but in quite different ways.

2. Divine action at the quantum level and general providence

God creates *ex nihilo* and sustains the existence of quantum systems as they undergo causal time evolution, governed by the deterministic Schrödinger equation, and as they undergo irreversible and indeterministic interactions (that is, quantum events) with other micro- and macro-systems whose existence God also sustains. The time evolution of quantum systems applies to isolated systems, such as elementary particles traveling through relatively empty intergalactic space, or to the very early universe. It also applies to elementary particles bound together, as atoms and molecules undergo time evolution in conformity with the Schrödinger equation. Quantum events, and the indeterminism associated with them, arise when micro-systems interact irreversibly with each other or with more complex, molecular or macroscopic systems. (Here I am not considering those irreversible interactions that lead indirectly to significant changes in the world, and are thus interpretable in terms of special providence.)

The point here is that during both time evolution and irreversible interactions, particles and systems retain their FD or BE properties, and these properties account for the classical properties of bulk matter that we experience as the ordinary world of nature and describe in terms of classical physics. It is to this world of ordinary experience that we attribute God's general providence (or continuous creation), namely the ongoing creation and sustenance of the general features of the classical world of physics, geology, chemistry, meteorology, evolutionary biology, and so on. Thus what we routinely take as general providence arises *indirectly* from God's *direct* action of sustaining in existence quantum systems and their properties during both their time evolution and their irreversible interactions. In short, God (indirectly) creates macroscopic structures and interactions, as well as classical chance, as a result of quantum processes and statistics. Murphy writes that "the laws that describe the behavior of the macro-level entities are consequences of the regularities at the lowest level, and are indirect though intended consequences of God's direct acts at the quantum level . . . I am proposing that the uniformity of nature is a divine artifact."[106]

Murphy provides an intriguing comparison of her work with that of Pollard. She sees her proposal as coming close to, but actually being preferable to, that of Pollard since hers, unlike Pollard's, allows for human freedom by insisting on both top-down and bottom-up causality and by stressing God's underdetermination of the outcome of events. But she leaves open several key questions: "What, exactly, are the possibilities for God's determining the outcomes of events at the macro-level by governing the behavior of sub-atomic entities? What exactly are the limits placed upon God's determination of macro-events by his decision not to violate the natures of these entities?" or what she calls their "natural rights."[107] This leads us to the next issue: the relation between God as acting i) in general at the level of quantum physics to create the ordinary characteristics and properties of the classical world, and ii) God as acting in particular quantum events to produce, indirectly, a specific event at the macroscopic level—one which we call an event of special providence.

3. Divine action at the quantum level and its relation to special providence[108]

This approach to NIODA views the domain of quantum mechanics as giving rise to the general features of the ordinary macroscopic world (that is, general providence/continuous creation) as well as particular events within it (that is, special providence).

We have just seen how, from a theological perspective, God's non-interventionist action at the quantum level gives rise to the creation of the general features of the classical world described above, as well as to their sustenance and physical development in time, or what we would routinely call general providence (or continuous creation).[109] It is widely asserted, however, that individual quantum events always "average out" at the macroscopic level, thus making quantum mechanics irrelevant to special providence and human free will. On the contrary, it is quite clear that quantum processes also underlie and give rise to specific effects in the macroscopic world in several ways, and that these may be particularly relevant to a theology of special providence via a quantum-based approach to NIODA.

One way is through those phenomena, such as superfluidity and superconductivity, which, though found in the ordinary classical world, are really "bulk" quantum states—what Ellis calls "essentially quantum effects at the macro level."[110] Another, and quite different, way is through specific quantum processes, which, when amplified correctly, result in particular classical effects in the classical world. It is the latter that will be the focus of this section and will be thought of in terms of special providence. Obvious examples range from such jury-rigged situations as "Schrödinger's cat" to such routine measurement devices as a Geiger counter. But the production of specific effects in the macroscopic level from quantum processes includes a whole range of phenomena *in nature* such as the animal eye responding to a single photon, mental states resulting from quantum events at neural junctions, or the phenotypic expression of a single genetic mutation in an organism (resulting, for example, in sickle-cell anemia or cancer). Regarding mental states and neural firings, Ellis discusses two possibilities: (i) coherent firings in large arrays of neurons leading to a holistic response in a region of the brain (here "amplification" is an almost inappropriate term), and (ii) localized firings in microtubules that are amplified to macroscopic effect, following the suggestions of Roger Penrose.[111] I have even argued that the evolution of life on earth over the past 3.8 billion years depends in part on what can be called "biological amplifiers"—the genotype-phenotype relation which expresses the effects of quantum mechanics within genetic mutations at the macroscopic level of individual organisms and populations.[112] I will argue in chapter 6 that a quantum-based NIODA is enormously relevant, then, to deploying a robust account of "theistic evolution" in which God's non-interventionist objective divine action works in and with nature to produce the phenomena of life. Moreover, the amplification of microscopic to macroscopic states in most of these processes does *not* rely on chaos theory. Therefore, contrary to the claim by some scholars such as John Polkinghorne, we need *not* deal with the unresolved problem of "quantum chaology" in this approach to divine action.[113]

In previous writings, I pointed to a watershed accomplishment in theology and science when, in the 1970s, Arthur Peacocke[114] shifted the discussion of chance from a conflict model, "law versus chance," as urged by atheists such as Jacques Monod (unfortunately, a formulation all too often accepted by Christians who reject evolution) to an integrative framework, "law and chance." As a result of this shift, Christians could claim that God acts through both law and chance to create physical, chemical, and biological novelty in nature. Still, the meaning of chance in this context may not be adequate for a genuine sense of non-interventionist divine action in specific events in time.

I suggest that we now face a more fundamental shift in our discussion of "law and chance" in light of quantum physics: a shift from chance in classical physics (where chance as mere epistemic ignorance of underlying causal processes precludes NIODA) to the meaning of chance in quantum physics (where chance as ontological indeterminism is open to NIODA). Rather than saying that God deistically watches the endless unfolding of the potentialities built into nature at the beginning, we can now say that God indirectly creates order in the classical realm by 1) directly creating a quantum mechanical universe with FD/BE statistics that give rise to the classical world and 2) by acting directly in time as the continuous creator in, with, and through the indeterminism of quantum events to bring about novelty in the classical world. God is thus truly the God of both order and novelty in the physical and biological realms. As Tracy writes, quantum physics is relevant to theology because it provides a way to describe God's action as playing "an ongoing and pervasive role" in contributing to the world's regular, ordered structure and as making a difference in "the direction of events" in the world through the "providential determination of otherwise undetermined events."[115]

In summary, then, God's action at the quantum level can be seen as bringing about, in a non-interventionist mode, both the general features of the world we describe in terms of *general providence* (or continuous creation) and those specific events in the world to which *special providence* refers.

4. Is divine action local or global?

Before proceeding, we should inspect an implicit assumption, namely that God's action in relation to ψ should be thought of as an unambiguously "local" action. Instead I will propose two claims.[116]

First, the mathematical features of the wave function ψ used in elementary quantum mechanics, and the parametric role of both space and time variables in defining ψ, suggest that God's action in relation to ψ occurs globally in space and time.[117] To see this we start with the general[118] wave function ψ such that $\psi = \psi(x,t)$. In principle, ψ is defined for $-\infty \leq x \leq +\infty$ and for $-\infty \leq t \leq +\infty$, with x and t both serving formally as parameters of ψ. We can view this in at least three ways: (i) We can stipulate the spatial shape of the wave function everywhere along the x-axis at a given moment of time; (ii) we can describe the spatial shape everywhere along the x-axis as it changes in time; (iii) we can specify its amplitude (height) at a particular point in space as it changes in time. Now (ii) is probably the closest we come, in very rough terms, to the classical conception of a particle with a well-defined location in space at a moment in time, such that we can write $x = x(t)$. Thus, right from the outset, an important aspect of the nonlocality of the quantum conception of matter is built in. Our conception of divine action in relation to ψ must reflect this view. We must take care not to presuppose an unambiguous locality to God's action when it is conceived in relation to ψ. We may think about divine action as "localized" by thinking of it in relation to the region in space where ψ is relatively large, somewhat in the way we refer to the "location" of the particle represented by ψ, as long as we keep in mind the fact that this is a rough way of speaking and do not fall tacitly into the classical conception of matter—or divine action.

Second, the concept of God as acting to bring about a quantum event (that is, the collapse of the wave function) is as much a global as a local event, regardless of whether this event leads indirectly to an instance of special providence. Consider a simple physical process: A particle is emitted at time t_0

and propagates freely through space until it is detected at time t_1, let's say one hour later. The motion of the particle between t_0 and t_1 is governed by the Schrödinger equation, and its wave function ψ is a uniformly expanding sphere centered on the source. (To be more precise, the particle is described by a wavepacket whose maximum value, ψ_{max}, describes a uniformly expanding sphere, but one that is everywhere nonzero.) Now, at t_1 the particle is detected and its wave function collapses instantaneously and unpredictably to a state representing the particle at the detector. (We might make the additional assumption that its detection has significant consequences in the world, which we interpret theologically in terms of special providence via mediated and indirect divine action.) What then can all this suggest about the relation between God's action at the quantum level and the collapse of the wave function?

In responding we should keep in mind the previous point: God is active everywhere in space and time in relation to ψ as it extends throughout space and evolves in time. Indeed, one might say that the "general action" of God is God's action in maintaining the regular time development of ψ as described by the Schrödinger equation, much as we understand God's general providence as maintaining the world in its bulk, macroscopic configurations. Still for convenience let us think in terms of the peak in ψ (ψ_{max}) as it expands spherically, since for all practical purposes this represents a spherical wavepacket about to "collapse."

Now, at the moment of collapse, ψ changes discontinuously from a light-hour sphere, ψ_s, to a fully localized wavepacket ψ_x. Thus the irreversible interaction or quantum event involving the particle and the detector is represented here by the juxtaposition of, and discontinuous transition between, the global ψ_s and the local ψ_x that co-characterize and co-constitute what we mean by the collapse of the wave function. If we are to think of God's action in relation to this event, then it, too, must have both a global and a local character: God acts *globally* on ψ_s to bring about the "collapse" by causing a *local* transition from a nonzero to a zero amplitude everywhere on a sphere one light-hour in radius except at the location of the detector. Finally, if we then assume that the detection of the particle leads to a macroscopic event that we interpret as an act of special providence, then the concept of special providence, which refers to significant local macroscopic events in history and nature, comes about by God's action at the quantum level globally *and* locally.[119]

5. Divine action, quantum physics, and the challenge of special relativity[120]

So far we have discussed several general issues related to divine action and quantum physics. Before turning to more detailed issues, we should note that this discussion has tacitly assumed the classical view of space and time found in Newtonian-Galilean physics. Special relativity (c. 1905) poses important issues for quantum physics and thus for our discussion of divine action. It would be good to mention these briefly before turning to more detailed issues. Indeed, we shall see that some of the reasons given for not pursuing divine action in terms of quantum physics stem from the problems with special relativity and not from the issues that we will later consider. I will discuss scientific issues first, and then theological issues raised by them.

From a scientific perspective, the Copenhagen interpretation in particular is challenged by special relativity in several ways. First, special relativity undercuts the classical assumptions of a global present and a universally unique rate of time's flow. Both the Schrödinger equation and the measurement problem presuppose these assumptions. Thus, in light of special relativity, it becomes crucial to ask how we are to pick out the physically correct surface of simultaneity on which the Schrödinger equation governs ψ and on which ψ collapses, as Jeremy Butterfield[121] and Raymond Chiao[122] stress. Second, special relativity can be given alternative ontological interpretations—much as alternative interpretations pervade quantum physics—namely, the "block universe" and "flowing time" views.[123] Which of these ontologies are we to adopt in a relativistic reformulation of the Copenhagen interpretation? These are serious problems for quantum physics. On the other hand, however, it is crucial to note that quantum mechanics is consistent with special relativity in a specific way: Violations of Bell's inequalities need not violate relativity's "first signal principle" (that is, instantaneous causal action-at-a-distance). This is a subtle point, since space-like correlations do exist and their presence undercuts local realism, as we shall discuss briefly below.[124] Additional insight is also shed on the relation between present and future by the "temporal nonlocality" that Chiao describes[125]. Here once-related events in the present and the future display a Bell-like correlation, which undercuts the classical relation between present and future.

Theologically, special relativity challenges the problem of "time and eternity" that lies behind what I have proposed about divine action and quantum physics. How, for example, does God know what action to take in the present to bring about events of special providence in the future in light of special relativity? There are actually a variety of nested problems and issues here. One will suffice for the present discussion, namely the "block universe" versus "flowing time" interpretation mentioned above. Chris Isham represents one widely held view: the "block universe" perspective in which the future (and the past) are as real as the present. We may not know what the future holds, but from the perspective of eternity, God's knowledge of the future is perfect. But can God—or can we—act to change things in the present, and thus the future, in this scenario, and does quantum indeterminism make a difference to our answer here? John Polkinghorne, like many others, rejects the "block universe," with its apparent contradiction of our experience of time and free will, and opts instead for a "flowing time perspective" in which the future has no ontological status and thus cannot be known by us or God. Here God's providential involvement in a genuinely open world is more like the "master chess player" who may not know the outcome of a specific game in advance but who is certain to win. But again, how do we make physical sense out of the "present" or uniformly flowing time in light of special relativity?

I think both of these options are valuable but problematic. Hence I am attempting to construct a third alternative that draws on the strengths of the previous scenarios. I call it an "*event/world-line* flowing time" interpretation of special relativity. The project includes a relationally-based ontology of events in which the status of "present," "future," and "past" is attributed to relations between events rather than to the events themselves. It then uses this ontology to explore the conception of time and eternity as developed in trinitarian doctrines of God. I believe this move will alleviate some of the problems raised by the block universe versus flowing time debate. In any case, though, one can always argue that God does not foresee the future in the sense of seeing the future from the present, but rather by seeing the future in its own state as present.

B. Crucial theological issues

We are now ready to move directly to the key questions in the debate on divine action and (nonrelativistic) quantum physics. My central thesis is that God acts in quantum events to bring about, or actualize, one of several potential outcomes; the collapse of the wave function occurs because of divine and natural causality. But does God act in every quantum event or only in some? And what are the theological implications for human freedom and the problem of evil in nature? To respond to these questions, it will be helpful to focus carefully on the responses given by Murphy, Ellis, and Tracy as they have explored these and other crucial issues.

1. Does God act providentially (general and/or special) in all, or only in some, quantum events?

Murphy supports the claim that God acts intentionally in *all* quantum events. In Murphy's view, all quantum events involve a combination of natural and divine causality; they are determined, though only in part and not solely, by God. "To say that each sub-atomic event is solely an act of God would be a version of occasionalism, with all [its] attendant theological difficulties."[126] Instead, a quantum event happens in part by God "activating or actualizing one or another of the quantum entity's innate powers at particular instants . . . these events are not possible without God's action." A crucial reason is that this claim keeps God from becoming a "competitor with processes that on other occasions are sufficient in and of themselves to bring about a given effect." Another reason is to avoid any sense of God's action as intermittent; instead, God's action is "a necessary but not sufficient condition for every (post-creation) event." If God is a participant in each event, then the charge of intervention is avoided because God acts everywhere, not just occasionally, yet since God acts only as a participant, the charge of divine determinism is also avoided.[127]

Murphy points to the close relation between her work and that of Pollard. Unlike Pollard, however, Murphy claims that her approach does not portray God as unilaterally determining, and thus dominating, all events in the world, nor does it undercut human freedom. Instead it limits bottom-up divine action by allowing for top-down causation and it stresses God's respect for the integrity and rights of creatures. In doing so, Murphy sees her approach as steering a path between two extremes: making God responsible for all the randomness, purposelessness, and evil in the world, or undercutting any possibility for divine action within the course of nature and history.[128]

Tracy[129] questions Murphy's position. In order for Murphy's argument to work, he contends that she must provide a developed account of top-down causation. But because the effects of wholes on parts are mediated by the bottom-up interactions of the parts, it remains unclear how freedom can appear as a top-down effect within a system of deterministic bottom-up causal relationships. Accordingly, Tracy explores the option that God acts in some but not all quantum events. On the one hand this option seems to violate the principle of sufficient reason, since some quantum events would occur without sufficient prior conditions, constraints, or causes. On the other hand it underscores the "special" character of "special providence": God's direct acts in key quantum events are special not only because their indirect outcome is special, but also because God normally does not act in other quantum events beyond creating them and sustaining them in being. Moreover, Tracy's approach provides a fruitful basis for thinking of God's occasional, special action in terms of self-limitation: God *could* act together with nature to codetermine all quantum events, but God *abstains* from such action in most cases.[130]

I find Murphy's approach helpful for several reasons. The idea of God acting in all quantum events supports the theological claim that God does more than sustain the existence of all events and processes; in fact, God sustains, governs, and cooperates with all that nature does. This idea offers us a subtle but compelling way to interpret God's action as leading to both general and special providence. Schrödinger's cat makes it clear that God's action at the quantum level results in two quite different kinds of macroscopic effects. It produces the *ordinary* world of the cat and Geiger counter (the ordinary physics of solid matter and Ohm's law, the routine biology of metabolism, and so on), which we describe as general providence. But it also results in *specific differences* in the ordinary world—the cat living instead of dying—when God acts in one way instead of another in a specific quantum event. For example, God acts with nature so that the particle is emitted now and not later, or it is emitted in the $+x$ direction rather than $-x$, and so on. Which way God acts determines (indirectly) a specific result in the ordinary world. Thus we may attribute special providence to the cat being spared from death and granted life in the crucial moment.

The chief virtue of the option Tracy is exploring is that it provides a more intuitive connection between the idea of God's occasional action at the quantum level and God's special providence in the everyday world. Still, it seems less clear how God's general providence could be based on God's occasional action at the quantum level. Actually, however, we may be able to combine Murphy's pervasiveness of divine causality with Tracy's concern for the event to be objectively special because of the nature of quantum statistics: God acts in this event as in all events (God's action is never "more" or "less" but the same, equally causative). Still in this occasion, with two states superposed before the event, God will choose one state in particular and not the other, the one destined to promote life, thus conveying God's intentionality in this particular event. We can thus interpret this particular event, in which the cat lives instead of dying, in terms of objective special providence without restricting God's action to that event, and yet still maintain the objectively revelatory character of that particular event.

In sum, both Murphy and Tracy deliver just what is needed for non-interventionist objective, special providence. It involves *objective* special providence—for the actual fact is that the cat lives when it might have died; it is objective special *providence* since it truly conveys God's intentions through the event of the cat living; and it is *special* providence because it is that event that we use to refer to God's providence against the assumed backdrop of the general situation itself: the cat purring, the sun shining, the apparatus functioning routinely, and so on. Most importantly, it is *non-interventionist* objective special providence because it is an act of objective special providence that God achieves without violating or suspending the ongoing processes of nature and the laws that describe them. So in short, God causes all the processes of the ordinary world (general providence), but a few of them genuinely convey special meaning because the choices God makes in causing them, and not the other options available to God, bring them about.

I am not persuaded, however, that either Murphy's or Tracy's approach deals adequately with the problems of human freedom and theodicy. In the following two sections, I will sketch an approach I have been developing as a third option that attempts to combine the advantages of their views.

2. Quantum physics, divine action, and the problem of human freedom.
The problem of free will, as formulated in the modern period, is the following: How are we able to act freely in the world if, as in the classical science picture, deterministic laws govern us somatically? Actually the problem only arises on an *incompatibilist/libertarian* account of free will (which I adopt here). Many scholars have seen quantum indeterminism as a way out of the impasse: Perhaps the human mind, through some form of top-down causality (for example, mind/brain causality), can objectively influence the movements of the body, making the enactment of free choices possible. Ian Barbour notes that as early as the 1920s physicists Arthur Eddington and Arthur Compton sought to relate quantum indeterminism to volition.[131] This idea is pursued in various ways by George Ellis.[132] This, however, raises a concern I have pointed out previously: How do we allow God's action to determine the quantum events that occur in my body and still allow for my own mind/brain to determine them? I will call this the problem of "somatic overdetermination."[133]

Before turning to it, though, I want to focus on the sub-problem of free will and quantum indeterminism. It is important to note here that Murphy does not see quantum indeterminism as essential to human freedom. She does appeal to the self-limitation of God in respecting the "natural rights" of creatures and of thus creating a dependable environment necessary to human agency. However, she argues that top-down causation does *not* depend on quantum indeterminacy at the bottom level. She cites Donald Campbell's example to show how top-down causation could work even if all biological processes were deterministic.[134] I am not convinced by her response. In my view, the somatic enactment of incompatibilist human freedom requires lower-level indeterminism, and thus when we add the possibility of divine action we return to the problem of somatic overdetermination.

Tracy, too, is concerned with the issue of free will, asking how freedom can "appear as a top-down effect within a system of deterministic bottom-up causal relationships."[135] It was precisely this concern that led him to explore the alternative option regarding divine action. Unfortunately, Tracy does not provide a detailed response there, either. Ellis, too, has stressed the problem of free will and quantum indeterminism to the extent of "inverting it" in a beautiful way: Starting from his assumption of divine kenosis and the intention of God to create a universe where moral action is possible, Ellis argues that there must be openness in physical laws, so that morality and special divine action are possible. Thus, just as Murphy and others insist that the macroscopic world must be regular for moral agency to function, Ellis demands there be causal gaps, using Tracy's term, at the microscopic level for it to be enacted.[136] But this takes us back to the larger problem: somatic overdetermination.

My suggestion is to start with the scenario that God acts in all quantum events in the universe until the evolution of organisms capable of even primitive levels of consciousness.[137] God then increasingly refrains from determining outcomes we call conscious choices, leaving room for top-down, mind/brain causality in conscious and self-conscious creatures. This would be a version of the standard "solution" to the problem of free will, namely God's voluntary or metaphysically necessary self-limitation, but seen now as a temporal development of the limitations, from minimum to maximum. In particular, God also abstains from acting in those quantum events underlying bodily dispositions, thereby allowing the developing levels of consciousness to act out their intentions somatically.

This approach combines aspects of Murphy's and Tracy's approaches, it includes the idea of divine self-limitation, and it gives to them all a temporal character. God bequeaths us not only the capacity for mental experience via God's special action in evolution and the resulting rise of the central nervous system, but God also bequeaths to us the capacity for free will and the capacity to enact our choices by providing at least one domain of genuine indeterminacy in terms of our somatic dispositions.[138]

3. Quantum physics, divine action, and the challenge of theodicy.

The problem of theodicy is stunningly exacerbated by all the proposals, including my own, that God acts at the level of genetics—certainly much more so than either Tracy or Murphy allow. The development of an adequate theological response is an important goal for future theological research.

The problem of theodicy, of course, is a perennial issue for theism: If God is purely good and if God can really act in history, why doesn't God minimize the evil done by humanity (that is, moral evil)? When we expand the scope of divine action to include the evolutionary history of life on earth, the question becomes: Why doesn't God act to minimize suffering, disease, death of individual organisms, and extinction of species (that is, natural evil)?[139] Theodicy has been discussed extensively in the "theology and science" literature,[140] where its subtle connection to the problem of human freedom has frequently been stressed. Arthur Peacocke provided an elegant example of this connection as far back as 1979, when he wrote: "[I]t seems hard to avoid the paradox that 'natural evil' is a necessary prerequisite for the emergence of free, self-conscious beings."[141] But theodicy becomes a particularly intense issue in light of the present thesis regarding a non-interventionist approach to objective, special divine action. In 1995, for example, George Ellis put the problem eloquently: "[T]here has to be a cast-iron reason why a merciful and loving God does not alleviate a lot more of the suffering in the world, if he/she has indeed the power to do so."[142] Does the approach of either Murphy or Tracy in relating divine action and quantum physics provide such a reason?

In response to the challenge of theodicy, Murphy calls on her notion of God's respect for the integrity or "natural rights" of all creatures. Being noncoercive, God's action is consistent with human freedom and thus addresses, in part, the issue of theodicy as "moral evil." But what of theodicy as "natural evil"? I am not entirely clear how Murphy would respond here. She makes a passing reference to the "free-process" defense proposed by Polkinghorne in analogy with the traditional "freewill" response.[143] Nevertheless, it raises several concerns. One is that it may be irreducibly tied to other concepts, such as top-down causality, which cannot fit, even analogously, at the much less complex domain of physics and early biology. Another is that, while it accounts for why God does not interfere in cases of natural evil where God's interference would undermine the conditions for the possibility of human freedom (that is, regularity/predictability), it may not be able to account for why God does not interfere in those cases where human freedom is unaffected, including the vast sweep of pre-human (and pre-sentient?) evolution.[144]

Since her 1995 essay on quantum physics, Murphy has worked with Ellis to develop a detailed theodicy in their work on the "moral universe."[145] There they explicitly reject the Augustinian response to theodicy, arguing instead for an Anabaptist approach grounded in a kenotic view of God's action that takes natural evil seriously, utilizes Murphy's work on quantum physics and divine action, and moves to the suffering of Christ on the cross. Clearly, Murphy and Ellis offer a promising approach to the challenge of theodicy.

Tracy, as we saw, explored the alternative view of divine action, citing the problem of theodicy encountered by Murphy's approach as a reason for his choice. But does Tracy's option help us here? It is not clear to me how restricting God's action really helps matters. Why does God not act in those events, or refrain from acting in others, if this would alleviate suffering, and so on? Tracy has also discussed the impossibility of assessing the extent of suffering compared to the goals met by these processes.[146] I find this helpful in showing the difficulty of such an assessment, and the naïveté with which such difficulty is normally overlooked, but the search for an acceptable response to theodicy must move beyond the philosophical framework of this approach to a fully developed theology of redemption. I believe it is only here that we will find the "cast-iron reasons" that Ellis so rightly demands—reasons that will have the form of the cross and the empty tomb.

4. Embedding "divine action and quantum physics" in a broader theological framework.
In essence, the question now is how to locate our work on divine action and quantum physics in the context of a fully developed and robust systematic theology. At this point, a number of promising options are available. With Murphy and Ellis, Barbour, Peacocke, Polkinghorne, Edwards, Peters, and many others in the "theology and science" conversation, I believe we must look to a kenotic theology that respects human freedom and focuses on the passibility and suffering of God. Through the cross and the atonement of Christ, God redeems the world, suffering with and taking on the pain and death of all creatures. We could explore the route Murphy and Ellis have taken, or pursue the "theologies of nature" articulated by Peacocke and Polkinghorne, or explore the directions taken by other scholars in "theology and science." However, I am still persuaded by Barbour's argument some thirty years ago that "an elaborated metaphysics is needed if we want to relate rather than simply juxtapose divine causation, natural causation, and free human causation."[147] Owen Thomas has recently underscored the lasting centrality of this problem, asserting that the most promising options are the metaphysical systems of neo-Thomism and Whitehead;[148] I would add to these the metaphysical framework of Wolfhart Pannenberg and other theologians exploring the doctrine of the Trinity.

It would be natural to explore divine action and quantum physics from the perspective of process theology. Ground-breaking research in "theology and science" has already come from a variety of scholars who work in differing ways within the broad outlines of process theology, including Ian Barbour, Charles Birch, John Cobb Jr., David Griffin, and John Haught. These scholars draw on a crucial aspect of Whiteheadian metaphysics—namely, that reality consists of "actual occasions" that perish as they come to be, an idea highly reminiscent of "quantum events." Such actual occasions experience the causal efficacy of the past by prehension, are characterized by inherent novelty, and respond freely to God's inviting, subjective lure. Process theology views God as active in all levels of nature, stressing God's respect of human free will and God's kenotic and redemptive suffering with all creatures.

Process scholars argue that the inclusion of God's subjective lure to evoke a response from creatures offers a creative new approach to non-interventionist divine action at various levels of organization and complexity in nature.[149] The problem—seldom acknowledged by process advocates—is that one has to explain how divine agency is effective in the domains of chemistry, biology, and early evolutionary life, if the result of a succession of actual occasions is described classically by *deterministic laws and epistemic (not ontological) chance.* Even with the metaphysical richness of the subjective lure, I believe we need quantum mechanics to offer the indeterministic framework in which actual occasions can "make a difference"—and then we have to face the apparent discrepancies between process philosophy and quantum mechanics discussed immediately below.[150] (For the record, I part company with most process theologians in the way they treat such crucial issues as the bodily resurrection of Jesus, the eschatological perspective of a new heaven and earth, and of course creation *ex nihilo*. These concerns would remain even if the issues to be discussed between Whitehead and quantum physics were settled.)

The similarity between "actual occasions" and "quantum events" may not be entirely surprising. One of the advantages attributed by process scholars to Whitehead's philosophical system is its compatibility with science.[151] Whitehead himself claimed to offer a conceptual framework suited to science in general and quantum mechanics in particular.[152] But, as Abner Shimony has pointed out, Whitehead may have been reflecting on very early stages in the development of quantum mechanics when he constructed his "philosophy of organism" in the mid-1920s, and not on quantum mechanics as we now know and use it. According to Shimony, Whitehead never refers to the new quantum theory in the exposition of his system.[153] Moreover, important differences appear to exist between Whitehead's philosophy and quantum mechanics. After a detailed comparison, Shimony has concluded that "the discrepancies . . . between Whiteheadian physics and current microphysics constitute strong disconfirmation of Whitehead's philosophy as a whole."[154] One discrepancy is particularly relevant here: From a Whiteheadian perspective, the temporal atomicity of actual occasions underlies and gives rise to what we take to be enduring objects, but from a quantum perspective, such atomicities are "quantum events" between which quantum systems undergo a continuous and deterministic time development governed by the Schrödinger equation.

The story, though, is far from over. In his attempt to reformulate quantum physics, Shimony has introduced a stochastic term that addresses precisely this discrepancy, making his proposal closer to Whitehead's view of indeterminism (where chance pervades each actual occasion and hence the trajectory of an isolated particle) than it is to the indeterminism of current quantum physics (where it is focused strictly on quantum events). Shimony also suggests that Whitehead's concept of the concrescence of an actual occasion may contribute to a clearer understanding of the collapse of the wave function.[155] Other scholars too, including Henry Folse Jr., Charles Hartshorne, William Jones, and Henry Stapp, have provided careful responses to the problematic relation between quantum physics and Whiteheadian philosophy.[156] Whether these suggestions and concerns will prove fruitful is an open and intriguing question, particularly as it suggests, once again, the creative role philosophy can play in the construction of new scientific theories (see endnote 40).

Rather than look to process theology, I propose we locate the problem of divine action and quantum physics in an explicitly trinitarian doctrine of God. In *The Crucified God*, which I take to be a landmark in twentieth-century Protestant theology, Jürgen Moltmann pointedly argues that only a move from a "weakly Christianized monotheism" to a fully articulated trinitarianism can respond to the theological problem of the cross.[157]

The challenge for this approach, however, is that this understanding of the cross is linked theologically to Christian eschatology, including the bodily resurrection of Jesus, the general resurrection in the parousia, and the transformation of this universe into the New Creation to come. Although Moltmann sees this, it is given a central place in the proleptic trinitarian theology of Wolfhart Pannenberg. It is only through the theology of reconciliation that the challenge of theodicy can be met, and reconciliation means both the end and the transfiguration of the world. "Only in the light of the eschatological consummation may [the verdict 'very good'] be said of our world as it is in all its confusion and pain."[158]

But we now find ourselves at "ground zero" of what is arguably the most powerful challenge to Christian theology in its encounter with science: How are we to understand eschatology in light of physics, biology, and Big Bang cosmology? I do not think that non-interventionist divine action will be of significant help with these issues. The resurrection of Jesus involves "more than a miracle," namely, the eschatological transformation of the fundamental conditions of nature, and not an extraordinary event within an unchanged natural backdrop, as described by this chapter on special providence through non-interventionist divine action. I am currently beginning a major research project aimed at these issues.

I do, however, expect quantum physics to play some role in the overall approach to this vast problem, particularly through the way Pannenberg reformulates the concept of divine action in both creation (and thus providence) and redemption in terms of the Spirit of God. He has suggested that we use the concept of field in modern physics in order to talk about the Spirit and divine action.[159] Pannenberg's promising suggestion invites a number of responses, the principal one here being that his understanding of field comes from the context of classical field theory, as seen in both Faraday's and Einstein's work. When we move to the context of quantum physics and then to quantum field theory, a number of dramatic new features occur, as we have seen already. John Polkinghorne has underscored several of these in his critique of Pannenberg's use of the concept of field: superposition, nonlocality, and entanglement,[160] to which I would add the relation (mentioned above and in the appendix) between determinism in Bohm's work and ontological indeterminism within the Copenhagen interpretation, the unification of such classically separate concepts as "matter" and "interaction" through the nonclassical nature of quantum statistics, and the concept of the "filled" quantum vacuum and its suggestion of a "meonic" view of spontaneous creation and annihilation.[161] Hopefully these discussions, in turn, will contribute at least indirectly to the central issue of eschatology and scientific cosmology, towards which our focus on divine action and quantum physics has slowly but inexorably led.

6. Directions for Future Research on the Philosophical Implications of Quantum Mechanics and Their Relevance for a Theology of Divine Action

In this chapter I have stressed the multiple interpretability of quantum mechanics and proceeded to work within one interpretation by using it as a hypothetical, a "what if" argument, thereby gaining insights about its implications in particular for a theology of divine action and bracketing for the time being the other, and often conflicting, implications from other viable interpretations of quantum mechanics. Even though this approach is evidently productive, it is necessarily limited by the relativism entailed by these conflicting philosophical implications. Thus the problem of multiple interpretability looms large over any approach that starts within a specific interpretation of quantum mechanics. Are there ways, then, to move out—or "above"—this multiplicity and get a broader perspective on the kinds of problems that will face *any* philosophical interpretation of quantum physics? Would this perspective offer a more promising set of implications for theology?

This question leads us well beyond the limits of this chapter. Here I will offer two suggestions for future research. First I will propose what can be called "an architecture of philosophical issues" which, while acknowledging that these interpretations and their respective insights often conflict with each other, succeeds in bringing us to a larger framework of ordered and prioritized philosophical implications which can contribute robustly to the conversations with theology. Secondly I will suggest that we already know something crucial about any future scientific theory which might eventually replace quantum mechanics. In specific any such theory must deal with certain specific features of the quantum world which seem already to transcend quantum theory and its quagmire of multiple interpretations, namely those features revealed by the Bell inequalities. These features in turn offer us a clue about such future theories since, regardless of their structure, these theories must deal with the Bell inequalities. This in turn implies that the philosophical implications of the Bell inequalities are arguably of more importance for a theology of divine action than the particular implications of specific interpretations of quantum mechanics, such as Copenhagen indeterminism. Thus even though the future theories which will one day replace quantum mechanics may not be available in full detail already, we can reflect theologically with reasonable confidence on these implications, and I propose that future research in the theological appropriation of quantum mechanics could best proceed in this way.

A. Architecture of philosophical issues

My first suggestion is to sort out which features are general enough to be found in most or perhaps all interpretations. Superposition and nonlocality are likely candidates. Raymond Chiao[162] distinguishes between quantum nonlocality as displayed in the Aharonov-Bohm effect, the tunnel effect, and the Einstein-Podolsky-Rosen effect. Each stems from the superposition principle (that is, quantum interference), but the first two involve single-particle interference, while the third involves an "entangled state" between two particles. Jim Cushing uses locality and separability interchangeably in his discussion of Jarrett locality, Jarrett completeness, and Howard's factorizability.[163] Cushing argues that either objective reality or locality must be given up. His option is for nonlocality, and he stresses the distinction between separability and locality, taking "relational holism" seriously.

Other issues and features seem to arise in closer association with individual interpretations of quantum physics. For example, the measurement problem and ontological indeterminism are integral to the standard Copenhagen interpretation, but there are a variety of attempts to resolve the measurement problem. Some work within the perspective of the Copenhagen interpretation broadly conceived, including those which propose to modify the Schrödinger equation, either through the introduction of nonlinear terms or through the inclusion of stochastic factors, and those which attempt to understand consciousness (the observer's mind) as bringing about the collapse of the wave function. Others seek to resolve the measurement problem by interpreting quantum physics in such a way that it simply does not arise. The most notable of these are Bohm's quantum potential interpretation and the branching of reality in the many-worlds and many-minds approaches discussed by Butterfield in the *Quantum Mechanics* volume of the CTNS/VO series.

This suggests that we can begin to lay out what I will call the "architecture of philosophical problems" in quantum physics. A first sketch might be as follows:

1. Generic features:
   - i. superposition (interference)
   - ii. nonlocality, including:
     - a. single-particle nonlocality (the Aharonov-Bohm effect; the tunnel effect)
     - b. multi-particle (entanglement) nonlocality (the Einstein-Podolsky-Rosen effect)
   - iii. nonseparability/relational holism

2. Interpretation-specific features:
   - i. Copenhagen: the measurement problem
     - a. accept the measurement problem and ontological indeterminism
     - b. overcome the measurement problem by:
       - 1. modifying the Schrödinger equation with
         - i. nonlinear terms
         - ii. stochastic terms
       - 2. von Neumann: introducing consciousness
   - ii. Bohm: the quantum potential/nonclassical determinism
   - iii. Everett: many-worlds, many-minds

The task will then be to see how the interpretation-specific features give particular expression to the generic features as we study the relation between each interpretation of quantum physics, philosophy, and finally, theology.

B. Implications of Bell's theorem independent of quantum theory

A second strategy is to unpack the implications of the actual data from quantum processes without getting entangled (!) in quantum formalism and its competing interpretations. One source is the data showing the violation of Bell's theorem, which may give us more direct access to these more general features of the quantum world, but without requiring us to get at them directly through the lens of quantum mechanics. These data will have to be accounted for by any future theory that replaces quantum physics. Thus any insights they give us regarding divine action will be less vulnerable to the problems of multiple interpretability and historical relativism.

For the purposes of the interaction with theology, this view of Bell's theorem suggests that we need not wait for the philosophical controversies to be "settled" regarding quantum physics before engaging with it. We might use the "leverage" of Bell's results to pursue the conversation and allow some of the philosophical uncertainties to play themselves out on their own.[164]

Acknowledgements

I wish to thank Nancey Murphy, John Polkinghorne, and Kirk Wegter-McNelly for their helpful comments.

Appendix B: Comparison of the Meaning of Nonlocality and (In)determinism in Bohm's Formulation and the Copenhagen Interpretation

A final suggestion for further work is to compare the approach to quantum physics by Bohm and Bohr in order to uncover a clearer understanding of the similarities and differences in the meanings they give to such key terms as (in)determinism and nonlocality and the resulting hints about quantum ontology. There are several reasons for such a comparison. First, the mathematical route from the Schrödinger structure of Copenhagen to the semi-classical context of Bohm is so straightforward that one can almost view them as formally equivalent, though the ontologies differ remarkably. Thus to compare quantum (in)determinism and nonlocality to classical determinism and locality, we will first move from Schrödinger to Bohm (who is close to Newton), and then from Newton to as close to Schrödinger as possible. Second, comparison helps us avoid the tacit assumption that Bohmian determinism is more like the classical worldview than is Copenhagen indeterminism. Clearly Bohm does limit the fundamental role of indeterminism in the Copenhagen approach by offering a deterministic alternative. However, as Jim Cushing and others[165] have stressed, Bohmian determinism is highly nonclassical in several important ways, making an explicit comparison with Newtonian determinism crucial. Third, the meaning of Bohmian nonlocality differs from that of Copenhagen nonlocality. Thus a comparison of Bohm and Bohr should help clarify just what the Bohmian "deterministic alternative" really involves, what one means by Copenhagen indeterminism, and how nonlocality comes to play in both approaches. Let us begin with the mathematical route from the Copenhagen formulation to that of Bohm, and compare the results with classical mechanics.

1. From Schrödinger to Bohm.

As is well known,[166] we can start with the Schrödinger equation (1)

$$-\left(\frac{\hbar^2}{2m}\right)\nabla^2\psi + V\psi = i\hbar\frac{\partial\psi}{\partial t}$$

(1)

and show that an additional term, which Bohm called the quantum potential *U* (2)

$$U = -\left(\frac{\hbar^2}{2m}\right)\left(\frac{\nabla^2 R}{R}\right),$$

(2)

is added to Newton's law to give a modified form of classical mechanics: (3)

$$\frac{d\mathbf{p}}{dt} = -\nabla(V + U)$$

(3)

This move requires us to change ontologies from Copenhagen to Newton, with the crucial addition of a de Broglie-like pilot wave ψ that governs the particle's motion. Bohm considers a particle of mass m following a well-defined trajectory with position x and momentum $p = mv$. Here x and p are the "hidden variables" in Bohm's account, and our knowledge of them is statistical in the classical sense: The probability $P(x,t)$ of finding the particle at x and t is given by $P = |\psi|^2$. We assume that P is conserved. For the purposes of calculation, it is convenient to represent ψ as $Re^{iS/\hbar}$ where $R(x, t)$ and $S(x, t)$ are real functions. In a crucial move, Bohm defines the momentum p in terms of the partial phase S through the "guidance condition" $p = \Lambda S$.

2. From Newton almost to Schrödinger.

We could also reverse the process and see how close we can get to the Schrödinger equation using classical mechanics as our starting point.

Thus, if we start with Newton's second law: (4)

$$\frac{d\mathbf{p}}{dt} = -\nabla V$$

(4)

and follow Bohm in setting $\psi = Re^{iS/\hbar}$ $p = mv = \Lambda S$, P = $*\psi*^2$, and in assuming that probability P is conserved, we will obtain: (5)

$$-\left(\frac{\hbar^2}{2m}\right)\left[\left(\frac{i}{\hbar}\right)\left(R\nabla^2 S + 2\nabla R\cdot\nabla S\right) - \left(\frac{R}{\hbar^2}\right)\left(\nabla S\right)^2\right] + VR = -R\frac{\partial S}{\partial t} + i\hbar\frac{\partial R}{\partial t}.$$

(5)

This is a *truncated* version of the Schrödinger equation. When written in terms of R and S, the full Schrödinger equation takes the following form: (6)

$$-\left(\frac{\hbar^2}{2m}\right)\left[\nabla^2 R + \left(\frac{i}{\hbar}\right)\left(R\nabla^2 S + 2\nabla R\cdot\nabla S\right) - \left(\frac{R}{\hbar^2}\right)\left(\nabla S\right)^2\right] + VR = -R\frac{\partial S}{\partial t} + i\hbar\frac{\partial R}{\partial t}.$$

(6)

We can summarize our results as follows:

- Schrödinger equation (1) → Bohm's modified classical mechanics (3)
- Standard classical mechanics (4) → truncated Schrödinger equation (5)

In one sense this result is completely obvious: If we know that the Schrödinger equation leads to the addition of the quantum potential U, then leaving it out of the Newtonian picture means it will be "subtracted" from the Schrödinger picture (6) leaving us equation (5). To emphasize this point, we can rewrite (5) as

$$-\left(\frac{\hbar^2}{2m}\right)\nabla^2\psi + V\psi - \left[-\left(\frac{\hbar^2}{2m}\right)\left(\frac{\nabla^2 R}{R}\right)\psi\right] = i\hbar\frac{\partial\psi}{\partial t}.$$

(7)

This is clearly the Schrödinger equation minus the quantum potential U.

In another sense, the result is intriguing, for it explicitly shows how the sources of the nonlocal and nonmechanical features associated strictly with the quantum potential U in the context of Bohm's interpretation carry over and are placed within the context of the Schrödinger equation when one moves to the Copenhagen interpretation. In particular, the quantum potential U, which acts as a *separate* factor in Bohm's "$U + V$" picture, is built into the $\nabla^2\psi$ term in the Schrödinger picture. In essence, if the Newtonian picture were correct, we could get a Schrödinger-like equation and still have classical physics, but the equation would not be a complete wave equation, since the $\nabla^2\psi$ term would be incomplete: it is missing the crucial term, $\nabla^2 R$.

I propose we view this result in the following way. The Bohmian formulation, with its delineation between and linear addition of $V + U$, allows us to separate out quantum (nonlocal and nonmechanical) aspects from the classical (local and mechanical) aspects of the governing equation $dp/dt = -\nabla(V + U)$; all of the uniquely quantum aspects of this equation are carried in one term, ∇U. The Schrödinger formulation, on the other hand, seamlessly combines the term U with the rest of the mathematical "machinery" available from the classical picture to produce one term, $\nabla^2\psi$. In this sense all of the nonlocal and nonmechanical aspects of U are hidden in and mingled with the classical aspects to yield the term $\nabla^2\psi$.

This allows us to make a further point. One could ask how many of the "quantum" features of the Copenhagen picture are carried by the wave function ψ and how many by the Schrödinger wave equation. The answer, regarding ψ, is straightforward: features such as superposition, entanglement, quantum statistics, and so on. We know this answer immediately because we explicitly and intentionally build them into the wave function. But which quantum features does that leave out? Now, from a comparison with the Bohmian picture we can conclude that the Schrödinger equation carries all those quantum aspects that we attribute to the quantum potential U; moreover, they are carried precisely within the $\nabla^2\psi$ term. This is all the more interesting since the usual motivation for the Schrödinger equation in physics textbooks, and particularly for the $\nabla^2\psi$ term, is so straightforward.[167] Thus it is all the more surprising to see how much of the overall quantum picture arises from these seemingly minimal assumptions.

In summary, then, the Bohmian formulation is highly nonclassical, involving nonlocal and nonmechanical features simply not found in the Newtonian picture. Bohm does not offer a return to classical determinism in comparison with the quantum indeterminism of Bohr. Instead both Copenhagen quantum indeterminism and Bohmian quantum determinism are highly nonclassical. The use of either view in a discussion of divine action thus requires a thorough rethinking of the conversation compared to its traditional context.

Finally, we may analyze the significance of the quantum potential's contribution to the "nonclassical" aspects of Bohm's formulation. Here I will follow the illuminating discussion by Greenstein and Zajonc.[168]

Consider the double-slit experiment from Bohm's perspective. The trajectory of each particle is influenced both by the slit through which it passes (note that it passes through only *one* slit!) and by the quantum potential U. The quantum potential, in turn, depends on the "pilot wave" ψ, which is conditioned by the entire experimental arrangement, including the fact that there are *two* slits. U has broad plateaus cut by "deep valleys . . . where U changes quickly, leading to a strong quantum force [which] guides the particles into the interference maxima and away from the minima."[169] Now, close either slit and the wave function—and thus the quantum potential—changes instantaneously, causing a force that alters the particles motion. But the nonlocality of U is even more complex that this.

The quantum potential does not fall off with distance, because U depends on R, which appears in the numerator and denominator. In this sense, the quantum potential U brings the influence of the whole system to bear on each part with an intensity and immediacy that we do not see with the classical potential V, even though the influence of either U or V can come from arbitrary distances.

Consider also a many-particle problem: Here ψ is a function of the coordinates of all n particles ψ $(x_1, x_2, \ldots, x_n, t)$. The force on the ith particle is a function of the gradient of the total potential $V + U$ at the particle's coordinates, x_i, making the problem seem like ordinary mechanics. But the force on each particle due to U depends on the position of *all* the particles in the system through the factor R because

$$U = -\left(h^2/2mR\right)\left(\nabla_1^2 + \nabla_2^2 + \ldots + \nabla_n^2\right)R.$$

Thus it depends on the coordinates of all of the particles, both through the ∇^2 terms and through the factor $R = R$ $(x_1, x_2, \ldots, x_n)$, and not just on the coordinates of the particle at x_i. As Cushing stresses, "the many-body quantum potential entangles the motion of the various particles."[170] In essence, the force is a function of a *local* gradient on a *nonlocal* potential U as well as on a *local* potential V. It thus combines both classical and nonclassical features in producing the net acceleration of each individual particle.

Finally, quantum nonlocality is highly *nonmechanical* in the sense that the quantum potential U depends not only on the positions of the other particles, but also on their wave functions and thus on the state of the entire system. As Greenstein and Zajonc note, Bohm's interpretation "goes beyond simple nonlocality, and calls upon us to see the world as an undivided whole. Even in a mechanical world of parts, the interactions between the parts could, in principle, be nonlocal but still mechanical. Not so in the quantum universe."[171]

Endnotes: Chapter 5

[1] This is a revised version of the original paper, "Divine Action and Quantum Mechanics: A Fresh Assessment," in *Quantum Mechanics: Scientific Perspectives on Divine Action* (hereafter *QM*), Robert John Russell, Philip Clayton, Kirk Wegter-McNelly and John Polkinghorne, eds. (Vatican City State: Vatican Observatory and Berkeley: Center for Theology and the Natural Sciences, 2001), 298–328.

[2] For an introduction to quantum mechanics for science undergraduates, see P. C. W. Davies, *Quantum Mechanics* (London: Routledge & Kegan Paul, 1984). Technical sources include Eugen Merzbacher, *Quantum Mechanics* (New York: John Wiley & Sons, 1961); Kurt Gottfried, *Quantum Mechanics* (New York: W. A. Benjamin, 1966); and the classic work, P. A. M. Dirac, *The Principles of Quantum Mechanics* (Oxford: Clarendon, 1958, revised fourth edition). Recent works for the general reader include J. C. Polkinghorne, *The Quantum World* (Princeton, N.J.: Princeton Scientific Library, 1989).

[3] Some of the key works include: Nancey Murphy, "Divine Action in the Natural Order: Buridan's Ass and Schrödinger's Cat," in *Chaos and Complexity: Scientific Perspectives on Divine Action,* Robert John Russell, Nancey Murphy, and Arthur Peacocke, eds. (Vatican City State: Vatican Observatory Publications; Berkeley, Calif.: Center for Theology and the Natural Sciences, 1995), 325–58 (hereafter *CAC*); Thomas F. Tracy, "Particular Providence and the God of the Gaps," in ibid., 289–324, and George F. Ellis, "Ordinary and Extraordinary Divine Action: The Nexus of Interaction," in ibid., 359–96; Ian G. Barbour, "Five Models of God and Evolution," in *Evolutionary Molecular Biology,* ed. Robert John Russell, William R. Stoeger, S. J and Francisco J. Ayala (Vatican City State: Vatican Observatory Publications; Berkeley, Calif.: Center for Theology and the Natural Sciences, 1998) (hereafter *EMB*), 419–42; see as far back as idem, *Issues in Science and Religion* (New York: Harper & Row, 1971). Other sources include Mark W. Worthing, *God, Creation, and Contemporary Physics* (Minneapolis: Fortress Press, 1996), esp. 130–46; Christopher F. Mooney, *Theology and Scientific Knowledge: Changing Models of God's Presence in the World* (Notre Dame: Notre Dame Press, 1996), esp. chap. 3, 108–10; Philip Clayton, *God and Contemporary Science* (Edinburgh: Edinburgh University Press, 1997), esp. chap. 7, 8. Some scholars have raised objections to the approach taken by these scholars. See, for example, Arthur Peacocke, "God's Interaction with the World: The Implications of Deterministic 'Chaos' and of Interconnected and Interdependent Reality," in *CAC*, 279–81. For an interesting recent response to Peacocke in terms of quantum indeterminacy, see John J. Davis, "Quantum Indeterminacy and the Omniscience of God," *Science and Christian Belief* 9.2 (October 1997): 129–44, and Peacocke's reply in the same volume. See also John C. Polkinghorne, "The Metaphysics of Divine Action," in *CAC*, esp. 152–3; articles in Niels H. Gregersen et al., eds., *Studies in Science & Theology 1996: Yearbook of the European Society for the Study of Science and Theology*, vols. 3 and 4, *The Concept of Nature in Science & Theology, Parts I and II* (Geneva: Labor et Fides, 1997); articles in *Science and Christian Belief* 7.2 (October 1995); and George Murphy, "Does the Trinity Play Dice?" *Zygon* 51.1 (March 1999).

[4] Karl Heim, *The Transformation of the Scientific World* (London: SCM, 1953). For a lucid discussion of Heim and others, see John Y. Fenton, "Random Events and the Act of God," *Journal of the AAR*, 25 (March, 1967): 50–57.

[5] Heim, ibid., 156.

[6] E. L. Mascall, *Christian Theology and Natural Science: Some Questions in their Relations*, The Bampton Lectures, 1956 (London: Longmans, 1956), 200–1. I am grateful to Kirk Wegter-McNelly for calling my attention to Mascall's ideas.

[7] William G. Pollard, *Chance and Providence: God's Action in a World Governed by Scientific Law* (London: Faber and Faber, 1958).

[8] Ibid., 86.

[9] Ibid., 92, 97.

[10] Ibid., 56.

[11] Ian Barbour, *Issues in Science and Religion* (New York: Harper Torchbook, 1966), 428–30.

[12] Donald M. MacKay, *Science, Chance and Providence* (Oxford: Oxford University Press, 1978), 33.

[13] Mary Hesse, "On the Alleged Incompatibility between Christianity and Science," in *Man and Nature*, Hugh Montefiore, ed. (London: Collins, 1975), 121–31; see 128 for the quotation.
[14] Ibid., 130.
[15] It is increasingly clear, in my opinion, that Arthur Peacocke presupposes a compatibilist view of divine action and therefore does not see NIODA as genuinely "non-interventionist." (See chapter 4.)
[16] Robert John Russell, "Creation and Modern Cosmology: Conflict or Synthesis?" (CTNS: unpublished, 1982); see also Andrew J. Dufner, S. J., and Robert John Russell, "Foundations in Physics for Revising the Creation Tradition," in *Cry of the Environment: Rebuilding the Christian Creation Tradition*, ed. Philip N. Joranson and Ken Butigan (Santa Fe, NM: Bear & Company, 1984), 163–80.
[17] Robert John Russell, "Beyond Dialogue: The Mutually Constructive Interaction of Science and Theology" (Annual Meeting, The American Association for the Advancement of Science, New York City: unpublished, 1984), 13.
[18] The text was the George Hitching Terriberry Memorial Lecture at Tulane University, September, 1988. It was published in Robert John Russell, "Christian Discipleship and the Challenge of Physics: Formation, Flux, and Focus," in *Reasoned Faith: Essays on the Interplay of Faith and Reason*, The George Hitching Terriberry Memorial Lecture, ed. Frank T. Birtel (New York: Crossroad, 1993), 25–55; with previous versions published in Robert John Russell, "Christian Discipleship and the Challenge of Physics: Formation, Flux, and Focus," *CTNS Bulletin* 8.4 (1988) Autumn; and Robert John Russell, "Christian Discipleship and the Challenge of Physics: Formation, Flux, and Focus," *Perspectives on Science and Christian Faith* 42.3 September (1990).
[19]Werner Heisenberg, *Physics and Philosophy: The Revolution in Modern Science* (New York, N.Y.: Harper & Row, 1958), 185.
[20]The invitation to give the inaugural lecture in the new Templeton/ASA lecture series in 1994 provided an opportunity to expand these themes in more detail. See Robert John Russell, "Cosmology and the New World of Faith," Templeton/ASA Lectures Series ([unpublished], 1994), 12–13.
[21] Robert John Russell, "Cosmology from Alpha to Omega," *Zygon: Journal of Religion & Science* 29.4 (December 1994): 567–68.
[22] See the discussion in R. J. Russell, "Quantum Physics in Philosophical and Theological Perspective," in *Physics, Philosophy and Theology: A Common Quest for Understanding* (hereafter *PPT*), Robert J. Russell, William R. Stoeger, and George V. Coyne, eds. (Vatican City State: Vatican Observatory, 1988).
[23] How macroscopic phenomena first arose out of the quantum processes of the very early universe remains a profound problem. Here I simply take it for granted that we can describe both our ordinary experience using classical science and our subatomic data using quantum physics, and look to their relation.
[24] FD and BE statistics are intimately connected to the indistinguishability of fundamental particles ("all electrons are identical") and their spin: □ is anti-symmetric for fermions (which carry odd spin) and symmetric for bosons (which carry even spin). Indistinguishability and spin are strictly quantum features, and yet they too give rise to the ordinary features of the classical world. The space-like correlations in these statistics are also intimately related to the problem of nonlocality in quantum physics, as Bell's theorem reveals (discussed below). A full discussion of spin-statistics requires a relativistic treatment of quantum physics. Thus, in a strict sense, it lies outside the confines of the present topic, nonrelativistic quantum physics, although quantum statistics can be warranted at least in part on the basis of indistinguishability.
[25] Technically, superfluidity and superconductivity involve both FD and BE statistics, as Carl York pointed out (private communications).
[26] FD statistics, $n(E) \sim 1/(e^{E/kT} + 1)$, and BE statistics, $n(E) \sim 1/(e^{E/kT} - 1)$, both approach Boltzmann statistics, namely $n(E) \sim 1/e^{E/kT}$, at energies $E >> kT$. Here n(E) is the average number of particles with energy E, k is Boltzmann's constant and T is the equilibrium

temperature of the system. Even at low energies, BE statistics still resemble the classical form, but FD statistics are strikingly different. See for example Figures 11:1–3 and Table 11:1 in Robert Eisberg and Robert Resnick, *Quantum Physics of Atoms, Molecules, Solids, Nuclei, and Particles* (New York: John Wiley & Sons, 1974), chap. 11.

[27] For an early example of the subtleties involved here, see Barbour, *Issues in Science and Religion*, 308, and compare with 309, including footnote #4. For a more recent example, see John Polkinghorne, "The Quantum World," in *PPT*, 334.

[28] See my "Quantum Physics in Philosophical and Theological Perspective" in *PPT*, endnote 2, 369.

[29] Here the life of a cat hangs in the balance over a single radioactive decay event. If the event does not occur, the cat is spared; if it does, it triggers a Geiger counter whose voltage spike causes lethal gas to be released into a chamber holding the cat. For a readable account and a helpful discussion of the underlying philosophical issues, see John Gribbin, *In Search of Schrödinger's Cat* (New York: Bantam, 1984); idem, *Schrödinger's Kittens and the Search for Reality* (Boston: Little, Brown and Co., 1995). I dislike this story for obvious reasons, but it has become too famous to easily "sanitize."

[30] Even this statement needs careful qualification. See Michael Berry, "Chaos and the Semiclassical Limit of Quantum Mechanics (Is the Moon There When Somebody Looks?)," in *QM*.

[31] George F. R. Ellis, "The Thinking Underlying the New 'Scientific' World-Views," in *EMB*, 251–80.

[32] In 1966, Ian Barbour provided what is still one of the most helpful surveys of these interpretations. Barbour, *Issues in Science and Religion*, chap. 10, sec. 3. See also Barbour, *Religion in an Age of Science*, 101–4. For a more recent and accessible account see Nicholas Herbert, *Quantum Reality: Beyond the New Physics* (Garden City, N.Y.: Anchor Press; Doubleday, 1985). See also R. J. Russell, "Quantum Physics in Philosophical and Theological Perspective," in *PPT*; Sheldon Goldstein, "Quantum Theory Without Observers," *Physics Today* (March and April, 1998); and John Polkinghorne, "Physical Process, Quantum Events, and Divine Agency," in *QM*, 181–90. For a technical survey of the philosophical problems in quantum physics see Max Jammer, *The Philosophy of Quantum Mechanics* (New York: Wiley, 1974); Michael Redhead, *Incompleteness, Nonlocality, and Realism: A Prolegomenon to the Philosophy of Quantum Mechanics* (Oxford: Clarendon Press, 1987); James T. Cushing and Ernan McMullin, eds., *Philosophical Consequences of Quantum Theory: Reflections on Bell's Theorem* (Notre Dame: University of Notre Dame Press, 1989); Abner Shimony, "Conceptual Foundations of Quantum Mechanics," in *The New Physics*, Paul Davies, ed. (Cambridge: Cambridge University Press, 1989); James T. Cushing, *Quantum Mechanics: Historical Contingency and the Copenhagen Hegemony* (Chicago: University of Chicago Press, 1994); C. J. Isham, *Lectures on Quantum Theory* (London: Imperial College Press, 1995).

[33] Cushing, *Quantum Mechanics*, 24.

[34] In his famous 1927 Como Lecture Bohr argued that "the spacetime coordination and the claim of causality, the union of which characterizes the classical theories, [are] complementary but exclusive features of the description, symbolizing the idealization of observation and definition respectively." For a convenient source and translation, see Jammer, *The Philosophy of Quantum Mechanics*, 86–94. See also Cushing, *Quantum Mechanics*, 28.

[35] See Cushing, *Quantum Mechanics*, for a discussion of Leslie Ballentine's arguments about Bohr versus Einstein. Cushing views Stapp's interpretation as close to Ballentine's statistical approach.

[36] Werner Heisenberg, *Physics and Philosophy: The Revolution in Modern Science* (New York: Harper, 1958); idem, *Physics and Beyond* (New York: Harper & Row, 1971). Heisenberg apparently had a "two truths" view of the relation between science and religion, with religion as a set of ethical principles. See for example idem, *Across the Frontiers*, Peter Heath, trans. (New York: Harper & Row, 1974/1971), chap. 16. He also argued that "the extension of scientific methods of thought far beyond their legitimate limits of application led to the much deplored division" between

science and religion; idem, *Philosophic Problems of Nuclear Science* (Greenwich, Conn.: Fawcett, 1952), chap. 1.

[37] Henry Margenau, "Advantages and Disadvantages of Various Interpretations of the Quantum Theory," *Physics Today* 7 (1954), quoted in Barbour, *Issues in Science and Religion*, 303–4. For earlier sources and references on the ontological interpretation of indeterminacy, see H. Margenau, "Reality in Quantum Mechanics," *Philosophy Science* 16 (1949): 287–302; Heisenberg, *Philosophic Problems of Nuclear Science*; K. Popper, *Quantum Theory and the Schism in Physics* (London: Hutchinson, 1956).

[38] Cushing, *Quantum Mechanics*, 32.

[39] C. J. Isham writes: "The most common meaning attached to probability in classical physics is an epistemic one. However, unless hidden variables are posited, the situation in quantum theory is very different. In particular, there are *no* underlying microstates of whose precise values we are ignorant. If taken seriously, such a view of the probabilistic structure in quantum theory entails a radical departure from the philosophical position of classical physics . . ." (*Lectures on Quantum Theory*, 131–32). According to Paul Davies, "Prior to quantum theory, physics was ultimately *deterministic*. The quantum factor . . . implies that we can never know in advance what is going to happen. We shall see that this indeterminism is a universal feature of the micro-world" (*Quantum Mechanics,* 4). Ian Barbour writes: ". . . [*A*]*lternative potentialities* exist for individual agents. We urged, in accordance with critical realism, that the Heisenberg Principle is an indication of objective indeterminacy in nature rather than the subjective uncertainty of human ignorance." (*Issues in Science and Religion*, 315–16; see also his *Religion in an Age of Science* [New York: HarperCollins, 1990], 123).

[40] Shimony not only argues for one philosophical interpretation against its competitors, but that he allows his philosophical commitments (that is, to realism) to drive his scientific research program in new directions that seek to revise current physics; Shimony, "Search for a Worldview Which Can Accommodate Our Knowledge of Microphysics," in *Philosophical Consequences of Quantum Theory*, Cushing and McMullin, eds., 25–37, esp. 34. Shimony's work exemplifies what I call the "creative mutual interaction." I use this term to emphasize the bidirectional ways that theology, philosophy, and science relate: Not only do we have the usual way—the critical analysis and incorporation of scientific results in constructive theology—but we also see, in Shimony's case and others, the positive role played by theological and philosophical commitments in the construction of new theories in science. Obviously, for such theories to count as scientific, they must be delimited by the assumptions of methodological naturalism and prove their worth empirically. See Robert John Russell, "Eschatology and Physical Cosmology: A Preliminary Reflection," in *The Far Future: Eschatology from a Cosmic Perspective*, ed. George F. R. Ellis (Philadelphia: Templeton Foundation Press, 2002), 276–79, 284–87; and Robert John Russell, "Bodily Resurrection, Eschatology and Scientific Cosmology: The Mutual Interaction of Christian Theology and Science," in *Resurrection: Theological and Scientific Assessments*, ed. Ted Peters, Robert John Russell and Michael Welker (Grand Rapids: Eerdmans, 2002), 3–30. Please note a confusing term in the figure: The term "observation/observation" appears in the upper half marked "theology." What I meant is that in theology our "data" is subject to a double hermeneutic: we are interpreting the interpretations of people about their experience. Thus our "observations" are really "observations about observations." Please note an error in the figure, too: Instead of "theory" the word "model" should occur at the top of the left-hand movement from data to theories in both upper and lower portions of the figure. I wish to thank Nancy Wiens for pointing out these errors to me. They will be corrected in future publications.

[41]See for example Redhead, *Incompleteness, Nonlocality, and Realism*; Cushing & McMullin, eds., *Philosophical Consequences of Quantum Theory*; Isham, *Lectures on Quantum Theory*.

[42]John Polkinghorne stresses this concern frequently, citing Bohm's deterministic account frequently as a reason not to use quantum physics for an indeterministic metaphysics within a theory of divine action.

[43]See again Shimony, "Conceptual Foundations of Quantum Mechanics," 34.

[44]Nicholas T. Saunders offers an overview of several interpretations of quantum physics and of various theological notions of providence and divine action. He then delineates four ways of relating divine action and quantum mechanics. The first three are that God alters the wavefunction between measurements, that God makes measurements on a quantum system, or that God alters the probabilities of obtaining a particular result. Curiously they do not describe the actual positions of *any* of the principal scholars that I know of in theology and science, nor does Saunders claim that they do, so their enumeration seems more of an academic exercise than a substantive argument.

I agree in a limited way with Saunders that several of us do fit into his fourth approach. As Sanders rather brashly puts it, "God ignores the probabilities predicted by orthodox quantum mechanics and simply controls the outcomes of particular measurements." I would rather more carefully say that God knows the probabilities predicted by orthodox quantum mechanics, since these after all describe what are ultimately the acts of God, and that rather than unilaterally controlling nature God acts with nature—since this is mediated divine action— to bring about the outcomes of particular measurements consistent with the probabilities given before the event occurs and consistent with the fact that specific outcomes might have an indirect effect at the macroscopic level which God wants to bring about and which those of faith would take correctly as acts of God's special providence.

[45] See Nicholas T. Saunders, "Does God Cheat at Dice? Divine Action and Quantum Possibilities," *Zygon* 35.4 (September 2000): 517–44.

[46]Isham, *Lectures on Quantum Theory*, chap. 8.

[47] Jeremy Butterfield, "Some Worlds of Quantum Theory," in *QM*.

[48]Note here the crucial role of irreversibility in defining "measurement." In order to distinguish a measurement from the ordinary time development of a quantum system as governed by the Schrödinger equation, we must refer to the process as irreversible. Recent research on decoherence sheds some light on the way irreversibility in quantum mechanics comes about, but the problem of defining "measurement" is far from settled. For a helpful discussion see Polkinghorne, "Physical Process" and Berry, "Chaos."

[49]In the example of a Geiger counter, a charged particle passes through a cylindrical ionization chamber filled with gas and containing a wire stretched along its center axis. The chamber walls are negatively charged, the wire charged positively, and a counter measures their relative voltage. The passage of the charged particle triggers a cascade of ionized gas which eventually produces a voltage spike on the counter.

[50]Although phenomena such as superfluidity and superconductivity are not specifically what I mean by "micro-macro" interactions, they do represent essentially quantum effects at the macro level. The same point is made in George Ellis, "Quantum Theory and the Macroscopic World," in *QM,* 259–91.

[51]Barbour, *Issues in Science and Religion*, 304; note his reference to Northrop.

[52]In a similar way Ellis acknowledges the unsettled issues surrounding measurement but proceeds to discuss quantum physics and divine causality; see Ellis, "Ordinary and Extraordinary Divine Action," 369.

[53]Yet another aspect of the measurement problem involves the so-called collapse of the wave function. When we represent elementary particles as interacting with each other, the wave function which describes them evolves continuously in time. Yet when we consider them as interacting with a classical system—such as the charged particle and the "macroscopic" Geiger counter—the wave function describing the quantum system changes instantaneously and discontinuously, a change often referred to as the collapse of the wave function. But if the classical system—here, the Geiger counter—is itself composed of fundamental particles, why doesn't the wave function for the entire system—particle plus Geiger counter—evolve continuously? Alternatively, when and where does the wave function of the entire system collapse? The options range all the way from the first interaction between the elementary particle and a gas molecule to the conscious observation of the Geiger counter. Any careful attempt to answer this question leads us directly into complex and unsettled issues in the philosophical foundations of quantum mechanics, and they are made even

more complicated when Bell's theorem and its implications about nonlocality and nonseparability are considered. The theoretical issues lying behind the measurement process thus form one of the most subtle and most controverted topics in all of quantum physics. A full treatment would take far more space than is possible here.

[54]In 2001 Michael Ruse provided a thoughtful and often conciliatory approach to the relations between Darwinism and theism. Unfortunately, though, he reiterates the charge that the appeal to quantum mechanics is an epistemic form of the "gaps" argument without discussing previous published responses by Tracy, Ellis, Murphy, and myself in which we argue in detail why we believe it is not a gaps argument. He also points out that it leads to the problem of theodicy as I stress here and elsewhere. See Michael Ruse, *Can a Darwinian Be a Christian? The Relationship Between Science and Religion* (Cambridge: Cambridge University Press, 2001), 86–8, 91–2.

[55]Thomas F. Tracy, "Particular Providence and the God of the Gaps," in *CAC*, 289–324.

[56]Dietrich Bonhoeffer, *Letters and Papers from Prison*, Eberhard Bethge, ed., enlarged ed. (New York: MacMillan, 1979), 311.

[57]Tracy defines "causal gaps" as "breaks in the order of what is commonly called 'event causation' . . . which occur when events are not uniquely determined by their antecedents. Where causal gaps occur, later events cannot be deduced from a description of their antecedents and deterministic laws of nature"; "Particular Providence and the God of the Gaps," in *CAC*, 290.

[58]Finally to what degree does one wish to relate God's action in nature and the actual events and processes in nature? The answers to this crucial question arise out of the early differences between Augustine's omnimiraculous view of nature and Aquinas's austere distinction between primary and secondary causality, with the latter (arguably) providing a crucial element in the intellectual climate out of which modern science grew—and with it the concept of the laws of nature as it first flourished in the age of Newton and his mechanical view of both terrestrial and celestial causality. My own view marginally favors Aquinas.

[59]"To say that each sub-atomic event is solely an act of God would be a version of occasionalism, with all [its] attendant theological difficulties." These include: exacerbating the problem of evil, verging on pantheism, and conflicting with the belief that God gives the world an independent existence. Murphy, "Divine Action in the Natural Order," *CAC*, 340.

[60]Ibid., 342.

[61]Once again, this approach differs radically from that of "intelligent design" since, unlike ID, it does not introduce "agency" into physics, biology, or cosmology. Instead it is a theological account of divine action that appropriates an indeterministic interpretation of quantum mechanics and, in chapter 6, shows the significance of this for giving evolutionary theory a theistic interpretation within Christian theology, thus bringing the natural sciences into Christian theology.

[62]Tracy, "Particular Providence," *CAC*, 318–319. Note his reference to Barbour in footnote #66 where Barbour discusses Pollard's views about how divine action at the quantum level would not violate science.

[63] Murphy, "Divine Action in the Natural Order," *CAC,* 331, 338.

[64]Arthur Peacocke, *Creation and the World of Science* (Oxford: Clarendon, 1979), 95–96.

[65]Again at the time it may not have been entirely clear to all writers to make the distinction I am stressing here between compatibilist and incompatibilist views of divine action and the distinct meanings of non-interventionism which follow from these views.

[66]See for example *God and the New Biology* (San Francisco, Calif.: Harper & Row, 1986), 62, for a reference to Monod but no reference to Pollard. See also *Theology for a Scientific Age: Being and Becoming—Natural, Divine, and Human*, enlarged edition (Minneapolis, Minn.: Fortress Press, 1993), 117–18; there is no reference to Pollard.

[67]Arthur Peacocke, "God's Interaction with the World: The Implications of Deterministic 'Chaos' and of Interconnected and Interdependent Complexity," in *CAC*, 279. In the mid-1980s, David Bartholomew provided a careful analysis with special attention to Peacocke's views, but he too downplayed the role of quantum physics, claiming that "from the theological point of view, it matters little whether or not all chance can be expressed in deterministic terms." See *God of Chance*, (London: SCM Press, 1984), 68.

[68]See chapter 6, section 4A.
[69]John Polkinghorne, *One World: The Interaction of Science and Theology* (London: SPCK, 1986), 72.
[70]John Polkinghorne, *Science and Creation: The Search for Understanding* (London: SPCK, 1988), 58; idem, "The Quantum World," in *PPT*, 339–40.
[71]John Polkinghorne, *Science and Providence: God's Interaction with the World* (Boston: New Science Library, 1989), 27–28.
[72]John Polkinghorne, *Reason and Reality: The Relationship between Science and Religion* (Philadelphia: Trinity Press International, 1991), 40–41.
[73]Polkinghorne, "The Metaphysics of Divine Action," in *CAC*, 147–56; see 152–3 in particular.
[74] Robert John Russell, "Special Providence and Genetic Mutation: A New Defense of Theistic Evolution," in *EMB*, 204, footnote #39, see also 211–12.
[75]Unfortunately, Polkinghorne has continued to use the term "episodic" to describe what he considers to be the limitations of this approach in very recent work. See Polkinghorne, "Physical Process," secs. 4, 5.
[76] I have been urged by a number of colleagues to include this section here even though it was written several years after this chapter was published in *QM* because Saunders's—in my view erroneous—criticism of the QM-SDA project, and Wildman's—in my view 'off the mark'—assessment of them, have—unfortunately—received so much attention.
[77] Nicholas Saunders, *Divine Action & Modern Science* (Cambridge: Cambridge University Press, 2002), see especially chapters 5, 6. See also Saunders, "Does God Cheat at Dice?" *Zygon: Journal of Religion and Science*, 35.3 (September 2000): 517–544.
[78] Saunders, *Divine Action & Modern Science*, 215, author's italics.
[79] Arthur Peacocke, "Editorial: Problems in Contemporary Christian Theology," *Theology and Science* 2.1 (April 2004): 2–3.
[80] Saunders, "Does God Cheat at Dice?"
[81] See *QM*, 296, footnote #11.
[82] Saunders, *Divine Action & Modern Science.*
[83] Ibid., 110–115.
[84] Ibid., 155.
[85] Ibid., 156.
[86] William Stoeger, S. J., "Contemporary Physics and the Ontological Status of the Laws of Nature," in *Quantum Cosmology and the Laws of Nature,* eds. Robert J. Russell, Nancey C. Murphy, and Chris J. Isham, Scientific Perspectives on Divine Action Series (Vatican City State/Berkeley, Calif.: Vatican Observatory Publications; Center for Theology and the Natural Sciences, 1993), 468, 209–34.
[87] Frankly it never even occurred to me that someone would take the view that quantum mechanics' statistical laws are 1) ontological *and* 2) govern each and every quantum event. Saunders, *Divine Action & Modern Science*, see especially chaps 5, 6.
[88] Wesley J. Wildman, "The Divine Action Project, 1988–2003," *Theology and Science* 2.1 (April 2004): 31–75.
[89] Ibid., 57.
[90] Ibid., 41, my italics.
[91] Wildman admits that "no [Divine Action Project] participant accepts this four-fold criterion as the desirable goal for a theory of SDA." Nevertheless he constructs his assessment of the SDA proposals, including ibid., Table 2, 43, as though the tetralemma were a credible criterion and the proposals are constructed to avoid being evaluated by it—neither of which I agree with.
[92] Ibid., 56; see Saunders, *Divine Action & Modern Science*, 155.
[93] Wildman, "The Divine Action Project, 1988–2003," 72, endnote #54.
[94] Philip Clayton, "Wildman's Kantian Skepticism: A Rubicon for the Divine Action Debate," *Theology and Science* 2.2 (October 2004): 186–90; see also Philip Clayton, *The Problem of God in Modern Thought* (Grand Rapids, Mich.: Eerdmans, 2000).
[95] Thomas Tracy, "Scientific Perspectives on Divine Action? Mapping the Options," *Theology and Science* 2.2 (October 2004): see especially 199.

[96]A previous version appeared in Robert John Russell, "Barbour's Assessment of the Philosophical and Theological Implications of Physics and Cosmology," in *Ashgate Science and Religion Series*, ed. Robert John Russell (Aldershot, UK: Ashgate Publishing Company, 2004), 148–50.
[97] Barbour, *Religion in an Age of Science*, 101–04, 123.
[98] Ian G. Barbour, "Five Models of God and Evolution," in *EMB*, 432.
[99] Barbour, "Five Models of God and Evolution," 432.
[100]Barbour's response to Pollard is found in slightly different versions in several sources: Barbour, *Issues in Science and Religion*, 428–30; Barbour, *Religion in an Age of Science*, 117–18; Barbour, "Five Models of God and Evolution," 432–33; and so on. I have cited the most significant ones here. The issue about "gaps" in Barbour's earliest critique of Pollard seems to me to be more of a verbal than a substantive disagreement since Pollard is aware of the implications of ontological indeterminism for a "gapless" form of divine action.
[101] Barbour, *Religion in an Age of Science*, 222–4.
[102]Admittedly I part ways with process theology over a variety of theological issues. These range from creation *ex nihilo* to the bodily resurrection of Jesus of Nazareth and an eschatology of the transformation of the universe.
[103]They may not be theologically necessary for NIODA; indeed I believe Barbour would concur that non-interventionist divine action as such can be defended without intrinsic novelty.
[104]See for example Alfred North Whitehead, *Process and Reality*, Corrected Edition, ed. David Ray Griffin and Donald W. Sherburne (New York: Free, 1978), 3.
[105] Barbour, "Five Models of God and Evolution," 436.
[106] Murphy, "Divine Action in the Natural Order," 346–8.
[107] Ibid., 356.
[108]God may act at other levels in nature should they, too, be open to an indeterministic interpretation. This would apply most clearly in the domain of neurophysiology and thus involve an analysis of the neuro- and cognitive sciences. See Robert J. Russell, Nancey Murphy, Theo Meyering, and Michael A. Arbib, eds., *Neuroscience and the Person* (Vatican City State/Berkeley, Calif.: Vatican Observatory/Center for Theology and the Natural Sciences, 1999), hereafter *NAP*.
[109] Russell, "Quantum Physics," 344–6; Ellis, "Determinism Versus Indeterminism in Quantum Mechanics," Sec. 1.2; Murphy, "Divine Action in the Natural Order," sec. 4.3; Russell, "Special Providence and Genetic Mutation," sec. 2.3.2 (ch. 6 in this volume).
[110]Ellis, "Quantum Theory and the Macroscopic World," 261.
[111] George F. R. Ellis, "Intimations of Transcendence: Relations of the Mind and God," in *NAP*, 472; idem, "Ordinary and Extraordinary Divine Action," in *CAC*, 369–71.
[112] For an extended discussion of quantum mechanics, evolutionary biology, and divine action see chapter 6 of this volume. See also Barbour, "Five Models of God and Evolution," in *EMB*, 426.
[113]Polkinghorne, "Metaphysics of Divine Action," section 4.1. Also see Polkinghorne, "Physical Process," secs. 4 and 5, esp. 189. Quantum chaos *is* a serious problem when one tries to relate chaos theory, at least in its present state, to divine action as Polkinghorne does—particularly when an appeal is made to quantum physics to provide those variations in initial conditions of specifically chaotic systems that give rise to the appearance of "openness" in deterministic, closed systems.
[114]See in particular Arthur Peacocke, *Creation and the World of Science* (Oxford: Clarendon Press, 1979).
[115]Tracy, "Particular Providence and the God of the Gaps," in *CAC*, 318, footnote #64.
[116]Note: These claims presuppose a realist interpretation of quantum mechanics in general, and of ψ as referring, even if only partially, to the physical world. But a variety of profound problems are associated with any such realist interpretation of ψ . A striking example is given by the wave function ψ. On the one hand, ψ can be thought of as a mathematical function defined on a multi-dimensional configuration space; for *n* particles, configuration space is $3n$-dimensional. From this perspective, a realist interpretation of ψ is problematic at best. On the other hand, elementary texts on quantum mechanics routinely treat ψ as a physical wave in ordinary three-dimensional space, and not without precedent. Louis de Broglie favored a physicalist interpretation of quantum

"waves." Schrödinger too began with a realist interpretation of the wave function, but quickly ran into the problems posed by its configuration space context. For an excellent discussion and references, see Cushing, *Quantum Mechanics.*

[117] However, see Cushing, *Quantum Mechanics*, footnote #33, 251–2.

[118]For simplicity, we will work strictly in configuration space, although a momentum-space formulation is certainly an option, too. Again, for simplicity, we restrict the discussion to one spatial dimension, *x*.

[119]At the same time, God's action in regard to both ψ_s and ψ_x is fully global in the general sense that both wave functions, in principle at least, extend infinitely in both space and time.

[120]I will not extend this essay to include relativistic quantum mechanics, the union of quantum physics and special relativity, but leave it for future work.

[121]Jeremy Butterfield, "Some Worlds of Quantum Theory," in *QM*, 111–40.

[122]Raymond Y. Chiao, "Quantum Nonlocalities: Experimental Evidence," in *QM*, 17–39.

[123]See for example Chris J. Isham and John C. Polkinghorne, "The Debate Over the Block Universe," in *QCLN*, 134–44; Robert J. Russell, "Time in Eternity," *Dialog: A Journal of Theology* 39.1 (Spring 2000): 46–55.

[124]Cushing claims that Bohm gives us a preferred frame for instantaneous action, and thus allows for "true becoming"—even though Bohm works with a completely deterministic theory in which what becomes is fully predetermined. He has also argued that Bohm's approach allows for action-at-a-distance but without remote signaling either, and that it offers a unique solution to the problem of simultaneity in special relativity. Michael Redhead, however, claims that Bohm's approach is inconsistent with a stronger requirement, Lorentz invariance. See James T. Cushing, "Determinism Versus Indeterminism in Quantum Mechanics: A 'Free' Choice," in *QM,* 99–110; and Michael Redhead, "The Tangled Story of Nonlocality in Quantum Mechanics," in *QM,* 141–158.

[125]Chiao, "Quantum Nonlocalities: Experimental Evidence."

[126]These include: exacerbating the problem of evil, verging on pantheism, and conflicting with the belief that God gives creates a measure of independent existence. Murphy, "Divine Action in the Natural Order," 340.

[127]Ibid., 342–343.

[128]Ibid., 355–6.

[129]Tracy, "Particular Providence." Tracy clearly indicates that his opinion on this issue is not settled. Here he is merely exploring an interesting option to test its strengths and weaknesses.

[130]Ibid., 321–2.

[131]Barbour, *Issues in Science and Religion*, 133, 305–14, particularly 308; Arthur Eddington, *The Nature of the Physical World* (Cambridge: Cambridge University Press, 1928); Arthur Compton, *The Freedom of Man* (New Haven, Conn.: Yale University Press, 1935).

[132]See for example, Ellis, "Intimations of Transcendence," *NAP*, 469–473, and "Quantum Theory and the Macroscopic World," *QM*, esp. 266–268.

[133]Russell, "Special Providence and Genetic Mutation," 215, point 2.

[134]See Nancey Murphy's careful discussion in her "Supervenience and the Downward Efficacy of the Mental: A Nonreductive Physicalist Account of Human Action," in *NAP*, esp. 154–7. If Murphy adopts a compatibilist view then it would be clearer why she doesn't need quantum indeterminism.

[135]Tracy, "Particular Providence," 316–9.

[136]Ellis, "Ordinary and Extraordinary Divine Action," 393.

[137]See Russell, "Special Providence and Genetic Mutation," secs. 3.3, 4.

[138]I wish to note that Ted Peters rejects the use of "divine limitation" in general as a "zero-sum" view of freedom. Instead he argues for a "both-and" view theologically. In future work I wish to consider the issue of quantum physics, divine action, and human freedom from the perspective that Peters offers.

[139]It is one of the most powerful arguments used by atheists in their rejection of attempts to accommodate Christianity and Darwinian evolution. See for example Richard Dawkins, *A River Out of Eden* (New York: Basic, 1995). In fact, the argument goes back to Darwin's own writings. For the pertinent reference to Darwin's letter to Asa Gray, May 22, 1860, see Ruse, *Can a*

Darwinian Be a Christian?, 130. It is noteworthy that, even while suggesting some creative ways in which Christianity and Darwinism might find a bit of common ground (or at least some appreciation for their respective positions), Ruse underscores the fundamental problem for that common ground raised by pain and suffering in the natural world; (91–2). See also Russell, "Special Providence and Genetic Mutation," sec. 5.2.

[140]Barbour, *Religion in an Age of Science*, chap. 8, pt. 4; Denis Edwards, "Original Sin and Saving Grace in Evolutionary Context," in *EMB*, 377–92; Gary Emberger, "Theological and Scientific Explanations for the Origin and Purpose of Natural Evil," *Perspectives on Science and Christian Faith* 46.3 (September 1994): 150–8; David Ray Griffin, *God, Power, and Evil: A Process Theodicy* (Philadelphia: Westminster, 1976); John F. Haught, "Evolution, Tragedy, and Hope," in *Science & Theology: The New Consonance*, Ted Peters, ed. (Boulder, Colo.: Westview Press, 1998); Philip J. Hefner, *The Human Factor: Evolution, Culture, and Religion* (Minneapolis: Fortress Press, 1993), 271; Nancey Murphy and George F. Ellis, *On the Moral Nature of the Universe: Theology, Cosmology, and Ethics* (Minneapolis, Minn.: Fortress Press, 1996), sec. 4.1; Ruth Page, *God and the Web of Creation* (London: SCM, 1996), esp. 91–105; Peacocke, *Theology for a Scientific Age*, chap. 8, sec. 2e; Polkinghorne, *The Faith of a Physicist*, esp. 81–7, 169; Robert J. Russell, "Entropy and Evil," *Zygon* 19.4 (December 1984): 449–68; Worthing, *God, Creation, and Contemporary Physics*, 146–56. A frequent source for these ideas is John Hick, *Evil and the God of Love*, rev. ed. (San Francisco: Harper & Row, 1966).

[141]Peacocke, *Creation and the World of Science*, 166.

[142]Ellis, "Ordinary and Extraordinary Divine Action," 360, 384.

[143]Murphy, "Divine Action in the Natural Order," 342.

[144]For a helpful discussion, see Daniel Howard-Snyder, "God, Evil, and Suffering," in *Reason for the Hope Within*, M. J. Murray, ed. (Grand Rapids, Mich: Eerdmans, 1999), esp. 96–8, and his references to Peter van Inwagen, William Rowe, and, interestingly, Quentin Smith. His conclusion should give us pause: "My sense is that we have no idea how God would be justified in permitting the isolated suffering of nonhuman animals at Nature's hand." For a classic version of the challenge of theodicy involving animal pain, see John Stuart Mill, *Three Essays on Religion* (London: Longmans, Green, Reader & Dyer, 1875).

[145]Murphy and Ellis, *On the Moral Nature of the Universe*, chap. 10, sec. 4. See my response in Robert J. Russell, "The Theological Consequences of the Thermodynamics of a Moral Universe: An Appreciative Critique and Extension of the Murphy/Ellis Project," *CTNS Bulletin* 19.4 (Fall 1998): 19–24.

[146]Tom Tracy, "Evolution, Divine Action, and the Problem of Evil," in *EMB*, sec. 3. Also see the extensive discussion in Howard-Snyder, "God, Evil, and Suffering," sec. 6, of what he calls "the argument from amount."

[147]Barbour, *Issues in Science and Religion*, 430.

[148]Thomas, "Recent Thought on Divine Agency," in *Divinie Action,* B. Hebblethwaite and E. Henderson, eds. (Edinburgh: T&T Clark, 1990), 35–50.

[149] See Barbour, *Religion in an Age of Science*, 232–4; John F. Haught, "Darwin's Gift to Theology," in *EMB,* 402–5; Charles Birch, "Neo-Darwinism, Self-Organization, and Divine Action in Evolution," in *EMB,* secs. 4, 8.

[150] For the related problem of sentience, top-down causation, and consistency with science, see Barbour, *Religion in an Age of Science*, 224–7.

[151]For a careful and balanced assessment of this compatibility, see ibid., chap. 8, esp. pt. 3.

[152]Alfred North Whitehead, *Science and the Modern World* (New York: The Free Press, 1925), chap. 8; idem, *Process and Reality*, corrected ed., David Ray Griffin and Donald W. Sherburne, eds. (New York: The Free Press, 1978), 94–5, 238–9, 254.

[153]See Abner Shimony, "Quantum Physics and the Philosophy of Whitehead," in *Search for a Naturalistic World View: Volume II, Natural Science and Metaphysics* (Cambridge: Cambridge University Press, 1993/1965), chap. 19, esp. 291–2.

[154]Ibid., parts II and III, and 303.

[155]Ibid., 309. Shimony proposes a hybrid between elements in quantum theory and Whitehead's philosophy of organism (chap. 19, esp. 303–4). Shimony also points to Whitehead's treatment

of an *n*-particle system as being at odds with a quantum treatment and leading to "revolutionary philosophical implications" (300–2).

[156]Henry P. Stapp, "Quantum Mechanics, Local Causality, and Process Philosophy," *Process Studies* 7.4 (Winter 1977): 173–82; Charles Hartshorne, "Bell's Theorem and Stapp's Revised View of Spacetime," *Process Studies* 7.4 (Winter 1977): 183–91; William B. Jones, "Bell's Theorem, H. P. Stapp, and Process Theism," *Process Studies* 8.1 (Spring 1978): 250–61; Henry J. Folse Jr., "Complementarity, Bell's Theorem, and the Framework of Process Metaphysics," *Process Studies* 11.4 (Winter 1981): 259–73. See also the two recent issues of *Process Studies*, vols. 26.3–4 (1997), guest edited by Timothy Eastman and devoted to the question of the relation between process thought and physics.

[157]Jürgen Moltmann, *The Crucified God: The Cross of Christ as the Foundation and Criticism of Christian Theology* (Minneapolis: Fortress Press, 1993), 236. At the same time, he claims that only a theology of the cross can extricate us from the perpetual warfare over the problem of evil between theism, which is "tantamount to idolatry," and its "brother" atheism. Ibid., 250, 221.

[158]Wolfhart Pannenberg, *Systematic Theology*, 3 vols., G. W. Bromiley, trans. (Grand Rapids, Mich.: Eerdmans, 1998), 3:ch. 15, sec. 5, 645. See also Pannenberg's comments on Barth's response to eighteenth-century theodicies.

[159]Ibid., 1:382ff; idem, "The Doctrine of Creation and Modern Science," in *Cosmos as Creation: Theology and Science in Consonance*, Ted Peters, ed. (Nashville: Abingdon Press, 1989), esp. 162–7; idem, *Toward a Theology of Nature: Essays on Science and Faith*, Ted Peters, ed. (Louisville, Ky.: Westminster/John Knox, 1993), esp. chaps. 5, 6, 7.

[160]See for example John Polkinghorne, "Pannenberg's Engagement with the Natural Sciences," *Zygon* 34.1 (March 1999): 151–8.

[161]Ernest Simmons has developed this approach in relation to divine kenosis in "Toward a Kenotic Pneumatology: Quantum Field Theory and the Theology of the Cross," *CTNS Bulletin* 19.2 (Spring 1999): 11–16.

[162] Raymond Y. Chiao, "Quantum Nonlocalities: Experimental Evidence," in *QM*.

[163]Cushing, *Quantum Mechanics*, 56–60; here he also discusses nonlocality in Bohm's theory.

[164]An instructive example is the Mermin machine, which shows how quantum data challenge local realism without explicitly invoking quantum mechanics; N. David Mermin, "Is the Moon There When Nobody Looks?" *Physics Today* 38 (April 1985): 38. See also idem, "Can You Help Your Team Tonight by Watching on TV? More Experimental Metaphysics from Einstein, Podolsky, and Rosen," in *Philosophical Consequences of Quantum Theory*, Cushing and McMullin, eds.

[165]Cushing, *Quantum Mechanics*; see also George Greenstein and Arthur G. Zajonc, eds., *The Quantum Challenge: Modern Research on the Foundations of Quantum Mechanics* (Boston: Jones and Bartlett, 1997); John Polkinghorne, in *QM*.

[166]See for example Cushing, *Quantum Mechanics*, Appendix 1.1, 60–63.

[167]For example, in light of the Davisson-Germer experiment, we represent the state function of a particle as a superposition of de Broglie waves and construct the Schrödinger equation such that its solutions are these state functions (that is, its second partial derivative in $\boldsymbol{r}$ varies as its first partial derivative in t).

[168]Greenstein and Zajonc, *The Quantum Challenge*, chap. 6.

[169]Ibid., 145 and figures 6–11, 6–12.

[170]An important exception arises with independent systems in which the wave function factors out and the quantum potential reduces to a linear sum of terms for each system. See Cushing, *Quantum Mechanics*, 62–3.

[171]Greenstein and Zajonc, *The Quantum Challenge*, 148. In a helpful example, Greenstein and Zajonc show how even in Bohm's case the motion of electrons in an atom is not mechanical in the way the motion of the planets is.

Chapter 6

Special Providence and Genetic Mutation: A New Defense of Theistic Evolution[1]

> The phenomenon of *gene mutation* is the only one so far known in these sciences which produces gross macroscopic effects but seems to depend directly on changes in individual molecules which in turn are governed by the Heisenberg indeterminacy principle.[2]
>
> —William Pollard

> γευηθήτω τὸ θέλ ημά σου
> ("let it come about the will of thee")
> —Matthew 6:10b

1. Introduction

For well over a century, Christian theologians have found ways to accommodate or even integrate the Darwinian theory of biological evolution into systematic and philosophical theology.[3] Clearly, antagonism to evolution by many theologians has also characterized this period, in part as a defense against those voices of atheism which have sought to use Darwinian evolution to attack Christianity. Richard Dawkins, Carl Sagan, Daniel Dennett, and Jacques Monod, to name just a few of the more prominent voices, have claimed that since chance pervades biological evolution any claim about God's action in evolution is unintelligible.[4] Nevertheless, the majority of scholars who take seriously the constructive interaction between theology and science have found evolution compatible with the core conviction that the God of the Bible is the creator of the universe and all life within it. Evolution, in short, is God's way of creating life. God is both the absolute, transcendent Creator of the universe and the continuing, immanent Creator of biological complexity. God gives the universe its existence at every moment *ex nihilo* and is the ultimate source of nature's causal efficacy, faithfully maintaining its regularities which we describe as the laws of nature. God provides the world with rich potentialities built into nature from the beginning, including the combination of law and chance which characterize physical and biological processes. God also acts in, with, under, and through these processes as immanent creator, bringing about the order, beauty, complexity, and wonder of life in what can either be called God's general providence (appropriate to a more traditional, static conception of nature) or continuous creation (*creatio continua*, emphasizing the dynamic character of the universe). This broad set of views frequently designated as "theistic evolution" has representatives spanning across the conservative/liberal, Catholic/Protestant spectrum. Prominent among these thinkers are Francisco Ayala, Ian Barbour, Charles Birch, Philip Clayton, Denis Edwards, George Ellis, Niels Henrik Gregersen, John Haught, Martinez Hewlett, Wentzel van Huyssteen, Kenneth Miller, Nancey Murphy, John Paul II, Ted Peters, John Polkinghorne, Bill Stoeger, Howard van Till, and B. B. Warfield. For his vigorous reply to Jacques Monod as early as 1979, I offer special gratitude to Arthur Peacocke,[5] and for his pioneering vision of the redemption of nature amidst the confines of the pre-Vatican II era, my lasting thanks go to Teilhard de Chardin.

In this chapter I will start with a discussion of theistic evolution and attempt to press the case for divine action further. I will draw on the current and prevailing theories in evolutionary biology, namely the neo-Darwinian theory of evolution often referred to as the "Modern Synthesis."[6] Given this theory, I will explore whether we can think of God as acting not only "in, with, and through" the routine processes of evolution, to use Peacocke's rich metaphor, but also with specific intentions in particular biological events. In other words, can we think in terms of general providence as focused on both human and natural history as a whole and special providence as concerned with the individual lives of all creatures? And can we do so without being forced to argue that God's special action constitutes an intervention into these processes and a violation of the laws of nature which God has established and which God maintains? To many theologians, the connection between special providence and intervention has seemed unavoidable, leaving them with a forced option. Liberals usually restrict language about God's action to our subjective response to what is really only God's uniform, general action. Yes God creates through the combination of chance and law; indeed this combination reflects God's intentions in creating the universe as it is in the first place. But this strategy, unfortunately, does not really settle the matter. Chance in biology, from cell to organism to population and the environment, usually stands for our ignorance of what are in fact underlying, though exceedingly complex, deterministic processes. In essence, "chance and law" really only amounts to "unknown deterministic law" and "known deterministic law," and thus a causally closed mechanistic system at the level of biology. If chance is therefore mere epistemic ignorance and nature is really a closed causal system, then the claim by theistic evolutionists that God acts through chance in evolution unavoidably devolves back into the notion that God's only real actions are to have created the universe "at the beginning" and to uphold it in existence. This strategy may avoid interventionist ideas of God violating the laws of nature to act in particular events, but by reducing the meaning of God's action to a uniform and single "enactment of history," even if history is filled with apparent chance events, leads us back ontologically to what I often call "statistical deism."

Conservatives argue for special providence as the particular and objective acts of God in history and nature attested to by biblical faith, but at the price of viewing God's action as interventionist. This option threatens to undercut the conversation with science and minimize their credibility in a scientifically informed culture. At worst it can move Christians in the direction of creation science or, more beguilingly, "intelligent design."[7] In any event, interventionism is objectionable to many theologians since it seems to pit special providence against general providence. Moreover both liberal and conservative options must still face the question of theodicy: What do we say about the pain, disease, suffering, and death which pervade the long history of life on earth?

The purpose of this chapter is to move us beyond these options to a new approach: a non-interventionist understanding of special providence as a form of objective divine action (NIODA). As I have suggested in chapter 4, this approach is only possible theologically if nature, at least on some level, can be interpreted philosophically as ontologically indeterministic in light of contemporary science. This would mean that nature, according to this interpretation of science, is not an entirely closed causal system. Instead, the laws which science discovers at least at one level would suggest that nature is open. There are what could be called "created natural gaps" in the causal regularities of nature, and they are simply part of the way nature is constituted by God's creative action *ex nihilo*.

In chapter 5 I argued that quantum mechanics provides a scientific theory which is both capable of such an interpretation and passes the criteria for qualifying as a science-based approach to NIODA. In the present chapter my claim is that chance in evolution, at the level of genetic mutations, involves quantum mechanics in a crucial way. If this claim is sustained, we can view nature theologically as genuinely open to objective special providence without being forced into interventionism. God can then be understood theologically as acting purposefully within the ongoing processes of biological evolution without disrupting them or violating the laws of nature or—put more carefully theologically—without God's special providence seeming to countermand God's general providence. God's special action results in specific, objective consequences in nature, consequences which would not have resulted without God's special action. Because of the irreducibly statistical character of quantum physics, these results would be entirely consistent with the laws of science, and because of the (*ex hypothesis*) indeterminism of these processes, God's special action would not entail their disruption. Essentially what science describes without reference to God is precisely what God, working invisibly in, with, and through the processes of nature, is accomplishing. Moreover, although these results may originate *directly* at the quantum level underlying genetics, they could lead eventually to *indirect* effects on populations and species. This insight is crucial if we are to make good on our claim that this non-interventionist approach is centered on *special* and *objective* providence.

I want to emphasize the importance of this approach. It offers a synthesis of the strengths of both liberal and conservative approaches by combining special providence and non-interventionism. It undercuts the atheistic claim that evolution makes divine action impossible as well as the assumption that to defend divine action we must attack evolution. It may thereby lead to a new period of creative discussions of evolution and Christian faith as represented broadly by the term "theistic evolution." The latter is particularly important if we are to "make good" the promissory note regarding the cogency of theistic evolution made by scholars since the early 1960s and 1970s, since most approaches in the past have tended towards a kind of "statistical deism," lacking a convincing interpretation of God really acting in time in biology. It also undercuts the rationale of intelligent design as an approach to God's action in evolution by arguing for such action without divine intervention, by describing it as a theological and not a scientific theory, and without calling for a "new science" that includes an appeal to "agency" within biology. I do, however, want to acknowledge and stress the way NIODA exacerbates the problem of theodicy. My response will be that we place the topic of biological evolution within a broader theology of both creation and New Creation/redemption instead of focusing narrowly on creation alone—for God is not the source of pain and death but its redeemer.

This chapter is divided into four sections. In section 2, the claim is elaborated as a hypothesis expressed in five steps. Section 3 discusses scientific questions regarding the role of genetic mutation in biological evolution and the role of quantum mechanics in genetic mutations. Finally, section 4 turns to the question of divine purpose in evolution and the challenge of theodicy.

2. Special Providence and Genetic Mutation: A Theological Hypothesis

The theological hypothesis to be explored in this paper can be expressed in five steps:

1. The basic perspective of the hypothesis is theistic evolution: Grounded in Christian faith and life, systematic theology speaks of the Triune God as Creator: the absolute source and sustainer of an intelligible and contingent universe (*creatio ex nihilo*), and the continuing Creator who, together with nature, brings about what science describes in a neo-Darwinian framework as the biological evolution of life on earth (*creatio continua*). Thus the 3.8 billion years of biological evolution on earth *is* God's way of creating life (that is, theistic evolution).

2. Theistic evolution is explicitly expanded to include providential divine action; God is not only the ultimate cause of all existence, God is also the source of its meaning and ultimate purpose. Thus, God not only creates but guides and directs the evolution of life towards the fulfilling of God's overall, eschatological, purposes.

3. Providence includes both general and special providence, and both are taken here to be objective; God's action is here understood not only in terms of general providence, that is, not only in terms of God's providing evolution as a whole with an overall goal and purpose. It is also understood in terms of special providence—God's special action having specific and objective consequences for evolution. These consequences would not otherwise have occurred within God's general providence alone, though they can only be recognized as due to God's action through faith. Note: here I am assuming that God's special action, though special and objective, is mediated through the natural processes with which God works. Thus God's action is neither unilateral or unmediated, nor is it reducible to a natural process. Finally, I am assuming that God may act directly in particular ways at one level in nature, that this action may have indirect consequences at another level, and that these indirect consequences may be identified as acts of divine objective special providence.[8]

4. Now in a crucial move responding to the problem of rendering our theological program intelligible in light of science, I require that objective special providence be understood as non-interventionist. God does not act in a way which violates or suspends the known laws of nature but rather in a way which is intelligible from a theological perspective in light of them (though without such a theological perspective we cannot recognize the effects of God's actions as, in fact, the effects of God's action). This account of divine action does not rely on a gap in our current scientific knowledge but on the positive content of that knowledge. Because of that knowledge, our account of divine action does not require God to create gaps in an otherwise closed causal order but relies on the intrinsically open character of natural processes.

5. With these requirements in mind, I present the core hypothesis: The non-interventionist effects of God's special action occur directly at the level of, and are mediated by, those genetic variations in which quantum processes play a significant role in biological evolution. Admittedly it is possible, as others argue, that God's creative and providential action may occur directly and in a non-interventionist manner at many—perhaps even every—level of biological complexity when and as these levels emerge in natural history. Moreover, if these direct effects occur at various levels of complexity they may in turn initiate sequences of subsequent, indirect effects both via top-down and whole-part patterns of interaction between and within these levels. Nevertheless, the current hypothesis is that if divine action within evolution is to be both direct and non-interventionist, the most likely locus of these effects, and perhaps the *only* such locus, is the level of genetic mutation. It is specifically at this level that I claim such direct effects may arise in a non-interventionist way, that is, in a way entirely consistent with the known laws of physics, chemistry, and molecular biology. Moreover, if the effects of God's action do indeed occur directly at the level of genetic variation as I claim they do, they may have bottom-up consequences which indirectly affect the course of evolution. However, for this claim to hold, one must show that quantum processes may be interpreted philosophically in terms of ontological indeterminism (see chapter 5) and that quantum processes are relevant scientifically to genetic variation.

3. Genetic Mutations and Quantum Mechanics: A Scientific Question[9]

A. What role does genetic mutation play in biological evolution?

According to contemporary biological science, life on earth extends back approximately 3.5–3.9 billion years. All living species have evolved from extremely simple and small organisms whose origin is barely understood. According to the theory of evolution,[10] the vast biological complexity we see in the fossil record along with the two million species we now know to exist can be explained in terms of two fundamental principles: variation and natural selection. It starts with the fact that variations occur in the hereditary material which alter the chance for survival and procreation of organisms carrying that material. Those variations which happen to be favorable to the survival of the organism tend to spread throughout the species from generation to generation while less favorable or harmful variations tend to decrease. This process of natural selection, or "the differential reproduction of alternative hereditary variants," results in the species being increasingly adapted to its environment.[11] Hereditary variation, in turn, involves both spontaneous mutations which change one variant to another and sexual reproduction, during which these variations are recombined in countless ways. With the discovery of the molecular structure of DNA by Watson and Crick in 1956, we know that hereditary information is carried by the sequence of nucleotides whose groupings as genes form the DNA molecule. Mutations in DNA during replication can involve a substitution, an insertion, or a deletion of one or a few pairs of nucleotides in the DNA. For its consequences to be hereditary, the mutation must have occurred in the germ-line of an organism, after which it can be passed on to its progeny.[12]

Mutations can occur spontaneously in DNA, or they can be induced by ultraviolet light, X-rays, or exposure to mutagenic chemicals, often as the result of human activity. Because genetic mutations occur at random with respect to the environment of the organism, their consequences for progeny are more likely to be neutral or harmful. Occasionally, however, they increase the adaptive fit of an organism to its environment, and the mutation is subsequently passed on through successive reproduction. "Natural selection keeps the disorganizing effects of mutations and other processes in check because it multiplies beneficial mutations and eliminates harmful ones."[13] Although the rate of variation in a population can occur due to a variety of factors including mutations, genetic drift, gene flow, sexual reproduction, and non-random mating, variation per se is ultimately due to genetic mutation. According to W. F. Bodmer and L. L. Cavalli-Sforza, "mutation in its broadest sense is, by definition, the origin of new hereditary types. It is the ultimate origin of all genetic variation; without it there would be no genetic differences, and so no evolution." Masatoshi Nei claims that "mutation is the driving force of evolution at the molecular level. I have also extended this view to the level of phenotypic evolution and speciation. . . . I have challenged the prevailing view that a population of organisms contains virtually all sorts of variation and that the only force necessary for a particular character to evolve is natural selection." Francisco J. Ayala argues that "the science of genetics has provided an understanding of the processes of gene mutation and duplication by which new hereditary variations appear. . . . Gene mutation and duplication [are] the ultimate sources of all genetic variability."[14]

B. What role does quantum physics play in genetic mutation?

In this chapter I am adopting the *theological* view that God's special action can be considered as objective and non-interventionist if the quantum events underlying genetic mutations are given an indeterminist philosophical interpretation. If it can be shown scientifically that quantum mechanics plays a role in genetic mutations, then by extension it can be claimed theologically that God's action in genetic mutations is a form of objectively special, non-interventionist divine action. Moreover, since genetics plays a key role in biological evolution, I can argue by inference that God's action plays a key role in biological evolution, and my hypothesis is warranted.

Thus it is of central importance to this chapter that we discuss the precise role of quantum mechanics in certain types of genetic mutation. In specific, we must ask: 1) To what extent is variation the result of classical processes such as hydrodynamics, thermodynamics, statistical mechanics, chaotic dynamics, chemistry, geology, ecology, and so on, with their presupposition of classical chance? And 2) to what extent is variation the result of quantum physics acting at the atomic and subatomic levels, principally in genetic mutations? I believe a reasonable answer to these questions is the following:

1. Classical sources. Sources of variation in organisms which probably have an entirely classical explanation include: chemical mutagens, mechanical/physical mutagens (including physical impacts), and chromosome segregation. Sources of variation in species include genetic drift, gene flow, and non-random mating.

2. Quantum sources. Sources of variation in organisms which may include a quantum process, or at least involve a semi-classical (classical/quantum) process, include: point mutations, including base-pair substitutions, insertions, deletions; spontaneous mutations, including errors during DNA replication, repair, recombination; radiative physical mutagens, including X-rays and ultraviolet light; and crossing over.

There are, however, some very interesting and as yet unsettled questions here. Further scientific research is required for us to gain a clearer understanding of the relative importance of quantum processes and classical processes in variation, including such specific topics as chromosome number mutation (aneuploidy and polyploidy), chromosome structure mutation (including deletion, duplication, inversion, and reciprocal translocation), transposons, and DNA mutagenesis. Some of the outstanding questions yet to be explored include:

1. To what extent do point mutations arise from the interaction of a single quantum of radiation and a single proton in a hydrogen bond in a specific base?

2. How important are quantum effects in the phenomenon of crossing over?

3. To what extent does cooperativity, being a semi-classical effect extending over several base pairs, minimize the quantum aspects of genetic variation?

4. Do discrete changes in phenotype, from more interwoven macroscopic changes (for example, single versus multiple insect wings and gross macroscopic changes such as the proverbial "wings to arms" change), to changes traceable to a point mutation of a single base-pair of DNA, result in turn from a single quantum interaction, or from a series of separate base-pair mutations, each the result of a single quantum interaction?

5. What is the relative importance of monogenetic effects compared with the polygenetic effects and/or effects of the entire genome in phenotypic expression? Here "polygenetic" includes gene-gene interactions either within the same chromosome or between different chromosomes, the role of the physical structure of chromosomes, the effects of ploidy or segmental rearrangements, and one could add the interactions between clusters of adjacent genes, and so on.

6. To what extent are the linkages between genes and expression so nonlinear that the possibility of an analysis of the genetic basis of expression is seriously impaired?

7. Which are the most crucial factors leading from a point-mutation or a series of point-mutations to significant changes in the population? Clearly the amplification of the mutation to the level of the phenotype, the survival and reproduction of the phenotype, and its adaptive advantage in the population, are complex and pivotal factors. However, two other very specific factors seem particularly important. 1) The mutation must occur in the germ-line. Somatic mutations will not affect progeny, and cannot be amplified by population increase through reproduction. 2) Amplification requires the faithful replication of the DNA mutation, producing billions of copies of the original mutation. Further research may help clarify the relative importance of these specific factors to the overall process of genotype-phenotype amplification.[15]

8. To what extent do environmental factors, from such quantum factors as radiation to such classical factors as chemical and physical effects at the sub-cellular level and ecological factors at the level of populations contribute to evolution?

Thus, it is hoped that further scientific research will clarify the roles of classical and quantum sources of genetic variation and shed further light on the central theological hypothesis of this paper regarding a non-interventionist, objective interpretation of special divine action in the evolution of life.

4. Divine Purpose and Theodicy: Two Promising Issues for Further Research

A. Chance and the challenge to purposeful divine action

"Chance" in evolution raises at least two distinct challenges to divine action: 1) to the possibility of divine action as such, and 2) to the possibility of God achieving a *future* purpose by acting *in the present.* So far I have focused on the first challenge; here I will turn, briefly, to the second. The challenge arises because "chance" in evolution, as Jacques Monod notably stressed, involves more than genetic variation. In addition we must consider a variety of domains which involve random factors: the multiple paths leading to the expression of genotype in phenotype, processes influencing the survival and reproduction of progeny, changes in the ecosystem in which natural selection plays out. Finally, we must consider the juxtaposition of these two streams: the stream of (ontological) chance events at the molecular level and the second stream of (epistemic) chance events at the environmental level, where natural selection occurs. Since these streams are uncorrelated, *their* juxtaposition is random. It is in *this* sense in particular that evolution is often called "blind." How, then, can God anticipate the eventual consequences of God's action at the quantum level of genes given all these varying factors?

To respond we must first locate these questions within the perennial issue of the relation of time and eternity. Specifically, I would start with the claim that *God can know what are for us the future consequences of God's actions in our present.* In the spirit of the non-interventionist approach of this paper, I would add: *God having such knowledge must not entail a violation or suspension of the laws of nature.* Next, this claim assumes that God does not *foresee* our future from our present or *foreknow* our future by calculating the outcome from our present. Instead, God as eternal *sees* and *knows* the future in its own present time and determinate state. Such a view was given a highly nuanced formulation in classical theism, and it has been reshaped in important new ways during the twentieth century by a number of Roman Catholic and Protestant theologians.[16] The basic point, however, is that God's knowledge of what is for us the indeterminate future is God's eternal knowledge of an event in what is its own present, determinate state. Thus theologically, God can have knowledge of the future consequences of God's actions in the present.

But the commitment to non-interventionism raises an additional issue here: How are we to think about the ontological status of the future which God is to have knowledge of in light of special relativity? There are two alternative interpretations of special relativity.[17] According to one view, the flow of time is real. However, this view undercuts the reality of the future from the point of view of the present, and thus seems to undermine our claim for God's knowledge of it. According to the other view, the flow of time is an illusion (the so-called block universe view). But this view undercuts the purported indeterminism of the future from the point of view of the present, and with it, some would say, free will. My response would be to argue that both alternatives fail to do justice to the actual implications of special relativity. Instead, an ontology of events and a relational definition of time can allow for the reality of time's flow consistent with special relativity. Weaving this model eventually into the contemporary trinitarian understanding of eternity promises to add further credibility to the claim that God can indeed act purposefully in the context of biological evolution.

B. Theodicy and the need for a theology of redemption

If God is intimately at work at the level of the gene, is God not also responsible for the disease, pain, suffering, and death brought about by these genes? Why does God allow the overwhelming majority of genetic mutations to end in failure of the organism? This is, of course, the perennial problem of theodicy—Why does a just, good, and powerful God allow real evil?—but now with the domain extended beyond the human world to include all of life on earth.[18]

My first response is that to stress that pain, suffering, disease, death, and extinction are facts which any theological interpretation of evolution must deal with; it is not unique to this approach. An all-too-frequent response is to remove God from the detailed history of nature. Instead God created the universe with certain potentialities, and the history of life is the mere unfolding of these potentialities, at least until humanity comes along to respond to God's personal revelation. Pain and suffering are seen strictly as the result of human sin, whose consequences ravage humanity and an innocent environment. Disease and death are simply the natural prerequisites for the evolution of life. But restricting God's action in this way does not resolve the problem of theodicy or the question of the origin of sin. It simply raises these problems to the level of cosmology: Why did

God choose to create this universe with this particular set of laws of nature and their unfolding consequences? Could God not have produced a universe in which life evolved without death, pleasure without pain, joy without sorrow, free will without moral failure?[19] Moreover, a world thus stripped of God's special providence and tender, constant attention seems a much more troubling one to me—since its suffering would be *both* real and beyond God's care—than a world in which God is genuinely, even if inscrutably, at work, caring for every sparrow that falls. By keeping God at a distance from the suffering of nature, we thereby render that suffering all the more pointless, its outcome all the more hopeless.

A more fruitful response begins with the insight that God created this universe with the evolution of moral agents in mind. In such a universe suffering, disease, and death are in some way coupled with the conditions for genuine freedom and moral development. A variety of promising responses to this question are being pursued in the current literature. For example, those offered by Ian Barbour, George Ellis, Philip Hefner, David Ray Griffin, Arthur Peacocke, John Polkinghorne, Bill Stoeger, and Thomas Tracy, while differing in important ways, mostly tend to stress the (either voluntary or metaphysical) limitation on God's action required by genuine creaturely freedom—a theme I suggested above (section 3.3)—with a corresponding emphasis on the suffering of God with nature. More recently, Nancey Murphy and George Ellis have drawn on the Radical Reformation/Anabaptist tradition to develop a "kenotic ethic" closely connected with a "fine-tuning" response to the Anthropic Principle.[20] But can these responses account for the magnitude of suffering in nature across billions of years and the essential role of death in the evolution of biological complexity and, in at least one species, moral agency?[21]

I can only suggest ways in which my own response to theodicy seeks to incorporate these themes and ground them in the central biblical insight that the God who creates is the same God who redeems,[22] particularly as it has been developed in twentieth-century trinitarian theologians such as Karl Barth, Denis Edwards, John Haught, Catherine Mowry LaCugna, Elizabeth Johnson, Jürgen Moltmann, Wolfhart Pannenberg, Ted Peters, and Karl Rahner.[23] Redemption, in turn, takes as its cornerstone the cross of Christ, in which the power of God is revealed through suffering as transformative love. That such love will ultimately—eschatologically—overcome the evils of this world is a wager Christians make in the wake of often overwhelmingly contradictory evidence, as the history of this century's human anguish bespeaks. Now as we extend the scope of history to include the billion-year drama of life on earth, this means that evolution must somehow provide the occasion, albeit hidden, not only for *creatio continua* but even more profoundly for healing, cruciform grace to continuously *redeem* creation and guide it along with humanity into the New Creation. In a formal sense, what I am proposing is that the doctrine of creation, and with it providence, offers a necessary but, in the final analysis, inadequate framework for responding to the problem of theodicy. Instead, theodicy and the implicit problem of evil can only be addressed (though never "resolved") within the framework of a theology of redemption and New Creation. In fact, I would venture a further step. The long sweep of evolution may not only suggest an unfinished and continuing divine creation but even more radically a creation whose theological status as "good" may be fully realized only in the eschatological future.[24] If these ideas are at all sound, they underscore how their further development is not only a daunting task, but an imperative one if we are to answer not just the critics of Christian faith, but also our own internal criticisms over the inadequacy of generic theistic evolution.

I will explore the problem of suffering in nature and the eschatological response to it in the remaining chapters of this book.

Acknowledgements

I wish to express my gratitude for the careful reading of an early draft by A. Durwood Foster. I also wish to thank Ian Barbour, Dave Cole, Wim Drees, Nancey Murphy, Mark Richardson, Tom Tracy, and Kirk Wegter-McNelly for their incisive comments on more recent drafts.

Endnotes: Chapter 6

[1]Published in *Evolutionary and Molecular Biology,* Robert John Russell, William Stoeger, S. J., and Francisco Ayala, eds. (Vatican City State: Vatican Observatory Publications; Berkeley, Calif.: Center for Theology and the Natural Sciences, 1998). Hereafter *EMB.* This paper is a development of ideas previously published in "Cosmology from Alpha to Omega" *Zygon* 29.4 (1994): 557–77; "Theistic Evolution: Does God Really Act in Nature?" *Center for Theology and the Natural Sciences Bulletin,* 15.1 (Winter 1995): 19–32; "Does the 'God Who Acts' Really Act?: New Approaches to Divine Action in Light of Science," *Theology Today* 54.1 (April 1997): 43–65.

[2]William G. Pollard, *Chance and Providence: God's Action in a World Governed by Scientific Law* (London: Faber and Faber, 1958), 56, my italics.

[3] Claude Welch, "Evolution and Theology: Detente or Evasion?" in *Protestant Thought in the Nineteenth Century* (New Haven, Conn.: Yale University Press, 1985), 2:183–211; David C. Lindberg and Ronald L. Numbers, eds., *God and Nature: Historical Essays on the Encounter Between Christianity and Science* (Berkeley: University of California Press, 1986); Ian G. Barbour, *Issues in Science and Religion* (New York: Harper & Row, 1971 [originally published in 1966 by Prentice-Hall]), chapters 4, 12; Ian G. Barbour, *Religion in an Age of Science,* Gifford Lectures, 1989–1990 (San Francisco: Harper & Row, 1990), ch. 6; John H. Brooke, *Science and Religion: Some Historical Perspectives* (Cambridge: Cambridge University Press, 1991); David J. Bartholomew, *God of Chance* (London: SCM, 1984).

[4]Jacques Monod, *Chance and Necessity: An Essay on the Natural Philosophy of Modern Biology,* trans. Austryn Wainhouse (New York: Vintage Books, 1972), 112, 180. For a recent and balanced assessment see Michael Ruse, *Can a Darwinian Be a Christian? The Relationship Between Science and Religion* (Cambridge: Cambridge University Press, 2001).

[5]In his 1979 Bampton Lectures, Arthur Peacocke gave what David Bartholomew called "the most extensive and convincing reply to Monod." See A. R. Peacocke, *Creation and the World of Science: The Bampton Lectures, 1979* (Oxford: Clarendon, 1979), and Bartholomew, *God of Chance,* 34.

[6]A brief historical overview: Near the end of the nineteenth century, research into the evolution of species split into two distinct programs: evolutionary biology, including systematics, ecology, and comparative anatomy; and developmental mechanics. Out of the former grew the "modern synthesis" or what is often termed "neo-Darwinian evolution." Today this has become the most predominant field of research. The latter, developmental mechanics, led to the study of genetics on the one hand and experimental embryology on the other. The study of genetics bifurcated, with one strand reconnecting with neo-Darwinian evolution through population genetics and the other developing into molecular genetics. Experimental embryology in turn led to developmental biology which combined with molecular genetics to produce the field of developmental genetics. Evolutionary and developmental biology have recently merged into the burgeoning subdiscipline of evolutionary developmental biology known as evo-devo. Today biologists face three broad issues: the egg-to-adult transformation, the brain-to-mind transformation, and the ape-to-human transformation. Perhaps all three can be "solved" at the conjunction of evolutionary and developmental biology plus the rapidly advancing disciplines of neurobiology and genomics. I am grateful to Oliver Putz for his assistance with this overview. I am also grateful to Joshua Moritz for pointing out that the term "neo-Darwinian" as used in the history and philosophy of biology often refers not to the "Modern Darwinian Synthesis" but specifically to George John Romanes's term for the understanding of evolution later exemplified by German zoologist/cytologist August Weismann. In light of his experimental evidence, Weismann argued against Lamarckian inheritance—maintaining the separation of the germ cell line and the somatic cell line ("Weismann's Barrier"). Ernst Mayr, in particular, finds the use of "the term Neo-Darwinism for the Synthetic theory" as "problematic." See Ernst Mayr, *PSA: Proceedings of*

the Biennial Meeting of the Philosophy of Science Association, 1984, Volume Two: Symposia and Invited Papers (1984), 145–156.

[7]Unfortunately, when Christians attack Darwinian science and seek to replace it with "creation science" or to modify it with "intelligent design," they play directly into the hands of the atheist, since they implicitly agree that it is Darwinism, and not its atheistic interpretation, which must be attacked. In doing so they ignore the fact that theistic evolution offers the real attack on atheism by successfully giving a Christian interpretation to science—thus undermining the very assumption they share with atheists, namely, that a Darwinian account of biological evolution is inherently atheistic. Not only does this abandon vast realms of biology to the atheistic camp, it implicitly undercuts the integrity of those Christians who faithfully pursue research in mainstream biology, as well as the vast number of Christians who, while not biologists as such, accept it and give it a Christian interpretation. How much better it would be if those attacking evolution would attack atheism instead!

[8]In the context of this paper, I am considering the possibility that when we view events at the level of the phenotype as acts of God they are actually the indirect acts of God. According to the idea being explored here, God acts directly at the level of the genotype, and the sequence of events so initiated may result in an effect in the phenotype.

[9]Disclaimer: This section is taken from the original materials written in 1996 and, unfortunately, it has not been revised in light of scientific progress made since then.

[10]See Francisco J. Ayala, "The Evolution of Life: An Overview," in *EMB*, 21–57. Also see Neil A. Campbell, *Biology*, 2nd ed. (Redwood City, Calif.: Benjamin Cummings, 1987/1990). Dawkins, Wilson, Gould, Mayr, and others have sought to expand the Darwinian Synthesis, while others such as Kauffman, Wicken, Goodwin, and Ho suggest we move outside the neo-Darwinian paradigm. For a helpful discussion and references, see the paper by Ian G. Barbour in *EMB*. I will leave a theological response to these suggestions to another essay.

[11] Ayala, "The Evolution of Life," 36.

[12]"Chance" in evolution thus involves *both* genetic variation and the juxtaposition of these variations with complex changes in the environment of the species; Arthur Peacocke, "Biological Evolution," in *EMB,* 361–64.

[13]Ibid.

[14]W. F. Bodmer and L. L. Cavalli-Sforza, *Genetics, Evolution and Man* (San Francisco, Calif.: W. H. Freeman and Company, 1976), 139; Masatoshi Nei, *Molecular Evolutionary Genetics* (New York, N.Y.: Columbia University Press, 1987), 431; Francisco J. Ayala, "The Theory of Evolution: Recent Successes and Challenges," in *Evolution and Creation*, Ernan McMullin, ed. (Notre Dame, Ind.: University of Notre Dame Press, 1985), 78, 82. See also Ayala, "The Evolution of Life."

[15]I am indebted here, and elsewhere, to very fruitful comments and corrections from David Cole.

[16]Here I am drawing on an understanding of the relation of time and eternity generally found, though with important differences, in the writings of Karl Barth, Karl Rahner, Wolfhart Pannenberg, Jürgen Moltmann, Ted Peters, and others. The essential claim here is that eternity is not a timeless point (Augustine's *nunc*) or unending, creaturely time but rather the endlessly rich supratemporal source of creaturely time.

[17]For a recent discussion see C. J. Isham and J. C. Polkinghorne, "The Debate over the Block Universe," in *QCLN*.

[18]Indeed, if evidence of even primitive life is ever found on other worlds—and current discussion of the "Martian meteor" raises this possibility—the domain could be extended almost without limit. See the papers by Paul Davies and Julian Cela-Flores in *EMB*.

[19]One could try to answer these questions, of course, by a "many-worlds" strategy, a "these laws are the only possible ones" strategy, or a "best of all possible laws" strategy, and so on. My point is simply that removing God from the detailed history of nature

does not automatically eliminate the challenge of theodicy since it remains at the global level of cosmology: Why did God create *this* universe?

[20]Nancey Murphy and George F. R. Ellis, *On the Moral Nature of the Universe: Theology, Cosmology, and Ethics* (Minneapolis, Minn.: Fortress Press, 1996), esp. chap. 10, section 4.

[21]See, for example, Holmes Rolston III, "Does Nature Need to Be Redeemed?" *Zygon* 29.2 (June, 1994): 205–29; see also Thomas Tracy in *EMB* and Ellis in *CAC*.

[22]In Christian theology, the link between creation and redemption is made very explicit: The Word made flesh, the Word through whom all things were made, is also the same Word whose self-emptying kenosis in revealed in the Incarnation and through the Cross. The Logos and Wisdom of creation is the slain Lamb who atones for all human sin. The Alpha Logos, whose "trace" is the laws of physics, is the mothering healer of the suffering and death of all that lives and the eschatological hope of the New Creation, the Omega of the universe.

[23]For a helpful perspective on the many voices, see Ted Peters, *God as Trinity: Relationality and Temporality in Divine Life* (Louisville, Ky.: Westminster/John Knox Press, 1993); see also Edwards and Haught in *EMB*.

[24]Pannenberg stresses this point at the close of his systematics. See Wolfhart Pannenberg, *Systematic Theology*, vol. 3 (Grand Rapids, Mich.: Eerdmans, 1998), chap. 15, esp. 645–46. See also Karl Barth, *Church Dogmatics*, vol. 3.2, *The Doctrine of Creation*, G. W. Bromiley and T. F. Torrance, eds. (Edinburgh: T. & T. Clark, 1958), esp. 385–414. Peters makes the point indirectly by setting it within a broader holism in which the term "creation" includes the whole history of the universe. See Ted Peters, *God, the World's Future: Systematic Theology for a Postmodern Era* (Minneapolis, Minn.: Fortress Press, 1992), 134–39, 307–9; idem, ed., *Cosmos as Creation: Theology and Science in Consonance* (Nashville, Tenn.: Abingdon, 1989), 96–97.

Chapter 7

Entropy and Evil: The Role of Thermodynamics in the Ambiguity of Good and Evil in Nature[1]

Introduction

The power of evil is tragically self-evident. The domain of the second law of thermodynamics extends throughout science. Is there any substantive relationship between entropy and evil? Before responding to this question, one must first acknowledge the methodological problems introduced by the very nature of a field as inhomogeneous as religion and science.

Faced with similar procedural questions, others have compared scientific and religious theories in terms of a hierarchy of levels of theories,[2] a relationship of consonance of concepts,[3] or a formal correspondence as communities characterized by paradigms and research programs.[4] In this chapter, I have chosen to frame the discussion in terms of *metaphor,* following the work of Ian Barbour and Sallie McFague.[5] I will define "metaphor" as an analogy between the normal context in which a word obtains its meaning and a novel context in which some new aspects of the concept are emphasized. As Paul Ricoeur and others stress, metaphors are more than mere similes, since they include a negative as well as a positive analogy: both an "is" and an "is not." According to Ian Barbour, a metaphor is extendable to other new contexts, beckoning us with a "suggestive invitation to the discovery of further similarities."[6] I would add that metaphors ought to draw on concepts which have some independent justification in each field and should produce some new insight about the novel context in which they operate.

With this notion of metaphor as my working methodological assumption, this chapter will be something of an initial survey, a reconnaissance project looking for general areas for future inquiry. I will begin with an overview of the physics of entropy, restricted primarily to classical thermodynamics, and the theological interpretation of evil as found within representative periods of the Christian tradition. Then I will explore similarities and dissimilarities in the proposed metaphorical relationship between evil and entropy. Finally I will analyze the Augustinian-Niebuhrian understanding of sin as "unnecessary yet inevitable" to see whether it bears a precursor in nature at the level of physics, specifically thermodynamics, where we find "universal contingent" processes throughout nature. Some tentative conclusions then follow.

Two Conflicting Worldviews in Physics

Dynamics and reversibility in a world without history

Seventeenth-century Newtonian dynamics viewed the material world in terms of absolute space, absolute time, strict causality, and temporal reversibility. All material processes were reduced to matter-in-motion through strictly reversible mechanical and gravitational interactions. Whether one considers a ball rolling along a plane, a planet revolving elliptically about the sun, a swinging pendulum, or a spinning top, these processes are such that they could occur "backwards" without violating the laws of dynamics. More accurately, one should say that the laws of dynamics cannot provide any parameter by which to distinguish physically allowable states of affairs from those in which cause and effect are reversed. Alternatively, the form of the dynamic equations is preserved if for time t one substitutes $-t$. Past and future are reciprocally deterministic. Many philosophers have objected to the implications of dynamics concerning the reality of the passage of time and the actuality of the future, but Newtonian physics has remained a formidable opponent to an opposing scientific treatment of time.

Thermodynamics and irreversibility—and "the talons of time"

The nineteenth century was an age in which *time's direction* took on a fresh meaning via classical thermodynamics. Although space and time remained absolute in the strict sense, temporal irreversibility became the central characteristic of the physical processes studied. Examples of such irreversible processes include the diffusion of an aroma from the kitchen throughout the house, a dark ink staining a clear liquid, mixing paint in a pail, ice melting in the sun, a roaring waterfall giving off clouds of spray and mist, ice cracking, mechanical gears heating, hot air rising. Such a world is marked by a radical, undeniable difference between past and future, by a statistical quality to its predictions, and by arbitrariness and contingency. A system is characterized by more than its present state; the path taken also counts, the process is part of the product. How fast ice forms contributes to its structure and fractures; the loudness of a waterfall depends on how steep the drop, not just the height from top to bottom. This world is one where nature is inherently historical, where matter at even the inanimate level displays an indelible sense of evolution. In this world the future state cannot be predicted in detail from the present, even with the governing equations. The character of the present is dependent on the path from the past: Although "all roads lead to Rome," the actual journey influences the quality of arrival. It is a world in fluctuation, filled with unpredictable novelty.[7]

Yet it is a world of dissipation, decay, and destruction. In this world time has an arrow and a claw, and the talons of time lacerate lived experience with a breaking of symmetry, a fracturing of structure, a loss of an irretrievable past, and a staining of the present with the marks of its birth through successive passage and epiphanies.

In Isaac Newton's world the future is always a version of the past; such a world seems irreconcilable with our experience of time's arrow and the inactuality of the future. In thermodynamics, as time passes the world changes irreversibly; nothing can be done to ever quite recover the way things were, and nothing can be done to condition entirely the way things will be next.

A closer look at entropy: two definitions

Entropy as a measure of available energy. Thermodynamics, the study of energy transformations, originated with the study of the bulk properties of matter such as pressure, volume, and temperature. Newtonian dynamics had already provided a framework for the mechanical interpretation of material processes, centered around the definition of work as the result of forces causing a body to move through a distance. Mechanical energy is the ability to do work: to lift a rock, accelerate an arrow, move the planets in their orbits. Central to mechanics was the law of energy conservation: In all mechanical processes the total energy of a closed system is constant, although it might be changed from potential energy to kinetic energy. Thermodynamics was related consistently to mechanics by treating heat as a form of energy. Energy conservation then included the transformation of mechanical energy into heat. For example, as we rub our hands together on a cold day, friction transforms mechanical energy into heat.

It is useful to define the state of *thermodynamic equilibrium* as one in which the macroscopic properties of the system do not change in time, for example, gas in an insulated bottle or water in a closed container. All parts of such a system and its environment must be at the same temperature, T. If external forces are applied to the system, such as a change in volume or pressure, or if heat is applied, the system will change until a new state of equilibrium is attained. If these forces are sudden and sharp, the system will change wildly and imprecisely, like bursting a balloon or tossing grease on a hot skillet. If gradual forces are applied, changes in the system will proceed slowly, even imperceptibly, like simmering a meal over a slow fire. If a system evolves smoothly from one state of equilibrium to the next, then in principle the process could be reversed, returning the system to its original state without incurring other net effects. For example, a piece of ice could melt so gradually that, if the air temperature began to cool, it might re-freeze to nearly its original shape. Reversible processes are also the only ones for which a precise description is possible, since they are limited to states of thermodynamic equilibrium and it is only for such states that the bulk parameters are well defined.

However, in nature such reversibility is an ideal and limiting case of actual processes which often involve abrupt, even catastrophic changes that drive the system far from equilibrium. Like surf breaking on the beach, the cracking of an iceberg, the diffusion of an aroma, the melting of snow, or the fermenting of sugar, they cannot be undone by somehow merely reversing the environmental factors. There will always be some other effect in the total system. Just as the concept of energy served to limit the kinds of processes which are allowable in principle, so the concept of entropy fixes the direction in which actual processes tend to go. Hence, although energy would be conserved whether an aroma diffused out from its source or, somehow, back to it from throughout the environment, entropy would increase in the former but decrease in the latter.

In general, then, entropy and the irreversibility which we expect of most physical processes are fundamentally linked, as expressed by the second law of thermodynamics: The entropy of an isolated system remains constant during a reversible process or increases during an irreversible process; the entropy of a system interacting with its environment can decrease only if the entropy of the system and its environment remains constant or shows a net increase. Hence the second law of thermodynamics tells us that all natural processes take place in such a way as to increase the entropy of the whole, that is, the system plus its environment.

The second law was given various formulations by Rudolph Clausius, Lord Kelvin, and Sadi Carnot. Studying the conversion of mechanical energy to heat, they found that in each case mechanical energy which would otherwise have been available for useful work was lost to heat. For example, friction drains the usable kinetic energy of a moving cart, turning it into heat. Hence the increase of entropy in irreversible processes was initially understood in terms of the loss of energy available for mechanical work. We say that systems run down, that entropy measures the dissipation of energy, the degrading of the environment, the irreversible conversion of work into heat.

Entropy as a measure of disorder. In the kinetic theory of gases, the bulk properties of gas are related statistically to the random motion of an enormous number N of gas molecules. Precisely because of the extraordinary size of N (typically a million billion billion molecules), statistics apply extremely well, and the molecular ensemble can be characterized by a few variables. For example, pressure is associated with collisions of the gas molecules with the container's walls; temperature is related to the kinetic energy of the molecules. How is entropy, defined macroscopically, that is, as a "state variable," related to the microscopic events underlying bulk phenomena?

Suppose we have a container with two compartments, *A* and *B,* separated by a partition, and imagine that there are two balls in compartment *A*. Clearly this is a unique state for the system of container and balls. If we remove the partition and shake the container, each ball could be in either *A* or *B*, or both in either *A* or *B*. The number of possible states of the system has therefore increased fourfold. In addition, note that this process is irreversible: Merely by replacing the partition we will not ordinarily find both balls in their original state in compartment *A*. The second law of thermodynamics tells us that the entropy of this system has increased during this process. Since the number of states of the system has also increased (fourfold), we might try identifying entropy with the number of states of the system. Such an idea was proposed by Ludwig Boltzmann in the late nineteenth century, and it turned out to work with enormous success. It provided a bridge between statistical mechanics and classical thermodynamics by giving analytic precision to the conceptual correlation of macroscopic and microscopic description.

In addition, statistical mechanics suggests a probabilistic interpretation of entropy which accounts for the sense that systems evolve irreversibly in time even though their underlying mechanical interactions are time invariant. We may equate the number of equivalent microscopic states of a system with a measure of the probability that the macroscopic state will occur which corresponds to it. Suppose, for example, that in the previous example there had been ten balls. Although there would still be only one way in which all the balls were in compartment *A*, there would be many ways to arrange the balls and still have, say, five balls in each compartment. Hence we would say that it is much more likely to find five balls in each compartment than all ten balls in compartment *A*. Notice too that, if we started with all the balls in compartment *A* and then shook up the container, as time proceeded, ordinary mechanical, time-reversible processes between the balls (bouncing off each other or the walls of the container) would tend to distribute them evenly between the compartments. It would be a long wait indeed before they would all happen to be back again in compartment *A*! We may legitimately say that the initial state is well ordered and the later states are disordered. Hence entropy can be considered as a measure of the disorder of the system, or as a parameter linked to the probability of finding the system in a particular state. Here an increase in entropy is equivalent to an increase in the disorder of a system, or an increase in the likelihood of finding that state over the previous ones.

Christian Thought Concerning Evil

Although the presence of evil seems unassailable, witnessed by the atrocities committed by our species to its own kind and to nonhuman nature, no universally accepted definition of evil exists. Each value system or worldview defines what it considers to be the good; the thwarting of this good is usually defined to be "moral" or "intrinsic" evil. For a Stoic evil is unreason, for a hedonist it is pain. For a Utilitarian it lies in the denying of the greatest good to the greatest number, while for a theist evil occurs as opposition to the will of God.

Evil can be taken to pertain only to human behavior as discussed in moral theology, or its presence can be extended into the natural dimensions of the world, in earthquakes, plagues, lightning, hurricanes, and the relentless struggle of predator over prey. In the past, natural events in the world were usually taken as morally neutral, neither good nor evil in themselves, but combined with human moral choice they could become occasions of natural or "extrinsic" evil. Yet might there be a more deeply ingrained connection between the evils common to our species and the whole of nature? It is certainly part of the program I envision for relating religion and science that we ask just such a question.

Before exploring this further, however, we must recognize that in asserting the reality of evil a critical paradox is forced onto traditional Christian theism. Often called "theodicy" from the Greek words for God *(theos)* and justice *(dikaia),* the theist's fundamental concern is to understand how the reality of evil in the world does not force us to abandon belief in the biblical God. The *locus classicus* of this issue is to be found in the threefold paradox attributed to Epicurus: How can one believe in a powerful and good God if evil is real? Alternatively, how can a loving God permit human suffering which through God's power could be avoided?

Christian theology has struggled perennially with this problem, seeking neither to deny the reality of evil (as in monism) nor to assert the ultimacy of evil (as in dualism)—either of which would resolve the Epicurian paradox at the cost of abandoning fundamental biblical faith. In a deep sense, the history of Christian thought from the apostle Paul to the present represents a profound wrestling with this single, central paradox of evil. Moreover, from the Genesis saga of the creation of the world, where God is pictured as brooding over the waters of chaos, to Calvary, where the forces of betrayal and abuse reach a pinnacle of expression in a wooden cross and rusted nails, evil as moral sin and evil as natural decay have seemed intimately joined.

The responses by Christian theologians to the problem of evil have varied strikingly across the centuries, so much so that it would take an extended essay to introduce them with real precision. Still, as John Hick has suggested, these responses can be grouped in terms of two basic points of view, rooted in the theologies of Augustine and Irenaeus. Here are the two parts of Hick's argument.[8]

Evil as the privation of good

According to Augustine, being as such is good since it reflects the goodness of the divine Creator. However, as it was made from nothing, being is mutable and hence capable of being corrupted. The primary agent of corruption is our free will, the cause of human suffering. In Augustine's view, evil is the corruption of natural form. Having no independent reality or material content, evil is like a brokenness in the nature of things, an abuse of the full being of each created thing, and a self-destructiveness caused by a corrupt free will. Evil is therefore to be found both in the human realm and in nature. In a similar vein, Thomas Aquinas identified evil as a defect which deprives things of their full potential. Although free will is an essential part of the goodness of God's creation, it too is defective, the defect being moral evil.

In Protestant thought, doctrines such as John Calvin's divine predestination and Karl Barth's emphasis on God's sovereignty over evil through the divine "No!" underscore the restrictions laid on the power of evil to work against the will of God. Paul Tillich affirmed the basic goodness of finitude, of freedom, and hence of finite freedom. It is only through the abuse of such freedom that sin, or existential estrangement, arises. Existence is thus a broken form of being, estranged from and contradicting its essential structure, and the human person is a particularly fragmented and self-contradicting creature. Yet for Tillich, too, such fragmentation is not brought about by an external agent, "but it is the consequence of the structure of estrangement itself," or as he called it, the "structure of destruction."[9]

Evil as developmental obstruction
In the theodicy of Irenaeus we find the roots of a second, and earlier, tradition.[10] Irenaeus distinguished between the *image* and the *likeness* of God in humankind. Although it is basic to human nature to express the divine image in the form of moral freedom and responsibility, this is only part of our inheritance from God. Through spiritual growth and struggle we have the possibility of maturing into the full manifestation of our relationship to God and of ultimately taking on a genuine likeness to God. In this view, evil is a stumbling block to our spiritual progress, an obstruction to our development into full spiritual maturity. Clement of Alexandria (died c. 220) wrote that we were "adapted to receive virtue." Although our nature may be disordered, this weakness is only a childlike immaturity which can be overcome by the Spirit. Perfection lies in the future, not in the broken past.

In nineteenth-century Protestant thought, Friedrich Schleiermacher took up this same insight by stressing that the purpose of God should come about through the human species, in which world-consciousness and God-consciousness can at last coexist and develop together. According to Scheiermacher, human perfection is rooted in human nature since this is where God-consciousness is both possible and actual, as we experience it in moments of pain and ecstasy. Perfection no longer means something found only in the distant past; it is a characteristic that is ever present and evolving toward greater realization. Sin is a preoccupation with the world, and it occurs as an obstruction in the otherwise smooth development of God-consciousness. While Scheiermacher grants that "sin is unnecessary but inevitable," he says that our personal responsibility for sin is in no way diminished.[11] Moreover, personal and community responsibilities for sin are blended in a suggestive way: "Sin is, in each, the work of all, and in all, the work of each."[12]

Pierre Teilhard de Chardin continued this tradition, though with occasional reference to an original perfection and the Fall. Teilhard stressed the evolution of *Homo sapiens* from other primate species, and within this evolutionary framework saw evil (both moral and natural) as an inevitable experience in the growth and spiritual maturing of people. We are creatures, he wrote, "who already exist, but are not yet complete." Thus we move toward a supremely good future, characterized by the emergence of a new global humanity and a final unity in the Omega point.[13]

Evil and Entropy: A First Look

Clearly the concepts of evil and entropy present, at face value, several similarities, suggesting our initial metaphor of entropy as a prefiguring of evil on the physical level. After briefly describing three of these similarities in this section, I wish to examine in the following section ways in which the metaphor produces new insights about both evil and entropy. Hopefully these observations will lend some justification for mixing the language of two separate fields of inquiry by showing the heuristic value of the metaphor.

First, throughout the history of theology the dominate instinct has been that God creates order out of disorder, ruling and overruling chaos, building up a world of harmony and a community of covenant. Whether cast in classical or modern metaphysics, God creates all that is through processes aimed at a dynamic peace. Evil is likened to a disorder, a dysfunction in an organism, an obstruction to growth or an imperfection in being. Entropy refers to such disorder, measuring the dissipation of a system, the fracturing of a whole. In religious language, sin is universal and it inevitably leads to despair, war, and death. Even though we grow in our relationship with God and each other, evil thwarts us. Similarly, our wasted energy scars our world and pollutes our environment. More generally, we need only to think of the pain and cost of natural disasters like famines, hurricanes, earthquakes, lightning, tornadoes, accidents of all kinds, or of plagues and diseases, to recognize the extent of suffering in this world. All these are rooted in the press of entropy, the relentless disintegration of form, environment, organism; all are an affront to hope and peace.

In a primal sense, entropy gives to time its "talons." Time passes, and in time we do what we should not do while we leave undone those things we should do. In time entropy increases, fires burn low, and night encroaches upon our momentary shining day. Our bodies age and die, and even the universe cools. How can the future be filled with hope in an inexorably dissipating cosmos? Perhaps a very distant future in a recontracting universe would allow some margin of promise, but the character of this present age seems to be one of remorseless unwinding.

In an Augustinian sense nature is marred by chaos and destruction; in an Irenaean sense the hope for a better future must do battle with the drain of usable energy. It is as though an overall increasing degree of chaos in nature is a global characteristic of the universe—from beginning to end.

Second, both evil and disorder are dependent on being, lacking independent existence. Is it the razor-sharp edge or the steel of the knife that cuts? Is it the vitality or the disorganization of cells reproducing without bounds that gives cancer its deadly power? In the language of Tillich, evil "has no independent standing in the whole of reality, but . . . it is dependent on the structure of that in and upon which it acts destructively."[14]

Like evil, entropy is a function of the processes of nature, not an autonomous entity in nature. As in theodicy, entropy is parasitic to natural processes, not a participant in those processes. Moreover, entropy represents an inevitable limitation on the varieties of processes which could occur according to the laws of physics, and as such it measures the distance of actual processes from their ideal. In Augustinian theodicy, evil arises as the mark of brokenness of being, while in Irenaean theodicy the processes of spiritual growth are characterized by regress and diversion, the power of sin.

Third, in thermodynamics entropy represents a function which never decreases in closed systems. In systems contained as subsystems in larger ones it can decrease in the subsystem, but the entropy of the system as a whole must not decrease. Cast in religious language, we would expect to find an inevitable increase in the power of evil in communities that cut themselves off from the needs of the rest of humanity and the challenge of global pluralism, or among those who view the human species as fundamentally separate from the rest of nature. Of course, if we press the metaphor we would expect that any closed community could contain additional internal communities which could evolve toward virtue and blessedness, but at the cost of the inclusive system. In a broader sense, if applied to our planet even with all of its species, we are still isolated, at least culturally, from the rest of the universe. Perhaps only if we venture out into the universe to other worlds will we find temporary release from the inevitability of the second law at the personal and cultural level.

Entropy and Evil: A Closer Look

We have listed some parallels between evil and entropy which suggest as a metaphor that entropy prefigures evil on the physical level. In order to test the fruitfulness of this metaphor and to show how this kind of interaction between science and theology can have more than poetic interest, we must see whether we can use the metaphor to suggest new avenues of thought in both theology and physics. I will briefly discuss three possibilities.

First, along with its functioning power, the *form* of evil is a central aspect in theology. Tillich, for example, discusses the form of evil in terms of the "structure of destruction," suggesting that evil contains within it an order, which, though destructive, embodies a remorselessness and a directionality: "Even destruction has structures. It aims at chaos, but as long as chaos is not attained, destruction must follow the structures of wholeness; and if chaos is attained, both structure and destruction have vanished."[15]

Tillich leaves this tantalizing metaphor before us, without pursuing the details of its structure. Yet the fact that he refers to it is significant in itself. In classical statistical models of entropy one finds the familiar bell curve form (the Gaussian distribution function) as the mathematical structure of chaos. This form acts as an identifying signature of randomness. Thermal equilibrium, the physical paradigm of a system in a state of maximum entropy, is precisely one whose states are governed by a Gaussian distribution function. The mathematical structure of entropy could suggest something about the specific form Tillich's "structure of destruction" might take and, thus, in turn open Tillich's metaphor for evil to further interpretation and extension. The detailed dynamics of systems approaching thermal equilibrium could magnify Tillich's suggestion of the "aim" of chaotic behavior. Finally, if modern thermodynamics is brought into the discussion, new mathematical structures occur which drive our theological inquiry about disorder into areas still to be explored.

Second, the cost of life in terms of entropy extends our metaphor into the context of biology. How can living organisms survive given the inexorable dissipation and disordering of a closed system? Clearly, as pointed out by Erwin Schröedinger (1956) and others, biological organisms are open systems, exchanging energy and matter with their environment. Hence living things develop themselves as local centers of order by causing greater disorder in their environment, and hence a net increase in disorder of the organism plus environment. Life flourishes in spite of the overall increase of entropy—but at a cost to the environment and, ultimately, to itself. In this sense the coupling of individual life to the ecological whole presses home with new significance Schleiermacher's characterization of sin as "in each the work of all and in all the work of each."

Third, continuing to explore the cost of living systems in terms of entropy we come upon another instance of the dark side of existence. This foreboding dimension of life seems to me to be underestimated in religion, where life is generally of supreme value as a gift of, even a form of, the living God. In this century, the work of Henri Bergson, Samuel Alexander, Teilhard de Chardin, Jürgen Moltmann, Arthur Peacocke, Ian Barbour, Charles Birch, John Cobb, and numerous others underscores the theological significance of evolution. Although they express quite different interpretations of the relationship between God and the world, the writings of these men have in common an underemphasis on the *cost* of life and evolution. Yet it is here that entropy and evil seem to conspire on a grand scale.

The Irenaean view of evil as a hindrance to growth returns now to signify the role of entropy in evolution and civilization, while the Augustinian insight underscores the brokenness of existence as our modes of interdependence—food, clothing, warmth, work—cost more than they yield. What could be a more appropriate interpretation of the communal cost and responsibility of sin, and the power of sin to grow and extract as its wages, than death? Not only individual life, but evolution itself, is like a plague devouring the order of the world; and humankind through its complicated civilization is the most insatiable consumer of all. This can actually be extended plausibly to a cosmic scale. Stars radiate light energy at a vast cost in entropy. Stars produce heavy elements via nucleosynthesis, then explode to fertilize the interstellar regions with these life-giving elements—all the while entropy counts the cost. Even the universe in its global expansion seems to grow at the expense of greater entropy.[16]

In a striking passage in his Pulitzer prize-winning book. *The Denial of Death,* Ernest Becker forces the point Rifkin and others are making about life:

> What are we to make of a creation in which the routine activity is for organisms to be tearing others apart with teeth of all types—biting, grinding flesh, plant stalks, bones between molars, pushing the pulp greedily down the gullet with delight, incorporating its essence into one's own organization, and then excreting with foul stench and gases the residue. Everyone reaching out to incorporate others who are edible to him. . . . Creation is a nightmare spectacularly taking place on a planet that has been soaked for hundreds of millions of years in the blood of all its creatures. . . . Science and religion merge in a critique of the deadening of perception of this kind of truth, and science betrays us when it is willing to absorb lived truth all into itself.[17]

All of Becker's examples hinge on the relentless and universal second law. Life is suddenly dethroned from its pedestal of value. How should theology respond to this massive *Gestalt* switch?

One place to begin would be with Teilhard de Chardin in whose writings the power of God is interpreted as working throughout nature in terms of the "within" of things.[18] Entropy now seems to me to emerge as a foreboding symbol connected with this within. For Teilhard, radial energy works to center, structure, and develop the within of things from the atom to the human, bringing matter forth to life and mind, and finally to Christ as Omega. I would propose that we add a new metaphor to that of Teilhard's, namely the notion of a "radial entropy" which measures the consuming of our center, the dissipation of our structure, and the paying of wages to the insatiable foe. Entropy in this metaphor is the natural basis for evil, the prerequisite for personal sin—even as physical indeterminacy is, arguably, the prerequisite for human freedom. It is the enemy within, the sword hidden in the wings of the angel, turning us constantly back from a lost paradise to the world of war and ashes.

The Value of Entropy as a Dissimilarity in the Metaphor

The essential tension of a creative metaphor arises from the dual affirmation of similarity and dissimilarity. Having looked for some correspondence between evil and entropy, we will now begin to consider several reasons which suggest that entropy is instead a component of growth and change, providing the basis by which the development of new orderliness occurs, and in so doing belonging partly to the *goodness* of creation.

First of all, many of life's most valuable moments—those of genuine excitement, awe, a quickening sense of numinous mystery, the rustling of the divine presence in one's deepest self-understanding—come during moments of radical change in a life situation. One's first walking step, first encounter with the Thou of another, the birth of one's children, death of a relative or friend, moments of great personal fear, the prospect of one's own death—these bring the depth of being into the course of living. Such sudden changes, such breakthroughs, take us far from "equilibrium" into a strange land of discovery and danger.

In thermodynamics, it is precisely these sudden changes in the macroscopic state where entropy grows rapidly. Although reversible processes evolve with a minimal increase in entropy, dramatic, irreversible processes are characterized by large increases in entropy. Is entropy, or something like it in the personal and spiritual realm, intimately coupled to the cataclysms in our life? Many of these are religious rites of passage, marked by sacraments and considered as sacred times in which eternity enters into the ordinary present with a transformative and salvific power. We cannot describe those personal moments of sudden growth or insight very well, except to say that they really are not like the periods of gradual, smooth living. Interestingly, in thermodynamics as well, it happens that we cannot describe in tight analytic formulas the changes in the state of a system during rapid alteration. An important research area of physics is actively investigating such "critical phenomena," searching for new mathematical methods for analyzing the anomalies and singularities associated with sudden gross changes in the state of the system.

Seen in this light, the irresolvable and paradoxical nature of evil itself takes on new, *positive* significance; like the ambiguity inherent in descriptions of catastrophic physical change, life crises too seem to transcend the limits of tight linguistic formulas or verbal accounts. A divine mystery lurks in the cauldron of our wrestling with the deepest moral ambiguities of conscience, and the very inexpressible nature of such experiences testifies to their genuinely religious dimension, laced with the mysterious divine/human encounter. Perhaps there is a theological parameter, like entropy in physics, which is associated with the intrusions of the Spirit in such deep moments where revelation, self-knowledge, and choice drive religious "state variables" such as confession, silence, and worship.

Second, although life and evolution cost the environment in terms of increased entropy, the value of life and indirectly the value of entropy as a necessary component to life cannot easily be dismissed. In C. E. Raven's 1951 Gifford Lectures, the biological reality of "new life through death of the old" was stressed as "the sublime law of sacrifice."[19] Through processes of physical evolution, the basis is ultimately laid for the evolution of planets, some of which develop atmospheres and oceans and revolve at reasonable distances around moderate suns. In some of these cataclysmic processes enough energy is released to produce macromolecules and an organic soup—the primordial womb of life. And in the case of at least one gentle green world the species which evolved includes humankind. As Peacocke points out, "Death, pain, and the risk of suffering are intimately connected with the possibilities of new life, in general, and of the emergence of conscious, and especially human, life, in particular. . . . It seems hard to avoid the paradox that 'natural evil' is a necessary prerequisite for the emergence of free, self-conscious beings."[20]

Although life inevitably involves disease and death, the New Testament vision is one of ultimate triumph. The apostle Paul wrote, "We know that the whole creation has been groaning in travail together until now. The creation itself will be set free from its bondage to decay and obtain the glorious liberty of the children of God" (Rom. 8:22, 8:21). Are we somehow to be freed from the tyranny of entropy, and is the universe to shine forever as the resplendent creature of God—a *new* heaven and earth?

Moreover, in the miracles of Jesus, filled with the promise of new creation and spiritual life, we hear of processes whose entropy—if one can speak of their physical dimension as surely an incarnation faith would wish to—must certainly diminish radically. Through themes of life and light, life abundant, loaves and fishes, water and wine, and life everlasting, a new order of nature is described; in such metaphors of God's continued creation, the power of new normative being seems to break the back of dissipating, destructive entropy.

The "Talon of Time": The Hidden Assumption Behind Both Entropy and Evil

Entropy in thermodynamics is linked with irreversible processes and hence with the direction of time in nature. In religion, the direction of the passage of time is an underlying, though normally tacit, assumption without which most personal experience and community history would be meaningless. We watch our children grow; we sorrow over lost friends and broken promises; we mourn the death of our loved ones; we can be tormented by the anticipation of suffering; we struggle for a better future; we believe in the promise of divine redemption; in short, we *know* the passage of time. Yet is the "arrow of time" a thoroughly established fact in all of physics? If not, would our human experience of its talons be, ultimately, an illusion? For me, victory can only be true, and defeat only bearable, if time will not one day erase the stages of my living. The reality of history, the values of our action, the power of evil, and the unending increase of entropy—all are based on an assumption lying prior to the level at which we have been exploring in our working metaphor between entropy and evil.

So now we must move to that deeper level. Recall that in Newtonian dynamics, the arrow of time is an illusion, although it is very real in thermodynamics. We are back at the conflict between the worldviews of classical physics: Newtonian, dynamic reversibility, and thermodynamic irreversibility (characterized by entropy). Our metaphors relating entropy and evil have tacitly assumed that entropy, or more generally thermodynamics, is an autonomous, irreducible description of the world. In physics, however, this is not generally accepted. Most adopt the view that thermodynamics can be reduced to dynamics by appeal to statistics, and that irreversibility is a result of initial, unusual conditions, not a fundamental fact based intrinsically in nature. For example, imagine continuously shuffling a deck of cards. The deck may momentarily start out ordered, but it gets quickly disordered. Still after a long time it will once again momentarily be ordered, then again disordered for another long time, till it is again momentarily ordered, and so on. Since the period of time between ordered states is so large, if we start from one such state, we never in practice get to the next one. Hence, although we would normally expect that only disorder could follow order, it is inevitable that ordered states appear during extended random sequences.

By reducing thermodynamics to statistical mechanics, physics reduces entropy and time's arrow to the characteristics of a small sample in a much larger ensemble with long-range periodicity over reversible fluctuations. This reduction leaves us with a cosmos which is too symmetric, too perfect, too absolute for evil—or redemption—to be real. T. S. Eliot captures a sense of this problem in his first lines from "Burnt Norton":

> Time present and time past
> Are both perhaps present in time future,
> And time future contained in time past.

If all time is eternally present
All time is unredeemable.[21]

Is there a way out? Although differing in other respects, the reality of time and duration and the difference between past and future are of central concern for philosophers such as H. Bergson, Alfred North Whitehead, and Milic Capek, for physicists including J. A. Wheeler, Freeman Dyson, and David Bohm, and for theologians such as Jürgen Moltmann, Langdon Gilkey, Wolfhart Pannenberg, Paul Tillich, and Karl Rahner. Certainly then, one would hope that in making scientific sense we can avoid talking nonsense theologically. Alpha and omega are simply not interchangeable theological symbols; a scientific cosmology which is based on the reversibility of time might thereby indicate its own transitory, limited value.

Should this theological criticism of time in physics be resolved by physics? This introduces a much broader question, whether one must not, for methodological, epistemological, and practical reasons, finally divorce theology from science, since to do otherwise could lead to some sort of perpetual conceptual contingency. But in this work we are concerned with bridge-building, and the flow of traffic—in both directions—is the purpose and warrant for a bridge. So again I turn to physics asking whether there is new light on this question at the scientific level. If thermodynamics is locked in desperate conflict with dynamics (a battle which in most physicists' opinion has been won in principle by dynamics, though skirmishes continue), perhaps modern physics can rescue the arrow of time.

Unfortunately, this does not seem likely—with one exception. Special relativity, general relativity, and quantum mechanics all are consistent with temporal reversibility at the formal level;[22] the direction of processes, including the expansion of the universe itself, is accounted for by appeal to special initial conditions. (In the cosmological case, for example, these conditions are called the "Big Bang" or "moment of creation.")[23] One can appeal to the arena of the weak interaction in which certain radioactive decay processes are not time-symmetric.[24] However, this effect is extremely small; the vast majority of elementary particle interactions are symmetric in time. In my opinion, trying to explain the arrow of time in this way is a bit like expecting the tail to wag the dog.

Recently, however, a new perspective on the ultimacy of temporal irreversibility is being developed, and surprisingly it comes from the area of modern thermodynamics! Normally dissipative systems evolve from states of order to disorder. Now the research of Ilya Prigogine and others suggests that, as one drives a system far from thermodynamic equilibrium, new forms of extraordinary order appear.[25] Moreover, they claim that thermodynamics cannot be resolved into statistical dynamics merely by appeal to special initial conditions. In ordinary thermodynamics, different complex states evolve into similar final states (everything consumed by fire turns to ash). Prigogine has studied the detailed evolution of new classes of physical systems far from the kind of physics normally explored. Using bifurcation theory, he now argues that in many cases two initially similar systems will eventually evolve into final states which differ drastically from each other. Cells, compartments, groups, vortices, inhomogeneities, clusters, lattices—these highly ordered spatial structures evolve in time through processes which seem to defy the law of entropy. Hence Prigogine suggests that temporal irreversibility is fundamental in nature, and that entropy plays a catalytic role during processes of unusual complexification.

If Prigogine is correct, the direction of time will find an irreducible foundation in modern thermodynamics, and the role of time in theological concepts like evil and history may be strengthened. Perhaps, then, the relationship between concepts of entropy and evil will be one of "consonance," as Ernan McMullin suggests in a similar vein regarding the problem of the origin of the universe and the Christian belief in divine creation.[26] I will venture to formalize this relationship in terms of the following working hypothesis: Although the characteristics of entropy and evil do not give direct support to one another, if evil is real in nature, entropy is what one would expect to find at the level of physical processes. Conversely, if a real arrow of time is coupled to entropy in physical processes, one would expect to find dissipative, disruptive, yet subtly catalytic processes in history and religious experience.

Conclusions Regarding the Metaphor of "Entropy and Evil"

We have explored a metaphorical relationship between entropy and evil, which has led to a discussion of time's arrow. The Augustinian interpretation of evil seems more akin to the negative sense of entropy—as a measure of increasing disorder, dysfunction, decay, destruction, and dissipation. Entropy is involved in the fragmenting of creation, even in those processes which form New Creation. The cost of industrialization in the pollution of the environment mirrors in a sociological context the staggering cost of biological evolution, borne by lower species in the food chain and finally by the cosmos itself which, while slowly dying, gives birth to its young. We eat, we grow, we explore, we destroy, we hope, we love, we die—some things increase beauty and compassion, others bring ruin and anguish; yet all in total increase the "heat death" of the whole. The disorder of the physical world, the cost of life and living, the inevitability of further disorder—these all reflect the dominion of sin as stressed by Augustinian theology.

The Irenaean interpretation may be closer to the dynamic sense of entropy as a characteristic of violent change leading, perhaps, to greater harmony, deeper insight, and broader structure. The Irenaean stress on the future, on development of the spirit, on growth toward full relationship with God clearly gives greater weight to time over the more static, structural Augustinian analysis. Moreover, "order out of chaos" is deeply consonant with the Irenaean theodicy: We grow spiritually from image to full likeness of the divine. This surprising feature of Irenaean theodicy suggests a striking parallel with the recent discoveries by Prigogine concerning temporal irreversibility and the development of novel structures in systems far from thermal equilibrium.

In sum, entropy seems a surprisingly pliable concept. It is related to processes of despair, decay, degeneration, and to the perfecting of creation as the signature of God's continuing creative participation in the evolving universe. The dynamic concept of entropy, rooted in the flow of time and characterizing processes throughout nature, embraces both the Augustinian and the Irenaean theologies and suggests a new conception of order evolving out of disorder.

Of course this level of inquiry is more of a first look, the suggesting of metaphors as signposts for further thought. There are numerous complexities in both the theological and scientific dimensions which have been barely touched on. For example, one would want to develop the traditional theological issues involved in much greater detail. The discussion ought to be expanded to include several broad areas of current theology, including Ricoeur's analysis of symbolism and evil; the theology of Moltmann, Pannenberg, Peacocke, Teilhard; and Whiteheadian, feminist, and liberation perspectives. In modern physics there are a variety of new aspects to be investigated for their relevancy to the theme of this chapter, including quantum statistics, thermal fluctuations, strange attractors, and Prigogine's continuing research in nonequilibrium thermodynamics. Also, since a metaphor is far from an identity statement, the dissimilarities in the metaphorical relationship between evil and entropy deserve fuller discussion. Still, with this first look, a form of consonance between the theology of evil and the physics of entropy seems to have been found. We shall see whether the consonance turns to a symphony.

Entropy and Evil: A Closer Look Within the Augustinian-Niebuhrian Paradigm on Original Sin[27]

Now we turn to a sharper proposed relationship between "entropy and evil": namely that there may be a similarity (even an isomorphism?) between the inner logic of the description of the physics of entropy and that of the description of human—and by extension natural—evil, at least from the Augustinian perspective. The discovery of such a similarity would go a long way towards making the case that human sinfulness does not arise entirely in a "vacuum" but that there are precursors not only in evolutionary biology but even in fundamental physics. We turn now to this discussion. For the purposes of this chapter, I will focus strictly on the Augustinian-Niebuhrian understanding of sin and "moral evil," leaving for future work a similar discussion of nineteenth- and twentieth-century reconstructions within a Schleiermachian framework.

The Augustinian-Niebuhrian "free-will defense": is it viable today?

In my opinion the key to the inner logic of Augustine's free-will defense can be found in Reinhold Niebuhr's analysis of the claim that *sin is "unnecessary but inevitable."*[28] Niebuhr traces this claim back to Augustine. In his struggle against Manicheanism, Augustine argued that it is not in our nature to sin, since our nature is created and therefore fundamentally good. Sin is in this sense *contingent*, the result of a truly free choice not necessitated by human nature. Yet in his struggle against Pelagius, Augustine also claimed that sin is pervasive, ultimately unavoidable, *inevitable*. This joint claim formed what Niebuhr called the "absurd paradox" of the Christian free-will defense, a paradox which Niebuhr defended against its historical and contemporary distortions.

Of course given his literal reading of Genesis, Augustine could locate the source of the paradox historically. The free choice of Adam and Eve represented a circumstance which was not necessary in principle but which, once done, would affect all humankind. Thus the paradox at the heart of the free-will defense could be, if not resolved, at least located through the logic of a *historical* event which, though contingent (unnecessary), would have universal ramifications for humankind (and thus operate inevitably on all future people). I will refer to this understanding of the logic of the free-will defense as the assertion that there exists at the origins of human history a "universal contingent."

The problem today, in an age of biblical criticism *and* evolutionary science, can be put rather sharply as follows: Is there anything about scientific anthropology which would allow us to ground the problem of moral evil in an empirically explicable universal contingent? If so, then the Augustinian insight into sin and free will might be maintained against contemporary Manichean and Pelagian tendencies (such as fatalism and "self-help" utopianism). Indeed it might allow a fresh basis for a revitalized critique of culture, something which Niebuhr clearly would have wanted.

Is there evil in nature?

A question must also be raised about the possible meaning of "natural evil." Granted there are such devastating physical events such as meteoroid impacts, earthquakes, and tsunamis, and that the history of evolutionary biology is replete with disease, death, and the extinction of species, and the suffering of sentient creatures, particularly animals. Do these kinds of physical and biological phenomena warrant the use of the term "evil"?[29]

Certainly no serious scholar would equate moral and natural evil. Clearly evil here means something less articulate than it does in the human realm, more of a precondition or prevenience of what is to come in the latter arena. Still the very subject leads us into immensely complicated issues which cannot be adequately dealt with here. From a biologist's standpoint, the cycle of life and death, of predator and prey, is part of the delicate balance of nature's ecology. One can hardly define life without death, nor the evolution of life without the "death" of whole species. Again, without physical "disasters," such as the meteorite which theoretically may have destroyed the age of dinosaurs, life along entirely different chains would never have come to prominence—including our own!

Yet it is hard to deny that nature "red in tooth and claw" is a suffering nature, full of agony, of pitiful and often senseless death, blind alleys, merciless waste, brute force. Is it entirely anthropomorphic to recognize in pre-human nature something which eventually becomes that which in the human realm is evil? Is it entirely inappropriate theologically to claim that there is something in pre-human nature which is related to such "pre-evil" as a form of "pre-sin"?

Is there in nature as a whole, and not just in the human realm, something like a "universal contingent"? What light *does* scientific theory shed on the theological problem of natural evil if we frame that problem in terms that are analogous to a "universal contingent"? If we are to assume that the human exercise of free will involves a paradox, namely that a universal contingent is the logical structure out of which free will operates, so that sin will on occasion arise in some not fully predictable way (that is, in a way which cannot be fully controlled and yet which is not entirely necessary), might it not also be the case that processes in nature at even the most fundamental level of physics involve a paradox, namely a universal contingent? One might even *start* with the theological assertion of the free-will defense and ask whether it could be used fruitfully as a heuristic device in science. The discovery of a universal contingent in nature would be highly satisfying.

To answer these questions we must first understand some basic concepts in thermodynamics and then ask whether there is something like a "universal contingent" in thermodynamics.

Universal contingent in modern thermodynamics

I would like to focus on the nature of chance in irreversible thermodynamics as developed by Ilya Prigogine and his colleagues. This field is coming more and more to include within its scope both classical thermodynamics (with its law of increasing entropy) and classical dynamics (with such topics as chaos theory, fractals, strange attractors, and so on).[30] The fundamental ideas of modern thermodynamics can be conveniently summarized as follows.

1) All closed systems conserve energy (the first law of thermodynamics). Those not in internal equilibrium degrade available energy, typically by chemical processes, and in the process move inevitably towards equilibrium from a state of higher order to a state of minimum, and thereafter constant, order (the second law of thermodynamics). The measure of increasing disorder is "entropy." Hence entropy is a monotonically increasing function in all closed systems.

2) Open systems (which exchange energy and matter with the environment) may be homeostatic, retaining their degree of order at the expense of increasing the disorder of their environment. Alternatively they may undergo a process of transformation, in which a lower degree of order is temporarily lost and the system fluctuates rapidly; then a much more complex level of order is obtained. This process is captured by Prigogine's famous phrase, "order out of chaos"; the systems capable of this process are called "dissipative systems." Of course the total system, with its open internal system together with the environment, when considered as a closed system will be characterized by a net increase in entropy. Eventually all closed systems will reach thermal equilibrium, or "heat death."

The "Thermodynamics of Natural Evil" as a Natural Precursor to Moral Evil

What might this tell us of any relevance to the theological problem of evil? As I argued earlier, the logic of the theological problem of evil, as expressed by the Augustinian-Niebuhrian free-will defense, entails the existence in *human history* of a "universal contingent." Accordingly it would be my contention that if we are to look for something in nature independent of the human realm, the logic of the free-will defense leads to the assertion that there exists *prefiguratively in nature*, a "universal contingent." But is there anything in nature which could be so characterized?

Interestingly, thermodynamics seems to contain a kind of universal contingent, but its exact nature is subtle. We know that both closed and open systems generate increasing entropy, so entropy by itself is not the target. But we also know that some open systems far from equilibrium operate in a highly contingent manner, occasionally managing to come out with a net decrease in entropy by exhausting it to the environment.[31]

What then determines whether an open system is homeostatic or whether it is subject to fluctuations and thence to greater order? Today this remains an unanswered issue in the kinetic theory of self-organization. However according to Prigogine and his colleagues,[32] what we do know is how to characterize the conditions under which a system can become, spontaneously, more complex. This may be what we are looking for. We are considering open systems far from equilibrium (that is, nonlinear irreversible thermodynamic systems). Will such systems resist the tendency to change their state or, when fluctuations occur, will they become unstable, undergoing a transition to a new, and often more highly structured, system? Arthur Peacocke provides a careful and highly illuminating response to this technical question.[33] According to Peacocke, we must first define the concept of entropy production, P, as the rate at which the entropy S of the systems changes in time (P=dS/dt). From this we define the excess entropy production E as the variation in the value of P *during a fluctuation and due to the fluctuation*. (Note that E is not the same as the change of P in time.) Now we are prepared for our result:

If E>0, the system is stable.

If E<0, the system may be stable *or* unstable.

In other words, if the value of E is positive, a fluctuation will not cause the system to change states (that is, the system is stable). If E is negative, a fluctuation may or may not cause the system to change states (that is, a new structure may emerge). Alternatively we can express the relations between E>0, E<0, and the necessary and sufficient conditions for (in)stability as follows:

	Necessary	Sufficient
For stability	—	E>0
For instability	E<0	—

Thus positive E is sufficient but not necessary for stability; negative E is necessary but not sufficient for instability. In sum, negative E is a step towards, but no guarantee of, instability following a fluctuation.[34]

What does this result mean? I suggest we interpret it as follows. *Contingency*: Open systems are subject to contingent features by their very nature: If their excess entropy production $E<0$ *they may or may not* resist change during fluctuations; moreover *these fluctuations are themselves contingent features* of such systems. *Universality*: Biologically, *all* forms of life that we know are *open systems*, and hence *all* are subject to these kinds of thermodynamic contingencies. Physically, most complex systems, from the earth's weather to stellar evolution and the plasma of the very early universe, are *open systems*. In this sense we have located, within the field of nonlinear, far-from-equilibrium thermodynamics, a form of universal contingent in physics and biology.

Conclusions Regarding the Inner Logic of Thermodynamics and of Natural Evil

Theologically we can conclude that the Augustinian free-will defense, focused as it is on the problem of moral evil and structured logically in terms of "inevitable but unnecessary," can be extended theologically to the problem of natural evil and, in doing so, leads us to discover something in nature by way of thermodynamics which carries much of its logical structure. The central claim of Niebuhr that the human condition articulates a paradox ("inevitable but unnecessary") has a counterpart in terms of the thermodynamic condition that *all* physical and biological open systems are subject to *contingent* factors leading to increased order or "heat death." The universality of the claim corresponds roughly to the Augustinian sense of "inevitability" (of applying to all humankind and to some acts of every human without exception), while the contingent features (both in the condition that $E<0$ and on the presence of contingent fluctuations) lead to the Augustinian sense of "unnecessary."

Yet in several important ways the logic of the thermodynamic problem is *not* isomorphic to the logic of the theological problem. 1) The future of open systems is "open": they may grow continuously towards complexity or they may decay towards equilibrium depending on the initial and governing conditions. However it would be the Augustinian claim that every human inevitably sins, that "sinlessness" never occurs in people (with Jesus as the exception, of course). In this sense the logic of thermodynamics and of the Augustinian position seem quite different. Yet to the extent that we might consider that all systems are ultimately closed, that every open system can be considered a subsystem of some greater, maximal environment, then thermodynamics predicts that *all* maximal systems eventually decay. Is this a "variant" of universal sin?

2) The contingency of thermodynamic systems is "instantaneous." At each junction a system may proceed along fork *A* or *B*; the past history of the system is not necessarily a constitutive factor, although some systems do display a "memory" of sorts. In human experience sin—and our resistance to it—entails

history in the form of memory and historically conditioned choice in the form of repentance, sanctification, and spiritual renewal.

Perhaps these similarities and differences, and others yet to be uncovered, will shed fresh insight on the uniqueness of human experience in the context of our evolutionary continuity. Even with these differences, it would seem we have uncovered in physical and biological processes something of a prefiguration of, or at least a precondition on, the phenomenon of evil in human experience. Nature is not divorced from the "human sphere" as our neo-orthodox, existentialist, and conservative colleagues urge. Rather what comes to fruition in human life has its initial instantiations, at least in part, in the pre-human world.

But wouldn't this be what evolution would teach us to expect? Theological reflection which takes evolution seriously must recognize that part of the human *sitz im leben* is terrestrial, even cosmological. Conversely a theology of the cross must take for its scope nature groaning for redemption, as the apostle Paul wrote. Though the differences remain, as here between the logic of the free-process and the free-will defenses, their similarity and continuity call out more forcefully. We will continue to learn theologically about the meaning of being human if we contextualize our species, as science teaches, within the frayed bounds of the organic and earthy matrix through which we arose.

Yet clearly the thermodynamic logic of theodicy does not carry anywhere near the complexity found in the human realm, where intentionality and self-transcendence are dialectically entangled with instinct and finitude. Some things—many things—remain a part of the ever-transcending mystery of evolved and evolving human nature. Without a more developed account of the mind/body problem, human subjectivity, the mystery of grace, and the theological meaning of free will conceived in terms of the *imago dei*, the problem of theodicy will continue to resist closer scrutiny. I can only hope this brief analysis sheds some light on my suggestion that, in physical and biological nature, there occurs something which might be called "natural evil."

Endnotes: Chapter 7

[1] This chapter is abridged and expanded from the essay, "Entropy and Evil," first published in the *CTNS Bulletin* 4 (Spring 1984): 1–12; and then in *Zygon: Journal of Religion and Science*, 19:4 (December 1984). That essay was based on a lecture presented at the Twenty-Ninth Summer Conference of the Institute on Religion in an Age of Science, "Disorder and Order: A Study of Entropy and a Study of Evil," Star Island, New Hampshire, 24–31 July 1982. I want to acknowledge the many helpful suggestions made by Nancey Murphy in preparing the previously published essay.

[2]See, for example, Harold Schilling, *The New Consciousness in Science and Religion* (Philadelphia: Pilgrim, 1973); and Arthur Peacocke, *Creation and the World of Science*, 1978 Bampton Lectures (Oxford: Clarendon, 1979).

[3]See, for example, Ernan McMullin, "How Should Theology Relate to Community?" in *The Sciences and Theology in the Twentieth Century*, ed. Arthur Peacocke (Notre Dame: University of Notre Dame Press, 1981), 17–57.

[4]See, for example, Ian G. Barbour, *Issues in Science and Religion* (New York: Harper & Row, 1971); Barbour, *Myths, Models, and Paradigms* (New York: Harper & Row, 1974); Hans Kung, "Paradigm Change in Theology: A Proposal for Discussion" (A public lecture delivered at the University of Chicago Divinity School, 1982); Nancey Murphy, "Revisionist Philosophy of Science and Theological Method" (A paper read at the March Meeting of the Pacific Coast Theological Society, Berkeley, Calif., 1983).

[5]Barbour, *Issues* and *Myths,* Sallie McFague, *Metaphorical Theology* (Philadelphia: Fortress Press, 1982).

[6]Barbour, *Issues and Myths*, 14.

[7]Whether thermodynamic novelty, including chaos theory, is a source of genuine (ontological) novelty is a question for another occasion, although I am highly doubtful that it is.

[8]John Hick, *Evil and the God of Love* (London: Macmillan, 1966). Hick includes a provocative evaluation of recent trends in theodicy and their positive relationship to Christian eschatology.

[9]Paul Tillich, *Systematic Theology*, 3 vols (Chicago: University of Chicago Press, 1957), 2:60.

[10]For references to Irenaeus and Clement, see the Ante-Nicene Library.

[11]Frederich Schleiermacher, *The Christian Faith*, H. R. MacKintosh and J. S. Steward, eds. (Edinburgh: T&T Clark, 1928), par. 68, 3.

[12]Ibid., par. 71, 2.

[13]Teilhard de Chardin. *The Divine Milieu* (New York: Harper & Row, 1969), 64. It would be interesting to analyze both the conflicting views in physics (thermodynamics versus dynamics) and the conflicting views in theology (Augustinian versus Irenaean theodicy) in terms of Imre Lakatos's methodology of scientific research programs (Imre Lakatos, *The Methodology of Scientific Research Programs*, vol. 1 [Cambridge: Cambridge University Press, 1978]).

[14]Paul Tillich, *Systematic Theology*, 2:60.

[15]Ibid.

[16]Whether entropy can be applied to an open cosmology is a controversial point which will not be explored in detail here.

[17]Ernest Becker, *The Denial of Death* (New York: Free Press, 1973), 282–83.

[18]Since writing this paper I have learned of a very thoughtful development of similar themes related to Teilhard by Juan Luis Segundo, *Guilt and Evolution* (Maryknoll, NY: Orbis, 1974).

[19]C. E. Raven, *Natural Religion and Christian Theology* (Cambridge: Cambridge University Press, 1953), 15; Raven attributes this remark to J. H. Fabre.

[20]Peacocke, *Creation*, 166.

[21]T. S. Eliot, *The Complete Poems and Plays, 1909–1950* (New York, NY: Harcourt Brace, 1952), 117.

[22]Eugene Wigner and others have suggested that the measurement problem in quantum mechanics necessarily involves consciousness as an actualizing agent in nature. This could provide a means of introducing time's arrow within physical processes. There are several arguments against such an approach, however, and it has not been widely adopted.

[23]See for example, James Trefil, *The Moment of Creation* (New York: Charles Scribner's Sons, 1983); and Ernan McMullin, "How Should Theology Relate to Community?"
[24]This result is linked with parity violations and PCT conservation. For a readable account, see John C. Polkinghorne. *The Particle Play* (San Francisco, Calif.: WH Freeman, 1979).
[25]Ilya Prigogine, *From Being to Becoming* (San Francisco, Calif.: WH Freeman, 1980).
[26]In a recent article McMullin argues that the Big Bang does not support the Christian doctrine of creation, nor does the Christian doctrine of creation support the Big Bang. "What one *could* readily say, however, is that if the universe began in time through the act of a Creator, from our vantage point it would look something like the Big Bang that cosmologists are now talking about" ("How Should Theology Relate to Community?" 39). It will be interesting to see whether McMullin's position can be sustained by a careful investigation of alternative physical cosmologies and their implications for present observational astronomy.
[27]This section is abridged and slightly rewritten from an early short article, "The Thermodynamics of 'Natural Evil': Response to Polkinghorne's Argument," *CTNS Bulletin* 10.2 (1990). I want to thank Wesley Wildman for a careful reading and insightful critique of an earlier draft of this article.
[28] Reinhold Niebuhr, *The Nature and Destiny of Man, Volume 1: Human Nature* (New York: Charles Scribner's Sons, 1964).
[29] Clearly a careful discussion of the meaning of "natural evil" is required here. Are physical processes, such as earthquakes, and biological phenomena, such as disease, properly considered "evil"? Evil in what sense and for whom: for the earth and for biological creatures? For humankind? Are they evil, or the preconditions of what is truly evil at the human level? Are they also somehow bound up with what we would also want to call good, such as life itself and the ecological cycles which produce and sustain it? What about the distinction between moral, natural, and metaphysical evil? Is there something about being itself which is "distorted," incomplete, an impediment to God-consciousness, something which one would want to call evil?
[30] From now on I will refer to nonlinear, nonequilibrium, irreversible thermodynamics as "modern thermodynamics."
[31] This is not meant as setting up an analogy such as "increasing order : decreasing order :: good : evil," but only to suggest that what may be of interest is the interplay of contingency and necessity in open systems.
[32] For helpful, though technical, introduction, see Ilya Prigogine, *From Being to Becoming: Time and Complexity in the Physical Sciences* (San Francisco: WH Freeman, 1980). For a nontechnical introduction, see Ilya Prigogine and Isabelle Stengers, *Order Out of Chaos* (Toronto: Bantam, 1984).
[33]A. R. Peacocke, *An Introduction to the Physical Chemistry of Biological Organization* (Oxford: Clarendon 1983), Part 1, ch. 2.
[34]See Ibid., 47.

Chapter 8

Natural Theodicy in an Evolutionary Context: The Need for an Eschatology of New Creation[1]

> In a universe of blind physical forces and genetic replication, some people are going to get hurt, other people are going to get lucky, and you won't find any rhyme or reason in it, nor any justice. The universe we observe has precisely the properties we should expect if there is, at bottom, no design, no purpose, no evil and no good, nothing but blind, pitiless indifference.
>
> —Richard Dawkins[2]

> There is every reason for a Christian of today to embrace both the theological teachings of Genesis and the theory of evolution. But holding together the Christian view of God and the insights of evolutionary science does demand a rethinking of our theology of the trinitarian God at work in creation.
>
> —Denis Edwards[3]

Introduction

Life is filled with beauty, joy, creativity, hope and peace. From an azure sky above a Tahitian atoll, whose coral reefs teem with abundant multicolored fish and plants, to the craggy Rocky Mountains and the soaring Swiss Alps, from the taste of delectable food to the ecstasy of sexual intercourse, from the glorious photos of stars being born in deep space to the astonishment at the birth of one's child, life is, as the first chapter of Genesis proclaims, "very good." But life is also torn by the pain of hunger, cold, and bodily wounds; threatened by hurricanes, drought, and earthquakes; vulnerable to bacterial and genetic diseases; a fierce combat zone in the Caribbean tropics and the African savannah. Most living creatures are caught up in the endless cycles of predation that compose the food chain, and most animals are fated to an agonizing death.[4]

The Bible is striking, compared to the views of its neighboring cultures of Greece and Babylon, in bringing both sides of life under the rubric of radical monotheism: God as the creator of the world, though working even through the tragedies of life, is the source of all that is and, ultimately, all that *is* is good. Suffering, disease, and death are the universal consequences of an inestimably tragic and singular event, the Fall. Yet they will be removed in the coming Reign of God when all living creatures are restored to their original, right, and harmonious relations (Isa. 11:1-9) and, even more so, when they will be transformed into creatures of everlasting life in the New Creation (Rev. 21–22:5).

This historical/theological explanation of the two sides of life as created good and only *consequentially* evil is severely challenged by Darwinian evolution, where natural selection, and with it death and extinction, is integral to what drives evolution and thus become *constitutive* of life. This chapter focuses on the "underside" of the picture of life on earth where "natural evil" (suffering, disease, death, and extinction) raises the immense challenge of "natural" or "evolutionary" theodicy:[5] How can we believe in the goodness and power of the God who creates life through the very processes of evolution which constitutively involve natural evil? This challenge is one which believers must address as we struggle with our faith in God, as we watch friends turn away from faith because of natural evil, and as we attempt to respond to the atheistic challenge to faith based on natural evil.[6]

This chapter is an elaboration of one theme—natural theodicy—in a previous paper delivered in Adelaide in 2002.[7] Both essays are sections of a large-scale research and writing program.[8] My overall argument is that diverse areas in contemporary theology drive us to construct an eschatology which entails the transformation of the universe into the New Creation and which addresses the challenges of both natural evil *and* Big Bang cosmology. Here I spell out in more detail the ways in which natural theodicy drives us to respond with such a robust eschatology.

At the outset, I want to underscore the apophatic context of theology. What little light we have to shed on theological issues is surrounded by the overwhelming mystery of God which we confess through faith. That there is such inevitable mystery should not be an excuse for sloppy thinking, of course. Instead the acknowledgment of mystery should drive us to pursue theology's fundamental task of reflecting self-critically on our encounter with God. This is particularly important for the task of theodicy: We should never seek to "solve" the problem of evil. As the Book of Job discloses, our fundamental response to evil must be faith in God and not rational argument. Karl Rahner writes that the deepest answer to the incomprehensibility of suffering is "the incomprehensibility of God in his [*sic*] freedom and nothing else."[9] This chapter is written with the hope that the kataphatic affirmation of God's ultimate goodness might have a place within the apophatic mystery of the world as God's creation including its trenchant and stunningly excessive moral and natural evil.

Evolution in Theological Perspective: Two Challenges and Responses

Challenge 1: evolution and chance—atheism or theism?

Before turning to theodicy, it is important to recall that evolutionary biology has been used repeatedly by atheists to challenge Christian faith and to support a dysteleological metaphysics of nature. The typical charge is that "blind chance" in evolution makes God's purposeful action as the Creator of life impossible, or more simply that evolution leads inevitably to atheism—or at most to a pale deism.[10] In the well-known words of Jacques Monod, "chance *alone* is at the source of every innovation, of all creation in the biosphere. Pure chance, absolutely free but blind, [lies] at the very root of the stupendous edifice of evolution." And so Monod concludes that "the ancient covenant is in pieces; man [*sic*] at last knows that he is alone in the unfeeling immensity of the universe out of which he emerged only by chance."[11]

The enormous cultural impact of Monod's views was stressed by D. J. Bartholomew in 1984: "The devastating attack on belief in a purposeful God made by Jacques Monod . . . is the most penetrating and damaging that has been launched in the name of science." If Monod were correct, it "would be sufficient to demolish Christianity and most of the other higher religions."[12] Theists such as Donald MacKay and Mary Hesse quickly responded to Monod. It was Arthur Peacocke, however, who in his 1979 Bampton Lectures,[13] gave what Bartholomew called "the most extensive and convincing reply to Monod."[14] According to Peacocke, the initial potentialities built into the universe by God are actualized in time through chance. Peacocke developed this into an elaborate theology of God's continuous creation (*creatio continua*). In creating the world *ex nihilo*, God bequeathed to it both lawfulness and chance, and God works continuously in time and immanently "in, with, under and through" the processes of nature. This view, which has frequently been termed "theistic evolution," contends, in short, that evolution is "how God creates life."

Initial response: theistic evolution—but is it more than "statistical deism"?

Today, theistic evolution is a view widely shared in the literature of theology and science. It represents a common starting point for a variety of distinctive and more fully developed positions about what it means to say that God acts immanently in nature. An enduring problem for this approach is that, without such further development, it could amount to little more than what I have termed "statistical deism." If "chance" refers to epistemic ignorance, namely our lack of knowledge of the underlying natural causes which deterministically produce apparently chance events, then the phrase "chance and law" really amounts to "(unknown) law and (known) law." God's action, in turn, then amounts to little more than the realization in time of potentials and possibilities written into the universe at its creation. Thus without further development, theistic evolution reverts to the deism of which Christians have been accused—even by Monod! Meanwhile even deism is on shaky grounds from recent challenges that undercut the claim that there was a beginning to the universe, denoted by t=0.[15] This coup for atheism is reflected with relish in Carl Sagan's caustic remark that Stephen Hawking has given us "a universe with no edge in space, no beginning or end in time, and nothing for a Creator to do."[16]

Developed response: "full-strength" theistic evolution via non-interventionist objective divine action (NIODA)

What is needed if theistic evolution is to flourish is an underlying account of God's *ongoing* action within the processes of nature that meets three stringent criteria[17]: 1) God's acts are objective and specific: without such action things would have turned out differently. (Claims about divine action involve counterfactuals.) 2) God's acts are hidden to science: science sees strictly random events. This entails that divine causality cannot be reduced to secondary or natural causality, the subject of scientific inquiry. 3) God's action is non-interventionist and both epistemic and ontological "gaps" arguments are rejected. (God acts in special events in nature without suspending God's general action which undergirds the regularities of nature. Moreover our claim that God acts is not based on what science does not understand but on what it does understand.)[18]

Such an account of divine action combines the commitment to objective divine action as found in conservative Christianity (but without paying the price of interventionism that conservatives bear) and non-interventionist divine action as found in liberal Christianity (but without our talk of divine action being merely our subjective, religious interpretation of regular natural causes). It has thus been labeled "non-interventionist objective divine action," or "NIODA."[19] NIODA offers to deliver on the "promissory note" of theistic evolution and in the process to undercut even further the atheistic attempt to co-opt evolution.[20] In my view, bottom-up causality, relying on quantum indeterminism, could hold for God's action throughout the entire history of the universe, including the evolution of life through genetic mutation and natural selection. Lateral amplification could become relevant once the domain of the "classical," ordinary world has emerged from the preceding domain where only quantum mechanics applies. Top-down causality in the form of divine action within the context of the mind/brain problem could be appropriated by God once the evolution of creatures capable of even primitive sentience has occurred. Divine causality as viewed by neo-Thomism and by process theology also applies throughout the entire history of the universe.

Challenge 2: evolution and suffering—theism or atheism revisited

An even more compelling argument for an atheistic interpretation of evolution than the appeal to "blind chance" is God's apparent creation of, complicity in, or at least allowance of suffering in nature. From Charles Darwin to Richard Dawkins, the sheer horror so frequent in the biological world has seemed to make Christianity unintelligible and even offensive. As Darwin wrote in a letter to Asa Gray, "I cannot persuade myself that a beneficent and omnipotent God would have designedly created the Ichneumonidae with the express intention of their feeding within the living bodies of Caterpillars."[21] More recently, Dawkins has pointed to the predator/prey cycle of cheetahs and antelopes to conclude, not that God is evil but that there simply is no God at all: "The universe we observe has precisely the properties we should expect if there is, at bottom, no design, no purpose, no evil and no good, nothing but blind, pitiless indifference."[22]

The bulk of this chapter is devoted to precisely this challenge, that is, how do we respond to "natural evil" and the question of theodicy that emerges from evolution. What I want to acknowledge and underscore at the outset is that NIODA makes the problem of theodicy more egregious than it would have been in earlier, "statistical deistic," versions of theistic evolution. If one chooses to move forward along the trajectory of theistic evolution via the strategy of NIODA, there is simply no way to avoid this problem.

"Theodicy Lite": Natural Evil Is Not Really Evil

We will first look at two important variations on the view that since what we call natural evil is just a normal part of biological evolution, "evolutionary theodicy" is a nonissue. I call positions such as this "theodicy lite." They represent one of three ways to undercut the paradox of theodicy: the denial (or at least de-escalating) of the reality of evil. (The other ways are in some way to deny or reinterpret God's goodness or power.)

Natural Theodicy Is Irrelevant

The most elementary response is to view natural evil as theologically irrelevant. Natural evil is "just natural" and it is inappropriate to call it "evil." What we take, erroneously, to be evil is in fact *a constitutive factor of life*; it is no more in need of theological attention/explanation than other biological features that reflect the way evolution works. Pain and suffering go hand in hand with sentience, and the death of organisms and the extinction of species are built into, and necessary for, the processes by which life evolves. In his illuminating article on theodicy, Christopher Southgate calls this response "The Problem Dismissed."[23]

One can find this view in much of the theology and science literature. According to Peacocke, "evolution can operate only through the death of individuals—'new life [arises] only through the death of the old.'"[24] Similarly, Denis Edwards writes that "natural selection is simply the differential reproductive success that is built into nature. When a theologian, biologist, or anyone else describes natural selection as 'selfish,' or nature as 'cruel,' that is an anthropomorphic way of speaking."[25] Of course theologians such as Peacocke and Edwards move on to robust theodicies, but more attention is then given to suffering and God's response to it without returning to the point about the irrelevancy of biological death.

Natural theodicy is marginally relevant

The previous response can be given a minimal theological gloss in two ways. Each focuses on the crucial scientific insight that natural evil is constitutive of life.

The first argument is that since natural evil is *constitutive of life*, it cannot be viewed as a *consequence* of a historical event, "the Fall" from paradise. Liberal Protestant theology from Friedrich Schleiermacher onwards has taken this more or less for granted; natural evil is not a consequence of human sin or of a prehistorical cosmic drama (the fall of the angels) as the traditional Augustinian "Fall" depicts it. Quoting Peacocke again, "Biological death can no longer be regarded as in any way the *consequence* of anything human beings might have been supposed to have done in the past, for evolutionary history shows it to be the very *means* whereby they appear and so, for the theist, are created by God."[26]

The second argument is that even God had "no choice" but to opt for Darwinian evolution if God was to create life by acting immanently through the processes of nature rather than by intervening in them. This means that adaptation by natural selection is unavoidable, and the resulting "natural evil" is an unavoidable consequence of God's action in creating life which even God could not eliminate. The "no choice" argument aims at lessening the intensity of natural theodicy by letting God "off the hook"—slightly. In an interesting turn of events, Michael Ruse actually offers the "no choice" argument in defense of Christianity against one of its most vocal critics, Richard Dawkins, by citing Dawkins's own reference to it: "Dawkins, however, argues strenuously that selection and only selection can do the job. No one—and presumably this includes God—could have got adaptive complexity without going the route of natural selection."[27]

Critique and implications of "theodicy lite"

Contrary to the idea that natural evil is just a part of the life process, I do not think that the constitutive nature of natural evil means that natural evil is theologically irrelevant. The New Testament narratives of the ministry of Jesus combine both physical healing and the raising of the dead with the forgiveness of sins.[28] They link the realm of natural evil (that is, disease, death) with the realm of moral evil (that is, sin) and the salvation offered by the ministry and resurrection of Jesus applies to both realms—although the latter only emerges with humanity. It would therefore be impossible to affirm the theological significance of moral evil while dismissing the theological significance of natural evil. Thus while rejecting the biblical framework in which natural evil is the result of moral evil (that is, the Fall) we must not reject the theological questions raised by natural evil, both in the context of humanity and now in the context of the evolution of all living creatures. The way forward, then, will take us along a more complex path than the dismissal of the relevance of natural evil per se.

In response to the idea that natural evil is marginally relevant, I would suggest two points. First, I agree, of course, that natural evil is not the consequence of the Fall, but this in itself is of tremendous theological significance since it sharply distinguishes liberal versus conservative interpretations of and responses to sin and evil. Second, the rejection of the Fall does not mean that traditional theologies which accept it have nothing to offer us towards constructing an evolutionary natural theodicy—as we shall see when we turn to the Augustinian theodicy. Neither does it mean that modern theology prior to Darwin in which the Fall is rejected has nothing to offer us—as we shall see in turning to Schleiermacher.

I would also point out that the "no choice" argument is based on a crucial assumption usually overlooked in these discussions: the assumption that the laws of physics underlying cosmology, astrophysics, geology, chemistry, molecular and evolutionary biology, and so on, are a "given." Admittedly if God were to create life by natural processes *and* if laws of physics which govern these processes are taken for granted, then God may have had "no choice" other than Darwinian evolution, and this approach to theodicy "eases the burden" of accounting for God's action in evolution as Ruse points out. But if we push it one step further, we see that this argument does not really help with theodicy since the question of whether God had a "choice" returns at a more fundamental level in what I will call *cosmic theodicy*. Since God created our universe *ex nihilo*, including the laws of physics and constants of nature, why did God choose to create *this* universe with *these* laws and constants knowing that they would then make Darwinian evolution unavoidable and with it the sweep of natural evil? Thus, the Ruse/Dawkins argument does not rescue God from blame, but merely places blame at a more foundational level, leading to the Leibnitzian challenge: Is this the best of all possible *universes* that God could have created with the intention of the evolution of life or could there be another kind of universe in which life evolved without natural evil? In the end we must choose to accept that an "agnostic cosmic theodicy" in which the problem of evil simply cannot be answered or we must continue to press for a more adequate response to the problem of theodicy that evolution and NIODA together raise. In sum, "theodicy lite" is ultimately a fruitless theodicy, and we must move ahead.

Robust Theodicies: Two Traditional Forms

Let us set aside these responses to natural evil and turn to more complex ones. I propose that any robust theodicy must meet at least three criteria:

i) it must ward off Manichean tendencies to "blame God" for creating natural evil or to view nature as unambiguously evil,

ii) it must ward off Pelagian tendencies to undercut the universality of moral evil,

iii) it must fully take on board Darwinian evolution, and in particular the constitutive character of natural evil to life.

Christian theology includes a variety of theodicies which meet these criteria. For the purposes of this brief chapter I will employ John Hick's analysis of this variety as falling within two broad types—the Augustinian and Irenaean. The task will be to reformulate these theodicies such that they meet all three criteria and then deploy them to the task of evolutionary natural theodicy.

The Augustinian theodicy: the free-will defense

Historical Christianity provided a framework which met the first two criteria via the Augustinian theodicy, drawn in large measure from New Testament/Pauline texts and the dominant context of Neoplatonism. Augustine's theodicy was profoundly influential to Aquinas, Calvin, and Luther and such contemporary theologians as Barth and Rahner.

According to Augustine,[29] both moral and natural evil are ultimately the result of free rational beings who sin: They willfully turn from God as the highest good toward a lesser good. Augustine avoids Manicheanism by affirming the goodness of all that God creates. Sin began with the premundane, cosmic fall of the angels. It continued with Adam and Eve who, though created "very good" by God, did of their own free will choose creaturely goods over God. The resulting corruption or bondage of the will is transmitted sexually from generation to generation to all humanity from the common human origin in Adam and Eve. On the one hand, then, human beings still have the power of free will, and are thus responsible for, and deserve punishment for, their actions by God. On the other hand, though in Eden it had been possible not to sin (*posse non peccare*), in human history free will is corrupt and without God's predestination of grace it is not possible not to sin (*non posse non peccare*). Augustine embedded his free-will defense in a Neoplatonic understanding of the plenitude of creation in which evil is a privation of being and in an overarching aesthetic in which God sees all things ultimately as "very good," including sin and its punishment.

Schleiermacher's theodicy: the moral growth argument

Liberal Protestant theology in the nineteenth century, and much of Catholic and Protestant theology in the twentieth century, have worked within an alternative framework provided by Friedrich Schleiermacher. The roots of Schleiermacher's theology lie in the eighteenth-century Enlightenment's rejection of biblical history and traditional theology as mythological. In the early nineteenth century, Schleiermacher's *Speeches* and *The Christian Faith*[30] provided a massive reformulation of original perfection and original sin in a developmental/proto-evolutionary framework. Briefly, the *original perfection of the world* according to Schleiermacher consists in the world being such that God's purposes can be achieved in and through natural processes. In particular, the world is such that our experience of our relative dependence on the world leads to our experience of our absolute dependence on God as the source of all that is. The *original righteousness of humankind* consists in our capacity for religious experience both as the personal experience of individuals and as communicated through culture.[31] *Sin* consists in the obstruction of our awareness of God due to our dependence on the world. It is virtually inevitable because we are "sentient animals" embedded in the world as physical and biological creatures, and because in our individual lives our physical character precedes the development of our individual cognitive and spiritual capacities. Yet sin is not necessary, since in Jesus the development of his consciousness of God was unobstructed; he was "sinless." Thus we are still personally responsible for our sins. *Original sin* is both individual and societal in character[32] leading to Schleiermacher's distinctive aphorism, "sin is in each the work of all, and in all the work of each." Finally, *natural evil* does not arise from sin. Still because of our sinfulness we experience natural evils as genuine evil, and for this reason natural evil can be considered a penalty of sin.

It is clear, then, that Schleiermacher's pivotal reformulation of original perfection and original sin in a time-independent, developmental/proto-evolutionary framework meets our three criteria for an evolutionary natural theodicy.

Retrieving and Extending the Augustinian Theodicy to Physics and Cosmology: Insights and Failures

At first glance it might seem clear that Schleiermacher's theodicy would be more compatible with our project of an evolutionary natural theodicy than would Augustine's. The latter is grounded in the framework of the Fall which Schleiermacher in many ways overcame, and Schleiermacher's approach, particularly through the lens of John Hick's revisions as we shall see below, has been highly influential in the "theology and science" community. However, I believe that there are resources in Augustine's theodicy which should not be overlooked.

Retrieval: Reinhold Niebuhr

The first task is to divest the Augustinian theodicy of its "creation/fall" framework by uncovering its underlying philosophical argument, and then reinterpret this argument in an evolutionary perspective. To do so I have turned, in previous writings, to Reinhold Niebuhr's immensely influential Gifford Lectures.[33] Here Niebuhr presented the underlying argument of the Augustinian theodicy stripped of its mythological language. Niebuhr showed that Augustine rejected the Manichean view which ontologizes evil; instead he argued that "all that *is* is good." Thus sin has no ontological status, and humans are not sinful because of their created nature. Augustine also argued against the Pelagian view that sin could be overcome by human will alone. Instead, redemption is due to God's grace, and this applies to all of humanity through Augustine's theory of the biological inheritance of sin and of the participation of all people in Adam. Finally against Neoplatonism Augustine located sin within the human will as corrupted by original sin.

Niebuhr then rendered the underlying logic of the Augustinian theodicy as asserting that sin is *unnecessary but inevitable*.[34] This phrase captures Augustine's argument without tying it to the Fall. It expresses in stark terms what Niebuhr called the "absurd paradox" of the Christian free-will defense. Augustinian theodicy rephrased through Niebuhr's formulation now meets our three criteria for an evolutionary natural theodicy.

Preconditions in physics that underlie the free-will defense

We are now in a position to extend the free-will defense to evolution and, in what I believe is more useful here, to the underlying laws of physics which shape the character of Darwinian evolution, as I pointed out previously in reference to Ruse and Dawkins. What, in particular, must physics be like for the reformulated Augustinian/Niebuhrian free-will defense to hold? Here we will explore two responses. *Diachronic method*: Search for those areas of physics and cosmology which underlie and make possible biological evolution. What, if anything, reflects the Niebuhrian logic of "unnecessary but inevitable" at the level of physics? *Synchronic method*: Search for the conditions in physics such that free will can be enacted physically.

Diachronic method involving thermodynamics. We must first reformulate Niebuhr's claim that "sin is unnecessary but inevitable" such that it can be more readily discussed at the level of physics. Previously, I have suggested that the underlying logical structure of Niebuhr's claim can be described by the term "universal contingent": that which is ontologically contingent but which holds in all cases.[35] The task, then, is to search for examples of a universal contingent in physics.

A prime example is found in nonlinear, nonequilibrium thermodynamics, with its concepts of "entropy" and "order out of chaos." In brief, the entropy S of all "closed" systems increases inevitably to a maximum according to the second law: $\Delta S/\Delta t \geq 0$. But as Ilya Prigogine and many others have shown, when a closed system contains "open" subsystems, they can spontaneously move to greater degrees of order by exhausting entropy to their environment, the closed system which contains them. In the process, the total entropy of the closed system increases, obeying the second law, even though its open subsystems may decrease in entropy. This simple fact underlies the homeostasis of life on earth through a thermodynamic "heat exchange" between the sun and the earth. It also underlies the processes of biological evolution in which vast increases in complexity over time are driven by the thermodynamics of the sun/earth system. Without thermodynamics, which applies *universally* to all physical and thus all biological systems, the evolution of life on earth would have been impossible.

Yet although thermodynamics applies to all physical systems, we cannot predict whether a given system will spontaneously fluctuate towards more complexity or dissipate and decay: Both paths are possible by the laws of nonlinear, nonequilibrium thermodynamics, but the details depend on other areas of physics such as kinetic theory. Thus the advancement to increased complexity in such systems, including biological ones, is entirely *contingent* on factors and processes beyond the limitations of these systems. Nonlinear, nonequilibrium thermodynamics thus carries both of the characteristics underlying Augustine's argument about the nature of sin: universality and contingency.

Synchronic method involving thermodynamics. A central theme of the NIODA project is that the enactment of (voluntarist/incompatibilist) free will requires ontological indeterminism at some level in physics. I believe a similar argument can be made that the enactment of human freedom and moral evil require something like thermodynamics in physics.

In previous articles I explored a metaphorical relation between entropy and evil that stressed both similarities and dissimilarities.[36] Here I followed Paul Ricoeur's understanding of metaphor as including a negative as well as a positive analogy (both an "is" and an "is not"), Ian Barbour's insight that metaphors are extendable to new contexts, and Sallie McFague's development of these resources into what she termed "metaphorical theology."[37] To summarize the idea briefly, we typically find beauty and goodness in the patterns of emergent complexity and creative novelty characteristic of life, while tragedy and sorrow play themselves out in terms of the dissipation and destruction associated with decay, disease, and death. Curiously, thermodynamics underlies and is entailed by all of these phenomena. The second law thus plays a *dual* role: It makes possible the physical and biological consequences of our moral action both for good and for ill. This metaphorical argument then led to a more pointed claim: that thermodynamics is needed if moral evil is to be actualized in the world. As I wrote almost two decades ago, "if evil is real in nature, entropy is what one would expect to find at the level of physical processes."[38] So thermodynamics provides an example at the level of physics of what is needed if the consequences of sinful acts are to be expressed physically, including dissipation and disruption, as well as the consequences of virtuous acts, including acts of beauty and goodness.

Extending the Augustinian/Niebuhrian free-will theodicy to cosmology

There are several ways to extend the Augustinian/Niebuhrian free will theodicy to cosmology. Here I will touch on one of them by returning briefly to the Ruse/Dawkins view, "theodicy lite." According to their argument, even God has "no choice" but to opt for Darwinian evolution if God is to create life by acting immanently through the processes of nature rather than by intervening in them. But in responding above, I pointed out that the question of whether God had a "choice" returns at a more fundamental level in what I called *cosmic theodicy*.

Now, in light of what has just been said about the logic of "universal contingent" and the complex relation between "entropy and evil" in thermodynamics, the problem of "cosmic theodicy" appears to be far more serious than it may have sounded initially. It now becomes: Why did God choose to create *this* universe with *these* laws of physics knowing that they would not only make Darwinian evolution unavoidable, and with it the sweep of natural evil in the biological realm, but that they would also contribute to *natural evil at the level of physics*—and thus to natural evil *throughout the universe* and not just within biological phenomena? Alternatively, if God intended to create life through the processes of Darwinian evolution, then not only is biological natural evil an unavoidable consequence, as Ruse and Dawkins argue, but *so is physical natural evil*—and *it* occurs *throughout the universe even where there is no possibility of life.*

With this in mind I have suggested renaming the "Anthropic Principle" the "thermodynamic Anthropic Principle" to underscore the irreducible but often overlooked role of thermodynamics in arguments about the Anthropic Principle in relation to the evolution of moral agents (for example, the Murphy/Ellis thesis[39]) and to stress its implications for cosmic theodicy.

Mutual interaction model: implications for eschatology and for contemporary physics

The Augustinian/Niebuhrian theodicy ultimately fails, not because it is tied to a mythical "fall"—which it clearly is not—nor because it views death as a consequence of sin instead of as constitutive of life—which it clearly does not—but because, like "theodicy lite," it leads to the recognition that underlying moral evil is natural evil that, in an implicitly Manichean way, characterizes the universe as a whole. I believe that this fundamental problem points at last to the impossibility of articulating an adequate response to theodicy in terms of the universe as it presently exists and thus in the theological context of the doctrine of creation. Instead it forces us to relocate the response to the context of eschatology and its portrayal of the New Creation.

But this failure brings with it an exceptional gift: It gives us a crucial insight into what eschatology must include if it is to address the failure of theodicy to account for natural evil. The insight is that if in the New Creation it will be impossible to commit moral evil since we will be liberated from the bondage of the will into true freedom (Augustine: *non posse peccare)*, then the New Creation will not include natural evil either. This claim could be taken in several ways.

In its most simple form it might mean that the New Creation will not include thermodynamics since it contributes to natural evil. In a slightly more complex form it might mean that the New Creation will not include thermodynamics to the extent that it produces natural evils, though it might include it to the extent that it produces natural goods. I am reminded by the apostle Paul that "the whole creation has been groaning in travail together until now. . . . The creation itself will be set free from its bondage to decay and obtain the glorious liberty of the children of God" (Rom. 8:22, 8:21). As I wrote in an earlier paper, "Are we somehow to be freed from the tyranny of entropy, and is the universe to shine forever as the respondent creation of God—a *new* heaven and earth?" As a Christian I answer "yes!"

What is even more interesting is the way this insight works "backwards" from eschatology to the universe as we now know it via the doctrine of creation. It implies that thermodynamics, as a "universal contingent" characterizing this universe, is itself "contingent" since it will not characterize the New Creation. This in turn carries *implications for current physics*. One question which has been discussed extensively is whether thermodynamics is a "fundamental" theory comparable to dynamics (quantum mechanics, quantum field theory, and so on). The implication here is that it is not a fundamental theory since it will not be part of the eschatological destiny of the universe, or at least not a part of it in the way in which it contributes to natural evil. If that is so, it could suggest interesting questions for future research in the foundations of physics regarding the relation of thermodynamics to fundamental physical theories.

Retrieving and Extending Schleiermacher's Theodicy to Evolution

Retrieval: John Hick

The legacy of Schleiermacher's theodicy can be found in John Hick's recent and profound treatment.[40] Hick's theodicy, in turn, has been widely influential among scholars in theology and science.

Hick's development of Schleiermacher's theodicy starting in the mid-1960s is "regarded generally as the first clearly defined alternative to the Augustinian-Thomistic perspective."[41] Hick names this type of theodicy after Irenaeus (c. 130–202 C.E.) who first brought together themes found in the sub-apostolic Eastern church, such as the distinction between the image and likeness of God in humanity, the understanding of our earthly life as one of gradual spiritual growth from image to likeness, sin as due to weakness and immaturity, and the world as a mingling of good and evil appointed by God for our growth towards perfection.[42] In the nineteenth century, Schleiermacher was to develop and systematize themes such as these into the rich framework we have just touched on.[43]

Hick provides a helpful comparison of both contrasts and agreements between the theodicies of Augustine and Schleiermacher.[44] Contrasts: The Augustinian theodicy looks to a created paradise in the past, focuses crucial importance on the fall of angels and humankind, and looks to a future last judgment which includes eternal punishment for the damned. The Irenaean theodicy accepts evil as an inevitable factor in a world suited for moral development. It does not deny the Fall but it rejects the ideas of lost righteousness and inherited sinfulness. It views an eternal hell as "rendering a

Christian theodicy impossible." The key difference, as I read Hick, is that the Augustinian theodicy seeks to protect God from responsibility for the existence of evil by stressing the Fall, while the Irenaean theodicy accepts God's ultimate responsibility for evil while showing why a world that includes evil is justifiable and inevitable.

Areas of agreement: These areas reflect "certain basic necessities of Christian thought concerning the problem of evil." Both affirm the aesthetic conception of the perfection of creation. For the Augustinian theodicy the world is "very good" as it is now, even including the reality of sin and evil. For the Irenaean theodicy the perfection of the world lies in the eschatological future where the end, the Kingdom of God, will justify the means of its achievement, the ambiguous historical process. Both theodicies attribute ultimate responsibility for the existence of evil to God, although the Augustinian theodicy does so only implicitly through the doctrine of predestination. Both affirm that the world is valuable to God independent of its fitness for humankind and that God may be at work elsewhere in the world to achieve divine purposes. Both affirm the *O felix culpa* (the "fortunate fall") theme: The Augustinian theodicy admits that bringing good out of evil is better than not permitting evil to exist, but such "greater good" or "means-end" arguments play a minor role in its overall structure while the Irenaean theodicy treats it as central and stresses the eschatological context of the "greater good."

Hick's contribution: the crucial role of eschatology

Hick develops his own theodicy within the Irenaean context through an extraordinarily careful, detailed, and judicious exploration of multiple problems involving moral and natural evil. In the second edition, he compellingly engages even his most severe critics who raise a variety of issues and objections, offering what I take as relatively persuasive logical responses as to why God does not act to remove or diminish the extent of suffering in nature. These include the impossibility of our doing the "means-end calculation," the limitations on the perspective needed for a "greatest good" argument, the relativity of the "worst evil," and so on. Recently, Tom Tracy has explored these in detail.[45] The arguments "do not seek to demonstrate that Christianity is true, but that the fact of evil does not show it to be false."[46] They do not constitute a theodicy as much as they clear the way for one to receive a fair hearing.

Central to Hick's robust theodicy is the argument that "pain and suffering are a necessary feature of a world that is to be the scene of a process of soul-making." Even their "haphazard and unjust distribution" and excess are ultimately beneficial, since "the right must be done for its own sake rather than a reward." Closely related is Hick's claim that "epistemic distance" is required if humans are to be capable of moral growth. "God must be a hidden deity, veiled by His [*sic*] creation" so that, unlike our physical surroundings, God's presence is not coercively imposed on us. The world must be *etsi deus non daretur* ("as if there were no God") because in such a world we have the necessary "cognitive freedom" by which faith and moral growth are possible. A great virtue of this claim is that it also goes a long way to accounting for moral evil, since the hiddenness of God makes evil a "virtually inevitable result" of the actions of a free agent.[47]

Let me pause briefly here to note an implication of "epistemic distance" which bears directly on the relevance of Hick's work for theology and science. First of all I contend that "epistemic distance" is also a requirement for science to be possible. Science is based on methodological naturalism: A scientific explanation of the processes of nature should rely on natural causes alone without the introduction of divine causation. Thus the world must be "as if there were no God" not only because this is necessary for faith and moral freedom, *à la* Hick, but also for scientific research. Secondly, this means that when we Christians encounter science, we should not see it as antagonistic to theology (although metaphysical naturalism certainly is) or try to replace methodological naturalism with a method that includes a "divine designer." Instead we should see science as a legitimate though limited method of knowing the world precisely because it is based on the way God created the world, and God's purpose in creating it this way was to make possible faith and moral freedom.

The gravest challenge, then, according to Hick, is excessive suffering and the attempt to justify it by a "means-end" argument: Can Christian theodicy respond to a world of "extreme and crushing evils . . . so severe as to be self-defeating when considered as soul-making influences . . . [A world] which seems at best to be utterly indifferent and at worst implacably malevolent"?[48] To underscore this challenge, Hick concludes the second edition of *Evil and the Love of God* with the agonizing quotation from Dostoyevsky's *The Brothers Karamazov*.[49] Hick's response is that eschatology provides the only context for addressing these challenges: "[W]e cannot hope to state a Christian theodicy without taking seriously the doctrine of a life beyond the grave."[50] Such hope is for a "future of infinite goodness." He connects this view of eschatology to a rejection of hell, an affirmation of universal salvation, and an understanding of heaven as an endless opportunity for continued spiritual growth. Hick ends with the *O felix culpa*; it lies "at the heart of Christian theodicy" and expresses the central paradox that while present-day evil is really evil, it will eschatologically "be defeated and made to serve God's good purposes."[51]

Expanding the Schleiermacher/Hick Theodicy into a Wider Theological Context and Applying It to Evolution via Kenosis *and* Eschatology

My goal will now be to appropriate the Schleiermachian theodicy through its reformulation by Hick, to expand and strengthen it theologically, and then to apply it to our evolutionary problematic. By adding the concept of *kenosis*—the self-emptying of Christ in taking on human life and, in turn, the suffering of God with humanity—to Hick's theodicy we can strengthen the connection between the suffering of creatures and God's suffering with creatures.

Background: kenosis and the suffering of God

> If you can accept the Christianity, then you can certainly accept the Darwinism. Conversely, if you are a Darwinian looking for religious meaning, then Christianity is a religion which speaks to you. Right at its center there is a suffering god, Jesus on the Cross.
>
> —Michael Ruse[52]

> The way of nature is the way of the cross; *via naturae est via crucis*.
>
> —Holmes Rolston III[53]

Overviews of kenosis are readily available.[54] One such overview by Sarah Coakley, focusing on kenosis in "theology and science," notes that exegetical, Christological, and trinitarian reflections on kenosis are often left out. She implies, instead, that they should be "in some sense normatively binding,"[55] and I share this opinion. Here I will highlight portions of Coakley's overview.

First, exegetical issues. In Paul's letter to the Philippians the Greek verb *kenoo* occurs in the phrase "he emptied himself" (2:7). The full text reads:

> Have this mind among yourselves, which you have in Christ Jesus, who, though he was in the form of God, did not count equality with God a thing to be grasped, but emptied himself, taking the form of a servant, being born in the likeness of people. And being found in human form he humbled himself and became obedient unto death, even death on a cross. (RSV)

But what does "emptied" refer to? According to Coakley,[56] there are two distinct interpretations. 1) Incarnation: Verse 6 provides the hermeneutical key to verse 7: "in the form of God" refers to Christ's divine pre-existence and "emptying" refers to the humility of Christ in becoming human. 2) Cross: Verse 8 offers the meaning of verse 7: "emptying" means "he humbled himself" through death on the cross. Here the phrase "in the form of God" simply refers to the humanity of Jesus which bears the *imago dei*. In short, the first, incarnational, reading leads to metaphysical issues in christology, while the second reading stresses the moral significance of self-sacrifice.

Second, kenosis as a christological issue. The first reading became the dominant view of the patristics, who presupposed the immutability of God and understood the incarnation to mean that Christ "became flesh" without a loss of his divine nature. The Chalcedonian formula, "one person in two natures" (451 C.E.), was used to affirm that Jesus suffered in his human nature though his divine nature remained impassible. Debates concerning the relations between his two natures, in particular the "communication of attributes" (*communicatio idiomatum*), continued through the Protestant Reformation and into the modern period. Ted Peters argues that Luther understood kenosis as referring to Jesus' "willingness to allow the pangs and pains of human despair to have an impact on his divine nature."[57] The resulting view was "theopassianism": God suffers in and through the life of Jesus, but this did not entail that God as Father suffers ("patripassianism").

Third, kenosis as a trinitarian issue. With divine passibility a broadly accepted agenda in the twentieth century, contemporary trinitarian theologians such as Jürgen Moltmann, Paul Fides, H. U. von Balthasar, and Denis Edwards have extended the idea of kenosis beyond christology to all three persons of the Trinity. Moltmann describes his own work as transforming the metaphysical attribute of divine impassibility into the biblical conception of the faithfulness of God such that we can now affirm that God not only loves but suffers with the world.[58] Finally, with kenosis now situated in a trinitarian context, kenotic self-surrender is seen as affecting all of God's acts *ad extra*, including the trinitarian creation of the world.

The road to a robust evolutionary natural theodicy: brief assessment of existing proposals

Many scholars in theology and science have appropriated a kenotic-based theodicy highly influenced by Hick's contributions and have extended it to evolution in response to natural evil. Just as God suffers with the experiences of people, God embraces the history of life on earth and suffers with it. If God enters into the physical and biological processes of the world through the Incarnation, it is the crucifixion through which God experiences the suffering of all life and offers it the possibility of redemption. Some scholars have, in turn, combined a kenotic theodicy with eschatology to one degree or another. Only a very few, however, have noted the challenge placed on eschatology, not only by evolution, but even more so by the scientific scenarios for the far future of the universe (that is, "freeze or fry").

Holmes Rolston provides a moving kenotic account of nature as "cruciform," the "passion play of God." However he does not connect this with a developed eschatology nor does he clarify whether his view of redemption includes all creatures or just some individuals or species.[59]

Arthur Peacocke bases his eschatology on his view of the resurrection of Jesus without necessarily including resurrection in the sense of materiality/physicality. This leads to a highly anthropocentric and "disembodied" eschatology; the *viseo dei* may await individual believers, but resurrection in the "bodily" sense and, in turn, the redemption of nature and its transformation into the New Creation are set aside.[60]

Process theology offers a striking way to affirm the redemption of every creature in the history of evolution: It builds into its metaphysics the crucial feature that God prehends every actual occasion during its concrescence, and thus every actual occasion is remembered forever in God's consequent nature. Moreover, some process theologians (such as Ian Barbour and Marjorie Suchocki) include the continuance of our subjectivity in God's memory. While Suchocki argues that process theology includes bodily resurrection—and, in a very creative argument, even justice and redress of evil—I am persuaded that process theology does not offer a concept for the resurrection of the body (*pace* Suchocki) which leads to a transformation of the universe into a New Creation.

John Haught draws on both Roman Catholic and process theology to insist that redemption should include all of life and not just humanity. Unfortunately, he offers three contrasting views of redemption: The first is clearly based in process theology's notion of objective immortality, the second is based on the power of nature, and the third is grounded in the bodily resurrection of Christ and the future transformation of the universe. In my opinion, the second view might be nested within either the first or third, but the first and third cannot be reconciled. In discussing the first view, Haught argues that cosmology and the far future of the universe are irrelevant to God's prehension of actual occasions and he dismisses potential conflicts with science. In the third view, however, he admits that cosmology poses a crucial challenge to his resurrection-based eschatology. This outright contradiction makes Haught's approach of marginal help.[61]

Christopher Southgate underscores the need for an eschatological response to natural theodicy. The Cross is both "*indicative* of God's co-suffering love of every entity in the cosmos . . . [and] *transformative* of that cosmos." He is critical of Moltmann who, while making a similar case about Christ as the redeemer of evolution, draws us away from the challenge of science.[62] I believe Southgate's writings on natural theodicy are extremely promising.

Denis Edwards offers a strikingly clear and robust trinitarian approach to theodicy and he recognizes the challenge posed by cosmology to a resurrection-based eschatology. He stresses the crucial importance of redeeming "every sparrow that falls" and not just humanity.[63]

John Polkinghorne is admirably clear about the challenge posed by cosmology to eschatology. He proposes that the future of creation is a new creation arising *ex vetere* out of the present world and he articulates this in full awareness of the challenges raised by science. Our first taste and grounds for hope in this new creation is the bodily resurrection of Jesus at Easter. The crucial feature that amplifies the challenge from science is the "embodied" character of Jesus' resurrection and the empty tomb.[64] I strongly endorse this approach and am developing a detailed response to eschatology and cosmology along similar lines. My concern is with Polkinghorne's kenotic response to theodicy. His "free-process defense" advocates divine self-limitation instead of divine coercion with regard to human freedom and the integrity of nature.[65]

The overall problem is that Polkinghorne's view that creaturely freedom requires divine limitation is widely shared in the theology and science community. I do not, however, think that human freedom in specific depends on limiting God's power, whether by self-limitation or metaphysical limitation. Instead I believe that God's grace is the condition for our true freedom from the bondage of sin. Many of these scholars make various *additional* connections between kenosis as divine limitation and the theology of creation which I also find questionable.[66] I expect that progress will be made when we begin to maintain the crucial distinctions between three separate but related topics: a) free will and physical determinism, b) grace and free will, and c) God's action and physical determinism.[67] I will simply state here that I would want to distinguish the problem of free will and its somatic enactment, where I too take an incompatibilist view, from both the problem of divine and human will and divine will and natural causality.[68] The latter two require considerable discussion and are not simply analogous to the first problem.

The path to a more robust natural theodicy and the challenge of both evolution and cosmology
Hence, as I see it, the real—and formidable—task is to construct an eschatology that meets both of these challenges: evolution and cosmology.

The challenge of evolution leads to the following criteria which eschatology must meet. First, it must include not only humanity and all the species in the history of life on earth, but more than that: not only every species but even and most importantly the individual creatures of each species. For creatures suffer, not species, and thus creatures individually—one by one—must be the focus of any genuine Christian eschatology. Second, it must include all creatures in terms of the concrete details of their own lives and in light of their own capacities and characteristics, and not as somehow included merely through human redemption. In particular, every moment of the time of evolution, and not just the "end" of historical time, must be taken up and transformed eschatologically by God into eternal life. Thus the "means-end" form of this theodicy must be such that *every means is also an end in itself.* I will call this a "nested means-end argument" (an "every sparrow that falls" theodicy). Third, and in sum, a "greater-good" argument must place this "good" within an eschatological context, for only such a context can offer a goodness sufficient to address the extent of evil in the history of the universe (the *Brothers Karamazov* problem).

In light of these criteria, my approach in specific will be to reformulate Hick's theodicy in an eschatology explicitly grounded in the Easter event, the bodily resurrection of Jesus. Only in this way, I believe, can we offer an eschatology appropriate to Hick's "means-end" argument,[69] and one which meets these stipulated criteria.

In addition, in order to move us beyond mere kenosis to genuine eschatology, I believe that both kenotic theodicy and eschatology must be structured on a trinitarian doctrine of God. The reason here is simple: it is the trinitarian God who will act to bring about the redemption of all of nature since it is this God who is revealed as God in and through the cross and resurrection of Jesus. A kenotic theodicy (that God suffers voluntarily with the world) in and of itself is not redemptive. Eschatology is required, in which the Father who suffers the death of the Son acts anew at Easter to raise Jesus from the dead. In turn, the involuntary suffering of all of nature—each species and each individual creature—must be taken up into the voluntary suffering of Christ on the cross (theopassionism) and through it the voluntary suffering of the Father (patripassionism).

The challenge from the far future of the universe, however, is much more severe than the challenge of evolution, and I will leave the details to future work.

Conclusions: The Failure of Evolutionary Natural Theodicy and the Need for a Robust Eschatology of New Creation in Light of Scientific Cosmology

> Does Darwinism make Christianity impossible?
> Dawkins, yes; Ruse, no.[70]

> [W]e cannot hope to state a Christian theodicy without taking seriously the doctrine of a life beyond the grave.[71]

How then do we respond to the problem of natural theodicy? My response is to recognize that the problem is generated in part by the fact that natural evil has been discussed in the context of the theology of creation. I believe, however, that we *cannot* answer the challenge of theodicy if the framework is creation—the universe as we know it and the laws that science has discovered, either through an Augustinian/Niebuhrian or an Irenaean/Hickian approach alone. Given science, we see ever more clearly and ominously the scale of the problem of natural evil: It extends back before and down under biology even to the physics of thermodynamics and outwards endlessly to cosmology as the scientific description of the universe as a whole. More ominously, we see that the challenge is immense: we have been forced to recognize "natural evil" as *constitutive of life* and *not just a consequence* of a historical event now taken as mythological.

Hence I propose that the only possibility for an adequate response to natural theodicy will be to relocate the problem of sin and evil beyond the theology of creation into a theology of redemption: the kenotic suffering of God with the world together with the eschatological transformation of the universe in the New Creation beginning proleptically with God's new act at Easter in the bodily resurrection of Jesus. This combined kenosis and eschatology might respond in a more helpful way to natural evil as well as moral evil than previous approaches. In doing so the implications we have found here should serve to help construct such an eschatology and the criteria should help assess its value. Conversely such a nuanced eschatology might shed light on contemporary physics, cosmology, and evolutionary biology as suggested by the methodology of creative mutual interaction. These observations, then, offer directions and criteria for future research in trinitarian eschatology and scientific cosmology.

Acknowledgement

I am very grateful to Christopher Southgate for his many insightful comments on an earlier draft of this chapter.

Endnotes: Chapter 8

[1] Based on a lecture given at a 2003 conference sponsored by the Australian Theological Forum in Melbourne and eventually published as: "Natural Theodicy in an Evolutionary Context: The Need for an Eschatology of New Creation," *Theodicy and Eschatology*, Bruce Barber and David Neville, Task of Theology Today, V (Adelaide: Australian Theological Forum, 2005).
[2] Richard Dawkins, *A River Out of Eden: A Darwinian View of Life* (New York: Basic, 1995), 133.
[3] Denis Edwards, *The God of Evolution: A Trinitarian Theology* (New York: Paulist, 1999), 13.
[4] I realize that this is a debatable point and can be seen as an anthropomorphic projection. Even if it were an overstatement, and I'm not convinced that it is, it could hardly be doubted that most animals experience real fear in the predator/prey cycle.
[5] A brief note on terminology: Most scholars make a basic distinction between "moral evil" and "natural evil." They use the term moral evil (or "sin") to refer to acts committed, or at least not subverted, by humans as free moral agents that are contrary to God's will and that subvert human flourishing. The term "natural evil" (or sometimes "physical evil") stands for phenomena which also subvert human flourishing but are not the result of human agency, such as earthquakes, tsunamis, disease, and their consequences including suffering and death, thus phenomena which are evil but not sinful. I wish to expand the latter term to include those phenomena which subvert the flourishing of life in all its varieties, and to encompass the phenomenon of the extinction of species as well as the death of individual organisms. Clearly a much more detailed set of terms is needed to make the careful distinctions one should eventually make in separating out physical evils that can afflict any form of life (human and nonhuman) but are not the result of agency, such as earthquakes, and biological evils that afflict sentient nonhuman life and are the result of nonhuman agency (and thus not moral agency), such as the suffering of animals during predation. Christopher Southgate has developed the term "evolutionary evil" in ways that are roughly parallel to my extension of "natural evil" to the pre-human realm. See Christopher Southgate, "God and Evolutionary Evil: Theodicy in the Light of Darwinism," *Zygon: Journal of Religion and Science* 37.4 (December 2002): 803–21.
[6] Other accounts of what drives evolution, such as punctuated equilibrium, panadaptionism, neo-Lamarkian effects, self-organization, cooperation, and symbiogenesis, may provide helpful critiques of the central role accorded to natural selection in neo-Darwinism. For an excellent overview see Ian G. Barbour, "Five Models of God and Evolution," in *Evolutionary and Molecular Biology,* ed. Robert John Russell, William R. Stoeger and Francisco J. Ayala (Vatican City State; Berkeley, Calif.: Vatican Observatory Publications; Center for Theology and the Natural Sciences, 1998), 419–42; hereafter *EMB.* Still, even if our understanding of what drives evolution "evolves," the facticity of natural evil will remain to be dealt with one way or another theologically, and no glib appeal to the challenges to neo-Darwinism will nullify the problem of evolutionary theodicy.
[7] Robert John Russell, "Sin, Salvation, and Scientific Cosmology: Is Christian Eschatology Credible Today?" in *Sin & Salvation*, eds. Duncan Reid and Mark Worthing (Adelaide, Australia: ATF, 2002).
[8] Sponsored in part by a grant from Philadelphia Center for Science and Religion #357.
[9] Karl Rahner, "Why Does God Allow Us to Suffer?" in *Theological Investigations*, Vol. 19 (New York: Crossroad, 1983), 206–8.
[10] Chance in the context of biological evolution occurs at and between many levels of biological complexity. There is random variation at the molecular level, including genetic mutation, crossing over, and the dissimilation of these changes through sexual reproduction. Some of these changes are eventually expressed phenotypically in individual organisms. There are also random changes at the macroscopic level in the environment of populations competing for finite resources. The changes at the molecular and macroscopic levels are themselves entirely independent of each other. Finally, if the characteristics expressed by individuals in the population increase the relative fitness (reproductive advantage) of the individuals holding them they may be passed on to future generations. This "filtering" process of the environment on phenotypic changes gives rise to natural selection.

[11] Jacques Monod, *Chance and Necessity: An Essay on the Natural Philosophy of Modern Biology*, trans. Austryn Wainhouse (New York: Vintage Books, 1972), 112, 180.

[12] David J. Bartholomew, *God of Chance* (London: SCM, 1984), 16. Bartholomew's book provides an excellent survey of theistic responses up to the mid-1980s.

[13] A. R. Peacocke, *Creation and the World of Science: The Bampton Lectures, 1979* (Oxford: Clarendon, 1979). See for example the discussion on 90 and following where Peacocke specifically refers to the two kinds of chance.

[14] Bartholomew, *God of Chance*, 34.

[15]See for example Robert John Russell, "Finite Creation Without a Beginning: The Spiritual and Theological Significance of Stephen Hawking's Quantum Cosmology," *The Way: Review of Contemporary Christian Spirituality* 32.4 (October 1992): 268–81.

[16] Stephen W. Hawking, *A Brief History of Time: From the Big Bang to Black Holes* (New York: Bantam Books, 1988), x. For a response to Hawking and an extended discussion of the changing role of t = 0 in Big Bang, inflation, and quantum cosmology in relation to creation *ex nihilo* see Robert John Russell, "Finite Creation Without a Beginning: The Doctrine of Creation in Relation to Big Bang and Quantum Cosmologies," in *Quantum Cosmology and the Laws of Nature,* eds. Robert J. Russell, Nancey C. Murphy and Chris J. Isham (Vatican City State: Vatican Observatory Publications; Berkeley, Calif.: Center for Theology and the Natural Sciences, 1993), 293–329, hereafter *QCLN*; Robert John Russell, "T=0: Is It Theologically Significant?" in *Religion and Science: History, Method, Dialogue*, eds. W. Mark Richardson and Wesley J. Wildman (New York: Routledge, 1996), 201–26.

[17]For detailed definitions and discussion of these terms see chapters 4–6.

[18] A non-interventionist account would depict God's regular action and God's special action as two modes of a single, coherent form of divine action. See for example Robert John Russell, "Divine Action and Quantum Mechanics: A Fresh Assessment," in *Quantum Mechanics,* eds. Robert John Russell, Philip Clayton, et al. (Vatican City State: Vatican Observatory Publications; Berkeley, Calif.: Center for Theology and the Natural Sciences, 2001), section 2, hereafter *QM.*

[19]For an overview see Robert John Russell, "Does 'The God Who Acts' Really Act? New Approaches to Divine Action in the Light of Science," *Theology Today* 51.1 (March 1997). The CTNS/VO series includes: Russell, et al., eds., *QCLN*; Robert John Russell, Nancey C. Murphy and Arthur R. Peacocke, eds., *Chaos and Complexity,* Scientific Perspectives on Divine Action Series (Vatican City State: Vatican Observatory Publications; Berkeley, Calif.: Center for Theology and the Natural Sciences, 1995), hereafter *C&C*; Robert John Russell, William R. Stoeger, S. J. and Francisco J. Ayala, eds., *EMB* (Vatican City State: Vatican Observatory Publications; Berkeley, Calif.: Center for Theology and the Natural Sciences, 1998); Robert John Russell, Nancey Murphy, et al., eds., *Neuroscience and the Person* (Vatican City State: Vatican Observatory Publications; Berkeley, Calif.: Center for Theology and the Natural Sciences, 1999), hereafter *N&P*; Russell, et al., eds., *QM.* For a brief description of these approaches, see the introductions to Russell, Murphy, and Peacocke, *C&C*, section 3.4, and Russell, Philip Clayton, et al., *QM,* section 2.1. Summaries of these papers can be found at http://www.ctns.org/books.html.

[20]There are at least four options which scholars are currently exploring: causality between different levels of complexity, including 1) top-down causality involving God's relation to the universe-as-a-whole and its effects on the macroscopic world, and God's relation to the mind/brain problem; 2) bottom-up causality involving God's action in relation to quantum physics and its effects on the macroscopic world; 3) causality within the macroscopic world, including God's relation to chaotic processes in the macroscopic world; and 4) neo-Thomistic and process philosophy-based discussions of divine action at every level in nature. Hopefully all forms of divine action can be integrated into one picture.

[21]The quotation is taken from a letter from Darwin to Asa Gray, May 22, 1860. References can be found in Dawkins, *A River Out of Eden: A Darwinian View of Life*, 95.

[22] Dawkins, *A River Out of Eden*, 133.

[23] Christopher Southgate, "God and Evolutionary Evil," 808–09.

[24] Arthur Peacocke, *Theology for a Scientific Age: Being and Becoming—Natural, Divine and Human*, enlarged edition (Minneapolis: Fortress Press, 1993), 63, 221.
[25] Edwards, *The God of Evolution*, 38.
[26] Peacocke, *Theology for a Scientific Age*, 222.
[27] Michael Ruse, *Can a Darwinian Be a Christian? The Relationship Between Science and Religion* (Cambridge: Cambridge University Press, 2001), 136. Here Ruse cites Richard Dawkins, "Universal Darwinism," in *Molecules to Men*, ed. D. S. Bendall (Cambridge: University of Cambridge Press, 1983), 403–25. In this book Ruse gives a very thoughtful and promising account of what he believes is really at stake in the Christianity/evolution controversy.
[28]Ron Cole-Turner makes a similar point in Ronald Cole-Turner, *The New Genesis: Theology and the Genetic Revolution* (Louisville: Westminster/John Knox, 1993).
[29] See for example Saint Augustine, Bishop of Hippo, *Confessions*, trans. Henry Chadwick (Oxford: Oxford University Press, 1991); and St. Augustine, *The City of God*, trans. Henry Bettenson (London: Penguin, 1984).
[30] Friedrich Schleiermacher, *On Religion: Speeches to Its Cultured Despisers*, trans. John Oman (New York: Harper & Row, 1958); Friedrich Schleiermacher, *The Christian Faith*, ed. H. R. Mackintosh and J. S. Stewart (Edinburgh: T & T Clark, 1968); most references can be found in Schleiermacher, *The Christian Faith*, paragraphs 58–89.
[31]Note: "Original" designates a timeless character of the world and of humankind, not a state in the past (Eden) from which we have "fallen": Schleiermacher rejects the Fall unequivocally.
[32] The original sinfulness of the individual (or "congenital sin") is grounded in our developmental phenomenology prior to any specific action or "acts of sin"; we are born this way, and yet we are personally responsible for our specific acts of sin. The original sinfulness of society (or "conditioning sin") is the distorted character of society into which each individual is born, which influences each individual in their lives, and to which each individual contributes by their own acts of sin.
[33] Reinhold Niebuhr, *The Nature and Destiny of Man: Volume I: Human Nature* (New York: Charles Scribner's Sons, 1941/1964).
[34] Ibid., 242. "Original sin, which is by definition an inherited corruption, or at least an inevitable one, is nevertheless not to be regarded as belonging to his essential nature and therefore is not outside the realm of his responsibility. Sin is natural for man in the sense that it is universal but not in the sense that it is necessary."
[35] Robert John Russell, "The Thermodynamics of 'Natural Evil'," *CTNS Bulletin* 10.2 (Spring 1990): 20–25. See also chapter 7 in this book.
[36] Robert John Russell, "Entropy and Evil," *Zygon: Journal of Religion and Science* 19.4 (December 1984): 449–68. I am grateful for the appreciative inclusion of these insights by Mark Worthing in his recent book, Mark W. Worthing, *God, Creation, and Contemporary Physics*, Theology and the Sciences Series (Minneapolis, Minn.: Fortress Press, 1996), ch. 4, "The Problem of Evil" and "Summary."
[37] Ian G. Barbour, *Myths, Models, and Paradigms: A Comparative Study in Science & Religion* (New York: Harper & Row, 1974); Sallie McFague, *Metaphorical Theology: Models of God in Religious Language* (Philadelphia: Fortress Press, 1982).
[38] Russell, "Entropy and Evil," 465. I compared Augustine's understanding of evil as privation of being with entropy in physics: Entropy does not refer to something physical (for example, matter) or even a property of something physical (like mass, which is a property of matter). Instead it is a measure of the loss of available energy or the increase in disorder. Hence neither evil nor entropy are "ontological"; both are dependent on being, lacking independent existence. In that paper and in chapter 7 in this book I compared entropy in physics to evil in Paul Tillich's theology. Tillich describes evil as having "no independent standing in the whole of reality, but . . . it is dependent on the structure of that in and upon which it acts destructively," and, his memorable phrase that the form of evil is the "structure of destruction." Thus evil "'aims' at chaos" and when chaos is attained, "both structure and destruction have vanished." See 457–459.

[39] Nancey Murphy and George F. Ellis, *On the Moral Nature of the Universe: Theology, Cosmology, and Ethics*, Theology and the Sciences Series (Minneapolis, Minn.: Fortress Press, 1996). See my response in Robert John Russell, "The Theological Consequences of the Thermodynamics of a Moral Universe: An Appreciative Critique and Extension of the Murphy/Ellis Project," *CTNS Bulletin* 19.4 (Fall 1998): 19–24.
[40] John Hick, *Evil and the God of Love,* revised edition (San Francisco: Harper & Row, 1966).
[41] Barry L. Whitney, *What Are They Saying About God and Evil?* (New York: Paulist, 1989), 38.
[42] Hick, *Evil*, 211–18.
[43]Hick notes that there is no evidence that Schleiermacher was influenced directly by Irenaeus or the early church, leading Hick to refer to this form of theodicy as a "type," not a 'tradition.' Ibid., 219.
[44] Ibid., 236–40.
[45] Thomas F. Tracy, "Evolution, Divine Action, and the Problem of Evil," in *EMB*, 511–30.
[46] Hick, *Evil*, viii.
[47] Ibid., 281–2, 353.
[48] Ibid., 327–31.
[49] Ibid., 385.
[50] Ibid., 339–40.
[51] Ibid., 364.
[52] Ruse, *Can a Darwinian Be a Christian?* 134.
[53] Holmes Rolston III, *Science and Religion: A Critical Survey* (New York: Random House, 1987), 146.
[54] Sarah Coakley, "Kenosis: Theological Meanings and Gender Connotations," in *The Work of Love: Creation as Kenosis*, ed. John Polkinghorne (Grand Rapids, Mich.: Eerdmans, 2001), 192–210; Jürgen Moltmann, "God's Kenosis in the Creation and Consummation of the World," in ibid., 137–51; Keith Ward, "Cosmos and Kenosis," in ibid., 152–66.
[55] Coakley, "Kenosis: Theological Meanings and Gender Connotations," 203.
[56] Ibid., 193–4.
[57] Ted Peters, *God: The World's Future: Systematic Theology for a Postmodern Era* (Minneapolis, Minn.: Fortress Press, 1992), 198–9.
[58] Moltmann, "God's Kenosis in the Creation and Consummation of the World," 142, esp. footnote 5.
[59] Rolston, *Science and Religion*, 144–46, 289–92; Holmes Rolston III, "Does Nature Need to Be Redeemed?" *Zygon: Journal of Religion and Science* 29.2 (June 1994): 227; Holmes Rolston III, "Kenosis and Nature," in *The Work of Love,* 58–65.
[60] Peacocke, *Theology for a Scientific Age*, 126–28, esp. endnote #72; Arthur Peacocke, "The Cost of New Life," in *The Work of Love,* see Russell, "Bodily Resurrection, Eschatology and Scientific Cosmology," 13–14.
[61] John F. Haught, *God After Darwin: A Theology of Evolution* (Boulder, Colo.: Westview, 2000), 43, 109–15, 160–64.
[62] Southgate, "God and Evolutionary Evil," 818. He cites Jürgen Moltmann. *The Way of Jesus Christ: Christology in Messianic Dimensions*, trans. by Margaret Kohl (London: SCM, 1990), 296–297. Christopher Southgate and Andrew Robinson, "Varieties of Theodicy: An Exploration of Responses to the Problem of Evil Based on a Typology of Good-Harm Analyses," in *Physics and Cosmology: Scientific Perspectives on Natural Evil*, ed. Nancey Murphy, Robert John Russell and William R. Stoeger S. J. (Vatican City State: Vatican Observatory Publications; Berkeley, Calif.: Center for Theology and the Natural Sciences, 2007), 67–92.
[63] Edwards, *The God of Evolution*, 39–44; Denis Edwards, "Every Sparrow That Falls to the Ground: The Cost of Evolution and the Christ-Event," *Ecotheology: The Journal of Religion, Nature and the Environment* 11:1 (March 2006), 103–123.
[64] John C. Polkinghorne, *The Faith of a Physicist: Reflections of a Bottom-up Thinker* (New Jersey: Princeton University Press, 1994), ch. 9; John Polkinghorne, "Eschatology: Some Questions and Some Insights from Science," in *The End of the World and the Ends of God: Science and Theology on*

Eschatology, ed. John Polkinghorne and Michael Welker (Harrisburg, Pa.: Trinity International, 2000); John Polkinghorne, "Eschatological Credibility: Emergent and Teleological Processes," in *Resurrection: Theological and Scientific Assessments*, ed. Ted Peters, Robert John Russell, and Michael Welker (Grand Rapids, Mich.: Eerdmans, 2002).

[65] Polkinghorne, *The Faith of a Physicist*, 83 ff; John C. Polkinghorne, *Science and Providence: God's Interaction with the World*, 1st ed. (Boston: Shambhala, 1989), 63–64; John Polkinghorne, "Kenotic Creation and Divine Action," in *The Work of Love*, 102–05.

[66] Peacocke, *Theology for a Scientific Age*, 123; Polkinghorne, *Science and Providence*, 66–68; see also Polkinghorne, *The Faith of a Physicist*, 83–85; Ian G. Barbour, *Religion in an Age of Science*, Gifford Lectures; 1989–1990 (San Francisco: Harper & Row, 1990), 241; Haught, *God After Darwin: A Theology of Evolution*, 111–12; Murphy and Ellis, *On the Moral Nature of the Universe.* Note: Murphy and Ellis add to the problem by using the term "non-inteventionist" in two very different ways: to refer to non-inteventionist divine action, as in the NIODA project (215), and to refer to God's self-restraint in the face of violence (247). The former suggests that God *does* act in the world but in such a way that it does not violate the laws of nature. The latter suggests that God does *not* act in the world even when God's action might seem highly desirable since that would be an "intervention," and such interventions might, in turn, undercut their arguments for pacifism.

[67] These distinctions have also been made in a very recent essay by Kirk Wegter-McNelly, "Reflections on the CTNS/VO Series, 'Scientific Perspectives on Divine Action,'" to be published in the CTNS/VO Capstone volume, *Scientific Perspectives on Divine Action: Fourteen Years of Problems and Progress,* (forthcoming 2007). He refers to them as "anthropo-physical in/compatibilism, anthropo-theological in/compatibilism, and theo-physical in/compatibilism," respectively.

[68]See Sarah Coakley's remarks on incompatibilism in Coakley, "Kenosis: Theological Meanings and Gender Connotations," 203.

[69] It could later be extended to the question of life in the universe (ET) and a "cosmic Christ."

[70] Adapted from the CTNS Spring Forum by Michael Ruse, in which Ruse gave what he takes to be Dawkins's answer and then his own.

[71] Hick, *Evil*, 339–40.

Chapter 9

The Transfiguration of the Cosmos: A Fresh Exploration of the Symbol of the Cosmic Christ[1]

> Christianity that is not entirely and altogether eschatology has entirely and altogether nothing to do with Christ.
>
> —Karl Barth[2]

> Then the human race as well as the entire world, which is intimately related to man [*sic*] and achieves its purpose through him, will be perfectly reestablished in Christ. . . . *The final age of the world has already come upon us.*
>
> —*Lumen Gentium*[3]
> (my italics)

1. Introduction

In the quiet dawn of Easter we Christians confess the threefold mystery at the center of our faith: "Christ has died, Christ has risen, Christ will come again." In daily prayer and weekly liturgy we combine this confession with faith in God's objective divine action and a rich doctrine of creation in the simple but stunning sentences lying at the heart of the prayer Jesus taught us: "The reign of God come, God's will be done, on earth as it is in heaven." In the documents of the church we teach explicitly a proleptic eschatology: "the final age of the world has already come upon us" based on a universal future: "the resurrection of the dead and the life of the world to come." In the theological research agendas of both Catholics and Protestants we find a renewal of eschatological thinking, foreseen by Karl Barth seventy years ago in the work which inaugurated the contemporary theological period, *Der Romerbrief*. In the practice of the church struggling for human liberation, eschatology is a central rallying point for solidarity with the poor and the oppressed. In the spiritual exercises of the faithful, eschatology brings home the promise that we shall experience personally the beatific *visio dei* as we are taken at our death into paradise (Lk. 23:43). But in its ability to make eschatology intelligible to Christians and nonbelievers alike in an age which takes for granted that our world is a tiny planet lost in the immensity of an unfeeling universe and that biological life is the unintended product of blind, evolutionary chance, we as theologians in service of the church have failed.

Why have we failed the test of intelligibility? Partly, I think, because of neglect. Within dogmatics itself, the doctrine is often presented in antiquarian form. For centuries most theologians have allowed the problem of the "last things" to take a last place, and a minor, muffled one at that, in most standard presentations of Christian dogmatics. It has not been the vigorous, centralizing theme around which to organize and interpret the full array of theological questions that a Karl Rahner, a Karl Barth, or a Wolfhart Pannenberg would insist on. In consequence, eschatology has become out of touch not only with the rest of church doctrine—God, creation, human nature, sin, redemption, christology, and the like—but also with the way Christians and non-Christians alike look at the world—the universe—around them.

One indication of the extent of this failure is the way the Evangelical and Fundamentalist segments of the church have been obsessed with eschatology for the last century—at least since John Nelson Darby and the C.I. Scofield Reference Bible. The American society, in turn and in large measure, has become captivated by the idea of the Last Things and the doctrine of the Rapture—as evidenced by the Left Behind series featured on the New York Times Best Seller List for almost a decade. This makes the intellectual failure of the church in these matters doubly disappointing because such gnostic notions of eschatology are not even native to Christianity but are imported from sectarian Adventism. It is all the more alarming because many of our nation's leaders subscribe to such doctrines—and even base their foreign policy on it. A recovery and heralding of a truly robust eschatology based on a scholarly reading of the New Testament has never been more important.[4]

Yet even when the cost of such failure is recognized and an earnest desire exists to remedy the situation, today's theologian—whether conservative or liberal—is extremely hard-pressed to interpret biblical language about resurrection, judgment, heaven and hell, and the beatific vision to either the secular world or the believing faithful when the scientific understanding of the history and future of the universe is taken squarely on board. It seems almost unimaginable how one should relate these terms to the worldview that reigns so prominently today, one derived from the natural sciences: cosmology, physics, biology, human genetics, and the rest.

Nor is there any easy to escape to this challenge: We cannot simply "write-off" eschatology as a pre-modern concern and then "de-mythologize" the text (*à la* Bultmann) in order to focus clearly on the "real" message of the New Testament. Instead, beginning with Albert Schweitzer's quest for the historical Jesus and continuing with today's biblical scholarship, we have discovered that the New Testament is irreducibly eschatological. Thus, as Lutheran theologian Carl Braaten argues, eschatological thinking among religious scholars is unavoidable, because of the biblical-critical discovery of the eschatological core of the New Testament *kerygma*. Moreover, Braaten urges that it be pursued aggressively because even the secular world is ready for it, given the recent philosophical and psychological discoveries of the phenomenon of hope in human existence.[5]

Thus the rediscovery of New Testament eschatology and the demand by society to provide grounds for hope in a frenzied age brings to Christian scholars and clergy alike a profound crisis: How can we interpret the primitive Christian *kerygma* to the contemporary mind if its content, though intended to provide real hope, seems unintelligible in light of science? If we are to avoid being isolated in a theological ghetto we must find a way to make our language intelligible so that faith can fulfill, and not obfuscate, reason, and so that our witness to the God of truth can make contact with the modalities of truth and authenticity of secular knowing. It is to this goal that this chapter is directed, although in a very preliminary and provisional fashion. It is meant to start the conversation afresh about Christian eschatological hope in light of contemporary natural science.

The present chapter is not an appropriate place to rehearse the many accomplishments already made by scholars who work in "theology and science" in treating other doctrines in light of science. While significant results have been achieved in relating such areas as the doctrine of God, the doctrine of creation, and theological anthropology to science, the efforts so far in reformulating the contents of eschatology in light of science have been, in my opinion, much less fruitful. Their documentation can be found in the literature; its detailed review here would be pedantic.[6] Arthur Peacocke offers an important exception, particularly in his 1978 Bampton Lecture.[7] There he surveyed several ways to explore eschatology and contemporary science. Among the most promising schools of thought Peacocke singled out the theologians of hope (principally Jürgen Moltmann), the process theologians (principally Cobb and Birch), and the Teilhardian theologians. Still, this was by and large a preliminary sorting out of possibilities and not a detailed development of the task at hand. Moreover, the results seemed meager, given the overwhelming prospect of a universe existing for billions of years after the extinction of all life, as Big Bang cosmology suggests (see below for details).

Here I shall try out a fresh approach, inspired by the vision of Teilhard, moved by its failure, and then hopeful about a new possibility based rather closely on the theology of Karl Rahner. In the process, I will note the movement from within science itself to construct a form of "physical eschatology," and assess its significance for Christian theology.

In order to sharpen the discussion, I shall pursue this approach through the stating and testing of a basic thesis. The basic thesis I will explore is that the resurrection of Christ, and thus of all those saved through him, entails the transfiguration of the cosmos, such that all of nature is taken up and made into the New Creation. This would mean that the spiritual body Paul speaks of (σῶμα πνευματικόν, for example, 1 Cor. 15:44-46) should not be thought of in isolation from the environment of the New Creation. Rather, just as we as people are at present psychosomatic unities with an intrinsic evolutionary and ecological relationship to the earth and ultimately to the universe as a whole, so our spiritual bodies, upon resurrection, will involve an intrinsic relationship to all of the universe transformed from its present status as Creation to its eschatological status as New Creation. The thesis carries with it the claim that an event in terrestrial history can equally be an event at the end of cosmic history. The resurrection of Christ, then, is the first instance of the end-times, and the event of the resurrection is the prolepsis of the eschatological future.[8]

This thesis is corroborated by three main streams of the biblical text. The Noahic covenant, alone among the Hebrew covenants, explicitly includes the rest of creation along with humankind in the covenant with God (Gen. 8–9, esp. 8:21-

22; 9:12, 13, 16). The Pauline text from Romans (8:18-24) speaks of nature's travail and its longing for God's revelation. The earlier strand in Revelation (5:13)[9] includes not only humans but all of nature in the eschatological event of the descent of the New Jerusalem and thereby picks up the vision of Isaiah (65:17-25, 66:22-23).[10] The heart of my thesis, therefore, is that *we must think in terms of a transfiguration of the entire cosmos in order to unlock the theological intelligibility of the resurrection of the faithful at the parousia*. The challenge, therefore, will be to seek coherence between this thesis and the knowledge we have about the cosmos from the natural sciences, specifically contemporary cosmology, physics, and biology.

To explore this coherence—or lack of it—I will start with the writings of Pierre Teilhard de Chardin. After assessing his vision of Omega and its problems, I will turn to the cold harsh light of secular thought, represented by Bertrand Russell and Steven Weinberg, whose writings span this century and for whom cosmology brooks little quarter for the ultimate significance of life. Next I will discuss the efforts by such philosophically-minded scientists as Freeman Dyson and Frank Tipler to construct what they call "physical eschatology" within the strict confines of reductionistic science. Finally, I will turn to the theology of Karl Rahner regarding eschatology, interpreted by the very insightful recent writings of Australian theologian Denis Edwards. Using Rahner's profound thinking on resurrection and eschatology, I will then explore two new possibilities for at least partial coherence between insights from cosmology and a Rahnerian type of eschatology.

2. Teilhard's Vision of Omega and Some of Its Problems

A thorough review of Teilhard's arguments as developed in *The Phenomenon of Man* would take us beyond the limits of this chapter. Moreover, many writers have already criticized Teilhard from the point of view of evolutionary biology, and this is not my central focus. Here instead I will lift up three themes which seem critical to Teilhard's theory and which, though they are challenged by science, seem to be themes worth further exploration in light of Rahner's work and very recent developments in science.

These themes are: i) the second law of thermodynamics undercuts evolution, leading to the claim that there is a hidden form of energy within matter which is ultimately responsible for the growth of complexity and the production of the biosphere and the noosphere. ii) This hidden form of energy, or radial energy, is characteristic of the "within" of matter. All matter has a within as well as a without to it, and though ultimately united, the within and the without are effectively independent. iii) The ultimate goal of this evolutionary process, and with it the complexification of life and thought, is the Omega point conceived in terms of the future of the earth. The universe is thus not the subject of teleology, but terrestrial life and, in specific, *Homo sapiens*. Each of these themes is subject to challenge by science now. To explore them I will closely follow the analysis by John D. Barrow and Frank J. Tipler in their monumental text, *The Anthropic Cosmological Principle*.[11]

A. Is the second law a problem?

Teilhard viewed the second law of thermodynamics as undermining the apparent complexification progressively achieved by the processes of evolution. Hence he needed to posit an entirely novel form of energy, the radial energy of the within, by which complexification can occur in spite of the constant dissipation of organic systems and the concomitant increase of entropy. This is understandable, given the state of research in thermodynamics in the late 1930s, when Teilhard was writing.

Over the past two decades, however, and increasingly in very recent years, we have turned attention to the study of nonlinear systems far from thermodynamic equilibrium, as well as to chaotic and self-organizing systems in classical mechanics. The work of Manfred Eigen in Germany and Ilya Prigogine in Belgium, in particular, has shown that it is precisely through the dissipation of energy in open systems undergoing rapid fluctuations that new, highly ordered states can occur spontaneously out of old, low ordered states. "Order out of chaos" has become the hallmark of our day! Thus it is due to the processes of thermodynamics that evolutionary biology works to produce increasingly complex systems over geological times and given the twin requirements of genetic variation and natural selection. We need not suppose orthogenesis, be it a vitalist principle, a teleological cause, or an interior energy, in order to account for the grounds of evolution.

Still, one might very well claim that God works through each event as primary cause, and that the very laws of nature and their dialectical relation to variation in genes and environmental pressures are God's way of continually creating living forms. Hence, while a predetermined final goal may be eliminated by evolutionary chance, a concomitant drive which is expressed by the option for order out of chaos may be God's actual interaction with the world in an ongoing sense.

B. Are the within and the without effectively independent?

Teilhard depicts a complex relationship between the within and the without.[12] On the one hand, they are ultimately unified, as can be seen from his discussion of "the two energies":

> Without the slightest doubt, *there is something* through which material and spiritual energy hold together and are complementary. In the last analysis, *somehow or other*, there must be a single energy operating in the world.[13] (author's italics)

On the other hand, Teilhard admits that a direct transformation between the energies of the within and the without is problematic:

> Yet, seductive though it be, the idea of the *direct* transformation of one of these two energies into the other is no sooner glimpsed than it has to

> be abandoned. As soon as we try to couple them together, their mutual independence becomes as clear as their interrelation.[14]

In this context he gives a wonderful example of the problem. We may need to eat bread in order to live and thus to think, but the energy physicists measure as contained in the bread, the tangential energy, seems to bear no "simple correspondence" with the energy used in thought processes, the organized energies of the within of consciousness. After all the same slice of bread can be used to produce an enormous variety of thoughts!

> A quantitative disproportion of this kind is enough to make us reject the naive notion of "change of form" (or direct transformation)—and hence all hope of discovering a "mechanical equivalent" for will or thought.[15]

Teilhard, here, is wrestling with one of the hardest topics in science. Often described as the mind/body problem or the mind/brain problem, it is one which continues to play a fundamental role in interdisciplinary research involving physics, biology, and neurophysiology on the one hand, and cognitive science, philosophy of science, psychological science, and even theology on the other. Current metaphors for the problem include those of "software/hardware" drawn from discussions of computers and artificial intelligence, and "double agency" drawn from philosophy of mind (and, ultimately, involving philosophy of religion and theology in the problem of grace and free will). The question might be posed in this way: How do we, as free, embodied agents, act in the world? Reductive approaches see the mind as the brain writ large, but minimize or eliminate mental agency in the process. Holists see the mind as a source of "top-down" causality in relation to the brain, but try to avoid a dualism (read vitalism, too) if the mind is ontologized separately from the brain. The problem is complexified when the question of divine action is mixed in with that of human agency.

In light of this extensive and ongoing discussion we might take Teilhard's argument to imply a particularly fecund insight. Before presenting it, we must recall some basic ideas in thermodynamics. In thermodynamics one distinguishes rather sharply between the concepts of energy and available energy. In all thermodynamic processes, total energy is conserved, though it is transformed from one form to another: this is the first law of thermodynamics. However, in the process of transformation, energy is degraded and dissipated, lost by the system to the environment. It is irretrievable without the expenditure of additional available energy of even greater amounts: This is the second law of thermodynamics. The second law is usually expressed in terms of entropy as a measure of the disorder or degradation of energy: Entropy never decreases in a closed system. Now we are ready to track the insight derived from Teilhard's writings.

First, is there a direct exchange of energy between the without and the within? Teilhard admits that if there is, it is minimal. Moreover, we know that if there were, the first law would have to be generalized to include the quantity of spiritual energy to offset the loss of physical energy, thereby preserving the overall unity of these energies (and in effect solving the problem of the "causal joint" between mind and matter). But in any case, my real claim is the following: *The loss of available physical energy in any neurophysiological process may place an upper bound on the gain in what we might call the level of organization of the mental (spiritual) energy.*[16] In other words, an increase in entropy in the without might be related to an increase in knowledge or complexity of the within. This claim is intelligible because physicists since Teilhard's time have developed a deep relation between what is called information theory and thermodynamics. (Once again, Barrow and Tipler provide a helpful summary of the physics involved here.)

If we want to learn a specific amount of information (I) we must process a specific amount of energy (E) at a specific temperature (T). The equation relating I, E, and T is quite simple:[17]

$$I < kE/T$$

Here we measure I in bits of information (where one byte equals eight bits, and we typically count computer memory in terms of megabytes), E in ergs (where one erg is the energy it takes to accelerate a particle at rest with a mass of one gram to a speed of one centimeter per second) and k is a constant (given as 10^{16} bits degree Kelvin per erg). For example, digesting the proverbial piece of bread provides enough energy to generate 10^{25} bytes of thought! Compare this with the standard hard memory of a personal computer, perhaps 100 gigabytes ($100 \mathrm{x} 10^9$ bytes), the energy dissipated in metabolizing a piece of bread is the equivalent of the information stored in one hundred million million personal computers![18] Hence although eating bread does not necessarily lead to thinking meaningful thoughts, we now seem to be in a position to predict the maximum capacity of the information contained in those thoughts based on the entropy produced when digesting the bread which energizes them.

Again, Teilhard's point is that well taken, for even if we know how much available energy is used up when we process information (that is, when we think), that amount does *not* determine the content of our thoughts, only the measure of the information thereby contained. One could say with Teilhard that the structure or content of the within is *underdetermined* by the processes of the without: Thinking requires energy processing, but what exactly one thinks transcends the notion of the quantity of information achieved.

C. The terrestrial omega point as a crucial problem for Teilhard's entire approach

The Omega point, representing a convergence of life and the coalescing of humanity, seems tied to the earth in Teilhard's thinking. It is true that Teilhard ultimately understood the Omega point as lying beyond the cosmos, with the hyperpersonal converging on God. Still the earth, and not the cosmos, is a pivotal focus for the successive convergences in evolutionary history, including the biosphere and the noosphere. To what extent does this raise a problem for Teilhard's vision, given that the earth is a tiny part of an immense universe, given the possibility of life elsewhere in the universe, and given the fate of extinction for the earth in the supernova of the sun and the immensity of the far future of the cosmos stretching beyond the extinction of the earth?

First of all, the universe as we now know is enormously larger than Teilhard could have realized, given the date of his writing. In the visible universe alone there may well be a hundred billion galaxies with hundreds of billions of stars in each galaxy ranging over a volume twenty billion light-years in diameter.[19] How are we to think of the convergence of life on earth as affecting the destiny of a universe of such magnitude? Second, how are we to understand the cosmic significance of terrestrial life in light of the possibility of life throughout the universe? On the one hand, it could be that life on earth is of cosmic significance merely by the fact of its existence and independent of whether there is other life in the universe. On the other hand, it seems hard to avoid deciding on the cosmic significance of life on earth without interpreting the problem in terms of the possibility of life elsewhere. If life were spread throughout the cosmos, in what ways would the terrestrial life, and with it Christ, be related to extraterrestrial life, and with it, their evolutionary outcomes, including, possibly, other Christs? If life were nowhere to be found in the universe except on earth, would this increase its significance (as with the parable of the coin) or decrease its significance (as though it were a curious anomaly)? Finally, we must remember that the future of the earth is that of extinction in the supernova of the sun five billion years from now. What does this mean in terms of the terrestrial location of Omega? What is the theological implication of a universe continuing on for countless ages after life has expired, at least on earth?

Clearly what is needed is to rethink the entire problem of Christian eschatology in terms of a cosmic perspective. What we need is a truly *cosmic* interpretation of the Omega point.

3. The Cosmic Christ Versus the Standard Bleak Scientific Picture

Even before the development of current cosmology, prospects for life having any ultimate significance in the universe seemed bleak to many writers. One need only recall Bertrand Russell's moving prose in "A Free Man's Worship" written in 1903. Russell concludes with these words:

> That Man [*sic*] is the product of causes which had no prevision of the end they were achieving; that his origin, his growth, his hopes and fears, his loves and beliefs, are but the outcome of accidental collocations of atoms; that no fire, no heroism, no intensity of thought and feeling, can preserve an individual life beyond the grave; that all the labours of the ages, all the devotion, all the inspiration, all the noonday brightness of human genius, are destined to extinction in the vast death of the solar system, and that the whole temple of Man's achievement must inevitably be buried beneath the debris of a universe in ruins—all these things, if not quite beyond dispute, are yet so nearly certain that no philosophy which rejects them can hope to stand. Only within the

scaffolding of these truths, only on the firm foundation of unyielding despair, can the soul's habitation henceforth be safely built.[20]

A contemporary expression of nihilism drawn, at least nominally, from the worldview of science comes from Steven Weinberg:

> It is very hard to realize that this [world of ours] is just a tiny part of an overwhelmingly hostile universe. It is even harder to realize that this present universe has evolved from an unspeakably unfamiliar early condition, and faces a future extinction of endless cold or intolerable heat. The more the universe seems comprehensible, the more it also seems pointless.[21]

Both Bertrand Russell and Steve Weinberg reflect the mood which infiltrates much of the scientific community when it ponders the contemporary scene in cosmology. To understand this more fully, we should review a few basics here.

Contemporary cosmology arises out of Albert Einstein's theory of general relativity (c. 1915) and general relativity, in turn, presupposes Einstein's theory of special relativity (c. 1905). In special relativity, the space and time of classical physics are combined into a flat four-dimensional spacetime via the Lorentz transformations.[22] Over the following decade, Einstein worked to extend special relativity to include the gravitational interaction. In the resulting theory of general relativity (GR), the gravitational interaction, which Newton understood as a force acting in flat space, is reinterpreted in terms of the curvature of spacetime. Einstein achieved this result by making spacetime and matter into two theoretical concepts which, though referring to ontologically irreducible elements in nature, mutually condition one another.[23] Thus, according to Einstein, the distribution of matter in the universe affects the curvature of spacetime, and the motion of matter is affected by the curvature of spacetime, matter always moving along the shortest path (geodesic) of the local spacetime surface.

Einstein's equations were solved almost immediately for two particularly simple cases. In one case, we consider a single massive point particle as the source of the gravitational interaction, and we look for the kind of orbits surrounding it as predicted by Einstein's equations. The results are the famous Schwarzschild equations which, when applied to our solar system, lead to the standard tests of GR: the precession of the perihelion of Mercury, the deflection of star light as it passes close by the sun, and the redshift of light as it travels away from the gravitational source. Moreover, it turns out that when the gravitational source has a mass greater than twice the mass of the sun, a "horizon" develops around the mass. This means that observers falling through the horizon towards the mass can never escape, and light generated from sources within the horizon is forever trapped within the horizon. The situation is known popularly as a black hole.

In the second case we solve Einstein's equations for matter in the form of dust, that is, a pressureless collection of point particles moving freely about and interacting only by gravity. What makes this problem particularly relevant is that it applies beautifully to cosmology! Astronomers since the mid-1920s, beginning with Edwin Hubble, have discovered that if we conceive of the universe as composed of clusters of galaxies and plot their positions in space, these clusters are, in fact, scattered much like a uniform cloud of dust—but here the mass of each dust particle is the mass of a cluster of galaxies, each with hundreds of billions of stars per galaxy! Now according to Einstein's equations, the particles of dust (read clusters of galaxies) must be expanding apart from each other at tremendous speeds—and yet their expansion is slowing, due to gravitational attraction.

One of three scenarios is possible: In all three models, the universe starts from a singularity of zero size and infinite temperature about 15 billion years ago. The singularity is usually denoted as t=0.[24] In the "closed" model, the universe has a finite size. It will expand to a maximum size roughly 100 billion years from now and then recollapse to a singularity of zero size and infinite temperatures. In the "open" model, the universe has an infinite size, and, moreover, one which increases in time! It will expand forever and cool eventually to absolute zero. In the "flat" model, the universe is also infinite in size and it will expand forever, but at a slower rate.[25]

Thus cosmology depicts a universe vastly bigger than we ever imagined before this century, literally billions of light-years in just the visible universe alone! Moreover the universe *as a whole* is expanding in time—what John Wheeler calls the biggest discovery in the books of science! Finally cosmology tells us something amazing about the future: it's HUGE! The universe may continue to exist forever (if the universe is open), or for at least 100 billion years (if the universe is closed). In either case, life will surely cease to exist on earth at the solar supernova in the "near" future (5 billion years), and if constrained by the speed of light as an upper limit on migration to and communication between the stars, will undergo a diaspora of unthinkable dimensions. Moreover, the universe will darken as stars like ours turn into dwarf stars, and in the far future, all complex states of matter decay into elementary particles. The far, far future is, apparently, either "freeze" (open universe expanding and cooling forever) or "fry" (closed universe recollapsing to a final black hole of infinite temperatures). (Table 1.1[26] lists these eventualities along with their associated timescales. As Wolfhart Pannenberg once remarked to me, if the Big Bang scenarios are correct, they could well represent a falsification of Christian eschatology.

4. Eschatology as a Subset of Scientific Cosmology: The Birth of "Physical Eschatology"

According to the Friedrich Schleiermacher, the "father" of Protestant liberal theology, "one cannot be truly scientific without being pious." It is this piety, common to all humankind, that leads to our encounter with the universe, since "true religion is sense and taste for the Infinite."[27] It is perhaps not surprising that into the cognitive vacuum of theological eschatology the secular community has moved to erect its own visions of what seems to amount to humankind writ large (who after Feuerbach would be surprised, as Barth himself foresaw?). Still the vision so raised, that life might in fact succeed in "colonizing the universe," undergo all possible experience, and obtain all possible knowledge, is a striking claim given the stringencies of Big Bang cosmology. What is extraordinary is that this vision comes not from New Age pseudoscience (the words of science, the metaphysics of the occult), but from scientists themselves—indeed often the very scientists whose research area is theoretical cosmology! Moreover these scientists tell us that they are co-opting religion, and giving it—at last—a reliable foundation! These are claims which must be heard by us, even as we ask scientists to take the time to hear the claims of theologians (Teilhard, Peacocke, Birch, Cobb, and others) about the course of nature. Here I shall pick up the conversations among Frank Tipler and Freeman Dyson.[28]

A. Dyson's open universe eschatology

Freeman Dyson is well known for his outstanding contributions to theoretical physics. Recently, however, he has turned his attention to the problem of the far future in Big Bang cosmology, making the first contribution to what he and others now term "physical eschatology" with his ground-breaking paper, "Time Without End: Physics and Biology in an Open Universe."[29] As Tipler puts it: "The study of the survival and the behavior of life in the far future became a branch of physics with the publication [of Dyson's paper]."[30] According to Dyson, life *can* continue indefinitely into the far future of the open universe, even though the temperature approaches absolute zero and the structures we know of—galaxies, stars, planets, even atoms—eventually decay to fundamental particles. Dyson's scenario depends on accepting the premise that a living creature is (at least) a type of computer, imputing, processing, storing and exporting information. As Dyson starkly puts it in his 1985 Gifford Lecture:

> Life resides in organization rather than in substance. I am assuming that my consciousness is inherent in the way the molecules in my head are organized, not in the substance of the molecules themselves. If this assumption is true, that life is organization rather than substance, then it makes sense to imagine life detached from flesh and blood and embodied in networks of superconducting circuitry or in interstellar dust clouds.[31]

Here then is the important insight Dyson renders us: If organization can be achieved through *any* material substrate, not just that of terrestrial biochemistry, then computation by appropriately organized matter can beat the second law indefinitely.[32]

B. Tipler's closed universe eschatology

Tipler locates the search for physical eschatology within what he calls the "Final Anthropic Principle" (FAP): The universe must be such that intelligent life will continue to exist forever. For the FAP to hold in Dyson's approach, the universe must be open spatially (that is, infinite in size) and it must continue forever in time. In contrast, Tipler's model of the FAP depends on a closed universe, both finite in size and with a finite future. Tipler makes a crucial distinction, however, between the passage of physical time (in terms of which the future will be finite) and mental time (the rate at which information is processed by our minds/a computer). He is able to show that, though the future physical time of the closed universe is finite, its mental time need not be. Indeed, in Tipler's model, life can process an infinite amount of information before the "Big Crunch." This leads Tipler to propose that for the FAP to succeed, the universe must be closed. In his more recent writings, Tipler in particular claimed to treat a variety of theological concerns, including God, resurrection, and immortality, in terms of his "Omega point theory."[33]

Still, although Tipler and Dyson require contrasting cosmologies (closed versus open, respectively), Tipler concurs with Dyson about the prognosis for life in the far future of the universe:

> When atoms disappear human bodies will disappear, but programs capable of passing the Turing test need not disappear . . . The basic problem of physical eschatology is to determine if the forms of matter which will exist in the far future can be used as construction materials for computers that can run complex programs, if there is sufficient energy in the future environment to run the programs, and if there are any other barriers to running a program.[34]

C. Critical scientific, philosophical, and theological assessments

It may be unsurprising that Tipler's work in particular, and to a lesser extent that of Dyson, have been subject to critical scientific, philosophical, and theological assessments. Tipler's scientific claims have been attacked aggressively by other scientists.[35] Willem B. Drees has given a particularly careful and extensive scientific analysis of Dyson and Tipler's works.[36]

While Tipler and Pannenberg have engaged in an interesting and creative interaction,[37] this too has been critically assessed.[38] Finally, both Dyson's and Tipler's reductionist philosophies, as well as their theological assumptions, have been criticized by a variety of scholars including Polkinghorne, Barbour, Peacocke, Clayton, and Worthing.[39] In essence, life cannot be reduced completely to information processing, and eschatology cannot be merely the outcome of the routine processes of nature as described by scientific cosmology. Instead, life involves emergent properties and processes which transcend the competence of the natural sciences to fully explain, and the New Creation will come about as a radical transformation of the universe by a new act of God found proleptically in the resurrection of Jesus.

In short, the scenarios of "physical eschatology" may capture little more than a celebration of life or even a "whistling in the dark." Still, two things should be borne in mind. First, it was a scientist—Dyson—who squarely answered the pessimism of another scientist—Weinberg. Dyson specifically states his intentions:

> The universe that I have explored in a preliminary way in this book is very different from the universe which Weinberg envisaged when he called it pointless. I have found a universe growing without limit in richness and complexity, a universe of life surviving forever and making itself known to its neighbors across unimaginable gulfs of space and time. Whether the details of my calculations turn out to be correct or not, there are good scientific reasons for taking seriously the possibility that life and intelligence can succeed in molding this universe of ours to their own purposes. Twentieth-century science, when it looks to the future, provides a solid foundation for a philosophy of hope.[40]

And we should remember that, according to Carl Braaten, it was *precisely* the search for such a foundation that drove theologians to rework the doctrine of eschatology. But who among us, even those busy at the task of thinking eschatologically, has done so with the specific intention of responding to the crisis in worldviews stemming from scientific cosmology?

Secondly, we should remember instead that, until the work of Dyson and Tipler, the choices that *theologians* accepted for relating eschatology to cosmology seemed fruitless at best: either ignore science and accept a "two worlds" view, as in neo-orthodoxy, existentialist theology, narrative theology, biblical/traditional theology, or liberation theology (all of which lead to the isolation of theology from the universe); reject science and attempt to substitute a pseudoscience built out of a literal interpretation of the Bible as in "scientific creationism" (which leads to a warfare with secularity and divides Christians from secular culture); construct a theology within the confines of existing science and culture (which leads to liberalism or, as Michael Buckley demonstrated so powerfully with the Newtonian settlement, to atheism[41]); or follow other strategies that marginalize the cognitive and empirically relevant content of theology.

We may not think that eschatology is reducible to unending life in *either* a closed[42] or an open universe, but these attempts to honor and celebrate life in a cosmic perspective *should* prompt us to rethink the cosmological implications of just what is at stake about the transfiguration of the empirical universe through the resurrection of Christ—both for the sake of intelligibility for those who believe, and for the sake of communication with those who do not. To pursue this task we turn to Karl Rahner.

5. Eschatology as Cosmic Transformation: Hints from Karl Rahner

In my opinion, the problem we face is actually more theological than scientific. That is, what we need is an aggressive and creative new approach to the doctrine of eschatology which can be used to engage the scene laid before us by the natural sciences. I propose we begin afresh by turning to the theology of Karl Rahner. In the following discussion I hope to offer some initial points of departure for further reflection.

There are diverse sources in Rahner for our themes of eschatology, Christology, and soteriology in relation to the universe. In his recent and highly creative book, *Jesus and the Cosmos,*[43] Denis Edwards brings together a diverse selection of these writings around the problem of the cosmic significance of Christ. I will use Edwards to probe two passages in Rahner's thought.

A. Humanity as the cosmos become conscious of itself

Rahner is clearly committed to the thesis which I gave as the thesis of this chapter, that the resurrection has cosmic significance in terms of the transfiguration of the universe, a transfiguration in which the destiny of the world is proleptically decided. A subset of this thesis is Rahner's argument that humanity is in a profound sense the self-expression of the cosmos in which the cosmos becomes conscious of itself:

> If man [*sic*] does exist, and precisely if he is the "product" of nature, if he appears not just at any time at all, but at a definite point in this development, a point at which he himself can even direct this development at least partially by the fact that he now objectifies it and stands over against what has produced him, and transforms the producer itself, then this very nature becomes conscious of itself *in him.*[44]

How might science support the claim that human beings are the cosmos "come to self-awareness"? As reported above, the standard approach to understanding the relation between terrestrial life and the universe of galaxies and stars is that life is an insignificant feature of nature overall. Given enough planets with a wide variety of physical conditions, life will emerge somewhere. Still life is seen to play a derivative role, a product of "blind chance" via biological evolution, and a marginal role, occurring on at most perhaps 1 percent of 1 percent of 1 percent of 1 percent of all the planetary systems in the Milky Way galaxy, and similarly throughout the universe.[45]

To the extent that Teilhard tended to minimize the relevance of the question of extraterrestrial life, he left the door open to the arguments such as these of the insignificance of terrestrial life. On the one hand, the fact that it would take a vast universe to produce *some* planet capable of life led Teilhard to recognize that the size of the universe need not make life on earth anomalous. Quite the contrary it can be seen as making terrestrial life precious. Still Teilhard did not seem to think of terrestrial life as being integral to the cosmos, a clue to *this particular* cosmos, whether or not there is extraterrestrial life. In this sense he leaves open the rebuttal that if life is as extremely rare as it seems to be, it really lacks cosmic significance and is only the product of "blind chance."

Now, however, the occurrence of even terrestrial life in the universe together with recent insights into cosmology suggest that terrestrial life has a much more intimate relationship to the universe as a whole than was understood in Teilhard's day. Indeed these arguments seem to point to the "design" by God the Creator—where "design" refers to the character of the *universe as a whole*, and not of the specific features of living species. I am referring to the now-famous Anthropic Principle, which points to the uncanny fine-tuning of the fundamental constants which characterize the universe as a whole, constants such as the speed of light *c*, Planck's constant *h*, which governs the Heisenberg uncertainty principle, the mass and charge of the electron, and so on. We now know that, had the value of these constants been different than they are, by one part in a million or even a billion, life could never have arisen anywhere in the universe.

Of course the actual evolution of life is still entirely consistent with Darwinian biology which describes how life evolves. The point here is that had the constants been different, the universe would have been incompatible with the evolutionary process per se. The question then becomes why the constants should have these values out of all possible values. Some say this leads to a new form of the argument from design. God as Creator is both the cause of the existence of the universe and the author of its overall characteristics, described by the laws of nature and the values of the natural constants. God chose these values to be precisely what they are, in order that life would arise eventually and by "blind chance" on a planet such as ours. In this sense, the Anthropic Principle sidesteps the Darwinian counterargument to Paley and relocates the question of design at the cosmic level.

Needless to say, there are strong reactions from naturalists who turn, most often, to a "many-worlds" argument. Here "world" means "universe." The idea is that all possible *universes* exist, each manifesting a different set of values of the fundamental constants and perhaps of the laws of nature as well. Most of these universes are lifeless. One, in particular, is not: ours. Hence the problem of our existence in this universe is rendered a tautology: We have evolved in that particular universe whose global conditions (constants and law) are consistent with the possibility of our evolving.

In Figure 9.1 I have sketched the arguments in their simplest form.[46] Part (a) shows the possible values of two natural constants, c_1 and c_2, plotted on two axes. The ranges of values for each constant consistent with the possibility of the evolution of life, Δc_1 and Δc_2, are shown by the dotted lines. The cross-hatched region at the intersection of these dotted lines marks the joint constraints on the global characteristics of any universe consistent with life. Part (b) shows two reactions to part (a). According to the cosmic design argument, God chooses to create the only actual universe by fine-tuning it to lie within the cross-hatched region. According to the many-worlds argument, all possible universes exist, including the few universes consistent with life, as suggested by the cross-hatching of the entire diagram.

The details of the argument quickly become technical, and the verdict remains open between the two options and their variants, in my opinion.[47] Interestingly, however, the verdict itself is somewhat irrelevant to our thesis. Whether it's design or many-worlds, our thesis seems served by the anthropic character of the universe, since I take the real importance of this character to be as follows: We humans are far from being a fluke of nature, a detached phenomenon in the sea of galaxies. Rather, we are, even if we are alone in the Milky Way—or even the universe—a key to the kind of universe we live in, for our existence is intricately connected to the precise way in which our universe as a whole exists as it does. If we hold that God is the Creator of *this* universe, we

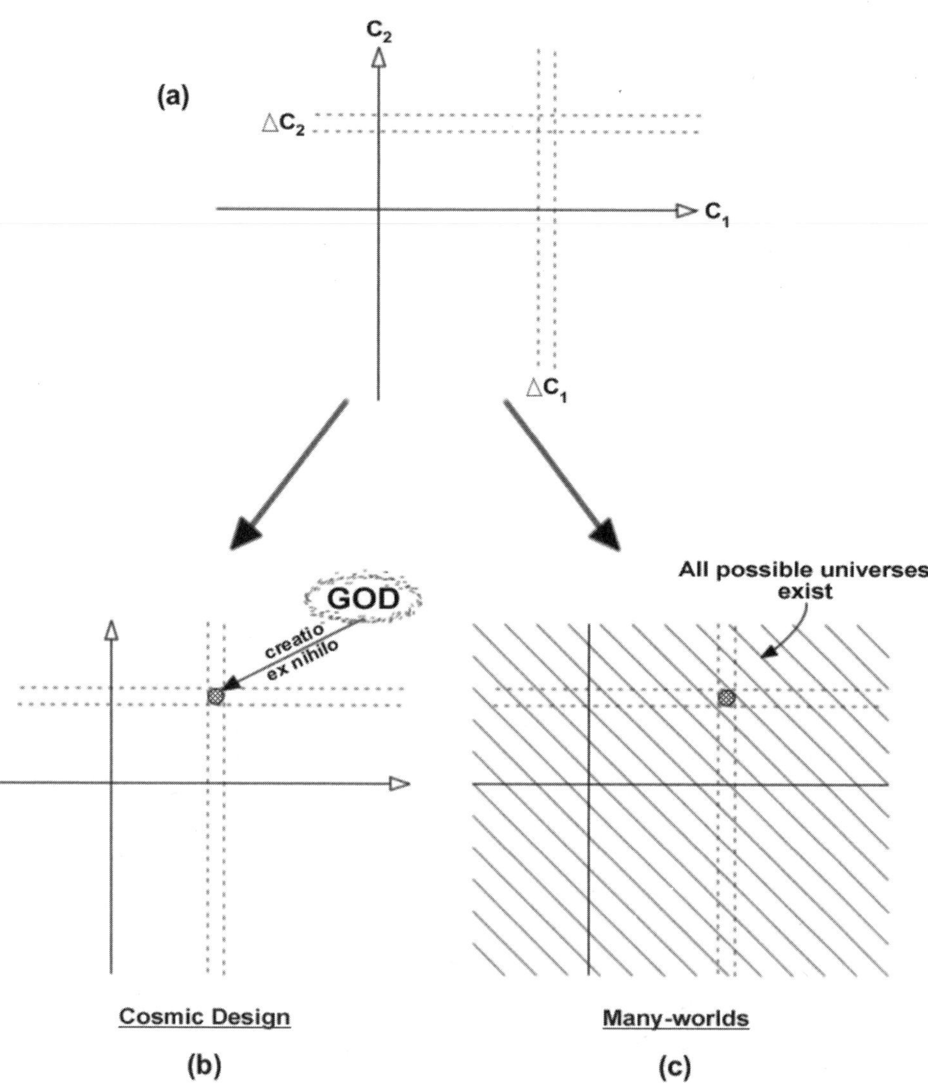

Figure 9.1: Does the fine-tuning of our universe (a) argue for God (b) or for many-worlds (c)?

are claiming something very special indeed, much more special and precise than we dreamed of before. We humans are not just tied to one particularly providential star with a propitious set of planets. Rather, we are somehow tied in with the entire cosmic scope of nature, for all of nature is governed by these "anthropic" constants: *c*, *h*, and so on. On the most remote whiff of interstellar dust is the faint impress of Teilhard's "hominization" in ways he may never have dreamed of!

B. The resurrection as prolepsis: the beginning of the end in historical time

The second theme I want to lift up in Rahner's writings is that in the resurrection we have the beginning of the end-times already occurring in history. This gives to eschatology its proleptic character, a view shared by several contemporary theologians working on Trinity and eschatology notably Wolfhart Pannenberg, Jürgen Moltmann, and Ted Peters. We see this theme in Rahner's discussion of the resurrection:

> Jesus' corporeal humanity is a permanent part of the one world with its single dynamism. . . . Consequently Jesus' resurrection . . . objectively is the beginning of the transfiguration of the world as an ontologically interconnected occurrence. In this beginning the destiny of the world is already begun. At all events it would in reality be different if Jesus were not risen.[48]

How is one to make sense of this, given the linear concept of time which is generally taken without a second thought in both theology and the natural sciences?

To bring this issue to as sharp a focus as possible I will put the options as contentiously as possible: Either a) *physics and cosmology are right*, and the universe will continue to exist for billions of years beyond the end of all biological life and (*pace* Dyson and Tipler) all forms of matter whatsoever which allow for the complexity and unity necessary for life, consciousness, and self-consciousness. If so, what do we mean by claiming that the resurrection of Jesus is "the beginning of the transfiguration of the world"? Or b) *theology is right*, that something radically new really happened *to the universe* at Easter. If so, then there must be some other way to construct a scientific cosmology consistent with all we know today but one which grows out of this theological claim and thus one in which the future is different from what standard cosmology predicts (that is, from "freeze or fry").[49]

However, if theology does have cognitive content, and I believe it does, then it too must somehow be taken seriously as making empirical, even competitive, claims about nature. Part of my warrant comes from the philosophy of science, where it is assumed that scientific theories are underdetermined by the data and that aesthetic and philosophical elements serve as sources for theories as well as criteria for theory choice. Given this, I see no reason why the cognitive component of theological doctrine could not serve as a source for certain metaphysical elements out of which to construct a testable alternative scientific theory. I would of course insist that such a theory be judged strictly by the standard criteria of scientific rationality, including the impartiality of empirical evidence assessed by the scientific community. Hoyle's steady state cosmology would serve as an example of such a project. For religious reasons (namely his commitment to atheism), Hoyle constructed a viable cosmology which did away with the embarrassing "beginning of the universe" in Big Bang cosmology, and one which survived two decades before its falsification. I take this to be an excellent example of a scientific theory constructed from theological roots. If after all this a theory could be constructed and tested, and if it were not clearly falsified, then its interpretation of the far future should be taken as seriously as that of Big Bang cosmology.

For the purposes of this chapter, I will assume case b). In this case, we can either start from scratch and try to construct an entirely new theory, or we can search for clues in alternative approaches within contemporary science itself which might get us beyond linear time. In either case it seems that a linear concept of time, although arguably essential in breaking with ancient cyclic views of time, is inadequate to the full eschatological vision. Somehow we must picture time as more complex than a linear view allows, such that an event within the historical sequence can also be an event at the end-times, and that the temporality of the post-Easter future differs from the linear projections of physics. Before taking the step of starting from scratch, I suggest we try seeing what might already be available on the blackboards of science. First, however, we have to have a clearer idea of what we are looking for theologically.

We get a glimmer of the "golden fleece" in Rahner's interpretation of death. Here Rahner seems to reject the notion of eternity as unending linear time as a basis for understanding life after death. "Christian eschatology . . . does not mean that things continue on after death as though, as Feuerbach put it, we only change horses and then ride on."[50] Thus he rejects the simplistic picture of a soul surviving on into this sort of unending time. On the other hand, he rejects the opposite conclusion that "with death everything is over because human time does not really continue on." Instead of viewing eternity in terms of simple linear time, Rahner describes eternity as "subsuming" the time we now know, the time

> which came to be temporarily so that freedom and something of final and definitive validity can be achieved. Eternity is not an infinitely long mode of pure time, but rather it is a mode of the spiritual freedom which has been exercised in time.[51]

Thus to treat eschatology we have to gain some insights into a more complex understanding of time which allows for the prolepsis of the resurrection and the temporality of divine eternity.

Can science help at all here? What we can say is still scanty, but there are signs from two quarters that a strictly linear view of time is inadequate to science, and thus its inadequacy to theology may be demonstrated *pari pasu*.

First, in cosmology, one finds that the topology of singularities (that is, "black holes") requires the splitting of time into several "strands." Basically, we think of two observers, one of whom (unfortunately) falls into a black hole, the other who avoids the trap and continues on into the indefinite future. Ted signals his observations while falling into the trap to Sara who floats free of the singularity. According to Sara, Ted falls into the hole in a matter of seconds. Once inside the event horizon surrounding the hole, contact is forever lost with Ted and his fate is unknown to Sara. However, to her partial appeasement, Sara finds it takes forever for Ted to actually fall into the hole. From his perspective, however, Ted is not so amused. In seconds he is trapped in the singularity and within milliseconds encounters the essential singularity lurking at its core. It might comfort him a bit to know that the event of his demise at the singularity is topologically, though not experientially, identical with Sara's approach to what can be called the Omega point of this model: the absolute infinite future event.

Roger Penrose[52] has developed a diagrammatic approach which helps tremendously with this sort of physics (see Figure 9.2). Ted and Sara both travel forward in time from the infinite past, denoted by α. Ted's path diverges from Sara's and crosses the horizon, after which it inevitably encounters the singularity at the heart of the black hole, indicated by a double horizontal line. Sara continues into the infinite future, approaching the ultimate event, Ω. Note that the double line of the singularity *within* the black hole is connected topologically, though not causally, to the event Ω in Sara's infinite future.

The point of this bizarre but mathematically true story is that a model universe consisting of even one singularity has to be described in what amounts to at least two different temporal perspectives. The remote future remains remote for some observers (like Sara) but enters into the immediate future, that is, the present, of others (like Ted). A model of prolepsis? Perhaps only extraordinarily crudely, but what is surprising is that physics on its own should even be speculating this way.

Thus, if we really believe that the end-times have already appeared in the events of Easter, we theologians ought to insist that *the universe has a more complex temporal topology than that of linear time, and that this might even be prefigured in some way by the musings of theoretical physics and cosmology.*

The second argument comes once again from Ilya Prigogine. Recall his discovery that nonlinear systems far from equilibrium can spontaneously move into states of greater order. Recently this has led him to speculate on the metaphysics of time and to think in terms of time as a discrete, as opposed to a continuous, variable. This would mean that the age of a system, that is, its location in time, would be more like an average over many internal time values than a single specific value. The comparison he gives is with Rome, a city which exists in the present but which, through its architecture and history, is an amalgam of many eras all co-existing at once. How would we date a building, after all, whose walls are nineteenth-century, whose exterior is current, but whose corner pillars are ancient Roman? Prigogine uses this as a metaphor to suggest that living systems, such as we, are a composite of current, recent, and older structures, which trail off into the distant past. The present contains the past even while transcending it. If so, we see another way in which the final eschaton, for which we cling in Christian hope, is present in us: *Since when the eschaton's time is the present, our distant time, its far past, will be contained in the complex but gentle structures of its omni-present.*

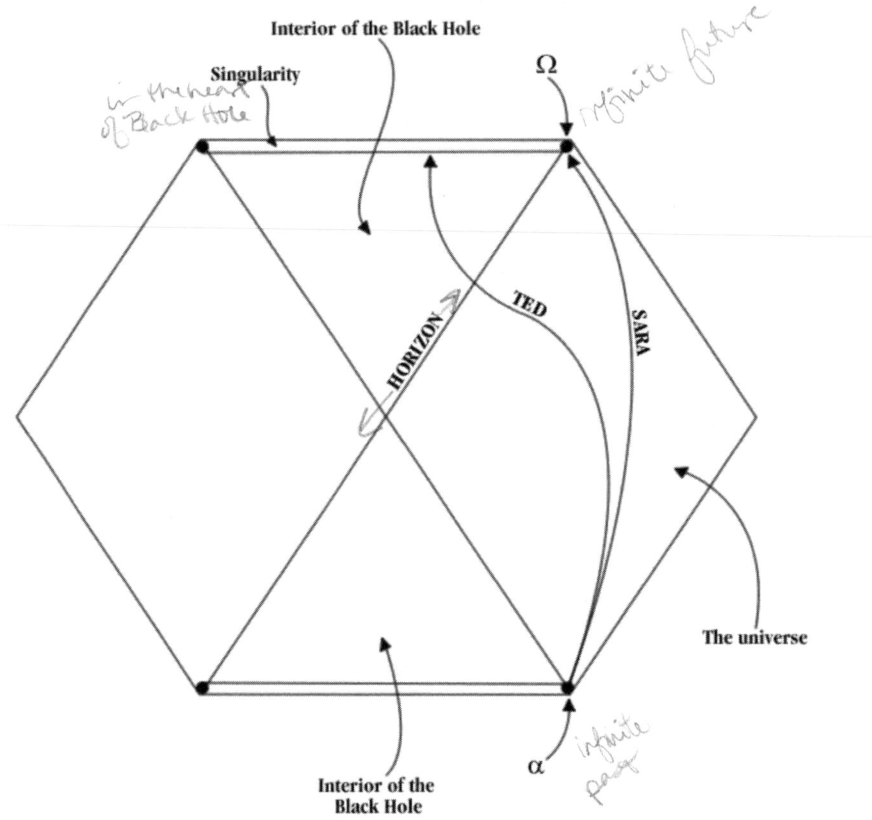

Figure 9.2: Penrose Diagram for a Schwarzschild Black Hole

6. Closing Remarks

In closing we return to our fundamental thesis, that eschatology entails a transfiguration of the entire cosmos based on the bodily resurrection of Jesus at Easter such that all of nature is taken up by God and made into the New Creation. Eschatology does not lead to a new creation *ex nihilo*. What it entails is a new creation out of the old, such that there is both continuity and discontinuity, as well as the proleptic appearance of that new creation already within the history of the present creation in Jesus Christ, such that every event in terrestrial history can also be an event at the end of cosmic history. Teilhard pioneered a way forward by which Christian faith can encounter science, but some of his steps were problematic. Science continues to challenge our understanding of faith, but new insights in science might open the discussion along lines of the Anthropic Principle and the diverse meanings of time in physics and cosmology. In the end, of course, faith is a divine mystery and a gift of grace. Our task is to think through the entailments of faith in the clearest light of reason possible, and today, that at least means in light of science. Perhaps then, we can add a new level of intelligibility and a deeper sense of hope to our confession of faith: "Christ has died, Christ has risen, *Christ will come again*."

Acknowledgements

I would like to thank John Wright, Denis Edwards, Mark Richardson, and Chris Mooney for stimulating conversations regarding this chapter.

Endnotes: Chapter 9

[1]Original title: "A Fresh Exploration of the Symbol of a Cosmic Christ: Eschatology and Scientific Cosmology." Unpublished lecture delivered to the Catholic Theological Association, 1993.

[2]Karl Barth, *Epistle to the Romans* (London: Oxford University Press, 1933), 314.

[3]Walter M. Abbott, S.J., ed., *The Documents of Vatican II* (New York: America Press, 1966), #48, 78–79.

[4]I am greatly indebted to Joshua Moritz for stressing this insight and I appreciatively acknowledge his participation in wording this paragraph.

[5]Carl E. Braaten, "The Kingdom of God and Life Everlasting," in *Christian Theology: An Introduction to Its Traditions and Tasks*, edited by Peter C. Hodgson and Robert H. King (Philadelphia: Fortress Press, 1982), 328–352, esp. 329.

[6]A representative sample would include: Ian G. Barbour, *Religion in an Age of Science* (San Francisco: Harper & Row, 1990); D. J. Bartholomew, *God of Chance* (London: SCM, 1984); Paul Davies, *God and the New Physics* (New York: Touchstone, 1983); John Dillenberger, *Protestant Thought & Natural Science: A Historical Study* (Nashville: Abingdon, 1960); Jan Fennema and Iain Paul, eds., *Science and Religion: One World—Changing Perspectives on Reality* (Dordrecht: Kluwer Academic, 1990); George S. Hendry, *Theology of Nature* (Philadelphia: Westminster, 1980); Stanley L. Jaki, *The Road of Science and the Ways to God* (Chicago: The University of Chicago Press, 1978); Christopher Kaiser, *Creation and the History of Science* (London: Marshall Pickering, 1991); Ernan McMullin, ed., *Evolution and Creation* (Notre Dame: University of Notre Dame Press, 1985); James B. Miller & Kenneth E. McCall, *The Church and Contemporary Cosmology* (Pittsburgh: Carnegie Mellon University Press, 1990); Iain Paul, *Science, Theology and Einstein* (New York: Oxford University Press, 1982); Ted Peters, ed., *Cosmos as Creation: Theology and Science in Consonance* (Nashville: Abingdon Press, 1989); John Polkinghorne, *Science and Providence: God's Interaction with the World* (Boston: Shambhala, 1989); Holmes Rolston, *Science and Religion: A Critical Survey* (New York: Random House, 1987); Robert John Russell, William R. Stoeger, and George V. Coyne, eds., *Physics, Philosophy and Theology: A Common Quest for Understanding* (Vatican City State: Vatican Observatory, 1988), hereafter *PPT*; Gerd Theissen, *Biblical Faith: An Evolutionary Approach* (Philadelphia: Fortress Press, 1985); Thomas F. Torrance, *Divine and Contingent Order* (Oxford: Oxford University Press, 1981); N. Max Wildiers, *The Theologian and His Universe: Theology and Cosmology from the Middle Ages to the Present* (New York: Seabury, 1982).

[7]A. R. Peacocke, *Creation and the World of Science* (Oxford: Clarendon, 1979).

[8]In this chapter I am not suggesting that Christians must choose between the doctrines of the resurrection of the body and the immortality of the soul as though they were mutually exclusive. Clearly both of these doctrines have strong roots in scripture and tradition. What I am suggesting is that the resurrection of the body, which I take to be the primary doctrine and which can include the immortality of the soul as a subsidiary doctrine, leads to the claim that the universe as a whole is transfigured in the eschatological future. I am indebted to John Wright for clarifying the relation between these doctrines in private discussion, and to Ted Peters for his insistence of the importance of the Corinthian passage here noted.

[9]But compare this with the vision of Revelation 21:1, devoid of the previous ecological theme.

[10]For recent discussions of these strands, see Richard Cartwright Austin, *Hope for the Land: Nature in the Bible* (Atlanta: John Knox, 1988); and George H. Kehm, "The New Story: Redemption as Fulfillment of Creation," in *After Nature's Revolt: Eco-Justice and Theology*, ed. by Dieter T. Hessel (Minneapolis: Fortress Press, 1992), 89–106.

[11]Oxford: Clarendon Press, 1986.

[12]I am indebted to John Wright for pointing out to me that Teilhard does not keep the within and the without entirely separate. Instead Teilhard relates them while not simply

equating them. Barrow and Tipler cite the same passages in Teilhard, but focus specifically on his rejecting "all hope of discovering a "mechanical equivalent" for will or thought." Thus, when they turn to the recent connections between information theory and thermodynamics (which I cite below), they take this as an instance of a "mechanical equivalent" for will or thought, and thus as a refutation of Teilhard's theory: "Information theory thus removes a cornerstone of Teilhard's theory, and *qua* scientific theory it crashes to the ground." Given Wright's clarification I realize that Barrow and Tipler are actually wrong in this claim. To their credit, however, they point out that since Teilhard's theory was falsifiable it counts as a scientific theory.

[13]Pierre Teilhard de Chardin, *The Phenomenon of Man* (New York: Harper & Row, 2nd ed., 1965), 63.

[14]Ibid., 63–64.

[15]Ibid., 64.

[16]This might be closely related to Teilhard's law of complexity and consciousness, ibid., 61.

[17]Barrow and Tipler, *Anthropic*, 198 and eqn. 10.39, 661.

[18]Barrow and Tipler continue the calculation in fascinating detail. If one used the total mass-energy of the earth in a thermodynamic process, and if one worked at the coldest environmental temperature we know of—that of the universe itself, which is characterized by the background radiation at 3 degrees K left over from the Big Bang, the most information that could be generated is 10^{64} bits. The mass-energy of the entire solar system would support the production of 10^{70} bits. The galaxy would produce 10^{81} bits. The mass-energy of the entire visible universe would produce 10^{98} bits (see ibid., 662).

[19]One light-year is the distance light travels in one year, approximately three thousand billion kilometers. For comparison, the moon is 1.5 light-seconds away, the sun about eight light-minutes.

[20]Bertrand Russell, "A Free Man's Worship," in *Mysticism and Logic, and Other Essays* (London: Allen & Unwin, 1963 eds), 41.

[21]Steven Weinberg, *The First Three Minutes* (New York: Basic, 1977), 154–155.

[22]Here spacetime is flat in the sense of being Euclidean, but it possesses a causal structure called the light cone which limits velocities to the speed of light. The causal structure is represented mathematically by the Lorentz metric which, technically, makes spacetime pseudo-Euclidean. The result of the light cone structure is that events which are not causally related to the present can appear to be in the future, the present, or the past depending on the velocity of differing observers, leading to the famous paradoxes of special relativity.

[23]Later work by Einstein anticipated what is now a widely pursued research goal in theoretical physics, the move to reduce matter and field to a single principle, the unified quantum field as a curved spacetime carrying all physical interactions.

[24]The prediction of an absolute beginning, t=0, has inspired rather extensive theological discussions. See my article, "Theological Lessons from Cosmology," in *Cross Currents: Religion & Intellectual Life* 41 (Fall 1991), 308–321, which includes extensive references. See articles in Ted Peters, *Cosmos as Creation* and Russell, et. al., *PPT*. See also *Quantum Cosmology and the Laws of Nature,* edited by Robert John Russell, Nancey Murphy, and C. J. Isham (Vatican City State: Vatican Observatory Publications; Berkeley, Calif.: Center for Theology and the Natural Sciences, 1993). Hereafter *QCLN*.

[25]In addition, in the flat universe the global metric is the same as that of special relativity: pseudo-Euclidean.

[26]This is reproduced from Tipler, *Anthropic*, 653.

[27]Friedrich Schleiermacher, *On Religion: Speeches to Its Cultured Despisers* (New York: Harper & Row, 1958), 38–39.

[28]Others who should be included but for space restrictions are Paul Davies, John Barrow, Stephen Hawking, Carl Sagan, E. O. Wilson, and many more.

[29]F. J. Dyson, *Rev. Mod. Phys.*, 51, 447 (1979).

[30]Tipler, *Anthropic*, 658.

[31]Freeman Dyson, *Infinite in All Directions* (New York: Harper & Row, 1988), 107.

[32]One might well insist that a principle of unity, or unity in being, seems required for consciousness. The argument being advanced by Dyson would seem to be that the principle of unity can be achieved in a variety of ways. Certainly one is the biological organization of terrestrial life-forms, including the molecular biology of genes, the biochemistry of cells, the physiology of organs structured in bodies, and the ecology of food-chain systems under the conditions of evolution. But other means for the principle of unity might be the structures of a neutron star, the self-replicating structures of an android, or even the loosely interconnected features of a highly complex interstellar cloud (see Fred Hoyle's *Black Cloud*).

[33] Frank J. Tipler, *The Physics of Immortality: Modern Cosmology, God, and the Resurrection of the Dead* (New York: Doubleday, 1994). For earlier reflections see Frank J. Tipler, "The Omega Point Theory: A Model of an Evolving God," in *PPT*, 313–32.

[34]Tipler, *Anthropic*, 659.

[35]W. R. Stoeger and G. F. R. Ellis, "A Response to Tipler's Omega-Point Theory," *Science and Christian Belief* 7.2 (October 1995); Hyung Sup Choi, "A Physicist Comments on Tipler's 'The Physics of Immortality'," *CTNS Bulletin* 15.2 (Spring 1995).

[36] Willem B. Drees, *Beyond the Big Bang: Quantum Cosmologies and God* (La Salle, Ill.: Open Court, 1990), ch. 4. See also Fred W. Hallberg, "Barrow and Tipler's Anthropic Cosmological Principle," *Zygon: Journal of Religion and Science* 23.2 (June 1988).

[37] Frank J. Tipler, "The Omega Point as Eschaton: Answers to Pannenberg's Questions for Scientists," *Zygon: Journal of Religion & Science* 24.2 (June 1989): 217–53. Wolfhart Pannenberg, "Theological Appropriation of Scientific Understandings: Response to Hefner, Wicken, Eaves, and Tipler," *Zygon: Journal of Religion & Science* 24.2 (June 1989): 255–71.

[38] Willem B. Drees, "Contingency, Time, and the Theological Ambiguity of Science," in *Beginning With the End: God, Science, and Wolfhart Pannenberg*, ed. Carol Rausch Albright and Joel Haugen (Chicago: Open Court, 1997). Robert John Russell, "Cosmology and Eschatology: The Implications of Tipler's 'Omega Point' Theory to Pannenberg's Theological Program," in ibid. See also Robert John Russell, "Cosmology, Creation, and Contingency," in Peters, ed., *Cosmos as Creation,* 201–04. Robert John Russell, "Cosmology from Alpha to Omega," *Zygon: Journal of Religion & Science* 29.4 (December 1994): 570–72. See also the responses in the March 1999 issue of *Zygon.*

[39] Polkinghorne, *Science and Providence*, 96; Barbour, *Religion in an Age of Science*, 151–52; Arthur Peacocke, *Theology for a Scientific Age: Being and Becoming—Natural, Divine and Human*, enlarged ed. (Minneapolis, Minn.: Fortress Press, 1995), 345; Philip Clayton, *God and Contemporary Science* (Grand Rapids, Mich.: Eerdmans, 1997), 132–36; Worthing, *God, Creation, and Contemporary Physics*, ch. 5. See also the Book Symposium in the June 1995 and September 1995 issues of *Zygon: Journal of Religion and Science*, 30.2, 30.3.

[40]Dyson, *Infinite*, 117.

[41]Michael J. Buckley, S. J., *At the Origins of Modern Atheism* (New Haven, Conn.: Yale University Press, 1987).

[42]It should be noted that Tipler, in particular, has aggressively pursued the theological implications of FAP both in *Anthropic* and elsewhere. (See, for example, "The Omega Point Theory: A Model of an Evolving God" in Russell, *Physics*.) I stand at some distance from his theological conclusions, since in my opinion he gives science far too normative a role in their foundations and he constructs them with a strongly Fundamentalist style. Nevertheless I respect the fact that he has attempted to take science very seriously in the theological discussion, unlike many professional theologians today.

[43]Denis Edwards, *Jesus and the Cosmos* (New York: Paulist, 1991).

[44]Karl Rahner, *Foundations of Christian Faith* (New York: Crossroad, 1978; 1992), 188.

[45]There are, however, some important exceptions to this general rule of thumb. Some scientists of a more philosophical bent have taken a line not entirely unlike Rahner's, though without an explicit theological framework. John Wheeler, for example, has argued that quantum physics leads to self-consciousness in the universe, since conscious observers are necessary to bring to actuality quantum events including all of the past of the observable universe. Paul Davies argues from the Anthropic Principle (see below) that the universe is more of a home for humankind than a barren stage. Freeman Dyson describes mind at three levels in nature: quantum, macroscopic, and cosmological, and remarks delightfully that "the universe in some sense must have known that we were coming." (Freeman Dyson, *Disturbing the Universe* [New York, Harper & Row, 1979], 250.) Of course, other writers who carry both scientific credentials and are working explicitly in theology, such as Arthur Peacocke, Ian Barbour, John Polkinghorne, and Charles Birch, have argued strongly for a theological anthropology which takes scientific anthropology, and with it cosmology, very seriously.

[46] Figure 9.1 also appears in chapter 1 as Figure 1.3.

[47]For details and an extensive discussion, see John Leslie, *Universes* (London: Routledge, 1989). Bill Stoeger has written an impressive criticism of the many-worlds argument. If as he insists the laws of physics are merely descriptive, they cannot be legitimately generalized to serve as the basis for an argument to the existence of other universes. See his article in Russell, Murphy, and Isham, *QCLN*.

[48]Karl Rahner, "Resurrection," in *Sacramentum Mundi: An Encyclopedia of Theology* 5 (New York: Herder and Herder, 1970), 333.

[49]I hasten to add that I want to avoid any charges of proposing a cousin to "scientific creation" based, here, on a literal reading of theological doctrine. Instead I insist that theology must be critically assessed in light of contemporary science to rid it of superstition and pseudoscience.

[50]Rahner, *Foundations*, 436.

[51]Ibid., 437.

[52]See Charles Misner, Kip Thorne, and John A. Wheeler, *Gravitation* (San Francisco: WH Freeman, 1973).

Chapter 10

Resurrection of the Body, Eschatology, and Cosmology: Theology and Science in Creative Mutual Interaction[1]

> Blessed be the God and Father of our Lord Jesus Christ! By God's great mercy we have been given a new birth into a living hope through the Resurrection of Jesus Christ from the dead.
>
> 1 Peter 1:3

1. Introduction

The defining *kerygma* of Christian theology is the resurrection of Jesus of Nazareth. For many biblical scholars and systematic theologians, the resurrection is understood as "bodily": the transformation of the total person of Jesus into a new form of existence—eternal life with God. The resurrection of Jesus, properly understood, is more than the "resuscitation" accounts of the raising of Lazarus or the daughter of Jairus. Instead it is "bodily": It was experienced by the disciples as recorded in the Easter appearances and delimited from all "spiritualized" or, more reductively, all "subjectivised" interpretations by an insistence on the empty tomb traditions. The resurrection is also more than a "miracle" confined to the person of Jesus and played out against the backdrop of a totally ordinary surrounding world. Instead the accounts of the risen Lord include the disciples and their surroundings in what appears to be an environment already showing signs of radical transformation as suggested by the accounts of his appearances and ascension. This view of the resurrection, for those biblical scholars and systematic theologians who pursue it, leads to an eschatology in which all of creation is to be transformed into the New Creation, the "environment" called the "new heaven and the new earth." This New Creation was instantiated by God's proleptic act at Easter, signaling what will become the future for all creatures when Christ "comes again in glory."

Ironically, for all the hard-won progress in the constructive engagements termed "theology and science" over the past half century, the challenge raised by science in general and scientific cosmology in particular to bodily resurrection and New Creation eschatology has received, with only a few exceptions, strikingly little sustained attention. Throughout the theology and science literature, the concept of "creation" refers unequivocally to the expanding Big Bang universe some 13 billion light-years in size (or, if one follows quantum cosmology, the "Universe" or "megauniverse" of endless inflation) and not, certainly, just to planet earth. Hence, in this literature at least, the "creation" which will be transformed into the New Creation must unequivocally refer to that same universe (or "Universe"). But this claim runs directly up against scientific cosmology for, regardless of the model chosen (again Big Bang, inflationary Big

Bang, quantum cosmology, and so on) the future of the universe is certainly not anything like the biblical/theological New Creation. Indeed, at least one very prominent scholar in theology and science has acknowledged that "should the final future as forecasted by the combination of big bang cosmology and the second law of thermodynamics come to pass . . . we would have proof that our faith has been in vain. It would turn out to be that there is no God, at least not the God in whom followers of Jesus have put their faith."[2]

The purpose of this chapter is to take some additional steps in the process of constructing a response, following on previous work where I have initially begun to sketch some of these steps.[3] After a brief overview of Big Bang cosmology, I will report a bit more fully on the positions taken in New Testament (NT) research regarding the bodily resurrection of Jesus. My intention is not to enter into the NT debates as a NT scholar, which I certainly am not. Instead it is to adopt the "worst case" scenario, the one which makes Christianity the most vulnerable to its atheistic critics, namely the bodily resurrection of Jesus and its implications for eschatology, since this position, as I have already claimed, raises serious, and perhaps unsolvable, conflicts and contradictions with science. It is this position—and not those already "jury-rigged" to fit with science—that is worth pursing, since it represents a "test case" of the highest order for those of us who urge that "theology and science" should be in a posture of "creative mutual interaction" and not in one of conflict or irrelevance.

I will then turn to theology and science to suggest why such an engagement is actually unavoidable, and report on the work of one scholar, John Polkinghorne, whose approach seems to me to be uniquely promising. I will then suggest that an expansion of the current methodology in theology and science is required, and out of this I will develop a series of guidelines for reconstructing eschatology in light of science and for exploring new approaches to science and cosmology in light of eschatology. These guidelines lead to some suggestions for future research programs in theology and in science.

2. The Challenge of Big Bang Cosmology

> [I]f it were shown that the universe is indeed headed for an all-enveloping death, then this might . . . falsify Christian faith and abolish Christian hope.[4]
>
> —John Macquarrie

To consider the universe from a scientific perspective, we must turn to physics with its theory of gravity and thus Big Bang cosmology.

A. Big Bang cosmology and the far future[5]

By 1915, Albert Einstein had constructed his general theory of relativity (GR) using his special theory of relativity (SR) as its basis and applying it to the problem of gravity. Here he extended Newton's principle of the relativity of motion to include not only electromagnetism (as in SR) but now gravitation as well. Instead of matter moving within a three-dimensional absolute, container-like space with time flowing uniformly and independently, Einstein's radically new approach combines space and time into spacetime,[6] sets it on an equal ontological footing with matter, and allows for their nonlinear interaction. As a famous interpretation goes, in general relativity "space tells matter how to move and matter tells space how to curve."[7] During the 1920s, astronomers such as Edwin Hubble discovered that the spectrum of distant galaxies was shifted towards the red end of the electromagnetic spectrum, and that the amount of redshift was linearly related to the distance to the galaxy. These observations, in turn, could be interpreted as showing that galaxies in all directions in space are receding from us at a velocity v proportional to their distance D, as given by Hubble's law: v=HxD.[8] The implication taken by most scientists was that the universe itself is expanding in time as described by Einstein's general theory of relativity!

There are three possible types of expansion. 1) Closed model. In this model the universe has the shape of a three-dimensional sphere of finite size. It expands up to a maximum size, approximately 100–500 billion years from now, then recontracts. 2) Open models. In both the "flat" and "saddle-shaped" models, the universe is infinite in size and it will expand forever. All three came to be called "Big Bang" models because they describe the universe as having a finite past life of 10–15 billion years and beginning at time t=0 in an event of infinite temperature and density, and zero volume.

B. Inflationary Big Bang and quantum cosmologies[9]

Since the 1970s, a variety of technical problems in the standard Big Bang model have led scientists to pursue "inflationary Big Bang" and "quantum cosmology." According to inflation, at extremely early times (roughly the Planck time, 10^{-43} seconds after t=0) the universe expanded exponentially, then quickly settled down to the slower expansion rates of the standard Big Bang model. During inflation, countless domains may arise, separating the overall Universe into many universes, each huge portions of spacetime in which the natural constants and even the specific laws of physics can vary. In most quantum cosmologies, our universe is just a part of an eternally expanding, infinitely complex megauniverse. Quantum cosmology, however, is a highly speculative field. Theories involving quantum gravity, which underlie quantum cosmology, are notoriously hard to test empirically.

C. Big Bang and the far future: "freeze or fry"

Even if inflationary or quantum cosmologies prove of lasting importance, the far future of the visible universe in which we live is described by Big Bang cosmology. There are two scenarios for the far future of the universe according to Big Bang cosmology: "freeze or fry." If the universe is open or flat, it will expand forever and continue to cool from its present temperature (about 2.7^{0}K), asymptotically approaching absolute zero. The presence of "cosmological constant," Ȼ, could either accelerate its expansion or, possibly, close the universe. If it is closed, it will expand to a maximum size in another one to five hundred billion years, then recollapse to arbitrarily small size and unendingly higher temperatures somewhat like a mirror image of its past expansion.

What about the future of life in the universe? It turns out that the overall picture is bleak, regardless of whether it is open or closed/"freeze" or "fry." A reasonably well-agreed-upon account of both closed and open scenarios has been given by Frank Tipler and John Barrow:[10] In five billion years, the sun will become a red giant, engulfing the orbit of the earth and Mars, and eventually becoming a white dwarf. In 40–50 billion years, star formation will have ended in our galaxy and others. In 10^{12} years, all massive stars will have become neutron stars or black holes.[11] In 10^{19} years, dead stars near the galactic edge will drift off into intergalactic space; stars near the center will collapse together forming a massive black hole. In 10^{31} years, protons and neutrons decay into positrons, electrons, neutrinos and photons. In 10^{34} years, dead planets, black, dwarves, and neutron stars, will disappear, their mass completely converted into energy, leaving only black holes, electron-positron plasma, and radiation. All carbon-based life-forms will inevitably become extinct. Beyond this, solar mass, galactic mass, and finally supercluster mass black holes will evaporate by Hawking radiation. The upshot is clear: "Proton decay spells ultimate doom for life based on protons and neutrons, like *Homo sapiens* and all forms of life constructed of atoms."[12]

Now we can return to our key question: *Can Christian eschatology be seen as consistent with either of these scientific scenarios?*

2. New Testament Debates Over the Bodily Resurrection of Jesus

In this paper I will adopt as a working hypothesis or "test case" that interpretation of the resurrection of Jesus which poses the most profound challenges for theology when scientific cosmology is taken seriously: namely the bodily resurrection of Jesus (including the empty tomb traditions) and thus eschatology as the transformation of the universe (the creation) into the New Creation. This position is well-defended by NT scholars and theologians, so that the option to adopt it as a test case for the encounter with cosmology is far from arbitrary or easily avoidable.

A. Objective interpretation of the resurrection of Jesus

The resurrection of Jesus has been given what can be called "objective" and "subjective" interpretations. According to those holding the objective interpretation, something happened to Jesus of Nazareth after his crucifixion, death, and burial such that he is risen, he lives forever with God, and is present to us in our lives. In short, God raised Jesus from the dead. In the objectivist view, the "resurrection of Jesus" refers to something which happened to Jesus of Nazareth which cannot be reduced entirely to the experiences of the disciples.[13] According to Raymond Brown, "our generation must be obedient . . . to what *God* has chosen to do in Jesus; and we cannot impose on that picture what we think God should have done."[14]

B. Subjective interpretation of the resurrection of Jesus

The "subjective interpretation" focuses strictly on the experiences as reported in the appearances and empty tomb (ET) traditions. These experiences caused the first disciples to know and believe something new about Jesus of Nazareth after his crucifixion. Here, however, language about the "resurrection of Jesus" is only a way of speaking about the experiences of the disciples and not about purported events in the new life given to Jesus by God after his death and burial.[15] According to Willie Marxsen: "All the evangelists want to show is that the activity of Jesus goes on. . . . They express this in pictorial terms. But what they mean to say is simply: 'We have come to believe.'"[16]

The objective interpretation of the resurrection of Jesus emphasizes elements of continuity (or identity) and of discontinuity (or transformation) between Jesus of Nazareth and the risen Jesus, holding these in tension by such phrases as "identity-in-transformation." These elements of continuity include everything about the human person of Jesus: There is at least a minimal element of physical, material, personal, and spiritual continuity between Jesus of Nazareth and the risen Jesus. Because of this, most scholars following the objective interpretation use the term, "the bodily resurrection" to emphasize the significance of the empty tomb traditions, and thus the inclusion of the physical in the overall meaning of the resurrection.[17]

Scholars who support the bodily resurrection of Jesus connect his resurrection with the general resurrection "at the end of time" and the New Creation consisting of a "new heaven and earth" but they tend to overlook the challenge from cosmology. They view the New Creation as a transformation of the world as a whole and all that is in it; it is a return of the risen Christ to *this* world in order that this world be *transformed* into an eternal world. Curiously, the challenge raised by scientific cosmology to this claim is seldom inspected.

For the purposes of this paper I will work with the "bodily resurrection of Jesus" interpretation of the resurrection texts since it constitutes the "test case/worst case" approach to the conversations with science.

3. Resurrection, Eschatology, and Cosmology Within "Theology and Science": The Surprising Lack of Engagement

Against competing claims for outright conflict or radical independence between theology and science, there has been enormous progress over the past fifty years in the approach that places theology and science in dialogue and interaction.[18] Physics, cosmology, evolutionary and molecular biology, and other areas of the natural sciences have been introduced into ongoing theological discussions. Particular attention has been given to the goal of articulating objectively special but non-interventionist divine action in particular by searching for genuine openness in nature (ontological indeterminism).[19] Little attention, however, has been given to the resurrection of Jesus and its eschatological implications in light of the natural sciences.[20] This lack of attention is particularly ironic since the same methodological framework which has played an essential role in making it possible for the field of theology and science to grow so richly prevents us from "side-stepping" the crucial issues raised by cosmology for Christian eschatology.

To see this we need to summarize two of the central claims of this methodology briefly:[21] 1) a nonreductive/holistic view of epistemology and 2) an analogy between the methodologies of the sciences and the humanities. Here I will be drawing directly on the pioneering writings of Ian Barbour[22] as well as on those of Arthur Peacocke,[23] Nancey Murphy,[24] Philip Clayton,[25] John Polkinghorne,[26] and many others:

A. Epistemic hierarchy

The sciences and the humanities, including theology, can be placed in a series of levels which reflect the increasing complexity of the phenomena they study. In this "epistemic hierarchy," lower levels place epistemic *constraints* on upper levels (against "two worlds"), but upper levels cannot be reduced entirely to lower levels. Thus, physics, as the bottom level, places constraints on biology. On the other hand, the processes, properties, and laws of biology *cannot be reduced* without remainder to those of physics.

B. Methodological analogy

Within this hierarchy, each level involves similar methods of theory construction and testing. Thus theological methodology is analogous to scientific methodology (though with several important differences).[27] This claim is both a *description* of the way many theologians actually work and a *prescription* for progress in theological research. Theological doctrines are seen as theories, working hypotheses held fallibly, constructed through metaphors and models, and tested in light of the data of theology, now including the results of the sciences.

C. Five paths from science to theology: SRP → TRP

In order to clarify the ways in which science can (and should) influence theology, I will combine these two ideas—epistemic hierarchy and analogous methodology—into a single framework, as indicated by Figure 10.1 (see below, p. 319 and paths 1–5). For simplicity I'll limit the conversation to physics and its effects on theology.[28] Thus there are five paths by which the natural sciences can affect constructive theology. Path 1: Theories in physics can act directly as data which place constraints on theology. So, for example, a theological theory about divine action should not violate special relativity. Path 2: Theories can act directly as data either to be "explained" by theology or as the basis for a theological constructive argument. Thus t=0 in standard Big Bang cosmology was often explained theologically via creation *ex nihilo*. Path 3: Theories in physics, after philosophical analysis, can act indirectly as data for theology. For example, an indeterministic interpretation of quantum mechanics can function within philosophical theology as making intelligible the idea of non-interventionist objective divine action. Path 4: Theories in physics can also act indirectly as the data for theology when they are incorporated into a fully-articulated philosophy of nature (for example, that of Alfred North Whitehead). Finally, path 5: Theories in physics can function heuristically in the theological context of discovery, by providing conceptual or aesthetic inspiration, and so on. So biological evolution may inspire a sense of God's immanence in nature. For convenience, I will use the symbol, SRP → TRP, suggested by George Ellis[29] to indicate these five ways scientific research programs (SRPs) can influence theological research programs (TRPs).

D. Why the challenge of cosmology cannot be avoided

We are now prepared to see clearly why the problem of eschatology and cosmology is "forced" on us by the same methodological framework which has played an essential role in making the field of theology and science possible: Scientific cosmology (Big Bang cosmology, inflationary Big Bang, quantum cosmology, and so on) is part of physics (that is, a solution to the field equations of general relativity). Therefore the predictions of "freeze or fry" must place constraints on and challenge what theology can claim eschatologically. No appeal to contingency, quantum physics, chaos theory, Whiteheadian novelty, emergence, the unpredictibility of the future, or metaphysics alone will be sufficient to solve this problem.[30]

E. Polkinghorne's approach as a starting point and the need for an expanded methodology

John Polkinghorne is among the very few scholars who have attended in detail to the challenge of cosmology to an eschatology. His work is based on the bodily interpretation of the resurrection of Jesus.[31] Just as Jesus' body was transformed into the risen and glorified body, so the "matter" of this new environment must come from "the transformed matter of this world." "[T]he first creation was *ex nihilo* while the new creation will be *ex vetere* . . . the new creation is the divine redemption of the old. . . . [This idea] does not imply the abolition of the old but rather its transformation."[32] Clues to what the "new heaven and new earth" will be like come from the themes of continuity and discontinuity found in the gospel accounts of the resurrection and in the Eucharist. Moreover, science "may have something to contribute" to our understanding of this transformation: The continuities might lie within the province of science (or, more precisely, what Polkinghorne calls "metascience").[33]

I will use Polkinghorne's ideas as a starting point. But before we can attempt to proceed, we must develop an extended new methodology in order to address the severe challenge placed by the existing methodology on such attempts as described above.

4. Methodology and Guidelines for New Research in Scientific Cosmology and in Eschatology

I see that you believe these things are true because I say them.
Yet, you do not see how.
Thus, though believed, their truth is hidden from you.
—Dante Alighieri[34]

If it is impossible, it cannot be true.
But if it is true, it cannot be impossible.

It seems clear that if one assumes the current methodology in "theology and science" and if one assumes the "test case," the bodily resurrection of Jesus and an eschatology of cosmological transformation, then one *seems* forced into a direct contradiction with the predictions of contemporary scientific cosmology. To move forward, I propose we expand our methodology to allow for genuine interaction between theology and science. I also believe that an expanded method is, from an informal point of view, already in place. Making it explicit should be helpful for a variety of problems in theology and science, possibly including our current problem.

A. A new methodology to meet the challenge: the creative mutual interaction between christian theology and natural science

Let me describe the expanded methodology by referring to three paths in Figure 10.1 which represent the possible influences of theology on the philosophical assumptions which underlie science and/or for individual scientists or teams of scientists in that initial phase of research are often called the "context of discovery." I will again use Ellis's suggestion to represent these paths as TRPs → SRPs. At the outset, however, I want to stress that by "influence" I am *not* assuming that theologians speak with some special kind of dogmatic authority. Quite the contrary; the overall context should be an open intellectual exchange between scholars based on mutual respect and the fallibility of hypotheses proposed by either side.

1. Three new paths from theology to physics.

Path 6: It is now abundantly clear that, historically, theological ideas provided some of the philosophical assumptions which underlie scientific methodology. Historians and philosophers of science have shown in detail how the doctrine of creation *ex nihilo* played an important role in the rise of modern science by combining the Greek assumption of the rationality of the world with the theological assumption that the world is contingent. Together these helped give birth to the empirical method and the use of mathematics to represent natural processes.[35]

Path 7: Theological theories can act as sources of inspiration in the scientific "context of discovery," that is, in the construction of new scientific theories. An interesting example is the subtle influence of atheism on Hoyle's search for a steady state cosmology.[36]

Path 8: Theological theories can lead to "selection rules" within the criteria of theory choice in physics. For example, if one considers a theological theory as true, then one can delineate what conditions must obtain within physics for the possibility of its being true. These conditions in turn can serve as motivations for an individual research scientist or group of colleagues to choose to pursue a particular scientific theory.

2. The method of creative mutual interaction (CMI).

The asymmetry between theology and science should now be quite apparent: Theological theories do not act as data for science, placing constraints on which theories can be constructed in the way that scientific theories do for theology. This, again, reflects the prior assumption that the sciences are structured in an epistemic hierarchy of constraints and irreducibility. It also safeguards science from any normative claims by theology. Together these eight paths portray science and theology in a much more interactive mode. I suggest calling this *the method of creative mutual interaction*. Given this method, we can begin to delineate the conditions needed for real progress in theology and science.[37]

B. Guidelines for moving forward: revising eschatology in light of cosmology (SRT → TRP) and cosmology in light of eschatology (TRP → SRP)

Given the expanded methodology described above we are prepared to engage in a twofold project: Following paths 1–5, we construct a more nuanced understanding of eschatology in light of physics and cosmology (indicated by the symbol: SRP → TRP). Following paths 6–8, we search for a fresh interpretation of, or possibly revisions of, current scientific cosmology in light of this eschatology (indicated by the symbol: TRP → SRP). If such a project is at all successful, it might eventually be possible to bring these two trajectories together at least in a very preliminary way to give a more coherent overall view, than is now possible, of the history and destiny of the universe in light of the resurrection of Jesus and its eschatological completion in the parousia.

This project is clearly a long-term undertaking, requiring the participation of scholars from a variety of fields in the sciences, philosophy, and theology. How do we then to proceed? My sense is that we first need some guidelines that will help point us in a fruitful direction. Using them, we can begin to explore specific ways to enter into the research.

1. SRP → TRP: Guidelines for constructive theology in light of contemporary science.

a. *Guidelines 1-4: General philosophical guidelines for constructive theology.* We begin with guidelines for constructive theology in light of contemporary science. Our first four guidelines deal with overall philosophical and methodological issues.

***Guideline 1**: Rejection of two philosophical assumptions about science: the argument from analogy and its representation as nomological universality.* The first guideline deals with the fundamental challenge physical cosmology poses to the kind of eschatology we are considering here: namely, one based on our choice of the "hardest case"—the bodily resurrection of Jesus. In bare form, the challenge is stark: If the predictions of contemporary scientific cosmology come to pass then the parousia will not just be "delayed," it will never happen. And if this is so, then the logic of Paul in 1 Corinthians 15 is then inexorable: If there will never be a general resurrection, then Christ has not been raised from the dead, and our hope is in vain. The challenge can also be seen as coming from theology to science: If it is in fact true that Jesus rose bodily from the dead, then the general resurrection cannot be impossible. This must in turn mean that the future of the universe will not be what scientific cosmology predicts.

We seem to be at loggerheads. How are we to resolve this fundamental challenge? My response is that the challenge is not technically from science but from a philosophical assumption which we routinely bring to science, namely that scientific predictions hold without qualification. It is quite possible, however, to accept a very different assumption about the future predictions of science while accepting all that science describes and explains about the past history of the universe. The first step is deciding whether the laws of nature are descriptive or prescriptive and, as Bill Stoeger argues, science, alone, cannot settle the matter.[38] A strong case can then be made on philosophical grounds that the laws of nature are descriptive. The second step is to claim on theological grounds that the processes of nature which science describes in terms of the laws of nature are actually the result of God's ongoing action as Creator and not of nature acting entirely on its own. The regularity of natural processes is ultimately the result of God's faithfulness, even if God bequeaths a significant degree of causal autonomy to nature. (Here one thinks of the traditional debates between Augustinian and Thomistic interpretations of natural causality: the former viewing nature as highly contingent upon God and natural events as "omnimiraculous," and the latter viewing nature as gifted by God with relative autonomy and a high degree of causal efficacy.) Finally, if this is so, and if God is free to act in radically new ways (which of course God is!) not only in human history but in the ongoing history of the universe, then the future of the cosmos will not be what science predicts. Instead the cosmic far future will be based on a radically new kind of divine action which began with the resurrection of Jesus, and this new act of God cannot be reduced to, or explained by, the current laws of nature, that is, by God's action in the past history of the universe.[39]

In short, we could say that the "freeze" or "fry" predictions for the cosmological future might have applied had God not acted in Easter and if God were not to continue to act to bring forth the ongoing eschatological transformation of the universe. Because of Easter and God's promise for its eschatological completion, however, the freeze or fry predictions will not come to pass.

Guideline 2: *Eschatology should embrace methodological naturalism regarding the cosmic past and present.* Any eschatology which we might construct must be "scientific" in its description of the *past* history of the universe. More precisely, it must be constrained by methodological naturalism in its description of the past: It should not invoke God in its explanation of the (secondary) causes, processes, and properties of nature. Indeed there is a strong theological reason for making methodological naturalism the basis for the natural sciences. To put it all briefly we start with the doctrine of creation *ex nihilo* and the Greek *logos* tradition as incorporated into classical christology. From this we come to understand the universe as ontologically different than God (that is, the universe is contingent) and as God's free creation through the divine Word (that is, the universe is intelligible). The contingency and intelligibility of the universe means that divine and natural causalities are distinct (that is, all natural causes are secondary causes through which God works), that genuine knowledge of it must be empirical, and that such knowledge can be represented by mathematics. This guideline separates my proposal as sharply as possible from movements such as "intelligent design" which criticize current theories in the physical and biological sciences for *not* including divine agency in science.[40]

***Guideline 3**: "Relativistically correct eschatology": constructing eschatology in light of contemporary physics (paths 1, 2).* Although we will set aside the predictions Big Bang offers for the cosmic future, we must be prepared to reconstruct current work in eschatology in light of Big Bang cosmology and contemporary physics—specifically relativity and quantum physics—and thus what cosmology tells us about the history of the universe, following primarily path 1 (science places a "limiting condition" or constraint on theology) but also path 2 (theology explains a scientific question which transcends science; confer David Tracy's concept of a "limit question"). I will refer to this project as the attempt to construct a "relativistically correct Christian eschatology."

***Guideline 4**: Big Bang and inflationary cosmology as a "limit condition" on any revised eschatology (path 1): the material argument.* Guideline 4 follows path 1 by stating that standard and inflationary Big Bang cosmologies, or other scientific cosmologies (such as quantum cosmology), place a "limiting condition" on any possible eschatology. All we know of the history and development of the universe and life in it will be data for theology.

***Guideline 5**: Metaphysical options: limited but not forced (paths 3, 4).* In revising contemporary eschatology there are various metaphysical options from which we may choose; they are not determined by science. These options include physicalism, emergent monism, dual-aspect monism, ontological emergence, and panexperientialism (Whiteheadian metaphysics).[41] Here we follow paths 3 and 4, deploying either a specific philosophical interpretation of a given scientific theory, or an entire philosophy of nature constructed with science in mind.

b. *Guidelines 6-7: Arguments for specific theological construction in light of both theological requirements and scientific findings (paths 1–4).* We must now begin the enormous job of reconstructing eschatology in a way that takes up and incorporates our theological requirements (that is, the resurrection of Jesus as bodily transformation and New Creation, and the problems of theodicy raised by evolution) as well as all the findings of science, and particularly scientific cosmology, without falling back into the philosophical problem guideline 1 is meant to address.

***Guideline 6**: Eschatology in light of the "resurrection of the body."*

***Guideline 6a**: "Transformability" and the formal conditions for its possibility (the "such that"[42] or "transcendental" argument):* Our starting point, based on the bodily resurrection of Jesus, is that the New Creation is not a replacement of the old creation, or a second and separate creation *ex nihilo*. Instead, God will transform God's creation, the universe, into the New Creation *ex vetere*, to use Polkinghorne's phrase. It follows that God must have created the universe *such that it is transformable*, that is, that it can be transformed by God's action. In particular, God must have created it with precisely those conditions and characteristics which it needs as preconditions in order to be transformable by God's new act. Moreover, if it is to be transformed and not replaced, *God must have created it with precisely those conditions and characteristics which will be part of the New Creation.* Since science offers a profound understanding of the past and present history of the universe (guidelines 2, 3), then science can be of immense help to the theological task of understanding something about that transformation if we can find a way to identify, with at least some probability, these needed conditions, characteristics, and preconditions. I will refer in general to these conditions and characteristics as "elements of continuity." Science might also shed light on which conditions and characteristics of the present creation we do *not* expect to be continued into the New Creation; these can be called "elements of discontinuity" between creation and New Creation. Thus physics and cosmology might play a profound role in our attempt to sort out what is truly essential to creation and what is to be "left behind" in the healing transformation to come.

Guideline 6a gives to the terms "continuity" and "discontinuity," found in the theological literature on the resurrection of Jesus, *a more precise meaning and a potential connection with science.* It can be thought of as a *transcendental* or "such that" argument because it spells out the conditions necessary in principle for the possibility of the transformation of the universe.[43] With it in place we can move eventually to a material argument and ask just what those elements of continuity and discontinuity might be.

***Guideline 6b**: Continuity within discontinuity: inverting the relationship.* Closely related to the previous guideline is a second formal argument about the relative importance of the elements of continuity and discontinuity. So far in theology and science, discontinuity has played a secondary role within the underlying theme of continuity in nature as suggested by the term "emergence." Accordingly, irreducibly new processes and properties (that is, discontinuity) arise within the overall, pervasive, and sustained background of nature (that is, continuity). Thus biological phenomena evolve out of the nexus of the physical world: the organism is built from its underlying structure of cells and organs, the mind arises in the context of neurophysiology, and so on. Now, however, when we come to the resurrection and eschatology, I propose we *invert* the relation: The elements of continuity will be present, but within a more radical and underlying discontinuity as is denoted by the *transformation* of the universe by a new act of God *ex vetera.* With this inversion, discontinuity as fundamental signals the break with naturalistic and reductionistic views such as "physical eschatology," while continuity, even if secondary, eliminates a "two-worlds" eschatology.

This has important implications on our search for candidate theories. It *eliminates* "non-interventionist objective special divine action" as a candidate since it does not involve a transformation of the whole of nature. Indeed, these approaches presuppose that it is the continual operation of the "usual" laws of nature which make objective special divine action possible without the need for their violation or suspension. But the bodily resurrection of Jesus directs us towards a much more fundamental view: the radical transformation of the background conditions of space, time, matter, and causality, and with this, a permanent change in at least most of the present laws of nature.[44]

Together, guidelines 6a and 6b can be thought of as representing what I previously called "first instantiation contingency" or FINLON, the "first instance of a new law of nature."[45] In a "weak" sense, FINLON refers to first instances of phenomena within creation, such as the emergence of life on earth. Here, however, in the context of the resurrection of Jesus, FINLON refers to the first instance of a radically new phenomenon. Nevertheless within the context of the coming New Creation the resurrection of Jesus will be the first instance of a general, regular phenomenon, the general resurrection from the dead and life everlasting. It might better be termed "the first instance of a new law of the new creation" (FINLONC).

Guideline 7: *Eschatology in light of the challenge of evolutionary theodicy.* In previous writings[46] I have studied the problem of theodicy raised by evolution and with it the billion-year history of natural evils on planet earth. In response I have explored two approaches. The first is based on the Augustinian tradition as developed in the twentieth century by Reinhold Niebuhr. The second is based on John Hick's appropriation of the theodicy of Friedrich Schleiermacher. Both lead to insights and problems. These problems in turn were used to generate criteria which any acceptable eschatology must address, and in this sense they were changed from problems to criteria of theory choice in theology.

Guideline 7a: *Drawing on the Augustinian/Niebuhrian theodicy:* The severe problems arising in the Augustinian/Niebuhrian theodicy in light of the challenge of thermodynamics and cosmology bring with them an exceptional gift: They give us a crucial insight into what eschatology must include if it is to address these problems. The insight is based on the idea that in the New Creation it will be impossible to commit moral evil: We will be liberated fully from the bondage of the will into true freedom (Augustine: *non posse peccare*). Then by analogy the New Creation will not include natural evil either, and this in turn has implications for the role of thermodynamics not only in creation but in the New Creation.

This insight could be taken in several ways. 1) In its most simple form it might mean that the New Creation will not include such processes as thermodynamics since it contributes to natural evil. I am reminded by the apostle Paul that "the creation itself will be set free from its bondage to decay and obtain the glorious liberty of the children of God" (Rom. 8:22, 8:21). As I wrote in an earlier paper, "Are we somehow to be freed from the tyranny of entropy, and is the universe to shine forever as the respondent creation of God—a *new* heaven and earth?" As a Christian I answer "yes!" 2) In a slightly more complex form it might mean that the New Creation will not include thermodynamics to the extent that it contributes to natural evil but that to the extent that it contributes to natural good.

Guideline 7b: *Drawing on the Schleiermacher/Hick theodicy:* We saw that the gravest challenge raised by the Schleiermacher/Hick trajectory in theodicy is the combination of excessive suffering in the world *and* the attempt to justify it by a "means-end" argument.[47] In this context Hick pointed to Dostoyevsky's *The Brothers Karamazov.*[48] Hick's response was that only eschatology can provide a context for addressing the challenge of theodicy. The overall goodness of creation—its truly "greater good"—must lie not in the present, as with Augustine, but in the eschatological future.

As before, then, this implies that the eschatological new creation must include not only humanity, but all the species and individual creatures in the history of life on earth. Specifically, it must include them in terms of the concrete details of their own lives and in light of their own capacities and characteristics, and not merely as included through the *human* experience of redemption. In particular, every moment in the history of the evolution of life, and not just the "end" of historical time, must be taken up and transformed eschatologically by God into eternal life. One might say that, rather than a "means-end" eschatology it must be such that *every means is also an end in itself.* Ultimately, this eschatological vision must include the redemption of all life in the universe.[49]

It also must be structured on a trinitarian doctrine of God since it is the trinitarian God who will act to bring this about as we know based on the revelation of the cross and resurrection of Jesus. Thus the involuntary suffering of all of nature—each species and each individual creature—must be taken up into the voluntary suffering of Christ on the cross (theopassianism) and through it the voluntary suffering of the Father (patripassianism).

2) TRP → SRP: Guidelines for constructive work in science.
Our project also involves the question of whether such revisions in theology might be of any interest to contemporary science—at least for individual theorists who share eschatological concerns such as developed here and are interested in whether they might stimulate a creative insight into research science.
Guideline 8: *Theological reconceptualization of nature leading to philosophical and scientific revisions (path 6).* Here we move along path 6 in discovering whether a richer theological conception of nature both as creation *and* as new creation can generate important revisions in the *philosophy of nature* that currently underlies the natural sciences, the philosophy of space, time, matter, and causality in contemporary physics and cosmology.
Guideline 9: *Theology as suggesting criteria of theory choice between existing theories (path 7).* We can also move along path 7 to explore philosophical differences in current options in theoretical physics and cosmology. The theological views of research scientists might play a role in selecting which theoretical programs to pursue among those already "on the table" (for example, the variety of approaches to quantum gravity).
Guideline 10: *Theology as suggesting new scientific research programs (path 8).* Finally we can move along path 10 and suggest the construction of new scientific research programs whose motivation stems, at least in part, from theological interests.

In closing this section I want to stress once again that all such programs in science would have to be tested by the scientific communities (what is often called "the context of justification") without regard for the way theology or philosophy might have played a role in their initiation ("the context of discovery").

5. Suggestions for Research Programs in Theology and Science

In order to move ahead and in light of our guidelines, I suggest the following directions first for theological research in reconstructing eschatology.

A. SRP → TRP: Reconstructing Christian eschatology as "transformation of the universe"
1. Continuities, discontinuities, and their preconditions for the transformation of the creation. Following guidelines 6 and 7 in particular, we start by focusing on continuities, discontinuities, and their preconditions that are part of that transformation. These may be found in certain suggestive eschatological hints gleaned from the resurrection of Jesus and the reign of God depicted in the New Testament and its glimpses in the living body of Christ, and the church, keeping clearly in mind the apophatic character of this material.

a) Continuities and discontinuities (G7).

i) Hints of continuity from the *resurrection of Jesus:* He could be touched, he could eat, break bread, be seen,[50] heard, and recognized. These instances of "realized eschatology" are suggestive of an extended "domain" of the New Creation prolepticly within the old, a domain which ceases with the ascension, but which, when present, includes Jesus, the disciples, and their surroundings.[51] Hints of discontinuity: These encounters with the risen Lord break with a mere resuscitation and with normal limitations on "physicality." ii) Hints of continuity from the *reign of God* in the NT and in the church: The New Creation will include persons-in-community and their ethical relations.[52] Hints of discontinuity: In the reign of God, it will "not be possible to sin," compared with the present creation in which it is "not possible not to sin," to use Augustine's apt formulation. iii) Hints of continuity from the problem of *personal identity* between death and the general resurrection in historical and contemporary theology: a) Paul's analogy of the seed;[53] b) numerical, material, and/or formal continuity between death and general resurrection in historical Christian thought.[54] Hints of discontinuities: Though death awaits all people now, the general resurrection, like that of Jesus at Easter, will not be a resuscitation; Paul's fourfold contrast.[55]

b) Preconditions for these continuities and discontinuities (G6).

Next, following guideline 6, we look for epistemically "prior" elements of continuity by moving "down" the disciplinary hierarchy, focusing on those characteristics which make possible the elements of continuity touched on above. For now, I will set aside the many levels to be found in the social, psychological, and neuro-sciences, and move directly to physics. A central theme underlying a) and b) above is temporality; thus we would expect that time as understood by physics is not only a characteristic of this universe as God's creation, but that it will in some ways be a characteristic of the New Creation. Yet we would expect that in the New Creation, our experience of temporality will no longer be marred by the loss of the past and the unavailability of the future. So there will be an element of discontinuity during the transformation as well. We could make a similar case for ontological openness as the enduring precondition for persons-in-community to act freely in love, so that this too might be an element of continuity during the transformation of the universe. Other examples include ontological relationality/holism, the role of symmetries/conservation laws, and so on.[56] Presumably mathematics, too, will be an element of continuity, and in this case, perhaps without discontinuity.[57]

2. The theological research program (TRP): reconstructing eschatology.

The next step is to undertake a reconstruction of Christian eschatology in light of these arguments and, following guidelines 3 and 4, in light of contemporary science and cosmology, at least regarding the past history and present state of the universe. This will clearly require extensive research far beyond the limits of this volume. Nevertheless, some hints of the way forward can be found in focusing, briefly, on one aspect of that project: the relation of time and eternity.

A crucial argument shared widely among contemporary theologians[58] is that eternity is a richer concept of temporality than timelessness or unending time. In essence, eternity is the source of time as we know it, and of time as we will know it in the New Creation. Eternity is the fully temporal source and goal of time. Barth calls it "supratemporal." Moltmann calls it "the future of the future," and Peters refers to the future as coming to us *(adventus)* and not merely that which tomorrow brings *(futurum)*. Pannenberg claims that God acts prolepticly from eternity: God reaches back into time to redeem the world, particularly in the life, ministry, death, and resurrection of Jesus. In this approach the relation between "time and eternity" is modeled on the relation of the finite to the infinite. Here the infinite is not the negation of the finite (as in the Platonic/Augustinian view of eternity as timelessness); instead the infinite includes while ceaselessly transcending the finite.

In my opinion, this view of eternity includes at least five distinct themes:

1. co-presence of all events: I will define the term "co-presence" to mean that distinct events in time are nevertheless present to one another without destroying or subsuming their distinctiveness
2. "flowing time": each event has what I will call a "past/present/future structure" (or "ppf structure"); this structure is that of an "inhomogeneous temporal ontology"
3. duration: each event has temporal thickness in nature as well as in experience; events are not point-like present moments lacking an intrinsic temporal structure
4. global future: there is a single global future for all of creation so that all creatures can be in community
5. prolepsis: the future is already present and active in the present while remaining future, as exemplified by God's act in raising Jesus from the dead

Note: The combination of flowing time and co-presence in eternity means that all events can be "simultaneously present" and available to each other (*à la* Boethius) and yet each event retains its own unique identity. Thus *in the New Creation, "flow" keeps "co-presence" from reducing to* "nunc" *while "co-presence" keeps "flow" from reducing to a stream of isolated moments.*

Our guidelines now lead to three questions: 1) Which of these themes are already present in creation and thus are elements of continuity in its transformation into the New Creation? 2) Which themes are not yet present in creation but instead represent elements of discontinuity, emerging only in the New Creation? 3) And regarding the latter, does the universe at present include the preconditions for the possibility of their coming to be in the New Creation? The answer to these questions will require a careful discussion of time in physics and cosmology. It will also require us to reformulate these theological themes in terms of our current understanding of time as drawn from twentieth-century physics and cosmology.

Though the reformulation is only begun, I can nevertheless anticipate possible responses to the three questions. To the first, I would argue that *flowing time and duration* are objective features in nature, though this is debatable. Time in special relativity is subject to conflicting interpretations (for example, "block universe" as well as flowing time). Moreover, lacking co-presence, flowing time for us means an isolated present with a vanishing past and a not-yet-realized future. Following path 3 I would introduce a "co-present flowing time" interpretation of special relativity into the theological discussion of time and eternity. Duration is a harder problem, since contemporary physics assumes a point-like or durationless view of time. I believe, however, that a case can be made for duration in nature by drawing on Pannenberg's arguments.[59]

To the second and third questions, I would identify what I am calling "co-presence," prolepsis, and the global future as elements of discontinuity, and thus search physics for their preconditions in nature. For example, the transformation of flowing time into co-present flowing time would seem plausible if one could argue that the inhomogeneous ontology of flowing time does not logically exclude the possibility of distinct temporal events being co-present. Preconditions for prolepsis could include backward causality, violations of local causality, and violations of global causality. Finally, a global future, while excluded by special relativity, is theoretically possible in general relativity where the topology of the universe is contingent on the distribution of matter.

The theological task will now be to reconstruct eschatology with these insights in mind and with our theological concepts reformulated in light of contemporary physics. For example, time and space are treated as independent quantities in classical physics. Similarly, theological treatments of eternity and omnipresence typically take for granted independent treatments of time and space. But time and space are placed in a complex inter-relationship in special relativity and further linked with matter in general relativity. Our task then will be to reformulate such theological categories as eternity and omnipresence in light of special and general relativity with an eye to "co-present flowing time" and time as duration. Similar theological reconstructions will hold for the treatment of time and space in quantum mechanics, and so on.

B. TRP → SRP: Directions for potential research programs in physics and cosmology

Our methodology of mutual interaction includes a second agenda: explore ways in which a revised eschatology as suggested above leads to a revised philosophy of nature as it underlies science, to criteria of theory choice among current theories in science, and to the construction of new scientific research programs.

The first project, revising eschatology in light of science, is still in its very early stages. Until more has been accomplished, we might pursue the second agenda by a more limited approach: Following paths 7 and 8 we begin with our existing eschatology and the *same* elements of continuities, discontinuities, and their preconditions as listed above, and then we ask what SRPs they might suggest. Once again, since temporality is such a predominant theme here, we could start with the theme of "time and eternity,"[60] but now we will explore its implications for current physics and cosmology in two ways: 1) We begin with those aspects of temporality in nature, such as flowing time and duration, which constitute elements of continuity and of discontinuity in respect to the eschatological transformation of the world. This time, however, the analysis should lead to interesting questions about time in current physics. 2) We will also consider aspects of temporality that physics may have overlooked but which, from the perspective of eschatology, might be expected to exist at present, such as co-presence, prolepsis, and global future. If physics were reconsidered with them in mind, could it generate concrete suggestions for research programs in physics?

1. Flowing time and duration vis-à-vis *special relativity and quantum mechanics.*
Let us return to the debate discussed above regarding flowing time versus the "block universe" in special relativity. Here the absence of any physical meaning for absolute simultaneity (that is, a universal and unique present moment) seems to challenge most approaches to the idea of flowing time. This leads to two SRPs:

> SRP (1): Construct a new interpretation of special relativity which is consistent with flowing time but which avoids these problems, as William Lane Craig and others suggest.[61]
>
> SRP (2): Revise special relativity to support a flowing time interpretation over a block universe interpretation, as John Lucas proposes.[62]

Note: SRP (1) follows path 7 if the new interpretation of special relativity leads to SRP (2), a revision of special relativity. Otherwise SRP (1) is more like path 3 from science through its philosophical interpretation to theology. SRP (2), however, clearly follows path 7.

The standard formalism of quantum mechanics presupposes flowing time, but the interpretation of this formalism is highly debated. The Copenhagen interpretation, although widely accepted among physicists and philosophers of physics, does presuppose flowing time.[63] However, given such internal problems as the "measurement problem" and given the vitality of competing interpretations one cannot rely on the Copenhagen interpretation to warrant an "objective arrow of time" in nature. Again we are led to consider two distinct SRPs:

> SRP (3): Construct a new and more competitive interpretation of quantum mechanics which more definitively supports flowing time.

SRP (4): Explore modifications of the actual formalism of quantum mechanics which support flowing time such as nonlinear or stochastic versions of the Schrödinger equation.

Note: The same remarks about path 7 above apply here as well.

Finally, one might pursue Pannenberg's arguments that duration should be found in nature through the following SRP:

SRP (5): Search for mathematical ways to represent time as duration, such as set theory or quantized time, and then by exploring their implications for research physics.

This approach follows path 7 in constructing a new research program in physics and path 8 by serving as a criterion for choosing a mathematical representation for time among existing ones that reflects Pannenberg's arguments more fully.

2. Co-presence, prolepsis, and global future in physics and cosmology.
We now turn to the preconditions for the possibility of continuity: co-presence, global future, and prolepsis. I will touch on the first two briefly, leaving more room for extended comments on the third precondition.
i) ***Co-presence.*** By this I mean the "temporal" (or, perhaps more accurately, "trans-temporal") presence to one another of distinct events in time, a presence which does not destroy or subsume their distinctiveness (for example what I have termed their unique ppf structure).[64] It is challenging to think of positive preconditions on the nature of flowing time which make its transformation into co-presence possible. We might, however, be able to formulate a "negative" precondition: There should be nothing about flowing time that makes its transformation into co-present flowing time intrinsically impossible or the concept of such a transformation entirely unintelligible.
ii) ***Global future.*** By "global future" I mean that all events lie in the causal future of some future set of events. A common theme in Christian eschatology is the unity of the future: The creation will be transformed into a single global domain so that all creatures in the New Creation can be in community. Is there a unique global causal future which could serve as a precondition for the transformation by God of the predicted future into the eschatological future of the New Creation?

According to SR, there is no unique global causal future. The causal futures of any two events P and Q will share some events in common, but there will always be other events which lie either in the causal future of P but not of Q, or of Q but not of P. GR, however, provides a possible precondition for the theme of the eschatological global future: It shows that the topology of the universe is contingent on the distribution of matter, and it allows for a variety of topologies for the future, including ones in which geodesics do not separate to arbitrary distances.

iii) ***Prolepsis.*** The theological meaning of prolepsis is that God acts from the eternal future in the present. The primary instance is God's act in raising Jesus from the dead and, in turn, the ongoing transformation of creation into new creation. Clearly the theological meaning of "future" is distinct from the scientific meaning; yet the attempt here is to find ways to bring them into a more fruitful relationship. Thus there may be features in physics and cosmology which were created by God *ex nihilo* such that they might function as physical preconditions for the possibility of proleptic action of God; they might do so by pointing to or indicating the intelligibility of "reverse causality" already present in nature. In essence, the causal structure of the universe might be more subtle than the "arrow of time" discussion allows; it might not be entirely inconsistent with the idea that the future transformation of the universe by God affects the present through reverse causal processes already at work in nature. For brevity, I will simply list examples of how these features have been discussed in physics:

a) Backward causality in time symmetric formulations. The equations of electromagnetism are "time symmetric": Mathematical solutions to these equations can describe the propagation of light forward in time, as we expect from experience, or backward in time, which is contrary to experience. Nevertheless mathematical models of the propagation of photons based on various combinations of such forward and backward solutions (or, as they are technically called, "retarded" and "advanced" solutions, respectively) have been explored for decades following the catalytic papers by Richard Feynman and J. A. Wheeler.[65] They illuminate several technical problems in electromagnetic theory, and they also provide a very simple model of how "the future could affect the past" without propagation at speeds greater than light.

Ironically, Fred Hoyle's steady state cosmology was the result of a modification of GR based, in part, on the idea of advanced and retarded gravitational potentials.[66] Although the Big Bang models based on GR "won the day" in the 1960s, the time symmetric approach begun by Hoyle still has scientific advocates today.[67] Thus a direction for research programs motivated in part by theological views about prolepsis and designed along these lines is at least in principle viable.

b) Violations of local causality (propagation at speeds greater than light). The expansion of the universe now appears to be accelerating instead of decelerating the way the standard open Big Bang models predicted. The acceleration might be explained by adding the so-called "cosmological constant," Λ, to Einstein's field equations. This addition represents a "pressure" term typical of an incompressible fluid and suggests a "physical" reason for the increasing acceleration of the universe's expansion.[68]

What is surprising is that Einstein's equations with the inclusion of $\not\subset$ allow, at least formally, for the propagation of sound exceeding the speed of light and thus possibly backwards in time. Such backward waves represent one possible way that causality within small regions of spacetime might be violated. In a recent work, George Murphy has discussed the potential significance of such backward waves for eschatology.[69] (Backwards waves are also allowed in the de Sitter static spacetime).[70]

c) Violations of global causality (closed paths in spacetime). It is well known that Gödel's universe allows for time-like paths (paths along which matter can move) that are closed but that do not violate the speed of light.[71] Essential singularities in spacetime allow passage from one portion of our universe (for example, "the future") to another portion (for example, "the past")[72] or another universe. To pursue these questions requires the use of global techniques in the analysis of such topics as time/space orientability; the chronology condition; the causality condition; the future/past distinguishing condition; the strong causality condition; the stable causality condition; the existence/nonexistence of a Cauchy surface (or a partial Cauchy surface); and so on.[73]

Features i), ii), and iii) can be explored through yet another SRP, now stated in more general terms than the previous five:

> SRP (6): Guidelines 8–10: Consider and develop ways in which the complex character of time and time's arrow in the eschatological conceptualities of co-presence, prolepsis, and the global future, hint at the existence of preconditions in creation and ways in which these features in physics and cosmology point to the existence of these preconditions.

SRP (6) can be pursued through path 6, in which eschatology rather than the doctrine of creation provides a conception of nature in which science flourishes more fully path 7 in which it inspires the construction of new scientific theories of time taking advantage of these already-existing resources in science; and path 8 in which we choose between existing scientific theories by their ability to articulate these preconditions in nature.

6. Conclusions

Many distinct areas in biblical studies and systematic theology require us to give central attention to eschatology, including the bodily resurrection of Jesus and its implications for the New Creation, the problem of suffering both in humanity and in the whole sweep of biological evolution, the "crucified God" as a response to suffering and its demand for an eschatology of new creation, and indeed the very meaning of a relational understanding of the trinitarian doctrine of God, not to mention the program of "theology and science" itself. But eschatology of this sort, with its unavoidable cosmic horizons, faces the severe challenge of the scientific prognosis for the far future: freeze or fry. Even if scientific cosmology changes, as indeed it will do (and is doing), the strictly scientific changes will never be capable of providing on their own a basis for such an eschatology. Instead of challenging science, however, we recognize that we need not make the strictly philosophical assumption that what science predicts must come to pass. Instead we can think about the future of the universe in theological terms, though terms which have been heavily engaged and reconstructed in light of what the sciences tell us validly about the past and present of the universe. Such a reconstructed eschatology might, in turn, offer new insights about the present creation which could be fruitful for those engaged in scientific research. In sum, we are asking what an expanded scientific conception of nature would be like if we were to inherit it from eschatology instead of creation theology, and what ramifications this might have for current science. Taken together—the reconstruction of eschatology in light of science but based on its theological/biblical resources, and the indication of directions for potential research in science from out of this new eschatological perspective on the universe at present—the relation represents an instance of the methodology of creative mutual interaction between theology and science. The extensive development of this and other representations of this interaction is currently in process. The value of the results of this interaction can only be judged when those results have been more fully articulated, but I do believe that in principle the laying out of such a new methodology is in itself of lasting value and provides an open invitation to a variety of scholars and a diversity of theological and scientific interests and views.

I believe that theology and science interact in a variety of creative ways. In Figure 10.1, I suggest that there are at least eight distinctive paths that move us between science and theology. The eight paths divide into two sets: those currently routine paths which describe the movement from science to theology and those more controversial ones which describe the movement from theology to science.

1. *From science to theology*. There are at least five ways or paths by which the natural sciences can affect constructive theology. (I will focus on physics and cosmology for specificity, but my comments would apply to the other sciences as well.) In the first four, theories in physics, including the key empirical data they interpret, can act as *data for theology* both in a direct sense (paths 1 and 2) and indirectly via philosophy (paths 3 and 4).

(1) Theories in physics can act directly as data which place constraints on theology. So, for example, a theological theory about divine action should not violate or ignore special relativity.

(2) Theories in physics can act directly as data either to be "explained" by theology or as the basis for a theological constructive argument. For example, t=0 in Big Bang cosmology could be explained theologically via creation *ex nihilo*. Such an explanation can serve to confirm the theological theory, although proof is out of the question. Note: The theological explanation should be considered a part of theology, and not as a scientific explanation.

(3) Theories in physics, after philosophical analysis, can act indirectly as data in theology. For example, an indeterministic interpretation of quantum mechanics can function within theology of divine action (special providence) by providing a non-interventionist approach.

Appendix: Discussion of the Method of Creative Mutual Interaction

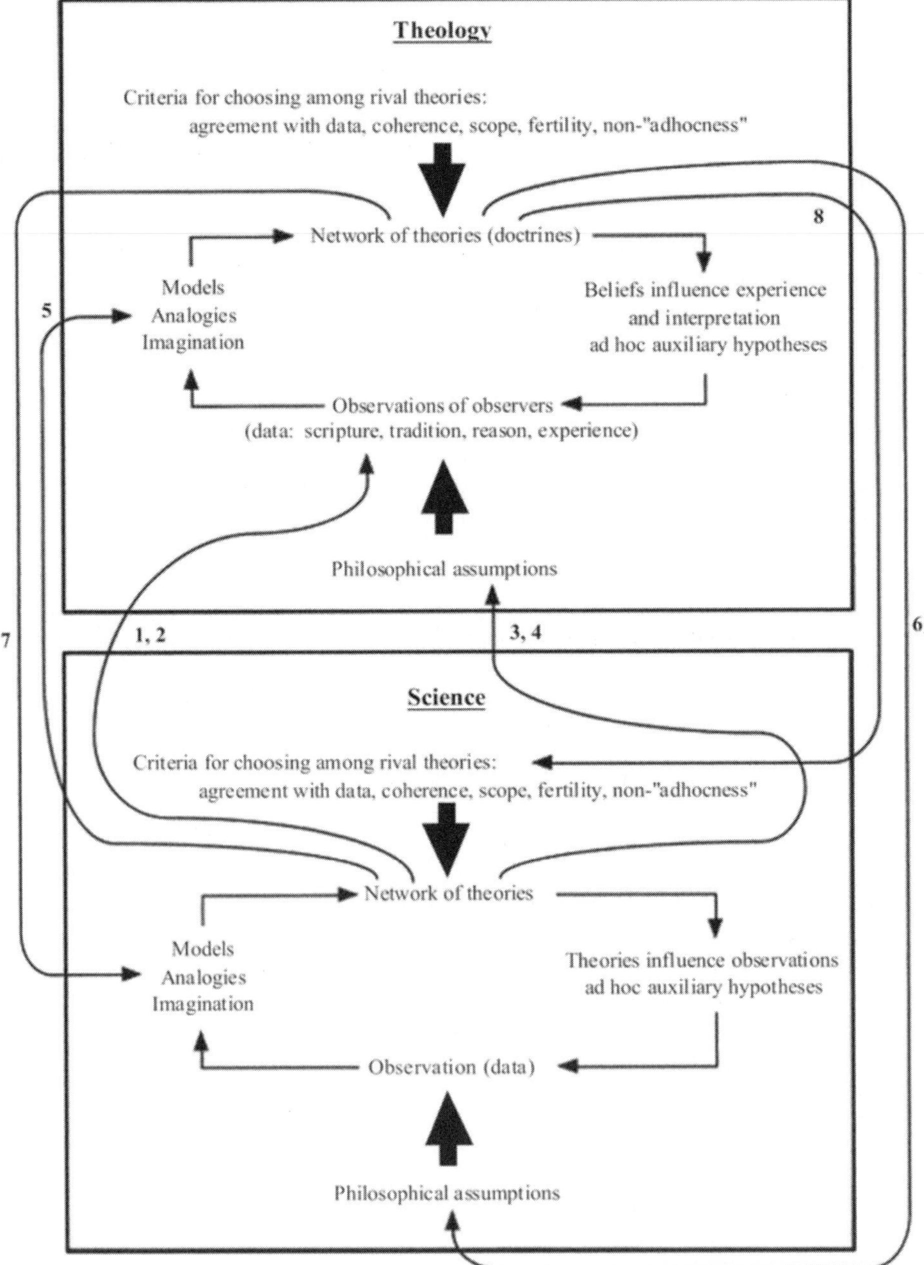

Figure 10.1: The Method of Creative Mutual Interaction (CMI)

(4) Theories in physics can act indirectly as the data for theology when they are incorporated into a fully-articulated philosophy of nature (for example, that of Alfred North Whitehead).

(5) Theories in physics can function heuristically in the theological context of discovery by providing conceptual inspiration, experiential inspiration, moral inspiration, or aesthetic inspiration. So Big Bang cosmology may inspire a sense of God's immanence in nature.

2. *From theology to physics.* To see the genuinely interactive, but asymmetrical, nature of the relations I am proposing, I will suggest at least three paths by which theology can influence science.

(6) Theology provides some of the philosophical assumptions which underlie scientific methodology. Historians and philosophers of science have shown in detail how the doctrine of creation *ex nihilo* played an important role in the rise of modern science by combining the Greek assumption of the rationality of the world with the theological assumption that the world is contingent. Together these helped give birth to the empirical method and the use of mathematics to represent natural processes. Other assumptions grounded in the *ex nihilo* tradition, however, were not carried over into the scientific conception of nature, including goodness and purpose. It would be interesting to reopen the question of the value of these assumptions for contemporary science. Is there a sense in which neo-Darwinian evolutionary biology includes teleonomy? Do values have a partial, evolutionary grounding in nature? Would scientific theories which incorporate such ideas be more fruitful than those which do not?

(7) Theological theories can act as sources of inspiration in the scientific "context of discovery," that is, in the construction of new scientific theories. For example a variety of theologies and philosophies influenced many of the pioneers of quantum theory in the period 1900–1930, including Vedanta for Schrödinger, Spinoza for Einstein, Kierkegaard for Bohr. Another example is the subtle influence of atheism on Fred Hoyle's search for a steady state cosmology.

(8) Theological theories can lead to "selection rules" within the criteria of theory choice in physics. If one considers a theological theory as true, then one can delineate what conditions must be obtained within physics for the possibility of its being true. These conditions in turn can serve as reasons for an individual research scientist or group of colleagues to pursue a particular scientific theory. For example, according to theological anthropology, humankind bears the *imago dei* which includes libertarian free will and with it the possibility of enacting our choices bodily. Thus we might prefer quantum mechanics to classical mechanics since the former is compatible with an indeterministic interpretation.

Together these eight paths portray science and theology in a dynamic, though asymmetric, interaction. I call this "the method of creative mutual interaction." It is first of all a description of the ways scholars allow science to influence theology and vice versa. But it is also prescriptive: I believe a more intentional exploration of such influences could be fruitful for science as well as theology. Most of all, it could be particularly fruitful for "theology and science" because it allows us to delineate the conditions and criteria for real progress in "theology and science." First, scholars in each field would need to find that such an interaction was fruitful according to the criteria of their own research field. So, would scientists feel that their research was more fruitful by having engaged with theology and philosophy in these ways? Would theologians consider their research to have benefited from engaging with science? Secondly, as major changes occur in one field and these changes are taken seriously by the other, would the corresponding effect of these changes be considered fruitful by scholars in that field? Finally a process such as this, once set in motion, could continue indefinitely. It might even be possible to compare these results with those of scientists and theologians who have chosen not to engage in mutual interaction and determine which methodology—interaction or "two worlds"—is indeed more fruitful.

Endnotes: Chapter 10

[1] This chapter is adapted from Robert John Russell, "Eschatology and Scientific Cosmology: From Conflict to Interaction," in *What God Knows: Time, Eternity and Divine Knowledge*, ed. Harry Lee Poe and J. Stanley Mattson (Waco, Tex.: Baylor University Press, 2006), 95–120; and in turn from: "Eschatology and Physical Cosmology: A Preliminary Reflection," in *The Far Future: Eschatology from a Cosmic Perspective*, ed. George F. R. Ellis (Philadelphia: Templeton Foundation Press, 2002), 266–315, with permission from the Templeton Foundation Press; from Robert John Russell, "Bodily Resurrection, Eschatology and Scientific Cosmology: The Mutual Interaction of Christian Theology and Science," in *Resurrection: Theological and Scientific Assessments*, ed. Ted Peters, Robert John Russell, and Michael Welker (Grand Rapids, Mich.: Eerdmans, 2002), 3–30, with permission from Eerdmans Publishing Company; and from Robert John Russell, "Sin, Salvation, and Scientific Cosmology: Is Christian Eschatology Credible Today?" in *Sin & Salvation*, ed. Duncan Reid and Mark Worthing (Adelaide, Austr.: ATF, 2003), with permission from the Australian Theological Forum.

[2] Ted Peters, *God as Trinity: Relationality and Temporality in the Divine Life* (Louisville, Ky.: Westminster/John Knox, 1993), 175–6.

[3] See endnote #1.

[4] John Macquarrie, *Principles of Christian Theology*, Second Edition (New York: Charles Scribner's Sons, 1977 [1966]), ch. 15, esp. 351–62.

[5] For a non-technical introduction, see James Trefil and Robert M. Hazen, *The Sciences: An Integrated Approach*, Second Edition/Updated Edition (New York: John Wiley & Sons, 2000), ch. 15; George F. Ellis and William R. Stoeger, S.J., "Introduction to General Relativity and Cosmology," in *Quantum Cosmology and the Laws of Nature,* ed. Robert J. Russell, Nancey C. Murphy, and Chris J. Isham, Scientific Perspectives on Divine Action Series (Vatican City State; Berkeley, Calif.: Vatican Observatory Publications; Center for Theology and the Natural Sciences, 1993), 33–48; hereafter *QCLN*. For a technical introduction, see Charles W. Misner, Kip S. Thorne, and John Archibald Wheeler, *Gravitation* (San Francisco: WH Freeman, 1973), Part VI.

[6] The reference to "spacetime" is actually based on Minkowski's geometrical interpretation of Einstein's SR. Although it is quite routine in scientific circles, it does not go entirely undisputed; cf. for example William Lane Craig, *Time and the Metaphysics of Relativity* (Dordrecht: Kluwer Academic, 2001).

[7] Misner, Thorne and Wheeler, *Gravitation.*

[8]Other interpretations of the magnitude/redshift data were also on the table which assumed a static universe. The debate between them constitutes a very interesting episode in the history of twentieth- century cosmology. See {Kragh 1996}

[9] For a non-technical introduction see Donald Goldsmith, *Einstein's Greatest Blunder? The Cosmological Constant and Other Fudge Factors in the Physics of the Universe* (Cambridge, Mass.: Harvard University Press, 1995), chs. 10 on. For a more technical introduction see Chris J. Isham, "Creation of the Universe as a Quantum Process," in *Physics, Philosophy, and Theology,* ed. Robert J. Russell, William R. Stoeger, S. J., and George V. Coyne, S. J. (Vatican City State: Vatican Observatory Publications, 1988), 375–408; hereafter *PPT*. Edward W. Kolb and Michael S. Turner, *The Early Universe* (Reading: Addison-Wesley, 1994).

[10] John D. Barrow and Frank J. Tipler, *The Anthropic Cosmological Principle* (Oxford: Clarendon Press, 1986), ch. 10; see also William R. Stoeger, S. J., "Scientific Accounts of Ultimate Catastrophes in Our Life-Bearing Universe," in *The End of the World and the Ends of God: Science and Theology on Eschatology*, ed. John Polkinghorne and Michael Welker (Harrisburg, Pa.: Trinity International, 2000).

[11] If the universe is closed, then in 10^{12} years the universe will have reached its maximum size and recollapse back to a singularity like the original hot Big Bang.

[12] Barrow and Tipler, *The Anthropic Cosmological Principle*, 648.

[13] Scholars who support an objective interpretation include Karl Barth, Raymond Brown, Gerald O'Collins, William Lane Craig, Stephen Davis, Wolfhart Pannenberg, Phem Perkins, Ted Peters, Janet Martin Soskice, Sandra Schneiders, Richard Swinburne, and N. T. Wright.
[14] Raymond E. Brown, *The Virginal Conception and Bodily Resurrection of Jesus* (New York: Paulist, 1973), 72.
[15] Scholars who support a subjective interpretation include Marus Borg, Rudolf Bultmann, John Dominic Crossan, John Hick, Gordon Kaufman, Hans Küng, Sallie McFague, Willie Marxsen, Rosemary Radford Ruether, and Norman Perrin.
[16] Willi Marxsen, *The Resurrection of Jesus of Nazareth*, trans. Margaret Kohl (Philadelphia: Fortress Press, 1970), 77, 156.
[17] Some scholars who refer to the resurrection as "objective" leave the question of physical and material continuity open-ended. For them, the objective interpretation of the resurrection of Jesus is compatible with the possibility that his body suffered the same processes of decay that ours will after death; indeed it may even be seen as necessary (for example, for his death to be like ours, and so on).
[18] Introductions to theology and science from a primarily Christian perspective include Robert John Russell and Kirk Wegter-McNelly, "Science," in *The Blackwell Companion to Modern Theology*, ed. Gareth Jones (Oxford: Blackwell Publishing, 2004), 512–56; Ian G. Barbour, *When Science Meets Religion: Enemies, Strangers or Partners?* (San Francisco: HarperSanFrancisco, 2000); Christopher Southgate, Celia Deane-Drummond, et al., eds., *God, Humanity and the Cosmos: A Textbook in Science and Religion* (Harrisburg: Trinity Press International, 1999); Ted Peters, "Theology and the Natural Sciences," in *The Modern Theologians: An Introduction to Christian Theology in the Twentieth Century*, 2nd ed., ed. David F. Ford (Cambridge, Mass.: Blackwell, 1997), 649–68.
[19] For an overview see Robert John Russell, "Does "The God Who Acts" Really Act? New Approaches to Divine Action in the Light of Science," *Theology Today* 51.1 (March 1997). Much of the research stems from the CTNS/VO series. Summaries of these papers can be found at http://www.ctns.org/books.html.
[20] Stoeger, "Scientific Accounts of Ultimate Catastrophes in Our Life-Bearing Universe," 19–20.
[21] Critical realists also claim that language is intrinsically metaphorical, and they defend a referential theory of truth warranted in terms of correspondence, coherence, and utility.
[22] Ian G. Barbour, *Religion in an Age of Science*, Gifford Lectures; 1989–1990. (San Francisco: Harper & Row, 1990).
[23] Arthur Peacocke, *Theology for a Scientific Age: Being and Becoming—Natural, Divine and Human*, Enlarged Edition (Minneapolis: Fortress Press, 1993). See particularly Fig. 3, 217, and the accompanying text.
[24] Nancey Murphy, *Theology in the Age of Scientific Reasoning* (Ithaca: Cornell University Press, 1990).
[25] Philip Clayton, *Explanation from Physics to Theology: An Essay in Rationality and Religion* (New Haven, Conn.: Yale University Press, 1989).
[26] John C. Polkinghorne, *The Faith of a Physicist: Reflections of a Bottom-up Thinker* (Princeton, N.J.: Princeton University Press, 1994).
[27] There are, of course, important differences between the methods of theology and the natural sciences, as Barbour and others stress carefully.
[28] One could do a more complicated diagram with physics, biology, and theology, for example, and one would need to include the influences of physics on both biology and theology, as well as the influences of biology on theology, and so on!
[29]This is a slight modification of George's actual suggestion (private communication).
[30]See for example the contradictory arguments about eschatology in John F. Haught, *God After Darwin: A Theology of Evolution* (Boulder, Col.: Westview Press, 2000); or the avoidance of the challenge of cosmology in Marjorie Hewitt Suchocki, *God, Christ, Church: A Practical Guide to Process Theology* (New York: Crossroad, 1982); Barbour, *Religion in an Age of Science.*

[31] John Polkinghorne, *The Way the World Is* (Grand Rapids, Mich.: Eerdmans, 1983), chapter 8; Polkinghorne, *The Faith of a Physicist*, ch. 6, 9, exp. 163–70; John C. Polkinghorne, *Serious Talk: Science and Religion in Dialogue* (Valley Forge, Pa.: Trinity International, 1995), ch. 7.

[32] Polkinghorne, *The Faith of a Physicist*, 167.

[33] John Polkinghorne, "Eschatology: Some Questions and Some Insights from Science," in *The End of the World and the Ends of God*, 29–30.

[34] Dante Alighieri, *The Divine Comedy*, trans. John Ciardi (New York: W. W. Norton, 1970), The Paradiso, Canto XX, vs. 88–90.

[35]To view nature as created *ex nihilo* implies that the universe is contingent and rational, and these are two of the fundamental philosophical assumptions on which modern science is based. See for example Michael Foster, "The Christian Doctrine of Creation and the Rise of Modern Science," in *Creation: The Impact of an Idea*, ed. Daniel O'Connor and Francis Oakley (New York: Charles Scribner's Sons, 1969); David C. Lindberg and Ronald L. Numbers, eds., *God and Nature: Historical Essays on the Encounter Between Christianity and Science* (Berkeley: University of California Press, 1986); Gary B. Deason, "Protestant Theology and the Rise of Modern Science: Criticism and Review of the Strong Thesis," *CTNS Bulletin* 6.4 (Autumn 1986): 1–8; Christopher B. Kaiser, *Creation and the History of Science*, The History of Christian Theology Series, No. 3 (Grand Rapids, Mich.: Eerdmans, 1991).

[36] Helge Kragh, *Cosmology and Controversy*.

[37]This diagram has appeared in various writings including Robert John Russell, "The Relevance of Tillich for the Theology and Science Dialogue," *Zygon: Journal of Religion & Science* 36.2 (June 2001): 269–308, Robert John Russell, "Eschatology and Physical Cosmology: A Preliminary Reflection," in *The Far Future: Eschatology from a Cosmic Perspective*, ed. George F. R. Ellis (Philadelphia: Templeton Foundation Press, 2002), 266–315; Robert John Russell, "Bodily Resurrection, Eschatology and Scientific Cosmology: The Mutual Interaction of Christian Theology and Science," in *Resurrection: Theological and Scientific Assessments*, ed. Ted Peters, Robert John Russell, and Michael Welker (Grand Rapids, Mich.: Eerdmans, 2002), 3–30. Other scholars have used similar terms to indicate their methodological approaches. Alan Padgett, for example, talks about "the mutuality of theology and science" in ways very similar to my own. His writings on time and thermodynamics are particularly helpful here. We seem to have developed our approaches independently, and it is wonderful to discover these common interests and hopefully to explore them together in the future. See Alan Padgett, "The Mutuality of Theology and Science: An Example from Time and Thermodynamics," *Christian Scholar's Review* 26 (1996) Fall: 12–35.

[38] William R. Stoeger, S. J., "Contemporary Physics and the Ontological Status of the Laws of Nature," in *QCLN*, 209–34.

[39]Another way of making this case is to recognize that all scientific laws carry a *ceteris paribus* clause, that is, their predictions hold "all else being equal." But if God's regular action accounts for what we describe through the laws of nature, and if God acts in radically new ways to transform the world, then of course all else is not equal. I am grateful to Nancey Murphy for stressing this point to me (private communication).

[40]Note: Unlike the claims of many in the ID movement, methodological naturalism does *not* entail metaphysical naturalism; it is not "inherently atheistic." On the contrary, metaphysical theism is an equally (I would say stronger) interpretation of methodological naturalism.

[41]Since eschatology starts with the presupposition of God, it rules out reductive materialism and metaphysical naturalism. By taking on board natural science, other metaphysical options become unlikely candidates, including Platonic or Cartesian ontological dualism.

[42] See in particular the articles by Noreen Herzfeld, Nancey Murphy, Ted Peters, Jeffrey Schloss, and Michael Welker in Ted Peters, Robert John Russell, and Michael Welker, eds., *Resurrection: Theological and Scientific Assessments.*

[43]I am grateful to Kirk Wegter-McNelly for suggesting the term "transcendental" here. (Private communications.)

[44]It is for this reason that I agree with O'Collins's criticism that previous work on non-interventionist divine action did not deal with the problem of the resurrection. It did not because it could not; it was never intended to deal with the resurrection. See Gerald O'Collins, S. J., "The Resurrection: The State of the Questions," in *The Resurrection: An Interdisciplinary Symposium on the Resurrection of Jesus* (Oxford: Oxford University Press, 1997), 21, footnote 52.

[45] See chs. 1 and 9 in this volume.

[46]See ch. 8 in this volume.

[47] John Hick, *Evil and the God of Love,* rev. ed. (San Francisco: Harper & Row, 1966), 327–31.

[48] Ibid., 385.

[49] In previous writings, I have assumed that the processes of evolution are applicable on all planets with the appropriate environmental conditions, and that evolution might (and probably will) lead to the capacity for reason and moral conscience—and the possibility (inevitability?) of sin. Cf. ch. 9 in this volume.

[50]O'Collins vs. Davis on "graced seeing" is a crucial issue here.

[51]Michael Welker offers a very imaginative formulation of the relation between the reign of God as already present and as apocalyptic in terms of "eschatological complementarity." See his paper in Ted Peters, Robert John Russell, and Michael Welker, eds., *Resurrection: Theological and Scientific Assessments.*

[52]For a very creative development of this theme, see the paper by Nancey Murphy in Ted Peters, Robert John Russell, and Michael Welker, eds., *Resurrection: Theological and Scientific Assessments.*

[53]First Corinthians 15:35 ff.

[54] Caroline Walker Bynum, *The Resurrection of the Body in Western Christianity, 200–1336* (New York: Columbia University Press, 1995); Sandra Schneiders, "The Resurrection of Jesus and Christian Spirituality," in *Christian Resources of Hope* (Dublin: Columba, 1995), 81–114. See the article by Brian Daley in Ted Peters, Robert John Russell, and Michael Welker, eds., *Resurrection: Theological and Scientific Assessments.*

[55]First Corinthians 15:42 ff.

[56] Polkinghorne, "Eschatology."

[57] Robert John Russell, "The God Who Infinitely Transcends Infinity." See chapter 1 in this book.

[58] For a helpful overview of trinitarian theologians on the problem of "time and eternity," see Peters, *God as Trinity*; and Robert John Russell, "Time in Eternity," *Dialog* 39.1 (March 2000). There are, of course, fundamental problems in contemporary discussions of the doctrine of the Trinity. These include the source of the doctrine (is it analytic or synthetic?), the meaning of the divine persons, their principle of unity, the relation of the economic and the immanent Trinity, and so on. Here I am not attempting to adjudicate between these issues. I am simply lifting up some themes which, arguably, most trinitarian formulations have in common in order to suggest ways to start the conversation with science.

[59] In brief, Wolfhart Pannenberg claims that duration was part of the biblical and early Western understanding of time, that it was lost in Augustine's separation of subjective and objective time, and that modern physics inherited the latter, durationless view. He then points to recent philosophy where attempts have been made to view physical time in terms of duration, as in the writings of Bergson, Heidegger, and Whitehead, whose roots lie, in part, in Christian theology. See Wolfhart Pannenberg, "Theological Questions to Scientists," in *The Sciences and Theology in the Twentieth Century*, ed. A. R. Peacocke (Notre Dame, Ind.: University of Notre Dame Press, 1981); Wolfhart Pannenberg, *Metaphysics and the Idea of God* (Grand Rapids, Mich.: Eerdmans, 1990); Wolfhart Pannenberg, *Systematic Theology*, trans. G. W. Bromiley (Grand Rapids: Eerdmans, 1991), 1; Wolfhart Pannenberg, *Toward a Theology of Nature: Essays on Science and Faith*, ed. Ted Peters (Louisville: Westminster/John Knox, 1993).

[60] The focus on "time and eternity" is particularly appropriate for our task here since most contemporary theologians root their eschatology within the framework of *creatio ex nihilo.* Thus

much of what they claim about time and eternity applies to the universe as the creation, and not only as it will be as New Creation.

[61]Scholars such as William Lane Craig insist that we should return to Einstein's original classical framework of matter moving in three-dimensional Euclidean space with time as an independent parameter. See Craig, *Time and the Metaphysics of Relativity*.

[62] J. R. Lucas, *The Future: An Essay on God, Temporality, and Truth* (Oxford; New York: Blackwell, 1989).

[63]Ironically, its most crucial technical problem, "the measurement problem," requires the assumption of a universal present and a flowing time.

[64] A possible mathematical model for the concept of co-presence is a non-Hausdorff manifold in which distinct events are not separable topologically.

[65] J. A. Wheeler and R. P. Feynman, "Interaction with the Absorber as the Mechanism of Radiation," *Review of Modern Physics* 17 (1945): 156; J. A. Wheeler and R. P. Feynman, "Classical Electrodynamics in Terms of Direct Interparticle Action," *Review of Modern Physics* 21 (1949): 424.

[66] F. Hoyle and J. V. Narlikar, *Action at a Distance in Physics and Cosmology* (San Francisco: WH Freeman, 1974).

[67] Fred Hoyle, Geoffrey Burbidge, and Jayant V. Narlikar, *A Different Approach to Cosmology: From a Static Universe Through the Big Bang Towards Reality* (Cambridge: Cambridge University Press, 2000).

[68]For a readable account see Goldsmith, *Einstein's Greatest Blunder?* For technical arguments see Lawrence M. Krauss, "The End of the Age Problem, and the Case for a Cosmological Constant Revisited," *CWRU_P6_97 / CERN_Th_97/122 / Astro_Ph/9706227 Preprint* (1997).

[69] George L. Murphy, "Hints from Science for Eschatology—and Vice Versa," in *The Last Things: Biblical & Theological Perspectives on Eschatology*, ed. Carl E. Braaten and Robert W. Jenson (Grand Rapids, Mich.: Eerdmans, 2002), 157–60.

[70] For a technical discussion see G. F. R Ellis, J. Hwang, and M. Bruni, *Phys. Rev. D* 40 (1989): 1819–26; Stephen Hawking and George F. R. Ellis, *The Large Scale Structure of Spacetime*, Cambridge Monographs on Mathematical Physics Series (Cambridge: Cambridge University Press, 1973), 88–96.

[71] K. Gödel, "An Example of a New Type of Cosmological Solution of Einstein's Field Equations of Gravitation," *Review of Modern Physics* 21 (1949): 447–50.

[72]For somewhat accessible background material see Misner, *Gravitation*, Part VII.

[73] Ibid., ch. 34. For technical material see Hawking and Ellis, *The Large Scale Structure of Spacetime*. Note: The discussion of these topics in the context of quantum cosmology is much more complex. See N. D. Birrell and P. C. W. Davies, *Quantum Fields in Curved Space* (Cambridge: Cambridge University Press, 1982); Isham, "Creation of the Universe"; Chris J. Isham, *Lectures on Quantum Theory: Mathematical and Structural Foundations* (London: Imperial College Press, 1995).

Appendix

A Complete Listing of Robert John Russell's Publications

Theology and Science

Books

Time in Eternity: Eschatology and Cosmology in Mutual Interaction, Robert John Russell (in process).

Physics and Cosmology: Scientific Perspectives on the Problem of Natural Evil. Robert John Russell Nancey Murphy, and William R. Stoeger, S. J., eds. (Vatican City State: Vatican Observatory Publications; and Berkeley, Calif.: Center for Theology and the Natural Sciences, 2007).

Scientific Perspectives on Divine Action: Twenty Years of Problems and Progress. Robert John Russell, Nancey Murphy, and William R. Stoeger, S. J., eds. (Vatican City State: Vatican Observatory Publications; and Berkeley, Calif.: Center for Theology and the Natural Sciences, 2007). To be distributed in the United States by University of Notre Dame Press, Notre Dame, Indiana.

Cosmology, Evolution, and Resurrection Hope: Theology and Science in Creative Mutual Interaction, Proceedings of the Fifth Annual Goshen Conference on Religion and Science, edited by Carl S. Helrich (Kitchener, Ontario: Pandora, 2006).

Fifty Years in Science and Religion: Ian G. Barbour and His Legacy. Robert John Russell, ed. (Aldershot, England: Ashgate, 2004).

Resurrection: Theological and Scientific Assessments. Ted Peters, Robert John Russell, and Michael Welker, eds. (Grand Rapids, Mich.: Eerdmans, 2002).

Science and the Spiritual Quest: New Essays by Leading Scientists. W. Mark Richardson, Robert John Russell, Philip Clayton, and Kirk Wegter-McNelly, eds. (London: Routledge, 2002).

Quantum Physics: Scientific Perspectives on Divine Action. Robert John Russell, Philip Clayton, Kirk Wegter-McNelly, and John Polkinghorne, eds. (Vatican City State: Vatican Observatory Publications; and Berkeley, Calif.: Center for Theology and the Natural Sciences, 2002). Distributed in the United States by University of Notre Dame Press, Notre Dame, Indiana.

The Neurosciences and the Person: Scientific Perspectives on Divine Action. Robert John Russell, Nancey Murphy, Theo Meyering, and Michael Arbib, eds. (Vatican City State: Vatican Observatory Publications; and Berkeley, Calif.: Center for Theology and the Natural Sciences, 1999). Distributed in the United States by University of Notre Dame Press, Notre Dame, Indiana.

Evolution and Molecular Biology: Scientific Perspectives on Divine Action. Robert John Russell, William R. Stoeger, S. J., and Francisco J. Ayala, eds. (Vatican City State: Vatican Observatory Publications; and Berkeley, Calif.: Center for Theology and the Natural Sciences, 1998). Distributed in the United States by University of Notre Dame Press, Notre Dame, Indiana.

Chaos and Complexity: Scientific Perspectives on Divine Action. Robert John Russell, Nancey Murphy, and Arthur R. Peacocke, eds. (Vatican City State: Vatican Observatory Publications; and Berkeley, Calif.: Center for Theology and the Natural Sciences, 1995). Distributed in the United States by University of Notre Dame Press, Notre Dame, Indiana.

Quantum Cosmology and the Laws of Nature: Scientific Perspectives on Divine Action. Robert John Russell, Nancey Murphy, and C. J. Isham, eds. (Vatican City State: Vatican Observatory Publications; and Berkeley, Calif.: Center for Theology and the Natural Sciences, 1993). Distributed in the United States by University of Notre Dame Press, Notre Dame, Indiana.

John Paul II on Science and Religion: Reflections on the New View from Rome. Robert John Russell, William Stoeger, S. J., and George Coyne, S. J., eds. (Vatican City State: Vatican Observatory, 1990). Distributed in the United States by University of Notre Dame Press, Notre Dame, Indiana.

Physics, Philosophy and Theology: A Common Quest for Understanding. Robert John Russell, William Stoeger, S. J., and George Coyne, S. J., eds. (Vatican City State: Vatican Observatory, 1988). Distributed in the United States by University of Notre Dame Press, Notre Dame, Indiana.

Books in Translation

Fisica, Filosofía, y Teología: Una Búsqueda en Común (Physics, Philosophy and Theology). Translated by Juan José Blásquez-Ortega, Alejandro González Sánchez, and Eugenio Urrutia Albisua, trans. Puebla, Mex.: UPAEP, 2002.

Essays/Chapters in Books

"The Bodily Resurrection of Jesus as a First Instantiation of a New Law of the New Creation: Wright's Visionary New Paradigm in Dialogue with Physics and Cosmology," *From Resurrection to Return: Perspectives from Theology and Science on Christian Eschatology*, James Haire, Christine Ledger, and Stephen Pickard, eds. (Adelaide: ATF PACT Series, 2007).

"Physics, Cosmology and the Challenge to Consequentialist Natural Theodicy" *Physics and Cosmology: Scientific Perspectives on the Problem of Natural Evil*, Robert John Russell, Nancey Murphy, and William R. Stoeger, eds. (Vatican City State: Vatican Observatory Publications; and Berkeley, Calif.: Center for Theology and the Natural Sciences, 2007).

"Problems and Progress: An Overview of the CTNS/VO Series" *Scientific Perspectives on Divine Action: Twenty Years of Problems and Progress.* Robert John Russell, Nancey Murphy, and William R. Stoeger, S. J., eds. (Vatican City State: Vatican Observatory Publications; and Berkeley, Calif: Center for Theology and the Natural Sciences, 2007).

"Arthur Peacocke on Method in Theology and Science and His Model of the Divine/World Interaction: An Appreciative Assessment," *All That Is: A Naturalistic Faith for the Twenty-First Century*, Arthur Peacocke (edited by Philip Clayton) (Minneapolis: Fortress Press, 2007), 140–51.

"Cosmology and Eschatology." In *Oxford Handbook of Eschatology*, Jerry Walls, ed. (Oxford: Oxford University Press, 2006).

"Quantum Physics and the Theology of Non-Interventionist Objective Divine Action," *Oxford Handbook of Religion and Science*, Philip Clayton and Zachary Simpson, editors (Oxford: Oxford University Press, 2006), 579–595.

"Eschatology and Scientific Cosmology: From Conflict to Interaction," *What God Knows: Time, Eternity and Divine Knowledge,* Harry Lee Poe and J. Stanley Mattson, eds. (Waco, Tex.: Baylor University Press: 2006).

"How Should Religion and Science be Creatively Related? A Christian Perspective," edited by Ryusei Takeda (Kyoto, Japan: Ryukoku University, 2005), 5–34.

"Beyond Dialogue: Toward a Mutual Transformation of Christianity, Buddhism and the Natural Sciences," edited by Ryusei Takeda (Kyoto, Japan: Ryukoku University, 2005), 71–100.

"Fruitful Interactions Between Scientific Cosmology and Christian Theology" *Faithful/Fateful Encounters: Religion and Cultural Exchanges Between Asia and the West,* Selected Papers and Presentations from the Graduate Theological Union/Chinese Academy of Social Sciences Beijing, October 21–26, 2002, edited by Judith Berling, Philip Wickeri, et. al. (2005).

"Science and Spirituality," *Blackwell Companion to Christian Spirituality*, Arthur Holder, ed. (Oxford: Blackwell Publishing, 2005).

"Natural Theodicy in an Evolutionary Context: The Need for an Eschatology of New Creation," *Theodicy and Eschatology*, Bruce Barber and David Neville, Task of Theology Today, V (Adelaide: Australian Theological Forum Press, 2005).

"Science and Spirituality," *SCM Dictionary of Christian Spirituality*, Philip Sheldrake, ed. (London: SCM Press, 2004).

"The Contributions of the Natural Sciences for the Academic Discipline of Christian Spirituality," *Festschrift* in honor of Sandra Schneiders (2004).

"Science," by Robert John Russell and Kirk Wegter-McNelly, *The Blackwell Companion to Modern Theology*, Gareth Jones, ed. (Oxford: Blackwell Publishing, 2004), Ch. 32, p. 512–556.

"Introduction," "Ian Barbour's Methodological Breakthrough: Creating the 'Bridge' for Science and Theology," and "Barbour's Assessment of the Philosophical and Theological

Implications of Physics and Cosmology," *Fifty Years in Science and Religion: Ian G. Barbour and His Legacy*," Robert John Russell, ed. (Aldershot, England: Ashgate Publications, 2004).

"Relativity," *Religion in Geschichte und Gegenwart*. German: RGG^4, 2004).

"Sin, Salvation, and Scientific Cosmology: Is Christian Eschatology Credible Today?" Task of Theology Today, IV, edited by Duncan Reid and Mark Worthing, (Adelaide: Australian Theological Forum Press, 2003).

"When Time Meets Eternity: Theology and Science in Mutual Creative Interaction," proceedings, C. S. Lewis Conference, 2002.

"Causality," "Contingency," and "Complementarity" *Religion in Geschichte und Gegenwart* (Germany: RGG^4, 2003).

"Special Providence and Genetic Mutation: A New Defense of Theistic Evolution" *Perspectives on an Evolving Creation*, edited by Keith Miller (Grand Rapids, Mich.: Eerdmans, 2003).

"Theology and Science: Current Issues and Future Directions," co-authored with Kirk Wegter-McNelly (Oxford: Blackwell, *Blackwell Companion to Modern Theology*, 2003).

"Bodily Resurrection, Eschatology and Scientific Cosmology: The Mutual Interaction of Christian Theology and Science" *Resurrection: Theological and Scientific Assessments*, Ted Peters, Robert John Russell, and Michael Welker, eds. (Grand Rapids, Mich.: Eerdmans, 2002).

"Eschatology and Physical Cosmology" *The Far Future: Eschatology from a Cosmic Perspective*, George F. R. Ellis, ed. (Philadelphia: Templeton Press, 2002).

"Forward," and "Methodology in Science and Religion," *Bridging Science and Religion,* Ted Peters and Gaymon Bennett, eds. (London: SCM Press, 2002). Also in the Chinese-language edition in simplified characters with Kang Phee Seng as a co-editor. To appear in Chinese-language edition in traditional characters, a Portuguese-language edition, a Spanish-language edition, and a Bahasa-language edition.

"Introduction" and "Divine Action and Quantum Mechanics: A Fresh Assessment," *Quantum Physics: Scientific Perspectives on Divine Action*. Robert John Russell, Philip Clayton, Kirk Wegter-McNelly, and John Polkinghorne, eds. (Vatican City State: Vatican Observatory Publications; and Berkeley, Calif.: Center for Theology and the Natural Sciences, 2002).

"Dialogo Science-Teologia, Metodo e Modelli," translation of Part 1, "Theology and Science: Current Issues and Future Directions," extended version. *Dizionario Interdisciplinare di Scienze e Fede*, Giuseppe Tanzella-Nitti, ed. (Città del Vaticano: Urbaniana University Press, 2002).

"The Doctrine of Creation Out of Nothing in Relation to Big Bang and Quantum Cosmologies" *The Human Search for Truth: Philosophy, Science, Theology*, International Conference on Science and Faith/Jubilee for Scientists, Rome (Philadelphia: Saint Joseph's University Press, 2002).

"Life in the Universe: Philosophical and Theological Issues" *First Steps in the Origin of Life in the Universe,* proceedings, Sixth Trieste Conference on Chemical Evolution, Julian Chela-Flores, Tobias Owen, and François Raulin, eds. (Dordrecht: Kluwer Academic Publishers, 2001).

"What are Extraterrestrials Really Like?" *God for the 21st Century*, edited by Russell Stannard (Philadelphia: Templeton Foundation Press, 2000).

"Introduction" and "Special Providence and Genetic Mutation: A New Defense of Theistic Evolution," *Evolutionary and Molecular Biology: Scientific Perspectives on Divine Action,* Robert John Russell, William R. Stoeger, S. J., and Francisco J. Ayala, eds. (Vatican City State: Vatican Observatory; and Berkeley, Calif.: Center for Theology and the Natural Sciences, 1998).

"How Should Religion and Science be Creatively Related? A Christian Perspective," Conference Proceedings, Ryukoku University, Kyoto (1997); *Hindu-Christian Studies Bulletin* (1997).

"Philosophy, Theology and Cosmology: A Fresh Look at their Interactions." *Scienze, Filosofia e Teologia di Fronte alla Nascita dell'Universo,* Padre Eligio, Guilio Giorello, Gioachino Rigamonti, Elio Sindoni, eds. (Como: Edizioni New Press, 1997).

"The God Who Infinitely Transcends Infinity: Insights from Cosmology and Mathematics into the Greatness of God." *How Large is God?* John Marks Templeton and Robert L. Herrmann, eds. (Philadelphia: Templeton Foundation, 1997). Also in Russian: *Dialogue between Science and Religion: Western and Eastern Christian Approaches* (Moscow, 2002).

"T=0: Is it Theologically Significant?" *Religion and Science: History, Method, Dialogue,* W. Mark Richardson and Wesley J. Wildman, eds. (New York: Routledge, 1996).

"Introduction" and "Chaos: A Mathematical Introduction with Philosophical Reflections" with Wesley J. Wildman in *Chaos and Complexity: Scientific Perspectives on Divine Action,* Robert John Russell, Nancey Murphy, and Arthur R. Peacocke, eds. (Vatican City State: Vatican Observatory Publications; Berkeley, Calif.: Center for Theology and the Natural Sciences, 1995).

"Cosmology: Evidence for God or Partner for Theology?" *Evidence of Purpose: Scientists Discover the Creator,* John Marks, ed. (Templeton, New York: Continuum, 1994).

"Christian Discipleship and the Challenge of Physics: Formation, Flux, and Focus," The George Hitching Terriberry Memorial Lecture, in *Reasoned Faith: Essays on the Interplay of Faith and Reason*, Frank T. Birtel, ed. (New York: Crossroad, 1993), 25–55.

"Introduction" and "Finite Creation Without a Beginning: The Doctrine of Creation in Relation to Big Bang and Quantum Cosmologies," *Quantum Cosmology and the Laws of Nature: Scientific Perspectives on Divine Action,* Robert John Russell, Nancey Murphy, and C. J. Isham, eds. (Vatican City State: Vatican Observatory Publications; Berkeley, Calif.: Center for Theology and the Natural Sciences, 1995).

"Theological Implications of Artificial Intelligence," *The Science and Theology of Information*, C. Wasserman, R. Kirby, and B. Rordorff, eds. (Geneva: Labor et Fides, 1992).

"Cosmology," *New Handbook of Christian Theology*, Donald W. Musser and Joseph L. Price, eds. (Nashville: Abingdon Press, 1991).

"Theological Implications of Physics and Cosmology," *The Church and Contemporary Cosmology*, James B. Miller and Kenneth E. McCall, eds. (Pittsburgh: Carnegie Mellon University Press, 1990).

"Cosmology, Creation and Contingency." In *Cosmos and Creation*, Ted Peters, ed. (Nashville: Abingdon Press, 1989).

"Agenda for the Twenty–First Century." *The New Faith–Science Debate*, John Mangum, ed. (Minneapolis: Fortress Press; and Genva: WCC Publications, 1989).

"Quantum Physics in Philosophical and Theological Perspective," *Physics, Philosophy and Theology: A Common Quest for Understanding*, Robert John Russell, William Stoeger, S. J., and George Coyne, S.J., eds. (1988).

"Technology, Ethics and Education in a Global Perspective," *Theological Education for the Future*, ed. Guy Fitch Lytle (Cincinatti, Ohio: Forward Movement, 1988).

"Whitehead, Einstein and the Newtonian Legacy," *Newton and the New Direction in Science*, George V. Coyne, S. J., Michael Heller, and Jozef Zycinski, eds. Citta Del Vaticano: Specola Vaticana, 1988.

"Evolutionary Understanding of Humanity and the Problem of Evil: Biological Evolution, Thermodynamics and the Problem of Evil," *Kooperation und Wettbewerb*, Hans May, Meinfried Striegnitz and Philip Hefner, eds. (Rehberg-Loccum, West Germany: Evangelische Akademie Loccum, 1988).

"The Meaning of Causality in Contemporary Physics," *Free Will and Determinism*, Viggo Mortensen and Robert C. Sorensen, eds. (Aarhus, Denmark: Aarhus University Press, 1987).

"A Response to David Bohm's 'Time, The Implicate Order and Pre-Space.'" In *Physics and the Ultimate Significance of Time*, David R. Griffin, ed. (Albany: State University of New York Press, 1986).

"Foundations in Physics for Revising the Christian Creation Tradition," with A. Dufner, S. J., in *Cry of the Environment: Rebuilding the Christian Creation Tradition*, Philip N. Joranson and Ken Butigan, eds. (Santa Fe: Bear, 1984).

Essays in Journals

"Evolution and Christian Faith" *America, The National Catholic Weekly*, Vol. 194, No. 6 (February 20, 2006).

"Five Attitudes towards Nature and Technology from a Christian Perspective," *Theology and Science*, Vol. 1, No. 2 (October 2003): 149–159.

Editorial: "Bridging Theology and Science: The CTNS Logo," *Theology and Science*, Vol. 1, No. 1 (April 2003): 1–3.

"Beyond Dialogue: Buddhism, Christianity and Science in Mutual Modification" (to appear in *Zygon: Journal of Religion and Science*).

"The Relevance of Tillich for the Theology and Science Dialogue" *Zygon: Journal of Religion & Science*, Vol. 36, No. 2 (June 2001).

"Did God Create Our Universe? Theological Reflections on the Big Bang, Inflation, and Quantum Cosmologies," *Annals of the New York Academy of Sciences*, Vol. 950: *Cosmic Questions*, ed. J. B. Miller (New York: New York Academy of Sciences 2001).

"Time in Eternity: Special Relativity and Eschatology" in *Dialog: A Journal of Theology*, Vol. 39, No. 1 (Spring 2000).

"Theology and Science: Current Issues and Future Directions," extended version, available on the CTNS website and on a CD from Counterbalance (2000).

"How the Heavens Have Changed!" *Ad Astra: The Magazine of the National Space Society* (November/December 1998) and *CTNS Bulletin,* Vol. 19, No. 3 (Summer 1999).

"Does Creation Have a Beginning?" *Dialog: A Journal of Theology* (Summer 1997).

"Does the 'God Who Acts' Really Act? New Approaches to Divine Action in Light of Science," in *Theology Today* (April 1997).

"Religion and the Theories of Science; Response to Barbour," *Zygon: Journal of Religion and Science,* Vol. 31, No. 1 (March 1996).

"Cosmology from Alpha to Omega," *Zygon: Journal of Religion and Science*, Vol. 29, No. 4 (December 1994).

"Finite Creation Without A Beginning," *The Way: Contemporary Christian Spirituality,* Vol. 32, No. 2 (October 1992).

"Contemplation: A Scientific Context," *Continuum,* Vol. 22, Nos. 2 and 3.

"The Human Genome Project: What Questions Does It Raise for Theology and Ethics?" With Ted Peters, *Midwest Medical Ethics,* Vol. 8, No. 1 (Summer 1992).

"The Theological-Scientific Vision of Arthur Peacocke," *Zygon,* Vol. 26, No. 4 (December 1991).

"Theological Lessons from Cosmology: Two Case Studies," *Cross Currents: Religion & Intellectual Life,* Vol. 41, No. 3 (Fall 1991).

"Contemplation in the Vibrant Universe: The Natural Context of Christian Spirituality," *CTNS Bulletin,* Vol. 11, No. 4 (Autumn 1991).

"Christian Discipleship and the Challenge of Physics: Formation, Flux, and Focus," *Perspectives on Science and Christian Faith,* Vol. 42, No. 3 (September 1990). Also *CTNS Bulletin,* Vol. 8, No. 4 (Autumn 1988).

"The Thermodynamics of 'Natural Evil,'" *CTNS Bulletin,* Vol. 10, No. 2 (Spring 1990).

"Bread of Life: A Communion Meditation." *CTNS Bulletin,* Vol. 9, No. 3 (Summer 1989).

"Contingency in Physics and Cosmology: A Critique of the Theology of Wolfhart Pannenberg," *Zygon: Journal of Religion and Science,* Vol. 23, No. 1 (March 1988).

"Science and Theology Today: A Fresh Appraisal of Peacocke's Thought," *Religion & Intellectual Life,* Vol. 5, No. 3 (Spring 1988).

"A Critical Appraisal of Peacocke's Thought on Religion and Science," *Religion and Intellectual Life,* Vol. 2, No. 4 (Summer 1985).

"How Does Modern Physical Cosmology Affect Creation Theology?" *Pacific Theological Review,* Vol. 18, No. 3 (Spring 1985).

"The Thought of David Bohm: Introduction," with Ian G. Barbour, *Zygon,* Vol. 20, No. 2 (June 1985).

"The Physics of Bohm and its Relevance to Philosophy and Theology," *Zygon,* Vol. 20, No. 2 (June 1985).

"Entropy and Evil," *Zygon,* Vol. 19, No. 4 (December 1984). Also *CTNS Bulletin,* Vol. 4, No. 2 (Spring 1984).

"Converging Streams," *San Francisco Examiner/Chronicle,* August 11, 1984.

"Computers: Altering the Human Image and Society," edited by Robert John Russell, *Computers & Society,* Vol. 13, No. 1 (1983).

"Energy and Values," *New Catholic World,* Vol. 224, No. 1341 (May/June 1981).

Reviews of Books in Theology and Science

"Book Worth Rereading," on *A Brief History of Time: From the Big Bang to Black Holes* by Stephen W. Hawking. *America,* Vol. 164, No. 4 (February 2, 1991).

A Brief History of Time: From the Big Bang to Black Holes by Stephen W. Hawking. *CTNS Bulletin,* Vol. 10, No. 1 (Winter 1990).

One World by John Polkinghorne. *Nature,* Vol. 321, No. 26 (June 1986). *Zygon,* Vol. 22, No. 1 (March, 1987).

The Miracle of Existence by Henry Margenau. *Zygon,* Vol. 20, No. 3 (September 1985).

The Sciences and Theology in the Twentieth Century, ed. by A. R. Peacocke. *CTNS Bulletin,* Vol. 4,

No. 1 (Winter 1984). Also *Zygon,* Vol. 20, No. 4 (December 1985).

The Dancing Wu Li Masters by Gary Zukav. *Zygon,* Vol. 15, No. 4 (December 1980).

Scientific Publications

"Kerr Solution to Whitehead's Theory of Gravity," with Christoph Wassermann. *Bulletin of the American Physical Society.* Vol. 32, No. 90 (1987).

"Systematic approach for comparing paraelectric tunneling models to resonance data." *Physical Review B.* Vol. 26, No. 6 (1982).

"Unusual Paraelectric System, KBr:Li^+," (with Frank Bridges), *Physical Review B.* Vol. 26, No. 6 (1982).

"Relative Magnitude of Tunneling Parameters Versus Energy Levels in Paraelectric Models," *Bulletin of the American Physical Society.* Vol. 26, No. 30 (1981).

"A New Paraelectric Center in NaCl:Li^+," (with Frank Bridges), *Bulletin of the American Physical Society.* Vol. 23, No. 18 (1978).

"Suppression of the Paraelectric Resonance of KBr:Li^+ by OH^-," (with Frank Bridges), *Bulletin of the American Physical Society.* Vol. 22, No. 332 (1977).

"A New Paraelectric Center in Lithium-Doped KBr," with Frank Bridges. *Solid State Communications.* Vol. 21, No. 1011 (1977).

"Isotope Effect on the Paraelectric Resonance of KBr:Li^+," (with Frank Bridges), *Bulletin of the American Physical Society.* Vol. 21, No. 265 (1976).

"Magnetic-Monopole Solution of Non-Abelian Gauge Theory in Curved Spacetime" (with F. A. Bais), *Physical Review D.* Vol. 11, No. 2692 (1975).

Index of Names

Index of Subjects